SERVICES MARKETING
MANAGEMENT

SERVICES MARKETING MANAGEMENT

AN INTERNATIONAL PERSPECTIVE

by

Hans Kasper
Piet van Helsdingen
Wouter de Vries jr

JOHN WILEY & SONS
Chichester • New York • Weinheim • Brisbane • Singapore • Toronto

GOVERNORS STATE UNIVERSITY
UNIVERSITY PARK
IL 60466

Copyright © 1999 by John Wiley & Sons Ltd,
       Baffins Lane, Chichester,
       West Sussex, PO19 1UD, England

       National   01243 779777
       International   (+44) 1243 779777
       e-mail (for orders and customer service enquiries):
       cs-books@wiley.co.uk
       Visit our Home Page on http://www.wiley.co.uk
                 or http://www.wiley.com

Other Wiley Editorial Offices

John Wiley & Sons, Inc., 605 Third Avenue,
New York, NY 10158-0012, USA

WILEY-VCH GmbH, Pappelallee 3,
D-69469 Weinheim, Germany

Jacaranda Wiley Ltd, 33 Park Road, Milton,
Queensland 4064, Australia

John Wiley & Sons (Asia) Pte Ltd, 2 Clementi Loop #02-01,
Jin Xing Distripark, Singapore 129809

John Wiley & Sons (Canada) Ltd, 22 Worcester Road,
Rexdale, Ontario M9W 1L1, Canada

British Library Cataloguing in Publication Data

A catalogue record for this book is available from the British Library

ISBN 0-471-98490-6

Design by Carol McCleeve, Middleton-on-Sea

Typeset by Dorwyn Ltd., Rowlands Castle, Hants
Printed and bound in Great Britain by The Bath Press, Bath

This book is printed on acid-free paper responsibly manufactured from sustainable forestry, in
which at least two trees are planted for each one used for paper production.

To our families:

Joke, Marnix, Rianne and Sigrid
Mila and Yara
Kerstin and Tobi

table of contents

foreword

As someone who has devoted his entire career to investigating, writing about, and teaching services marketing, I am pleased for those of you holding this book in your hands and preparing to study services marketing yourself. You are in for an exciting journey, learning about the special challenges and opportunities of marketing a performance – the essence of a service.

Services permeate everyday existence. They are a big part of your life so it makes sense to learn more about them as a consumer and as a present or future manager. Within the last 24 hours, you may have listened to the radio, watched television, taken a train, bus, cab or subway, made or received a telephone call, consumed a restaurant meal, used the campus library or gym, observed a sporting event, made a banking transaction, been warmed (or cooled) by electric power, gone to class, or contacted an insurance agent. In each case, you were a services consumer.

Because services pervade our lives, I always remind my students that improving the quality of service in society is more than just a market share issue, more than just a profit and loss issue, more than just a business issue. Improving service quality also is a quality-of-life issue; the better the service quality of our doctors, grocers, bankers, restaurants, government agencies, department stores, transportation services and other providers, the better the quality of our daily living.

Everyone wins when service is excellent. The customers win (because the quality of daily life is better). The employees win (because striving for excellence at work is more fun than accepting mediocrity). The owners of the company win (because the business will be more successful). And the community and country win (because their businesses are competitively stronger and the quality of everyday living is better).

Enjoy this book and profit from the lessons. Unearth and tuck away the many lessons for marketing and managing the more or less invisible products we call "services".

Leonard L. Berry
Author of *Discovering the Soul of Service*
and Distinguished Professor of Marketing
Texas A&M University, U.S.A.

preface

OBJECTIVES OF THIS BOOK AND TARGET GROUP

Today, the marketing discipline has become so mature that many sub-disciplines have been developed. Services marketing is one of those new fields. It has been actively researched for the past 15 to 20 years.[1] A vast number of articles and conference proceedings have been published and some books on specific topics in services marketing as, for instance, service quality, have been published. Most of the research is on consumer services, only a few studies are based on business to business services. The body of literature is growing at a fast rate. The need to provide an extensive overview of services marketing management, in international literature, becomes manifest. It is *the main aim* of Services Marketing Management to provide that overview for students, instructors, managers, employees and all other people interested in the service industry. Another important goal is to provide students and practitioners with information about managing service organizations. That knowledge can be applied to their future or present employers, or in their own company. So, *the benefits* of this book are threefold: the reader will

- Get a proper understanding of services marketing management in a national and international context;
- Be able to manage a market-oriented service organization; and
- Be able to deliver excellent service quality – leading to long-term relationships with customers and employees.

Textbooks encompassing a broad overview of existing literature are not yet present, at least not at a level that can be used by advanced undergraduate and graduate students. They are the *primary target audience* of this book. Consequently, the reader should be familiar with the basic knowledge of marketing and management.

This book provides an overview of the existing literature on services marketing management and it encompasses the latest developments in this field from Europe, Northern America and Australasia. It is based on our own view about the essence of marketing. For, in our opinion, the essence of marketing lies in concepts like market orientation, long-term relationships, quality and – ultimately – satisfaction.

The people employed at service organizations operating in dynamic national or international environments, have to implement these concepts and deal with the clients in the service encounters. Future employees of service organizations will be the students now studying this text. In this way, we hope to contribute to their effective and efficient performance in a market driven service organization.

We therefore shall attempt to provide students and practitioners with an overview of all the issues relevant to formulating and implementing marketing strategy in and by service organizations. Theory and practical applications will be given simultaneously.

GENERAL LINE AND PHILOSOPHY

Studying strategies and activities of a national/international operating service firm means it is not possible to target marketing specifically. A textbook on services marketing management has to have a broader scope. Rendering services is a "people to people" business. We will, therefore, examine the important role of the personnel, human resources management and the internal organization. Side steps will also be made into the domain of operations research. Rendering services is a dynamic process in an ever changing environment. To fully understand and control these processes, they have to be sectioned into various phases or parts. This will result in a better understanding and control of the service encounter and the back office support. This is an up to date advanced textbook on services marketing with a managerial and international outlook. However, issues regarding accounting and finance will be discussed to a limited extent.

FOUR THEMES

Our aim is to affect the way services marketing management should be dealt with. This is reflected in four themes central to this text and can be regarded as a "credo" for this book. Discussing them at the very beginning makes the reader aware of our vision on marketing.

The four themes are:

1. the fundamentals of services marketing management: concepts include, market orientation and the accompanying corporate culture, satisfaction, quality, relationships and personnel/human resources management;
2. a new classification of services based on an extensive overview of the existing taxonomies. This classification combines existing taxonomies into one overall framework and provides new strategic insights into ways in which service organizations can cope with the intangible nature of services, position themselves and implement the fundamentals of services marketing management;
3. the definition of four new types of services. The difference between customized services and standard services and the difference between core services and augmented services. The four types of services each have their own strategy and marketing mix; and
4. the increasing trend to the internationalization of services. This topic will be discussed not only in Chapter Nine, but throughout the whole text samples will be given of service organizations acting in various countries.

These four themes build up the foundation of the book and will be discussed in separate chapters and, if deemed relevant, recalled in every other chapter.

STRUCTURE OF THE BOOK

Services Marketing Management consists of 15 chapters grouped into four parts. These parts are called respectively: The Services Domain, At the Heart, Strategic Issues, and Services Marketing Mix.

Part One, The Services Domain, is built up of three chapters. The fundamentals of services marketing management, the ways in which services can be classified, and (trends in) the external environment are discussed, including the trend towards internationalization. The four themes that are the building blocks of this book will be discussed at length.

Since most of the existing books on services marketing or services management do not contain a chapter on "consumer behavior and services" or on buying industrial services, Part Two starts with such a chapter. Topics dealt with extensively are: attributes of services used in decision making processes; (dis)satisfaction with services; perceptions; perceived risk. They all contribute to creating long-term relationships (retention and loyalty). Evaluating and assessing the quality of services and service delivery processes are important topics dealt with in Chapter Five. Subjective evaluations of quality are decisive. So, we fully agree with Bateson (1992) who states: "It is the perceived service that matters, not the actual." Although the main emphasis is on consumer services in this book, business to business services will also be dealt with.

The specific consequences of the characteristics of services to market research (especially measuring service quality via expectations and perceptions), will be discussed in Chapter Six, the first chapter in Part Three on strategic issues. Our discussion on the various methods that can be used in measuring service quality goes further than the famous SERVQUAL model. Other methods are mentioned on how to collect data from the market and manage that information effectively and efficiently. The other three chapters contain the framework for strategic marketing planning in a service organization. They are based on the preceding chapters and our own experience in dealing with strategic development in service firms. The links with corporate strategy and corporate planning are shown in Chapter Seven. The relationship between planning the internal and external marketing strategy is shown in Chapter Eight. These chapters contain the basics for easier understanding of the internationalization strategies for service firms (Chapter Nine).

Part Four is on the Services Marketing Mix. The chapters have an operational nature and shorter term orientation. A service organization's personnel plays a crucial role in developing and delivering excellent service quality in a market-oriented way while developing and maintaining sustainable relationships with the customer. Therefore, the marketing mix in service organizations consists of more than the traditional four Ps. Some have added a fifth P, namely personnel, while others added three more Ps, namely participants (being personnel and – other – customers), physical evidence (surroundings where the service encounter takes place) and the process (of delivering the service). We have taken these viewpoints into account in the following way. In our opinion, the marketing mix in service organizations consists of six Ps: people, processes, products, promotion, place and price. We will not forget the P of physical evidence. However, we do not treat it as a separate P. This P has so many links with other areas that we prefer to discuss it in close connection with the processes, the products, the promotion and the place.

For practical reasons we have written the next Chapters 10 to 15 on the marketing mix in service industries. People, Organization and Processes are so intertwined that we have POPped them together. The traditional other Ps then follow: service (= product, the range of existing services as well as developing new services), communication (= promotion, including most of the issues on physical evidence, distribution (= place, availability and accessibility), and price.

It is obvious that the mix is needed to implement the strategy. However, just looking at the mix is not enough to properly implement a strategy. In practice (but also in teaching) the fundamental, underlying concepts as discussed in Part One, are overlooked quite often (or taken for granted). Then, a management style of – what Thomas Bonoma (1985) once called – "management by assumption", will result. Such a style should be avoided.

Most of the topics discussed in this book also apply to public services and other non-profit services, i.e. charities. Nevertheless, being not subjected to the laws of the market, these services have many specific features. The growing knowledge in this field requires special textbooks about these services. It would do no justice about their importance and way of managing them, to dedicate only one chapter to them.

THE PEDAGOGICAL STRUCTURE AND LAYOUT

Services Marketing Management can be used in classroom teaching as well as for self study activities.

Therefore:

• the goals of the whole book and the goals of each chapter are stated clearly;
• the book is easily accessible, well structured and attractive;
• it has a clear writing style;
• the link between theory and practice is present; and
• the text possesses incentives to test one's own knowledge and skills.

These pedagogical considerations are reflected in the layout of the book.

Every chapter:

- starts with a photograph of an event explaining the content of that chapter as much as possible;
- begins with a clear overview of the chapter's objectives;
- contains margin words, indicating the most important concepts in a section;
- contains real life examples clarifying the text when needed; the service practices;
- ends with a summary of the chapter's content;
- ends with questions and assignments;
- contains a 2 or 3 page case with a few questions in which the knowledge acquired in that and previous chapters can be applied.

We are eager to hear the comments from the market place, especially on the surface typology developed, in order to improve the book where needed. If you inform us, then we may have the opportunity to react quickly and carry out any amendments that may be required please use e-mail – H.KASPER @MW.UNIMAAS.NL.

ENDNOTE

1. Excellent historic overviews of the developments in services marketing in Europe and the USA are given in: Swartz, Bowen and Brown, 1992; Berry and Parasuraman, 1993; Fisk, Brown and Bitner, 1993.

acknowledgements

We would like to thank a great many people for helping us to complete this text and providing so many ideas.

First of all, our families. Our wives and kids encouraged us to finish the journey we were on. They accepted that we had to invest time into this book that could not be devoted to them. Now that the project is over, we will serve them more and better. That is why this book is dedicated to them.

In completing the text, our secretary Mieke Donders did an excellent job. With an everlasting energy, great competence and enthusiasm she always managed to meet our wishes and whims with great creativity, reliability and responsiveness. A warm "Mieke thank you" is here in the right place: the flowers are on their way!

At an art exhibition in one of the Maastricht art galleries, we were impressed by a wonderful etching Ineke Brummer had made. We are very pleased that this etching could be used on our front cover. It very much adds to the international dimensions of our book.

It was a wonderful service experience, writing about the intangibility of services and putting it into a tangible form (this book). Class discussion, management development programs, attending conferences on services marketing or quality in services, doing consultancy and actually working in the service arena, provided us with many theoretical and practical insights on services marketing management which we would like to share with many others.

Many of our students have contributed to this book by doing internships or writing master theses. Their work has proven to be very valuable to us. We would like to mention especially here (in alphabetical order) Miranda van Golde, Coos Groot, Robin Hattink, Hans Hijlkema, Judith van Hulst, Sander Jansen, Ringo Janssen, Alain Loosveld, Anjo Meurs, Monique Peters, Jean Pierre Schreurs, Jur Smit, Jolande Soons, Rob Thomas, Victor Tija, Rene Toet, Karin Verschuren, Rob Westgeest, Karin Zinken and Tatiana Zinken. Some of our students helped in translating text from our Dutch textbook on services marketing: Anita Nijssen, Mireille Paasen, Pascal Peeters, Hanneke Reys, Nancy Scheijven, Wink Versteegh, and Ellen Wen helped us greatly in speeding up the process of making this book come true. Danielle Francken helped in updating some tables with actual figures about the world wide service industries.

Moreover, what we learned in cooperating with our colleagues who were writing their PhD in the domain of services marketing and/or relationship marketing, was indispensable to our own understanding of service quality and long term relationships. We especially thank Marcel van Birgelen, Gaby Odekerken-Schröder, Jos Schijns, Mireille Suchanek, Karin Venetis and Martin Wetzels for the opportunity of sharing ideas. Moreover, the close cooperation with the other colleagues in marketing departments led to many stimulating ideas; many thanks to Gary

Bamossy, Josee Bloemer, Ruud Fontijn, Ignaas van Kooten, Jos Lemmink, Charles Pahud de Montagnes and Ko de Ruyter. A special word of thanks is for Jos Lemmink who gave wonderful support in writing Chapter Six on market research in service industries, for Luci Moorman whose contribution to the section on waiting and queueing in Chapter Ten was indispensable, for Peter Bollen, who taught us more about business process reengineering (Chapter Ten), and for Jos Ahlers in producing data on the Brand Asset Valuator.

This project started four years ago after we had published the first edition of our Dutch textbook on services marketing. Cathy Peck encouraged us to write an international edition. We did not realize at the time what an immense project we had got involved in, nor the dynamics of the publishing industry. Now that the project is finished, her ideas have come true.

We completed this project with the wonderful support of the Wiley team: Steve Hardman, Mary Seddon, Dawn Booth, See Hanson, Anne Wals, and many others from the production staff. They have had a thorough job meeting deadlines and correcting our English. The unknown reviewers provided us with many suggestions and ideas that we have used to improve the quality of the text. We hope we have met their stimulating demands in a sound way.

March, 1998

Hans Kasper, Maastricht
Piet van Helsdingen, Sofia
Wouter de Vries jr, Amsterdam

introduction to part one

THE SERVICES DOMAIN

This book is about services marketing management in an international context. The first part is devoted to elaborating on the fundamentals of services marketing management, defining services, developing a typology of services that can be used to structure all the knowledge in this field, market orientation and the service environment. Once these concepts are known to the reader, the framework is set for all the other topics that can be applied to be(come) a market-oriented service provider, creating service breakthroughs, delivering superior customer value with a high degree of employee satisfaction. Excellent service quality is a particular means to that end. This applies to companies working in a particular region or country, as well as for companies working in turbulent international environments.

The benefits from studying this part of the book are summarized in the next overview.

Part One: The Services Domain

FUNDAMENTALS OF SERVICES MARKETING (Chapter 1)

- define services;

- reproduce the basic characteristics of services;

- understand the concept of market orientation;

- distinguish between customer orientation and competitor orientation;

- understand the need of relationship marketing;

- define the essential features of a market oriented strategy in a service company;

- report on the importance of the service sector in many different countries;

- understand the complexity of internationalization in services; and

- circumscribe and argue the overall framework, perspective or marketing philosophy applied in this book.

CLASSIFYING SERVICES (Chapter 2)

- reproduce the specific characteristics of services;

- mention the main implications of these characteristics;

- recall the many criteria to be used in classifying services and service delivery processes;

- classify services and service delivery processes;

- understand the classification proposed by the authors;

- argue the relevance of the four types of services we have developed;

- explain why and how these four types of services can be used in describing and analyzing the strategies and actual performance of service organizations; and

- start analyzing the many service experiences you come across every day.

SERVICE ENVIRONMENT (Chapter 3)

- a structured and periodic external analysis by scanning the environment is of vital importance for a service provider in order to survive;

- the growth in the service sector is fuelled by various marketing related trends;

- a comprehensive framework of the external analysis consisting of sequentially examining the macro-environment, the environment of the service sector and the competition enables managers to make their own judgement of the risks and opportunities for their organizations;

- the insights from these separate analyses can be utilized in the process of strategic planning, marketing planning and in the development of new services; and

- major developments in selected service industries world wide make rapid changes in the business environment of individual companies.

Part Two: At The Heart

FROM BUYING BEHAVIOR TO RELATIONSHIPS
(Chapter 4)

SERVICE QUALITY
(Chapter 5)

Part Three: Strategic Issues

COLLECTING AND
MANAGING MARKET
INFORMATION
(Chapter 6)

STRATEGIC PLANNING AT
CORPORATE LEVEL
(Chapter 7)

INTERNATIONALIZATION
OF SERVICES
(Chapter 9)

SERVICES MARKETING
PLANNING IN STRATEGIC
BUSINESS UNITS
(Chapter 8)

Part Four: Services Marketing Mix

PEOPLE,
ORGANIZATION AND PROCESSES
(Chapter 10)

DEVELOPING AND PROVIDING
SERVICES
(Chapter 11)

COMMUNICATION
(Chapter 12)

DISTRIBUTION
(Chapter 13)

PRICING
(Chapter 14)

IMPLEMENTATION
AND CONTROL
(Chapter 15)

CHAPTER ONE

FUNDAMENTALS OF SERVICES MARKETING

After studying this chapter you should be able to:

- *define services;*
- *reproduce the basic characteristics of services;*
- *understand the concept of market orientation;*
- *distinguish between customer orientation and competitor orientation;*
- *understand the need of relationship marketing;*
- *define the essential features of a market-oriented strategy in a service company;*
- *report on the importance of the service sector in many different countries*
- *understand the complexity of internationalization in services; and*
- *circumscribe and argue the overall framework, perspective or marketing philosophy applied.*

LEFT: *Care in 'Swansational' services*

1.1 INTRODUCTION

Service practice 1-1 One day we'll fly away?

The airline industry is a very important part of the service sector, nationally and internationally. More and more people fly these days. Competition is fierce, especially in the US after deregulation. Did it really benefit the customer, the employee and the shareholder? See what Bill Saporito reports about it in Fortune, April 3, 1995 (p. 38). under the heading "GOING NOWHERE FAST".

"Here's all you need to know about the operating logic of the airline industry: they use really big jets, capable of carrying hundreds of passengers. They use one door to board them. Why does this industry act as if it has 100,000 seats and no brains? What other industry gets caught price fixing twice and still manages to lose $12 billion in five years? What other business intentionally puts the customer last?

You don't really fly today, as much as climb a salmon ladder of anxiety. From ticketing to bag claim, you fight to get upstream, only to become sushi at any moment to one of the airline grizzlies – suspicious flight cancelations, scant comfort, bad attitude at high altitude, or schedule lotto in the hub-and-spoke network – a clever system for collecting a lot of very angry people in one location.

Airlines and passengers each want the same thing: a pleasant experience for a fair price. But there is a mean dialectic at work. The worse it is for you, the better it is for them. They want to fill every seat on every jet – you want a row to yourself so you can move your leg an inch without the person next to you mistaking your intentions. Airline marketeers spin service fantasies, while their operations managers search for new ways to cut back."

Airlines have to be on time with respect to departure and arrival. Flight attendants have to serve their customers well on board. Insurance companies should have the right policies for their insured passengers, then serve their cleint well, for instance, by giving the right information on the phone or via their agents. The after sales departments of manufacturers of heavy equipment like, John Deere or JCB, should be able to serve their customers immediately in order not to disturb the customers' processes when one of the machines has a break down. They have to satisfy their customers, delivering quality in goods and services, thus creating brand loyalty. The local real estate agent has to fulfil the needs of those planning to buy or sell a house; (s)he has to do that personally. A university has to offer the right courses that students want to take and which employers consider relevant. Moreover, these universities must give the professors who are developing and teaching those courses, complete research facilities on a fundamental level and not forget the practical application.

magic How can this servicing, adding value or creating value, be achieved? Can only magic accomplish it? Or, is it really possible to achieve these goals for the two parties (the customer and the company) simultaneously? We believe it is possible. We argue why and how in this book. It is not a matter of magic, although it is a great challenge to be(come) market oriented, motivate the company's employees to serve the customer well, deliver excellent service quality, satisfy the customers and even keep them for life.

make the intangible service as tangible as possible

To explain the essence of services it is possible to compare a service provider with a magician. Where the magician is well trained and skilled in making visible and tangible things disappear, service providers work in quite the opposite direction. They try to make the intangible service as tangible as possible. The customers then know what the service is all about. They may then be willing to invest time and money in buying something that is considered to be worthwhile.

domain of services marketing

This chapter contains a brief overview of the domain of (international) services marketing management. The domain of services marketing is becoming more and more important within the whole discipline of marketing. This holds true for the academic world (the theoretical side of this field) as well as for the practical side (business life, public sector). Therefore it is necessary to have the words "services" and "marketing" well defined. Sections 1.2 and 1.3 deal with the definition of services and the basic characteristics of services. Sections 1.4 and 1.5 contain a short summary to give some general ideas about marketing and forms an overview of what we consider important building blocks of market-oriented services including amongst others the key success factors in service marketing. Since the service sector's part of the national economy in many countries is growing rapidly, ample attention is paid to the internationalization of services. Another argument for doing so is the fact that many service organizations have branches in many other countries nowadays. Section 1.6 shows in global terms the complexity of internationalizing services. In the last section 1.7 we present our perspective about market-oriented

managing services is more than magic

services marketing management. After reading this chapter it transpires that managing services is more than magic.

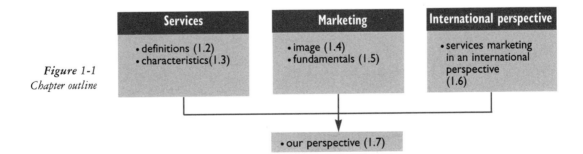

Figure 1-1
Chapter outline

1.2 WHAT ARE SERVICES?

The German word "Dienstleistung" and the French word "service" are translated simply into the English word "service". But then, a wide variety of other connotations are given, for the word "service", for instance:

- O.H.M.S. (like James Bond, On Her Majesty's Secret Service);
- no service today (churches);
- one good turn deserves another;
- render a person a service;
- be on duty;
- refuse orders;
- put one's knowledge at the service of ...;
- what can I do for you?;
- we shall be happy to oblige you.

Many of these issues can be detected at the Ritz Carlton hotels.

Service practice 1-2 Ladies and Gentlemen of the Ritz Carlton

The Ritz Carlton Hotel Company has a comprehensive service quality program that is integrated into marketing and business objectives. Hallmarks of the program include participatory executive leadership, thorough information gathering, coordinated planning and execution, and a trained workforce that is empowered "to move heaven and earth" to satisfy customers. Of these, committed employees rank as the most essential element. All are schooled in the company's "Gold Standards". which set out Ritz-Carlton's service credo and basics of premium service.

The corporate motto is "ladies and gentlemen serving ladies and gentlemen" according to one of the brochures of the company.

This way of looking at providing services is completely different from the experience we all have once in a while (and hopefully not more often) when employees at other service organizations consider serving the customer as an awful obligation. The Ritz Carlton shows it really can be different.

DEFINING SERVICES

definitions   The services marketing literature will come across several definitions. We will mention a few of them and stress the commonalities.

Christian Grönroos[1] (1990b) defines a service as:

> "...an activity or series of activities of more or less intangible nature that normally, but not necessarily, take place in interactions between the customer and service employees and/or physical resources or goods and/or systems of the service provider, which are provided as solutions to customer problems."

Philip Kotler[2] (1991) defines services as:

"...any act or performance that one party can offer to another that is essentially intangible and does not result in the ownership of anything. Its production may or may not be tied to a physical product."

John Bateson[3] (1992) argues:

"The goods/service dichotomy is a subtly changing spectrum, with firms moving their position within this spectrum over time. A good example of a good/service dichotomy is Domino's Pizza, a home-delivery pizza chain. Is the customer buying goods (a pizza) or a service (a guaranteed arrival within 30 minutes).

"The word service should be read with the following caveat: to the extent that the benefits are delivered to the consumer by a service rather than a good".

Valarie Zeithaml and Mary Jo Bitner[4] (1996) hold that:

"in the most simple terms, *services are deeds, processes and performances.*"

Their broader definition, which is in line with this simple one, is:

"services include all economic activities whose output is not a physical product or construction, is generally consumed at the time it is produced, and provides added value in forms (such as convenience, amusement, timeliness, comfort or health) that are essentially intangible concerns of its first purchaser."

So, in talking about services we have to deal with something that is intangible, whose buying does not necessarily result in the ownership by means of a physical transfer of the object but still creates benefits during (or after) a particular interaction and experience. Before we can give a proper definition of services, first we have to discuss in the next section a few questions about some key elements, which can be defined from all these definitons:

- are services really intangible ?
- what is a bundle of benefits?
- what does the experience mean?
- what does the interaction mean? and
- the physicical transfer of title: yes or no?

SOME RELEVANT QUESTIONS ABOUT SERVICES

Are services really intangible?

demarcation line between tangibility and intangibility

In principle, services are indeed intangible. However, the demarcation line between tangibility and intangibility will not always be that easy to draw. Sometimes, a particular activity can be a service such as, e.g. teaching; sometimes it can be part of a tangible product (e.g. teaching and training employees how a new copying machine works). To a certain extent this is in line with the three types of products Kotler (1994) distinguishes: the core product, the tangible product and the augmented product. Here, the augmented product is seen as the comprehensive product embracing the other two plus all the additional services provided (like installation, after sales, repair and maintenance, etc).

This made us believe that it is important to distinguish between core services and augmented services, the latter being the core service plus the additional services. The core service is mostly intangible, while the additional service may give the impression to the customer that the service becomes more tangible. However, many of those additional services still remain intangible. Moreover, when the additional services are closely related to a physical product, they may also be perceived as partly tangible (see the definiton of Bateson and the goods/service dichotomy).

What is a bundle of benefits?
Fitzsimmons and Fitzsimmons (1994, p. 24) discuss the "service package" concept and define it as "a bundle of goods and services provided in some environment". This bundle consists of supporting facility, facilitating goods, explicit services and implicit services.

bundle of benefits

The phrase "bundle of benefits" is important in understanding consumer behavior. It is a reflection of what consumers expect from a service. What is in it for me? How will it satisfy my needs and wants? How will it solve my problem or contribute to maintaining or improving my life style or status? So, it has to do with the functional and psychosociological consequences of buying services.[5] If these consequences are positive we can talk about the benefits of a service. If consequences are negative the term perceived risk is used. So a service may have

perceived risk

positive (benefits) as well as negative consequences for a consumer. Perceived risk will turn out to be one of the core issue in the analysis of consumer behavior with respect to services.

excellent service quality

customer satisfaction

The bundle of benefits and the way services are delivered are aimed at creating customer satisfaction. Excellent service quality is a crucial means to accomplish customer satisfaction.

What does the experience mean?
Some services, like physical goods, should provide benefits. Customers experience those benefits in an intangible form. This takes place during a process of interaction, the service encounter. Then customer and service provider meet and both contribute to (or: participate in) the production of the service. For the customer, it can be said

the service experience

that (s)he perceives what is going on and what the result will be: the service experience.

meet expectations

The consumer will also have expectations about the service experience. It is important for service organizations to meet, or exceed, those expectations.

Service practice 1-3 The foundation of services[6]

"...the essence of service marketing is service. Service quality is the foundation of services marketing."

What does the interaction mean?

In many cases, the production and consumption of services take place at the same moment. Production and consumption occur simultaneously; they cannot be separated. So, consumer and service provider interact during the service experience.

servuction process

Eiglier and Langeard (1987) have developed the concept of the "servuction process". This word is a combination of services and production, indicating the simultaneous production and consumption of services.

A part of this servuction process is visible to the customer. Here the customer interacts with personnel which are called the "front office personnel". These persons and their activities are supported by the invisible part of the service provider: the back office personnel. In general, the servuction process differs from a production process of a tangible good in the following respects:

the moments of truth

- interaction between front office personnel and the client. The direct contact between service provider and customer is essential. During these events, the actual service delivery takes place. These are "the moments of truth" where the organization actually shows what they can do and how they meet expectations set;

physical surrounding

- certain degree of relevancy of the physical surrounding to the customer; and,

interaction

- mutual interaction between customers during the production process. Customer A will be affected by the presence of customer B and C (see Figure 1-2).

The borderline between front office and back office is not fixed forever within a particular service organization. It may change over time. Thus, it may be subject to the marketing policy of a service provider.

service encounter

The servuction process refers to human encounters in both a profit and a non-profit setting. People interact with one another, unless a (large) part of the service encounter is substituted by machines (like the automated teller machines in banks). This offers the opportunity for people to start building some kinds of relationships

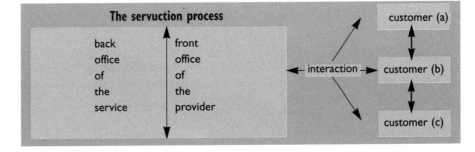

Figure 1-2 The servuction process

*Service
practice
1-4
Waiting:
where, with
who and for
how long?*

The difference between a servuction and a production process can be explained by one possible (negative) consequence or effect of the interaction between people: waiting times. Normally, people do not appreciate it if they have to wait, but there are some situations, depending on where, how long and with whom you have to wait, in which people do care less. For example, if the environment is nice and pleasant (a restaurant, stadium or amusement park), if the people around you are amusing (your child or girlfriend) and if the waiting time is acceptable (people sometimes perceive a certain waiting time as an indication of quality in a restaurant or a hospital).

relationships

with one another in these service encounters. Building these relationships is important for several reasons:

- it offers the opportunity to learn about each others' wishes, whims, preferences, capabilities, opportunities, etc. This may sharpen the knowledge of the expectations about the other "party involved in the interaction"; and
- secondly, existing relationships may function as a means to keep customers.

The physical transfer of title: yes or no?

*no physical delivery
of title*

As we have stated, services are intangible. This implies that they cannot be stored or transferred. Therefore, no physical delivery of title can occur with respect to chairs in a theater, seats in an aeroplane, or rooms in an hotel. This is not always the case, however.

Quite often, the result of the service encounter may be that the customer has something of a tangible nature, like airline tickets, money from the bank, insurance policy or the marketing consultant's report. It should be realized that the prime goal of these transfers is not the possession of something tangible. With insurances, the possession of a policy is not the prime target, but the security provided in case of illness or a fire at home. The marketing consultant's report as such is not important, as its content is the consultant's advice written down (for instance to reread, to store, or to convince others).

When services are added to a physical product (like the after sales services of a car) the customer possesses the car and knows what will be provided when necessary. These services may look more tangible but in fact there is no difference, just the car is tangible. Then, it may seem that a physical delivery takes place.

So, in principle, a service is intangible but in many situations the outcome of the service process may be partly of a tangible nature. Then, there seems to be a transfer of title but in essence the nature of most core services makes the transfer of title superfluous.

OUR DEFINITION OF SERVICES

We can now construct a broad definition of services, in which the reader will recognize the relevant topics:

> Services are originally intangible and relatively quickly perishable activities whose buying takes place in an interaction process aimed at creating customer satisfaction but during this interactive consumption this does not always lead to material possession.

delivering excellent service quality and creating value to the customer

A wide variety of activities can be labelled as services. We can think of tourism, education, health care, protection, retailing, repair, maintenance, national and local public services, etc. Some of these services are practised by profit oriented organizations like tour operators, shops and private hospitals, while others are practised by non profit organizations like the police, university hospitals or local government. Nevertheless, in all instances delivering excellent service quality and creating value to the customer is the corner stone of success.

In the Western world, it appears that in many countries more than 50% of their Gross National Product is "produced" in the service sector. Also, a very large number of people are employed in the profit and non profit service sector. The importance of the service sector is also reflected in the proportion of household income spent on services. The figures are now much higher than 10 or 20 years ago, let alone compared to 50 years ago.

Service practice 1-5 Some figures about American services[7]

- In the USA the service industry grew as a percentage of total GNP from 43.4% (1970), 46.3% (1980) to 51.3% (1990).
- The same picture can be given if services are related to the Total Personal Consumption in the USA: 44.3% (1970), 48% (1980) and 55% (1990).
- The American service industry became also more important in employing people: 63.5% (1970), 67.3% (1980) and 71.8% (1990) of total employment.
- Some examples of large American companies in different service categories are:
  - commercial banking: Citicorp (81,000 people) and BankAmerica (79,225);
  - retailing: Wal-Mart (520,000), Sears (308,500), Kmart (344,000);
  - transportation: United Parcel (286,000) and AMR (118,900).

1.3 THE BASIC CHARACTERISTICS OF SERVICES

intangibility

In general, services are intangible. The intangibility feature is the most dominant one in defining services, determining the other three characteristics: simultaneous production and consumption, heterogeneity and perishability. Consequently, transferring the service usually requires the presence and participation of the customer during the production and consumption of the service which take place simultaneously. This *human influence* human influence of the service, including the employee and the customer in the whole process of producing and consuming a service, often leads to a fluctuating quality of the service. That is why we have cited Berry and Parasuraman (1991) (see Service practice 1-3) with their view on service quality, just to show how important it is to control this service quality and motivate your personnel. Then, the heterogeneity in service quality could be avoided. Of course, as we will see in later chapters about the Services Marketing Mix, there are more ways to enhance the homogeneity of delivering services.

In order to better memorize these four characteristics, some authors[8] talk about the four I's of services. These are intangibility, inseparability, inconsistency and inventory.

relative concepts

This section shows that the four aspects of services should be considered as "relative concepts". For all concepts may come to the fore to a certain degree (and not always for 100%). So:

intangibility
inseparability
inconsistency
inventory

- intangibility: as a degree of (in)tangibility:
- inseparability: as a degree of simultaneous production and consumption;
- inconsistency: as a degree of heterogeneity; and
- inventory: as a degree of perishability.

INTANGIBILITY: THE DEGREE OF (IN)TANGIBILITY

This feature has been already introduced. Originally, services are intangible. Services are an activity, an experience and not a thing. Looking at services this way, the demarcation line between goods and services becomes rather diffuse. In daily life, service organizations are trying to make their intangible offer as tangible as possible, while many manufacturers (for instance, of fast moving consumer goods) try to create an (intangible) image around their goods instead of focussing on the tangible aspects of their goods in advertising. Also, many services cannot be provided without tangibles. How could transportation services be provided when there were no planes, trucks, cars, boats or trains? How could a hospital function without advanced technological equipment and beds? In that manner one could even challenge the traditional notion that services are intangible. However, we will stick to the common notion of intangibility in this book. In fact, we believe that intangibility determines the three other basic characteristics of services.

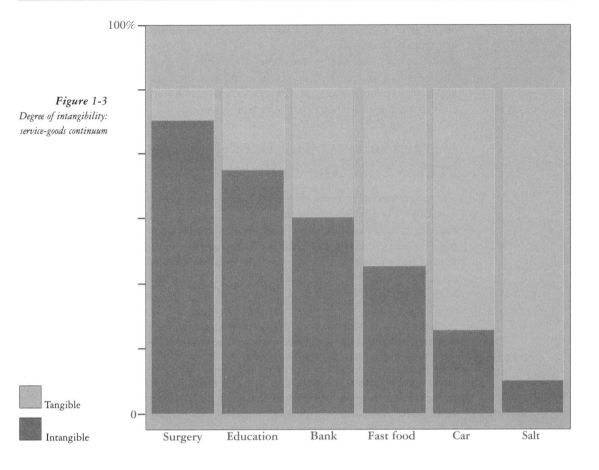

Figure 1-3
Degree of intangibility:
service-goods continuum

Tangible

Intangible

Service practice 1-6 Core services with tangible aspects and core products with intangible components

The financial services provided by universal banks like UBS, Deutsche Bank, Barclays, ABN Amro, Crédit Lyonnais or the Bank of America do not only consist of intangible services like capital investment, monetary transactions and receiving money, which activities are quite invisible. The banks' services also include tangible daily accounts, files, and folders explaining financial issues.

Computer firms like Digital, IBM, Olivetti and Tulip used to be the firms building all kinds of tangible computers, from main frames to PC's. In the eighties, many of them realized it was hard to earn a profit on their computers. The market for computer services was much more attractive. This service aspect has been used on many occasions to position the computer firms. They also started "computer clubs" in order to promote the (home) use of computers. At the same time, they tried to build a relationship with the computer owner through these clubs. Now some computer suppliers say: we offer a total concept in solving information problems.

The degree of tangibility or the goods/services dichotomy can be visualized by the intangibility continuum, (Figure 1.3) based on Shostack's (1977) idea of the goods–services continuum. Her continuum ranges from goods to services; our continuum ranges from services to goods. In this way, the figure better demonstrates the importance of services and the service sector in the Western economies. It also makes clear that services are not a particular kind of goods.

INSEPARABILITY: THE DEGREE OF SIMULTANEOUS PRODUCTION AND CONSUMPTION

consumer has to participate

The consumer has to participate in the production of services on many occasions, sometimes even without knowing it. This is in sharp contrast to the production of durables or non-durables. As a consequence, typically consumers do not know who makes a particular tangible product. For instance, not many readers will know in which country or city the toothpaste they use, or fast-moving consumer goods like magarine, washing powder detergent or marmalade, are produced. On the other hand, they often know exactly who served them at the bank, taught them in school, styled their hair, or served them in a pub. In many cases, the consumer can not only pinpoint who served him/her, but knows him/her personally. Mostly, the service process can only start when the customer is present. It is difficult to provide a hair cut when no one is in the barber shop.

customer is present

interaction

This personal contact is meant by the the words "interactive consumption" and "interaction process" in our definition of services. This interaction may be referred to as "the service encounter"[9]. When both parties – physically – meet, the production of the service can take place. Both, the customer and the employee have to perform particular activities. In other words, they have to apply particular roles. In order to

the service encounter

Service practice 1-7
Which role am I supposed to play?

The script for the service encounter in a fast food restaurant is quite clear to almost everybody. TV commercials show how people behave at McDonalds, Burger King or Wendy's. People know they have to stand in line and order at the counter. The customer may decide then whether (s)he eats the meal in the restaurant or takes it home. There will be no waiter serving you at your table. (However, recently, in the US McDonalds are experimenting with waiters in one of their restaurants. This is a kind of differentiation to the traditional formula.) Probably, the meal will take just 20 minutes to eat.

When you go to a two star Michelin restaurant, you know you will be seated, the menu will be offered to you by the waiter or waitress, and sometimes your (female) company will receive the menu without prices on it. You know the role which you are supposed to play: tell your choice to the waiter and they will serve you. The meal will take longer than 20 minutes and probably you will be out dining for a whole evening. It is very unusual in this kind of restaurant to order and take the meal home. In American restaurants you may ask for a doggy bag when you are finished; in Europe that is very unusual and in some countries even impolite.

script

roles

know exactly what is expected from both parties, it could be helpful if a particular script existed indicating the roles to be played. Then, it is - hopefully - clear what each party is expected to do. These scripts can become clear through experiences with the service provider or can be communicated in advance.

This simultaneity in production and consumption implies services can be affected by human beings at three levels:

1. the environment in which the process of producing and consuming the service takes place;
2. the personnel involved; and
3. the consumer/customer.

physical environment

behavior of personnel

customer's mood and needs

The greater a service's intangibility the more important the physical environment in which the service takes place and its physical closeness will be. The atmosphere and ambiance in a restaurant is one of the issues determining a dinner's total quality. The behavior of a restaurant's personnel may affect this quality in a positive as well as in a negative way. The role of these persons should not be underestimated. They provide added value and security or safety to people who are dining at that particular restaurant for the first time. Those guests coming regularly to that restaurant will be welcomed personally and not posed questions about entrees or main courses they do not like (the waiters should know that). On the other hand, most service business is people's business. Therefore, the Dutch expression holds: Making mistakes is always possible when you are working.[10] And finally, the customer's mood and needs are relevant here. These moods or needs are not always recognizable or controllable by the service provider. Although a waiter will have difficulties in detecting the capricious behavior of customers quickly, it should be taken into account that different states of mind will count at different moments in time. The design and layout of a restaurant or theater may help customers coming in to reach the right mood. The chairs in a church are different from those in a movie theater; the same holds for the layout of a fast food restaurant and a two star Michelin restaurant. Music is quite often used to bring people to a particular mood. This applies to waiting rooms in airports, restrooms in restaurants or shopping malls.

All these issues are relevant in shaping the required participation of the customer to the process of producing services.

INCONSISTENCY: THE DEGREE OF HETEROGENEITY

customer is an essential part of this whole process

It will be clear that the customer is not only subject to the service provider, but actively participates in the process of producing the service. The customer is an essential part of this whole process. This means that standardizing services is quite difficult on many occasions. It raises questions like:

- who controls the customer?
- who tells the customer what (s)he is expected to do? and,
- what is the influence of time on service quality?

controlling people and time

A service provider should try to find the optimum in controlling people and time

*Service
practice
1-8
Getting your
own money
back*

Remembering the pin-code, typing the right amount of money one wants to fetch from the ATM, indicating whether one wants a receipt or not, etc. are still activities to be carried out by the customer who feels the line growing and growing behind him/her when he does not succeed in this service encounter with a machine. Also, the weather (wind, snow, sunshine, etc.) plus the length of the waiting line, will all co-determine the quality of fetching your own money from the ATM.

output

with respect to these quality evaluations. The chance of heterogeneity in the final output of service delivery processes will still be large, even when companies try to standardize their service operations, provide manuals and train their employees. Automation and reducing the role of people in these processes cannot completely reduce the impact of people and environment on service quality. The automated teller machine has largely contributed to this but still depends on some activities the customer has to perform himself.

*objective and
subjective criteria*

A complication in controlling the role of people is the fact that not only objective and/or technical issues are evaluated. The subjective preference will be relevant as well and in some cases even more relevant. The customer will use objective and subjective criteria to evaluate service quality and the whole service process of which (s)he is part of. This makes this evaluation a complicated issue and hard to grasp for

quality control

a service provider. Part of the quality control of certain airlines on their flights is measuring the temperature of the coffee. The standard is that the coffee should have a certain temperature. This is an objective standard and therefore measurable. But some people like it hot, while others prefer their coffee at a lower temperature. The subjective norms are deciding whether the coffee tastes good or not.

One objective as well as subjective criteria is time. With respect to time, the presence of the customer in participating in the servuction process implies that the amount of time used will be evaluated as well. For consumers cannot allocate this time to other activities. So, it is important for service providers to know:

*the opportunity
cost of time*

- what costs the customer has to make (see also the chapter on pricing); and,
- with what other activities the participation of the customer competes.

Some consumers will, for instance, consider the various ways they may allocate (use) their time: the opportunity cost of time – this will hold especially when people have to wait. This waiting time will have an objective aspect (how many minutes does one have to wait?) and an subjective aspect (how long is the waiting time perceived?). If these two differ, there is a problem when the subjective waiting time is perceived to be longer than the objective one. One simple solution is to make waiting more attractive than just sitting or standing in line.

It will be clear that people and time cannot be separated from one another here. They are interrelated. At one moment consumers may have more time to spend than at another moment. This affects their willingness to participate extensively in a service process. All this means that the work of a service provider is quite complicated. The

*Service
practice
1-9
Waiting is an
attraction?*

Waiting for attractions in Disneyland in California, Walibi in Belgium, De Efteling in the Netherlands, Futuroscope in France or Phantasialand near Cologne (Germany), is not a pleasant way of spending your time in such a park. Especially not when you are queueing there with your kids. One way of making it more attractive to the customers is providing them with entertainment and information. Providing information on how long it will take to get from a particular spot to the entrance, gives an indication about the length of the waiting time: you know when it will be over.

Also, providing some kind of entertainmennt and letting things happen around the queue (like dancers on a platform, a movie on a TV screen) reduces the chance of negative feelings about waiting and decreases the subjective waiting time.

moods of the customer which may change per situation and lead to different preferences are partly due to this. This calls for a proper understanding of consumer behavior with respect to services and how satisfaction can be created. It also shows that the degree of heterogeneity in the quality of service is affected by many variables and depends on many situational factors.

INVENTORY: THE DEGREE OF PERISHABILITY

If a service becomes more and more intangible, the opportunities to store the service become less and less. In other words, the degree of intangibility is increasing the degree of perishability. Often, services which are perishable cannot be kept in stock. That is why the cost of warehousing and storage are quite often low or completely lacking in service companies. This may be seen as a positive result of perishability. However, not having the possiblity to store services creates the complicated issue of "yield management". Frequently, managers in service organizations have to face fluctuations in demand or in capacity. That is why many service providers deliberately strive for minimizing un-used capacity in quiet times and "no sales" in busy times. Although, to a lesser extent, it even counts for electronic services such as the Internet, i.e. in Europe if America starts working at approximately 3.00 AM Greenwich time. Information technology may dramatically change this "distribution-

perishability

yield management

*Service
practice
1-10
How free is a
free Air Mile?*

In the United Kingdom, Canada and the Netherlands it is possible to save Air Miles by buying goods and services at certain banks, stores, petrol stations, etc. Each consumer joining the program has a personal account on which the miles are registered automatically. Most people "sell" their loyalty to the store or the product to get a free ticket. After saving and buying for an average period of two years, many people can fly free to a number of destinations. They are not completely free, because. Air Mile flyers are only allowed to sit on un-used capacity seats. The main goal of the airlines participating in the program for Air Miles is the filling of capacity rather than giving loyal people a free ticket.

problem" of services and create new opportunities to better serve the customer.

Now that we have discussed the most important characteristics of services and managing services in broad terms, it is time to turn to the marketing side, for that is the other corner stone in "services *marketing* management". Firstly, let us have a look at what is marketing all about basically.

1.4 THE IMAGE OF MARKETING

The word marketing is often used these days. Sometimes, it is supposed to be the cure for all problems organizations face in the market place. Marketing knowledge and skills are required in many jobs. However, many organizations do not always make clear exactly what is meant by that. Many misunderstandings about this concept and discipline exist, not only in business life but also in academia. This implies that personal norms, values and opinions on marketing will be reflected in the way the *domain of marketing* is defined and discussed. Therefore, it is necessary to pay attention to this topic before we can even start a discussion on service marketing in an international perspective.

domain of marketing

In discussions about marketing, one often finds people who consider marketing as a trick to sell goods and services. Sometimes, people even think it is a trick designed to sell products people do not even want to buy or use. Marketing, then, is very much associated with pushing people to buy goods and services they do not really want or need. Such an opinion was quite common in the seventies and early eighties. Those opinions appeared in studies about consumer attitudes towards marketing and *marketing philosophy* consumerism.[11] They are quite opposite to the real content of marketing philosophy.

marketing philosophy

A research project among students taking the basic course in marketing was done to test for these popular misunderstandings. It showed that these students associated the word marketing mainly with:

- advertising (38% of the 205 students);
- consumers (29%);
- market research (18%);
- sales (17%);
- products (15%); and
- marketing strategy (12%).

image of marketing

That was the short list of concepts determining the image of marketing. These findings were in line with common beliefs. It is interesting to see whether this image is a universal one, is it typical, or does it exist in other countries as well? The same topic was studied at various business schools all over the world to decipher what students think about marketing (Kasper, 1993). These answers are an indication about what the universal image of marketing is. The findings are presented in Figure 1-4.

Figure 1-4
The image of marketing

Items	University of Lund, Sweden	Swedish School of Economics & Business Administration Helsinki, Finland	University of Ghent, Belgium	University of Groningen, The Netherlands	Technical University Delft, The Netherlands	University of Innsbruck, Austria	Carleton University, Canada	Marquette University, USA	Purdue University, USA
Advertising	57.3%	69.2%	83.8%	74.1%	35.1%	61.9%	31.4%	48.2%	43.0%
Sales	30.9	46.2	57.3	33.0	28.9	37.0	51.4	47.0	54.0
Products		11.5	15.4	14.3	22.8	16.6	14.3	25.3	16.0
Promotions	16.8		17.9				24.5	12.1	
Market research			16.2	17.8	16.7	21.5			
Market			12.8	11.7	10.5	12.7			
Money	24.1	11.5			25.4				19.0
Commercials			16.2				17.1	19.3	
Consumers								13.3	
Price				13.3					
Public relations	13.2	13.5							
Customer contact		15.4							15.0
Buying									
Communications							14.3		
Segmentation							14.3		
Business			12.8						14.0
Influencing									
Distribution								12.1	
Positioning			10.3					12.1	
Sales representatives									
Number of respondents (=100%)	220	52	117	540	114	181	35	83	100

*These findings given here are the result of the following question: "What do you think of immediately when you hear the word marketing?"
Name three key words: ....
Only those answers counting for more than 10% of the respondents at each university are presented here

communications, Now it appears that all kinds of communications, especially advertising, sales and products, are the most frequently mentioned attributes of the image of marketing. A number of items are also present but not so dominantly, namely market research, market and the consumer.

1.5 FUNDAMENTALS OF MARKETING

Our main conclusion from these findings, regarding the marketing image, is that there are minimal associations with items like market orientation, quality, segmentation, need satisfaction, relationships or servicing, in the image of marketing. These fundamentals do not come to the fore, while very visible operational issues are dominant. In our opinion, the important long(er) term issues, upon which every mar-

fundamentals of marketing keting strategy should be based, are lacking in the image of marketing. Therefore, we will pay ample attention to the following fundamentals of marketing in the first chapter of our book:

- market orientation;
- customer expectations and quality perceptions;
- internal organization and personnel; and
- key success factors in services organizations.

MARKET ORIENTATION

Simply stated, marketing is based on three benchmarks in the market. This fits into the strategic marketing concept as developed by George Day and Robin Wensley (1983). These are:

- the customer;
- the competitor; and
- the organization itself.

They all (inter)act on a particular market. The organization should provide services which actually satisfy the needs, wishes, whims and preferences of present and future customers. In order to accomplish this difficult and complex mission, an organization should select a proper target group. Focussing on these customers is called the

customer orientation organization's customer orientation. Customer orientation may lead to different services for different customers. In terms of Michael Porter's strategies (1980), it is possible to speak here about differentiation strategies and/or focus strategies.

The organization's own services should be better than those services offered by competitors. The customer should then ascribe a higher quality-price ratio or added

competitors value to the organization's service than to the competitors'. In order to realize this, a company should know:

- which services are perceived as competing by the customer;
- which organizations "produce" these services;
- in which way are they produced (how much and what kind of customer participation is required);
- what are competitors likely to do in the near future, etc.

In short, the organization should know when, where and how consumers perceive them as different from their competitors. Only then, can a company position itself properly on the grounds of quality or price. Quality-price ratios quite often have to do with the costs and cost structure of the company. So, to a large extent, this item has to do with Michael Porter's strategy and ideas about cost leadership.

George Day[12] took a similar way of reasoning when he argued that "competitive superiority is revealed in the market as some combination of superior customer value and lowest delivered cost." and "The essence of competitive advantage is a positioning theme that sets a business apart from its rivals in ways that are meaningful to the target customers. The most succesful themes are built on some combination of three thrusts:

- better (through superior quality or service);
- faster (by being able to sense and satisfy shifting customer requirements faster than competitors); and
- closer (with the creation of durable relationships).

The task for management is to simultaneously find a compelling theme and ensure continuing superiority in the skills, resources, and controls that will be the source of this advantage over target competitors."

market orientation

The combination of the visions of customer orientation and competitor orientation ends up in the concept of market orientation.[13] Market orientation, then, is a

Figure 1-5
Market orientation:
better, faster, closer

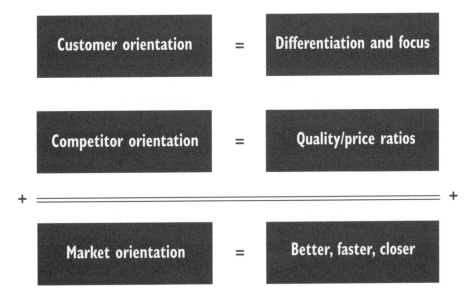

| Customer orientation | = | Differentiation and focus |
| Competitor orientation | = | Quality/price ratios |

+ ═══════════════════════════════════ +

| Market orientation | = | Better, faster, closer |

combination of these two concepts and also a combination of the two kinds of strategies mentioned (see Figure 1-5). Market orientation is a first operationalization of the marketing concept. It is still at a very fundamental level. Therefore, the overall starting point is set for developing the marketing strategy, policy and plan. Each of these is concrete and operational, as Chapters Seven to Fourteen show.

So, what is new about it? Is market orientation indeed more than just the summing up of looking at the customer and the competitor? Of course, it is![14]

Not all organizations that look at both are able to formulate standards to translate the results of this external research into internal activities. Employees should be aware of the fact that it is crucial to use this information in all their activities and decision making processes and – of course – in the way they deal with customers and competitors on a day to day basis.

When information is considered as a crucial asset, market orientation can be defined as: "the organizationwide generation of market intelligence pertaining to current and future customer needs, dissemination of the intelligence across departments and organizationwide responsiveness to it."

generation of intelligence, dissemination of intelligence

The generation of intelligence focusses on collecting relevant information. The dissemination of intelligence spreads out the information across the departments. In fact, every employee should have relevant market information and an external orientation toward the market instead of only having a perspective on internal procedures.

cooperation

The result of the generation and dissemination of the relevant information has to be departments and people who work closely together or at least cooperate in a sound way. When the information is available, a corporate strategy, a marketing strategy and a positioning strategy can be formulated for each target group of customers. The resulting marketing plan should pay attention to the expectations of the customer, the quality of the services to be delivered, the internal organization, and the employees' relationship with the customers. The key success therefore lies in services and creating a market oriented culture as well. Based on all these studies, we will use the following, broad definition of market orientation in this book:

definition

"Market orientation is the degree to which an organization in all its thinking and acting (internally as well as externally) is guided by and committed to the factors determining the market behavior of the organization itself and its customers. The right internal and external actions, then, will create the benefits and value for the organization and their customers."

CUSTOMER EXPECTATIONS AND QUALITY PERCEPTION

Beside the market orientation, marketing has to pay attention to the expectation of customers and how they perceive quality.

customers' expectations

The first issue of customers' expectations is dealing with the fact that customers should know in advance what the service organization can do for them or may mean for them.

Service practice 1-11 Do borders change expectations?

In an international perspective, it is important to know that expectations on the same service may differ per country. What is considered appropriate in one country can be considered insufficient in another country.

A couple of years ago, a study on the quality of postal services was conducted in many countries in Europe. It appeared that Dutch people considered a proper mail delivery an overnight delivery. If we cross some borders in Europe this expectation is changing; the Italians were satisfied when a letter arrived three days after it was put in the mail box.

managing customer expectations, providing fair and honest information

Creating proper expectations is important for the service provider in order to avoid customers having expectations that cannot or will not be met. The service provider, therefore, has to communicate to customers what to expect from this organization and what not to expect. This is not a matter of manipulating the market but a matter of providing fair and honest information. Often, wrong, false or unjustified expectations will lead to dissatisfaction. In turn, dissatisfaction will perhaps lead to brand switching, complaining or negative word-of-mouth communication. Certainly, it will not lead to a high degree of brand loyalty or repeat purchases, let alone long lasting relationships between company and client. Managing customer expectations and providing fair and honest information, therefore, are important features of services marketing management.

asymmetry of information

When customers do not have any experience with or sufficient information from a particular service or service organization, it is hard to know in advance what to expect or how to judge the service provider. The lack of experience and information can be described as an asymmetry of information. An information asymmetry exists between the customer (having no information about the new service) and the service provider (having all the information about the service). This asymmetry can be solved mainly by providing information or building up a good reputation or brand name. In searching for information, consumers may use various characteristics, attributes or qualities of services. Often three kinds of search attributes or search qualities are distinguished. Zeithaml and Bitner (1996) maintain that search attributes are attributes which are quite easy to judge by the consumer before the service delivery actually takes place. They can be evaluated in advance. Usually, they involve tangible aspects, they are physically visible and are more related to the equipment than to the person delivering the service. Credence attributes, on the contrary, can only be judged a long time after the actual service delivery (only a long time after an operation do you know whether it has been succesful or not) and are therefore based on trusting people delivering the service. Experience attributes are positioned in between these two extremes of the (in)tangibility of service attributes. They are also quite difficult to evaluate in advance and mostly they can be experienced only during or shortly after the service delivery.

search attributes

credence attributes

experience attributes

quality perception

The issue of quality perception is important because the customer's evaluation of the service and hence the customer's quality judgment about the service is determined to a very large extent by the employee's behavior. Various models show that there is some relationship between expectations and the quality of the delivered service.

Everybody – front as well as back office employees – contributes to the service quality as perceived and experienced by the customer. The final quality is determined by the weakest part of the – quality – chain. It is possible to distinguish between three kinds of quality. The first two in the list were mentioned by Christian Grönroos (1990b), we have added the third one:

technical quality:
functional quality
relational quality

1. the technical quality: WHAT is being delivered?;
2. the functional quality: HOW is it delivered?; and
3. the relational quality: BY WHOM is it delivered?

Research into service quality often reveals that functional and relational quality are much more decisive in determining the overall quality than the technical quality. This finding is sometimes hard to accept for people working in professional organizations like hospitals, universities, etc.

subjective evaluations

Putting the customer at the center of services marketing implies the subjective evaluations of the customer are decisive in his/her evaluation of the organization's performance. Of course, these subjective evaluations can (and will) be based on technical and objective facts. Still, they are interpreted and evaluated subjectively. Those subjective evaluations will determine whether customers want to do business with a firm or not. This is also the reason why the customer and his/her need satisfaction is at the center of our definition of services. His or her judgment is the only opinion that really counts.

Internal Organization And Personnel

trust and
understanding

The service industry is an industry where people can have very intense relationships with each other. Client and service provider then have intense contacts in their relationship. Quality is mostly determined by WHOM the service is delivered: the relational quality. Trust and understanding are very important in service delivery processes. Relationship marketing is a crucial topic in services marketing management: that will lead to establishing strong relationships based on trust in delivering customized services.

at arm length

On the other hand, relationships can also be very loose. These are services called "at arm length" services (services provided without interaction between provider and customer) or fully standardized services. A fully standardized service, provided without any possible chance to meet any deviation in the needs and wants of a individual client, is called a standard core service. Of course, many other situations in between these two extremes – core versus customized – will exist.

the start of the
relationship life cycle

service attitude

But in spite of differences in the kind of service each employee has to realize that out of a first contact a lifelong relationship can be born. The first contact is the start of the relationship life-cycle. During this life cycle, the intensity of the relationship may change due to requirements in needs, preferences, whims and external contingencies. This has to be reflected in the employee's service attitude. If employees do not act according to the strategy formulated and claims offered in the external

Service practice 1-12 Customized versus core services: do I have to know you?

A typical example of a customized service is a lawyer knowing a lot about a suspect's life. The lawyer will know to a certain extent what the accused has done and why, when and how. The same requirements hold for consultants: they will have to know a lot of things about the company asking for their advice. This is especially true in times of severe problems or when a consultant is hired to restructure the company and guide change processes. Here, quite often, 1:1 relationships are at stake.

A standard core service is delivered by the railway. Railways assume it is not possible or necessary to know the clients on a personal basis when they are buying a railway ticket. The front office employee and the customer do not know each other and the customer uses one of the standard train rides between two destinations together with many other passengers.

communications, the consumer will be disappointed, dissatisfaction will occur and the relationship life cycle may end. Therefore, a service provider (like any other organization) should have organized the important issues internally first before they can claim externally that they will meet particular needs or demands.

establishing a close relationship

The importance of the relationship implies that the focus is not on a one-off transaction, where customers switch from one service to another, but on establishing a close relationship between the service provider and the customer. With increased information and knowledge about each other's preferences and capabilities, the quality of the service provided will be improved because the information assymmetry changes. This will result in more satisfied customers and better services.

KEY SUCCESS FACTORS IN SERVICE ORGANIZATIONS

key success factors in marketing, focussing on the service industry

Figure 1-6 reveals the results of an international research project on the key success factors in marketing, focussing on the service industry.[15]

The key success factors for all the UK service companies are competitive pricing, quality, performance, close links with key customers, company/brand reputation, and personal selling. The study conducted in Hungary, Poland and Bulgaria revealed a different pattern. Now only two factors are mentioned very often as the key success factors of service firms: competitive pricing and quality. The Dutch service companies indicated quality would be the key success factor in their competitive markets, followed by close links with the key customers, reputation of the company or brand, a competitive price, personal selling, performance, speed and reaction.

quality and pricing

These findings show that, in an international context, specific contingencies should be taken into account. Moreover, it shows that success factors in one country need not be the success factors in another country. The service firms in all three areas report a key factor as quality and pricing. In other words, both factors reflect the

Figure 1-6
Key success factors in
service firms*

	United Kingdom	Central and Eastern Europe**	The Netherlands
Product/service quality	32.9%	28.8%	53.6%
Close links with key customers	29.7	14.9	46.4
Company/brand reputation	29.0	18.4	46.4
Competitive pricing	34.8	37.4	44.2
Personal selling	28.4	8.2	31.2
Product/service performance	32.3	12.0	30.4
Speed of reaction to customer requirements	20.6	17.7	30.4
Distribution coverage and/or uniqueness	18.1	6.1	23.2
Product/service range offered	11.6	7.9	18.1
Advertising and promotion	11.0	15.5	13.8
A cost advantage in production/delivery	11.6	9.2	13.0
After sales service	20.0	4.3	10.9
Prior market research	20.0	9.9	9.4
Close links with industry suppliers	14.8	4.3	5.8
Superior marketing information systems	11.6	3.4	5.8
Finance and credit offered	7.7	7.2	5.1
Superior packaging	4.5	2.2	1.4
Product (service) design	20.0	5.0	1.4
Number of responding firms (=100%)	155	683	138

* Self reported key success factors; multiple answers (max. 5) could be given
**Based on samples in Hungary, Poland and Bulgaria during 1992

value

value their customers perceive (or hope to get) from these service offerings. Referring to the market orientation, these findings are comparable with the customer and market orientation which has to result in better and faster services that are closer to the customer than competitors'. Close links with the customer are needed, based on relationship marketing. These studies also indicate the importance of a service firm's image or reputation. A good image profile can be of great help to the insecure, first time service buyers.

close links with the
customer
image or reputation

Services
practice
1-13
On Great
Service

In his book "On Great Service", Len Berry (1995) sets out a framework for great service. The service company must (1) develop service leadership skills and values; (2) build a service quality information system; and (3) create a comprehensive service strategy based on the four principles of great service: reliability, surprise, recovery, and fairness. This leadership issue was not taken into account in the studies just mentioned. We consider it crucial to being or becoming a market oriented service organization.

1.6 Services Marketing In An International Perspective

The International Perspective

following the client

In short, there are two strategies for service organizations to internationalize.[16] The first step is "client following" and next step is called "market seeking".

If an organization is using the strategy of following the client, the service provider will serve the foreign subsidiaries of the customer in their own country. The existing relationship and familiarity will reduce the risk for the foreign subsidiary: they already have information about the way this service firm operates. The information asymmetry is solved in this way and perceived risk is reduced. Clients that are satisfied about the service quality delivered will recommend such a service provider to their subsidiary. So, being market or customer-oriented in one country pays off for market entry in another country.

seeking new markets

If the company is seeking new markets, the service provider enters into new international markets to expand and serve new customers in foreign countries. These customers have to become familiar with this new entrant and new relationships have to be built. This is more complex than the "client following" scenario.

location bound

Due to the nature of services, an interaction between service provider and customer takes place. This puts special requirements on the service delivery system in international services[17] as services usually have to be produced in close proximity to the customer. It is therefore important to know whether services are location bound. This will co-determine whether they are tradeable or not. These issues should be taken into account when a service firm wants to internationalize.

Market-Oriented Cultures In An International Service Organization

corporate culture

Corporate culture has been a widely studied issue the past fifteen years, since Peters and Waterman (1982) concluded that a customer orientation is one of the characteristics of excellent companies and their culture. Other authors use two dimensions to describe the culture of a corporation, namely the risks implied in the business activities (which may be high or low) and secondly, the speed of obtaining feed back on the results of decisions made (this feed back from the market may be fast or slow).[18] A corporate culture has to do with the norms and values deeply rooted in an

shared values

organization. They are the shared values or shared beliefs. These are about how people do things around here. Quite often they are taken for granted, in the sense that it is self evident that employees behave in a particular way although these norms and shared values can differ between countries. Managing the service organization's culture is therefore an essential issue for a market-oriented culture in an international service organization.

Hofstede (1991) defines corporate culture as "the collective programming of the mind which distinguishes the members of one organization from another".[19] This conceptual definition is operationalized by looking at culture via "the shared perceptions of daily practices". His research depicted six dimensions to describe organizational cultures:

1. process orientation   versus   results orientation;
2. employee orientation   versus   job orientation;
3. parochial   versus   professional;
4. open system   versus   closed system;
5. loose control   versus   tight control; and
6. normative   versus   pragmatic.

a market-oriented corporate culture

In the empirical studies that we have carried out (Kasper, 1995), a market-oriented corporate culture appeared to be results oriented, employee-oriented, professional, open and pragmatic. We have not found clear evidence about the kind of control in the culture of the organization (dimension 5). It appears that, partly, control should be tight: goals and targets should be set and well communicated to employees. Then their performance can be compared to these goals. On the other hand, service providers should also be empowered. This requires a loose(r) control system. Obviously, people can only be empowered when they are aware of the overall framework (=strategy) and goals set.

care for people

A great care for people (customers as well as employees) is a dominant feature of a market-oriented culture in an international context. These companies also possess high ethical standards and do business accordingly. They are very results driven or goal directed. Meeting customer preferences is much more important than applying the rules (for the sake of the rules only). Consequently, many governmental bodies and bureaucratic agencies have to make big changes in this respect when they want to become (more) market-oriented. A mindshift for the employees and top management is then needed. Market-oriented firms also stress a long term orientation (over a short term orientation). Such an organization is open and the employees accept risk taking. They are empowered and are able to accept the responsibility to act accordingly.

marketing strategy

These cultural characteristics are the foundation for the marketing strategy in these organizations. Such a marketing strategy is dominated by a strong drive to be the best, thorough knowledge about present and potential customers and competitors (= the market), clear marketing goals and a positive attitude towards risk taking in developing new services. Moreover, such a culture is characterized by meeting the needs of the customers via target group specific marketing policies (customized offers), and setting marketing goals accordingly. These goals are clear and well communicated throughout the company in which (top) management provide an "example function" in showing how

role model

employees should work and treat the customer (= role model). The company's offering is perceived to be of better quality than competitors'. A market-oriented company is permeated with marketing philosophy and is aware of providing excellent after sales services. Within this company, the various departments cooperate and exchange market information deemed relevant to other departments (almost) automatically.

Such a culture is hard to accomplish overnight.

*Service
practice
1-14
Some efforts of
an
international
market
orientation*

According to a recent issue of the Wall Street Journal Europe:

- Ford Germany encourages its dealers to give their customers a "special feeling" when they come to pick up their new car. Women get a bunch of flowers when they get into their new car or a glass of champagne is offered on closing the sale;
- Rover UK has adjusted its distribution system to assure a faster delivery of new cars;
- GM Europe, based in Cadiz, Spain, started a training center to teach their European dealers the basics of customer orientation and teamwork. This is based on experiences in the US;
- the Korean brand Daewoo sells its cars in Europe via "stores like Ikea". In these stores, the whole family will find interesting things.

All these things, and many more, are performed in order to make clear to the customer: who provides the best service for your money (= highest added value, or, best quality price ratio)?

1.7 MARKET-ORIENTED SERVICES MARKETING MANAGEMENT: OUR PERSPECTIVE

*market-oriented
culture of service
organizations*

The previous sections contain the fundamental basics upon which our book about services marketing in an international perspective will be built the market-oriented culture of service organizations.

culture

Such a *culture* is characterized by a sincere concern and care about people, ethics, results/goals, long term orientation, risk taking, empowerment and – pragmatically – meeting customer needs. This is "translated" into thorough market knowledge, clear and internally well communicated target group specific marketing goals, developing new services, manager's role model, better quality of services and after sales services, and an excellent cooperation and exchange of market information between departments.

*service
quality*

From a service perspective, the word *quality* is crucial. It is important in dealing with the intangibility of services and the accompanying characteristics like inseparability (simultaneous production and consumption), inconsistency (heterogeneity) and not having possibilities to store the service (inventory or perishability).

*marketing perspective
market orientation*

From our marketing perspective, we believe the concept of *market orientation* should be at the heart of this book. This contains the norms and values determining what the organization defines as its mission, strategy, policies and actions. It also sets out a framework for how employees will think, act, and consequently treat their customers in giving meaning to their external orientation and service attitude. An excellent and close relationship between service provider/employee and the customer/client is important to understand customer expectations and meet them by providing the right information. Quality in services and performance, the organization's reputation, close relationships and competitive pricing are the key success factors of a service organization, next to leadership, in having the service organization function as it should. All these can reduce the customer's perceived risk with regard to the intangible service.

To make it as concrete as possible, we will use two types of services throughout this book:

core service
- one is the core service, being the bare minimum of a particular service without any bells or whistles or specific features. It is the heart of the service; and

augmented service
- the augmented service, being the core service plus all the bells, whistles and other features.

With this kind of offering (and, of course, all kind of services can exist in between these two extremes) the service organization may meet customer needs. Meeting these needs can be done in two ways. First of all, very specific customized services can be offered. Usually, these kinds of services are complex. Secondly, services can be provided in a very standardized way as a mass service. Often, these services are not so complex. Combining these kinds of services, allows us to sketch four strategic types of services:

customized services

standardized service

1. standard core services;
2. standard augmented services;
3. customized core services; and
4. customized augmented services.

This typology – as shown in Figure 1-7 – will be applied in many chapters of this book. These four strategic types of services also show a link with the previously mentioned ideas about market orientation – the combination of cost leadership and differentation/focus. Core services will be offered most of the time to the lowest cost possible while augmented services will be the negotiated result of decisions about the differentiation in services to be provided by the company.

Service practice 1-15 Is it all magic?

In this chapter's introduction we discussed "The Magic of Services Marketing Management". We hope to have shown that market-oriented services marketing management in a local and international setting is complex and challenging. It is not only magic to accomplish the goals set – a well thought strategy will help. Or, as Lawrence Weinback, CEO of Arthur Andersen, has defined it: "There is no magic, just hard work".

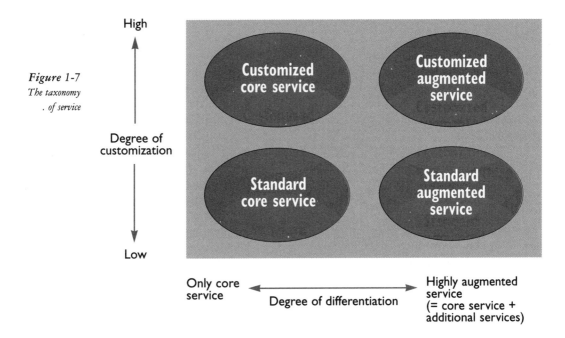

Figure 1-7
The taxonomy
. of service

In this way we have made explicit what we consider as marketing and how we think about "market oriented marketing" in service organizations. It is important to know these thoughts in advance in order to understand our way of reasoning.[20]

SUMMARY

This chapter is the introduction to this text on services marketing management. The basics of services marketing in an international perspective are briefly highlighted. Therefore, this chapter contains our philosophy about:

- services;
- marketing; and
- internationalization.

We define services as: "originally intangible and relatively quickly perishable activities whose buying takes place in an interaction process aimed at creating customer satisfaction but during this interactive consumption this does not always lead to material possession".

Services have, therefore, four basic characteristics. Intangibility is the main feature of services. This determines the other three important characteristics of services: inseparability, (simultaneous production and consumption), inconsistency (heterogeneity) and inventory (perishability). The intangibility also implies an information asymmetry between the customer and the service provider, especially when a customer "buys a service" for the first time and no prior experience exists. All these issues may vary to a certain degree. Some services are more intangible than others.

The part about marketing first creates a picture of the image of marketing and some popular misunderstandings. Research shows that marketing is mostly associated with advertising and selling. Aspects like market orientation, customer expectations, quality, the internal organization and personnel are hardly mentioned, although we like to describe them as the fundamentals of our vision about marketing. From a marketing perspective, it is important to manage the relationship between the customer and the service provider. Close links appear to be one of the key success factors in service companies. Other factors, such as competitive pricing, quality and reputation also count in determining the success of market oriented service organizations. A combination of cost leadership and differentiation/focus strategies is then at stake. This may also be called a combination of competitor orientation and customer orientation. Such market-oriented companies have a specific corporate culture: care about people (customers and employees) is one of the features of such a culture.

The third part of this chapter is about internationalization. Internationalization in services is complex. Two different strategies can be distinguished: "client following" and "market seeking". The complexity refers to the information asymmetry, the location (physical closeness to the customer to co-produce the service) and cultures which may differ inside (organizational culture) or outside (culture in a country) the service company.

In such an internationalization perspective, the service provider may expand one of the four types of services it can implement:

- standard core services;
- standard augmented services;
- customized core services; and
- customized augmented services.

QUESTIONS

1 What are the key elements in defining services?
2 What is market orientation all about?
3 Summarize the characteristics of a market-oriented service company. Do you know examples of companies resembling these characteristics the most?
4 What are the key success factors of the service companies you meet regularly? How do these KSF's fit into the results of the studies reported in section 1.6?
5 How is market orientation related to the marketing concept, the marketing strategy and the marketing mix?
6 What are the four I's? Are services really always intangible?
7 Why is service quality so important to a service company to achieve customer satisfaction and its own goals? How does it fit into the key success factors of service firms and their market orientation?
8 What does it mean to say that all four characteristics of services are relative concepts?
9 How could information technology improve the service delivery process and "solve the inventory problem"?
10 What do you consider as the proper image and fundamentals of marketing?

ASSIGNMENTS

1 Make an overview in which you show how large the present proportion of the service sector is in Gross National Product and in the total number of employment in some of the following countries:
Brazil, Colombia, Mexico, United States of America, United Kingdom, The Netherlands, Sweden, Italy, Greece, Egypt, Morocco, Nigeria, South Africa, Saudi Arabia, India, Malaysia, Indonesia, Japan, South Korea, Australia.
What do you conclude from the figures found with respect to the magnitude of the service sector and the wealth of each country? What can you say about the service sector in your own country relative to the data for the other countries found? What do you conclude when you compare the figures found with data from 1975 and 1955?
2 What are the three kinds of service quality? Apply all three of them to the performance of (1) your favorite professor; (2) your favorite sports team (basketball, soccer, baseball or hockey); or (3) airline. Explain.
3 Give examples of what you consider as an excellent service company and a very bad one. Explain what you consider as excellent and bad and why.

Case: JACK WELCH'S ENCORE[21]

How GE's chairman is remaking his company – again

It started out simply enough. For years, the US's General Electric Co sold CAT scanners, magnetic resonance imagers, and other medical imaging equipment to the 300-plus hospitals run by Columbia/HCA Health-care Corp. Then in March, 1995, GE persuaded Columbia to let it service all of the chain's imaging equipment, including that made by GE's rivals. And early this year, it added managing virtually all medical supplies to the deal – most of them product lines GE isn't even in.

But the pièce de résistance was still to come. As the new contract evolved, Columbia executives invited a team of GE managers to help improve the way they run hospitals. GE is now providing Columbia with a big dose of its well-known management skills. From GE's fabled "workouts" to seminars on supply-chain management and employee training, GE execs are working with Columbia to boost productivity.

For Columbia, which has saved tens of millions of dollars, it was medicine well worth swallowing. But for GE, the benefits go well beyond added revenue. The open-ended relationship is a smart gambit to gain a greater lock on one of its biggest customers – and a sign of a profound shift now gaining steam at the world's most successful conglomerate. As GE faces slow domestic growth and cut-throat pricing abroad for its big-ticket manufactured items, Chairman and CEO John F. Welch is again transforming the global giant.

GOLD STANDARD. Call it Jack Welch's Third Revolution. Since the hypercompetitive Welch took the reins at GE 15 years ago, he has relentlessly reshaped this icon of the American economy. Through the 1980s, Welch barnstormed through GE shutting factories, paring payrolls, and hacking mercilessly at its lackluster old-line units. Welch's tough tactics presaged much of the reengineering that followed across Corporate America. But he was hardly done. At the businesses he kept, Welch pushed his managers to become ever more productive. Inventories were trimmed, bureaucracies dismantled, and inefficiencies attacked with a vengeance.

Today, Welch oversees a vastly more competitive company than the one he took over. And Welch himself has become the gold standard against which other CEOs are measured. With its stock up 86%, to 95, since early 1995, GE has become the most valuable company on the globe, with a total market capitalization of $157 billion. And with earnings expected to hit $7.4 billion this year, GE is now poised to become America's most profitable company.

But Welch isn't resting on his laurels. Just 15 months after undergoing triple bypass surgery – and four years from his expected retirement – he's turning up the heat again. The goal: to remake GE into what may be the world's only $70 billion growth company. In what could well be Welch's final legacy, the 60-year-old executive is hard at work assuring that GE builds on the strengths it has gained in his reign.

Over the last year, Welch has launched two huge company-wide initiatives aimed at revving GE's growth up to a steady double-digit clip. Early this year, he announced a drive to boost GE's quality that could one day yield billions in added earnings. But perhaps most surprising from one of America's premier manufacturers is a push launched roughly 12 months ago to bolster revenue by pushing GE ever deeper into services. Like everything Welch does, the effort is being closely watched – this time – as a pattern for the refashioning of an industrial company in a postindustrial economy.

In businesses as far afield as health care and utilities, Welch foresees tremendous growth providing sophisticated services that spring from GE's core industrial strengths. In a world without borders, Welch is telling his troops, GE can no longer prosper on manufactured goods alone. "Our job is to sell more than just the box," he says.

To sell more than the box, GE executives have hatched plans over the past year to do everything from helping utilities run power plants more efficiently to running engine service ships for airlines. GE even wants to set up and run corporate computer networks. Says Welch simply: "We're in the services business to expand our pie".

HIGH OCTANE. In fact, with revenue growth slowing in its traditional industrial units, the manufactured products that GE has long made have increasingly come to resemble the classic loss leader. They just get the customer in the door. And a big part of the service GE is selling is itself. Flaunting its skills at boosting efficiencies and squeezing costs, GE is increasingly positioning itself as a sort of consultant. "The question is can we create a business helping customers take costs from their operations?" says John M. Trani, CEO of GE Medical Systems. "It's a question mark now, but [potentially] an awful lot of money." To customers struggling to cut their own costs and boost efficiency, GE's knowhow is a pretty seductive inducement – one few rivals can match. "They've become part of our team," enthuses Columbia/HCA's CFO Sam Greco.

For Welch, the thrust into services represents the culmination of a long career at the giant conglomerate. The son of a Boston & Maine Railroad conductor and a housewife, Welch began as a chemical engineer. But his scrappy competitiveness moved him quickly up the ranks. In 1981, at 45, he was CEO.

In his tenure at the helm, Welch has thoroughly dominated the company. So when he underwent the surgery in May, 1995, it immediately raised questions about who would replace him. But

today, he seems fitter than most men his age. Welch walks five miles on a treadmill most mornings, and his gruelling travel schedule regularly takes him to Europe and Asia. "I feel great," he says.

An intensely private man, Welch refuses to speak of his illness or succession. He returned to work full-time after Labor Day, 1995. And those who work closely with him say that, if anything, he appears to have more energy than ever. "He's about 120%," says Walter Wriston, the former Citibank chairman who served as a GE director for three decades before retiring in 1993. "I think he's actually better than before." Indeed, inside the company, managers joke that Welch's furious pace is likely to give them, not him, the next heart attack.

Welch sits on no outside corporate boards and devotes virtually all his energy to running GE. Living quietly with his second wife Jane – he has four adult children from his first marriage – Welch has a house across the street from the Country Club of Fairfield, the better to indulge his biggest passion next to running GE: golf. He and his wife, a former mergers-and-acquisitions lawyer, also frequently spend spare time golfing at their second home on Nantucket. And since his operation, company officials note pointedly, Welch's game is stronger than ever. This year, he broke 70 for the first time.

Yet if Welch refuses to talk about the transition ahead, he is clearly preparing for the home stretch. Although GE is one of

America's most competitive companies, its revenues grew an average of around 5% a year between 1990 and 1994. Sure, GE boosted a 17% revenue hike in 1995, and earnings rose 11%, to $6.6 billion. But few expect that one-time spike to be repeated, coming as it did largely because of big acquisitions, a booming economy, and a turnaround at NBC. Still, Welch argues GE can do far better than in the early 1990s: He's aiming for steady growth upwards of 10%.

This year, anyway, he looks well on his way to delivering. For 1996, analysts expect sales to hit $78 billion, an 11.4% rise. Even better, profits should jump 12.1%, to $7.4 billion. To keep up the pace, Welch is pushing forward on three fronts. His early 1990s push into global markets is already yielding huge dividends. International revenues soared 34% last year, to $27 billion.

Down the road, Welch is also counting on big gains from a multiyear program to boost quality launched early this year. From installing a gas turbine at a power plant to quickly answering a service call for a faulty washing machine, Welch wants GE to become virtually flawless in all it does. GE is also applying its engineering mind-set to the far squishier notions of service productivity and business processes. That should allow GE to trim its working capital needs and best productivity. If it succeeds, Welch's quality push could cut $7 billion to $10 billion from operating costs over several years.

But to fuel revenue growth, Welch is increasingly looking

towards services. Of course, it's hardly a new arena for GE. Almost from the day Welch took the helm, he has preached the need to shift from manufacturing. "All I talked about was the drive to get into services," he recalls. Nearly 60% of GE's profits now comes from services – up from 16.4% in 1980. "I wish it were 80%," he says.

Much of that shift is the result of the stunning growth of GE Capital Services. The financial-services unit has grown sevenfold since 1985, from revenues of $3.8 billion to $26.5 billion today, while operating profits leapt from less than $500 million to nearly $3.5 billion. Today, GE Capital provides nearly a third of total operating profits of $11 billion. GE's move into broadcasting with its 1986 acquisition of NBC has also cut manufacturing's role. NBC's revenues have doubled to $4 billion, while earnings have hit $738 million.

Now Welch is moving to the next stage of his services drive. He's pushing managers in GE's core industrial units to grab a bigger share of related services. Reengineering guru Michael Hammer sees GE as a bellwether. "This is the next big wave in American industry," he says. "The product you sell is only one component of your business."

The new approach is needed because many of GE's manufacturing markets rumble along with single-digit growth. Moreover, as product life cycles shorten and technology becomes easy to emulate, companies end up with few real competitive advantages. With

Welch seeking returns on capital of 15% to 20%, says Aircraft Engines services chief William Vareschi, "we have to participate in more of the food chain".

HUGE POTENTIAL. So far, many of GE's efforts are fledgling. But the potential is huge. Nicholas P. Heymann, a GE-watcher at NatWest Securities Corp., estimates that today GE brings in $7.8 billion-roughly 11% of its revenues – servicing its huge installed base of industrial equipment. By 2000, Heymann expects service revenues to more than double, to $18 billion. Moreover, margins typically run 50% higher on services than on product sales.

Of course, GE is far from alone. After watching its hardware margins shrink, IBM has aggressively moved into outsourcing in recent years. At Otis Elevator, two-thirds of its $5 billion revenues now comes from service and maintenance, since software-controlled elevators are far more reliable than older, electromechanical models. Xerox Corp. reorganized its Business Services unit in 1992 to chase the growing outsourcing market for corporate copy centers. And since winning the Malcolm Baldridge National Quality Award, Xerox has also been selling its quality-enhancement skills along with its products to customers such as Volvo and Amoco Corp.

Yet because of the size and scope of its operations, GE faces perhaps the biggest challenge. Insiders say the move got a big push a year ago, when a cadre of rising executives were named to develop services in many of the

industrial units. At the same time, Welch asked Vice-Chairman Paolo Fresco to set up a Services Council through which top managers can exchange ideas.

A trip to the Milwaukee headquarters of GE Medical Systems, traditionally little more than a maker of high-tech imaging gear, offers a clear idea of where Welch wants GE to head. As with its multiyear deal with Columbia/HCA, servicing the products of rivals is already a key initiative. Altogether, services – including looking after GE's own huge installed base – account for 40% of Medical's $3.5 billion in revenues.

ULTIMATE PITCH. To spur double-digit growth, Thomas Dunham, Medical's head of services, is acquiring independent medical service shops. In February, GE Medical bought National Medical Diagnostics, a leading independent servicer of imaging equipment. Six months later, GE added a private equipment maintenance insurance company. The moves have rivals riled. "I am not sure you keep competition when you lock everybody else out," says Carl Reilly, vice-president of Philips Electronics" medical imaging unit.

Yet that's just the beginning. GE Medical spent $80 million building a state-of-the-art training center, complete with a TV studio, to develop educational programming. For fees ranging from $3,000 to $20,000, hospitals can tune in to live broadcasts on subjects such as proper mammography techniques. Dunham is also trying to use GE's own management expertise to help its customers better run their businesses. And then there's the ultimate sales pitch for hospitals that buy a certain amount of equipment and maintenance: Recently, the top brass at Medical Systems gave the executive team of a regional hospital chain a half-day management seminar on topics such as strategic planning, employee evaluations, and time management. "They probably got $100,000 to $200,000 worth of consulting," says Trani.

Even in the company's more tradition-bound units, similar change is under way. Ernest Gault, an engineer recently named to head a new global services unit at GE Power Systems, says the Services Council meetings have helped him realize the value of strategic acquisitions. Gault now expects 50% of his growth to come from acquisitions and joint ventures, moves he wouldn"t have considered a year ago. In May, 1995, GE signed a joint venture with the Milan-based power company Societa Nordelettrica. The pair will offer utility maintenance and operation services throughout Europe.

Back in the US, Gault is also aggressively chasing what he foresees as a $1 billion market managing power plants for independent power producers and coordinating fuel purchasing for deregulated utilities. In one typical deal, GE is running a 500-megawatt gas-fired power plant for Ocean State Power in Rhode Island. Of course, many utilities and independent energy companies also see power plant management as a big

growth opportunity. One rival argues that, in the U.S. at least, few utilities will want to buy equipment and services in a single package that may make pricing hard to judge. "You can question whether it will be that competitive," he says.

At GE's Cincinnati-based Aircraft Engines, Vareschi also now sees servicing engines as more of a growth business than making new ones. He envisions more deals like the 10-year, $2.3 billion contract GE signed with British Airways PLC in March under which GE will now do 85% of the engine maintenance work on BA's entire fleet – including engines made by rivals Rolls-Royce PLC and Pratt & Whitney.

Today, GE is busy transforming the carrier's maintenance practices. It's moving BA to a just-in-time inventory system for parts, and instituting self-directed teams and other advanced management practices from its own plants. David J. Kilonback, who oversees the deal for BA, says the shift saved the carrier money and management time, in addition to speeding engine turnaround. Building on the BA deal, GE inked a $1 billion, multiyear contract in September to service US Air Inc.'s GE engines. And to broaden its global base, GE acquired Celma, a Brazilian repair shop with about $140 million in revenues.

GE's moves haven"t gone unnoticed by rivals. Pratt & Whitney has also begun promoting its servicing capabilities for its own engines, although it lags well behind GE and Rolls-Royce – which has built a $300 million

servicing unit since 1993 – recently formed a joint venture in Hong Kong to do servicing for Asian-Pacific carriers.

Managers throughout GE's industrial units are developing similar new markets. Executives at Transportation also recently signed a deal for roughly $550 million to sell and service 150 new locomotives for Burlington Northern Santa Fe Corp. And they've formed a joint venture with electronics specialist Harris Corp. to design and sell global-positioning systems similar to those used in air-traffic control. In a pilot project, the GE/Harris system has enabled the railroads to run twice as many trains over the same length of track.

Much of Welch's new services drive has been geared toward revving up GE's industrial units. Yet even within GE Capital there is a new aggressiveness. "You can't make money selling money anymore," says GE Capital CEO Gary Wendt. By far the biggest sign of GE Capital's new turn is its rapid build-up of a $5 billion global computer outsourcing business. Although GE has long financed computer purchases and run help desks for corporate clients, it now wants to compete head-on with IBM and EDS for multimillion-dollar deals running computer networks for others. In May, it bought Ameri-data Technologies Inc, a $2 billion Stamford (Conn) company that sells PCs to corporate buyers. In July, it added CompuNet, a fast-growing German outsourcer. **REGULATORY HACKLES.** So far, rivals seem more dismissive than threatened. "Moving from being a product company to a service company is much more difficult than some of these folks think," sniffs one EDS exec. Adds Perot Systems CEO James A. Cannavino: "We haven't bumped into them yet."

But as corporate customers start turning to GE, they might soon. In a 1995 deal that CE execs hope will prove typical, GE and Andersen Consulting – a software-services leader – joined forces to beat major competitors for a 10-year, $350-million contract to manage LTV Corp.'s mainframe-based computer needs.

Still, GE's moves to get more deeply involved in its customers" operations have raised regulatory hackles. In August, the Justice Dept. charged GE with placing illegal restrictions in hospitals that use its remote diagnostic software for CAT scans. GE doesn't let customers use its software to service rivals" equipment. This has raised fears among independent service providers. "Customers want choices," says Claudia Betzner, executive director of the Independent Service Network, a trade group. GE says the suit is "meritless."

Yet the greatest challenge facing Welch in redirecting GE may well be human. Service was always a backwater in a company with a rich engineering heritage. As the hot shots from services gain influence, the shift has brought tension. "It's been hard for the old equipment businesses, where building the latest high-efficiency this and high-efficiency that was the route to epaulets on your shoulder," says Welch.

With customers unwilling to pay for engineering perfection, there's not going back. And as the differences among GE units blur and old-line manufacturing businesses begin to more closely resemble its fast-moving services units, Welch is pushing all of GE to take on a more entrepreneurial mind-set. That has clearly been his aim since he began reconfiguring the company 15 years ago. Welch's GE is still a work in progress, but there is no doubting its direction. Welch will leave behind a company that remains synonymous with the ever-changing American economy.

QUESTIONS

1 Why is GE pushing deeper into services?
2 In what respect(s) is GE becoming a service firm?
3 Why is it important that GE considers itself a service firm?
4 What implications may this shift have for the company's employees and its culture?
5 Elaborate on the role model each manager now has to perform for their sub-ordinates.

ENDNOTES

1. Grönroos, 1990b, p. 27.
2. Kotler, 1991, p. 455.
3. Bateson, 1992, p. 8.
4. Zeithaml and Bitner, 1996, p. 5.
5. Peter and Olson, 1993.
6. Berry and Parasuraman, 1991, p. 4.
7. US Department of Commerce; Bureau of the Census and The Service 500 in Semenik and Bamossy, 1993, pp. 597-601.
8. Berkowitz et al., 1986, pp. 608-610.
9. Bitner, Booms and Tetreault, 1990.
10. In Dutch: Waar gehakt wordt, vallen spaanders.
11. Barksdale and Darden, 1972; Barksdale et al., 1982; Interview/IPM, 1974 and 1981; Gaski and Etzel, 1986; Varadarajan and Thirunarayana, 1990.
12. Day, 1990, p. 29.
13. Narver and Slater, 1990; Slater and Narver, 1994a and 1994b.
14. Kohli and Jaworski, 1990; Kohli et al., 1993; Jaworski and Kohli, 1993; Diamantopoulos and Hart, 1993.
15. Hooley, 1992; Alsem and Hoekstra, 1994; Prof. Hooley provided additional data about the Eastern European countries on our request. We are very grateful for that.
16. Erramilli and Rao, 1990; Post, 1992. Chapter Nine will reveal more about such strategies.
17. Normann, 1984; VanderMerwe and Chadwick, 1989; Buckley et al., 1992.
18. Deal and Kennedy, 1982.
19. Hofstede, 1991, p. 180 and pp. 182-183.
20. De Vries jr., Kasper and Van Helsdingen, 1997.
21. Smart, 1996.

CHAPTER TWO

CLASSIFYING SERVICES

After studying this chapter you should be able to:

- *reproduce the specific characteristics of services;*

- *mention the main implications of these characteristics;*

- *recall the many criteria to be used in classifying services and service delivery processes;*

- *classify services and service delivery processes;*

- *understand the classification proposed by the authors;*

- *argue the relevance of the four types of services we have developed;*

- *explain why and how these four types of services can be used in describing and analyzing the strategies and actual performance of service organizations; and*

- *start analyzing the many service experiences you come across every day.*

LEFT: *The many sides of one service.*

2.1 INTRODUCTION

*Service
practice
2-1
What service
am I in?*

Different answers to this strategic question will create different services. Each service organization has to focus on different issues in providing its service: decisions about which market to enter (national versus international), what kind of goals (profit or not-for-profit), which service will be delivered in what kind of delivery process (customized or standard service in a people or equipment based process), etc.

Ader, Jolibois & Associés (Paris); Baileys, Shaw & Gillett (London) and Sarda, Calomarde, Castelo y Asociados (Spain) are law firms in different countries linked in a network called "Legalliance". By joining this international network each individual firm had to face many strategic questions or changes, for example:

- do we want to change the customer orientation ? This orientation had to be broadened from being local/national one-man enterprises to multinational corporations;
- do we want to accept a different relationship between the customer and our firm;
- do we want to cross borders? The physical site appeared to become a multi site distribution in different countries instead of a single site distribution in one country;
- are we prepared to confront customers with new questions (new tasks) instead of ongoing relationships characterized by modified or straight rebuys?

To classify services in a structural way will help the service provider to react proactively to the actions of a competitor or major developments in the environment. This chapter provides an overview of the issues, questions and existing literature on services marketing with respect to changes in:

- the environment of the services provider. What is the present situation and which role does our organization play now? Classifications can help in describing the present state of a particular service or service organization in order to decipher and analyze the actual situation;
- the competition now or in the future. Classifying services allows one to compare the status quo of one's company with its (main) competitors';
- the strategy of the company. Organizations may find niches in the market given its own market position, activities, service delivery processes, skills and capabilities versus the competitors';
- developing new core or additional services; and
- the behavior of the customer.

taxonomies of services   Our taxonomies of services offer in a simple way an overview of the issues deemed important in defining, describing and analyzing services. The difference between a core service and the additional services can be formulated easily in terms of the *degree of differentiation*

difference between a core service and an augmented service. The augmented service becomes more complex, for it encompasses the core service plus all the additional services. This may be labelled as the degree of *differentiation*. Those additional services can be used by service providers to offer a service that is more appealing to a customer. From the supplier's point of view, a wide or small choice of services may be offered. The degree of differentiation is the result of a service organization's decision about its offering. On the other hand, the customer's point of view should

degree of customization

also be taken into account. Here, it is useful to make a distinction between the degree of *customization* required by the customer. Is the offer developed solely to meet the special needs of one particular customer or are the services (core or augmented) the same for all customers? These dimensions are reflected in Figure 2-1.

Figure 2-1
Our taxonomy of service

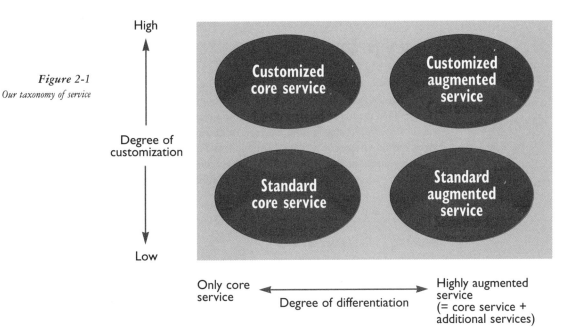

Figure 2-1 differentiates between various types of services. This classification is based on the two issues just described, the degree of differentiation and the degree of customization. Four extreme forms of services can be distinguished. These are:

Four forms of services

1. standard core services like dry cleaning, take home pizza, Mister Minit;
2. standard augmented services like Pizza Hut, McDonald's, toll free numbers;
3. customized core services like doctors, accountants as long as the "traditional services" are concerned;
4. customized augmented services like academic hospitals, specialized lawyers and other niche players.

Here, in this chapter, we want to widen the knowledge about classifications by showing a systematic order and structure in the many ways services occur in our world. These insights can be used, for instance, in developing strategies for service organizations, in positioning service organizations and in differentiating their offerings. These insights can be applied in the process of implementing and controlling strategies. This overview will not only provide a better understanding of services as such, but also deepen the understanding of relations between service firms and their customers, the marketing strategy and the marketing mix. We have defined nine categories of subjects useful in classifying services.[1] Each of them will be elaborated upon. The first ones to be discussed cover broad and more or less strategic issues while the latter are more concrete and operational by nature.

2.2 NINE CATEGORIES FOR CLASSIFYING SERVICES

Many classifications of services exist. Quite often, authors have developed their own classification, best suited to the specific topic they want to deal with in services marketing. This means that a common opinion on how to classify services does not exist, yet. It also means that a long list of criteria or subjects utilized while classifying services would emerge if we listed them all. We have put them into nine categories. This will give some structure to the subjects deemed relevant in rendering services and organizing service delivery processes. The nine categories are labelled as:

nine categories

1. services and goods;
2. profit versus non profit;
3. markets and industries;
4. internal or external services;
5. the consumer/customer/client and his/her service buying behavior;
6. the relationship between the service provider and the customer;
7. the service provider's knowledge, skills and capacity;
8. the service delivery process; and
9. the physical site of the service delivery.

strategic outlook
operational side

These nine topics are also the sections of this chapter, as Figure 2-2 reveals. The outer ring in this figure refers to concepts with a more strategic outlook, while the inner part of the figure relates to the operational side of the service delivery process. Each box in Figure 2-2 will now be elaborated upon in separate sections.

SERVICES AND GOODS

With respect to the classical distinction between goods, people usually say services are different from goods in the sense that they are intangible. As stated in Chapter One, this intangibility determines the other basic characteristics of services: simultaneous pro-

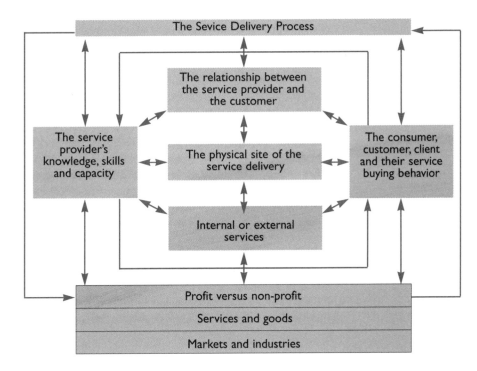

Figure 2-2
The overall classification
scheme of services:
chapter outline

duction and consumption (during the service encounter), heterogeneity and

intangibles and perishability. The difference between services and goods, therefore, can be formulated
tangibles in its most extreme form as the difference between intangibles and tangibles.

The services/goods that fall between the two extremes are composed of varying combinations of tangible and intangible attributes. Goods or services in the middle contain a mixture of intangible and tangible elements. Classifying these products as either goods or services may be misleading unless the classification is accompanied by a clear understanding on the part of the marketeer about which attributes (tangible or intangible) are decisive from the customer's perspective.[2] Therefore, two issues are important in interpreting the integrative framework and the scales which are used:

a continuum 1. it appears that all concepts used in classifying services should be regarded as
phenomena to be viewed on a continuum instead of in a discrete way;
all concepts 2. in our framework, we will sketch a picture in which all these concepts come to
simultaneously the fore simultaneously.

A combination of intangibility and tangibility often occurs when services are offered in addition to goods. Then, services play a role in the total offering by such a manufacturer. There is a distinction between the various roles of services in the total offering:[3]

- a pure service exists where there is little (if any) evidence of tangible goods;
- services adding value to a tangible good;
- services adding value to goods more fundamentally by making them available in the first place.

the services-goods continuum

As the first way of classifying services is determined by the degree of intangibility, each service can be positioned on a continuum ranging from very intangible to very tangible. Then, the services-goods continuum ranges from:

- pure services; via
- services with supporting services and goods; and
- goods with accompanying services; to
- pure goods (being the very tangible or "canned" services).

no exchange of title

In other words, pure services are immaterial while pure goods are very material. Buying goods results in the transfer of a "material object": an exchange of title. This is not the case with services. When services are bought no exchange of title takes place. Such an exchange is always at stake when buying goods.

Consequently, it is the difference between simultaneous production and consumption versus very distinct production and consumption (in place and time) and therefore between non-storable services and perfectly storable products. If services can be stored, they can be transferred or transported as well.[4] Figure 2-3 summarizes the differences between services and goods mentioned in this section.

Figure 2-3
The intangibility continuum and the implications for the other basic characteristics of service*

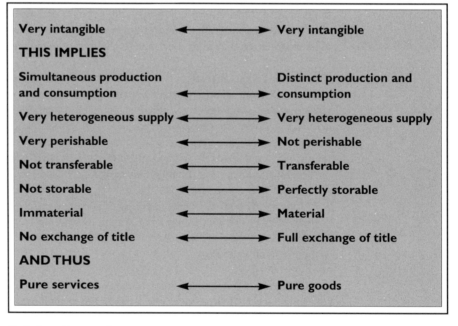

Very intangible	←→	Very intangible
THIS IMPLIES		
Simultaneous production and consumption	←→	Distinct production and consumption
Very heterogeneous supply	←→	Very heterogeneous supply
Very perishable	←→	Not perishable
Not transferable	←→	Transferable
Not storable	←→	Perfectly storable
Immaterial	←→	Material
No exchange of title	←→	Full exchange of title
AND THUS		
Pure services	←→	Pure goods

*All these tables (2-3 till 2-12) should be read line for line. Although we tried in each column to have more or less issues with a similar meaning, this will not always be the case. Therefore, the issues in one column should not be considered as (perfect) symonyms

Lovelock (1983) formulated 5 matrices providing a series of classifications illustrating the complex nature of services. One matrix reveals the difference between:

- intangible actions to people or things; and
- tangible actions to people or things.

Tangible actions to people are, for example, services directed to the human body, like health care or hairdressing. If the service is mainly a combination of tangible actions to things, Lovelock talks about maintenance, freight transport or laundry services.

Examples of intangible actions are education and musea (museums of art, natural history etc) (people) or financial and assurance services (things).

PROFIT AND NON PROFIT

*profit and the non-
profit sector*

Traditionally, a distinction can be made between the profit and the non-profit sector. To a certain extent, this is almost similar to the distinction between marketable and unmarketable services or regulated (and protected) service markets versus deregulated service markets.[5] Unmarketable services consist of many public or governmental services.

pricing issues

A more detailed classification relevant in this section is the classification which has been developed with respect to pricing issues and services.[6] In essence, it refers to questions like: "who sets prices" or "who regulates the service offering"?:

- is it done by the market place (as is mostly done in the profit sector);
- is it done by public regulation (as usually holds for governmental and non-profit services); or
- is it done by formal self regulation in the industry?

Today, quite often non-profit organizations have to earn part of their revenues themselves. Phenomena like privatization are becoming well known in the public sector. Governments are not subsidizing all kinds of institutions any longer. Sometimes, parts of the activities of a public agency are privatized. Also, in some countries particular services are provided by the government while that is not the case (or to a lesser degree) in an other country.

Moreover, the emphasis on organizations' social responsibilities may force them to rely more on self regulation than on the market place as the instrument to set prices, determine the features of a specific service and guide the organization's behavior.

profit non-profit
continuum

Figure 2-4 is about the profit non-profit continuum in which the well known services like public services, merit services and private services can be positioned.

Figure 2-4
The profit non-profit
continuum of services

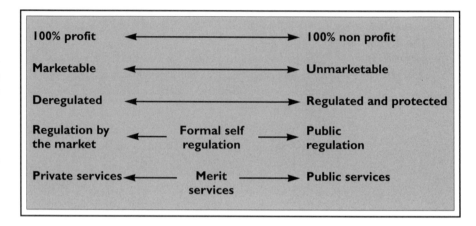

MARKETS AND INDUSTRIES

markets and specific
industries

The third group of topics used to classify services refers to the markets and specific industries. This can be used in defining markets and hence consumers and competitors. Classifying the service industry can be a first step:

- to demarcate the "playing field" of the company; and
- to define the organization's mission and goals.

user's perspective

SIC codes

With respect to the markets, two main criteria can be distinguished. The first relevant aspect is the difference between customer markets and industrial markets. The difference is determined mainly by the user/buyer of the service: is it a household or a service company, manufacturer, governmental agency or any other organization. We define competing industries as industries providing those type of services which end users (consumers or organizations) perceive as substitutes. This user's perspective is the most important point of view for a marketer, also in the service sector. The second main issue of the market is the scope of the market. Here, the term "market" is used from a geographical perspective. Is the organization active in a small local area, country wide or internationally? For a more detailed classification with respect to industries, one can think of SIC codes or other classifications of industries, giving a description of a region's or country's service sector. The international Standard Industrial Classification (SIC) of all economic activities labels each industry by a unique code. The more digits used, the more specific the industry. Such codes can be used to describe some characteristics of an industry; it does not reveal what kind of benefits they provide to the customer. Industries like agriculture, hunting, forestry, fishing, mining, quarrying and manufacturing have codes between 01 and 40. The SIC-codes for the service industries are presented in the next overview.

Figure 2-5
Markets and industries

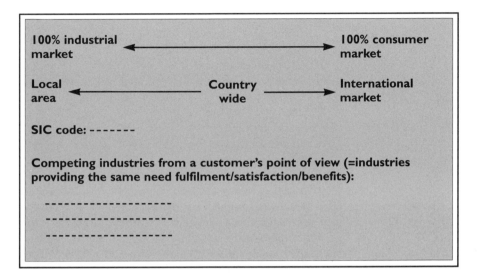

100% industrial market ←——————————————→ **100% consumer market**

Local area ←——————— **Country wide** ————→ **International market**

SIC code: - - - - - - -

Competing industries from a customer's point of view (=industries providing the same need fulfilment/satisfaction/benefits):

- - - - - - - - - - - - - - - - - - - -
- - - - - - - - - - - - - - - - - - - -
- - - - - - - - - - - - - - - - - - - -

Service practice 2-4 SIC for services

Electricity, gas and water supply
    40: Electricity, gas, steam and hot water supply
    41: Collection, purification and distribution of water
Construction
    45: Construction
Wholesale and retail trade; repair of motor vehicles and motorcycles and personal and household goods
    50: Sale, maintenance and repair of motor vehicles and motorcycles; retail sale of automotive fuel
    51: Wholesale trade and commission trade, except for motor vehicles and motorcycles
    52: Retail trade, except of motor vehicles and motorcycles; repair of personal and household goods
Hotels and restaurants
    55: Hotels and restaurants
Transport, storage and communications
    60: Land transport; transport via pipelines
    61: Water transport
    62: Air transport
    63: Supporting and auxiliary transport activities; activities of travel agencies
    64: Post and telecommunications
Financial intermediation
    65: Financial intermediation, except insurance and pension funding
    66: Insurance and pension funding, except compulsory social security
    67: Activities auxiliary to financial intermediation
Real estate, renting and other business activities
    70: Real estate activities
    71: Renting of machinery and equipment without operator and of personal and household goods

72: Computer and related activities
73: Research and development
74: Other business activities
Public administration and defence; compulsory social security
   75: Public administration and defence; compulsory social security
Education
   80: Education
Health and social work
   85: Health and social work
Other community, social and personal service activities
   90: Sewage and refuse disposal, sanitation and similar activities
   91: Activities of membership organizations
   92: Recreational, cultural and sporting activities
   93: Other service activities
Private households with people employed
   95: Private households with people employed
Extraterritorial organizations and bodies
   99: Extraterritorial organizations and bodies

INTERNAL AND EXTERNAL SERVICES

One way of looking at the functioning of organizations is to analyze the cooperation between individuals and departments as if they were each other's customers. This idea of internal customers has been developed in the literature on internal marketing and total quality management.

The price of internal services has to be based on some kind of transfer pricing. If such

Service practice 2-5 Inside out or outside in

internal customers

In the seventies a song by the rock and roll band Yes had the same title: Inside out or outside in. It is a perfect way to describe both tendencies. There are plenty of organizations which have taken some actions in one of these directions. For instance:

- restaurants in hospitals start some kind of catering service for external customers (inside out);
- universities sell their lecture halls to outside customers for conferences (inside out);
- a middle sized company in the financial sector is closing down the market research department and will buy the market information in the future (outside in); or
- a large travel agent selling their hotels and apartments to concentrate just on the core service travelling. The accomodations will be hired instead of being owned.

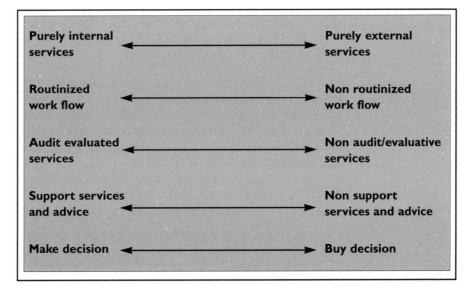

Figure 2-6
The internal - external
services continuum

prices are lacking, other signals should be incorporated to improve the allocation of resources within an organization and/or to encourage the cooperation between departments and individuals. Recently, two trends are becoming common practice:

- to offer internal services to the external market as well; and
- at the same time, a trend in which internal services are being dispersed with and bought on the market.

outsourcing

This last trend is called outsourcing. Currently, many kinds of internal services are very vulnerable to outsourcing. Both trends (offering internal services to new outside clients, and outsourcing) seem to stem from the same tendencies, like: organizations opting to become leaner and meaner; developing business units and profit centers (indicating which costs are made when and where); back to the core business; and privatization of public bodies.

continuum of internal versus external services and their clients

Most of the services can be offered internally in the firm to other departments as well as outside to the market. Therefore, we might speak of a continuum of internal versus external services and their clients. With respect to internal services, a further specification of internal services is developed[7]:

- routinized work flow services, referring to activities that can be done by different employees in a relatively fixed sequence, such as for instance, the transferral of data in an administrative protocol;
- audit/evaluative services, being the services directed at controlling operations (e.g. accounting and control);
- support service and advice are services relating basically to the many traditional staff functions in an organization that may or must be consulted in particular circumstances (personnel department, mailing department, house keeping, etc.).

Here, dynamics may occur as well. Especially, business services and infrastructure services may be provided to internal and as well to external clients (inside out) or bought outside the company (outside in).

This way of reasoning can be applied to organizations like companies as well as to non profit organizations and individual households. Members of a household provide services to one another. Some of these services could be carried out by outside help as well (e.g. catering, housekeeping). In total, it means that for companies as well as for households the difference between internal and external services is closely linked to the well known "make or buy-decision". Then services provided to the external market are subject to a "buy-decision" of the customer while internal services are the result of a "make-decision".

make or buy-decision

CONSUMER SERVICE BUYING BEHAVIOR

consumer services and industrial services

(bundles of) benefits

degree of customer participation

Here, the main distinction to be made is between consumers and other organizations. This hinges upon the difference between consumer services and industrial services. It is also reflected in another classification criterion, namely that of consumer or industrial markets. Both industrial customers and individuals may have different needs or wants and may be looking for different (bundles of) benefits. Therefore, it is necessary to define the target group carefully. This, in turn, will affect the degree of customer participation in the service delivery process: what are the customers in this segment willing to do, at what price and how should they participate?

patterns of buying behavior and problem solving behavior

The customers will also have different patterns of buying behavior and problem solving behavior. Sometimes, just one individual is involved in buying services and the service encounter while in other instances many people are involved in this buying process. It is important to note the difference between a completely new situation in which a service is "bought" and a repeat service encounter. So, here we would like to position services on a continuum ranging from a new task situation via a modified rebuy to a straight rebuy. In other words, the problem solving behavior ranges from very extensive via limited to routine problem solving behavior. This distinction goes along with the degree of perceived risk a consumer experiences when buying a service. Most of the time the degree of perceived risk present during the interaction in the service encounter will be larger in new task situations than in straight rebuys. In line with the previous two issues, the degree of perceived risk may vary between very high and very low (or even to situations lacking any risk) and can be reduced by, e.g. information gathering, stressing the tangibles of the service provider or developing a strong brand.

degree of perceived risk

seeking information

Other terms that may be applied in positioning the service from a consumer's point of view are the speciality, shopping or convenience services. This well known classification of goods has to do with the degree to which consumers are deliberately seeking information about the product they would like to buy: are many pre-purchase activities involved or not? With respect to evaluating the service on the basis of the information that can be collected at a particular moment of the service experience, one can make a distinction between the search, experience and credence attributes.[8] These attributes may also differ as to the degree in which the customer is familiar

attributes

with the service provider and the service delivery process. In other words, whether little pre-purchase activity exists or not, or, whether decision processes are short or long. Each of these attributes may vary from high to low (or zero). Finally, the degree to which the customer is willing to participate in the service delivery process, may

domain specifity

be domain specific.[9] Domain specificity means depending on the specific purposes at a particular moment, the wealthy customer may buy cheap or expensive services for different occasions/domains. This issue of domain specificity is partly related to the degree of commitment and involvement to the service: both may differ between high and low, but will be unique to a particular customer and particular occasions.[10] This

value of the service

will depend partly on the value of the service to the customer.

Figure 2-7
The consumer's
continuum

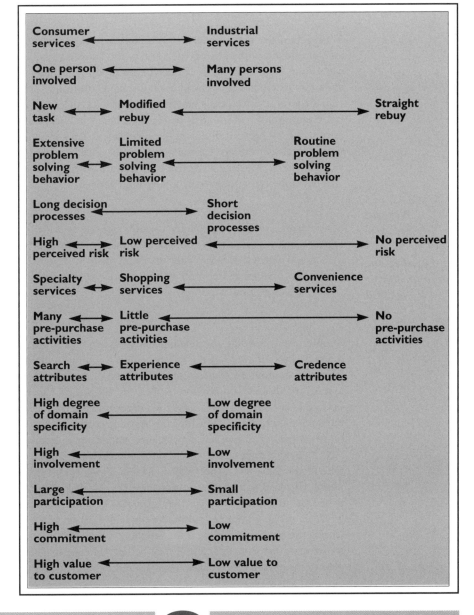

*Service
practice
2-6
The customer
in different
domains*

Due to specific wishes, needs, etc. a consumer may be willing to eat in a self service restaurant when little time is available, while the same person may want to be fully served in a five star restaurant when going out to dinner on a special occasion. So, one cannot say that each customer always wants self service. It is contingent to the purpose (=domain) whether some services are consumed rapidly or not.

THE RELATIONSHIP BETWEEN THE SERVICE PROVIDER AND THE CUSTOMER

kind of relationship

This section discusses issues determining the kind of relationship between the service provider and the customer. In one of the famous classifications of Lovelock[11] the question is raised: "Does the service organization enter into a "membership" relationship with its customers or is there no formal relationship?". The second criteria in the classification of Lovelock is whether the service is delivered on a continuous basis or not. Examples of continuously delivered services in a membership relation are: insurance, cable TV subscription or college enrolment. Less or no formal relationships with discrete transactions are: car rental, restaurant or toll highway. Of course, for many service providers it is very attractive to find ways – utilizing the service marketing mix – to develop continuous formally delivered services.

no formal relationship

continuous basis

*Service
practice
2-7
Loyal to the
newspaper or
not*

According to the percentages of subscriptions and the percentages of home delivery, switching between journals on a day to day basis is much easier in some countries (Greece, Italy or Spain) than in other countries (USA, Japan, Russia, Luxemburg or South Korea). Formal relationships (subscriptions) form the basis for more loyal behavior.

*one time discrete
transactions and long
term continuous
relationships*

Another issue defining the relationship between a customer and a service provider refers to another view on the difference between one time discrete transactions and long term continuous relationships.[12] Between discrete and contininuous relationships a series of discrete transactions will show up which can be called the difference between the "episode level" and the "relationship level". Episodes refer to one time interactions, while a relationship consists of a number of such episodes. The distinction between these two levels is, for instance, important in evaluating the quality of a service. Episodes refer to the whole service experience during one particular period of time (a moment), like a short visit to a bank, a long evening dinner in a restaurant or a rafting trip lasting a week. Relationships consist of a (large) number of episodes in time. This "time perspective" is the distinction between services supplied quite casually versus services supplied within an ongoing relationship between buyer and seller. During the service experience, the interaction between the service employee and customer may vary. This interaction may be very intense or very loose and may require sometimes personal interaction (cashier at the bank) and sometimes not (ATM).

episodes

Figure 2-8
Newspaper delivery

	Percentage on single copy sales	Percentage on subscriptions	I.D.	I.D.
		total	home deliveries	postal deliveries
Belgium	62%	38%	-	38%
Brazil	35	65	65	-
Chile	40	60	na	na
Cyprus	82	18	18	-
Czech Republic	45	55	55	-
Denmark	30	70	61	9
Estonia	38	62	62	-
Finland	13	87	69	18
France	70	30	na	na
Germany	35	65	na	na
Greece	96	4	4	-
Ireland	85	15	14	1
Israel	85	15	na	na
Italy	93	7	-	7
Japan	7	93	93	0.5
Luxemburg	10	90	na	na
Netherlands	11	89	87	2
Norway	32	68	na	na
Peru	95	5	na	na
Russia	6	94	na	na
Singapore	45	55	na	na
Slovak Republic	70	30	30	-
South Korea	4	96	91	5
Spain	91	9	5	5
Sweden	24	76	68	8
Switzerland	12	88	70	18
Tunisia	90	10	8	2
Turkey	90	10	10	-
USA*	18	80	75	5

na=not available
* =the data do not show why it does not add up to 100%*
I.D.=Idem
Source: Fédération Internationale des Editeurs de Journaux, Paris, 1994

loyalty

All these "relationship issues" will affect the customers' loyalty to the service provider. Consequently, the way a service provider wants to practise relationship marketing[13] will be determined largely by the planned positions on the continua mentioned in this section. It will be affected also by the positions held in the various phases of the relationship life cycle.

Probably, the most stable and profitable relationships will be the ones that can be labelled as formal and continual. For example, publishers, monopolistic telecom providers, suppliers of repair and maintenance services, insurance companies, they all

contracts

strive for formal and continual relationships, most of the time formalized in contracts. A quite stable cash flow will result and less marketing effort has to be put into keeping these customers. The one time, discrete transactions with customers shopping around to find the best service will not create a strong bond between the two. The same will hold for those customers buying a particular service, just from a perspective of variety seeking; they will show no or hardly any loyalty to the service provider because of lack of commitment.[14]

Figure 2-9
The continuum of
the customer service
provider relationship

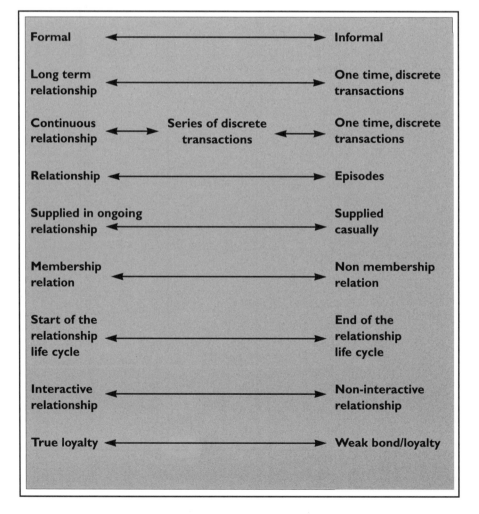

Formal	⟷	Informal
Long term relationship	⟷	One time, discrete transactions
Continuous relationship	⟷ Series of discrete transactions ⟷	One time, discrete transactions
Relationship	⟷	Episodes
Supplied in ongoing relationship	⟷	Supplied casually
Membership relation	⟷	Non membership relation
Start of the relationship life cycle	⟷	End of the relationship life cycle
Interactive relationship	⟷	Non-interactive relationship
True loyalty	⟷	Weak bond/loyalty

THE SERVICE PROVIDER'S KNOWLEDGE, SKILLS AND CAPACITY

the service provider's point of view

Now that a wide variety of issues used to describe the customer of the service and the relationship between customer and provider have been discussed, some issues to be used in classifying services from the service provider's point of view will be presented. Because of the many discussions in relevant literature on quality of services and market orientation, one of the issues here could be labelled as the organization's personnel's ability to be market-oriented and therefore provide excellent service quality. We have therefore mentioned the topic here first before other internal organizational issues.

ability to be market-oriented

Another important subject that can be used in classifying providers of services is the degree to which the organization's service rendering activities depend on one particular person (or a group of interchangeable persons). It affects the way in which other people may replace a colleague in the service encounter. Moreover, the degree of loyalty of the customer to a particular member of the contact personnel is relevant here. This loyalty may vary from very high to very low. A high degree of loyalty to a certain member of an organization can be a main strength against competitors but it may be also dangerous when that person leaves the company. Perhaps the clients will be so loyal that when such a person leaves the company he is accompanied by his clients.

loyalty

Service practice 2-8 What happens if Maurice is leaving?

A high degree of loyalty occurs quite regularly in the advertising industry. One of the most striking examples is Maurice Saatchi leaving Saatchi and Saatchi in 1994 and with him some very important employees and clients. The case was even been brought to the High Court in London. Maurice Saatchi was planning to start a new ad agency. This would be a competitor to the former Saatchi and Saatchi. The judge said Maurice may search for new clients and may even "recruit" some of his former Saatchi and Saatchi employees.

people bound services, knowledge based services

Quite a lot of these "people bound" services can be characterized as knowledge based services (sometimes called the "professional service providers" like lawyers, consultants). This bonding need not be based on knowledge or personal capabilities alone. Some service providers are not offering just knowledge, they also provide facilities to be used. Examples of service providers which offer knowledge and facilities are television studios, construction equipment used to build houses, highways or fly overs. In line with this distinction is the question whether the service is directed at people, property or information.

capacity

Some other issues can be raised in the classification of service providers. They deal with matching demand and supply and thus with the capacity of the service provider. The capacity of the service organization has to do with the ability to react properly to temporal changes in demand. Are these fluctuations in demand small or large, do they occur regularly or not, is the variation considerable, is it easy to cope with these

Figure 2-10
The service provider's
knowledge, skills
and capacity

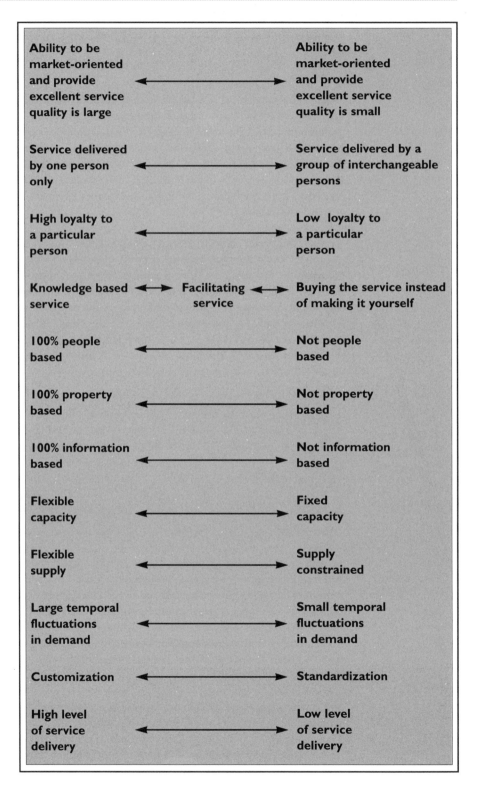

Ability to be market-oriented and provide excellent service quality is large	**Ability to be market-oriented and provide excellent service quality is small**
Service delivered by one person only	**Service delivered by a group of interchangeable persons**
High loyalty to a particular person	**Low loyalty to a particular person**
Knowledge based service ←→ **Facilitating service** ←→	**Buying the service instead of making it yourself**
100% people based	**Not people based**
100% property based	**Not property based**
100% information based	**Not information based**
Flexible capacity	**Fixed capacity**
Flexible supply	**Supply constrained**
Large temporal fluctuations in demand	**Small temporal fluctuations in demand**
Customization	**Standardization**
High level of service delivery	**Low level of service delivery**

fluctuations or not? In short, is it crucial for a service organization to investigate to what extent the capacity is flexible or fixed?[15]

ability to customize or differentiate

With respect to the relevant service provider's skills, it is necessary to make a distinction between the degree of customization and differentiation. In other words, to what extent is the service provider able to customize its offerings to individual preferences or differentiate in its offerings between core services and the augmented service? This distinction holds for a service organization's activities within one country as well as in an international context. It is self evident that the capacity affects storage, waiting times and queueing, the organization of the internal processes and consequently whether the quality level of services delivered is high or low.

THE SERVICE DELIVERY PROCESS

actual operations of delivering services

In our search of the literature we came across a wide variety of topics used to classify services related to this important part of the service encounter. It hinges upon the way in which the services are rendered to the customer. In fact, it refers to the process of delivering the service. The physical sites where the service delivery takes place (the scenery) will be discussed in the next section. Here, we deal with topics referring to actual operations of delivering services. Partly, it has to deal with:

- the role of the customer: what the customer is expected to do; and
- the way the process of "creating" the service delivery within the company is organized.

In other words, many issues here have to do with the technology applied in the dialogue relevant to the particular service encounter and the internal rules and structure of the internal processes.

human involvement

The well known distinction between capital-intensive and people-intensive services is also phrased in terms of equipment-based versus people-based services or in terms of large or little (or no) human involvement in the delivery of services. Moreover, it can also be phrased in terms of whether the customer really interacts with a representative of the organization or whether the customer interacts only via technology with the service organization: so, a continuum can be constructed of the combination of persons and technology in the service encounter.

number of contacts

The number of contacts during the service encounter may be just one or may be many. For the service experience may take place at just one moment in time or during a longer time period. In line with this distinction is the way in which people experience the service encounter: it may differ between a very superficial contact and a very deep and intensive contact. To a certain extent, this is related to the difference between relationships and episodes in services.

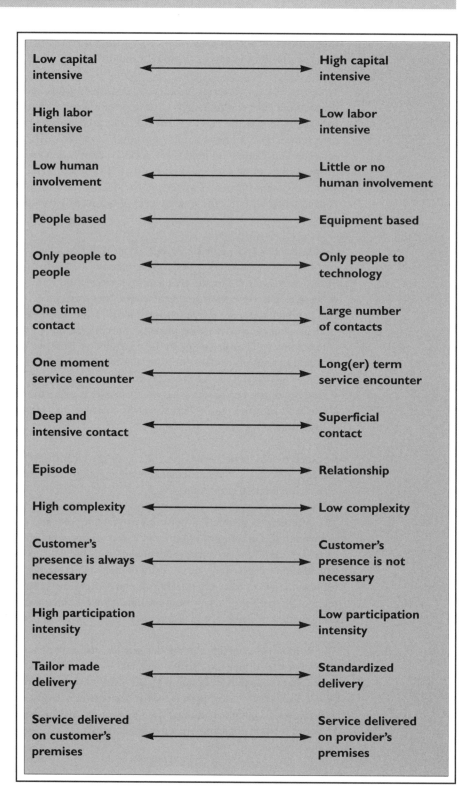

Figure 2-11
The service delivery
process

*Service
practice
2-9
How deep is
your contact?*

Some customers have a very superficial contact with the bank employee when they change foreign currency at the counter, but have a longer and more intense contact during a discussion on mortgages. In corporate and private banking, account managers have a strong bond with their clients.

The intensity of contact may also vary with respect to discussions a holiday traveller may have with his/her hostess during a fortnight's, stay in a hotel, a one week rafting trip, or during an eleven hour flight.

complexity

The process of delivering services will differ in its complexity. This is partly reflected in the way the service providers's knowledge, skills and capacity are applied. The complexity of the service delivery process may vary from very high to very low. It affects the script and roles to be played by both parties in the service encounter. The complexity is partly reflected in the degree of differentiation (see Figure 2-1).

presence

It is also possible to describe service delivery processes in terms of the presence of the customer during this process. This presence can vary between 100% (doctor or hair dresser) and zero (deciding on the customer's claim at the headquarters of an insurance company). Slightly differently, this topic can be expressed in terms of the

participation intensity

"participation intensity" during the service encounter. Has the customer come to participate actively and intensively or is the mere presence of the customer just sufficient and would it be detrimental to the customer if (s)he become active during the service encounter (surgery)?

Finally, one can think of very standardized service delivery processes versus customized ones. To a certain degree, this distinction refers to the question whether services are delivered on the provider's premises or on the customer's premises.

THE PHYSICAL SITE OF THE SERVICE DELIVERY

physical site

The last issue of the complex overall classification is the heart of Figure 2-2: the physical site of the service delivery. This issue deals with all operational aspects with respect to the physical place (scenery) where the service delivery process takes place. It can also be labelled in terms of the physical distance or physical proximity of the service encounter.

distribution network

With respect to the distribution network of the service company, one may think of intensive, selective or exclusive distribution. So, the density in the distribution can differ from very low to very high: from a few (a local pub) to many outlets or sites (banks, shops, etc.).

Figure 2-12
The physical site of the services delivery

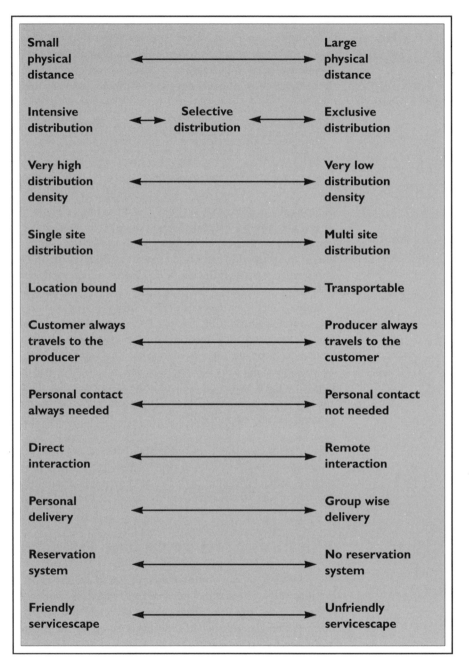

location bound   A second relevant question is: "Are services transportable or location bound?" In other words, is the service delivery taking place at one single site or at multiple sites? Another issue in this domain concerns the question: who is coming to who? Does the customer have to travel, will the representative of the service provider come to the client at home, do both parties come to a particular place, or, is the service encounter taking place without any personal contact (telephone calls). In this respect, the difference

The distribution intensity may differ in the different sectors of the service industry. Most of the retail banks have higher distribution intensity than postal agencies. Primary schools have more "outlets" than universities and the distribution intensity is very low for exclusive services like highly specialized lawyers. But, remember most services have a "distribution intensity which is so exclusive" that the multiple services are just delivered in one certain (local) spot (bakery, dentist, shoe repair, etc.).

between direct interaction in the service encounter versus remote interaction (i.e. interaction based on remote communication) is relevant.[16] Of course, a mixture of these options may exist.

It is also important to note whether the service is delivered to the client individually (private violin lessons) or to a group of customers at the same time (all passengers in the bus on their excursions to a particular site).

Finally, the existence of a reservation system should be mentioned. This allows for a better control of the service delivery system at the place where the service is being served and may prevent queueing problems and waiting times.

servicescape

Until now, many issues about the site have been discussed in terms of its geographical position. The internal part of it should also be taken into account in describing the actual service delivery. Is this "servicescape" friendly to the customer or not?[17] This refers to the right part of Figure 1-2 on the service encounter mainly (the waiting room, office, area where service is delivered).

2.3 SOME EXAMPLES OF THE COMPLEX CONFIGURATIONS

Now that we have discussed a large number of topics that can be used to define and circumscribe services, it is important to note that all these topics should not be regarded as separate ones. Many of them interact or are closely related to each other. Therefore, we will give some examples of such configurations. These examples can be positioned in the many boxes in Figure 2-2.

Service practice 2-11 What might happen if there is more contact?

As the contact between the service provider and the customer becomes more frequent, loyalty to the contact person will possibly increase. Customer and service provider will meet more often. Consequently, a relationship based on trust will emerge. Depending on the kind of service, the relationship can become more formal or more continuous. Continuous relationships may result in a personalized service delivery.

*Service
practice
2-12
A customized
service, please*

Customized service delivery processes will require personal treatment. The supply of services will then be differentiated to a very large extent. These speciality services are very domain specific to the customer, who is probably highly committed to the service provider (organization as well as employee). In many cases, a lot of interaction may take place during the service encounter and true loyalty will exist. In sum, the services will be delivered on the customer's premises.

*purpose of developing
the integrative
framework*

The purpose of developing the integrative framework in Figure 2-2 with all its continua offers the possibility to decompose the whole service offering of a company and its competitors at a particular moment and/or over time. Many issues are at stake and should be taken into account to analyze the dynamics of a service organization, its people, processes, policies, customers and competitors. In fact, Figures 2-3 to 2-12 contain detailed information about the boxes in Figure 2-2: the overall classification scheme of services. Combining that figure with those nine tables would lead to a very comprehensive and detailed overview of a particular service in all its aspects.

*most important
characteristics*

We believe that the most important characteristics to be used in a simple and pragmatic way of classifying services are, **the degree of differentiation and the degree of customization**.

The degree of differentiation reflects whether only a core service is supplied or augmented service. The capabilities of the service provider determine what will be offered and the cost associated with this service-production. This degree of customization balances the marketing concept. It refers to putting the customer first, taking into account the firm's positioning relative to its competitors. In essence, the organization's market orientation constitutes the underlying philosophy of the marketing concept. Simply stated, the customization continuum ranges from customized individual services to mass services. In this way, both aspects of our view on market orientation come to the fore (see Figure 1-5).

Our discussion about the basic feature of services (its intangibility) has led to four kinds of services, differing in their degree of intangibility. They range from fully intangible to fully tangible. These four kinds of services can be defined in terms of the extent to which services are the core of the offering, just an additional issue to a service or a product, or the very tangible product itself.

*evaluate the present
position*

*what should be
changed*

Now, every organization, and thus every service organization, can position itself simply, relative to its competition. They can evaluate whether the present position is the ideal position, and if not, what should be done to accomplish the new position. The positions held in the other tables presented in this chapter (Figures 2-2 to 2-12) may be useful in deciding what should be changed in those detailed features of the service package in order to accomplish the benefits and/or (subjective) quality desired by the customer.

SUMMARY

This chapter aims at providing a comprehensive overview of the many issues deemed relevant to understand services. It reveals that the basic characteristic of services (intangibility) has many consequences in developing strategies for service organizations and implementing specific service activities.

In classifying services, it appears that a distinction between a strategic and operational level is useful. This starting point led us to develop nine categories to be applied in providing a structured overview of the many characteristics of services. The first ones have a more strategic nature while the latter ones have a more operational (or concrete) nature:

1. services and products;
2. profit versus non profit;
3. markets and industries;
4. internal or external services;
5. the consumer and his/her service buying behavior;
6. the relationship between the service provider and the customer;
7. the service provider's knowledge, skills and capacity;
8. the service delivery process; and
9. the physical site of the service delivery.

Each of these nine categories could be subdivided into many characteristics of services. Figure 2-2 puts them all together and this could be used for a detailed description of a company"s own services or their competitors". A disadvantage of this integrative framework is its complexity. Therefore, we started with a more simple taxonomy (Figure 2-1) to be used throughout this book. It consists of four archètypes of services:

1. standard core services;
2. standard augmented services;
3. customized core services; and
4. customized augmented services.

Of course, these four types are extreme forms. Many other types of services will exist having two or more characteristics of these in common. However, for reasons of simplicity and for a better understanding of the "world of services" it will be useful to keep this taxonomy in mind. Since this taxonomy is based on the degree of differentiation in the service provider's offer and the degree of customization expected by the customer, it reflects our approach to market orientation (see Figure 1-5).

QUESTIONS

1 What is the most dominant feature in defining services?
2 What does "the simultaneous production and consumption of services" mean?
3 Which nine major categories can be found in order to describe and analyze services?
4 Why is it important
   a) to analyze; and,
   b) to stress,
   the relationships between a customer and a service provider in services marketing?
5 Figures 1-7 and 2-1 are the same. What arguments are given in sections 1.7 and 2.1 to develop these figures? How do they fit into one another?
6 Are services always intangible?
7 What is the use of classifying a particular phenomenon in general?
8 In what way can the classification of services be used for strategic purposes?
9 Why is it relevant to define all categories used in classifying services as continuous instead of discrete "variables"?
10 Explain why the box about "the physical site of the service delivery" is said to be the heart of Figure 2-2.

ASSIGNMENTS

1 Give more examples of some possible configurations (see Service practices 2-11/2-12).
2 Fill in all the boxes in Figure 2-2 with the details from Figures 2-3 to 2-12. Then use this comprehensive framework to describe the services provided by your bank, university or (most or least) favourite airline. In analyzing the description, please pay attention to the logic of this overall picture: do all the elements of the service offering fit logically together?

Assignments 3 and 4 are the basis of the "service diary" you could keep during your study in Services Marketing Management. You will discover more about it in subsequent chapters.

3 Provide an overview of the three most positive experiences you had with service organizations during the last month.
4 Provide an overview of the three most negative experiences you had with service organizations during the last month.
5 When you have completed assignments 3 and 4 and all your fellow students have reported on their findings, what general conclusions can be drawn about
   • the positive experiences;
   • the negative experiences;
   • the kind of service organizations involved (e.g. industry, size, labor intensity, perceived risk, the service delivery process);
   • the intangibility of the services involved;
   • the customization by the service organizations involved;

- the positioning of the services and the service organizations involved in Figures 2-3 and 2-4.

6 Mark the characteristics of services given in Service practices 2-11 and 2-12 in Figures 2-3 to 2-12.

7 In which figures do most of your positive and negative service experiences (see your service diary) fit? What can you conclude from that?

ENDNOTES

1. When the field of services marketing started to be developed in the 70's and early 80's many articles focused on defining and classifying services. Especially, the differences between services and goods were a hot topic. This explains why the references in this chapter seem to be rather old. Today, this topic is hardly discussed any more. This does not mean that a generally accepted classification of services exists. Therefore, we have provided this overview. See also Berry and Parasuraman (1993) or Fisk, Brown and Bitner (1993) for an historic overview of the services marketing domain.

2. Shostack (1977); Wright (1995).

3. Zeithaml and Bitner (1996); Palmer (1994); Kotler (1991).

   In a broader perspective, Mangold (1997) maintains that, at present, the development in society is not one from producing goods to producing services but rather a trend to adding more services to goods. Especially in the high tech industry Mangold (one of the Daimler-Benz top managers) stresses the need to combine high tech (industrial) products with complementary high tech services. Mangold expects this to be difficult in Germany since that country lacks a "service-culture".

4. Kostecki, 1994, pp. 205-208.

5. Palmer, 1994; Kostecki, 1994.

6. Cowell, 1984, pp. 149-151, citing Rathmell, 1974.

7. Stauss, 1994.

8. These concepts are further elaborated upon in Chapter Four.

9. Van Raaij and Verhallen, 1994.

10. See also Cunningham, Young and Lee, 1997.

11. Lovelock, 1991, p. 28; 1983.

12. Palmer, 1994; Strandvik, 1994; Liljander and Strandvik, 1995.

13. Grönroos 1990b; Gummesson, 1993.

14. Bloemer, 1993.

15. Lovelock, 1991, p. 32.

16. Kostecki, 1994, p. 206.

17. Bitner, 1992.

CHAPTER THREE

SERVICE ENVIRONMENT

After studying this chapter you will understand that:

- *a structured and periodic external analysis by scanning the environment is of vital importance for a service provider in order to survive;*

- *the growth in the service sector is fuelled by various marketing-related trends;*

- *a comprehensive framework of the external analysis consisting of sequentially examining the macro-environment, the environment of the service sector and the competition enables managers to*

- *make their own judgement of the risks and opportunities for their organizations;*

- *the insights from these separate analyses can be utilized in the process of strategic planning, marketing planning and in the development of new services;*

- *major developments, in selected service industries world wide, make rapid changes in the business environment of individual companies.*

BELOW: *The many faces of a strategic alliance*

Photograph printed with permission of Wilhelm Schultz © 1997.

3.1 INTRODUCTION

Service
practice
3-1
Trends
affecting
America's
future[1]

Forecaster Marvin Cetron, author of numerous books about the future, prepared a report listing 74 trends and forecasts affecting the United States approaching the 21st century. He and the editors of The Futurist worked together in filtering the trends. Each trend is the result of analysis and research findings. Reviewing the total future picture, Cetron foresees a "renaissance" for America in the years ahead. In one way or another, all of these so called societal trends will also influence businesses. We have selected the following forecasts which, if coming true, will have a profound effect upon major parts of the service sector.

Technology will increasingly dominate both the economy and society. The growth of the information industry is creating an extremely knowledge-dependent society. Software will become even more important. Expert systems will issue reports and recommend actions based on data gathered electronically. These systems will be incorporated in services as diverse as automotive diagnostics, medicine, commercial and consumer loans, insurance underwriting and legal services. By 2001, artificial intelligence (AI) and virtual reality will help most companies and government agencies to assimilate data and solve problems beyond the range of the mid 1990's computers. AI uses include robotics, machine vision, voice recognition, speech synthesis, electronic data processing, health and human services, administration and airline pilot assistance. Information technologies are promoting long-distance communication as people hook up with the same commercial databases and computer networks. Two-way cable television will accelerate this process. The very poor and very wealthy will decline in American society. Rural land is being colonized by suburbs and cities. In the transport industry, rails are on the way out, but trains are not. For journeys of 100 to 150 miles, high speed trains will begin replacing air travel in the airlines' existing hub-and-spoke system. The US economy is becoming integrated with the international economy. Imports continue to increase, international capital markets are merging and buying patterns around the world coalesce. All these factors promote the interdependence of business and government decisions worldwide.

Mass telecommunications and printing are continuing to unite the nations of the world. Mass media will be increasingly personalized as more consumers use pay-per-view television to select movies and entertainment.

With respect to education, demand for lifelong education will heat up throughout society. Telecommunications course work will open up new vistas in education. As education becomes more individualized (with the assistance of electronic tools and software), the "places" of learning will be more dispersed and the number of adolescents diminishing – the institutions of higher education are shrinking. However, adults' need for higher education will grow.

At the same time job mobility – changing location or firm, but doing the same work – will increase. People will soon expect to change jobs four to five times during their lifetime. Dual-career families, with both partners sometimes working in different cities, will require greater personal mobility. Two-income couples are becoming the norm. In 1970, only 43% of women worked. By 1990, the figure had grown to 57.5%. By 2000, 62% of women will be in the labor force; by 2005, 63%. More flexitime and flexiplace work opportunities will make it easier for women to enter the work force. As life expectancy increases, workers are retiring later. One of the consequences will be that pensions and pension funds continue to grow.

On the management front, information organizations are quickly displacing the old command-and-control model of management. Information technology is the driving force. Manual and clerical workers are increasingly outnumbered by knowledge workers. Information is the primary commodity in more and more industries today. Services are the fastest-growing sector of the American economy (and not only in the USA!).

The only thing that is certain about the future is that people keep trying to predict it.[2] Although, not every forecast will become fully realized, and not every American trend will apply to the rest of the world, the fact is that each organism that wishes to survive will have to suit itself to the environment and will have to adapt itself. Mapping sustainable societal changes or trends – such as the ones outlined in Service practice 3-1 – are an important tool to survival. It indicates opportunities and threats to the company. The same applies to service providers. Together with the analysis of the internal strengths or core competencies it will form the basis of the corporate strategy of a service firm just as any other organization.

mapping sustainable societal changes or trends

internal strengths or core competencies

By systematically charting the external factors influencing the service environment, this chapter provides a basis for the corporate and marketing strategy of a service provider. By doing so, we utilize the environment theory which sees the company as an open system interacting with its environment and striving towards survival of the organization.[3] The environment theory is based on the idea of periodically scanning the external factors surrounding the organization in order to develop, adjust and implement an adequate company policy. Scanning the environment means collecting and analyzing information about relevant trends in the environment of the organization. We have seen in Chapter One that market information is crucial to be market oriented. The external analysis first deals with each of the macro (DRETS) factors and their implication on the marketing strategy of services. Second, at the service sector level many of the tendencies in the outside world will be placed into several groups and considered as marketing-related trends which pertain to services. Then – third – the external analysis of the industry environment will result in an overview of developments shaping the future in various service industries. The whole scanning process of the service environment will be done from an international perspective. The out-

environment theory

external analysis

line of this chapter is given in Figure 3-1. The origin of external factors influencing the company stems from:

macro-environment
- the macro-environment, i.e. demographic, regulating, economic, technological and social factors (section 3.2 on DRETS factors);

service sector environment
- the service sector environment, consisting of marketing-related trends, specific to the service sector (section 3.3);

competitive environment
- the competitive environment, forces confronting the service provider, such as customers and supplier influence, or that of the industry one operates in (section 3.4).

Figure 3-1
Chapter outline

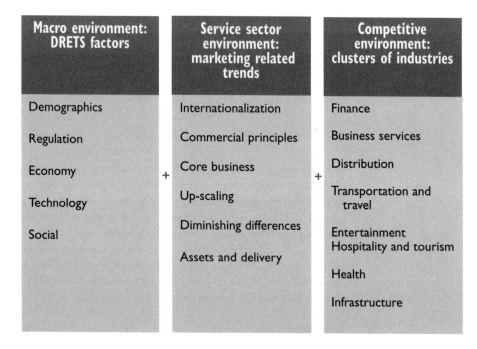

Macro environment: DRETS factors		Service sector environment: marketing related trends		Competitive environment: clusters of industries
Demographics		Internationalization		Finance
Regulation		Commercial principles		Business services
Economy	+	Core business	+	Distribution
Technology		Up-scaling		Transportation and travel
Social		Diminishing differences		Entertainment Hospitality and tourism
		Assets and delivery		Health
				Infrastructure

The results of the external analysis are vitally necessary as it should be applied on a regular basis, within various functional areas and at a number of organization levels. Top management uses the opportunity and risk analysis during the strategic planning process. Further, the information gathered can be used for functional long term-planning of divisions and/or sections or as input of strategic business units' (SBU's) plans. Ultimately, environment analysis data can be a stimulating source for developing new services. This chapter will go into the first three categories, the macro-environment, the service environment and that part of the competitive environment as far as it deals with developments of the particular industry. The other environment factors such as competition at an individual level and the micro environment will be discussed in Chapters Seven and Eight – covering the overall strategy and market planning process. All these factors are depicted in Figure 3-2.

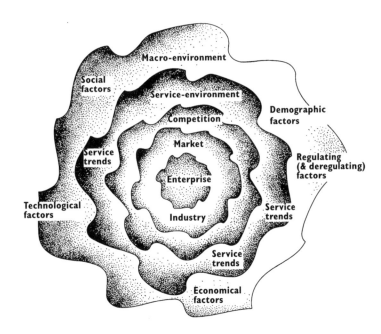

3.2 THE MACRO ENVIRONMENT: FACTORS THAT CANNOT BE INFLUENCED

All organizations are influenced by macro-factors in their environment. Although a combination of a few large companies or multinationals is sometimes able to influence a number of these factors, these forces remain invariable in most companies.[4] This section deals with five uncontrollable influences in the macro-environment of an organization. These are as follows:

- demographic (D);
- regulatory (R);
- economic (E);
- technological (T); and
- social factors (S).

DRETS   To simplify matters, all these factors combined will be abbreviated to DRETS. Each of them will be discussed.

DEMOGRAPHIC FACTORS (DRETS)

The demographic environment of the service sector has changed considerably during the past decades. Major demographic tendencies are: total population growth, increase in the number of households and decrease in the number of members per household in most industrialized countries; higher life expectancy, dejuvenation and population ageing; better education; multiracial societies in North America, Australia and major parts of Europe.

Total population growth, increase in the number of households and decrease in the number of members per household

In 1996 the world population was 5,800,000,000 (5.8 billion); for the coming years an actual annual growth of about 86,000,000 (86 million) persons is expected. In the industrialized countries, the number of households is expected to increase much *rise in number of households* more percentage wise. The increase is mainly due to the rise in number of households consisting of two persons and the explosive growth of the number of people living alone. In 2015, the majority of singles will be composed of elderly people, elderly women in particular, who live alone after the death of their spouse. On average, there is still a six-year gap in life expectancy between men and women, although this gap gradually diminishes.

On the other hand, in many Western, Central and Eastern European societies the total population will probably decrease within 10–20 years from now. In different regions across Europe (like France and Bulgaria) this is happening already or will happen within a few years.

Higher life expectancy, dejuvenation and population ageing

In most developed countries people live longer and the population continues to age. In 2010, 23% of the total European Union's population will consist of people who are *dejuvenation* 60 or over. At the same time, dejuvenation will take place, in the sense that relatively speaking (as a percentage of the total population) and speaking absolutely (in actual numbers), the number of young people is decreasing.

care for the elderly Higher life expectancy demands extra efforts in care for the elderly. Other companies will have new opportunities too. As the young can be classified as being Yuppies (Young Urban Professionals) or Dinkis (Double Income, No Kids), nowadays many elderly people can be defined as Grampies (Growing Retired Active Monied People In Excellent State). The amount of their financial resource is conspicuous, which has resulted in an ever decreasing dependence on others, of both the young as well as the elderly.

Service practice 3-2 Ageing, chances for service providers[5]

The "economics of ageing" is based on the idea that people (e.g. the Americans) are getting older. The Woodstock generation, the roughly 76 million baby boomers who where born from 1946 to 1964, is going grey. The elderly are living longer now. The predictions grow darker on fears that spendthrift Americans aren't saving enough and that their living standards will plunge when they retire. Social Security payments may not be there to help out as the system buckles with too few workers supporting too many retirees, and the swelling ranks of the elderly will send medical costs spiralling out of control. These days, the mantra "we can't afford it" echoes from Senate hearings rooms to corporate boardrooms. But there are strong reasons that suggest that the age apocalypse will never arrive. Instead, a series of broad, mutually reinforcing changes in the US economy will make an ageing population much more of an economic asset than before. One striking transformation is how companies now use information technologies to raise productivity, which makes it easier to fund the Social Security and health-care bills that are squeezing America's wallet today. People are also productive far longer in an information-and-services economy. Healthier lifestyles and medical advances should postpone disability among the elderly.

In the USA, until recently, a nursing home was one of the few alternatives for those who where finding it difficult to run their own households. In the past decade, however, "assisted" living centres for those who needed some help have been gaining in popularity. At the moment, many are quite expensive, although competition should bring prices down over time. The Heritage Club in Denver has both independent apartments and assisted living, and some of the homes also have nursing facilities. Jean A. Carson, 88, entered her two-bedroom apartment three years ago. She cooks her own breakfast and lunch but eats dinner in the dining room downstairs. To stay healthy she takes exercise classes and she works out in the weight room. "I'm better than I was 10 years ago. I've got muscles and joints I haven't used for years that are working again", she says.

Colleges see senior citizens as a market opportunity, too. The Academy of Senior Professionals at Eckerd College in St Petersburg brings retired professionals together with Eckerd's undergraduate student body as teachers and participants in classes. "It's very important for older people to pass on values and experiences in the hope these things will be helpful to tomorrow's leaders", says Arthur L. Peterson, director of the program. The age wave is sure to bring about plenty of upheaval. The ageing of America isn't a story about the imminent, or even distant, arrival of utopia. But there are many positive fundamental forces at work. The nation is more productive than any time since the 1960s. The elderly are more vital than before. Americans can afford to grow old. And they grow old gracefully.

Elderly Americans will live longer and be better educated as well as healthier.

As the elderly have come to live independently for a longer period of time, all sorts of perspectives have been opened for service sectors like the catering industry, care for the elderly, home care, tele-shopping and security services. Due to the growing number of elderly who are physically fit and financially well off, it becomes more and more interesting to introduce market segmentation for this group of "oldies but goldies" or "hale and hearty types".

Differentiation in products and services for this growth segment, however, will have to take place without using a specific "seniors label". After all, many senior citizens do not wish to be confronted with their true age.

Better education

better educated

Compared with thirty years ago, the world population is better educated. The percentage of the "age group enrolled in primary education" increased from 83% in 1970 to almost 100% in 1991. Percentages for secondary and tertiary education rose in this period from, 31% to 52% and 12% to 17% on average. The chances of receiving higher education for the young in North America, Israel, Hong Kong, Singapore, Australia, New Zealand, United Arab Emirates, most countries in Europe, all belonging to the so called high-income countries, is still much higher than in most other countries, as their figures are 73% to 93% for secondary and 36% to 50% for tertiary education. During that time, a great number of jobs in agriculture and industry were lost to other sectors. That is why professional grounding had to make way for general education. When projecting the concept of education onto the latter tendency, it will immediately be obvious that the number of elderly people being educated in the future will rise spectacularly. Estimates by planners in various industrialized countries indicate that the number of elderly people participating in education will double or triple over the coming decades.

general education

Multiracial societies

ethnic composition of the population

The final demographic factor mentioned in this context, is the change in the ethnic composition of the population in a number of countries such as the USA, UK, Germany, France, Belgium and The Netherlands. In Australia and New Zealand, the shift in immigration figures from European countries to Asian countries has resulted in a more diversified population. The change towards new minorities brings opportunities for service providers as diverse as cafés and restaurants (with the atmosphere from home), laundries and tax advisers speaking the language of the new immigrants.

REGULATORY FACTORS (dRETS)

influence of government

Both directly and indirectly, governments have a strong influence on the commercial policies of the service providers. The influence of government on the service industries may roughly be divided into a number of tendencies. We will discuss the following ones: political and legal (both regulation and deregulation); flexibility of the labor factor; commercialization of the educational system; and self-regulation and other regulating forces.

Regulation and deregulation

political/legal factors

Political/legal factors include the election results, legislature, jurisprudence, and decisions taken by various governmental bodies, including NAFTA and the European Union (EU). In the EU, for example, national acts or laws about shop closing times and selling in the evening and on Sundays have recently changed in many countries on the European continent. Other momentous legal developments embrace the advertising standards act and the conditions of tender that prevail in the EU. These examples also include the spreading-out or staggering of holiday periods in schools, sometimes considered to be one of the triumphs of the holiday industry, and the plans to relax or even revoke the licensing system for the temporary employment agency industry, or the introduction of legislation regarding day-care centre standards. For instance,

cutting into Europe's welfare state

cutting into Europe's welfare state is creating tremendous opportunities for all kinds of private service providers from temp services and insurers to health providers.

Due to regulatory measures that were mainly taken by governmental institutions, the marketeer's playground has changed radically over the last decades. Lately, however,

supra-national organizations

the tide has turned in a number of these fields. Supra-national organizations are setting the path. Increasingly, macro trade (de)regulations issues are decided upon at NAFTA, EU, and/or GATT level.

Service practice 3-3 Deregulation in the financial sector

From Jakarta to San José (Costa Rica) the trend in many service industries, including banking, is one clearly towards deregulation creating opportunities as well as risks for the financial establishment. As a result of deregulation, commercial banks established within the EU, can nowadays easily open a branch in another country within the Community. The central bank of the country where the main offices of the commercial bank are registered, is now obliged to supervise the proper conduct of the whole business. This is a form of geographic deregulation. Deregulation of services sèc also takes place. In an increasing number of countries it has proved to be possible to run an insurance company and a banking firm within the same institution ("banc assurance" or "all-finanz" concept). In the United States, similar tendencies can be observed.

Deregulation and liberalization are not the only tendencies in the financial world. As of a few years ago, the international markets have been dominated by financial derivatives such as options, swaps, futures, and every other possible combination or variant thereof. In 1986, one thousand billion dollars in loans, currencies, shares or goods were at stake on the derivatives market. To the great satisfaction of bankers, entrepreneurs and investors, this sum increased tenfold in 1992.

The International Monetary Fund, the Bundesbank and the Bank for International Settlements in Basle, Switzerland advocate regulation by establishing international rules for these financial derivatives. The need for it can be proved by the bankruptcy of one of the oldest merchant banks, Barings of London, due to the actions of one trader and loose control of the senior management in 1995. Moreover, big losses in some of the top companies and banks using these sophisticated techniques, are used as an argument for more regulation.

Flexibility of the labor factor

increase labor flexibility

The urge to increase labor flexibility in Japan, Europe, Canada and Australia manifests itself through all sorts of environmental factors. There is no doubt that governments will take action in this field in the future.

The role of government is expected to change considerably over the next decades. In an interesting study, two trends which are susceptible to government influence are

*Service
practice
3-4
Europe loses
its laborers*

The development of electronic communications such as computer, fax and modem no longer restrict labor to one place. The fall of communism, including the turn to capitalism by the Chinese government, will limit opportunities for routine labor which, by nature, is not restricted to locations in North America, Western Europe or Japan. For these regions, this implies that highly skilled industrial branches and the role of the service sector that is usually tied to a specific location, will gain in importance. For that reason, it is proposed that there should be flexible working hours and a legal right to work for two or three employers.

pointed out, which are interesting to several service sectors in many countries.[6] These are: the commercialization of education and limitation of publicly-financed health care. (The subject of health care will be dealt with under industry cases later in this chapter.)

Commercialization of the educational system

*educational
institutions*

An ever growing part of education fees are being paid by the clients. These clients consist of students, working and unemployed people, graduates, companies and others. Companies wishing to beat the competition and those who wish to continue to function in society, will need "education permanente" (life-long learning) to be able to keep up with the many developments within and outside one's own sector. It is essential for everyone to keep abreast of the times. In that process, training courses will be increasingly assessed for their quality. America's businesses have become some of the country's most important educational institutions. Spending on corporate education has grown 5% a year for the last decade. Besides training of their workers, grants or credits from corporations are another form of support to students. Some companies have gone as far as to award students with their own degree. For example, Arthur D. Little, a management consultancy, offers a degree in management consultancy. A survey of 100 companies with well developed education programs conducted in 1995 by Quality Dynamics, a New York based consultancy, found that a third of them planned to start granting degrees, up from a handful now. Others are establishing formal connections with local colleges or well established universities.[7] We would like to extend this commercialization to other government factors. Grants to community centres may be decentralized. The delegation of power to lower authorities or institu-tions often leads to an increase in the citizens' personal contributions.

Self-regulation and other regulatory forces

codes of conduct

The regulation of marketing customs, however, need not always be legislated or explicitly influenced by politics. Many sectors – particularly in the professional service business – have their own codes of conduct which affect market policy (self-regulation). Committees such as the Code of Advertising Practice, the Fraternity of Public Notaries, the legal practice, or the accountants see to it that the codes of conduct are abided by. Furthermore, it goes without saying that in an informal way, consumer organizations, institutions like Greenpeace and the media constitute a regulating force.

ECONOMIC FACTORS (drEts)

economic forces

Economic forces have an important influence on company policies. This third category of macro-factors encompasses among other things: the development of the Gross National Product (GNP) and the changes in consumer's income; the country's stage of economic development; the value of the national currency; and changing expenditure patterns.

Gross National Product and changes in income

steady growth

Steady growth of the Gross National Product naturally offers opportunities for new companies and promotes the growth of existing companies. The consumer is likely to be able to spend more, especially on services.

economic growth
flattens out
recession

However, opportunities also arise when economic growth flattens out, or during a recession. This is particularly true in countries that put comparatively few constraints on an individual wishing to start a private company. Then, an explosive growth in business service companies can be observed. For, the starting capital needed to set up such companies is relatively low. (Quite often a lot of them fail due to being insufficiently prepared.)

Furthermore it can be observed that some service sectors suffer from bad economic times while other sectors see opportunities to benefit from it. In this way some services (holiday-trips, retailers in durables and financial services, loans and mutual funds being amongst these) will suffer from a recession whereas financial services in the savings sector will thrive in such times.

The stage of economic development

stage of economic development of a country

The stage of economic development of a country is of particular interest to service providers operating in the international markets.

developing countries

basic customer-related services

About 75% of the world population lives in what the World Bank terms developing countries. In such countries, there are hardly any opportunities for highly specialized consumer services. There is a market, though, for rather basic customer-related services in the fields of infrastructure, the agricultural sector or in health care.

newly industrialized countries

emerging markets

Those countries with a rapid economic development and a strong GNP growth rate, the "newly industrialized countries" in the Far East and the "emerging markets" in South America and Central and Eastern Europe, offer excellent opportunities in particular for these customer-related services in the next few years. Chapter One indicated that key success factors will be price and quality in former Eastern Europe.

In consumer services, the fast-food sector is an example of an industry quick to spot new markets. Its growth partly depends on the demographic trends.

The value of the national currency

national currency

competing services from abroad

The value of the national currency is of particular interest to the importing/exporting service providers in non-dollar dominated countries (i.e. Yen) who make a great part of their profits in areas dominated by the dollar, or who are sensitive to the imports of competing services from abroad. International transportation companies, consultants and engineers can be hindered by their hard currencies in particular if they renumerate their staff in these currencies. This plays a key role in securing project assignments where the price, in addition to the quality offered, is a major consideration. Software houses, too, face increasing international competition. It is becoming more and more profitable to have computer programs developed or R&D done partly in Pakistan, India or China, as well as in Central and Eastern Europe. Highly educated young professionals, low salaries and a frequent devaluation of the local currency all go hand in hand. To promote business to business services such as software export or international finance services, countries like India and Ireland provide additional fiscal stimuli.

Changing expenditure patterns

expenditure of consumers

The expenditure of consumers change as time goes by. Amongst other things, this has to do with changing habits, altering preferences and the state in which the economy finds itself.

income development

well-off citizen

Current projections for income development in Europe and the US say that the net income for large groups of their population will increase only slightly over the next few years. Among other things, competition from countries with low wages and the different ways in which large companies organize themselves contribute to this. Nevertheless, typically the well-off citizen still maintains a preference for goods and services of better quality ("more of less"). It must be pointed out, however, that the price factor (by sheer necessity) will play a more dominant role in the customer's selection process.

baby boom generation

In many countries, the "baby boom" generation is increasingly saving for their pensions. No doubt, this change in expenditure pattern greatly influences the sale of financial services such as mutual funds and other investment vehicles. However, it has, in the short term, a negative impact on the turnover of many other goods and services.

TECHNOLOGICAL FACTORS (DRETS)

acceleration of technological developments

In the last few decades, the Western world has been flooded with all sorts of technological developments which have had a strong influence on the services environment. This century has seen an acceleration of technological developments: products like the PC, telefax and the services they provide were still unknown in the sixties, not to mention E-mail and the Internet which only developed during the nineties. Here, we distinguish between: technological developments; and the emergence of telematics, the integration of information technology and telecommunications.

Technological developments

chip

developing new services

A major technological breakthrough such as the development of the chip allows for the rapid manufacturing of numerous new goods which, in turn, form the basis for developing new services. To illustrate:

- personal/portable phones simplify the accessibility of professional service providers who are en route most of the time;
- modems make it possible for insurance agents to advise their clients or submit a quotation on the spot. While travelling, consultants or managers of large companies can remain informed on the latest company news through electronic mail (E-mail). The modem enables them to send memos to the head office's fax or electronic mailbox; and
- the Internet has created a total new way of distribution and communication, addressing world audiences with the push of a button. In Europe, 6.3 million households were connected to the Internet in 1997. This is twice as many as in 1996.[8] This growth is not expected to stop in the near future.

effect on the labor factor

effect on education

The technological development did not fail to have an effect on the labor factor. Numerous service jobs have disappeared in the past years. New functions introduced such as system designer, programmer, and a new generation of electronic maintenance operators, in part, have already vanished. The changes in computer technology also have an effect on education; instruction via the computer is growing.

telematics

The emergence of telematics

networks

life cycles of services

Telematics, the integration of information technology and telecommunication, opens a host of perspectives to service providers. Physically, company divisions can operate independently and still be connected to each other through a web of communication networks. When office rents in New York went sky-high in the eighties, banks and insurance companies moved their back offices to other parts of the country, where rents and wages were more moderate. Qualified, low-paid administrative staff in India, the Philippines and Central-America can now perform administrative tasks, e.g. in air-lines or banks, previously undertaken by higher paid employees elsewhere in the world. The progress in technological developments over the last decades has also attributed to the life cycles of services being shortened and led to intensifying the competitive environment. Services like private laundries, barbers and doctors who make house calls have all but disappeared in many countries. Merely the turbulence in the technological environment alone makes predicting the future, based on historic observations, a perilous undertaking.

teleworking

For companies and individuals alike, technology will increasingly change the way we work. It now facilitates teleworking. People can work from home or from regional teleworking centres and add value to the chain.[10] This counts especially in an age where information is becoming a key asset. Traffic jams are increasing around the globe and environmental issues (in this case pollution and scarcity of raw materials such as oil) are highly political and at the forefront of the thoughts of many people. Teleworking will change once-sleeping towns and the way parents and children as

*Service
practice
3-5
Stock
exchanges;
telematics and
services[9]*

The famous "Big Bang" in October 1986 on the London stock market has inspired major sellers, buyers and traders both now and in the future to deal with each other largely by way of screens using electronic information rather than operating solely at the actual stock exchange. The Nasdaq electronic based stock exchange which principally lists medium to small companies is growing rapidly. The Stock Exchange in The Netherlands, the oldest on the European continent and the Amsterdam options market ("European Options Exchange") was pushed to develop a less expensive and more efficient market system, as orders of institutional investors were shifting increasingly to London. Two other European countries implementing national market reform and innovation were Italy (1991) and Germany (1993), both long-hampered and delayed by a strong regional spirit. Both markets are promising as their equity markets are grossly underdeveloped in respect to their GDP compared with most other countries. Italy has opted for a transparent national screen market. Germany has linked up all regional market centres and member firms to its automated trading system, IBIS. Even its relatively young futures market, DTB, is in the process of being united with the new national Deutsche Börse.

well as neighbors interact, with people being at home more often. As a consequence, it will influence both the demand and supply of services. For example, teleworking together with the highly regulated labor market in major parts of the world will fuel the trend to so called Micronesian – long-life working relationships between organizations and their staff will give way to small companies or individuals delivering their services on request or contract. These once sleeping neighborhoods will become a birthplace of new service providers:

*delivering services on
request or contract*

- one type, servicing companies and individuals mainly located at a distance from the new working place; and
- the other type, providing services directly to the new teleworkers often staying at home or at a local teleworking centre.

The foregoing leads us to social factors, the last set of macro forces to be mapped.

SOCIAL FACTORS (DRET**S**)

*values, traditions and
trends*

The final DRETS-factor regards the social and cultural environment that encompasses the prevailing values, traditions and trends in society. Exploring the culture is, in general, more difficult than scanning the other environment factors. This can largely be explained by the social and cultural forces that cannot easily be recorded in statistics. Moreover, these tendencies are influenced by the four external environment factors mentioned earlier (demography, regulation, economy and technology).

The following social tendencies have also contributed to the growing need for services: women working outside the home; a shorter working year; the complexity of society; care for health; concern about environmental issues, and the trend towards more comfort.

Figure 3-3

Female labor force participation rate

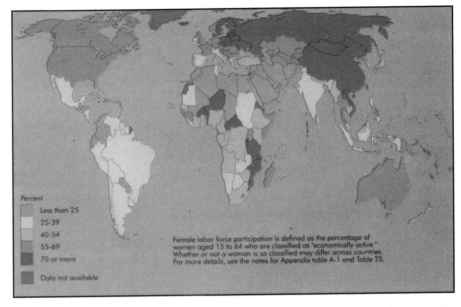

Source: World Development Report 1995; Workers in an Integrating World, Published for the World Bank, Oxford University Press, p. 161

Women working outside the home

female labor force participation

Although the degree of female labor force participation varies per country and was for a long time very high in Eastern Europe and Sweden, women working outside the home has now become a familiar phenomenon around the globe.[11] The increasing number of women now engaged in professional labor predominantly lies in the 20 to 45 years age group. Consequently, the buying power of multi-person households is increasing, inasmuch as the demand for so-called "time-saving goods/services".

time-saving goods/ services

Services responding to these developments mainly concentrate on activities the woman working outside the home, nor her partner, no longer can, or wishes, to do:

- go out for a quick meal – or have the food delivered at home;
- day care;
- shopping delivery service;
- house cleaning and dry cleaning, etc.

The growth in dry cleaning is also stimulated by the dress code used in offices. This growth may decline if the dress code changes.

Shorter working year

average number of hours per labor year

Most Europeans are working less and less. In the period between 1963 and 1995 the average number of hours per labor year decreased in some European countries by more than 25%. In addition, the rates of unemployment and of incapacity for work have also increased, limiting people's chances for paid labor.

The number of hours worked by employees in Japan has been coming down steadily

– from an average of more than 2,100 hours a year in 1978 to around 1,900 in 1996. The figure dropped in 1997 when small companies had to comply with the same maximum 40-hour week introduced for large- and medium-sized firms in 1994.

leisure As a consequence, people nowadays have much more leisure time than thirty years ago, leisure time that is filled with new activities. Services which appear specifically to profit from this are:

- tourism: travelling but also the so-called amusement-fairs and theme parks;
- education: self-improvement, night-school and adult education; and
- toys and sports.

Only in Japan is the leisure business expected to double from the year 1996 to 2010 (to more than Yen 20 trillion).[12]

a longer working year In Europe, the tendency to shorten working hours – at least for a period – seems to be coming to an end. External factors – the competitive position of Northern European states, for example, is threatened by Asian countries and the United States both, having (still) a longer working year. Internal European factors also seem to point to an end of this trend. In comparison with the past, the coming decade will bring fewer younger people to the job market. Also, the ageing population and the affordability of the public retirement schemes will more than likely lead to an extension of working hours rather than to their limitation. It will also imply a more flexible attitude to retirement, forcing the elderly to work beyond the current retirement age as fixed in many countries.

It should also not be forgotten that a growing number of unemployed people implies less working hours for them but also less income. So, not everyone with more leisure time will have a real opportunity to travel or spend less money then at current levels. On the other hand, even after the Asian economic turmoil in 1997/1998 we may expect in these countries, more than in the foregoing years, a larger group prepared to spend time and money on leisure.

Complexity of society

society is becoming *more complex* Society is becoming more complex. Structures that used to be transparent are disappearing and new forms of cohabitation are emerging. Unwed mothers are living beside earning couples who have living-apart-together relationships, and someone benefiting from a job release scheme plays cards with a father who is on parenthood leave.

The simplicity of times past, when in every village one could ask for advice from the vicar, the notary public, or the head-master, has had to make room for a broad range of organizations delivering these services more or less professionally. Nowadays, people address themselves to marriage counsellors, psycho-analysts, tax consultants or insurance agents. The interest in our health has also led to an explosive growth in those services.

Care for health and environment

healthy life The emphasis on leading a healthy life has tremendously stimulated industries in the fields of health foods, fitness and recreation. Service-wise, this trend has evolved into squash courts, weight loss centres (Weight Watchers, Slender You, Manhattan), aerobics and body-shaping schools.

*care for the
environment*
The increasing care for the environment is evident from, amongst other things, the stricter quality standards, for example, cleaning agencies, the search for alternatives in the transportation sector that are environmentally friendly, and the reactions of a hamburger giant such as McDonald's, in this field. In 1995, the Shell Oil company had to change its plans of sinking its used oil platform Brent Spar into the North Sea after tremendous pressures from consumers in Europe, in particular Germany, led by Greenpeace. Environmental issues are becoming more and more strategically incremental for many companies. Polls of younger age-groups in various industrialized countries also show an increasing care for the environment.

The trend towards more comfort

more comfort
Consumers want more comfort. They desire to order or consume their services at home. A number of services that go along with this are still in their infancy but will become more important as the 21st century draws closer: electronic banking, teleshopping, or studies by way of a modem, to name a few.

A number of things a household, a family, or a community used to do themselves is nowadays being done by others. By contracting out or outsourcing, one saves time to do other things (assuming that is what one wishes, can do and can afford to pay the service provider). It is paramount for a services marketeer to realize that as far as *do themselves or contract out* many services are concerned, people can either do them themselves or contract them out. When consumer spending power is decreasing many people will (be able to) do more maintenance of their houses themselves and no longer require the services of a house painter or a plumber.

EPILOGUE

These five social tendencies, in addition to the other four DRETS factors and specific trends in the service sector to be discussed hereafter, are the main causes for growth (and sometimes decline) of the service sector, growth that is not only caused by an increasing demand for existing services. Over the last thirty years, many new services have emerged. More and more, these have to do with services which require higher *services require higher standards of quality and productivity* standards of quality and productivity. It is noticeable that traditional all-round service providers must specialize themselves in one area whereby quality standards are not only aimed at the service's core activities but also at all sorts of additionally related matters. Standards are increasingly set to functional and relational quality and less to the technical quality alone.

*Service
practice
3-6
Additional
services
influenced by
time*
Some dentists have for years been aware of the fact that their profession has come a long way from a routine check-up or a lateral condensation-filled 2.5 (= a filling). As a result, they pay ample attention to tasks that are not specifically dental tasks in a group practice. This varies from putting toys in the waiting room to sending flowers to patients who have already been treated. In addition, in cooperation with the dental hygienist, much more time is spent on advice and prevention, to young(er) patients in particular.

3.3 THE SERVICE SECTOR ENVIRONMENT: MARKETING-RELATED TRENDS

The early nineties was a period during which large companies like IBM and American Airlines were struggling to survive. Enormous cost-cutting programs were swiftly executed by companies world-wide. Non-profit companies, too, were not able to avoid this development. Massive amounts of dismissal notices were the order of the day. "Back to the core business" was a slogan one often heard. The government had related questions. What are the core tasks of a government? How can government bodies operate more efficiently? How may they become (more) market oriented and deliver better quality? All types of service organizations had to react to the growing complexity surrounding them. Inspired by Lovelock's dynamics of change, many factors underlie the ongoing transformation of service management that is taking place in a highly developed economy.[13] This section examines the trends resulting from the interplay of macro-environmental factors in the world, which are especially pertinent to marketing, and, within the marketing arena, especially relevant to services marketing.

ongoing transformation of service management

These trends in the environment apply to the service sector as a whole. As a consequence, they have practical use for individual companies establishing their marketing policy or as input while developing new services. The services trends are accommodated in the following six groups and considered as marketing-related trends which pertain to services:

- internationalization;
- the raise of commercial principles: gaining self-sufficiency, privatization and unbundling of services;
- the implications of focusing on core business: contracting out, down-sizing and specialization;
- up-scaling in core activities: mergers, acquisitions, cooperation and franchising;
- diminishing differences between services and goods as well as between ownership and non-ownership; and
- changes in asset structure and delivery mode: delivery via technology, disintermediation and self service.

INTERNATIONALIZATION

internationalization

The internationalization of services has risen steeply. The same hotel chains, fast-food restaurants, airlines, rental companies, auditing firms, advertising agencies and financial services can now be found all over the world. This trend is reinforced by media and telematics.

All over the world more than four billion people watch American films and television programs or listen to English-language music. Every local culture, wherever it may

*follow the American
pattern*

be, is being Americanized as a result. Indirectly and locally, whether it is wanted or not, this opens perspectives to service providers who follow the American pattern. The viewer, through his television screen, has become familiar with this way-of-living.

This internationalization is not only fuelled by media and changes in technology. Deregulation, competition, financial markets and many other globalization drives have a major impact on the internationalization of services. In the business to business sector, chasing the client – following the manufacturer in his adventures – has been for many service suppliers, especially advertising agencies, a major force to internationalize. As we believe that the internationalization trend and it's underlying factors influence many service industries, we shall analyze this trend in detail separately in Chapter Nine.

THE INCREASE OF COMMERCIAL PRINCIPLES

*applying commercial
principles*

Applying commercial principles in both profit and non-profit service industries is on the increase. This trend is visible throughout the world. Accountable management and focused goals are key issues. In the private sector, offering profit services, this trend shows itself by a strong focus on creating shareholder value, and business units gaining more self-sufficiency or independency within a certain central framework of objectives and rules. More decisions are made at lower levels in the organization and closer to the market. Privatization and unbundling services for competition are expressions of this trend in the public sector.

Shareholder value

*impact on the value of
the company to its
shareholders*

In many instances, the focus is not only on the strategy or actions of the firm, but on the results obtained. Or, in financial terms, the impact on the value of the company to its shareholders. Nevertheless, it should not be forgotten that satisfied customers (based on excellent service quality) are a prerequisite to achieve profits and, hence, shareholder value.

Gaining self-sufficiency

*independence and
autonomy
streamline activities*

Business units that gain self-sufficiency by becoming autonomous units have led to the tendency towards independence and autonomy. A fruitful basis for gaining self-sufficiency seems to be at hand everywhere. On a world-wide scale large companies and governments are trying to streamline their activities. First of all, firms try to become more efficient by focussing on their core business, downsizing, or, "mean and lean" production. Two developments that go some steps further in this respect are privatization in case of a state company and unbundling of (public) services.

Privatization

Under this headline International Business Week (1993) made it clear to its readers that during the next few years, one hundred major government undertakings from several European countries are due to be privatized. It means that the treasurers of the various Western European countries are expecting to receive one hundred and fifty billion dollars. That is to say, if the world's capital markets co-operate. This massive sale of government undertakings includes many service companies, such as nearly all the telecommunication companies and banks such as the Banque National de Paris and the Swedish Nordbanken, Airlines (Lufthansa), electrical industries (ENEL Italy and British National Power) and insurance companies (the French UAP).

governments loosen their grip

Across the world, governments loosen their grip. Bureaucrats still run important segments of the economies, particularly in developing countries. In these countries, large state-owned sectors can be a significant impediment to growth. Rising debts and the need to compensate for the deficits of state undertakings tempt public authorities to sell their properties on a national, regional or local level. World-wide developments in the macro environment influence these decisions. These developments vary from financial pressure on state companies and non-profit organizations, the financing of growing investments, deregulation, multi-lateral organizations such as The World Bank and IMF advocating free enterprise, to technical and other macro-factors earlier discussed in this chapter. In many countries, it comes down to the inability of politics to secure what was often a government monopoly leading to the necessity of more efficient company management. Add to this the temptations presented by the prospective buyer, of the revenues of selling state-owned enterprises (when the coalition is in power) and the recurring interest income from the principal sum (provided the revenues are not, or not solely, used for a one-time clearing of government deficit), and it

sale of state-owned enterprises

is clear why the sale of state-owned enterprises (SOEs) is so attractive to governments and those in power. SOEs are defined here as government owned or controlled economic entities that generate the bulk of their revenue from selling goods and services.[14] The phrase "privatization" was first used in Britain to denote a policy in which

privatization

nationalized companies were sold off to private ownership. The World Bank has developed a decision tree (see Figure 3-4) which helps to organize the multitude of choices involved in SOE reform. To use it, begin with the first question on the left. Each answer leads to another question or recommended policy course.

Unbundling services for competition

Like privatization, unbundling services fits within the rapidly changing regulatory environment. Politics and governments think differently about public enterprises than a few decades ago. The unbundling of public services for competition attracts

unbundling of public services

global service providers. As the authors of the World Bank report (1994) question: should one company provide all telephone services – local, long distance, cellular, data transmission – or should the elements of the telecommunications business be unbundled into separate enterprises? Similar questions could be raised for the most efficient way to generate, transmit, and distribute power by utilities or public

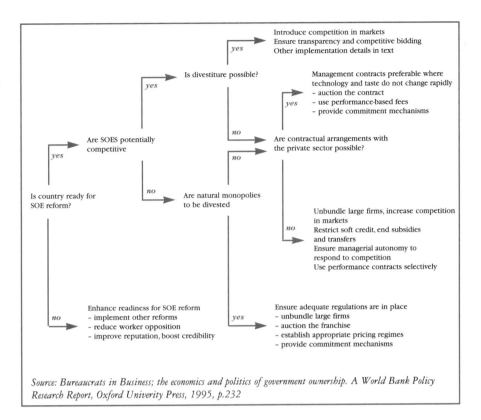

Figure 3-4
A decision tree
for state-owned
enterprise reform

Introduce competition in markets
Ensure transparency and competitive bidding
Other implementation details in text

yes

Is divestiture possible?

Management contracts preferable where
technology and taste do not change rapidly
- auction the contract
- use performance-based fees
- provide commitment mechanisms

yes

yes

no

Are SOES potentially
competitive

Are contractual arrangements with
the private sector possible?

yes

no

Is country ready for
SOE reform?

no

Are natural monopolies
to be divested

Unbundle large firms, increase competition
in markets
Restrict soft credit, end subsidies
and transfers
Ensure managerial autonomy to
respond to competition
Use performance contracts selectively

no

no

Enhance readiness for SOE reform
- implement other reforms
- reduce worker opposition
- improve reputation, boost credibility

no

yes

Ensure adequate regulations are in place
- unbundle large firms
- auction the franchise
- establish appropriate pricing regimes
- provide commitment mechanisms

Source: Bureaucrats in Business; the economics and politics of government ownership. A World Bank Policy
Research Report, Oxford Univerity Press, 1995, p.232

Service
practice
3-8
Taking
advantage of
the three:
unbundling,
deregulation
and
privatization[15]

The World Development Report of 1994, examines the link between infrastructure and development. Moreover, it explores ways in which countries and especially developing countries can improve both the provision and the quality of public services, especially infrastructure services and their actual delivery. The report states that the old paradigm implied that infrastructure services are best produced and delivered by monopolies because the unit costs of delivering an infrastructure service - a gallon of water, a kilowatt-hour of electricity, a local telephone call - typically decline as service output increases. Then, provision by a single entity seemed to make economic sense.

The trend from a public towards a private way of providing unbundled services, creates tremendous opportunities for reputable international service providers. Especially United States-based service suppliers have build up a track record as private operators and independent service enterprises. As a consequence, they are now well positioned to take advantage of these emerging opportunities.

Estimated gains from competition through deregulation of infrastructure sectors in the United States are presented in the next overview:

Sector	Extent of deregulation	Estimated annual gains from deregulation (billions of 1990 US dollars)
Airlines	Complete	13.7-19.7
Trucking	Substantial	10.6
Railroads	Partial	10.4-12.9
Telecommunications	Substantial	0.7-1.6
Natural gas	Partial	Substantial gains to consumers

transport. Typically, the unbundling of public services is accompanied by arrangements between public ownership and private operation in the form of leases, concessions and short-term contracting-out services or fully fledged privatization.[16]

The same advantage applies for French companies such as Generale des Eaux and Lyonnaise des Eaux who have a long-time experience in water supply as privately run but publicly quoted firms. Also, internationally operating law firms, surveyors, consultants, advertising agencies, PR-firms, securities brokers, investment and commercial banks, in turn, can profit from this international trend of privatization and unbundling. They may serve as adviser and/or financer to governments, the management, new owners or operators.

returning to the idea of bundling services

While it is true that much of the public sector is experimenting with unbundling, other industries - in particular once competition has been established - are returning to the idea of bundling services. A good example is the MCI in the USA, with the introduction of MCI ONE - offering all telecommunication services through one supplier.

FOCUSSING ON CORE BUSINESS

downsizing or downscaling

focussing on core business

Focussing on the core business is a trend that also can be observed in the service sector. It implies, typically, downsizing. Important ways to pursue downsizing or downscaling are: spinning off units which senior management view as not belonging to the core activities, specialization or outsourcing. During the last two decades the trend to focussing on core business has led in many other industries to spin-offs or outsourcing of such diverse activities as cleaning, security and information technology. This development creates tremendous opportunities for service companies to whose core business these activities belong. Even, within the service sector, organizations such as banks and hospitals follow this pattern of getting rid of their non-core activities. Thus, banks are outsourcing their cleaning, security and cheque handling to companies which specialize in these types of services.

Outsourcing or contracting-out

contracting-out

The essence of this trend is that an organization decides to stop executing a particular activity and to contract it out to another company. The contracting-out trend is encouraged by laws governing dismissal. In continental Europe and Australia, it is not easy for employers to dismiss permanent staff and to rehire them when things are going better. Although in some countries (as a consequence of, i.e. the globalization trend) changes in labor laws are under way, these options are available right now by contracting out activities.

downsizing and specialization

To many large companies the solution to the present problems may well be found in *downsizing*. The trend towards contracting-out seems to run parallel with this development of downsizing and *specialization*, i.e. by focussing on the core competencies of the firm and/or services with market potential.

Williamson's transaction cost theory

production costs and coordination costs

There are two organizational theories guiding the outsource decision making process.[17] These are Williamson's transaction cost theory and Pfeffer's political model. Williamson's transaction cost theory states that the only reason a company would consider outsourcing is to reduce costs. Here, managers must consider two types of costs, namely production costs and coordination costs. These two should always be compared to each other when outsourcing is being considered. Williamson proposes that outsourcing often accomplishes economies of scale that elude smaller, internal departments. Williamson warns, however, that outsourcers only have a production cost advantage over in-house production for products and services that are standard. When a high degree of customization is involved, in house production costs may be lower. Considering coordination costs, Williamson proposes that outsourcing causes higher coordination costs because the customer must monitor a vendor's behavior. In order to reduce coordination costs, the customer should pay particular attention to contract details. The contract may be the only mechanism for preventing coordination costs from escalating to a point of negating the savings from the vendor's production efficiencies.

Pfeffer's political model

power and political tactics

Pfeffer's political model offers a different interpretation of outsourcing decisions. He notes that objective cost figures, especially for long term decisions like outsourcing, are virtually impossible to predict. Instead, Pfeffer notes that power and political tactics play an important role in organizational decision making – an idea that rational, economic models ignore. This aspect should also be taken into account in decisions about outsourcing.

Commodity services such as security, cleaning, gardening and catering are commonly contracted out to specialized firms. During the 1980s, more complex speciality services like corporate information systems also became an outsource topic: in particular, since Eastman Kodak announced their outsourcing contracts with IBM, Businessland and DEC. Other examples include American Airlines, American Hospital Supply, Merrill Lynch, Enron, various regional banks and performing City administrations in the US or collecting local statistics in The Netherlands.

UP-SCALING IN CORE ACTIVITIES

In a number of sectors, however, we see scaling-up, often in combination with internationalization. Examples of the clustering in sectors are insurance, banking and professional services (accountants, consultants, lawyers and public notaries). A larger

up-scaling on or around core activities

size of operations can be reached by various ways, as we will see in Chapter Seven about strategy. Up-scaling in the service industry typically concentrates on or around the core activities of companies. In order to create scale advantages, mergers and acquisitions are in vogue in addition to internal growth. The emergence of dominant players in fragmented markets such as banking, insurance, waste-disposal, auditing, business consultancy and even funeral services is a well known phenomena across the world. Cooperation and franchising are two alternative ways to achieve an accelerated growth path in the service sector.

Cooperation

memberships network

strategic partnering and strategic alliances

In the last decade, the trend towards cooperation between companies has undeniably increased. Whereas McKinsey & Company is seeking expansion by establishing their own offices (and promoting their mutual cooperation), other local management consulting groups are tapping into their memberships network of independent bureaus abroad to carry out international assignments. Every week we may read about new strategic alliances between parties nobody ever expected to cooperate. Strategic partnering and strategic alliances are common in the airline and telecom industries.[18] Flight code sharing among airlines is an attractive option to optimize yields. At present, the cost of coordination and cooperation seem to be less than the "cost of competition".

Cooperation can be actively sought by parties or more or less compelled by the circumstances such as the high cost of R&D and the government. In the early 1990's, for instance, members of the public broadcasting system in some European countries were driven into each others arms, influenced by, amongst other factors, a down-scaling government and the competition of commercial broadcasting companies. Suppliers of business services also demonstrate a tendency towards more cooperation. In some countries, umbrella-organizations represent independent engineering firms, consultants and other service providers with partly overlapping fields of activities. It serves as a platform aiming to win joint contracts.

cooperation and competition

Whenever there is a public EU-tender, Brussels encourages companies from different countries to form a consortium. Cooperation and competition are no longer at odds with each other.

Franchising

A franchise chain attempts to present itself to the consumer as a unit by providing a consistent level of service. According to Lovelock (1991), the major growth is in the franchising of so-called "business formats", in which almost every aspect of the business is specified by the franchising organization – from the shop's design up to and including the training of its employees. A general prerequisite to a proper functioning of a franchise organization is that both parties are willing to cooperate and trust each other. Opportunistic behavior will be detrimental here.[19]

franchising chains

Most franchising chains direct themselves at consumers. Fast-food restaurants, barbers, DIY stores and photocopy centres are well-known examples. Other service providers – which do not necessarily operate from a shop or outlet – include Rentokil (pest control) and Dyno-rod (drain cleaning in the UK) who use vans, uniforms, etc. all in house colors.

Service practice 3-9 Franchising in Europe[20]

While driving through the different states of America, the franchise outlets are easily recognized. Franchising counts in that part of the world as the single most important business format to increase business in product and service retailing. In Asia and Europe, the picture is quite different. The European Franchise Federation notes that "the main characteristic of franchising in Europe is heterogeneity. It is perhaps the reason why there are mostly European franchising concepts in Europe, and very few American ones". The UK may be the exception to this rule. Franchising has recently become also the most dynamic form of distribution in Europe. With 3,000 franchisors and 120,000 franchisees among the Free Trade Agreement countries, the turnover is over ECU 55 billion (US 66 billion). The degree of franchising in number of outlets as well as turnover as a percentage of total (retail) sales differs throughout Europe. The sizes of the networks also vary. Concepts have developed in supermarkets, household appliances, personal equipment, restaurants, hotels, fast food, shoe repair, mortgage advisors and the like.

Some figures include

	Number of:	
Country	*Franchisors*	*Franchisees*
France	600	30,000
Great Britain	132	18,600
Germany	265	10,000
Austria	80	2,500
The Netherlands	300	11,000
Belgium	90	32,000
Italy	318	16,100
Spain	120	14,500

In the Scandinavian countries and Portugal as well as Central and Eastern Europe franchising is now growing. The importance of franchising measured in amounts and per cent of retail sales turnover differs strongly per country. France has a turnover in franchise outlets of over US$ 25 billion, representing 7.5 per cent of French retail sales. In The Netherlands, 12 per cent of retail sales is accomplished via franchising. In Italy, where in particular service franchising has expanded during the past decennia, the turnover of this business format represents only 1.2 per cent of the total retail sales. In most European countries, the growth figures of franchising are impressive. In the UK, where the American concepts represent almost 30 per cent of all those developed in the UK market for several years, the turnover in deliveries through franchising has increased about 25 per cent.

international franchising

To be successful in international franchising, the following ingredients are also indispensable: e.g. creating advertising campaigns for the national (or even worldwide) promotion of brand names, standardization of operational activities, formalized training programs, continuous emphasis on increased efficiency, and dual marketing programs aimed at clients as well as franchisees.

Franchising is more than an alternative in the service sector, as the chapter on distribution will show.

DIMINISHING DIFFERENCES

Is a computer company a supplier of goods or services? Is General Electric really becoming a service organization as Jack Welch intends it to be? (See also the GE case at the end of Chapter One.) How important is ownership? Can we enjoy the total usage of a good without owning it? Existing borders between services and goods as well as between ownership on one side and rental, leasing, or collective property are diminishing.

Diminishing borders between services and goods

service-profit centers within industrial enterprises
Service-profit centers within industrial enterprises are considerably changing the image of world-famous companies. Additional services, once designed to support the sales of physical goods – such as consultancy, credit, transportation and delivery, installation, training, maintenance and repair – are now offered by the manufacturer as independent profit-generating services.[21] The services are even sold to clients who opted for rival services.

Service practice 3-10 From goods to services

A computer supplier such as IBM or ICL retains nowadays a large part of its revenues from software, contracting, maintenance and consultancy. Hoogovens, a modern steel factory based on the west coast of The Netherlands, also has a technological service division that concentrates on activities in the field of engineering and contracting, consultancy, transportation and insurance.

Growth in leasing, rentals and collective property

leasing and rentals
Leasing and rentals represent a marriage between the service sector and the manufacturing sector.[22] An increasing percentage of business and individual consumers think that they can enjoy a physical product without necessarily being the owner. On the psychological side, friends and neighbors often will not notice that you are not the owner. In many countries, ownership does not necessarily enhance someone's satisfaction within what Maslow calls humans' hierarchical needs pyramid. The demand impetus of commercial leasing is tax-driven (costs are deductible while investments can only be depreciated), management focus on core business (instead of on their equipment or cars), access to capital (sometimes easier to lease than to borrow or to attract capital), convenience and incentives (i.e. for employees of a company). On the supply side, leasing attracts many banks and other companies as it accommodates financial institutions with higher margins than

traditional loans. Besides a nice return on investment, this type of financing offers producers of capital goods a (pricing instrument) route to enhance their market share. In some emerging countries, leasing may even be the only way to provide medium term financing.

Leasing companies have apparently increased their ownership shares in North-American and Western Europe's fleet of vehicles formerly owned by the companies. Nowadays, kitchens and even gardens can be leased. Tools, audio and video equipment rentals are available. Crockery and even toilets can be rented for special events. The rental section in the Yellow Pages provides an impressive array of articles people can rent.

CHANGES IN ASSET STRUCTURE AND DELIVERY MODE

Technology is dramatically changing the way services are purchased, processed and delivered. It has totally changed the asset structure in many service industries.

Delivery via technology

personal touch is replaced by the technological touch

Many of the services which were "personally based" in the past are now deliverable through "technology". The personal touch is replaced by the technological touch (partly). Sometimes it concerns add-on services; in other cases the complete core service is available with the assistance of technology. Examples of add-ons are information on balances of current accounts in banking by telephone or PC modem, information by telephone about the number of collected air miles or after-sales service for software or hardware problems. By means of spinning off, some companies have even made their core-business this kind of after-sales service. Core-services, via technical delivery, concern home shopping, direct-banking and insurance, or scanning of sales by market research firms at point-of-sales in supermarkets. The use of these

computerized services

"computerized services" is partly determined by consumers' willingness, capability and motivation to do so.[23]

improve the personal touch

Usually, it is assumed that technology is a substitute for labor. On the other hand, it may also improve the personal touch in services. In banking, the employees can provide customers with better information by using computers, which provide all the information on a client present in their records. So, the improved service at the counter is based on computers at the front office desk supported by an up to date computerized back office. Universities were already offering distance learning. Now, they may offer real-time learning for the real-time student.

dual distribution

Large service providers may even have various distribution channels for their service delivery existing next to each other (= dual distribution). An insurance company might sell through direct mail, bank branches and independent agents. The impact of the macro-environment factors such as developments in technology and deregulation, combined with the striving of companies to be cost-efficient, are major drivers of these alternative modes of delivery within that service sector. The alternative distribution modes may lead to disintermediation.

Disintermediation

disintermediation

Disintermediation implies the elimination of intermediaries in economic activity including agents, brokers, wholesalers, some retailers, broadcasters, record companies; in short anything that stands between producers and consumers. Within the company, it marks the end of the middle managers and internal agents. Outside the company, it means that middlemen, brokers or other agents passing information (mainly) may be surpassed by the consumer directly if they are not able to change and to add value in other ways. An example of industries that will be affected are travel agencies. As travellers are able to contact by the Internet, or directly telephone airlines or tour operators, waiting time should shorten and this would result in lower prices. Similar developments may take place with theatre ticket agencies and real estate brokerage. Even now, US customers seeking a used car can use the Internet to select a model and go to the dealer to buy their car. In this sense, dealers are "downgraded" to only a selling point.

Service practice 3-11 Disinter- mediation at work [24]

Under this heading Don Tapscott quotes in his book, *The Digital Economy*, *The New York Times* article containing examples of disintermediation.

The Condé Nast magazine publishing company eventually plans to create Web versions of all its fourteen core magazines. The first was a version of *Condé Nast Traveller* called CondéNet, offering detailed reports on more than 250 islands and 1,000 hotels. Eventually, users will be able to make airline, hotel and dinner reservations, check local conditions, and have on-line discussions with travellers who have visited the sites they're considering going to. The president of Condé Nast says that CondéNet is "a serious seven-figure investment" which will be an enormous business someday.

Changing asset structures

The times are gone for starting one's own service company with a capital of less than US$ 5,000 and only one's own labor force, at least in most service industries. This small amount of money and the owner's skills, capabilities and goodwill are no longer the only assets that count, even in small service firms.

asset structures
assets are substituted by information

Exceptions may be found in IT-services at the forefront of new developments such as Internet services and individual freelance consultants. As in other industries, not only are asset structures changing, but also assets are substituted by information. Of course, the increasing technology component in many service industries has changed the asset structure, but not alone. Consumer services based on franchising concepts, such as key cutting or shoe repairs, require investment in equipment, refurbishment, cash register and PC, also involving fixed costs such as rent, bookkeeping and (often) wages. Typically, in the mature markets of developed countries many business to business services require more investment than just after World War II. For many markets have reached a particular status quo with regard to competition and it is hard to fight with these well-established parties. To start successfully in industries such as cleaning, temps or advertising, entrepreneurs nowadays need higher investments (even when

investment

adjusted for inflation) than a few decades ago. However, exceptions can still be found in niches such as specialized software. The two extremely successful American founders of Netscape, an Internet software supplier, proved this view. Other examples include in the business to business sector – specialized consultancy or regionally operating firms, and emerging markets' service providers, which are still able to establish companies with limited funds.

Self-service

growing client participation

self-service

During the last twenty years numerous service sectors saw a development towards growing client participation. Again, technology (for example, allowing service delivery partly or wholly by technology, such as home-shopping or virtual banking via the Internet) is a major push behind self-service. Certainly, it is not the only one. Pricing (at the demand side), lower costs (at the supplier side), social acceptance and even the impression of a higher service level – as in the case of a breakfast buffet in a hotel where the guests may choose from a selection of foods in their own time – are other drives behind this service trend. The cash dispenser, direct insurance, electronic banking, as well as having the consumer collect his/her own tray in the school or company restaurant are forms of self-service. Copying one's own documents in photocopy centers is another example of client participation. The youth hostel concept was

people accept that they have to do more themselves

initially based on this principle of doing things for yourself. Many people accept that they have to do more themselves than in the past, even when it comes to "unpleasant and hardly valued services". For example, having to take your own garbage to a certain area, instead of having it collected door-to-door.

EPILOGUE

As noted before, these six trends, combined with the macro-factors discussed in section 3.2, account for the growth (or sometimes the decline) of the service sector to a great extent. Organizations that regularly assess their environment appear to be successful within their sector more often; be more aware of any changes in their environment; upgrade their strategic planning and decision making in a better fashion; operate more effectively in government matters; and, upgrade their sector and market analysis.

In Chapters Seven and Eight we will deal with most of these topics from a strategic point of view. Those chapters deal with the strategic and marketing-planning process in a service company. Whereas the influence of the macro-factors could be regarded as a far-away phenomenon by many (small) service providers, this is certainly not so for the competition and the market in their own industry.

3.4 THE COMPETITION ENVIRONMENT: FORCES SHAPING THE FUTURE IN SELECTED SERVICE INDUSTRIES

This section will give an overview of some important forces in an international shaping, competitive, environment. For practical purposes, an industry approach will be followed. The overview is aimed at giving the reader a global impression (and no more than that) of how some of the largest and most interesting service industries are converging world-wide. [25]

FINANCIAL SERVICES

The financial sector is one of the sectors that seems most in turmoil. The provision of financial services as a result of saturated markets, changing technologies, globalization, deregulation/liberalized markets and increased competition, is subject to many changes. Only the most dominating trends in retail banking, corporate banking, insurance and securities will be reviewed.

Retail banking

shift in retail banking

local personal presence

During recent years, a dramatic shift in retail banking has taken place in the USA, Western Europe and some countries in Asia. Whereas in the past retail banking was virtually impossible without having a local personal presence, other options are now becoming available. These options offer a more cost effective alternative for banks servicing the retail market internationally. As retail banking is a mature market in most countries, consumers have more information. Because these services are very much alike, the focus of retail banks is now on reducing costs in combination with a higher degree of automation. It proves that "bricks and mortar" branches have become an expensive way of expanding. Traditional discussions in banks about issues such as security, labor costs, rental costs, and expensive management time are gradually taken

technology

over by discussions about issues like "which technology is most user friendly" and "until what hours telephone-banking employees have to work at night (in shifts) and at weekends to back up the computer (voice)". Sophisticated bankomarts which can not only pay out but also collect money and initiate transfers are becoming more widely available. Point-of-sale terminals and retailers do allow clients to pay with their local bank cards or credit cards instead of cash. The growth of direct service provision either as an add-on to existing accounts or as a stand-alone operation is visible around the globe. Telephone banking, call-centres, Internet-applications, direct PC-

electronic banking

modem connections and other devices of electronic banking are nowadays in many instances an increasing alternative for paying bills by ordinary money transfers or cheques, trading securities, balance checking or information about financial services. Currently, E-banking is found across the world, while an increasing number of finance houses are introducing Web-sites.

The availability of software packages for direct banking and other types of electronic banking allows banks and non-bank competitors, such as retailers, software houses, credit card organizations, insurance companies and even car manufacturers or GE-Capital (to mention just one name) to avoid the (only) route of expensive expansion via branches. For example, recently GE-Capital acquired a major stake in Budapest Bank, Hungary. It is advancing all kinds of financial services, including wholesale activities such as aircraft leasing. In other words, established banks have become more vulnerable to leaner and more innovative competitors. Niche players try to conquer profitable slices of markets when they feel they have competitive advantages over the more traditional retail banks. By offering their services via different distribution channels, universal banks try to protect their business. Thus, the universal bank concept, financial supermarket or "one stop shopping" is only one of their channels. Leasing is one of the trends supporting the growth of the service industry. Consumer finance, international payments and residential mortgages have all proven to be attractive services in the past, both for universal banks and niche players (e.g. special companies or limited service providers).

leaner and more innovative competitors

different distribution channels

The outsourcing or contracting-out of non-core bank services including security, catering, transport and other facilities is, next to technology and distribution changes, the third major trend in retail banking. In recent years, discussions have started as to whether information-systems, or parts of it belonging to the core strategic strengths of banks, could be contracted out.

outsourcing or contracting-out of non-core bank services

A fourth trend clearly visible in the banking industry is deregulation. In the US, it offers more possibilities for interstate banking and in the EU to open branches in other countries.

deregulation

As a fifth trend, we notice the privatization of state banks, in particular in Asia, South America and Central and Eastern European countries.

privatization of state banks

Globalization, although not so visible in corporate banking, is the last major trend in retail banking to be mentioned. Outstanding examples of this strategy are American Express and CitiBank, both operating in many countries. Other global banks only select a few countries where they would like to expand their retail activities. Mature markets, technological developments and deregulation in many countries have led to increased competition. Consequently, banks operating in mass-markets will have to concentrate on cost-savings in order to stay competitive. These and other factors, have encompassed acquisitions and mergers throughout the industry. It has all resulted in major redundancies in the banking industry. In terms of employment, retail banking is a shrinking industry. Staff reductions in retail banks as high as 50% by 2005 will be no exception.[26] Much of the impetus for take-overs stems from the emotional forces of fear (to be left behind, unwanted, taken over), ambition (size and capital are the dominant forces) and/or the genuine desire to increase shareholder value (assumed economies-of-scale and synergies both in revenues and costs). In many countries, this has already led to oligopolistic market structures. In the future, it will prove that different distribution channels will appeal to different customers. Even one customer may prefer different channels at different times or for different services

globalization

increased competition

oligopolistic market structures

relationship

making the use of financial services domain specific. New technology – sometimes in combination with personal banking – will allow banks to strengthen their relationship with their clients. As a result, loyalty management will become a key marketing issue.

Service practice 3-12 Oligopolistic banking

> Across the globe, concentration in the financial sector is now taking place at a breath-taking pace. In 1995 the merger of Chemical Bank and Chase Manhattan was front page news of the financial papers. Just a few years after the two New York based banks, Chemical and Manufacturers Hannover, merged, a merger with Chase Manhattan was announced, making the combination the largest bank in the country. The fast growing Banc One gobbled up the large First USA (big in credit cards). Nobody can predict the outcome of all the consolidations taking place throughout the United States. In other parts of the world, from Scandinavia to the Philippines, shake outs and concentrations are much the same daily news. Commercial banks are taking over investment banks and/or asset management firms. In Central and Eastern Europe, banking crises have led to fewer institutions. In France, the insurance field was changed drastically when giants Axa and UAP decided to merge in 1996. In the UK, banks and building societies combine their strengths. Also, in the mid nineties the Misubishi Bank and Bank of Tokyo merged. In some instances, take-overs or mergers are triggered by failures, scandals or bad-debts. For example, in Japan, the immediate reason of the merger between Daiwa and Sumitomo Bank were the difficulties of Daiwa in New York - uncovered treasury positions causing a loss of US$1.2 billion. A similar motive triggered the sale of reputed British merchant bank Barings to the Dutch ING Bank.

Corporate banking

corporate or wholesale banking

Whereas the advantages of globalization are less profound in retail banking, they are certainly present in corporate or wholesale banking. To be on the shopping list as a relationship bank for a multinational, a bank should have enough financial muscles to finance the company around the globe. In addition, local presence – based on the axioma of chasing or following the customer – may then be an advantage. Other criteria to become one of the prime bankers of these companies (so called first tier banks) hinge upon the art to create "added value" for them, cheap (local) funding and placement power in case of securitization. Together, these requirements ask for strongly capitalized, knowledgeable and well reputed banks able to network with clients, other banks and financial advisers, as well as within their own organizations. For these reasons, we have seen lately the take over of several specialized merchant banks in the UK by European banks. Deutsche Bank acquired Morgan Grenfell in the 1980s. In the nineties, ABN AMRO Bank took over Hoare Govett, ING Bank rescued the troubled dignified Barings, Swiss Bank Corporation and Dresdner bought respectively Warburg and Kleinwort Benson. Technology has a major impact on the successful operation of these newly merged financial wholesale institutions. E-mail, and intranet connections between employees, sophisticated dealing rooms, video-conferencing in order to coordinate strategic activities, on-line information from data

first tier banks

network

technology

relationship marketing and networking

providers as Telerate, Reuters and Bloomberg are just a few of the most obvious developments. Relationship marketing and networking are crucial tools to survive in this highly competitive industry. As customized solutions are the key, highly qualified, well paid and strongly motivated staff are a condition *sine qua non* for long term success.

distributing sophisticated corporate banking "products"

In the area of distributing sophisticated corporate banking "products", a shift from head office to "centers of gravity" can be noticed. Corporate, investment and other specialized financial advisers believe that, in order to remain competitive, it is worth moving employees and other resources to London and New York, where it all happens. Examples of this approach include Deutsche Bank, ABN AMRO Bank and ING Bank shifting the main point of their investment banking and global securities related research to London (away from their home countries).

the Web

The Web offers both a threat and an opportunity to corporate banks and everyone involved in financial activities such as lawyers, accountants, venture capitalists and stock brokers. For example, small companies selling stock has always been a cumbersome undertaking. By appealing directly to investors via the Net, firms can raise money without spending a fortune on expensive underwriters such as banks or venture capital houses. Computer programs such as CapScape automate the tedious process of compiling an offer document. By using the program and then offering shares directly to investors over the Internet the cost of raising money is lowered substantially.[27]

Leasing

leasing

Leasing is a burgeoning business. As a vehicle for financing purchases of capital equipment and other items, leasing has been growing world-wide since the first independent leasing company was established in the United States in the 1950s. According to estimates provided in the IFC report in 1994, leasing supported global sales of vehicles, machinery and equipment valued at about $350 billion, or around an eighth of the world's private investment. Around the globe, including the emerging markets, leasing has now been percieved as an effective means to broaden the access to medium- and long-term financing.[28] However, the end of the growth of, at least, leasing vehicles may be in sight. Governments may put boundaries to car leasing, as lease companies providing unlimited mileage and (semi) gratis transport to (private) drivers is certainly not the way to stop traffic jams and air pollution all over the earth.

Insurance

Bancassurance All-finanz

integrated approach of all financial services

With "Bancassurance" or "All-finanz", one financial institution combines banking and insurance services. The putting together of a bank and an insurance company offers potential cross-selling based on vertical integration (especially when an insurance company starts using the whole bank's network as its distribution channel). This tendency towards an integrated approach of all financial services is visible in several European countries.[29] However, not every bank or insurer sees the advantages of such an integration. For instance, banks may choose to operate as an intermediary of insurances rather than as a producer, and thus position themselves as independent advisors. Much depends on whether customers prefer to have all these financial services performed by one company. This makes them very dependent on one

deregulation
internationalization

supplier. On the distribution side, direct marketing of motor policies has become enormously popular in the US and UK since the introduction of shopping-around for cut price deals by telephone in the mid-eighties. This new distribution trend in insurance will no doubt conquer new markets. As deregulation sweeps its way through the world, internationalization is another force changing the landscape of offering security. After the opening up of Japan's insurance sector in 1997, foreign insurers are in overdrive to move in to this lucrative market. It will press existing institutions to become more cost efficient. In theory, a fully deregulated Japanese market would lead to a 60% decline in profits.[30] Foreign competition in many countries will certainly heat up, bringing better deals to the consumers.

deals to the consumers

Securities

technology

trading house

The securities and commodities exchange markets are adding more technology, allowing members to trade, at distance, even from outside the country. This diminishes the operation to be location-bound. The pressure is on commodities exchanges to operate more globally. For example, the traditional trading house is disappearing around the world. Either they are acquired by big banks/fund managers, or will be pushed out of business by their larger competitors. At the same time, demand pressurizes them to change their strategy. Either trading houses have to concentrate their market focus if they are small or, as part of a large entity, have to integrate their activities and do more things for their customers. James Capel, the UK's largest stockbroker and part of HSBC Investment Bank (Capel's parent company), became also a market maker in 1995, as it experienced that "clients feel you can only deal in large sizes if you deal with a 'market maker'". A market maker is able to use its own capital to buy and sell shares.

market maker

internationalization

Not only banks intensify their international activities. Partly as a reaction to this internationalization, stock and commodity exchanges start a kind of internationalization process as well. As a consequence, some local exchanges start to cooperate. Various local exchanges have already established electronic links, or are discussing it. In 1994 Nymex and Comex, both located in the World Trade Center in New York, merged to form the largest commodities exchange. This one is now dominating the world futures trading in energy and precious materials.

As a whole, the international financial markets have changed and will further change the conditions for service businesses. Easier access to information about the credit worthiness of companies, deregulation, internationalization of both the financial institutions and their clients in the service sector and the increasing use of technology are the main reasons.

Business Services in General

business services

The business to business sector is one of the fastest-growing sectors of activity in the industrialized countries. In the European Community, business services accounted in 1990 for about 6% of the total GNP. During the period 1980-85, it achieved a higher annual growth (14.6%) than the average of all goods and services sector (10%).

Moreover, this growth rate was the highest among all market services. In 1990, business services accounted for 5% of the total European Community's employment.

function performed for the customer/firm

Business services can be classified in sub-sectors on the basis of several criteria. One of these criteria relates to the function performed for the customer/firm.[31] According to this classification, business services can be grouped as follows:

- management and administrative services (management consultancy, legal services, accounting, fiscal advice, etc.);
- production services (architectural, engineering, operational leasing, repair and maintenance, packaging, quality control, etc.);
- research-related services (contract research, R&D, etc.);
- personnel-related services (vocational training, labor-recruitment, supply of temporary labor, etc.);
- information and communication services (data banks, software services, technical computer services, advanced telecommunications services, express mailing, etc.);
- marketing services (advertising, sales promotion, market research, direct marketing, public relations, export promotion, fairs and exhibitions, etc.); and
- operational services (industrial cleaning, security services, linguistic services, etc.).

externally subcontracted

in-house

A company sample survey on the use of externally provided business services within the European Community, covering users from all economic sectors, revealed that 40% of business services are entirely externally subcontracted.[32] External (business) services pertain to industrial and other professional buyers outside the company. Almost a third of all business services are provided exclusively in-house. In other words, these are internal services pertaining to the customers within the company. The rest (27%) are provided as a combination of in-house and external services. The degree of externalization varies with type of business services, size and country.

degree of externalization

different factors

The importance of business services for the economy in the USA is similar to Europe. In Asia, the growth in this sector is impressive. Different factors explain the rapid growth of business services. First of all, total demand increases quickly as the whole economy expands. Secondly, as the business environment is becoming more complex, management needs specialists to cope with legislation, taxes, market research, personnel matters, etc. The ever-increasing complexity of the legislation, production/distribution systems, and the widespread adoption of information-related functions are the main factors here. However, many of the business environment factors and trends we discussed in the previous sections, also count for the rapid growth in business services.

temporary additional specialists

Even without hefty requirements of the environment, companies need various temporary additional specialists to carry out all the business tasks as they have an insufficient workload to keep these people busy permanently. So, for efficiency and expert reasons, the opportunity to hire skilled staff temporarily or on a semi-permanent basis, is welcomed. Therefore, bookkeeping, software development, waste management and cleaning may be done not in-house but performed by outsiders. It is also true that outsourcing strengthens this trend. Although in different degrees, the tendency towards *low barriers to entry*

externalization can be witnessed across the whole business spectrum, in large, medium-sized and small profit and non-profit organizations. Because of the relatively low barriers to entry at the supply side, the increase in the number of business to business firms may be explained by young entrepreneurs, free-lancers and people who are recently laid-off by their firms. A recent survey among former bank employees in the US, who were made redundant by their employers, shows that after finding a job with another bank, starting their own consultancy was what happened most.

Service practice 3-13 Business services in Europe[33]

Operational and engineering services show the highest degree of pure externalization. Financial review and advertising are above average. Supplied in-house, are mainly public relations and R&D. Combinations of internally and externally performed services are often found in computing and legal areas. Among the community member states, France and Italy show a high degree of service externalization, whereas Germany has the highest degree of internalization. The Netherlands and the United Kingdom show the lowest internalization pattern but they have a very high degree of combination between internal and external services. Concerning the size of the firms, the highest externalization is exhibited by medium-sized firms; small and large firms internalize business services.

However, since the time of the survey, we have indications that many large European companies follow the American example and outsource internal business services. Personnel function based services (vocational training and temporary staff) in Europe are by far the most important, both in terms of employment and turnover.

market structure

company size

In observing the market structure of business services, one should note that a large number of small units and, at the same time, a limited number of very big, mainly international companies, exist. In general, company size tends to be small for most business services, for which quality and specialization are overwhelmingly important and for which few scale economies can be identified. The sectors in which a large number of firms employ more than 50 employees are engineering consultancy, accountancy, market research, testing, inspection, quality control and some operational services. Many business firms operate on a regional or national scale. Some very specialized industrial and professional service firms are international by nature as the home country offers only a limited customer base. Moreover, they have to follow their clients when they internationalize. Although concentration in most world wide business services industries is still rather limited, the concentration phenomenon is undoubtedly growing. Smaller units are linking up within the country, trans-national across Europe or Asia and even more global as, e.g. the development of legal, management, accounting and advertizing services shows. This tendency is expected to continue as a "natural" consequence of deregulation and changing information technology. It will all lead to a growing interest in mergers, acquisitions, partnerships and alternative business formats such as franchising in this dynamic sector of today's Western economies.

concentration

TABLE 3-1 *Top ten European advertising agencies in 1992*

Company	Gross income (million $US)
1. Euro RSCG	620.9
2. Publicis	529.5
3. McCann-Erickson Worldwide	474.9
4. Ogilvy & Mather Worldwide	449.3
5. Young & Rubicam	445.5
6. DDB Needham Worldwide	445.0
7. Grey Advertising	401.6
8. BBDO Worldwide	364.5
9. J. Walter Thompson Co.	357.9
10. Ammirati Puris Lintas	325.7

Source: Advertising Age International, June 1997

TABLE 3-2 *World top ten management consulting firms in 1996*

Company	Main office	Revenues income (million $US)
1. Andersen Consulting	Chicago, IL	3,115.3
2. McKinsey & Co.	New York, NY	2,100.0
3. Ernst & Young	New York, NY	2,100.0
4. Coopers & Lybrand Consulting	New York, NY	1,918.0
5. KPMG Peat Marwick	New York, NY	1,380.0
6. Arthur Andersen	Chicago, IL	1,379.6
7. Deloitte & Touche	Wilton, CT	1,303.0
8. Mercer Consulting Group	New York, NY	1,159.0
9. Towers Perrin	New York, NY	903.0
10. A. T. Kearney	Chicago, IL	870.0

TABLE 3-3 *World top ten market research companies 1996*

Company	Worldwide research revenue (million $US)	Main office	Countries with office
1. A.C. Nielsen Corp. (incl. Nielssen Media Research)	1678	Westport Conn.	NA
2. IMS	604.4	Westport Conn.	NA
3. Information Resources Inc.	405.6	Chicago	18
4. SRI International	326	Menlo Park, Calif.	7
5. Research International	246.7	London. UK	59
6. VNU Marketing Information Services	200	New York	35
7. Gallup Organization	168.8	Princeton, NJ	NA
8. NPD Group	163.8	Port Washington, NY	14
9. Millward Brown International	155.8	Warwick, UK	17
10. Arbitron Co.	153.1	New York	6

Source: Advertising Age

DISTRIBUTION

distribution sector

The distribution sector is a very large services sector in terms of both output and employment. In 1990, the distribution sector accounted for nearly 40% of employment in the EU, USA and Japan. The role and structure of the distribution sector, which includes retailing and wholesaling activities, has changed dramatically over the past 40 years.[34] There is a wide diversity of retail formats ranging from speciality stores to hypermarkets, embracing supermarkets, department stores, discount stores and catalogue sales. They differ in their degree of providing services. Many service discussions in the USA seem to separate services into primary and secondary services, dependent upon whether the service was of initial benefit to the consumer in the primary case, and that the service "assisted the consumer" in buying other products in the secondary case. Obviously, the majority of retail situations are in the "secondary" category.

retail formats

primary and secondary services

Traditionally, the retail sector is distinguished from the wholesale sector by the fact that it sells to consumers. However, this distinction is becoming increasingly blurred. In many cases today, the function of the distribution sector itself may be partially or fully undertaken by the manufacturer. During the last decades large retail groups have emerged. This made it possible for manufacturers, especially large manufacturers, to *disintermediation* bypass the wholesaler and deal directly with the retailer (=disintermediation). Sometimes, the role of the wholesaler is split up between the manufacturer and the retailer. In other cases, such as the large retail buying groups, the wholesale and retail functions have been integrated, creating a seamless organization performing both *retail concentration* roles. Over the past 40 years, there has been a gradual increase in the degree of retail concentration in many countries. This has been most notable in food retailing, resulting in, e.g. a higher level of professionalization and management in that industry. *structure of the retail* However, the structure of the retail trade differs enormously between countries and *trade* even between neighbouring countries. Detailed data about the retail business in the European Union is presented in Table 3-4. On average, there were 96 retailers per *retail density* 10,000 inhabitants (= the retail density). Table 3-4 shows five countries with a retail density higher than this average number. This refers to a retail structure with many small "pop and mom shops", especially in the Southern European countries. Local *regulatory* planning laws and opening hours are two important regulatory differentiators *differentiators between* between countries. Local planning, strong relationships between manufacturers, *countries* wholesaler and distributor, strengths of established supermarket chains and local lobby-groups of established retailers also explain for a large part why the hypermar-

TABLE 3-4 *Retailing in the 12 member countries of the European Union, 1990-1994*

Country	Number of retailers	Number of retailers per 10,000 inhabitants	Number of persons employed per company	Total turnover (Mill ECU)	Year
Portugal	132,094	13.36	2.76	26,470	1993
Greece	175,000	17.40	1.90	NA	1990
Italy	888,330	15.65	2.69	230,000	1991
Belgium	121,912	12.07	1.94	43,803	1993
Spain	54,459	6.23	5.29	33,766	1994
Denmark	47,597	9.19	4.17	24,846	1992
Luxemburg	3,587	8.95	5.45	3,767	1993
Ireland	29,337	8.29	4.48	12,168	1991
France	451,800	7.84	4.48	239,448	1993
Germany	435,471	5.37	6.58	347,038	1993
Netherlands	102,900	6.69	6.19	69,280	1994
United Kingdom	330,491	5.76	6.66	283,152	1992

Source: Eurostat

ket is not widespread over Europe and Asia.[35] Regarding opening hours, recently a strong trend to extend opening hours on week days and at the weekend can be noticed in many countries where shopping is limited to 40 hours a week or less.

logistics

supermarkets

traditional entrepreneurs

specialized niche players

The drive towards cost-savings has increased the significance of logistics, including computer ordering by phone and lean production techniques invented by the manufacturing sector, such as "just-in-time" and "zero-stock" in distribution. These factors have a major impact on the lay-out as well as on the size of the shop. Supermarkets have taken business from the smaller shops, selling food and non-food convenience goods in the US and Western Europe. For most traditional entrepreneurs, the consequences were that they either had to adopt investing in larger sales units, joint procurement and selling formats, joint labelling of name and articles, become franchisee, specialize, sell-out or disappear. The others survived as small shop owners, delivering personal service by knowing their clients by name, offering a rather broad but limited assortment against relatively high prices resulting in lower annual sales. Some of them become specialized niche players located in the proximity of the large retailers. Remarkable is the start-up of immigrant entrepreneurs in many places around the western world, often filling in the gaps traditional shop owners leave after ending their own business or the gaps not met by the large retailers. In spite of the limiting forces in some countries the trend is towards larger and more specialized stores. Recently, the successful French hypermarket formula has been gaining ground abroad.

Service practice 3-14 New retail formats abroad [36]

Many people notice the entering of new retail formats to the market. Warehouse clubs, such as CostCo and Troika who are entering the UK market from the United States, offer significant discounts but with a relatively limited depth of products sold under wholesale conditions. It is too early to say if the format will catch on but it is certain that it will add to the already fierce price competition in the food sector. Teleshopping, or home shopping, is a promising format, as the developments in the US, experiments with Minitel system in France and the standardized offerings via broadcasting throughout Europe, show.

specialist discount chain

Not new, but an attractive growth area, also outside America as it appears, is the specialist discount chain format adopted by the American Toys-R-Us. Challenged by competitors, they had to restructure their business in 1998 (= deliver better service quality).

slowing growth rate

In the food sector, internationalization is slowly but gradually growing. At an aggregate level of retail sales, one may point out several factors which indicate an overall tendency towards a slowing growth rate in this sector, at least in Europe:

- the low population growth (or even decline) expected within the EU means that the volume of the market, measured in numbers of consumers, will not grow rapidly (or go down);

- despite the fact that the average purchasing power of the population will increase over time, such growth will probably be spent on the purchase of specific services, including tourism, eating-out and entertainment rather than retail goods; and
- with the ageing of the population and a government withdrawing social security, health and other sectors, people will spend more money on savings and pension funds.

internationalization in the retail sector

The advantages of internationalization in the retail sector are more difficult to obtain than in many other sectors. In retailing, and in particular the food sector, the expansion of leading firms outside their national home base has been limited for a long time. As mentioned earlier, this is now changing: logistics, low prices, strong competition, cultural differences, high investments and existing relationships with clients still create obstacles to enter the market.

TABLE 3-5 *Top ten retailers in the EU ranked by turnover in 1992 (Billion ECU)*

Firm	Country of origin	Turnover
1 Tengelmann	Germany	23.1
2. Spar International	Netherlands	19.6
3. Rewe-Handelsgruppe	Germany	18.2
4. Carrefour	France	17.1
5. Leclerc	France	16.6
6. Intermarché	France	16.6
7. J. Sainsbury	UK	13.2
8. Promodes	France	12.3
9. Otto-Versand	Germany	10.4
10. Tesco	UK	10.3

Source: Le Nouvel Economiste (November 1993)

During the 1990s, the interest among companies in the distribution sector for internationalization is growing. European firms are focusing their attention mainly on the neighboring markets of Central Europe and Southern Europe (both markets are near by, relatively easy to manage, benefit from economies of scale, while being fragmented markets). Large enterprises have a manifest interest in the US (many opportunities to buy retail and supermarket chains) and Asia (fast growing, emerging and fragmented markets). Some companies, such as the Dutch Ahold, have grown substantially in the US by taking over middle-sized supermarket chains, as they believe it is a far better way

expansion

to grow in this competitive and mature market than starting from scratch. Recently, they started joint ventures with local firms accelerating the scope of their operations in the Far East. Coming from the other side, the American owned Walmart has in 1997 acquired a local chain in Germany as a first step towards expansion.

Service practice 3-15 Different strategies to inter- nationalize [37]

The US based retailer Toys-R-Us first entered via own stores (organic growth) countries like Canada, the UK and Germany. Then they started franchise oper- ations in, for instance, Singapore, Hong Kong and Malaysia.

The Sweden based furniture and home decorating retailer IKEA have inter- nationalized their retail activities since 1963. In the first years, they export- ed their standard Swedish retail format to Norway, Denmark, Switzerland and (West) Germany. Then IKEA went, via franchising, to Australia, Hong Kong and Japan.

environmental issues

Environmental issues are becoming more important as the preference of consumers for "natural"/"green" is gaining momentum. The role of the national government (and EU) in the packaging industry is further proof of increasing environmental awareness among regulators. For example, in 1982 a study among 83 Dutch companies in the packaging industry (net response 67.2%) showed that anticipated measures of the government regarding non-returnable and excessive packaging had impact on their product policy,[38] an impact that has been increased since, by the introduction of new regulation and demand by the public for refills.

scaling-up and internationalization fun aspect of shopping

In brief, the future seems to be in scaling-up and internationalization. Formulae such as the French hypermarket and specialized retail formats have, seem to have good prospects for marketing across borders. The fun aspect of shopping will gain importance in face-to-face retailing and as a way to spend growing leisure time. On the other hand, where almost no personal contact with the service provider is needed, home shopping and (a little later) virtual shopping will gain market share. Clients – at certain times – will appreciate the convenience of not actually visiting the store.

TRANSPORTATION

freight and passengers

In the transportation industry, the two main subjects to be transported are freight and passengers. The transport options vary between road, rail, water and air. Increase in demand for transport services is, in general, strongly related to overall economic development around the world and the individual countries where companies are located.[39]

TABLE 3-6 *Road transport in Western Europe; volume, 1993*

Country	Billion passenger-km		Billion
	Cars	Bus and Coach	tonne–km
Belgium	86.9	4.7	35.0
Denmark	57.9	9.2	8.8
Germany (West)	741.9	69.9	210.0
Finland	49.9	8.0	24.1
France	627.0	41.8	115.3
Greece	NA	5.2	9.8
Ireland	NA	NA	5.5
Luxemburg	NA	NA	0.6
Italy	602.2	87.8	184.9
Netherlands	140.5	14.0	26.0
Norway	41.5	4.7	7.8
Austria	54.5	13.7	5.8
Portugal	75.8	11.8	11.0
Sweden	90.7	9.3	25.9
Switzerland	76.7	6.0	10.2
Spain	198.4	37.1	162.4
United Kingdom	582.0	42.0	132.3
Western Europe	3425.8	360.0	975.4

Source: Rick Gruber (1996)

Road transport

The general trend in this industry is that demand will increase gradually during the coming years. At the same time, growing liberalization in the EU market will sharpen the competition among the present suppliers. It will force them to operate more efficiently. The road transport industry is changing from a general haulage type of service towards modern logistic services, consisting of sophisticated transport and distributive services (physical distribution and materials management). This will involve several structural changes. On the one hand, a process of concentration and cooperation in this fragmented market will take place. On the other hand, a rise in market niches for specific specialized services by small companies will emerge. The real haulage rates have been falling in the European Community by about 20% between 1985 and 1990. Various factors underlie this trend: improved energy efficiency and stagnant oil prices caused a drop in fuel costs; the gradual deregulation brought about by the creation of the Common Market improved operating efficiency; and the impact of new transport. As a consequence of all these regulatory and technological factors, an increased professionalization of the sector is visible. Professionalization is also required by manufacturers and retailers either as they centralize their stock-holding - at national or European scale (depending on the size

modern logistic services

concentration and cooperation

market niches

professionalization

of their activities) - within value chains in order to achieve economies of scale or require reliable sophisticated transport partners to implement just-in-time techniques.

environmental regulations

Road transport is subject to various environmental regulations in North America and Europe. Although there is a trend to include external costs (like environmental taxes) in road transport prices, this may be offset by new technological developments which enable companies to minimize these costs and thus the effect on prices. Most governments around the globe are investing heavily in the road infrastructure to cope with the demands of the industry and consumers using private cars. In more and more countries, such as Switzerland, Austria and The Netherlands, the combination of transport via road and rail and/or water is more environmentally acceptable to the public than purely transport by road. Increasing congestion and pollution is making road transport unpopular. The EU road haulage industry both for passengers and freight is expected to increase at around 2% per annum.

Rail transport

Besides the US, where this tendency has long been visible, there is a world wide trend

privatize railways

to privatize railways. This can happen in different ways as in the UK where the authorities created a separate vehicle for the rail infrastructure management and (competing) train transport operators, by dividing freight and passengers (both approaches also involve unbundling) or by privatization of the whole formerly state-owned company. The railway industry may benefit from this trend. With the growing attention for the environment, its position versus road and air transport is improving.

flexibility

The flexibility of the train deserves special attention. Both passengers and freight need transport from door to door, which the train cannot offer. Therefore, efficient combinations with other transportation modes will make the train a more attractive alternative then at present. With substantial investments in (international) high-speed rail links, rail will become more attractive for medium range transportation needs in many countries. In the USA recently, the trend towards up-scaling via mergers and take-overs has become visible. The enlarged and combined railways are supposed to respond more effectively to the competition of road haulage in America. Also, trains can compete with planes over shorter distances. Total travelling time is almost the same by train as plane when you have to go from downtown Manhattan to downtown Boston.

Service practice 3-16 Dutch railways' efforts in door-to-door transportation

Dutch Railways (NS) have made agreements in many cities with local taxi firms to pick up passengers at their home address and bring them to the railway station at reduced prices. The same counts for bringing them from the railway station to their destination.

Arrangements with local and regional bus enterprises have been made to better coordinate arrival and departure time to avoid situations in which passengers would sigh: "I missed the bus again."

Inland waterways transport

In Europe, growth rates in inland shipping have been very marginal lately. The opening up of Eastern Europe will have positive effects on the traffic flows between the Benelux countries and Germany, on the one hand and the Danube states, on the other. *opportunity for inland shipping* Another opportunity for inland shipping lies with new services in container and roll-on roll-off cargoes and integrated logistics. In Northern America as in Europe, the services offered by inland waterways remain, by and large, unchanged: large fixed flows with a known volume on well-established routes. However, in China a whole new economic power bloc of 160 million people is emerging along the sides of the Chang Jiang river from Shanghai to Chongging, rapidly making the river a crucial traffic route for passengers and freight.

Shipping

Everyone who follows the share prices of major shipping companies at the stock exchanges has experienced that this trade is a very cyclical one. The shipping indus-*cyclical* try is highly fragmented with some large companies specializing in bulk or contain-*fragmented* ers. In particular, container shipping is characterized by an ongoing process of *container shipping* concentration. In 1993, the aggregate operating capacity of the top 10 liner companies (Maersk Line, Sealand Services, Evergreen/Uniglory, NYK Line/TSK Line, Mitsui OSK Lines, P&O Containers, K-Line, Hanjin Shipping Co., Nedlloyd Lines and Zim Israel Navigation) totalled 29% of the world's total slots in service. By definition, the shipping industry is an international one. The larger lines have to cope with low prof-*over-capacity and* itability as a result of over-capacity and fierce competition. Staff reductions and the *fierce competition* flagging out of ships are meant to boost productivity. On some routes, cooperation between some of the principal line operators includes slot charter, joint marketing, *strategic moves* revenue/cost sharing and combined use of vessels. Strategic moves of shipping companies include: focussing on deep sea shipping; niche marketing such as specialized bulk transport; short distance shipping intended to cover many harbors with self-equipped vessels for container loading and unloading; door-to-door transport either self or by means of strategic alliances; and/or, heavy attention on logistics and added value for augmented services.

Some manufacturers have their own in-house shipping units. Besides pure transport, some companies specialize in rental or leasing of ships. The EU shipping industry has shown a considerable decline in capacity over the years. For the future, it is expected that the global competition in shipping (in particular from Far East companies) will heat up, leading to a shake-out and further concentration. In 1993, five Far Eastern companies were among the top ten shippers.

Air transport

more competition
shake-out

Whereas the American deregulation in the airline industry took place in the late 1970s, this process recently started in most other countries and trade blocs. Deregulation and liberalization of markets will no doubt lead to more competition and a shake-out of inefficiently operating airlines (e.g. PAN AM). Responses by existing airlines to the challenge of new, foreign entrants in, up till now, still heavily regulated home markets, will include cost reductions (personnel and operating), higher loading/occupancy rates both for passengers and freight, concentration (mergers and acquisitions), collaboration and partnerships, e.g. in maintenance of carriers, code-sharing, reservation systems, joint marketing, etc. The privatization of national airlines is just waiting around the corner as national governments and the EU will not fund these loss-making airlines continuously with public money collected by taxes from ordinary people and enterprises.[40] In Latin America, the privatization of national airlines is well underway; in Europe, the public are still waiting for major airlines to shift ownership.

privatization

cycles are shorter

In no other industry does fortune appear to change so quickly as in the air business. In 1993, the international airlines combined together made a loss of 5 billion dollars, in 1995 the profit was about 6 billion. The airline industry was always a cyclical one. Now, it seems that the cycles are all the time becoming shorter, making it more difficult to plan a long-term strategy. In the meantime, air transportation is one of the most rapidly developing industries in terms of foreign direct investment (FDI) with a surge of equity investments taking place since the second half of the 1980s. However, most countries continue to restrict FDI to minority stakes. The most active investors are airlines from Western Europe, pursuing different geographical strategies by means of equity links. Strategic alliances and mergers between airlines of different parts around the world are other well-known strategies to increase economies-of-scale and subsequently yield per mile (both in passenger traffic "seats" and freight "tonnage").

strategic alliances and
mergers

international business
traveller market

On the demand side, the recession of the 1990s has forced substantial change upon the international business traveller market, an increasing number of business travellers can now be found in the back of the plane. Even if the business passenger does fly business class, the company is more alert to the discounts and special packages offered by the airlines. The largest travel increase for the coming years is expected in the Asia-Pacific region. With the back-log of aircraft orders coming on to the market, the question will be whether the growth of passenger and freight traffic is enough to compensate for the new capacity. Unconventional "no-frills" new regional lines (limited instead of universal service providers) are appearing within America and Europe operating at lower costs and offering lower prices. Recently, by means of computer systems, existing airlines attempt to fill their planes as much as possible with high-yielding passengers. Loyalty schemes such as frequent flyer programs and personalized target marketing attempt to bind these high-yielding passengers to the airline. Although the tempo of change in culture and costs is still low in many of the major European airlines, we expect within the next ten years a major shake-out leading towards a few mega-carriers complemented with a limited number of small regional players and niche players.

"no-frills" new
regional lines

loyalty schemes

shake-out
mega-carriers

TABLE 3-7 *Top Ten Schedules Passenger and Freight Traffic Air Transport Enterprises, 1992*			
Carrier Passengers	Million passenger-km	Carrier Freight	Million Tonne-km
1. American Airlines	156,737	1. Federal Express	5,768
2. United Airlines	148,841	2. Lufthansa	4,284
3. Delta Airlines	129,541	3. Air France	3,284
4. Aeroflot	116,347	4. Japan Airlines	3,229
5. Northwest Airlines	94,345	5. Northwest Airlines	2,694
6. British Airways	72,491	6. Korean Airlines	2,656
7. Continental Airlines	69,317	7. British Airways	2,461
8. US Air	56,482	8. KLM	2,392
9. Japan Airlines	55,090	9. Singapore Airlines	2,306
10. Lufthansa	48,661	10. United Airlines	1,930

Source: IATA Yearbook 1992 (WATS); AEA Statistical Yearbook 1993; Ereco

Combined, the travel, tourism and hospitality industry is one of the largest business sectors. In the mid-nineties, it already counted for 10% of the world's economy. This figure is expected to double in the next ten years. At the same time, it is expected that some people who routinely travel to, e.g. standard business meetings within or outside the company, will be substituted by bits. The Internet, fax, modem equipped PCs and teleconferencing contribute to this tendency of moving bits instead of people.

ENTERTAINMENT

new commercial channels

All over the world, public broadcasters are in retreat from the onslaught of new commercial channels. For example, Germany's two public networks, ARD and ZDF, together lost 44% of their audience between 1990 and 1994. Spain's TVE lost almost 20%. NHK, Japan's public broadcaster, found in a survey a few years ago that, although 90% of people in their 50s and 60s watched its programs at least once a week, the "contact rate" dwindled with each succeeding age group to a mere 50% among people in their 20s. Perhaps with hindsight, public-service broadcasting will seem a freak of technology: for a rare half-century, it was possible for one medium to communicate the same material to most of a country's population. The BBC's share of the national television audience has already fallen to 42% (1995), from 50% in 1989. In the 20% of homes that receive cable or satellite television, the BBC accounts for only 28% of total viewing.[41] These observations indicate that public broadcasters which are heavily

public broadcasters

dependent on licence fee revenues have to change their business to survive. One could even ask how legitimate it is to request a licence fee from the public if people watch less and less of their programs. Cutting costs of overheads and production, diminishing bureaucracy, investment in programs, investment in digital transmission, increased broadcasting hours, expanded services, reducing over-capacity and increased cooperation between national public broadcasters, are only part of the answer to compete more successfully with commercial television and radio. They face an additional problem, as we see that financial muscle and income from advertising allows commercial broadcasters to successfully bid on major sport and other events, luring even more viewers from public television. Privatization, scaling down or focusing on core business on particular subjects (e.g. sports) may be the only solution in the long term. In the long run, of all the parties involved, satellite TV promises great opportunities with channels reaching pan-regional audiences in different parts of the world.

technology
competition

globalization of the
media industry

It is clear that major adjustments in the way public broadcasters operate are needed. Changes in technology (e.g. new digital television technology) will force a less wasteful and more rational allocation of broadcast frequencies. The competition in the industry will be stifled by the scaling-up, concentration and integration of production and distribution of entertainment. A combination of environmental changes and industry characteristics has resulted in the globalization of the media industry. In particular, large media companies have snapped up their rivals both in the entertainment industry and its distribution channels. Driven by saturation in their home markets, competition and changes in technology, US firms are very active in this concentration wave. Recently, we have seen the emergence of media empires such as Walt Disney and Viacom combining on the production of movies, with distribution via television stations, cable networks and satellite TV. In the case of Viacom, it also distributes via its Blockbuster video-rental unit. Sony and Philips have entered the entertainment market from the other end, namely from hardware. Both found it necessary in the eighties to ensure the sales of their electronics (hardware) by accessing the lucrative entertainment music and movie markets (software) as well as the potential higher revenues/margins of these industries. Both electronic firms now own large entertainment firms.

remain cyclical,
difficult to exactly
define the specific
market,
new and unexpected
competitors

On the production side, the game is still to find the creative talent and good scenarios. Talent scouts from Time Warner, PolyGram (largely owned by Philips), Sony, Bertelsmann, MCA and ThornEMI are scouting around the world snapping up talent. The big challenge for large entertainment conglomerates on the production side will be to understand the potential of artists and agencies and, once on board, to nurture and cultivate them. Flexible organizational structures need to cope with these requirements. The future outlook for globalization of the media and entertainment industry is prosperous. However, in spite of all its new resources this industry will remain cyclical, one of hits and misses. The examples in this section also indicate that it is very difficult to exactly define the specific market of a firm, especially as the entertainment market can be defined in a very broad way. Consequently, new and unexpected competitors emerge.

HOSPITALITY AND TOURISM

cyclical

The accommodation market is cyclical where firms benefit from the upturns in the economy but suffer in recessions. The hospitality industry includes tourism, hotels

fragmented,
trend to universal
business formats,
concentration

and restaurants. This industry is still fragmented. However, in accomodation (and to a lesser extent the restaurant business), we notice a trend to universal business formats. This takes place sometimes through full ownership, sometimes via joint ventures or franchising. Concentration, in particular in the hotel business, is noticeable.

highly segmented

The accommodation market is highly segmented. High-end segment names include Mariott, Four Seasons, InterContinental, Hilton (Europe) and Conrad. The target groups of Hilton in the USA are more dependent on market opportunities and the size/type/location of the hotel than on one single well-defined market segment. The Flamingo Hilton Las Vegas, for example, caters to middle market tour and travel patrons, while the Las Vegas Hilton targets conventions and high-spending guests. Hilton's Nevada properties serve different customer groups. Outside Las Vegas, the Reno Hilton targets the middle market and conventions, while the Flamingo Hilton-Laughlin targets the budget-market. Holiday Inn finds itself in the middle of the full service accommodation market.

occupancy rate
over-capacity

Accor, Europe's largest hotel company with 256,000 rooms (1995) spread across 65 countries, has principally used joint ventures to expand. With one of its hotel chains, the French hotel and travel group "Formule 1" focused on the low-(budget) end of the market. Also, in many Asian countries, the hotel market is dominated by local and foreign moguls. For example, in 1995 the American Radisson group exploited four hotels in Indonesia. The group belongs to the gigantic Carlson Hospitality Group in America, which operates 350 hotels in 39 countries. By the year 2000, the group plans to open 75 hotels in Asia. For many chains, the fee income from management and franchise contracts provide a stable earnings stream. The occupancy rate of rooms and beds is crucial in this industry. The over-capacity in many countries is driving down industry margins. Exceptions to this rule are often found in the emerging markets, including former Eastern-bloc countries, where prices for western-style rooms are very high, until more high-end hotels enter the market and occupancy rates start to fall.

tourism

Tourism has become an important source of income for many countries around the world. In Asia alone, Indonesia, Malaysia, Thailand, India, Sri Lanka to mention a few, are all well known holiday destinations. The same holds in the Caribbean, for Aruba, Barbados, etc. Less well-known is that since Vietnam opened to visitors international travellers have taken a keen interest in the country. Singapore now aims to transform itself into a culture-hub. In Hong Kong, the importance of the total service sector has been surpassed by that of the industrial one. Within the service sector tourism was and is important in terms of national income. Tourism spreads its wealth among many different people within the society, especially when tourists are not booked into holiday resorts owned by large companies or tycoons. Because the foreign buyer is visiting the service provider, it can be seen as a way of exporting services while staying at home. Projections of economists in Australia show that tourism, alongside manufacturing, will be the two main money-makers for the country in the coming years.

Countries cannot take income from tourism for granted. This has been experienced by the Mediterranean region. This center of the world's "sun, sea and sand" holiday lost its market share in the late eighties and early nineties. Bad service quality, too high prices and old facilities are partly to blame. Service innovation, promotion, investments in infrastructure, market segmentation and cooperation between private entrepreneurs and governments should provide an answer to this.

Service practice 3-17 Singapore's cultural hub [42]

Singapore hopes to become a culture hub. This city has grown wealthy by zealously courting big business. Now it hopes to enrich its cultural lifestyle by doing the same with the arts. The Singapore government is spending millions of dollars in an attempt to transfer the city-state into an arts hub of Asia. The goal isn't just to keep the Singaporeans entertained; officials also hope to attract art lovers from other parts of the region. "Recently we have been looking at cultural tourism as a distinct industry", says Tong Min Way, director of corporate affairs at the Ministry of Information and the Arts. The Singapore Tourist Promotion Board and the National Arts Council have joined forces to push art attractions in the city and the government is investing money to make that push pay off. In addition to wooing big Broadway plays and pricey art attractions with financial support, local authorities are investing more than 1 billion Singapore dollars (US$708.5 million) in two landmark projects to build up the city's art infrastructure. The Esplanade, a US$667 million complex of theaters, studio's and a concert hall, is due to open in 2001. The Singapore Art Museum has recently opened and three more new museums will follow. Singapore has a good chance to become the events capital of Asia.

Service practice 3-18 Bigger must be better, say cruise operators [43]

The cruise ship Carnival Destiny boasts the world's largest floating casino, four pools, seven restaurants and a 1,500 seat theatre. It breaks the cruise ship record held by the Princess Cruise Liners, part of the UK's P&O shipping group, with 77,000 tons. But Princess Cruises will retake the record in 1998 with the 104,000 ton Grand Princess. Both companies will be overtaken in 1999 when the Seattle-based Westin hotels launches the $1.2bn America World City. At 250,000 tons and with 8,600 passengers and crew, it will be more than twice the size of today's largest cruise ships. The new ships usually include large play areas and fun pools for children, health and fitness clubs for adults and more informal restaurants and bars.

Sheherazada Daneshkhu of the *Financial Times* examines where the cruise industry is heading. The trend towards ever bigger ships is driven by economies of scale which make large ships increasingly cost-effective in catering for the demands of a rapidly-growing industry. The number of passengers in North America, which accounts for three-quarters of the total cruise market, has risen from 3.6 million in 1990 to just under 5m in 1996. In Europe, the second largest market, passenger numbers have doubled from 530,000 to more than 1 million at the same time. Gone are the days of sea-faring cruise liners. Many of today's cruises compete with land-based resorts and are floating resorts with every facility you can find on land. The cruise industry has expanded from its traditional base of middle-aged couples to appeal to younger travellers, with prices and facilities which compete with land-based holidays. But there are signs that the 30 ships currently on order might lead to an oversupply. Mr Wild, a consultant and analyzer of the industry, believes that, as a result, the cruise market will be increasingly characterized by winners and losers in the next few years. "Heavy discounting and a downward pressure on rates would seem probable with survival depending increasingly on effective marketing, control of costs, improved efficiency and the maximization of marginal revenues."

The Carnival Destiny caters to a new kind of passenger – arriving by air for a week-long cruise around the Caribbean.

HEALTH SERVICES

increase of spending on health care

The ageing of the world population, breakthroughs in the medical diagnostic and research front, the increasing price of health services (often in relation to other goods and services) all contribute to an increase of (public and private) spending on health care. In 1990, the United States devoted 12.7% of its GNP to health, as against 9.1% in Canada, 8.9% in France, 8.0% in Germany, 6.5% in Japan, and 6.1% in the United Kingdom. The 2.7% annual increase in the health-to-GNP ratio for the United States during the 1980s was the highest among the OECD countries. US health expenditure of $2,800 per person in 1990 was nearly $1,000 above the average for the OECD countries.[44]

rate of medical inflation

In 1993 and 1994, the rate of medical inflation has begun to slow down, mainly as a result of cost-cutting initiated by the private sector. The findings concerning health cost escalation in the United States and other industrial countries are especially relevant for middle-income developing countries. Those countries are under pressure from medical professionals, manufacturers, and consumers to use new technologies, they also face difficult policy choices relating to insurance institutions and the compensation of health care providers. For example, Korea has already more sophisticated new medical equipment such as imaging machines and lithotripters (used to treat kidney stones) per capita than either Canada or Germany.

The authors of the World Bank paper, World Development Report (1993), propose a three-pronged approach to government policies in this sector which may have a dramatic impact on the providers of health services and its consumers:[45]

- foster an environment that enables households to improve health;
- improve government spending on health; and
- promote diversity and competition.

managed competition

The US form of managed competition – as we can learn from this World Development Report – has attracted widespread interest as a health-care services purchasing strategy, designed to promote competition and to reward those health-care providers with the best performance in terms of cost, quality and patient satisfaction. The strategy is designed to address the fundamental problems of the current health-care financing and delivery system in the United States.

Service practice 3-19 "Managed competition" and health care reform

Since the 1960s, most Americans have grown accustomed to first-class health coverage. Most working people got health insurance through their employer; the retired had Medicare, the poor Medicaid. Nearly everyone had free choice of doctors and hospitals, as Robert Kuttner, co-editor of *The American Prospect* and author of *The End of Laissez-Faire* writes.[46] "Some people had no insurance, but the government required hospitals not to turn anybody away, and hospitals simply shifted costs onto paying customers." For decades then, the increase in national cost of health care was much higher than the inflation rate. With managed care, which involves a higher involvement of the free market than in the past, fewer health plans allow doctors and hospitals to pursue treatments without insurer review. More consumers are in prepaid health maintenance organizations that sharply limit benefits. Acquisitions, mergers and consolidations by for-profit hospital chains are squeezing out excess capacity and putting hospitals and doctors under real competitive pressure for the first time. Insurance plans and health maintenance organizations (HMOs) with market power are negotiating contracts that shift the financial risk for the cost of treatment to doctors and hospitals. All of this ratchets down costs.

negative externalities

Despite these advantages, some negative externalities do occur. In the US health care, coverage is mainly employment based and is far from universal: approximately 37 million people under the age of 65 lacked insurance coverage in 1990. Costs are increasing rapidly. Under third-party providers, reimbursement methods often create financial incentives to provide more care. Insurers seek profits by excluding higher-risk individuals rather than aggressively pursuing greater efficiency in health services. A major indirect cost of the system is reduced labor mobility as a result of the risks of exclusion from insurance at a new place of employment. Under managed competition, a health insurance purchase cooperative (HIPC) would be formed to organize purchasers of health care within a region. The HIPC would establish standards for the region's health plan by, for example, defining a basic benefit package of comprehensive health services. Next, the HIPC would contact eligible providers for this basic package. The HIPC would provide the public with information about price and quality of the various suppliers. Universal coverage would be achieved through public subsidies to those not otherwise covered so they could purchase packages. One example of "managed competition" is the California Public Employees Retirement System, which operates like the proposed HIPC, arranging health coverage and managing competition on behalf of almost 1 million state employees and their families.

The World Bank reporters believe that, although the system has some weak points such as the costs of universal coverage and how to cover areas of low population density, this US model has a future and may well be applied in other countries. In addition, some other side effects of managed care must be pointed out, like the administrative burden to hospitals, doctors spending hours on the phone with insurance reviewers and the limits of personal freedom for doctors and patients. Finally, in The World Bank's view, coverage should be portable. In other words, the US like many other states is still trying to find an optimal way to finance and deliver health services. As it appears, neither option, private or public (fully or partly) seems to have it all. But definitely, the chances for private operators in this industry are rising around the world.

other side effects of managed care

During the coming years, we expect a more critical attitude of governments and other regulators towards expenditure on health services. However, consumers, manufacturers and health providers will form strong countervailing powers. No doubt, the call for more efficient and effective health care services will prevail. This will result in a concept where private care in addition to public (basic and essential) services will become an increasingly interesting option for both consumers and service providers. Governments should hurry, as in most countries the demographic time bomb is ticking. For health service and insurance companies the challenge will be how to respond to this structural change in providing health care, adjusting their ownership structure, service concept and package towards these new realities.

countervailing powers

INFRASTRUCTURE SERVICES

The reform of the provision of infrastructure services is under way around the world, both in industrial and developing countries. As this group of services is in such a turmoil and offers big opportunities for internationalization we will investigate infrastructure in more detail than some other industries. We use, following a recent World Bank report, infrastructure as an umbrella term for many activities referred to as "social overhead capital". We will focus on the economic infrastructure which includes services from:

reform of the infrastructure services

internationalization

- public utilities – power, telecommunications, piped water supply, sanitation and sewerage, solid waste collections and piped gas;
- public works – roads, major dam and canal works for irrigation and drainage; and
- other transport sectors – urban and interurban railways, urban transport, ports, waterways and airports.

Governments are changing their attitude toward their role in providing infrastructure. What seemed impossible twenty years ago is now becoming a reality. National flagships, such as airlines, and services, once thought solely to be operated by the "people", like telecommunications, door-to-door mail, water, gas, electricity, are about to drastically change in either type of operating, management, size or ownership. The World Development Report, Infrastructure for Development published in 1994 for the World Bank, shows the route for performance enhancement of these services.

governments are changing their attitude

performance enhancement

Although focussed on developing economies, the report signals the trends for delivering infrastructure services in most countries. For this reason, we will present the main recommendations to develop an infrastructure that responds to effective demand and does so efficiently. The following recommendations include incentives in order to ensure a more efficient, responsive delivery: introduce competition, promote commercial management and involve stakeholders. The expectation is that the implementation of these recommendations and the various options to carry them out will be typical of the infrastructure services provided in the future. The two recommendations are as follow.

The introduction of competition

"direct" competition
"indirect" competition

This will increase efficiency, volume and quality of infrastructure services as indicated by many studies. Where "direct" competition is not possible, efficiency can be increased by means of "indirect" competition ranging from simple contracts for specific services to long term concessions. Competition gives consumers choice for better meeting their demands and putting pressure on suppliers to be efficient and accountable to users. Competition can be introduced directly, by liberalizing entry into activities that have no technological barriers, and indirectly, through competitive bidding for the right to provide exclusive service where natural monopoly conditions exist and by liberalizing the supply of service substitutes.

Apply commercial principles of operations

infrastructure must be managed like a business

Infrastructure must be managed like a business and not like a bureaucracy. The provision of infrastructure needs to be conceived and run as a service industry that responds to customer demand. Poor performers typically have a confusion of objectives, little financial autonomy or financial discipline, and no "bottom line" measured by customer satisfaction. The high willingness to pay for most infrastructure services, even by the poor, provides greater opportunity for user charges. Private sector involvement in management, financing, or ownership will in most cases be needed to ensure a commercial orientation in infrastructure. To illustrate this approach, the report points out four options ranging from solely public to fully private.[47] These four options are:

A. public ownership and operation by enterprise or department;
B. public ownership with private operation;
C. private ownership and private operation; and
D. community and user provision.

EPILOGUE

The trends in the various industries discussed in this section reveal that many things are changing. Dynamics and uncertainty are at stake. Analyzing all the environmental factors may decrease the risks involved. We also saw as an underlying trend that the traditional borders between markets fade away. This is partly because of cooperation between firms from several industries. On the other hand, services from various *looking at markets from a customer's perspective*

industries can satisfy the same need. Then, looking at markets from a customer's perspective (what do they see as similar or competing services?) will define the relevant market for the service provider. Some of these changes are shown in our final Chapter Three Service practice.

Service practice 3-20 Convergence of industries

Mobile telephone services, the availability of cable networks and the Net are changing the landscape of telephone companies. Besides privatizations, deregulation and technological changes, the telecom sector is characterized by internationalization. Not only is the international telecommunications traffic fast growing and profitable, also international alliances are the order of the day. In the mid-nineties, strategic alliances, mergers and acquisitions were visible around the world. Many telecoms were eager to get a piece of the action abroad, as well as at home either to protect their share or enter the local transmission market. The development of mobile networks next to fixed transmission has further triggered concentration. All these changing circumstances have serious effects on the telecommunications sector. Some changes have effects that even go beyond the scope of the telecommunications sector. This process is called "convergence". The term convergence is used here to describe the amalgamation of three formerly separated industries: telecommunications, hardware (computer and consumer electronics) and content (entertainment, information). Digitization of information can be seen as the main catalyst of convergence. The computer industry was the first, and now the telecommunications industry is turning into a digital industry. As Van Soest and Van de Wal describe in their industrial sector report (1995), the content industry (yet the least digital of the three) will also follow this step from analogue to digital. Even the printed media will be part of this process. There is now little difference between, for instance, a magazine, a TV and a radio than one might think. Right now digital magazines (on CD-ROM) exist whose bits are convertible into printed text, video to be watched and music to be listened to. Nowadays, some of these services are offered on-line. A trend that will continue. It also implies that the creation industry (content) will be the most profitable and dominate, as there is only one movie *Jurrassic Park* but several ways to deliver it (network operating) such as the movie theatre, videocassette, in an aeroplane, public broadcasting or video on demand at home or elsewhere. As the lines between media blur, so do the lines between industries. Once all three sectors can handle information in a digital form, a truly single information industry can arise. As a consequence, companies operating in one of these industries have to analyze the external environment even outside the borders of their own industry in order to formulate a proper corporate strategy.

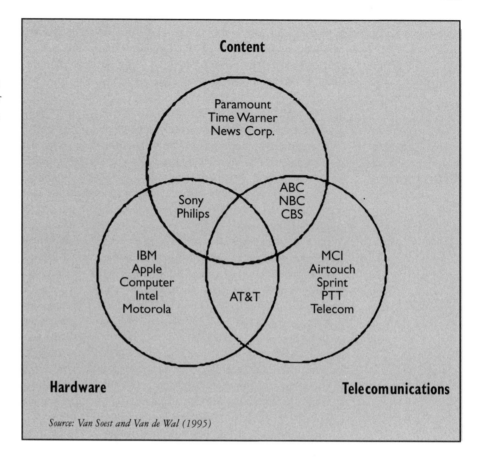

*Figure 3-5
Convergence of
industries*

Content

Paramount
Time Warner
News Corp.

Sony
Philips

ABC
NBC
CBS

IBM
Apple
Computer
Intel
Motorola

AT&T

MCI
Airtouch
Sprint
PTT
Telecom

Hardware

Telecomunications

Source: Van Soest and Van de Wal (1995)

SUMMARY

To service providing organizations, the environment consists of four components:

- the macro-environment (DRETS-factors);
- the marketing environment of the service sector environment (marketing related trends);
- developments within a particular service industry which also determine the degree of existing competition; and
- the market.

This chapter focussed on the first three components of the business environment. The brief analysis of selected service industries was centered on trends rather than on competition at an individual level. It became clear that both the marketing related trends

which hold in the service sector as the trends within each individual industry are subject to the developments in the macro-environment.

Dynamic changes in the macro-environment can be labelled as the DRETS-factors. They include:

- demographic factors such as the increasingly ageing population, changing ethnic composition of the population, etc.;
- regulation in some sectors (environmental issues) and further deregulation in other sectors (finance);
- economic factors like the phase of development and the state of the economic indicators;
- technological developments such as telematics,

the Internet and technological product improvements facilitating numerous new services; and
- social and cultural factors resulting in drastic changes to customers' daily life.

A number of marketing-related trends in the service sector indicate the possible direction of company growth in the next decade. Internationalization is the first, although to many service providers it is slippery ground to tread on. The need for more efficiency urges governments and companies to be(come) self-supporting (privatization and contracting-out). Service companies in various sectors from entertainment to banking and from tourism to auditing have reviewed their corporate and marketing strategies during recent years as a result of globalization, market and technological changes. In many service industries, we see the impact on the strategies (and employment) of major service firms caused by closely linked issues of privatization, deregulation and liberalization. In this chapter, these issues are combined under the phrase "the urge of raising commercial principles around the globe". Privatization alone is like a wave swamping many service sectors worldwide. Among the list of privatization candidates are many domestic services that to date have been shielded totally from open market conditions. Others, like national airlines, were protected in their home country, e.g. by limited landing rights or unattractive slots for their international competitors. After all, national airlines rely on state funds to supplement their losses. Privatization is well under way in the infrastructure. Technology, market and competition drive service industries into convergence. The amalgamation of telecommunication, hardware (computer and consumer electronics) and content (entertainment and information) is a well known example. Less known perhaps is the convergence of retail banking and insurance in many countries as well as shopping and entertainment. Throughout the world, low cost competitors are entering deregulated markets. Raising commercial principles, focussing on core business is a marketing related trend, often leading to downsizing e.g. by spinning off subsidiaries. On the other hand, scaling up in the same core business by means of internal growth, mergers, acquisitions, strategic alliances or strategic partnering is another

marketing related trend. It appears to be difficult to determine the optimum size of a business; both small and big can be "beautiful" in the service sector. Yesterday's competitors may well be today's partners. If necessary, strategic alliances are formed per project or market. Diminishing differences between products and services and changes in asset structure of service companies and the delivery mode they choose are the fourth and fifth service trends. The growth in leasing and rentals as well as collective ownership are interesting developments in the service sector. It is obvious that in many industries delivering services electronically (e.g. by telephone or the Internet) is dramatically changing the landscape. Where possible, the marketing related service trends should be translated into strategic policies and definite ideas on new services.

Rising costs may trigger a change in health industry legislation. Changes will also occur due to a withdrawing government, who focus on prevention rather than cure and set conditions on basic health care services for everyone. This may create opportunities for private health and service companies. Those firms that operate internationally and have greater experience in their home-country will be in the best position to take advantage of these opportunities.

After all, chances and risks are most likely to surface in the immediate environment of the organization: the competition and the market. As the influences are more direct and intensive, prompt action is called for in that respect. This argument is especially relevant to those service providers that did not act in a competitive market before.

The results of the external analysis of the service environment as worked out in this chapter will be utilized while carving the corporate strategy, the marketing strategy, developing new services and the planning of the other marketing instruments in chapters still to come. Issues that occur or have occurred in a particular service industry could be applied in another industry to get a competitive advantage. In this way, service firms can learn from one another to satisfy share holders, customers and other stakeholders by providing excellent service quality.

QUESTIONS

1 Which environmental factors together form DRETS? Give examples of each.
2 What type(s) of service provider(s) would be interested in the rate of fluctuation of the national currency?
3 Why should a service provider analyze macro-factors which are beyond the organization's control?
4 What social trends partly account for the growth of the service sector?
5 What other trends are relevant to the growth of the service sector?
6 Discuss briefly the major reasons explaining the explosive growth of leasing? State your opinion whether this growth will continue.
7 Give a description of disintermediation. In which service industries may this phenomenon play a role?
8 Why is information and information technology so important to service firms?
9 Outsourcing has been mentioned on various occasions in this chapter. What are the reasons for and consequences of outsourcing as mentioned in this chapter?
10 Why does privatization of governmental services take place?

ASSIGNMENTS

1 Make your own case study using tendencies, trends, and macro- and service sector factors that play a role in determining the strategy of a particular service provider you selected yourself.
2 Discuss the major developments in one of the following industries: financial services, business services in general, distribution, transport and travel, entertainment, hospitality, health services, or infrastructure services. What can be said about concentration in these industries? What is happening in those industries in your own country?
3 Is there a kind of convergence in the financial sector worldwide? If so, describe the convergence and its roots.
4 What kind of explanations can be found in this chapter for the positive and negative experiences noted in your service diary?
5 When firms define their markets in a different way, this may open up new opportunities. Give some examples for service industries defining their markets in a different way. Does the GE-case from Chapter One fit into this perspective? Explain. Do you see a comparable situation or company to GE in your own country?
6 Make an update of Table 3-7. What can you conclude in comparing your findings with those from 1992?

Case: THE GERMAN LIFE INSURANCE INDUSTRY: THE IMPACT OF DEMOGRAPHIC CHANGE

Background – private provision through life insurance

In 1992 the German state statutory pensions system was reformed. The changes in pension provision were the result of the growing pressure from rapid demographic changes which are particularly acute in Germany. The population is ageing rapidly and is putting significant pressure on state welfare and its ability fully to meet commitments given to the population. There is a growing awareness by individuals that self-provision for pensions is essential.

Forecasts show that the number of working persons is in decline, as the result of a continuous fall in the birth rate and the number of pensioners increasing, in comparison to the working population. This shortfall in active workers in the population will nearly double over the next 40 years because of longer life expectancies. Additionally people are spending longer in education and taking early retirement, resulting in a reduced period of time in which contributions to statutory pensions are paid. A study reported in the *Financial Times* (1993) predicts that by the year 2000 a quarter of the population will be over 60 and that by 2030 deaths will exceed births by 300,000 a year, resulting in a city the size of Frankfurt disappearing every two years. This decline in the working population and its ageing is having a dramatic impact on welfare provision.

Pension provision

Under this demographic pressure, pension reform in Germany has grown out of an increasing recognition that most people will now have to provide privately for their old age. To make provision for retirement it has been estimated that pension income to satisfy average needs has to be approximately 70% of gross income earned before retirement. In Germany three main forms of old-age pension provision exist; they are:

(1) statutory pensions which can provide, at best, 45% of gross income;
(2) company pension schemes which provide 12 to 20% of income;
(3) life insurance which provides 10 to 15% of old-age provision.

In addition it should be noted that as in most countries in Europe it is essential for the self-employed to provide privately for their old age as they will only receive either a small statutory pension or none at all. And SMEs, especially sole traders, make up one of the largest employers in Germany and the EU.

The demographic changes that have caused the pension system to be reformed are, on the one hand, good news for life insurers as provision will be needed by the working population to make up the shortfall of 10-15% in most people's pension income. However, the negative effect is that the declining, young, working population in Germany will inevitably lead to a decline in the traditional life insurance market.

Life insurance offered

There are many different types of life insurances and pensions on offer in the German life insurance market. The key types of products on offer break down into the following groups:

Endowment and whole-life insurance

This is the most common form of life insurance which offers cover for death and benefits on survival. The sum insured is based on sex, age at the start of the contract, the duration of the contract and the premiums paid. On taxation grounds it is advisable for the duration of the contract to be over 12 years (six years in Eastern Germany); the average duration of a life insurance contract in Germany is 28 years. This is the most important form of private provision for both the employed and self-employed as it fulfils the two crucial financial security functions:

• a capital provision for old age: when the policy matures it is paid out tax free with bonuses)
• immediate dependent provision should the insured die before the policy matures.

Annuities and pensions

This is the most common form of

private pension cover. One can pay either a regular premium so that pension benefits will be received in future years, or a lump sum so that pension benefits are received immediately. The lump sum may be all or some of the amount received from a mature life insurance policy. Pensions are usually paid until the death of the policy-holder and it is also possible to provide for dependents.

Risk insurance
This is insurance purely to cover the risk of death within a specified period. This type of insurance is often used as an insurance to cover loans and mortgages (endowment policies).

Supplementary insurances
The most common types of supplementary insurances are accident insurance and vocational disability insurance. Life insurers also offer vocational disability insurance for self-employed people.

Capital investment products
Capital investment products (unit trusts and unit-linked insurances) are not part of the German life insurers' portfolio, although many companies do offer such products through their sales representatives mainly for the reinvestment of capital received on mature policies (GDV, 1992). The availability of such products in the German life insurance market may increase if the market is deregulated. Additionally EU insurers entering the German market will be able to offer such products because of the development of single authorisation.

Life insurance for women
Following the revision of mortality tables, which, in 1986, for the first time separated life expectancy for the sexes and showed that women lived longer, life insurance for women has become a growth area. Insurers have been able to offer reduced premiums to women because of their longer life expectancy.

The German economy
Germany is under the increasing pressure and strain of economic and social integration following reunification. The costs of restructuring and refurbishment of the Eastern German economy and its infrastructure have meant that in addition to weathering the world economic recession it has had to increase public expenditure substantially which has meant that the overall economic situation remains difficult as we enter the mid-1990s.

In 1991 the employment situation improved in Western Germany, the number in employment rose by 2.8% and unemployment fell to 1.69 million. Conversely, unemployment has continued to rise in Eastern Germany due to the restructuring that is taking place. At the start of 1991 there were nearly 8 million gainfully employed persons; the number had decreased by 1.2 million to 6.8 million by the year's end and the number of unemployed continues to grow. In recent months the full impact of the downturn in the European economy has impacted upon Germany and major companies such as Mercedes-Benz, BMW and

Volkswagen have announced sizeable redundancies and planned further reductions in staff.

However, high real wage increases and transfers of funds to Eastern Germany have also stimulated consumer spending and the service sector in Eastern Germany has developed extensively, although the downturn in the German economy as a whole has clearly dampened down this growth.

Life insurance industry
Unification has opened up a new market for life insurers. The readiness of Eastern German citizens to make provisions for old age has risen considerably as a result of increased income and the uncertainty of the open market. This has also been fostered by life insurers setting up company pension schemes in small and medium-sized companies in Eastern Germany.

However, due to increasing unemployment in Eastern Germany it is likely that many life insurance policies taken out after reunification will lapse. This has been Aachener & Munchener Lebensversicherung's (A&M Leben) experience. Since reunification A&M Leben has sold many life insurance policies in Eastern Germany; however, its lapse ratio (i.e the number of policies cancelled expressed as a percentage of the average number of insurance contracts held in the financial year) rose considerably to 7.3% in 1991 (5.5% in 1990). In its annual report for 1991, A&M Leben stated that the increased amount of business in Eastern

Germany has contributed to the rise in the lapse ratio. In contrast less than 10% of GDV Lebensversicherung's new business came from Eastern Germany in 1991 and its lapse ratio has risen by just 0.2% to 3% in 1991.

This is a costly problem for the industry for if a life insurance policy lapses within two to three years of its inception the life insurance company will incur a loss due to the high start-up costs of policies to administration. Thus it is essential for life insurance companies to minimise the number of policies that lapse to avoid reducing margins.

Life insurance industry supervision

The German life insurance industry is closely supervised as one can see from Table C.8.1 which compares life insurance industry supervision in Germany and Great Britain.

Premiums must correspond to set guidelines and all German life insurance companies are liable to credit at least the mandatory interest rate (3.5% in 1991) to policy-holders on life insurance policies. Close regulation and supervision make it difficult for German life insurance companies

to be innovative in their home market, that is by developing new products, and there is little opportunity for them to compete by offering lower premiums to lower-risk groups, for example nonsmokers. Single authorisation will have the effect that from 1993 foreign companies may offer life insurance in the German market without having authorisation from the German supervisory authorities. This will almost certainly lead to an increase in competition from foreign insurers not bound by the rules. Additionally the market may be deregulated, allowing insurers to offer more products with varying premiums.

The Market

In 1991 Germans (West and East) spent DM 60.25 billion on life insurance, an increase of 12% on 1990 (1990 9.4%). This figure does not include the income of the former state-controlled life insurer in Eastern Germany (GDV Jahrbuch, 1991). Demand for life insurance is predominantly from private households with 70% of all households having life insurance and 90% in households where people are in full employment.

The growing importance of provisions for old age, vocational disability and dependents can be seen in the increase in insurance benefits paid: in 1980 benefits to policy-holders from life insurance totalled DM 11.3 billion and represented slightly more than 10% of income from statutory pensions; in 1991 payments totalled DM 39.5 billion and represented more than 21% of income from statutory pensions (GDV, 1991a).

Customer profile

Over 90% of all households with people in employment have at least one life insurance policy; it is a widely accepted form of old-age and dependent provision. Young people are also very aware of the need for such provisions as the largest proportion of life insurances was sold to the 20-29 age group. Nearly 65% of life insurances sold to men were in the 20–39 age group; this compares to nearly 58% for women.

One clear difference does, however, emerge: the number of insurances taken out by women over 50 was 18.8% in comparison to 11.6% for men. This reflects the increasing provision by women for a longer life expectancy (GDV Jahrbuch, 1991). The sum insured also varies with age group. The average age of people taking out an endowment insurance policy is 32 and provision for old age is the most frequently occurring important reason for taking life insurance protection.

Currently private households spend 3.5% of their disposable income on life insurance premiums. Over 85% of premiums paid

Table C.8.1 Life insurance supervision in Germany and Great Britain

	Germany	Great Britain
Regulations for calculation of:		
Mortality probability	Yes	No
Interest return	Yes	No
Costs	Yes	No
Regulations for profit participation	Yes	No

Source: GDV Lebensversicherungsmärkte in der Europäischen Gemeinschaft (1992).

are for endowment insurance, annuities and pensions; group insurances are of lesser importance. The total market for risk insurance is less than 3% of all money spent on life insurance premiums (GDV, Lebensversicherungsmarkte in der Europäischen Gemeinschaft, 1992).

Profit participation and surpluses

Surpluses are credited to the policy holder, so that the sum insured increases each year. The surplus arises from:

• The difference between actual current net return from capital investments and the minimum guaranteed (the mandatory interest rate). In 1991 the net average yield on capital investments in Germany was 7.2%, but this figure varied widely from company to company, being dependent upon the performance of the company's investments. In 1991 the mandatory interest rate was 3.5%.
• The risk surplus arises when fewer people die than was estimated. Risk surplus is the second most important source of

Table C.8.2 Germany and Great Britain: a life insurance sales channel comparison

	Germany	Great Britain
Sales representatives (employed by a company)	xx	xx
Sales representatives (independent)	—	xx
Direct insurers*	—	—
Banks	x	—

xx = very important; x = important; — = less well developed.
* Generally on the increase but still remain less well developed.
Source: GDV Lebensversicherungsmärkte in der Europäischen Gemeinschaft (1992).

surplus, after that on investment income, and is derived from prudent actuarial calculation.
• Effective cost control, that is, the provision for administration costs which are not fully utilised.

If current surpluses could be maintained in the future, a policy with a 27-year maturity would double in value by the time the policy has matured.

Life insurance sales channels

In many EU countries most life insurance is sold through sales representatives. In Germany sales representatives represent one particular company; they can be either employed full time by the life insurance company or self-employed. In the UK most life insurance is sold through inde-

pendent sales representatives.

Growth in integrated financial services: *Allfinanz*

Recently the growth in *Allfinanz* in Germany has opened new sales channels to life insurers (Wiedemann, 1992). Some examples are shown in Figure C.8.1

AMB Insurance, for example, is able to sell its insurance products through the BfG Bank and Badenia Building Society. This formation of companies offers the advantage of 'cross-selling' between the companies. Marketing life insurance through banks and building societies offers life insurers the opportunity to take advantage of an existing distribution system and the prime high street locations. Additionally, banks and building societies offer

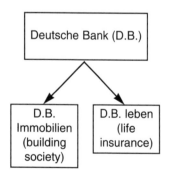
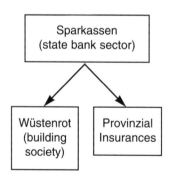
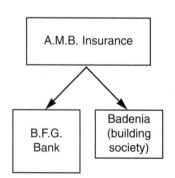

Figure C.8.1 Examples of *Allfinanz*.

a large customer base with a high frequency of customer contact and a strong, trusting relationship between the banks and building societies and their customers.

Allianz Insurance sells its insurance through the Deutsche Bank and it has been given permission to sell insurance through the Dresdner Bank; these are two of the largest banks in Germany.

Allianz Lebensversicherung A.G. is by far the largest life insurer in Germany, it also owns Deutsche Lebensversicherungs A.G. (successor to the state monopoly insurer in Eastern Germany) which ranked as number 11 with DM 1,428 million premium income in 1991.

The Eastern German life insurance market

The reunification of Germany opened up a significant new market for Western German life insurers. The market has its own unique features and is very different from the Western German market; following reunification the Western German pension system was introduced to Eastern Germany. In the former GDR all old-age provisions were made through the state and private life insurance as we know it did not exist in Eastern Germany. Due to low statutory pensions in the former GDR there was a voluntary, supplementary pension scheme, to which 85% of those liable to pay statutory pension contributions belonged. This supplementary pension scheme was abolished and all statutory pensions were transferred to the new system following reunification. A growing familiarity with the need to cover this shortfall and arrange supplementary pension cover is contributing to a rising demand for life insurance in Eastern Germany.

As in Western Germany demographic changes will also affect the Eastern German statutory pension system in the next decade. The demographic problems associated with old-age provisions cannot, from experience, be solved by statutory pensions alone, but it is necessary for people to make private provisions particularly through life insurance.

Life insurance will become an important element in old-age, invalidity and dependent provision in Eastern Germany. Its medium- and long-term development will be influenced by socio-demographic factors, incomes and the social and political environment (GDV, 1991b).

As in Western Germany demographic factors, such as an ageing population, will affect the sale of life insurance. Other factors such as employment, population and life expectancy will influence the sale of life insurance. It is estimated that there will be approximately 8 million gainfully employed persons in Eastern Germany in the year 2000. This figure depends, of course, on the development of the Eastern German economy. The number of households in Eastern Germany is expected to remain unchanged at 6.6 million. However, the number of persons per household should remain slightly above that in Western Germany, currently 2.2 persons per household. The average life expectancy in Eastern Germany for men and women is about two years shorter than in Western Germany. As the standard of living comes into line with that of the West, that is, wider choice of food, better healthcare and a better environment, life expectancy will increase. These socio-demographic factors point to market potential for life insurance, which may reach up to 25% of the Western German market.

The development of the market will depend on whether there will be a demand from older generations for life insurance, as is the case in Western Germany. Due to lower premiums and the length of time for which life

Table C.8.3 Major life insurance companies – market share

Rank	Company	Premiums 1991 (DM million)	Growth 1991/90 (%)	Market share 1991 (%)
1	Allianz Leben	7,915	9.76	12.73
2	Hamburg-Mannheimer	3,855	15.61	6.20
3	Volksfursorge	3,150	6.27	5.06
4	R&V Leben	2,468	12.01	3.97
5	Victoria	2,325	13.37	3.74
6	A&M Leben	2,063	27.00	3.32

Source: *Handelsblatt*, 3 August 1992.

insurance is taken out it tends to be a more attractive proposition for young to middle-aged persons. As there was not any private old-age provision in Eastern Germany before reunification the law allows tax relief for life insurances with a six-year maturity (12 years in Western Germany); this makes life insurance more attractive to older working people. This change in the law has opened up a new market segment for life insurers.

Income growth in Eastern Germany will also play an important role in the demand for life insurance. Wage increases tend to follow growth in the domestic product, therefore wages in Eastern Germany should increase as the two economies (West and East) converge. However, to encourage private old-age provision it is important that wage increases result from a competitive environment and not from transfers of money from the West.

Additionally one should not underestimate the effect that the general mood in Eastern Germany and the future expectations of the people will have on sales of life insurance. From the results of market research and actual demand that have been experienced one could assume that, after overcoming the problems associated with reunification, there will be demand for life insurance. In the long term there is a good market potential for the sale of life insurance in Eastern Germany. However the development of the life insurance market is very much dependent on the development of the economy; put simply – people need to be employed if they are going to take out life insurance.

German life insurance industry – the future

The life insurance market will continue to grow as the population as a whole becomes aware of the need to make increased private provision for old age, disability and dependents, as a result of declining state welfare and ageing populations. In addition the statutory pension reforms will encourage people to make more provisions for their old age through life insurance. Currently close state supervision gives the German life insurance market much protection from competitive practices. However, the market will change over the next few years because of increased competition from foreign insurers and the pressures for a deregulated market.

The way that life insurance is sold will change, particularly if the market is deregulated. The growth in Allfinanz offerings will lead to a larger volume of life insurance being sold through banks and building societies. Direct insurers would also benefit if the market were deregulated: it would allow them more leeway to be innovative and price competitive. Recently there has been a marked increase in direct sales; this trend looks set to continue in the future.

Eastern Germany offers a large market for life insurers. In the short term the economic situation will hinder growth as increasing unemployment will cause many life insurance policies to lapse because policy-holders will not be able to pay their premiums. However, the long-term view is that as the two economies even out there will be growth in the life insurance market.

References

Financial Times (1993), 25 October.

GDV (1991a), *Die Deutsche Versicherungs-wirtschaft Jahrbuch.*

GDV (1991b), *Die Deutsche Einigung und Versicherung-wirtschaft.*

GDV (1992), *Lebensversicherungsmärkte in der Europäischen Gemeinschaft.*

Wiedemann, A. (1992) *Verbundsstrategie Für Kreditgenossenschaften*, Paul Haupt, Berlin.

QUESTIONS

1   How is the changing structure of the German population likely to affect the German life insurance market?
2   How should the German life insurance industry respond to these demographic pressures?
3   What opportunities exist in Germany to develop new insurance products?
4   How is life insurance sold in Germany? How does this compare with the rest of the EU?
5   What will be the impact of single authorization on the German insurance market?

ENDNOTES

1. Cetron, 1994.

2. Example used by Margaret Crimp in *The Marketing Research Process*, 2nd edition, (1985).

3. In this view on the organizational theory – the external environment of the organization is viewed in its entirety as an "independent" source. As a consequence, the environment influences the organization.

4. In Chapter Seven, we will see that the most recent ideas of gaining a competitive advantage are based on the ability of a firm to shape its own external environment, e.g. trends in its own industry. The competitors have to follow. We will not elaborate on that idea at present.

5. *Business Week*, 19 September, 1994.

6. Van Beek et al., 1993.

7. *The Economist*, 28 October, 1995, p. 121.

8. Datamonitor results published in *Adformatie*, 5 February, 1998, p. 7.

9. The European Stock Exchanges, The Italian Stock Exchange Council, CBI, European Business Handbook, UNICE, Kogan Page, London, pp. 27-29, 1995, and own sources.

10. It turns out that social contacts among employees are still very important to perform well. That is why they need to be at the office regularly.

11. We do not refer here to some tribal societies where women usually do all the work and educate the children.

12. An UnMITIgated success, *The Economist*, 31 August, 1996, p. 59-60.

13. Lovelock, 1991, p. 2.

14. *Bureaucrats in Business*, 1995, p. 263.

15. *The World Development Report* (1994), Infrastructure for Development, p. 53-57, Oxford University Press, Oxford. The table at page 57 of the report is adopted from W. Kip Viscusi, John M. Vernon and Joseph E. Harrington (1992), "Economics of Regulation and Antitrust". Lexington, Mass.: D.C. Clifford Winston (1993). "Economic Deregulation: Days of Reckoning for Microeconomists", *Journal of Economic Literature*, 31, pp. 1263-1289.

16. Unbundling is even able to offset the advantages of economies of scale and scope. The latter occurs when it is cheaper for a provider to produce and deliver two or more services jointly than for separate entities to provide these services individually. Unbundling promotes new entry and competition. The benefits of cost-minimizing behavior under competitive pressures can easily outweigh the gains from economies of scope. Unbundling makes cross-subsidies between lines of business or customers within enterprises offering multiple services - more transparent. It identifies more precisely the subsidies needed to deliver services to the poor and/or remote customers, and improves management accountability. *The World Development Report* 1994, Infrastructure for Development is clear on this. The trend is unmistakable: unbundling of infrastructure services is proceeding at a brisk pace.

17. Lacity and Hirschheim, 1993, pp. 47-48.

18. Sometimes partnerships stop after a while. See, for instance, Qantas who sold their 19% share in Air New Zealand for strategic reasons in the beginning of 1997.

19. Kasper, 1994.

20. European Franchise Federation, Franchising in Europe, CBI, *European Business Handbook*, 1995.

21. Also, those who were initially service providers are increasingly entering into the production of tangible goods if the market demands them. Thus the success of the movie *Jurassic Park* by Steven Spielberg brought about a veritable craze of goods. So, the reverse trend can be seen as well.

22. Lovelock, 1991.

23. Kasper, 1997b, pp. 38-39.

24. Don Tapscott in *The Digital Economy* (p. 191) quoting the *New York Times*, 1 May, 1995, C8.

25. Many of these observations have been based on a joint study done by some of the leading European economic institutions, about Europe in 1998 (ERECO, Market Services and European Integration, 1993), the report Market Services and European Integration (1993), as well as various World Bank reports, OECD publications and our own personal experiences.

26. The projected staff reduction in retail banking of as high as 50% by 2005 draws on Coopers & Lybrand including more than 50 interviews with senior bank executives. It indicates not only a sharp reduction in staff but also a change in the skills employees will require, according to Richard Waters in the *Financial Times*, 17 September 1995.

27. Internet offerings, "On-line capitalism", New York, *The Economist*, 23 November, 1996, pp. 98.

28. "Leasing operations catalyze capital equipment purchases", Kathy Holzmann, *Development Business*, 16 October 1996, Volume 9, Number 448, page 1.

29. Not everywhere (yet), i.e. in the US, regulators allow banks and insurance companies to join forces.

30. New policy delights foreign insurers, William Dawkins, *Financial Times*, 21 January 1997.

31. Vogler-Ludwig and Hofmann, 1993, p. 383.

32. Commission of the European Community, 1988.

33. Vogler-Ludwig and Hofmann, 1993, p. 384.

34. Baker, 1994, pp. 306-310.

35. Nevertheless, the French Carrefour group is succesful with their hypermarkets in Taiwan; the same holds for the Dutch Makro group.

36. Baker, 1994.

37. Kasper and Bloemer (1997); Laulajainen (1991).

38. Van Helsdingen, 1982.

39. Most observations of this sector are based on the ERECO-report, (Baker, 1994.)

40. Still this can take a large time and large amounts of money as the continuous subsidizing of Air France by the French government shows.

41. In radio, where lots of new services have become freely available, BBC's share has dropped from 66% in l990, when commercial radio was deregulated, to just under 50%

42. Brady, *Asian Wall Street Journal Weekly*, 4 December, 1995.

43. GP Wild (International) projections, published in the *Financial Times*, Thursday, 24 October, 1996, p. 5.

44. World Development Report, *Investing in Health*, World Bank, 1993, p. 122.

45. Here, we report the titles of the main World Bank proposals. We consider that there may always be circumstances in which (increased) competition does not provide the best solution to cutting cost in health care.

46. Kuttner, *Business Week*, 7 August, 1995.

47. World Development Report, *Infrastructure for Development*, World Bank, 1994, pp. 8-9.

introduction to part two

AT THE HEART

Like any organization, a major "raison-d'être" for service providers is the degree to which customer needs are met. Consequently, it is important to understand consumer behavior and customer satisfaction. This would/should lead to relationships to various extents. Service quality is a major factor contributing to customer satisfaction. However, it turns out that mere quality is not enough. Excellent service quality is a prerequisite to really satisfy customers and create true loyalty to the firm and the services offered. A market-oriented service provider needs to adopt the customers' perspective in order to check whether they provide services customers perceive as better than those provided by other service providers. Summarizing services buying behavior, service quality, customer satisfaction and establishing relationships are at the heart of our book. These aspects will be integrated in the strategic issues (Part Three) challenging service firms and during the operationalization of the marketing mix (Part Four).

Part One: The Services Domain

FUNDAMENTALS OF SERVICES
MARKETING
(Chapter 1)

CLASSIFYING
SERVICES
(Chapter 2)

SERVICE
ENVIRONMENT
(Chapter 3)

Part Two: At The Heart

FROM BUYING BEHAVIOR TO RELATIONSHIPS
(Chapter 4)

- understand consumer behavior with respect to services;

- understand the buying of business-to-business services;

- reproduce differences in the consumption of services in different countries;

- understand the impact of culture on buying and using services;

- see the relevance of ethnocentrism and country-of-origin effect in marketing services internationally;

- understand the role of perceived risk in buying services;

- see through the function of services to the buyers and understand the impact of attributes, benefits and the functional and psychosocial consequences;

- reproduce and apply the ways in which markets for services can be segmented;

- explain the importance of positioning in services; and

- argue which factors are important to customers in the relationships with their service providers.

SERVICE QUALITY
(Chapter 5)

- know the basics of quality management;

- define the terms "quality of service" and "quality of service delivery";

- know the basics of service quality within service organizations;

- decipher the difference between quality and satisfaction;

- realize the importance of both expectations and perceptions;

- reproduce ways to express satisfaction and dissatisfaction about services and service providers;

- understand the SERVQUAL-model for measuring the quality of service delivery;

- understand the importance of the SERVQUAL-model for decision making in service organizations

- assess some of the criticisms of the SERVQUAL-model; and,

- argue how service quality may contribute to strengthening relationships between buyers and service providers.

Part Three: Strategic Issues

COLLECTING AND
MANAGING MARKET
INFORMATION
(Chapter 6)

STRATEGIC PLANNING AT
CORPORATE LEVEL
(Chapter 7)

INTERNATIONALIZATION
OF SERVICES
(Chapter 9)

SERVICES MARKETING
PLANNING IN STRATEGIC
BUSINESS UNITS
(Chapter 8)

Part Four: Services Marketing Mix

PEOPLE,
ORGANIZATION AND PROCESSES
(Chapter 10)

DEVELOPING AND PROVIDING
SERVICES
(Chapter 11)

COMMUNICATION
(Chapter 12)

DISTRIBUTION
(Chapter 13)

PRICING
(Chapter 14)

IMPLEMENTATION
AND CONTROL
(Chapter 15)

CHAPTER FOUR

FROM BUYING BEHAVIOR TO RELATIONSHIPS

After studying this chapter you will be able to:

ABOVE: *Only benefits count*

- *understand consumer behavior with respect to services;*
- *understand the buying of business-to-business services;*
- *reproduce differences in the consumption of services in different countries;*
- *understand the impact of culture on buying and using services;*
- *see the relevance of ethnocentrism and country-of-origin effect in marketing services internationally;*
- *understand the role of perceived risk in buying services;*
- *see through the function of services to the buyers and understand the impact of attributes, benefits and the functional and psychosocial consequences;*
- *reproduce and apply the ways in which markets for services can be segmented;*
- *explain the importance of positioning in services; and*
- *argue which factors are important to customers in the relationships with their service providers.*

4.1 INTRODUCTION

The famous author George Orwell wrote the phrase "all animals are created equal" in his book *Animal Farm*. We would like to change this to the question "are all people created equal and therefore behave the same"? The answer is clear: no. But why?

For example: why do people prefer one airline over another? Why is the decison making process of flying with an airline different for business travellers and people flying to their holiday destination? The business traveller wants to depart and arrive on time and cares about quality; price is not important. The holiday traveller selects an airline quite often only on price. Why?

Some people like to use one bank for all their financial transactions. Others use different banks. Also in insurance, some people are the "total client" of an insurance company meaning that they have all their policies with one insurance company. Others deal with a wide variety of insurance companies. Why?

Some nationalities like to stay at home or travel to a country with a climate and culture similiar to their own. For example, if Italians are going on holiday they travel to countries comparable with Italy. At the same time, German tourists travel over whole the world. Why?

Various ways of defining particular segments of clients in accounting firms exist. Clients may differ, for instance, with respect to the personal relationship or the speed of carrying out the audit. Whereas another group of clients may select an accounting firm on price only. Why?

All these examples show that in buying services many differences occur, dependent upon the subjects. In Chapter One, we found that in many countries of the Western world, more than 50% of Gross National Product is spent on services. In this chapter, we leave this macro perspective of the consumption of services and move to the micro perspective of individuals, households and organizations buying services.

In Chapter Two, we set up a complex scheme where the consumer was one of the main players in the classification of services. In this chapter, the specific characteristics of consumer behavior with respect to services will be discussed. The way different individuals, households and organizations buy and use services is the topic of this chapter. Consumer services as well as business to business services are discussed.

buy and use services

This textbook has an international flavor, implying the need to embrace some issues relevant to buying services in an international context. Therefore, we shall consider different cultures. The way we will deal with them affects the context of the strategy of service firms.[1] Ethnocentrism and country-of-origin will also be tackled. We

*an international
context*

consider these topics important to the international service firm which has to overcome national sentiments in order to get its own services accepted in the host country.

Next to such fundamental underlying factors determining consumer behavior, some interesting differences also occur on the surface of consumer behavior. Due to the intangibility of services, consumer behavior has a number of unique aspects. First, we shall discuss the impact of perceived risk in buying services. This will assist understanding, later in this chapter, the relationship between a consumer and a service provider (in general and in particular with respect to business to business services). Next, we will take a closer look at the buying process; the search activities of consumers and buying situations. Before coming to the last part of this chapter and one of the key issues of service marketing, namely "relationships", the unique aspects of market segmentation and positioning for service providers will be explained. Because expectations and actual experiences with services play a crucial role in shaping customer satisfaction and service quality, the concepts of expectations and perceptions will receive full attention in Chapter Five.

Figure 4-1
Chapter outline
(4.2)

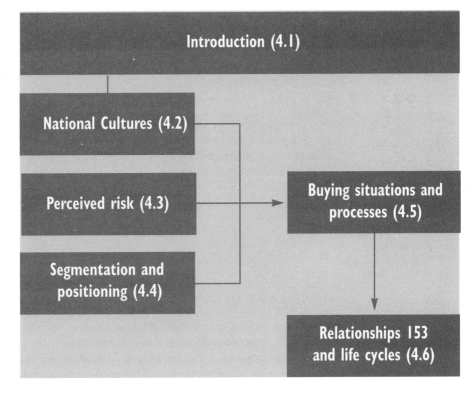

4.2 ON NATIONAL CULTURES

cultural environment

One of the forces affecting an organization in its functioning, is the cultural environment it is acting in. It is generally accepted that this force is extremely important when organizations are doing business in different countries in different parts of the world. Differences in national cultures should be taken into account. This applies with respect to developing a strategy as well as with respect to all kinds of day-to-day activities, like:

differences in national cultures

- different customs or rites;
- different connotations to colors, words, sounds or symbols; or
- different ways of looking at parents or authority.

All these (and many more) expressions of culture will affect a company's strategy and daily activities. It is important to analyze consumer behavior at this very basic level since norms and values seem to be one of the few segmentation criteria that can be applied successfully to define segments of "Euro-consumers".[2]

norms and values

Service practice 4-2 What is punctuality and what is the language of flowers?[3]

Punctuality may differ from country to country: people from Scandinavian countries, The Netherlands and Germany tend to be very punctual, while this is not the case in Southern Europe and Latin or South America. This may affect the planning of service encounters for instance.

Whoever dreamed up the phrase "the language of flowers" must have been dreaming. As a male guest, you can offer red roses to your host's wife if she's Italian, but emphatically not if she's German. Give her white lilies and she'll think you're trying to bury her – the same thing with chrysanthemums if, rather than German, she's French or Belgian (but not, incidentally, if she's an Australian mum). And, please, no carnations or hydrangeas (perish the thought) if she's French.

THE IMPACT OF NATIONAL CULTURE

Many authors, especially anthropologists, sociologists, etc., have carried out a lot of research with respect to differences in cultures. Sometimes it is hard to apply their theories adequately. One of the authors whose work is very accessible and applicable for our purposes, is Geert Hofstede. He reports on the national cultures of 53 countries and defines culture as:

"the collective programming of the mind which distinguishes the members of one group or category of people from another."[4]

The cultural differences manifest themselves in various ways. In his research, Hofstede has initially developed four dimensions that can be used to describe the culture of a

dimensions

nation. Later, he has added a fifth dimension. These dimensions are:

1. masculinity versus femininity (MAS);
2. individualism versus collectivism (IDV);
3. uncertainty avoidance (UAI);
4. power distance (PDI); and – the subsequently added dimension of –
5. long term orientation versus short term orientation (LTO).

These dimensions are defined as follows:

masculinity

femininity

1. "*Masculinity* pertains to societies in which social gender roles are clearly distinct (i.e. men are supposed to be assertive, tough and focussed on material success, whereas women are supposed to be more modest, tender, and concerned with the quality of life); *femininity* pertains to societies in which social gender roles overlap (i.e. both men and women are supposed to be modest, tender, and concerned with the quality of life)."

individualism

collectivism

2. "*Individualism* pertains to societies in which the ties between individuals are loose: everyone is expected to look after himself or herself and his or her immediate family. *Collectivism*, as its opposite, pertains to societies in which people from birth onwards are integrated into strong, cohesive in-groups, which throughout people's lifetime continue to protect them in exchange for unquestioning loyalty."

uncertainty avoidance

3. "*Uncertainty avoidance* can ... be defined as the extent to which the members of a culture feel threatened by uncertain or unknown situations. This feeling is, among other things, expressed through nervous stress and in a need for predictability: a need for written and unwritten rules."

power distance

4. "*Power distance* can ... be defined as the extent to which the less powerful members of institutions and organizations within a country expect and accept that power is distributed unequally. 'Institutions' are the basic elements of society like the family, school, and the community; 'organizations' are the places where people work."

long-term orientation

short-term orientation

5. Recent research indicated a fifth dimension should be added. This dimension came to the fore when questions referring to values being very important in the Far East were incorporated. The new dimension was composed of the following values: on the pole which could be labeled *long-term orientation* (persistence, ordering relationships by status and observing this order, thrift and having a sense of shame) and on the opposite pole *short-term orientation* (personal steadiness and stability, protecting your "face", respect for tradition, reciprocation of greetings, favors, and gifts).

The scores computed for each dimension may range from zero to a little over 100 when positions on the two extremes of each dimension are compared. The scores for several countries are presented in Figure 4-2. It is important to note that all these *relative scores*

scores should be interpreted as relative scores: one country's culture is, for instance, more individualistic than an other country's culture. Out of this figure can be concluded which countries resemble each other's culture on one of these five dimensions and how this might affect international marketing/management (see, e.g. Usunier, 1992).

Figure 4-2
Scores of 58 countries
on five dimensions
reflecting their national
culture as computed
by Hofstede (1991)

Country		MAS	IDV	UAI	PDI	LTO
Sweden	SWE	5	71	29	31	33
Norway	NOR	8	69	50	31	
Netherlands	NET	14	80	53	38	44
Denmark	DEN	16	74	23	18	
Costa Rica	COS	21	15	86	35	
Yugoslavia	YUG	21	27	88	76	
Finland	FIN	26	63	59	33	
Chile	CHL	28	23	86	63	
Portugal	POR	31	27	104	63	
Thailand	THA	34	20	64	64	56
Guatemala	GUA	37	6	101	95	
Uruguay	URU	38	36	100	61	
South Korea	KOR	39	18	85	60	75
Salvador	SAL	40	19	94	66	
East Africa	EAF	41	27	52	64	
Peru	PER	42	16	87	64	
Spain	SPA	42	51	86	57	
France	FRA	43	71	86	68	
Iran	IRA	43	41	59	58	
Panama	PAN	44	11	86	95	
Taiwan	TAI	45	17	69	58	87
Turkey	TUR	45	37	85	66	
Indonesia	IDO	46	14	48	78	
West Africa	WAF	46	20	54	77	
Israel	ISR	47	54	81	13	
Singapore	SIN	48	20	8	74	48
Brazil	BRA	49	38	76	69	65
Malaysia	MAL	50	26	36	104	
Pakistan	PAK	50	14	70	55	00
Canada	CAN	52	80	48	39	23
Arab countries	ARA	53	38	68	80	
Belgium	BEL	54	75	94	65	
Argentina	ARG	56	46	86	49	
India	IND	56	48	40	77	61
Greece	GRE	57	35	112	60	
Hong Kong	HOK	57	25	29	68	96
New Zealand	NZL	58	79	49	22	30
Australia	AUL	61	90	51	36	31
United States	USA	62	91	46	40	29
Equador	EQA	63	8	67	78	

Country		MAS	IDV	UAI	PDI	LTO
South Africa	SAF	63	65	49	49	
Columbia	COL	64	13	80	67	
Philippines	PHI	64	32	44	94	19
Germany FR	GER	66	67	65	35	31
Great Britain	GBR	66	89	35	35	25
Ireland (Republic of)	IRE	68	70	35	28	
Jamaica	JAM	68	39	13	45	
Mexico	MEX	69	30	82	81	
Italy	ITA	70	76	75	50	
Switzerland	SWI	70	68	58	34	
Venezuela	VEN	73	12	76	81	
Austria	AUT	79	55	70	11	
Japan	JPN	95	46	92	54	80
China	CHI					118
Bangladesh	BAN					40
Poland	POL					32
Zimbabwe	ZIM					25
Nigeria	NIG					16

scores on masculinity

The countries with the highest scores on *masculinity* are Japan, some countries on the European continent like Austria, Italy, Switzerland and West Germany and some larger Latin American countries around the Carribean.[5] The most *feminine cultures* can be found in Scandinavia, The Netherlands, Costa Rica and (the former) Yugoslavia.

individualism scores

With respect to the *individualism* scores, it can be seen easily that almost all wealthy countries score high on this dimension, while many poor countries score high on its opposite pole: collectivism. Countries with a very individualistic culture are the English speaking countries (USA on top, followed by Australia and Great Britain) and many European countries.

uncertainty avoidance

High scores on *uncertainty avoidance* can be found for Latin American, Latin European and Mediterranean countries, plus Japan and South Korea. Many other Asian countries and most of the English speaking countries score low on this dimension.

power distance

Countries with high scores on *power distance* can be found among the Latin countries (in Europe as well as in America) and in African and Asian countries. Low(er) scores on this dimension are found in the Scandinavian countries, in many of the English speaking countries, in Switzerland and West Germany. However, the lowest scores on power distance are found in Austria and Israel.

long-term orientation

Countries with a *long-term orientation* in their culture are especially China, Hong Kong, Taiwan, Japan and South Korea. Many European countries and English speaking countries are among the countries scoring high on a *short-term orientation*.

two patterns

It is also possible to see which countries look alike when their positions on all factors are taken into account simultaneously. This indicates in which countries consumers will have – on average – the same background in norms and values affecting their behavior. In Figure 4-3, we present the graphical results of a correspondence analysis performed on the data for the 53 countries and the four dimensions.[6] Now, all relative positions of the 53 countries on those four dimensions are taken into account simultaneously.[7] Two patterns can be found in the scores on the dimensions. First, we see a factor ranging from high scores on individualism to high scores on power distance. In fact, this factor represents the degree to which a culture is structured in terms of different institutions and the acceptance of their power. We call this factor "institutions and their accepted power". This acceptance of institutional power may range from high to low. The other factor ranges from high scores on uncertainty avoidance to high scores on masculinity. It represents the way in which a culture values care taken of each other. In masculine societies, this is done in line with the needs of the individual, only when needed, while this care should always be present in cultures high on uncertainty avoidance. So, this factor ranges from care "on call" to "always present".

perceptual map

In this perceptual map, four cultural "outliers" can be found: Denmark, Jamaica, Singapore and Costa Rica. These four have in common an extreme position on the original uncertainty avoidance dimension. Moreover, Denmark and Costa Rica also have an extreme position on other original dimensions (power distance and femininity for Denmark and femininity and collectivism for Costa Rica).

Roughly speaking, the left side of Figure 4-3 contains most of the European countries (exclusive of the economically weaker countries like Greece, Portugal and (the former) Yugoslavia) plus the other wealthy, English speaking countries of the world and Israel. They all score (quite) high on individualism.

The right part of Figure 4-3 contains the African, South and Latin American and Asian countries. One can also see that the cultures of Spain (not so wealthy), Argentina (many ex-Europeans are living there), Japan (wealthy and becoming much more "western") and India (fast growing GNP) are quite close to the borderline between these two groups.

cultural closeness

This map reveals, for instance, that the cultures of Germany and Austria are almost similar and that Switzerland deviates a little from the two. These countries also have a similar language to a large extent. Cultural closeness is related to similarity in language. Also, the Scandinavan countries are grouped together like the English speaking countries (Great Britain and its wealthy, former colonies). For Asian countries and South or Latin American countries similar patterns can be found.

geographical distances, cultural distances

This map also depicts that geographical distances may be completely different from cultural distances between countries, see, e.g. both types of distances between Belgium and The Netherlands, or, Hong Kong and Taiwan, or, Australia and the United States.

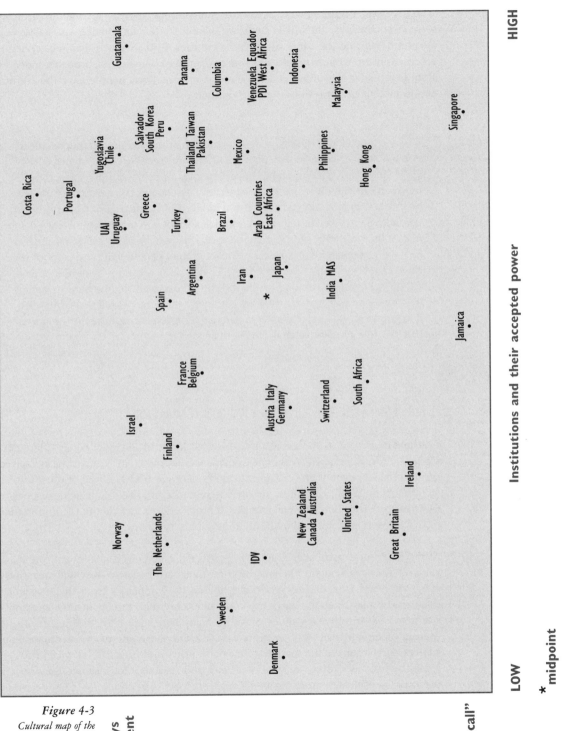

HIGH

Institutions and their accepted power

LOW

* midpoint

"on-call"

care

always
present

Figure 4-3
Cultural map of the
countries in the world

When we see the present trend towards substituting labor by technology in many service encounters, one may question whether the acceptance of self-service operations will be the same in different cultures. Today, we see that self-service is accepted in the Western world and other wealthier countries. So, probably, individualism is the most important cultural dimension here. Then, people have the cultural background to perform these services on their own.

Service practice 4-3 Where to go with self-service? [8]

> The acceptance of self-service will be greater probably in more individualistic cultures than in collectivistic cultures. These are wealthier, have higher educated people, more open to technological change, and will consider self-service as more efficient. With respect to uncertainty avoidance, the acceptance of self-service will depend on the degree of perceived self-control; probably the more technology involved in the servuction process, the less uncertainty involved. In high power distance cultures, self-service will only be accepted when it is in line with people's status; otherwise lower status people will have to perform this job. It is not clear how accepting self-service is related to feminine or masculine cultures. On the one hand, one could imagine it will be hard to accept it in feminine cultures, for they are stressing interpersonal relations. In masculine cultures, self-service may demonstrate achievement, but then it is required that the role of self-service is clear and accepted.

THE IMPACT OF COUNTRY-OF-ORIGIN

country-of-origin

Consumers as well as industrial buyers use all kinds of intrinsic values (like taste, design, performance, reliability, tangibles) and extrinsic cues (like brand-name, perceived quality) to assess goods and services. Country-of-origin (COO) is one of those extrinsic cues to be used.[9] Until now, hardly any research has been done with respect to COO and services. Here, we will attempt to provide some ideas about the importance of COO to services and to the internationalizing service firm.

attitudes

Attitudes about a particular country may affect the perceived quality and purchase value of services bought.[10] When these attitudes are negative, this will negatively affect the service quality of services rendered by companies from that particular country. This may then be a barrier to companies entering a foreign market. The opposite may hold in other instances. Since so many issues are hard to evaluate in the

attributes

domain of services, it can be expected that COO will be one of the attributes consumers use to evaluate the service from a particular – international – service provider.

proxy

It may be used as a proxy for quality or trust and reliability, for instance. Some countries may be evaluated more positively in this respect than others. So, COO may be a variable determining the perception of the technical, functional and relational quality of a service firm.

With respect to goods, it is important to make a distinction between the country of design and the country of assembly. This could imply for the international service sector that the country from which the service firm originates and where the services were/are designed is relevant and not the country of "assembly or production". For, the services are produced on location in a particular country. Then, it may become important whether the service is "produced" by local employees or by people from the exporting company's country. This may differ per service and the degree of labor intensity per service.

Service practice 4-4 How do you like US airlines? [11]

A small scale study about the effect of country-of-origin on the perception of services was done recently among students in the United States, Poland, The Netherlands and France. The seven-point semantic differential scale was used to depict the images of these countries for particular services. The first 12 items of the scale, presented here, belong to the traditional scale, as developed by Osgood and Tannenbaum in the late fifties. We added the other eight items for this specific purpose. The question raised was:

"You are asked to evaluate some concepts on the basis of a scale of values. Each scale contains a pair of words. If the concept, according to you, corresponds completely to one of the two ends of the scale, you mark that point. Otherwise you mark one of the other points reflecting your opinion the best. Please, use just a second to place a check mark. Place a mark on every scale."

It appeared that Polish, Dutch, French and American students evaluated the US airlines in many respects in the same way (see Figure 4-4): for example, pleasant, big, good, rather kind and quite flexible. On the other hand, the Dutch have the impression that US airlines are quite old, while the Americans (compared with students from the other three countries) have the image that their airlines are the kindest but also the most chaotic of these four. (This latter issue is in line with the examples about the American airline industry given in Chapter One.)

explanatory variables of COO

The most important issues that should be used as explanatory variables of COO mentioned in the literature, are: involvement or familiarity with the product category; knowledge about that particular country; experience and expertise in taking buying decisions; individual consumer or industrial buyer; presence of other extrinsic information cues; and education, income, gender, age. [12]

	US airlines evaluated in				
	Holland	Poland	France	USA	
pleasant	3.3	2.5	3.3	3.1	unpleasant
small	6.0	5.5	6.3	5.7	big
active	3.2	2.8	2.3	3.3	passive
sad	4.0	5.3	4.0	4.5	happy
strong	2.5	3.0	2.0	3.2	weak
slow	5.9	5.5	5.8	5.0	fast
good	2.9	3.0	3.3	3.2	bad
light	4.4	3.1	5.0	4.8	heavy
fascinating	3.4	3.0	3.9	4.0	dull
cruel	4.3	4.0	4.5	4.7	kind
hard	3.4	3.3	4.0	4.1	soft
relaxed	4.6	3.0	4.0	4.4	tense
formal	4.0	4.3	4.0	4.8	informal
young	4.2	3.4	2.5	3.7	old
unkind	4.8	4.5	5.0	5.1	friendly
modern	2.6	2.8	2.3	3.3	old-fashioned
flexible	3.9	3.3	3.5	3.9	inflexible
safe	2.5	2.8	3.1	3.6	risky
aggressive	3.0	4.0	3.8	3.6	resigned
ordered	2.9	3.3	3.5	3.7	chaotic

Figure 4-4
Airlines in the US
evaluated in different
countries

THE IMPACT OF ETHNOCENTRISM

ethnocentrism

Studying ethnocentrism is a more sophisticated investigation of the country-of-origin issues.[13] We will define ethnocentrism in this book on services as: "the beliefs of consumers in a particular country about the appropriateness, indeed morality, of purchasing foreign made services."

Non-ethnocentric consumers will evaluate services on their own merits without taking into account the country from which the service provider originates. Highly ethnocentric consumers will consider buying foreign services as wrong: it will hurt the domestic economy, it is unpatriotic, or, "... consumer ethnocentrism gives the individual a sense of identity, feelings of belongingness, and... an understanding of what purchase behavior is acceptable or unacceptable to the in-group".[14] In general, one could say, ethnocentrism is a way of valuing the "in-group" (the group with which an individual identifies) and not valuing the "out-group" (those regarded as the opposite of the in-group). This distinction on in-groups and out-groups is similar to the Hofstede dimension of collectivism and individualism. Belonging to the in-group is a very important issue in the cultural dimension of collectivism. A study in Europe revealed average ethnocentrism scores for the following countries as: Belgium (28.7); Great Britain (30.3); Spain (34.1); and Greece (37.8).[15] Comparing the Hofstede scores on collectivism for these four countries to the ethnocentrism scores computed, shows that a higher ethnocentrism score goes with a higher score on collectivism.

valuing the
"in-group"

ethnocentrism scores

The findings also indicated that the degree of ethnocentrism may vary per region in a country and that older people are more ethnocentric than youngsters.

We would like to emphasize[16] that the concept of consumer ethnocentrism can improve the understanding of how consumers and corporate buyers compare domestic with foreign-made services and how and why their judgements may be subject to various forms of bias and error. Highly ethnocentric consumers are probably most prone to biased judgements by being more inclined to accentuate the positive aspects of domestic services and to discount the virtues of foreign-made items. Therefore, we like to conclude from this whole section on culture, country-of-origin and ethnocentrism that it is very important to use these concepts and scales to understand the willingness or resistance to buy services offered by companies originating from other countries than the home country.

understand the willingness or resistance to buy services

Service practice 4-5 Measuring ethnocentrism[17]

Shimp and Sharma have developed a 17 item scale: the Consumers' Ethnocentric Tendencies-Scale (CETSCALE). The scale is very reliable and studies have been done in various countries. In Europe, a sub-set of ten of the original 17 items is used. This scale also has excellent scores on statistics about reliability and construct validity. Five-point Likert scale items are used (1=strongly disagree and 5=strongly agree) instead of the seven-point Likert scale in the US. This means, on the European scale, that a maximum score of 50 (10*5) can be obtained while the minimum score can be 10. The questions are phrased in such a way that a higher score denotes a higher degree of ethnocentrism. In measuring ethnocentrism in France, the following items can be used in research among French citizens:

1. Only those services that are unavailable in France should be imported.
2. French services, first, last, and foremost.
3. Purchasing foreign-made services is un-French.
4. It is not right to purchase foreign services, because it puts the French out of jobs.
5. A real Frenchman should always buy French-made services.
6. We should purchase services produced in France instead of letting other countries get rich off us.
7. The French should not buy foreign services, since it hurts French business and causes unemployment.
8. It may cost me in the long-run but I prefer to support French services.
9. We should buy from foreign countries only those services that we cannot obtain within our own country.
10. French consumers who purchase services made in other countries are responsible for putting their fellow Frenchmen out of work.

4.3 PERCEIVED RISK

perceived risk,
uncertainty avoidance

Elaborating on the previous section, perceived risk is one of the issues relevant in consumer behavior related to the uncertainty avoidance dimension of national cultures. Here, we continue with individuals' behavior by stating that the perceived risk hinges upon the risk consumers perceive in buying and using particular services. Due to

intangibility

intangibility, it is hard to evaluate services in advance in many instances. Nor is it always known in advance what will be the outcome of the service experience. These two items make up the most important issues within the concept of perceived risk in the context of services. In general, one could say perceived risk will be greater the less search attributes and the more experience and credence attributes are at stake. We can also say that perceived risk refers to what kind of service will be offered, in what way and by whom.[18]

DIFFERENT TYPES OF PERCEIVED RISK

two factors

With perceived risk two factors play an important role. On the one hand, is the uncertainty about the answer to the question whether one has bought the right service. On the other hand, is the uncertainty about the answer to the question what will be the consequences of this buy. We will discuss such positive and negative consequences in section 4.5.

In the literature, different types of perceived risk are mentioned, next to the ones mentioned at the beginning of this section, namely:[19] financial uncertainty; functional uncertainty; physical uncertainty; social uncertainty; psychological uncertainty; life style uncertainty; time uncertainty; and, environmental uncertainty.

financial uncertainty

Financial uncertainty concerns uncertainty as to whether consumers pay more than they should pay. So, there is doubt about the price-quality relation. Among others, consumers cannot always overlook all the costs of a service. Sometimes it is difficult to make a comparison between the performance of an intangible service and the money they have to pay for the service delivery. Besides, it is possible that the consumer is willing to pay a certain amount of money just for "the name of the service provider", without an actual performance.[20]

functional uncertainty

Functional uncertainty refers to uncertainty as to whether the service really offers what it should provide. This has, among others, to do with the question of whether the service is in line with expectations: does the fire insurance policy really cover what one hoped for when being confronted with fire damage now?[21] Because it is often difficult to standardize services, consumers cannot always rely on their own experiences with comparable services to reduce functional uncertainty. Then, they need help or advice from others: family, friends or independent bodies like consumer unions or consultants (e.g. brokers).

physical uncertainty   Physical uncertainty concerns questions about the safety of the service delivery. Might the service or the service delivery process cause any damage to others or the consumer himself? This can play a role when taking skiing lessons or learning to parachute.

social uncertainty   Social uncertainty concerns the way in which the environment of the consumer will react to the choice of a certain service or particular service provider: will the reaction be disapproving or approving; does the choice match my reference groups, etc?

psychological uncertainty   Psychological uncertainty is a special extension of social uncertainty. It concerns the uncertainty that a bad choice will damage the image of the consumer. The hesitating consumer may ask himself: do I really deserve it? With services, one can also think about the uncertainty that the consumer and service provider might not like each other personally.

life style uncertainty   Life style uncertainty of the consumer is much like the social and psychological uncertainty, but especially concerns the expected or actual consequences for one's own life style: can it be maintained when the consumer is going to use a certain service?

time uncertainty   Time uncertainty refers to the uncertainty that the time spent searching for a service is wasted when the chosen service or service provider does not perform according to expectations. This also has to do with the customers' decision about their allocation of time available, based on the costs of their time.[22] Another time uncertainty concerns the time in which a consumer has to make a decision about the intangible service or the unknown service delivery process. Is that time enough or must a choice be made in a short time?

environmental uncertainty   Environmental uncertainty concerns the uncertainty of consumers about the possible damage the service or service delivery process may cause to the environment (energy and materials used during the service delivery process; environmental pollution when going to the service provider, etc.). Nowadays, this uncertainty is becoming increasingly important in the decision making process of consumers. Its role will be bigger with more environmentally conscious consumers than with less environmentally conscious consumers.

Service practice 4-6 Services friendly to the environment   The impact of a consumer's behavior on the environment is also an issue in the hotel industry. Is it really necessary to clean up all the towels every day and use a lot of washing powder? The SAS-hotels in Gothenburg, Sweden, and elsewhere, solved the problem. They make clear to their guests what they should do (an example of managing expectations in the service encounter); put the towels to be cleaned on the floor or in the bath tub.

total perceived risk   A consumer's total perceived risk in certain purchase situations or in the participation in the service delivery process consists, in principle, of a mixture of these eight different kinds of uncertainty. Because of the intangible nature of service, this uncertainty may be considerable. This uncertainty not only concerns the choice of the right service and/or service provider, but also the expected positive and negative consequences of this choice: the benefits and risks.

Although the total perceived risk could be constructed from the earlier mentioned eight kinds of uncertainty, this does not imply that every part will always occur to the same extent or is equally important. Of course, this can vary among services or service delivery processes. Stated differently, perceived risk is a relative concept: it can occur to a certain extent. As with the services classification, whereby often the occurence of a certain extent of a particular characteristic of services is mentioned, this also holds in this regard. In this context, it is even possible to speak of a correlation, for example: raising the tangibility of the service may reduce perceived risk.

a relative concept

So, the perceived risk does not always have to be equally high. For an individual customer it can vary among services or service delivery processes. Among other things, it is dependent upon earlier experiences. Therefore perceived risk may diminish over time when more experiences have been achieved.

the extent of perceived
risk varies
The notion that perceived risk is not necessarily equally high for every customer has several implications. For example, the extent of perceived risk varies among customer groups; different kinds of services; different buying situations and various cultures.

Groups of customers with a high perceived risk will only choose from a limited amount of familiar services; often they will be highly brand loyal. In contrast, customers with low perceived risk will experience no difficulty in choosing from many different alternatives and more often show variety seeking behavior. The perceived risk towards different kinds of services can vary; it will be different in the case of life insurances compared to a cinema ticket. Perceived risk also varies among different kinds of buying situations, such as:

- extended problem solving behavior;
- routine buying behavior; and
- limited problem solving behavior (modified buying).[23]

In certain countries and cultures, people have a high aversion to uncertain situations and occurrences. Then, one cannot cope with uncertainty in comparison with other countries and cultures. Moreover, within a particular country subcultures of uncertainty avoidance may exist. This was elaborated on in section 4.2.

segment the market
The foregoing means that a service organization has to be well informed about the perceived risk of its customers. This has, for example, consequences on pricing policy, the market segmentation and the services offered. The differences in perceived risk for different groups of customers imply that several kinds of service packages could be offered. In other words: the extent of perceived risk offers a way to segment the market. Therefore, perceived risk determines what customers will, could and want to do themselves during the service delivery process. It is to be expected that customers who experience high perceived risks will not participate too much in the service

delivery process. They would like everything to be offered in detail and they would wish everything to be clear.

How Can Customers Reduce Perceived Risk?

reduce perceived risk; information; reputation and image; advertisements; consumer unions

Consumers can reduce perceived risk in many ways.[24] The most common behavioral strategy is the search for (more) information. This can range from consulting friends and acquaintances, to being informed by sales and front office personnel. Often, the service organization's reputation and image are used. Advertisements or research findings published by consumer unions (comparative testing) are also used.

Service practice 4-7 Searching for information [25]

In buying services, consumers often engage in extended decision making processes in which the role of personal sources of information is noteworthy. Personal sources are preferred over impersonal sources of information. Consumers indicate greater confidence in personal sources when contemplating a service purchase. Personal independent sources are more effective for services than for goods. Internal sources, like own experiences, are particularly relevant to service consumers.

To reduce perceived risk can be difficult, because a customer does not always know exactly where to look or what the cost and benefits of the service delivery will be. Furthermore, a customer does not know for sure whether all the communication initiated by the service organization is a proper reflection of reality; usually advertising presents an idealized view.

loyalty

In the case of a first time buy (a new task), this uncertainty will be higher than in the case of a rebuy situation. Therefore, brand and/or store loyalty are behavioral strategies suitable in reducing these uncertainties.

price

Customers can also use the price as a quality indicator and thus, as a measure to reduce the perceived risk. Most customers assume a higher price indicates a better service. Sometimes, an uncertain consumer searches for the most expensive service as a solution. This customer assumes that you don't get something valuable cheaply. This is not always the case, especially in less informed markets. The price does not always have to be the best indicator of the perception of quality. It may even be the case that consumers fool themselves by only buying the more expensive services. It may also be that the mere change of a name to a "higher status brand name" makes consumers willing to pay a higher price for the same service. This even happens to the "rational" industrial buyer who is supposed to know as much as his professional counterpart in the business to business area.

*Service
practice
4-8
A higher
status brand
name pays
off* [26]

A study among a wide variety of firms has been carried out to find the way in which accounting firms charge for their auditing services. It appeared that - on average - the large, international well known accounting firms charged a premium fee of about 4% in a very competitive market. Moreover, it appeared their customers were willing to pay this premium, despite the fact that the service was exactly the same as offered by a less known, local auditing firm.

*warranties and
guarantees*

Finally, consumers may ask for warranties and guarantees. That provides security and safety in case the service is disappointing or does not meet expectations (the warranty the dealer or plumber gives after repairing).

When initially perceived risk is higher and therefore the uncertainty of the customer is higher, it is realistic to believe that the chance of uncertainty during or after the service delivery process will be higher. For, in this case it is understandable that expectations are more difficult to formulate, just as the factual observations. Because of this, we will also focus on the evaluation of services and the existence and expression of dissatisfaction (see Chapter Five). With respect to new services, the intangibility and great uncertainty will probably imply that the adoption and diffusion of new services may take some time (see the chapter on services and new service development).

4.4 MARKET SEGMENTATION AND POSITIONING

*many different market
segments*

Customers of services can differ from each other in many ways and at many moments. For example, customers can have different perceptions, attitudes or expectations in the different stages of the buying process. It is also conceivable that one customer group is more willing or able to participate largely in the service delivery process than another group (some prefer a self-service gas station and others prefer being served). Therefore, many different market segments can be found, which are based on the specific characteristics of services. In fact, the different criteria used in describing and classifying services in Chapter Two, can be used to segment the services market.

*criteria used in
describing and
classifying services*

strategic choices

The segmentation will (have to) correspond to the strategic choices made by the service provider about the way he wants and is able to offer the services and what is expected from the customer (i.e. the extent of participation). Thus, segmentation of the services market based on, for example, the degree of perceived risk, must be feasible as well. Because of this, a service provider can focus on one or more groups consisting of customers with a comparable degree of perceived risk toward the service.

socio-economic and demographic variables; psychological variables, psychographic variables and life styles; domain specific segmentation

However, in segmenting the market for customer services, traditional segmentation variables (such as socio-economic and demographic variables) can also be applied. A prerequisite is, however, that this also ends up with homogeneous groups of customers, which can be clearly separated from other customer groups. Also, on the basis of psychological variables, psychographic variables and life styles, the market can be segmented. A new development in this area is the domain specific segmentation, in which the specific use of a particular service in a certain situation and in a specific moment is the segmentation criterion.[27] In fact, this has to do with specific behavior in specific situations. By that, we have returned – perhaps unnoticed – to another basic issue in this chapter. This domain specific segmentation deals with the specific need fulfilment that the customer is searching for. In other words, it deals with the segmentation of the required consequences in a functional and psychosocial respect. These

benefits; risks

consequences can be positive ("benefits") and negative ("risks").

time perception

Another development in segmentation is related to the different ways people perceive time and to the marketing implications of these differences.[28] The concept of time perception refers to the attitudes people show towards the past, present and the future. Although each individual spends his mental time in all three dimensions, psychologists have proven that some of them spend more time in memories and past situations, others concentrate on current issues and others still turn their thoughts to events that may, or may not, take place in the future. This issue also has a cultural background (see section 4.2).

Past-orientated people are more conservative, sentimental and brand loyal. Present-orientated people have a quick reaction/stimulus process and are therefore more impulsive and uninterested in long-term projects. Future-orientated people are likely to be more adventurous, creative and risk-takers. The equal combination of these three temporal dimensions produces people who follow a balanced decision making process with careful evaluation of all possible buying alternatives. However, this is not always the case.

In our opinion, "benefit segmentation" and segmentation based on the observed uncertainty/perceived risk or time perception corresponds more closely to the actual behavior of customers toward services than segmentation on the basis of criteria, such as income and family size. The service provider should realize that cultural differences with respect to uncertainty avoidance will affect such a segmentation procedure in different countries. The advantage of this approach is that these criteria reflect individual factors which – in turn – determine the decision process of a customer. A market-oriented service provider should, as a result of this, preferably, segment the market in this way. This applies to industrial services as well.

Service practice 4-9 Client types in the accounting business

Two types of clients of accounting firms can be found: the phlegmatics and the involved.[29] They differ in their importance of rating issues relevant to selecting an accounting service provider and in the way they evaluate the performance of the accounting firm.

The involved consider the competitive advantage (efficiency) items, the personal service items and the external recommendation items as much more important than the phlegmatics. Both groups do not differ significantly on the issues of image and "product range".

The phlegmatics were substantially larger in size than the involved, but did not differ in terms of average market share, their representation by industry sector, years in business, or annual billings with their current CPA firms. Greater proportions of involved versus phlegmatic clients are either experiencing, or perceive that they are experiencing, higher performance for some services.

Another study in one of the European accounting markets in the early nineties depicted that two broad groups of clients exist.[30] However, each group can be split into other sub-groups. All give different degrees of importance to the criteria used in selecting their CPA.

The first group consists of firms stressing service quality and the wide range of services offered in their selection process. However, they differ from one another on the next three issues:

- the personal relationship between client and CPA;
- the cost of the auditing activities; and
- the accountant's expertise.

The second group of clients have in common that they pay great attention to the accountants' knowledge of or familiarity with the client's industry. They differ as to

- the time necessary for doing the auditing;
- the international image of the accountant;
- the accessibility of the accountant (as a person); and
- the brand awareness and the international image of the accounting firm.

positioning

Segmenting the market is often mentioned in the same breath as positioning. In this book about the marketing of services, positioning means the place a service has compared to other competitive services for subjects who belong to a certain market segment:

"Positioning is not what is done to the service, it is what is created in the minds of the target consumers; the service is positioned in the minds of these consumers and is given an image".[31]

This subjectivity is not only expressed in the specific position of a service relative to other services, but also in the way and in the number of competitive services which are deemed important to a customer. After all, customers subjectively determine what and who are viewed as each other's competitors. Therefore, it is important to know *what customers perceive as competitive services* (and not what the service organization assumes the competitors are). Perceptual mapping is a tool to visualize the relative positioning of different services on specific attributes. This results in the familiar positioning maps.

what customers perceive as competitive services; perceptual mapping

Positioning maps show current positions. A service provider can consider, on strategic grounds, whether this positioning is the desired one and what position one should aim to accomplish. If such an aim is known, the policy can be planned to reach this goal.

We would like to emphasize that market research for such positioning maps should start with *qualitative research*. In this qualitative research, the customer should be asked for the relevant attributes of services; the services which are familiar to him/her; and the services which are seen as competitive to him/her. Customers should make this clear, because their perception of the environment is important. Once qualitative research has depicted which services consumers consider as competitive and which attributes (or benefits and risks) are relevant, this can be presented to greater numbers of customers in a large-scale *quantitative research* project. Market-oriented service organizations should proceed in this way instead of basing it on their own ideas of the market.

qualitative research

quantitative research

image

When we discuss positioning, image is also at stake. Within service organizations, it is important to realize that the image is not only determined by the communication policy of the service provider, but in particular by the behavior of the contact personnel during the total servuction process.

impression

An *image* can be defined as the total impression a customer or group of customers has about an object (a service or service provider). Such a total impression consists of more than just a set of facts. Facts, feelings, customs, attitudes, expectations, perceptions and the like, plus associations of a person or group with these, result in the final image of a service. Therefore, such an image can be based on a quick first impression of a service or service provider, but also on thorough analyses of all attributes, experiences and the like with the service or service provider. This means that the service or service provider's image can differ between target groups. Image or reputation is considered as one of the *key success factors* of service organizations. Therefore, it is necessary for service organizations to pay ample attention to this topic. Mistakes can be very detrimental to both firms and customers.

key success factors

4.5 BUYING SITUATIONS AND BUYING PROCESSES

BUYING SITUATIONS

different buying situations

Consumers can face different buying situations. There is, for example, an essential difference between an initial purchase and a repeat purchase. This difference concerns the knowledge that the buyer of the service has of the characteristics of the intangible service or about the presumed participation in the service delivery process. At an initial purchase, everything is new, relatively unknown, and therefore, a high perceived risk exists. During a decision about a repeat purchase, for example, experiences in previous service encounters can play a role. The extensive search process with a new task buying situation, by which the consumer tries to reduce uncertainty and the consequences of a purchase as much as possible, will receive particular attention in this chapter about consumer behavior.

BUYING PROCESSES

bundle of attributes

bundle of benefits

Services can be considered as a bundle of attributes. Services have a number of characteristics, attributes or features, which have a certain benefit or use for the consumer. At an even more abstract level, services can also be considered as a bundle of benefits. This perspective is taken from the viewpoint of the consumer, client or buyer. These benefits can have both a positive and negative meaning for the consumer. In this perspective, consumers judge the buying process of a service in terms of its consequences with respect to the service outcome and the service process. Peter and Olson defined these consequences as "the specific outcomes that happen to a consumer when the service is purchased and used or consumed".[32]

need fulfillment

These consequences are determined by the many attributes of services and service delivery processes; and these attributes are aimed at achieving a particular need fulfillment.

functional consequences; psychosocial consequences;

positive and negative

Here, it is possible to make the distinction between functional consequences (for example, satisfying one's hunger by eating a hamburger) and psychosocial consequences (the reaction of friends, reference groups, etc. at eating a hamburger). The consequences of buying services and participating in service delivery processes can also be classified as positive consequences (perceived benefits) and negative consequences (perceived risks). These consequences ultimately make sure that the consumer can accomplish certain - more or less abstract - values, which he or she believes are important.

instrumental values

Those values can be instrumental or terminal. Instrumental values are "the cognitive representations of preferred modes of conduct or behavior (having a good time, being independent and self-reliant)". Examples in the service sector of these instrumental values are: competence, compassion, integrity, politeness and the like, reflecting

terminal values

desirable behaviors. Terminal values are representing "preferred end states of being (happy, at peace, wealthy)". These terminal values can be, for instance, in the service sector social harmony, security, self realization and personal contentedness. They represent desired final goals of the life of the consumer.[33]

In order to find out how the consumer interprets all these notions, a simple market research will not be sufficient for the service provider. Perhaps qualitative research can help to make the motivating factors more clear when questions are asked about the reason why the consumer gives a particular answer. A new market research method, called laddering, has been developed to measure these "means-end-chains". This laddering technique can be used when asking consumers in personal interviews to indicate how the attributes are connected to the functional or psychosocial consequences, whether those are positive or negative consequences and what the contribution is to the realization of instrumental and/or terminal values. After every answer given, the respondent is asked for "the reason why". The answers to these "why" questions provide possibly a better understanding of all the consequences and values of the buying process.[34]

laddering; means-end-chains

FROM FIVE STAGES TO THREE STAGES

Basically, the well-known model of buying processes is also applicable to the services sector. This model distinguishes the following stages:

- problem recognition;
- information search;
- evaluation of alternatives and the purchase decision;
- actual purchase; and
- evaluation after purchase (resulting in satisfaction or dissatisfaction, which influences the next purchase).

EPS, RPS, RBB

The structure and size of this process will vary with respect to the buying situation: extensive problem solving behavior (EPS), restricted problem solving behavior (RPS) or routine buying behavior (RBB). With EPS, all stages will be passed through, with RBB only the final two stages. If this model of buying process is matched by the characteristics of services (interaction between consumer and producer) the buying process of services can be described by three stages, namely:

three stages

1. the pre-purchase stage, which comprises the first three of the five stages mentioned above;
2. the consumption stage, which agrees to the fourth stage. Here, it consists of the servuction process of the service delivery (see Chapters One and Two), in which the customer participates; and
3. the post-purchase evaluation stage, which partly determines the satisfaction or dissatisfaction of the customer about the complete service delivery (the fifth stage).

Those three stages are shown in Figure 4-5. We will elaborate on them in the next sections.

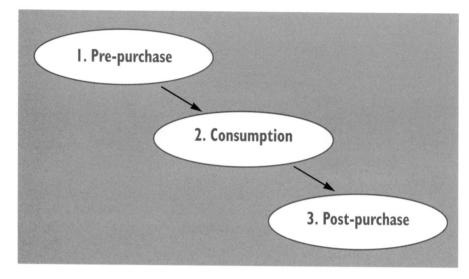

1. Pre-purchase

2. Consumption

3. Post-purchase

PRE-PURCHASE STAGE

pre-purchase stage

The pre-purchase stage is the stage in which the consumer is searching for information about the service provider, the services and the service delivery process. Because services are intangible and the market is not so transparant, the consumer does not always know exactly which aspects are important in choosing a particular service or service provider. In choosing, the consumer may rely on, amongst others:

1. his own needs, wishes and experiences from the past with this and other service providers;
2. word-of-mouth (from both consumers and service providers); and eventually
3. objective sources like advice or results of comparative testing by (national or international) consumer groups.[35]

image or reputation

Besides this, the image of the service provider plays an important role in the decision making process. Chapter One indicated that the firm's reputation is considered to be one of the key success factors for service providers. The image or reputation of a service provider can give the consumer a sense of trust and security. A logical business consequence is that organizations (i.e. profound in the case of banks and insurance companies) invest in guarding their image. This image/reputation issue is also relevant in starting a relationship in professional business to business services.[36]

Service practice 4-10 What is important in a pre-purchase? [37]

A New Zealand study about the issues being important to clients in selecting international accounting service providers, revealed five factors:

1. competitive advantage (fees competitive with other firms, reputation for fast and efficient service);
2. personal service (key staff always accessible, able to offer personal "one-to-one" service;
3. external recommendations (recommended by bank, solicitors or other business people);
4. image (has overseas links/expertise, advertising/promotion); and
5. "product range" (wide range of services offered).

In the pre-purchase stage of the buying process, it is essential for the service provider to realize that the consumer is looking for an answer to the question where he can get the best benefits (especially the positive functional and/or psychosocial consequences) to solve his question/problem. The essential matter is which service provider is superior in realizing the desired function or need fulfillment, given the budget and wishes of the customer.

attributes, search attributes

So, in searching for information the consumer (being an individual, a household or a firm) uses own information sources and experiences of others for judging the several alternatives. Another way of looking at this search behavior is determined by the kind of attributes used. Here, we can apply the already mentioned search attributes, experience attributes and credence attributes. Search attributes are attributes quite easy to judge by the consumer before the service delivery actually takes place. They can be evaluated in advance. Usually, they involve tangible aspects, they are physically visible and are more related to the equipment than to the person delivering the service.

credence attributes

Credence attributes, on the contrary, can only be judged a long time after the actual service delivery (only a long time after an operation do you know whether it has been succesful or not) and are therefore based on trusting people delivering the service.

experience attributes

Experience attributes are positioned in between these two extremes of the (in)tangibility of service attributes. They are also quite difficult to evaluate in advance and mostly they can be experienced only during or shortly after the service delivery. Both the experience and credence attributes are more people based than equipment based, contrary to the search attributes. [38]

relationship starts at first stage of the relationship life cycle

At the end of this section on pre-purchase, it can be said that the relationship between the service provider and the customer starts at this stage. Therefore, it is the first stage of the relationship life cycle. It is also the first stage in which the moments of truth come to the fore. These will determine whether the consumer wants to continue the relationship or not. A consumer who enters such a relationship with a service provider for the first time will therefore hardly be able to use his/her own experience or credence attributes. At best, the consumer can try to find information on search attributes himself; for information about the other attributes, (s)he will be dependent on the judgement of others.

CONSUMPTION STAGE

consumption stage;
service encounter

The consumption stage is the stage in which the actual service delivery occurs. In other words, it is where the service encounter or interactive consumption takes place. Consumer and service provider interact with each other and the consumer participates in a certain way in the servuction process. There will be many moments of truth because consumption and production during the service delivery process coincide.

(dis)satisfaction
judgement;
continue the
relationship

This is the stage in which the service is evaluated for a different part of the whole process than in the pre-purchase stage. Therefore, the next part of the (dis)satisfaction judgement of the consumer is being made. With services, one does not wait in making a satisfaction judgement until the actual purchase is over. So, also in this phase, the consumer may determine whether or not to continue the relationship, and if so, in what way? One may think, for instance, of changing the relationship to a more intensive one than before.[39] This evaluation already happens during the servuction process and the eventual waiting before this process actually starts. The satisfaction evaluation is based on both the technical, functional and relational quality of the whole service experience.[40]

Service
practice
4-11
What is the
quality of
after sales? [41]

The customers of a manufacturer of copying equipment maintained that the after sales services consisted of three factors determining the service quality:

1. the hard core elements of the augmented product bought (office equipment: the machine as such *plus* paper, ink, availability of spare parts during the service call, service contract options, price performance ratio of services rendered, quality of spare parts and instruction, etc.);
2. the general attitude of the customers about the relationship with the manufacturer (relations with the vendor's sales staff, administrative services, complaint handling, etc.);
3. the relations with the technical services staff and their way of working (attitude of the technician, availability of technical services staff, repair time, dispatch of break down call, response time).

In this stage, it becomes clear whether the consumer really gets the benefits (or positive consequences) (s)he was hoping for or expecting.

"The benefits bought by a customer consist of the experience that is delivered through an interactive process."[42]

In other words, it becomes clear what the functional and psychosocial consequences of the purchase and use of the service are. The actual moments of truth may appear to be very short ones, nevertheless, the experience attributes now become visible to the consumer.

POST-PURCHASE STAGE

post-purchase stage

In the post-purchase stage, the consumer can review and evaluate the complete service delivery. As far as applicable, probably only the credence attributes for evaluating a service are being put forward. For, only at this very point, can it be checked whether the consumer indeed has received the desired functional and psychosocial benefits. That may take some time. Consequently, the outcome of this evaluation may not be "available" right after the service experience. Finally, after this whole evaluation, it will become totally clear whether the consumer is satisfied or not. Or, in other words, whether excellent service quality has been provided or not.

consumer is satisfied or not

Now, all stages of the service delivery process have been passed. The final judgement will consist of positive and negative aspects. In turn, this has consequences for the next purchase situation: will the consumer continue the relationship with the service provider or not? In other words: will the consumer become brand loyal and/or loyal to the service provider?

Service practice 4-12 Are you satisfied?

Mercuri Urval is a Swedish based recruitment and selection agency with offices in many countries in Europe and the United States, etc. Companies ask them to recruit and select people for specific jobs. Most of the time these are high-level jobs in management, marketing, quality management, production, etc.

Whether companies will use Mercuri Urval again is determined by one overall factor representing the evaluation of the cooperation between the company and Mercuri Urval. This may sound self evident. However, this overall evaluation of the cooperation depends on three other factors all representing a particular kind of satisfaction with parts of the service encounter, namely:

1. the evaluation of the kind of contact with the Mercuri Urval consultant;
2. the evaluation of the final outcome; and
3. the evaluation of the unique Mercuri Urval way of working.

4.6 RELATIONSHIPS AND LIFE CYCLES

degree of temporarity

All different kinds of relationships throughout the world have in common a certain degree of temporarity. This degree of temporarity in the relationship has already been discussed in our classification (Chapter Two) where a relationship (the heart of the scheme) could be: formal or informal; and, continue/long term or one time/short term. For this reason, we would like to place the relationship and the life-cycle of it here as a fundamental issue, whereby the marketing strategy and mix may be of help in giving content and meaning to that relationship.[43]

the relationship and its life-cycle

RELATIONSHIPS BETWEEN SERVICE PROVIDERS AND CUSTOMERS OR CLIENTS

starting, developing and maintaining relationships

Market-oriented service providers are not focussing on a single transaction with consumers. Their main objective is starting, developing and maintaining relationships with customers. In some situations, it may also mean that relationships are ended, e.g. when the service provider cannot meet customer's specific demands (any longer). Or:

> "Relationship marketing concerns attracting, developing, and retaining customer relationships. Its central tenet is the creation of 'true customers' – customers who are glad they selected a firm, who perceive they are receiving value and feel valued, who are likely to buy additional services from the firm and who are unlikely to defect to a competitor. True customers are the most profitable of all customers. They spend more money with the firm on a per-year basis and they stay with the firm for more years. They spread favorable word-of-mouth information about the firm, and they may even be willing to pay a premium price for the benefits the service offers."[44]

Companies with such customers will have lower marketing costs. Such relationships are favored by customers. For in the service business, customers often want to have a partner whom they can trust and who cares about them. This allows for closer and more personalized contacts; in the extreme situation: one-on-one very personal contacts. It is within this framework that Berry and Parasuraman (1991) distinguish between three kinds of bonds that may exist between the service firm and the customer:

three kinds of bonds

financial bonds
1. *financial bonds*, when the customer is approached by means of financial incentives only;

social bonds
2. *social bonds*, emphasizing personalized service delivery and the transformation of customers into clients by keeping in close contact with one another in order to learn much about each other's needs, wants, and possibilities; and

structural bonds
3. *structural bonds*. These are offered in addition to the former two types of bonds. These bonds are created by providing services that are valuable to clients and not readily available from other sources. Quite often, they are technology based and intended to make the participation of the customer in the service delivery process more efficient and effective.

Service practice 4-13 What kind of relationship do you want?

basic, reactive, accountable

Kotler (1994) defines five different levels of relating to customers. Redefined in terms of services they can be circumscribed as follows:

1. *basic*: the salesperson sells the service but does not contact the customer again;
2. *reactive*: the salesperson sells the service and encourages the customer to call if he or she has any questions or complaints;
3. *accountable*: the salesperson phones the customer a short time after the sale to check whether the service is meeting the customer's expectations.

proactive

partnership

The salesperson also solicits from the customer any service improvement suggestions and any specific disappointments. This information helps the company to continuously improve its offering;

4. *proactive*: the company salesperson phones the customer from time to time with suggestions about improved service use or helpful new services;

5. *partnership*: the company works continuously with the customer to discover ways to effect customer savings or help the customer to perform better.

These five types of relationship were used in a study with respect to the relationships car owners have and would like to have with their car dealer.[45] In a study among 1,038 car owners of the Japanese brand Mitsubishi the researchers found that:

- 55% of the Mitsubishi car owners wanted to keep the relationship in the future as it was now;
- 40% wanted to have a more intense relationship than at this very moment; while only
- 5% wanted to have a less intensive relationship.

The study also indicated that car owners having (or preferring) a less intensive relationship were less brand loyal, less dealer loyal but more price sensitive than those car owners having (or preferring) a more intensive relationship.

In the services sector, many relationships between customers and service providers have a long term history. Many people not only have the same doctor, dentist or physiotherapist for years, but also have the same bank or insurance company for years. In the last case, they have to, because insurance contracts are mostly for a long period. Life insurance, for example, has a contractual duration of thirty years and can only be terminated between times at very unfavorable terms for the consumer. Although the relationship lasts for a long time, it does not say anything about the nature of that relationship, nor about the satisfaction with that relationship.

inertia   Sometimes, people stay for reasons of inertia.

true loyal customers   What kind of relationship will finally determine whether we can speak of true loyal customers (transferred into real clients) or about customers having a weak bond with the service provider who may switch easily to another supplier when their offer is a little better? In our opinion, it is not only important to look at these relations from the point of view of the service provider but also from the point of view of the customer. A market-oriented service provider will often have to check what kind of relationship customers have right now and what kind of relationship they would like to have in the future, as the Mitsubishi example shows.

dynamics   Relationships are not static phenomena. Rather, they are characterized by dynamics and change over time. They go through a certain development, comparable with the well-known life cycles of products or organizations. So, there is a life cycle for services and a life cycle for service providers.

LIFE CYCLES OF ORGANIZATIONS AND RELATIONSHIPS

three different types of life cycles

Within the life cycle of a service we like to distinguish three different types of life cycles: the traditional life cycle; the relationship life cycle; and the family life cycle.

traditional life cycle

The first one is the traditional life cycle. The change points or transition points are the critical moments of choice at which the organization moves from one stage to the other. The following stages can be distinguished: introduction and survival in the short-term, expansion, consolidation, further growth, maturity and decline.

stages in the relationships

The second life cycle shows us stages in the relationships of (business to business) services:[46]

selection

1. *selection* (interest, pre-relationship phase, getting to know each other, pre-purchase);

development

2. *development* (purchase, repeat purchase, development, initiation, post-pitch, test stage, initial phase);

maintenance

3. *maintenance* (involvement, integration, continuation, maturity, growth phase, troubled phase, constant phase); and

termination

4. *termination* (end relationship, decline phase, termination phase).

factors contributing to the success of a relationship

Commitment, trust (to reduce perceived risk), satisfaction, quality and various kinds of bonds are all factors contributing to the success of a relationship.

family life cycle

The third life cycle is the family life cycle, meaning that a household will have different needs for services in time as a consequence of, for example, family composition, wishes, income and the like. Service providers should take that into account when developing marketing strategies to suit particular segments and households. Insurance companies or brokers, knowing their insured very well, can really benefit from such a family life cycle approach. A lot of relevant data can often be detected very easily from their own records.

transition points

continue the relationship

In all cases of the three life cycles mentioned, it is important to realize which are the important moments in the life cycle: the change or transition points. These are the moments at which important decisions have to be made, at which important happenings and changes take place. Transition points are also often the moments to think about continuing the relationship. Also, other points or experiences may determine whether one wants to continue the relationship. In fact, activities of the service firm and its personnel may make or break the relationship. Sometimes, front office personnel may be the cause of this. That is why Richard Buchanan (1996) talks about the enemy from within. In many cases, employees' crude behavior makes customers decide not to come back.

Service
Practice
4-14
How to ruin a
beautiful
relationship

First, let's look at how a very local customer relationship was created.

A small, failed bookstore in a suburban shopping center was bought by an enterprising young woman. She understood people who loved books.

In just a couple of years this bookstore had grown so prosperous that it moved into the space vacated by a regional supermarket. The store was designed with wide aisles and benches where people could sit and read the books. Most bookstores discourage this. But this bookstore owner knew that people who loved books would buy more books if they were allowed to browse through them.

This bookstore owner made customer service a specialty. She hired salespeople who also loved books and could get as excited about newly published archaelogical findings as they could the latest bestselling novel.

With inventory zooming from 35,000 to more than 150,000 titles on almost every subject, selection became a drawing point for people all over the state.

A bimonthly newsletter with book news and reviews and a lively schedule of special events, from author signings to mini-art shows, was mailed to everyone who signed up at the store. But there was something else in that newsletter that kept customers consistently buying books: coupons. Every two months, customers received a coupon worth $1 off a $5 purchase, $5 off a $25 purchase or $10 off a $50 purchase.

As a regular customer, I grew to expect those coupons and planned my book purchases around them. Over a period of several years, I spent about $25 every two months to get the $5 discount. Occasionally, I spent only enough to get $1 off. But I also occasionally spent at least $50 in order to get $10 off.

On average, I was buying about $150 worth of books a year at this store. That is almost double the national average of $80 for consumer books purchases in 1994, according to the Statistical Abstract of the United States, 1994.

This relationship strategy apparently worked just as well with other customers, because the inevitable happened. The store became so successful that the owner sold it at a profit and went traveling. While she was sailing the South Seas, the national chain that bought the store began quietly eliminating the very things that built those loyal relationships and made the store so profitable in the first place.

I can just see it. Corporate says, "We can't afford to keep so many different kinds of books in stock. They don't sell in big enough quantities". Pretty soon I couldn't find books on the shelf as I used to. I had to special-order them. So, with less selection on the shelves, I stopped browsing.

Next Corporate says, "We make more money on publishers' remainders. Stock more bargain books". When I came in to pick up my special orders, I noticed more and more tables of bargain books. Now there's nothing wrong with bargain books. But I doubt most customers had been going to this store for bargain books, which could be found almost anywhere else.

Of course, Corporate could not allow those over-generous coupons to continue eating away profits, either. But I'm sure Corporate insisted, "We've got to wean them off those coupons". So now I was asked to pay $10 to join a club. That would give me a 10% discount on any book in the store and a 40% discount on current best-seller list books, which I almost never buy. When the newsletter came out, it contained a coupon for $1 off a $10 purchase or $5 off a $50 purchase in addition to the club discount.

Let's do a little math here. My purchases totaled about $150 retail the previous year. With coupon discounts, this would be about $129 in actual sales. The new owners gained my $10 club fee. But with fewer books to choose from, I shopped less often and did not buy as many books. With the discount that motivated me to buy all my books from this store severely reduced, there's no longer any advantage to buying only from there.

So my purchases dropped to about $65 retail. Subtract $6.50 for the 10% club discount, then subtract $8 in additional discount coupons. Add the $10 club fee for a grand sales total of $60.50.

As a markting person, I found it fascinating to watch this retailer not only cut my purchases to less than half in the space of one year, but also destroy my bonds of loyalty. This is only my experience. How many other loyal customers have similar stories?

The final chapter? Not unexpectedly, the additional discount coupons in the newsletter disappeared altogether. And I joined the Book-Of-The-Month Club.[47]

Summary

Consumer behavior with respect to services has several unique aspects, all emerging from the intangible nature of services. The internationalization of service industries makes this even more complex. Now, differences in consumer behavior in various countries have to be taken into account. This requires analyzing the different cultural characteristics in these countries and assessing the cultural distances (which are often different from the geographical distances). Partly, this is important because of the fact that coping with uncertainty (inherent to the perceived risk going along with intangible services) will differ per culture, partly because the barriers to entry can be caused by ethnocentrism ("preferring a country's own goods and services over imported ones"). Moreover, the "country-of-origin" effect may play a role in accepting services offered by foreign companies. This all may impact on the many (eight) types of perceived risk.

The services market cannot only be segmented on the usual socio-economic and demographic variables, but also on the basis of the four typical characteristics of services and on our classification criteria. The benefits and perceived risks can be used as segmentation variables especially when these segmentation variables match the policy of a market-oriented service provider.

The image of a service or service provider can differ per segment. The positioning of services can be shown by a perceptual map. From these positions, strategic consequences can be drawn.

In order to be able to analyze the buying process of services, the following classification has been made:

- pre-purchase stage;
- consumption stage; and
- post-purchase stage.

The interaction between a service provider and a customer can be analyzed within the framework of ongoing relationships. The focus then is not on one short term transaction but on a long(er) term relationship, and the bonds between service providers and their clients. The dynamics in these relationships should be analyzed carefully in order to be a truly market oriented service provider. This relationship paradigm is preferred over a strong and sole focus on the marketing-mix. In our view, the different service marketing-mix instruments should support and enhance the relationship between the client and the service provider. The relationship concept also applies to analyzing the modified and straight rebuy situations. This paradigm can be applied also to the issues of starting, developing and maintaining relationships in case of new task buying situations. Building relationships is one of the many ways to reduce customers' perceived risk. In the next chapter, we will see that consistent quality while delivering services is also a next step in strengthening relationships between the two parties.

QUESTIONS

1 Why should one distinguish between search, experience and credence attributes in services?
2 What kinds of perceived risks can be found?
3 Summarize the arguments why service organizations should pay much attention to their reputation and image. What are the consequences with respect to consumer behavior?
4 Summarize the ways customers can reduce perceived risk with respect to their buying and using services. Apply this to your own decision process about going to your present university and your bank.
5 What is meant in this chapter by functional and psychosocial consequences? Why is it important to make that distinction? How does perceived risk fit into these concepts?
6 What is benefit segmentation and why could it be useful to service providers?
7 Why should market oriented service organizations primarily not use their own ideas about the market (competitors and consumers) but customers' perceptions about service attributes and competitors?
8 How can you define and operationalize national culture?
9 What might be the link between COO and ethnocentrism?
10 In what way might COO affect the new task of buying services?

ASSIGNMENTS

1 Describe the culture of your own country with the data from Figure 4-2. Where is your country's culture positioned in Figure 4-3?
   In those figures, you will see countries with similar countries close to your own. Does that positioning make any sense to you? Why/why not?
2 In this chapter, some examples/Service practices hinge upon accountants, CPA's or auditing firms and their clients.
   Put these separate issues together into a one page summary. What can you conclude from that summary? What does that mean for developing, and maintaining relationships between a CPA and its client? From a strategic point of view, where do you position CPAs and their service offering in Figure 2-1?
3 In this chapter, we stated the classification criteria from Chapter 2 could in fact be used in segmenting the market, especially the basic characteristics of services. Give some examples.
4 Do you know other examples of the events and history described in Service practice 4-14? Explain.
5 Based on Service practice 4-13, for which service would you like to have stronger or weaker relationships? Why?

Case: FEDEX PRACTICES WHAT IT PREACHES ABOUT SEGMENTS

When Federal Express first took flight, it practically created an industry. It became the first company to go from zero to $1 billion in sales in ten years without the aid of mergers or acquisitions, and has dominated the fast-growing overnight-cargo field ever since.

Today, however, the field has grown. Shippers, such as UPS, DHL, TNT and Emery, battle FedEx daily for market share around the world. But instead of emphasizing product or firing the first shots in a price war, the courier opted to maximize growth by emphasizing service to customer segments.

"We found an opportunity to improve customer satisfaction and profitability by defining the needs of customer segments in a more meaningful way", said James Sellers, manager global distribution marketing at Memphis-based FedEx.

Sellers spoke recently at the AMA's Attitude and Behavior Research Conference in Palm Springs, California.

"We wanted to focus on customer behavior, generate better return on investment, and better integrate our product and service offerings", he said. "Our objective was world-class segment management marketing."

Segment management marketing (SMM) was a new way for FedEx to look at its business. Until 1993, the company had pursued an ad hoc marketing strategy, Sellers said. Marketing staffers developed programs on a case-by-case basis around FedEx service offerings. It was a more traditional method of product management, conducted independently of company operations.

The old-fashioned approach hadn't harmed customer satisfaction. The company was the first winner of Malcolm Baldrige National Quality Award in 1990, became an inductee into the AMA's Marketing Hall of Fame, and is one of the most often benchmarked companies in the world.

"We were already seen as very good at managing our customer relationships", Sellers said. "The success that we have had has always come from an intense focus on what our customers want and delivering value to them."

But FedEx knew that satisfaction alone wasn't enough to keep it on top in terms of sales. It needed a strategy comprehensive enough to deliver extra value to all customers.

The new method does that by researching current consumer behavior to tell the company when additional service investments can fill a customer segment's needs more completely. For instance, customers who use FedEx only for overnight letter service and use another company for boxes might be approached or enticed to make FedEx their exclusive freight service under segment marketing.

Other goals might be as fundamental as increasing customer retention or as ambitious as designing a specialized logistics-support system like the one FedEx furnishes to computer-chip manufacturer Intel.

"Intel has no warehouses in China", Sellers said. "Our planes are their warehouses."

Reebok also has an exclusive agreement with FedEx to overnight athletic shoes from factories to retailers.

"We evaluate a consumer's behavior, then we put together marketing programs that include value propositions to see if we can increase the value of the consumer", Sellers said. "We need to compete on an intense basis, and the only way we can do that is to build on these customer relationships and increase our profits."

The pilot test, targeting some of FedEx's huge base of smaller clients, showed the profit potential of SMM. From $4.5 million invested in telemarketing and discount offers, the company estimated incremental returns of $49 million. The pilot also helped develop FedEx's popular package-tracking service and Web site.

Anticipating further applications for segment marketing, the company appointed cross-functional teams to formalize the new methodology. FedEx has since moved into research with national clients and had defined 14 distinct customer segments in domestic and international markets whose full worth to the company is, as yet, unrealized.

With SMM, an initiative's returns can be forecast in advance of full rollout, so executives can see the benefits of a segmented approach before approving any related investments. "Rather than just saying we can make a profit, we can go to the finance people and say, 'Hey, it's worth it, because it will bring in millions in profits'", Sellers said.

"We're preaching the segment management marketing message throughout the company. As a result, we're able to bring innovations to our customers."

Source: Ian P. Murphy, 1997

QUESTIONS

1   James Sellers stated "We wanted to focus on customer behavior, generate better return on investment, and better integrate our product and service offerings". Why is this a crucial statement?

2   "But FedEx knew that satisfaction alone wasn't enough to keep it on top in terms of sales." Explain.

3   James Sellers said "We need to compete on an intense basis, and the only way we can do that is to build on these customer relationships and increase our profits". How can this statement be explained with what we said about relationships in this chapter?

ENDNOTES

1. Riddle, 1992.
2. Steenkamp et al., 1993.
3. Axtell, 1991, p. 87; Hill, 1992, p. 326.
4. Hofstede, 1991, p. 5. The definitions of the first four dimensions can be found respectively on pp. 82-83, 51, 113, 28.
5. The research was carried out in the early seventies, long before the unification of Germany.
6. Kasper and Bloemer, 1997.
7. The analysis revealed three new factors explaining 100% of total variance. Here, we show the perceptual map based on the first two factors, explaining 62% respectively 24% of total variance. For a more detailed analysis, see Kasper and Bloemer, 1997.
8. Kapoor and Sautter, 1995.
9. Papadopoulos and Heslop, 1993.
10. This section is based on Ahmed and d'Astous, 1994 and Papadopoulos and Heslop, 1993.
11. Meurs, 1995.
12. Since the COO is a representation of a particular image of a country, we believe several scaling techniques may be applied. To us, the semantic differential scale can be used to that end. It will indicate the underlying feelings of consumers with respect to services from a particular country. Given the words used in the semantic differential scale, this technique will reveal also something about the norms and values attributed to services from a particular country. The semantic differential scale usually ranges from 1 to 7.
13. Shimp and Sharma, 1987, p. 287.
14. Shimp and Sharma, 1987, p. 280.
15. The maximum ethnocentrism score obtained could be 50 in this study by Steenkamp, 1993 (see also Service practice 4-5).
16. This is in line with the conclusion of Shimp and Sharma (1987) p. 287.
17. Steenkamp, 1993b.
18. This refers to the three parts of service quality that can be distinguished (see Chapters One and Five).
19. Gemünden, 1985; Suchard and Polonsky, 1991.
20. In our chapter on pricing, we will return to the question how price can act as an indicator for quality of services.
21. Note that this is a different use of the word functional than at the beginning of this chapter.
22. The monetary and non-monetary cost of the consumer involved in searching for services will be discussed in our chapter on pricing.
23. Hutt and Speh, 1992; Peter and Olson, 1993.
24. Assael, 1987; Schiffman and Kanuk, 1987.
25. Murray, 1991.
26. Firth, 1993.
27. Van Raaij and Verhallen, 1994.
28. Morello, 1988 and 1993.
29. Van der Walt, Scott and Woodside, 1994.
30. Leeflang et al., 1992.
31. Similar to the definition of positioning products provided by Dibb et al., 1994, p. 89.
32. Peter and Olson, 1993, pp. 92, 93, 97.
33. Peter and Olson, 1993, pp. 92, 93, 97.

34. This will be elaborated upon in Chapter Six.

35. See also the SERVQUAL-model of Parasuraman, Berry and Zeithaml (1988), discussed in our Chapter Five.

36. Venetis, 1997.

37. Scott and Van der Walt, 1995.

38. This shows the usefulness of applying our classification of services from Chapter Two here.

39. An example of a shift to more intensive relationships is given in section 4.6.

40. The relationship between quality and satisfaction will be discussed in Chapter Six.

41. Kasper and Lemmink, 1989.

42. Bateson, 1992.

43. These and similar ideas have been developed to a large extent in Scandinavia by Grönroos (1990a) and Gummesson (1987a) with respect to services and by the Industrial Marketing and Purchasing (IMP) Group with respect to business to business marketing (see, for instance, Häkansson, 1982 and Ford, 1990).

44. Berry and Parasuraman, 1991, p. 133.

45. Lemmink, Rohs and Schijns, 1994.

46. Karin Venetis' overview (1995, 1997) is based on studies in the business to business services sector, like Grönroos (1982a,b), Wackman et al., (1987), Yorke (1988), Szmigin (1993), Sharma (1994) and Halinen (1994). Within brackets we mention the terms used by other authors than Venetis.

47. Spoon, 1996.

CHAPTER FIVE

SERVICE QUALITY

After studying this chapter, you should be able to:

- *know the basics of quality management;*

- *define the terms "quality of service" and "quality of service delivery";*

- *know the basics of service quality within service organizations;*

- *decipher the difference between quality and satisfaction;*

- *realize the importance of both expectations and perceptions;*

- *reproduce ways to express satisfaction and dissatisfaction about services and service providers;*

- *understand the SERVQUAL-model for measuring the quality of service delivery;*

- *understand the importance of the SERVQUAL-model for decision making in service organizations;*

- *compare the SERVQUAL-model with some other models used to study service quality;*

- *assess some of the criticisms of the SERVQUAL-model;*

- *argue how service quality may contribute to strengthening relationships between buyers and service providers.*

BELOW: *Keeping promises is essential*

5.1 INTRODUCTION

*Service
practice
5-1
Excellent
quality:
mission
impossible?*

The legendary basketball player Michael Jordan is famous for "flying" under the basket. Perhaps even more legendary in the US is baseball player "Babe" Ruth, who in 1927 held the home run record of 60 in a 154 game season.

Emile Zatopek, marathon runner from the former Czechoslovakia, was called the "locomotive". He was known for his revolutionary constant speed. Now, fifty years after his sporting career, Zatopek plays the key role in an Adidas' advertising campaign.

In June 1988, the Dutch Football Team played in the European Championship Final in Munich. Russia was the opponent. During the second half of the game, Marco Van Basten scored an almost impossible goal. The Dutch press described this goal as the "miracle of Munich".

All these sportsmen have in common is that they have achieved the seemingly impossible. In sports terminology, this is often associated with quality. Fortunately, in service delivery, quality does not necessarily relate to the impossible. However, accomplishing unexpected things contributes to quality to a great extent.

From the previous chapter, it has become clear that the service sector is subject to many trends and changes. In addition, the consumer's attitude is changing. Customers are becoming more conscious of their rights. More and more, customers want to be involved in deciding on the quality of a service. In making a choice, customers will take into account their own past quality experiences as well as the experiences of friends and acquaintances. Of course, specific experiences throughout the whole process of service delivery and the communication strategy of a service provider also play a role.

It is important to understand that customers do not all have the same wishes with regard to their ideal quality level. Consumers can also differ in the extent to which they "tolerate a certain lack of quality". Not everybody is dissatisfied right away when the service is not delivered 100% perfect. In this context, we should emphasize it is most likely that different market segments, each of them having comparable desired service-quality levels for standard services and customized services, might exist. Market-oriented service providers try very hard to meet the individual expectations of their customers: an additional challenge is that if customers have once experienced the excellent quality of the firm or its competitor, they expect this to be repeated. The organization (and in particular its contact personnel) face the difficult task of identifying each customer's expectations with respect to the quality level and the nature of the service delivery. In order to understand these complexities, we will consider them in this chapter:

- characteristics and definitions of quality (section 5.2);
- service quality and quality management in general (section 5.3);
- the relationship between expectations and perceptions when studying quality as well as satisfaction (sections 5.4, 5.5 and 5.6); and
- service quality and quality management in services and service organizations (sections 5.7, 5.8 and 5.9).

This all is depicted in Figure 5-1.

Figure 5-1
Chapter outline

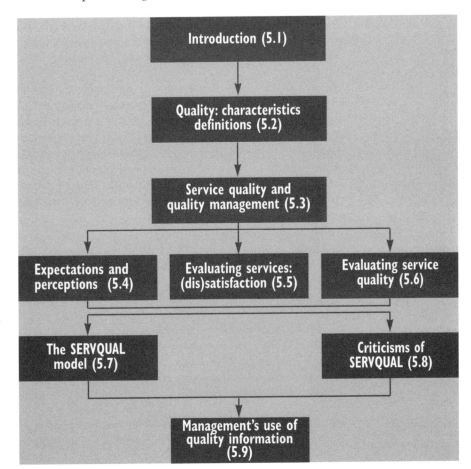

5.2 QUALITY

In many service organizations today, quality is considered the magic word in competition. Offering quality has a magical impact on present and future customers. "Quality is the best weapon to fight competitors" is the new-born slogan.

Unfortunately, just as with King Arthur's magic sword, Excalibur, it is not enough to carry the "quality sword". Only one person was able to draw the Excalibur sword from a massive stone and use it as a weapon. Therefore, it is essential to clearly understand the meaning of "quality", before using it for the fight, whether it be in medieval times or in the present market place.

CHARACTERISTICS AND DEFINITIONS

Quality is an ambiguous term. On the one hand, everybody knows (or think they know) what quality is. On the other hand, formulating a comprehensive and uniform definition is a big – if not unsurmountable – problem.

philosophical approach

In a philosophical approach to the term quality, quality is a characteristic of thoughts and statements, which are believed to be taken for granted or self evident.[1] Because definitions are the results of abstraction and formal thinking, quality cannot be defined. Pirsig (1987) adds to this: "Although we cannot define quality, we know what quality is." In his opinion, it is thus impossible to give a definition of quality, because quality can never be considered independently, but only in relation to what is per-

some definitions

ceived. Nevertheless, we will try to clarify the term by presenting some definitions. Otherwise, it would be impossible for managers in service industries to formulate a quality strategy.

- "Quality is fitness for use, the extent to which the product succesfully serves the purpose of the user during usage" Juran (1974).

- "Quality is conformance to requirements" Crosby (1983).

- "Quality is zero defects – doing it right the first time" Parasuraman, Zeithaml and Berry (1985).

- "Quality is exceeding what customers expect from the service" Zeithaml, Parasuraman and Berry (1990).

five approaches to quality

The great number of definitions already shows that opinions on quality strongly differ. To express the meaning of quality, five approaches to quality have been formulated.[2]

FIVE APPROACHES TO QUALITY

Quality can be viewed from many different points of view. We can think of economics, marketing, psychology or operations research. Partly based on the viewpoints of these fields, Garvin (1988) formulated five approaches to studying quality:

- transcendent approach (psychology);
- product-based approach (economics);

- user-based approach (marketing and operational management);
- manufacturing-based approach (operational management); and
- value-based approach.

When studying this section, one should be aware of the fact that Garvin's approaches are based on the tangible product. In the choice of our examples, we have translated these approaches into the field of the intangible service.

Transcendent approach

innate excellence

Pirsig's philosophical approach is a clear example of the transcendent approach. According to his way of thinking, quality is synonymous with *innate excellence*. Here, quality cannot always be defined and is partly a matter of experience. This approach claims that quality cannot be defined precisely, that it is a simple, unanalyzable property we learn to recognize only through experience. The sports examples at the beginning of this chapter illustrate this approach.

Service practice 5-2 All or nothing?

> Everything is quality. The people you hire, the work you deliver, and your understanding of what people need. It is like music. Music composed by Beethoven is high quality, but we still do not know exactly why.

Product-based approach

quantity of features or attributes

The product-based approach maintains that differences in quality are caused by the quantity of features or attributes of a product.[3] This results in a ranking of attributes, which are required by all consumers. This approach views quality as a measurable variable and thus also as an objective and absolute term.

In a sense, this approach could be looked at in terms of the level of services offered; the features attached to the core service. Thus, a budget family room in a hotel would differ in quality from a luxury executive suite, while the (technical) quality of each (quiet room, perfect bed and bathroom) might be perfectly acceptable to the customer in terms of value for money.

User-based approach

customer's judgement

In this approach, quality is determined by the customer. The customer's judgement is always right. It needs no explaining that this approach is subjective to a large extent, because every user has different thoughts and ideas about what quality is. In this approach, quality corresponds with Juran's definition: "Quality is fitness for use." This approach fits very well into the marketing philosophy (which also has a strong focus on the customer). It hinges upon the functionality of a good or service to the customer: what are the benefits received? This is closely linked to the customer oriented perspective to quality: the perceived service quality.

"In our organization, quality of service is a vague term. How can you know whether you are doing the right thing if you don't check with the customer?"

"To me as a customer service quality is getting exactly what I want. And that doesn't necessarily mean that it has to be expensive."

Manufacturing-based approach

the supply-side

In this approach, quality is considered from the supply-side point of view and mainly concerns conformance to requirements. Every product must meet a fixed number of specific requirements. Any divergence from these requirements is considered a decrease in quality. As in the product-based approach, quality here is viewed as an objective and measurable term, for the requirements are mostly stated in technical terms/specifications.

A fast food chain may operate this type of conformance quality: rigorous quality checks on all supplies, exact uniform portion measurement, staff trained to greet customers in standard way, service to be delivered in specific time scale, etc. (When we look at the way customers actually assess these service activities, then the perceived service quality approach is applied.)

However, even the number of "technicalities" taken into account may differ in determining service quality in different societies when assessing the same service. In determining the quality of British Rail or the Deutsche Bundesbahn, it is mainly the arriving and leaving on schedule that really matter. In other countries, just arriving and leaving is enough in assessing quality, like with the taxi-brousse, matatu, jeepney, bemo or colectivo.[4]

Value-based approach

quality is considered in relation to cost and price

Here – simply stated – quality is considered in relation to cost and price. Product quality is only considered good if the price is acceptable for (potential) buyers or costs are low. In this approach, services or products which are judged not as poor according to the product-based approach, may be qualitatively judged excellent, because the price and costs relate better.

value for money

This concept reflects the point that customers seek value for money, whereas the main question is: "What do I get for the sacrifices I make?" Value is seen as a broad concept (utility, need satisfaction, supply in relation to the price paid, investments in time, other psychological costs, etc.). Here, an example will illustrate our point.

"A return ticket Sydney–London for only $500, that is what I call quality. Okay, I know I have to bring my own food and drinks, because they are not served on board."

THE NEED FOR A USER-BASED APPROACH TO SERVICE QUALITY

Parasuraman, Zeithaml and Berry (1988) assume that the product- and manufacturing-based approach refer to the objective quality, whereas the user-based approach runs parallel to the subjective, perceived quality. This point of view, however, leads to two problems:[5]

- how should widely divergent individual wants be linked up to create a workable concept of quality?; and
- how should a distinction be made between attributes leading to quality and attributes leading to higher customer satisfaction (see also section 5.5)?

Some examples will illustrate these questions. Parasuraman et al. (1988) found that consumers use basically similar criteria in assessing services regardless of the type of service. American Airlines and British Airways, for example, aim mainly at reliability, care and friendliness because their passengers deem these topics as important. The question remains as to whether or not this results in real quality. In fact, what these airlines do is give priority to particular quality attributes.

Service practice 5-5 Satisfaction versus quality

In the user-based approach, quality is synonymous with maximum customer satisfaction. Although these terms may seem to be closely related, they do not necessarily mean the same.

Many teenagers travel through Europe hitchhiking. Often, public property is used as a sleeping-place, for example the railway station of Venice or the bridges of Paris. Research shows that these travellers are very satisfied with this alternative. However, a "concrete-bed" may be satisfactory, but absolutely not of high-quality.

In spite of these drawbacks, Garvin's classification provides insights into the many approaches to studying the quality of tangible products. The basic characteristics of services make some approaches unsuitable for determining the quality of a service. In products, a clear distinction can be made between production and the good itself. In services, it is harder to draw a line between the servuction process and the service itself. Usually, services cannot be stored and production and consumption of a service take place at the same time. In addition, services are often characterized by a certain

differentiation in quality

extent of heterogeneity. Differentiation in quality or deviations away from the quality standards are common practice. If not, these standards must be made very elastic. However, this contradicts the manufacturing-based approach.

marketing theory

Garvin positions the user-based approach clearly within the field of marketing theory. Therefore, it seems obvious to base the rest of this book on this approach. Apart from the above-mentioned arguments, several other reasons support the use of this approach.

First, the quality of a service is often, because of the intangibility of the service itself, a perceived quality.[6] The way a service is perceived depends not only on products or manufacturing aspects (*what* is in it?) but more on expectations and the way the service is brought to the customer (*how* is it done and *by whom*?). These last aspects are mainly based on the user's perception. The characteristic of the interactive consumption in the service encounter makes this even more important. That is why we discussed in Chapter One the concepts of technical, functional and relational quality.

what, how,
by whom

perceived risk

Second, the consumer is generally facing a higher perceived risk in his or her consumption of services. This is caused by services' intangibility. For example, this fact influences consumers in the way that they accept the price (both the economic price as well as the psychological price), or consider price as a quality indicator. The last reason why the user-based approach is selected is the fact that this philosophy supports the basic principles of marketing and the perspective of relationship marketing.[7]

relationship
marketing

Therefore, we like to define quality here as:

> Quality is the extent in which the service, the service process and the service organization can satisfy the expectations of the user.[8]

zero defects

One should, however, not forget that customers expect in most cases the best from the service provider. Mistakes or faults are not appreciated. Therefore, zero defects should be strived for. These zero defects should be accomplished with respect to the technical part of the service, as well as to the functional and relational part of it. These zero defects should also apply to all the attributes or dimensions of the service and service delivery process. In other words, all aspects of the service encounter should be organized in such a way that no defects might occur. This puts pressure not only on the employees but also the customer (as part of the servuction process), who should also not give rise to any defects in his participatory behavior in the service encounter.[9]

Also, we would like to stress here that the user-based approach is compared to the standards professional service providers set for their profession. Quite often doctors, professors, lawyers and teachers assume that customers cannot assess the quality of their services. For, customers or students would lack knowledge about the field or discipline. We maintain that these customers can evaluate the service rendered. They will have a feeling as to whether the service provider really does do a technically perfect job, and, they may actually understand how the service is delivered. It is in our own experience that students complain, for instance, when "what we teach them or expect them to do is too easy". Nevertheless, it is often very difficult for these professionals to accept the customers' judgement in evaluating their service.[10]

5.3 SERVICE QUALITY

total quality control

Now that we know how to define the term quality in service industries, we will take a closer look at service quality itself. Japanese service-quality theory and practice in particular tells us that total quality control (TQC) is a prerequisite to compete and survive. TQC is defined as "an efficient system to integrate the efforts of several groups within an organization to develop, maintain and improve quality in order to organize the production process and service delivery in the most economic way, totally satisfying the customer".

everyone in the organization is responsible for delivering quality

customers also contribute to the level of service quality

From this definition, it is clear that TQC is based on the view that everyone in the organization is responsible for delivering quality. The Japanese especially are clearly opposed to hiring service-quality specialists. Hiring specialists gives the other employees the impression that specialists are responsible for service quality instead of themselves.[11] In services, we should realize that customers also contribute to the level of service quality accomplished. Quality standards and perceptions may differ per industry as Service practice 5-6 shows.

In our view, the customer should perceive the offered service as high quality. This means that the core service and the augmented services must be – separately as well as together – high quality services. In fact, the definition of TQC is part of the strategic quality management vision (see the next section). To give a clear understanding of this approach, we will now present a summary of the evolution of ideas about quality.

THE EVOLUTION IN THINKING ABOUT QUALITY

Over the years, quality control has seen a shift from a production process focus to a mainly organizational focus, in which the market plays an important role in determining product (or service) quality. To get a clear understanding of the role of service quality within a service organization, we will now firstly pay attention to the development of quality in manufacturing.

four phases

Four phases can be distinguished in the historical development of the quality concept: inspection; statistical quality control; integral service quality and strategic quality management.[12]

Inspection (before 1920)

mass production

output inspection

When mass production evolved, an increasing need for inspection of ready-for-use products emerged. Using specified checklists, quality inspectors had to trace incomplete or wrong products. Such an inspection guaranteed standardization and product-uniformity to a certain degree. Quality was an operational matter and more or less synonymous with output inspection. Nowadays, some products are still inspected before they are put on the market. However, there is more.

Service practice 5-6   Quality drops in first quarter

First quarter results of the American Customer Satisfaction Index show that there was a decrease in quality of goods and services in the two key sectors measured during this period. The sectors updated during the first quarter were the Transportation/Communications/Utilities sector and the Services sector. Business performance in the eyes of the consumer inched downward in this the second quarterly update since the ACSI was first released in October of 1994. The index has dropped overall from 74.5 to 74.1 (-.5%) on the ACSI's 100-point scale.

The transportation/Communications/Utilities sector shows an overall .5% drop in quality with airlines accounting for the largest share of the sector-wide decline, dropping 4.2%. Slight decreases were seen in the local telephone service, electric service, and network T.V. news broadcasting industries (all down 1.3%).

The services sector dropped from 74.4 at the end of 1994 to 74.2.

Of the three industries that comprise this sector, the motion picture and hospital industries were unchanged, while the hotel and motel industry dropped 2.7%.

The biggest surprise of the quarter was the U.S. postal service, which showed substantial improvement, up 13.1%. This was the only industry to show an increase this quarter. What is perhaps most shocking about this dramatic increase is that it came at a time when the postal service raised the price of first class postage. While the post office has made continuous efforts to improve its level of service, extended operating hours, and a refocused advertising campaign, it is important to point out that it started out with a comparatively low base rating of 61 in the initial ACSI.

"We need to keep an eye on this, because when customer satisfaction and quality decline, competitiveness declines," explains Jack West, chairman of the board of the American Society for Quality Control. "Industry needs to take notice of this so they can do something about it. Quality is a fundamental driver of customer satisfaction and competitiveness. If things turn around, consumers and business will benefit greatly."

The ACSI tracks the economy as a whole as well as, seven sectors, and 40 industries within those sectors. Changes within these sectors account for the overall change in the ACSI. Additional sectors of the economy will be updated quarterly. The index is co-sponsored by the American Society for Quality Control and the University of Michigan Business School.

AMERICAN CUSTOMER SATISFACTION INDEX
Consumer dissatisfied with goods and services

ACSI RESULTS

Quarterly Update for Transportation/Communication/Utilities and Services Sectors
Change in ACSI between baseline (Oct. 1994) and 1st quarter 1995.

Sector/Industry	Scores % Change	1st Q	Baseline
National ACSI	-0.5	74.1	74.5
TRANSPORTATION/ COMMUNICATIONS/ UTILITIES SECTOR	-0.5	75.1	75.5
Airline/Scheduled	-4.2	69	72
U.S. Postal Service (except express mail and package delivery)	+13.1	69	61
Parcel delivery/ express mail	0.0	81	81
Telecommunications/ local phone service	-1.3	78	79
utilities/electric service	-1.3	74	75
Broadcasting/TV (network news)	-1.3	76	77
SERVICES SECTOR	-0.3	74.2	74.4
Motion pictures	0.0	77	77
Hotels and motels	-2.7	73	75
Hospitals	0.0	74	74

Source: Services Marketing Today, vol. 10, no, 3, June 1995,

Statistical quality control (1920-1965)

control during the production process

As time went by, statistical methods were used for quality control. Partly, a shift from "end product" control, to control during the production process was observed. Consequently, the need for control of each final product no longer existed. Taking representative samples during the production process and a sample from end products was sufficient. In short: a shift from output to throughput in the production process occurred to check for quality.

Integral service quality (1965-1985)

coordination

Integral service quality emphasizes coordination between different departments. The main goal of this coordination is to be able to control cooperation in an organization and to achieve a more efficient interaction between functional units. This period is characterized by the fact that quality control does not only concern the product, but the production process as a whole. Now, more emphasis is put on throughput again. Although interfunctional cooperation is an important issue in the present literature about market orientation, it must be said that integral service quality does not yet pay enough attention to the customer and/or the market. The emphasis is more on the

internal side

internal side of the company. Thus, the need for a more external quality management vision was born.

Strategic quality management (1985-now)

strategic quality management

The present vision on quality management is reflected by the following definition of strategic quality management:

> "Strategic quality management is managing the process of continuous improvement of all internal processes, in order to fulfil the customer's need at the lowest possible costs."

This definition clearly expresses the relationship between service quality, marketing and market orientation.

These are also the years in which numerous quality awards were established, like the Deming Award in Japan, the Malcolm Baldridge Award in the USA and the European Quality Award. All these awards were aimed at stimulating managers to pay more attention to the quality of their products and services. The Malcolm Baldridge Award, was specifically designated to:

1. raise enterprise leaders' consciousness level regarding quality; and
2. provide a comprehensive framework for measuring business quality efforts.[13]

To apply for these awards, companies have to describe and analyze their own business, procedures and the like in a very detailed way. This goes further than the search for the mere presence of a number of procedures, which is one of the most important issues to qualify for one of the ISO 9000 certificates (International Organization for Standardization). Many more issues like leadership, planning and the like should be taken into consideration.[14]

*Service
practice
5-7
The Malcolm
Baldridge
Award*

In total, 1,000 points can be allocated to seven major categories for assessing applicants for the Award:

- leadership   90 points
- information and analysis   80
- strategic quality planning   60
- human resource development and
  management   150
- management of process quality   140
- quality of operational results   180
- customer focus and satisfaction   300

This division of points was used in the 1992 Malcolm Baldridge Award. It indicates a wide spectrum of issues is at stake, ranging from internal organization, internal quality and externally perceived quality.

Quality awards in countries like Sweden or The Netherlands or the award given by the European Foundation for Quality Management have more or less similar criteria and ratings. All awards have in common that a large number of points are allocated to the customers' point of view on quality and satisfaction.

It is self-evident that good quality has many advantages. But, how about the cost to achieve that quality level?

COST

It is our firm belief that the total quality cost of producing poor product or service quality is considerably higher than the total quality cost of producing good quality. We will argue why this is the case.

four components

The cost of quality is made up of four components: inspection costs, prevention costs, internal-failure costs and external-failure costs.

inspection costs
prevention costs

internal failure costs

external failure costs

Inspection costs are direct costs of testing, collecting and processing quality-control data. Prevention costs are the expenses incurred in avoiding poor quality. One can think of the cost of training programs, quality-improvement programs, process modifications and vendor-qualification programs. Internal failure costs are costs of scrapping or reworking faulty products, before they reach the consumer. If defective products are not intercepted before they reach the consumer, the consumer will become dissatisfied, may complain and external failure costs arise. Product liability claims may even arise for damage caused. These costs also include the possible expenses incurred to compensate for the inconvenience caused and to rebuild the positive image of the organization (e.g. a PR campaign). Stemming from poor-quality delivery, the highest cost of all probably – although expenses are not incurred *lost sales*

immediately – occurs when an unhappy customer never returns. These costs of lost relationships may be seen as lost sales, which can be very high if the lifetime of the relationship between consumer and supplier is taken into account. Then, the life-time value of a customer is lost.

Quality costs for delivering good quality consist of inspection costs and prevention costs only. If poor or inferior quality is produced, quality costs do not only consist of inspection and prevention costs. They also consist of internal-failure and external-failure costs as well as a share in the loss of sales, that the organization will suffer in the future because of dissatisfied customers. It is obvious that delivering poor quality *prevention strategy* will be more costly than delivering good quality. That is mainly why a prevention strategy aimed at avoiding poor quality is so important. The scheme illustrated in Figure 5-2 shows the total cost of quality.

Figure 5-2
Total cost of quality:
good quality versus
poor quality

Good quality	Poor quality
Inspection costs	Inspection costs
Prevention costs	Prevention costs
	Internal-failure costs
	External-failure costs
	Costs of lost sales
Total costs	Total costs

Poor service not only causes unnecessary costs for the service provider, but also for the customer.[15] The customer has to make extra efforts to have the poor service "repaired".[16] Often, these costs not only involve money but sacrifices like psychological costs (or other non-monetary costs) as well. A strategy aimed at improving the service now becomes a win-win strategy, as it is advantageous to both parties. The service provider even gets a chance to set a premium price, because the customer considers the service above average. Besides, it saves the customer the costs of seeking an alternative, as the relationship with the service provider is – for its continuous high service quality – mainly based on trust. Thus, this argument doubles the number of advantages of improving service quality.

Management should understand that service quality is a lot more than just sorting out good and bad products (= inspection of the output at the moment the product is finished) or preventing poor products and services from reaching the customers. For service-quality control, this means that the emphasis is now placed on the performance of the process control (throughput), instead of just on final inspection at the moment the service is delivered. By focussing on the various phases in the servuction process, management will see a range of possibilities to perform quality control effectively.[17]

By monitoring and supervizing the production process in steps, the inspector as well as the person inspected will find themselves in a much more pleasant situation. In addition, a lot of expenses (arising from reworking services or products which in the end appear to be of poor quality) can be saved. Monitoring and evaluating the production process is also known as a way of business process redesign (BPR) or business process re-engineering.[18]

Return On Quality

Until now, this section has indicated that quality pays off. Still, it is interesting to see whether these effects can be quantified. Roland Rust, Anthony Zahorik and Timothy Keiningham started a research program focussing on the Return On Quality (ROQ).[19] Their basic assumption is that "quality is an investment..." therefore it "is a conscious attempt to place quality improvement expenditures on an equal basis with other investment decisions". In order to compute the net present value of the quality investments, four assumptions are underlying in their model:

1. quality is an investment;
2. quality efforts must be financially accountable;
3. it is possible to spend too much on quality; and
4. not all quality expenditures are equally valid.

"The ROQ approach enables managers to determine where to spend on service quality, how much to spend, and the likely financial impact from service expenditures, in terms of revenues, profits, and return on investments in quality improvement – the return on quality."[20]

THE QUALITY AUDIT

Quality improvement aims at bringing an organization's service quality to a higher level. A quality audit can be used to determine whether a specified quality level has been achieved.

quality audit

A quality audit is a systematic examination of an organization's quality system with a view to determining whether objectives (the desired quality level) are (can be) achieved (by the quality system). In performing a quality audit, the end product/ service or the level of ROQ is not the only relevant issue. The emphasis is placed on

organizational processes

whether the organizational processes are managed in such a way that a constant quality level can be achieved (or even guaranteed).

internal audits

Three types of quality audits can be distinguished. Internal audits are conducted by the managers of an organization themselves to evaluate their own performance.

external audits
extrinsic audits

External audits are conducted by an organization to evaluate the activities of its suppliers, agents, licensees, etc. Extrinsic audits are conducted by a buyer, an independent authority or a regulatory agency to check whether an organization meets the standards applied by these bodies.

ISO 9000 certificate

Often, as a reward for the effort made, an organization obtains a quality certificate from an independent authority, for instance an ISO 9000 certificate

(Internationational Standards Organization). Such a certificate must provide consumers with certainty about the quality of procedures applied and products or services they buy. To receive such a certificate, an extrinsic audit must be carried out.

four phases   Four phases can be distinguished in quality audits:

planning the audit

1. *planning the audit.* During this phase, the schedule is determined as well as who is going to perform the audit. The persons involved are informed and the required information is gathered and studied. If necessary, questionnaires are prepared beforehand or standard questionnaires are adjusted to relevant target groups;

performing the audit

2. *performing the audit.* This phase starts with a meeting, during which the employees involved are informed about the procedure. After that, using extensive questionnaires, interviews are held. In this stage of the audit it is also useful to observe the organizational process. Weaknesses discovered are examined carefully and a corrective action-plan is made. The performance phase ends up with a meeting of all persons involved, during which the results of the audit are discussed;

reporting

3. *reporting.* Findings are recorded in a report. In this report, defects are presented as well as a plan to correct the shortcomings. Often, a deadline is set; and

follow-up

4. *follow-up.* After some time, a check is made as to whether the corrective actions recommended have been taken and whether they have lead to the desired results.

Thus, the effectiveness of service-quality activities can be determined objectively by a quality audit. However, a quality audit gives a temporary impression which does not guarantee a permanent high-quality level for the future. This drawback can be obviated by conducting periodic audits. A quality audit is indissolubly associated with customers' judgements about quality, for example as a part of an internal or external audit. Quality can be described as meeting the user's requirements or expectations of a product or service. Therefore, the user – the internal or external customer – is the best judge of quality. There are several ways to find out how customers experience quality. Two important sources of information are customer research and complaint registration.[21]

CUSTOMER RESEARCH

Traditionally, customer research has been applied mainly to map customer needs. Based on the outcome of such research projects, the service provider determines which services to offer. Today, more and more organizations practise customer-re-

customers are satisfied search to detect whether customers are satisfied with the service delivered. Evaluation of the service delivered can provide a lot of information, e.g. to change the service delivery, if needed. In this way, it is possible to really improve quality. Important indicators to be investigated are, for instance, loyalty, repeat purchases, cross selling, satisfaction, complaints and compliments received. Complaints always receive a lot of attention in quality programs. In order to get this kind of information, customers should express their opinions, attitudes, satisfaction, dissatisfaction, etc. This knowledge must then be collected. Different forms of relevant market research will be discussed in Chapter Six.

Marriott Hotels check whether customers are satisfied with the service by providing every room with a questionnaire. The gold-printed text "We need your assistance to help us provide the service you expect" captures the attention of the guests. The information gathered from the questionnaires is analyzed in Amsterdam and then sent to the Marriott headquarters in Washington. Here, the information is used to compare all Marriott hotels with each other. Averages are computed and standards set for the next period.

COMPLAINT REGISTRATION

*number and nature of
complaints*

Complaints are an important source of information. The number and nature of complaints give an indication of the quality perception of customers. If the registration and analysis of complaints are performed properly, the service provider can determine which aspects of the quality perception do not meet customer expectations. It can also be determined upon which aspects of quality management the focus should be set for the next few months.

However, a problem is that not everyone who has had bad experiences or was dissatisfied will voice a complaint. A high proportion, if not the majority, will not complain but simply never use the service again. Therefore, it is not possible to control quality on the basis of complaint registration only. In addition to other sources (for example, customer research), complaint information is essential: for dissatisfied customers, it is easy to express the reasons for their discontent. Satisfied customers will find it more difficult to describe why they are satisfied.[22]

5.4 EXPECTATIONS AND PERCEPTIONS

In the literature on quality and satisfaction, expectations and perceptions play a decisive role. That is why we will elaborate on these concepts.

EXPECTATIONS

expectations

The concept of expectations has been widely used in many studies about consumer behavior. However, very little is known about what determines expectations and how these expectations are formed. We do know that people make certain demands on certain services, which are based on their own norms, values, wishes, needs, etc., so, we do know expectations are very individualistic. Also, it is known that expectations are not stable in the sense that they may change over time due to changes in aspiration levels or needs at a particular moment in time. Therefore, expectations will be domain specific and may alter under the influence of all kinds of new situations. Changes in household composition (certainly when a first child is born), for example, lead to different expectations in certain areas (one will be going out less and prefer to stay at home). In other words, there will be a certain link between expectations in a household and the stage in the household life cycle.

Expectations are not only determined by individuals themselves, but also by reference groups, external situations, norms, values, time, service provider and the like. Therefore, expectations cannot always be predicted by individual households or consumers. Sometimes it is easier to predict them with a more aggregate level of groups of consumers.

With respect to service encounters, this discussion about expectations implies that consumers themselves have to know what is expected of them. In short, what role they are supposed to play. The whole service encounter will be more efficient if the service provider and the consumer both know what role they are supposed to play (and accept that role). In fact, one could say that the service delivery process is comparable with a theatre play which contains a certain "script" about the different roles of the actors (consumer and contact personnel) that have to be learned.[23]

Expectations are complex in many ways. What do people mean when they talk about their expectations? They may give different meanings to this word. This may cause serious problems in researching expectations. One can think of the most ideal situation one wants to accomplish, what can be expected normally, or what can be expected reasonably speaking. Generally speaking, expectations can be formulated in terms of "what should be done" and in terms of "what will be done". However, more and other performance standards can be formulated as well. In the literature on consumer (dis)satisfaction, some distinctions are made about the kind of performance standards *four performance* consumers apply. Four different performance standards can be distinguished: the *standards* equitable performance or deserved performance; the ideal performance or desirable performance; the expected performance; and the minimal tolerable performance.[24]

Berry and Parasuraman (1991) discuss two levels of expectations and conclude:

> "Our findings indicate that customers' service expectations exist at two different levels: a *desired* level and an *adequate* level. The desired service level reflects the service the customer hopes to receive. It is a blend of what the customer believes 'can be' and 'should be'. The adequate service level reflects what the customer finds acceptable. It is, in part, a function of the customer's assessment of what the service 'will be', i.e. the customer's *predicted* service level."[25]

The difference between the desired service level and the adequate service level can *zone of tolerance* be called the zone of tolerance: "the extent to which customers recognize and are willing to accept heterogeneity".[26] In their focus group interviews, these scholars not only found considerable variation in customers' tolerance zones between various services, or between various service attributes, but also that they vary (expand or contract) over time, even for one particular service. This depends on the specific situation or need to be fulfilled. In their conceptual model, they came up with four main sections determining service quality:

expected service 1. the expected service component, consisting of the desired service level and the adequate service level and – consequently – the zone of tolerance;

antecedents of desired service 2. the antecedents of desired service such as enduring service intensifiers (= stable factors that lead the customer to a heightened sensitivity to service) and personal needs;

antecedents of adequate service 3. the antecedents of adequate service such as transitory service intensifiers (= temporary, usually short-term, individual factors that lead the customer to a heightened sensitivity to service), perceived service alternatives, self-perceived service role (= customers' perceptions of the degree to which they themselves influence the level of service they receive) and all kinds of situational factors; and

antecedents of both 4. antecedents of both predicted and desired service such as the explicit service promises made in advertising or personal selling, the implicit service promises (e.g. derived from tangibles or price), word of mouth communications, and past experiences.

This is all depicted in Figure 5-3. It illustrates why it is of utmost importance to define very clearly in research about satisfaction and quality, the concept of expectations. Both are usually researched in terms of the difference between expectations and perceptions. When expectations are not clearly defined they can be interpreted *bias* differently by different respondents. That will cause a bias in the findings and may – eventually – lead to wrong conclusions.

Service practice 5-9 Expectations on banking differ across countries

Barbara Lewis reports in a study in the UK and US banking industry about consumers' expectations towards banking services. She concludes:

"...both UK and US respondents were found to have very high expectations of service from their banks across most of the dimensions which were investigated; in particular with respect to reliability elements, and the honesty, trustworthiness and discretion of contact staff. There were some differences between respondent groups: UK bank customers gave higher ratings to privacy, interior and staff appearances, and using customer suggestions to improve service; and US respondents were more concerned about locations and parking, opening hours, the number of staff available to serve (with associated perceptions of slow-moving queues), and several of the personal characteristics of bank staff they came into contact with."[27]

time A final point in researching expectations refers to time dimension. In many studies, consumers are asked for their expectations and perceptions about a particular service *at the same moment*. Then they have to go back into their memory to formulate their prior expectations. These expectations may be affected, for instance, by a loss of memory, their present perceptions and/or a rationalization of their expectations in terms of their perceptions. So, ideally, it would be best to ask for expectations at the beginning of a service experience and for perceptions at the end.

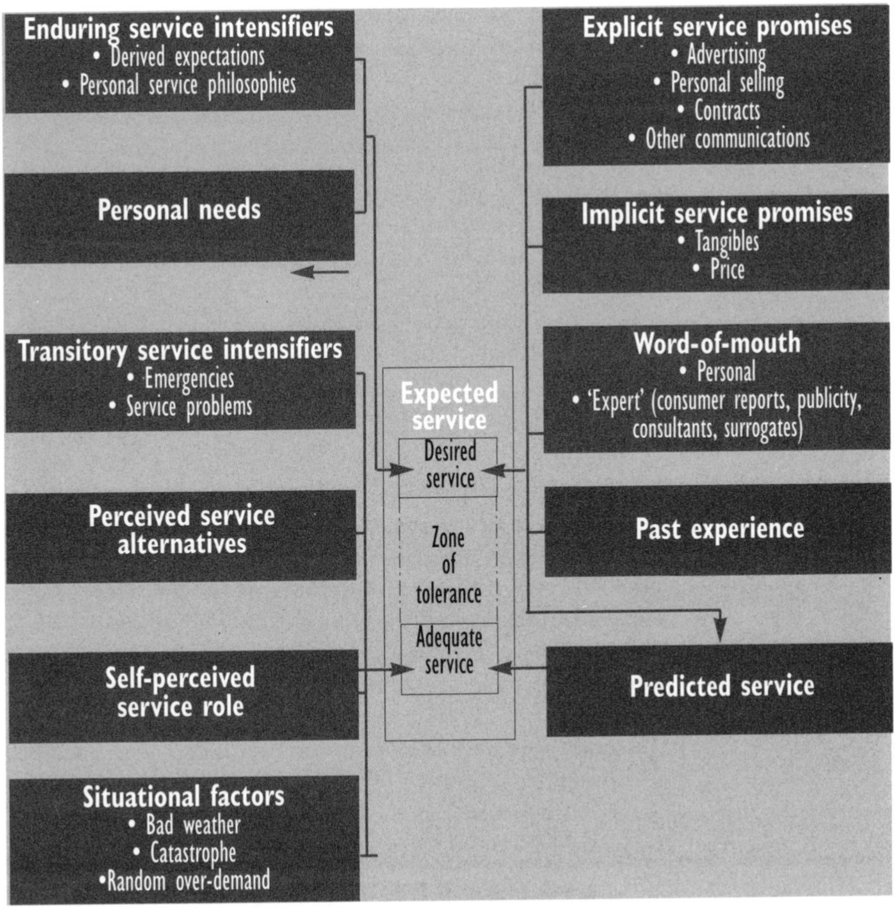

Figure 5-3
Nature and
determinants of
customer expectations
of service

PERCEPTIONS

perceptions

Perceptions are – translated literally – (the end result of one or a number of) observations. Perceptions can be based on the actual or supposed experiences. Schiffman and Kanuk (1987) define perceptions as follows:

> "Perception is defined as the process by which an individual selects, organizes and interprets stimuli into a meaningful and coherent picture of the world."[28]

subjective and selective
character

Service providers must be aware of the subjective and selective character of perceptions in general and of quality perceptions of consumers in particular. It not only concerns the perception of the service but also the perception of the service delivery process. The resulting attitudes about a particular service provider may change over time.[29] Changes over time in an individual customer's ratings of the components of service quality appear to be sensitive to the effects of a service change, but will result more in a long-term attitude change than in immediate attitude change. This partly explains why overall ratings of service quality are quite stable over time. Another explanation we came across is the fact that customers base their quality judgement on a number of experiences. Therefore, it is a more or less weighted score, or, in other words, it has been weighed out (see also Chapter Six).

Service practice 5-10 Perceptions on banking differ across countries

Barbara Lewis concludes in a study of the UK and US banking industry:

"...perceptions of service actually received were high: respondents were generally satisfied or very satisfied with most of the service quality criteria being assessed, with some significant differences between respondent groups. US customers were more satisfied with location and parking, and UK customers with appearance related physical features. Further, UK respondents were generally more satisfied with all the personal characteristics of staff and the elements of banks' responsiveness to their needs..."[30]

reputation and image

Perceptions partly determine the reputation and image of the service provider. This is important to realize since reputation is a key success factor in services and an issue consumers often use in their decison making process. In complex decision making processes about (new) services, consumers try to find some justification and knowledge of the service provider to make the right decision. This is especially true when they also have to consider experience and credence attributes besides search attributes in their decision process. Because of the importance of perceptions in evaluating services and service delivery processes we have discussed this issue here. Therefore, we can turn now to the final outcome of such processes: satisfaction or dissatisfaction with those services.

5.5 EVALUATION OF SERVICES AND (DIS)SATISFACTION WITH SERVICES

This section describes the ways in which satisfied and dissatisfied consumers can express their feelings. Also, the process of becoming satisfied or dissatisfied will be discussed in more detail. Finally, we will focus on the link between satisfaction and quality. The two resemble each other very closely. Both are based on comparing expectations and perceptions, but still there are some differences.

satisfaction and dissatisfaction

Many techniques can be used to detect satisfaction and dissatisfaction about services. Usually, questionnaires are used. The critical incidents technique may be used here as well.[31] The results of some of the CIT studies are presented in Table 5-1.[32] Three broad categories of incidents are found, namely:

1. employee response to service delivery system failures;
2. employee response to customer needs and requests; and
3. unprompted and unsolicited employee actions.

These three can be subdivided into other issues, as shown in Table 5-1.

TABLE 5-1 *Satisfaction and dissatisfaction about services*

Incidents	Percentage of satisfactory incidents in The Netherlands	Percentage of satisfactory incidents in the US	Percentage of dissatisfactory incidents in The Netherlands	Percentage of dissatisfactory incidents in the US
GROUP 1. Employee response to service delivery system failures				
Response to unavailable service	2.9	6.9	8.0	8.2
Response to unreasonably slow service	2.4	4.9	8.8	15.1
Response to other core service failures	6.6	11.5	25.2	19.6
Subtotal group 1	11.9	23.3	42.0	42.9
GROUP 2. Employee response to customer needs and requests				
Response to "special needs" customers	5.1	10.4	5.4	1.7
Response to customer preferences	19.3	14.7	19.6	10.5
Response to admitted customer error	7.3	5.8	5.4	2.3
Response to potentially disruptive others	1.5	2.0	1.7	1.1
Subtotal group 2	33.1	32.9	32.1	15.6
GROUP 3. Unprompted and unsolicited employee actions				
Attention paid to customer	17.3	13.8	6.9	13.6
Truly out-of-the ordinary employee behavior	19.3	6.3	7.5	11.6
Employee behaviors in the context of cultural norms	0.2	4.6	1.1	11.9
Gestalt evaluation	17.1	15.9	9.5	4.3
Performance under adverse circumstances	1.0	3.2	0.9	—
Subtotal group 3	55.0	43.8	25.9	41.5
Number of incidents per column (=100%)	411	347	464	352

satisfactory incidents

The results in Table 5-1 indicate that most of the satisfactory incidents in the two studies are related to the unprompted and unsolicited employee actions in delivering the service, especially the evaluation of the whole service and the attention paid to the customer. In both studies, the most unsatisfactory incidents refer to the employee's response to service delivery system failures, especially the incidents in aspects other than the core aspects of the service which do not meet basic standards for the industry. Table 5-1 also indicates some differences between the two studies. These are partly due to the different industries investigated.

unsatisfactory incidents

In the Dutch study, almost half of all the incidents were associated with "courtesy and understanding the customer": 52% of all the satisfactory incidents and 46% of all the dissatisfactory incidents.[33] Next, almost 20% of all the incidents could be labelled as dealing with "responsiveness"; this stands for almost a quarter of all the satisfactory incidents and almost 15% of all the dissatisfactory incidents. Communication is over-represented among the satisfactory incidents whereas "reliability" and "competence" are quality dimensions being over-represented among the dissatisfactory incidents.

These findings imply a few things for managing service quality. First of all, the most critical service quality dimension for satisfactory and dissatisfactory incidents refers to the service employee's courtesy behavior and their understanding of and responsiveness to the customer. Communication issues are thus important in accomplishing satisfactory service experiences. The negative experiences are caused mainly by lack of competence (knowledge, skills, etc.) and reliability (failures in delivering the service). Consequently, it is wise to have a thorough understanding of those determinants of service quality that can be labelled as satisfiers or dissatisfiers. In other words, which factors will especially increase satisfaction and which will affect dissatisfaction?[34]

satisfiers or dissatisfiers

Service practice 5-11 Satisfiers and dissatisfiers in banking

Another UK banking study has been carried out by Robert Johnston (1995b). He states, "Dissatisfiers represent the necessary but not sufficient conditions of product performance. There were also some satisfiers where unusual performance elicited strong feelings of satisfaction leading to complimenting behaviour, but typical performance or the absence of performance did not necessarily cause negative feelings."

For customers with a personal account at their bank, the satisfiers appeared to be attentiveness, responsiveness, care and friendliness. The typical dissatisfiers were integrity, reliability, responsiveness, availability and functionality. Note that responsiveness comes to the fore in both lists.[35]

ON (DIS)SATISFACTION IN GENERAL

after the process
during the process

Customers not only evaluate the service delivery after the process has taken place, but this also happens during the process. Consequently, it is necessary to look at the emergence of satisfaction or dissatisfaction about services in many ways. It appears to be useful to distinguish here between overall (dis)satisfaction and (dis)satisfaction with the service encounter. The overall (dis)satisfaction comprises of the (dis)satisfaction of the whole service delivery process or the evaluation of all the service encounters that have taken place in the past. The (dis)satisfaction with the service encounter may be comprised of two components, namely the (dis)satisfaction with discrete service encounter and/or the (dis)satisfaction with all the service encounters taking place during one service delivery process such as staying in a hotel for many days. Experiences with one part of the whole service process in hotels (check-in, hotel room, hotel restaurant, breakfast, and check out) affects other parts. That is why this process can be labelled as carry-over effects. A study done in a museum setting in Sweden and The Netherlands revealed carry-over effects between evaluating entrance, temporary collection, permanent collection, restaurant, museum shop, and wardrobe.[36]

overall (dis)satisfaction

(dis)satisfaction with the service encounter

carry-over effects

servicescape

The "servicescape" is also very important here.[37] This concept applies to the physical surroundings in which the service is offered. Their functionality and aesthetic appeal are relevant here. All these topics refer to unique aspects of the marketing mix in services: people, processes and physical evidence. A greater perceived control by the customer may decrease (potential sources of) customer dissatisfaction.[38]

perceived control

interaction

In general, it appears the interaction with the participants in the service encounter (customer, contact personnel, other customers and waiting) are dominant issues in becoming dissatisfied about services. This applies to the industrial buying process as well as the consumer. A US study in the business to business world revealed

> "... that expectations emerge and evolve as the purchasing process unfolds. A set of contingencies following initial expectations determines the extent to which an industrial buyer is satisfied or dissatisfied with delivery service. If the material arrives when expected, on the due date, purchasers are satisfied. Delay of an order can still result in a satisfied buyer when the seller (vendor) follows normative rules (= when the vendor could anticipate missing the due date, the vendor had an obligation to inform the purchaser of the problem and be responsive to any request that the purchaser made concerning the status of the order and due date) for late delivery, when the cause of the delay was not the vendor's fault, and when there was no loss (cost) to the buyer."[39]

We believe that consumers check whether the expectations are in line with the factual experiences of the service and service delivery. On the basis of such an evaluation of expectations and perceptions the customer will turn out to be satisfied or not. Cognitive as well as affective issues play a role in this process. Looking for gaps between expectations and perceptions is crucial to detect what should be improved (or not).

cognitive as well as affective issues

(dis)confirmation paradigm

This method of reasoning about the emergence of (dis)satisfaction is based on the (dis)confirmation paradigm.[40] The basic idea is about the confirmation or disconfirmation of expectations and actual experiences or perceptions. Satisfaction will emerge in two situations:

1. when an actual service meets the expectations; or
2. when the actual service exceeds the expectations (positive disconfirmation).

subjective evaluation process

Dissatisfaction will occur when the actual service is below the expected level (negative disconfirmation). So, satisfaction and dissatisfaction are the outcome of a subjective evaluation process. The degree of (dis)satisfaction and the past attitude about this service, in turn, will determine the "new" attitude towards the service, which will affect the intentions to rebuy the service. It should be noted however, that the sources of satisfaction are not necessarily the opposite of sources of dissatisfaction.[41]

action to express satisfaction or dissatisfaction

cost-benefit analysis

Consumers can undertake different kinds of action to express their satisfaction or dissatisfaction. The first decision consumers have to make is whether they really want to express this (dis)satisfaction. In order to do so, they must be motivated, capable and have the opportunity to really express that satisfaction or dissatisfaction. It is known that consumers do not make the effort to write a letter of complaint, for example. They do not consider it worthwhile or they think the costs of writing a complaint letter are more than the expected benefits.[42] Such a cost-benefit analysis will always be made one way or another in decision making processes about expressing (dis)satisfaction. These actions may be culturally bound. In some cultures, people will express their dissatisfaction more quickly and more overtly than in other countries. Also, differences may occur in what people consider as good and bad service themes.

Service practice 5-12 Good and bad services in retailing [43]

A study of what consumers consider good and bad service themes in retailing in Taiwan, the US and The Netherlands depicted some of those culturally bound differences. The most often mentioned good services themes were:

- Taiwan   polite, friendly, respect, feeling important, and competent/knowledgeable sales people;
- US   good merchandise/what I want is available, friendly, and good prices; and
- The Netherlands   personal approach, knowledgeable sales people, and helpful.

The most often mentioned bad service themes by customers are quite often the opposite of these good service themes. Nevertheless, the way they are formulated puts it sometimes in a slightly different perspective. These are:

- Taiwan   impolite/impersonal, and feeling ignored;
- US   doesn't have what I wanted, impolite/impersonal, not knowledgeable, and little selection; and
- The Netherlands   impolite/rude, no attention, and no information.

While in Taiwan and The Netherlands behavioral issues are at the top of the good service issues in retailing, US customers focus much more on the availability of the merchandise itself. This is reflected in the most often mentioned negative service themes. In all three countries impoliteness is detrimental to good service.

When we compare these findings to quality issues, we can say that US customers often mention topics related to the field of technical quality while the Taiwanese and Dutch customers mention topics related to the field of functional or relational quality. As mentioned in Chapter Four, these latter countries have a culture in which "people caring about other people" is more visible than in the US. That is reflected in these findings. Differences in national culture between the US and Taiwan (especially power distance) also come to the fore as explanatory variables in another study about differences in the intentions to express dissatisfaction in general and with respect to buying hamburgers, toasters, jackets, and vehicle repairs in particular. It was found that "... American respondents opt for direct confrontation; Taiwanese respondents take indirect routes in responding to a dissatisfying purchase." In fact, it appeared, "... American respondents are more likely to voice their complaints to the higher management of retail stores or to manufacturers than they were to stop buying the brand involved. On the other hand, respondents in Taiwan were more likely to stop buying the brand than to complain to the higher management of retail stores or to manufacturers."[44]

differences in national culture

EXPRESSING SATISFACTION

Satisfaction can be expressed in many ways, like positive word-of-mouth, giving compliments to the service provider and brand loyalty or loyalty to the service organization. Quite often, it is assumed that (all or most) satisfied consumers will be brand loyal. That need not be the case, especially when new entrants have come to the market or previous services are not available anymore ("out of stock", "not produced anymore"). Nevertheless, the notion that satisfied customers will show a higher repurchase rate than dissatisfied customers is an important one.

satisfied consumers brand loyal

repurchase rate

Customers can express their satisfaction by using the service or service organization again next time: the relationship is continued. In this case, a new phase in the relationship life cycle is started. After entering the relationhip, the phase of maintaining the relationship is begun. In this case, we can speak of a certain loyalty towards the service and/or service provider. Retention is at stake. The relationship will be longer and stronger when customers are more satisfied about the service delivery. This sounds very logical. However, certain conditions will have to be met in order to really understand it. As satisfied customers show a higher commitment to the service and the service provider, this service provider is seen as more attractive and switching to competitive service providers may mean there are higher costs; the relationship between satisfied customers and the service provider will thus be stronger.

relationship

retention

Mutual trust and responsiveness are important factors which determine the quality of the service delivery and the bond between the customer and the service provider. This all implies that it is more important to look further afield than stay at a superficial level of just looking at the phenomenon of satisfaction. It is important to analyze what is behind it, as Amex did.

bond

*Service
practice
5-13
Amex looks
beyond
satisfaction,
sees growth* [45]

Don't tell the researchers at American Express that customer satisfaction is important to business success – they know it. But there's another factor that the company rates as even more important.

"It's behavior that counts", said Doug Filak, senior director, marketing research for American Express Travel Related Services, the New York-based retail card-services division. Filak spoke recently at the ninth annual Customer Satisfaction & Quality Measurement Conference, sponsored by the AMA and the American Society for Quality Control.

"I don't know about your business, but in ours, what really matters is how we improve the bottom line", he said. "You have to look beyond satisfaction to what is happening in your business overall. A focus on improving customer satisfaction is critical, but by focusing on satisfaction, we learned more about our products' other dimensions."

Satisfaction research led the company to a better understanding of what customers wanted from the Amex cards in their pockets and purses. This understanding was the added benefit in a new quality strategy that helped American Express develop new products and direct positioning and promotion of its flagship charge card.

Before 1992, Filak said, American Express had no uniform method for customer satisfaction and quality measurement. Although the company had copious amounts of data on customers' card ownership and use – from who they were to what they bought – measurement programs "were *ad hoc* at best," Filak said.

Because methodologies differed from division to division, conflicting findings would appear. There was no way to share information. And satisfaction studies often focused on how Amex could improve internal processes, rather than looking to customers for information on their needs.

To change that, the company developed a total quality management program, American Express Quality Leadership (AEQL). Based on criteria set by the Malcolm Baldrige quality award, AEQL recognized that Amex had three constituencies that it must satisfy: employees, customers, and shareholders.

Satisfying shareholders depended on demonstrable improvements in business performance, profit and share value, and these depended on general excellence. American Express started improving from within. "Satisfied employees work harder, and produce better business results", Filak said. "We've seen strong links between employee satisfaction and overall satisfaction."

The company then began to study its relationships with two more traditional customer segments, American Express cardholders and service establishments. The goal? To define "moments of truth", or MOTs: crucial service points that made customers choose Amex over another card, or another card over Amex.

"We didn't really care about MasterCard or Visa as organizations," Filak said. "What we cared about was why you pull out that other card sometimes, and why you use American Express at other times. What we were really talking about was customer behavior."

Using primary customer research and a transaction-based survey sampling system, the company identified a number of quality attributes, out of which the MOTs grew. For instance, the accuracy, timeliness, and readability of a monthly statement made up a comprehensive "billing" MOT.

The nine final MOTs (customer service, billing, benefits, acceptance, advertising, fees, flexibility, rewards, and value) were incorporated into a relationship model as drivers of overall satisfaction for American Express cards. Overall satisfaction, in turn, was expected to be the force behind market behaviors such as card retention, share of spending, and actual spending.

More than a few attributes, however, proved to be strong enough factors in customer use that they affected retention and spending directly. American Express discovered that its original card's fees were a sticking point among both cardmembers and service establishments, discouraging its use despite a reputation for "great service, great billing, great everything else", Filak said.

The company also asked customers to rate competing cards on service MOTs, and used that information to develop a new product. The company had not yet offered a rewards card like Visa's American Airlines AAdvantage and United Mileage Plus cards. Today it has two, including the popular Delta SkyMiles Optima, an indirect result of its comparative satisfaction research.

"It led us to spend a lot more time working on a rewards-based product", Filak said. "Some of the major airline rewards cards were really not up to the service level that our customers expect, so their programs' satisfaction was actually very low. But card use was still high because of the rewards. It was an important piece of information for us in the development of our strategy."

The research helped identify the most important card attributes for new customer segments, permitting the company to differentiate and target individual card products. "Original card customers pay the annual fee and in return, expect status," Filak said. "For the Optima card, acceptance is more important, and we positioned it for retail use."

Amex continues to use AEQL research to back up strategic decisions. Using a one-point change chart, the company predicts the impact of any shift in customer satisfaction in a given quality attribute. For example, if certain cardmembers' satisfaction in customer service improves 1%, spending should go up approximately 8.5%.

"We've really been able to prove the linkage between improving customer satisfaction and business results," Filak said. "We've also shown that there are

> many components of a business that drive satisfaction of a product. But we couldn't look at satisfaction alone; we had to extend it to behavior."
>
> And consumer behavior has improved, he said. "We had a small share increase for the first time in 1996, and in our industry, one point is worth $1 billion in revenues. To American Express, these are big stakes."

commitment, involvement, elaboration

In most cases, it is too simple to state that satisfaction will automatically lead to repeat purchases or brand loyalty.[46] Satisfaction is a necessary condition to that end but it is not sufficient. Commitment to and involvement with that particular service will play an important role here too, as well as the elaboration on the choice made and experiences found. Consumers must have the motivation, the capability and the opportunity to evaluate the brand relative to the reference point employed. It is also important to make a distinction between two types of satisfaction in order to really understand the link between satisfaction and future buying behavior: manifest satisfaction and latent satisfaction. Manifest satisfaction will lead to true brand loyalty. Then, consumers are committed to the brand, have elaborated on their choice and do not want to switch. Consumers who are latently satisfied with a particular service or brand may repurchase that service but are also very open to other brands. They do not have a strong relationship with that particular service provider. They are not so motivated for that particular brand, nor did they elaborate on their choice. Therefore, they may switch easily.[47]

manifest satisfaction and latent satisfaction

Expressing Dissatisfaction

do nothing at all; express dissatisfaction

When customers are dissatisfied, they can undertake different kinds of action as well. It may sound strange, but the first action is, in fact, to do nothing at all. One can express dissatisfaction in many ways, for example by complaining to the service provider or to a consumer union. Another action could be to never visit the service provider again. Two models exist in explaining the ways to express dissatisfaction: the economic model and the behavioral model.[48] In the economic model, basically, the perceived cost, the perceived benefits and the probability of success determine whether consumers will express their dissatisfaction and how. In the behavioral model, this is determined basically by the ability and motivation to do so. The classical Day and Landon (1976) study reveals how dissatisfied Americans express their dissatisfaction about services (multiple answers could be given in Table 5-2).

economic model, behavioral model

switching

One of the other actions dissatisfied customers can apply is switching to another service provider. Recent studies showed which reasons induce such switching behavior in service industries.[49] These findings are again based on a critical incidents study. In interpreting the findings, one should bear in mind that multiple reasons for switching could be given. The most often mentioned reasons for switching were related to the core service failures (more than 44% of all critical incidents inducing switching). This group encompasses such issues as mistakes or a series of mistakes during one service encounter or over a period, decreases in service levels; billing problems (incorrect billing or failure to correct incorrect billings in a timely manner); and "service catastrophes" (service failures causing damage to the customer's person, family, pets, or belongings; or damage in terms of losing time or money). The second largest group (34%) consisted of issues about failures in the service encounter (uncaring, impolite, unresponsive and unknowledgeable). In this US study, the third largest group refers to pricing issues (30%): high price, price increases, unfair pricing and deceptive pricing. The fourth group of reasons to be mentioned here is labelled "inconvenience" (these counted for 21% of all critical incidents). The customer felt inconvenienced by the service provider's location, hours of operation, waiting time for service, or waiting time to get an appointment. The other reasons found (response to failed service, competition, ethical problems, involuntary switching) each counted for less than 20% of the switching incidents.

TABLE 5-2 *Americans being dissatisfied about services expressing this dissatisfaction*

I told my friends of my experience and urged them to avoid the product	47.3% of the respondents
I resolved to never purchase/use that service again	39.3%
I contacted the store to complain	34.5%
I returned the merchandise for a replacement	13.1%
I contacted the "manufacturer" to complain	9.1%
I contacted a local or state official	6.9%
I contacted my lawyer about possible legal action	6.2%
I contacted the Better Business Bureau	5.8%
I contacted a federal regulatory agency (like the Federal Trade Commission)	2.2%
I contacted my congressman or senator	1.8%
I contacted the officer of Consumer Affairs in Washington, DC	0.4%
I contacted a consumer advocate to suggest an investigation (someone like Ralph Nader)	0.4%

Service practice 5-14 Being dissatisfied about your CPA: what to do? [50]

In Canada, firms reacted in four different ways to express their dissatisfaction with their Certified Public Accountant (CPA). Most of the firms are "passives" (42%); they do not have the inclination to express their dissatisfaction in one of the three ways mentioned. Secondly, the "voicers" (34%) are a substantial group of firms. These firms will complain to the CPA and engage in negative word-of-mouth. Thirdly, the "activists" will engage in all three modes of actively expressing dissatisfaction (20%). Finally, the "irates" demonstrate above average private responses such as engaging in negative word-of-mouth or switching CPA (5%).

As explanations for being dissatisfied, it was found that many CPAs are not market or customer oriented. Most of the negative quality evaluations refer to problems about billing (unclear, not transparent pricing), value for money, giving advice, continuity in the auditing team, efficient cooperation with the client and speed of response.[51] To us, all these issues demand close relationships between the service provider and the client in order to understand the client and know the expectations the client holds. Then it is possible to deliver tailor made services.

lack of information

Summarizing the findings from several international studies about complaints in different service industries, the conclusion is that complaints are indeed industry specific. Many complaints about insurances can be attributed to a lack of information. In banking, a very contact-intensive service-industry, many complaints refer to contact personnel's behavior and waiting. Most complaints about medical services deal with the core service, the care provided, people's behavior, and incorrect or unclear billing. Also, in postal services, many complaints are about the technical quality of the service: the delivery of the mail on time and in good condition.[52]

ON SATISFACTION AND QUALITY

service quality as an antecedent of satisfaction

Recently, discussion arose regarding whether satisfaction leads to quality, or, whether quality results in satisfaction. The results were mixed.[53] Nevertheless, many authors posit very clearly that service quality is regarded mostly as an antecedent of satisfaction.[54] So, the satisfaction judgement is based on service quality. Others conclude that the two concepts resemble each other quite closely but are still different.[55] Both are an overall evaluation of a service provider and its offering. However, the service quality evaluation will be relatively more objective than the satisfaction evaluation which in turn impacts on behavior.

In assessing satisfaction, the decision process will be even more subjective than in the case of service quality. Now, additional cognitive and affective processes will be used in the comparison of expectations and actually perceived experiences. Here, one can think of attribution of the actual service delivery, a cost benefit analysis, and emotions. Moreover, other dimensions than the quality dimensions can be taken into account.

These differences imply satisfaction and quality may (but need not necessarily) differ from one another. High quality does not always coincide with high satisfaction. The reverse also does not always apply.

Therefore, one may conclude that quality judgement is just one of the many aspects determining customer satisfaction about services. In other words, "... service quality is the key driver of usage rates (just as it is the key driver of customer retention ...)...".[56] Stated differently, it is important to have a thorough understanding of the behavioral consequences of service quality.[57] Superior service quality will lead to more favorable behavioral intentions by customers to stay/remain which results in ongoing revenues, increased spending and referred customers. On the other hand, inferior service quality will lead to unfavorable behavioral intentions by customers (e.g. switching) leading to decreased spending, lost customers and additional costs to attract new customers.

5.6 EVALUATING QUALITY

In discussing how consumers evaluate service quality, we will pinpoint three topics. When used in combination, they provide valuable insights into the quality of service-delivery processes. We are talking about:

1. the five underlying dimensions of service quality;
2. the three types of quality; and
3. the three types of attributes consumers may use in evaluating the services and in the accompanying evaluative processes.

Understanding these issues is important since quality determines satisfaction to a large extent, which in turn will affect customer retention and the relationship lifecycle.

FIVE DIMENSIONS

overall performance

In evaluating service quality, an assessment of the overall performance of an organization is not enough. This provides little or no insight into the shortcomings and excellent parts of the service delivery. Managers cannot take any decision based on such an overall judgement. It is not specific enough for managerial purposes. It is therefore necessary to describe services by a number of characteristics, which can be applied deliberately to measure service quality. In the previous sections, many of those attributes have been mentioned already. Robert Johnston (1995b) discussed a large number of studies in which various service quality attributes had been used. He came up with 18 determinants of service quality for his own banking study.

18 determinants of service quality

Service practice 5-15 Eighteen determinants [58]

Access: the physical approachability of service location, including the ease of finding one's way around the service environment and the clarity of route.

Aesthetics: the extent to which the components of the service package are agreeable or pleasing to the customer, including both the appearance and the ambience of the service environment, the appearance and presentation of service facilities, goods and staff.

Attentiveness/helpfulness: the extent to which the service, particularly of contact staff, either provides help to the customer or gives the impression of interest in the customer and shows a willingness to serve.

Availability: the availability of service facilities, staff and goods to the customer. In the case of contact staff, this means both the staff/customer ratio and the amount of time each staff member has available to spend with each customer. In the case of service goods, availability includes both the quantity and the range of products made available to the customer.

Care: the concern, consideration, sympathy and patience shown to the customer. This includes the extent to which the customer is put at ease by the service and made to feel emotionally (rather than physically) comfortable.

Cleanliness/tidiness: the cleanliness and the neat and tidy appearance of the tangible components of the service package, including the service environment, facilities, goods and contact staff.

Comfort: the physical comfort of the service environment and facilities.

Commitment: staff's apparent commitment to their work, including the pride and satisfaction they apparently take in their job, their diligence and thoroughness.

Communication: the ability of the service providers to communicate with the customer in a way he or she will understand. This includes the clarity, completeness and accuracy of both verbal and written information communicated to the customer and the ability of staff to listen to and understand the customer.

Competence: the skill, expertise and professionalism with which the service is executed. This includes the carrying out of correct procedures, correct execution of customer instructions, degree of product or service knowledge exhibited by contact staff, the rendering of good, sound advice and the general ability to do a good job.

Courtesy: the politeness, respect and propriety shown by the service, usually contact staff, in dealing with the customer and his or her property. This includes the ability of staff to be unobtrusive and uninterfering when appropriate.

Flexibility: a willingness and ability on the part of the service worker to amend or alter the nature of the service or product to meet the needs of the customer.

Friendliness: the warmth and personal approachability (rather than physical approachability) of the service providers, particularly of contact staff, including cheerful attitude and the ability to make the customer feel welcome.

Functionality: the serviceability and fitness for purpose or "product quality" of service facilities and goods.

Integrity: the honesty, justice, fairness and trust with which customers are treated by the service organization.

Reliability: the reliability and consistency of performance of service facilities, goods and staff. This includes punctual service delivery and an ability to keep the agreements made with the customer.

Responsiveness: speed and timeliness of service delivery. This includes the speed of throughput and the ability of the service providers to respond promptly to customer requests, with minimal waiting and queuing time.

Security: personal safety of the customer and his or her possessions while participating in or benefiting from the service process. This includes the maintenance of confidentiality.

The number of attributes to describe and analyze a service may differ per service. However, there are a particular group of features which are always coming to the fore. The first results from the qualitative studies Parasuraman, Zeithaml and Berry conducted in researching service quality with their model named SERVQUAL, which depicted ten dimensions of service quality.

ten dimensions of service quality

Service practice 5-16 Ten dimensions [59]

Zeithaml, Parasuraman and Berry found these ten dimensions:

- *tangibles*: appearance of physical facilities, equipment, personnel, and communication materials;
- *reliability*: ability to perform the promised service dependably and accurately;
- *responsiveness*: willingness to help customers and provide prompt service;
- *competence*: possession of the required skills and knowledge to perform the service;
- *courtesy*: politeness, respect, consideration, and friendliness of contact personnel;
- *credibility*: trustworthiness, believability, honesty of the service provider;
- *security*: freedom from danger, risk, or doubt;
- *access*: approachability and ease of contact;
- *communication*: keeping customers informed in language they can understand and listening to them; and,
- *understanding the customer*: making the effort to know customers and their needs.

Further and more quantitative research led these researchers to the conclusion that consumers use five underlying dimensions in judging service quality. We see these five dimensions in all four types of service organizations, as mentioned in our service typology in Chapter One. They are general dimensions underlying the quality of many services. These five dimensions are a summary of ten dimensions, found in earlier studies. The dimensions we are talking about now express, to a certain extent, the benefits customers get from the service delivery. In other words, they reflect - customers' subjective judgements about the value received by service performance.

benefits

five dimensions

Here are the five dimensions:

1. *tangibles*: appearance of physical facilities, equipment, personnel and communications materials;
2. *reliability*: ability to perform the promised service dependably and accurately;
3. *responsiveness*: willingness to help customers and to provide prompt service;
4. *assurance*: knowledge and courtesy of employees and their ability to convey trust and confidence; and,
5. *empathy*: caring, individualized attention the firm provides to its customers.

Figure 5-4 shows how the ten dimensions are related to the five dimensions of SERVQUAL.

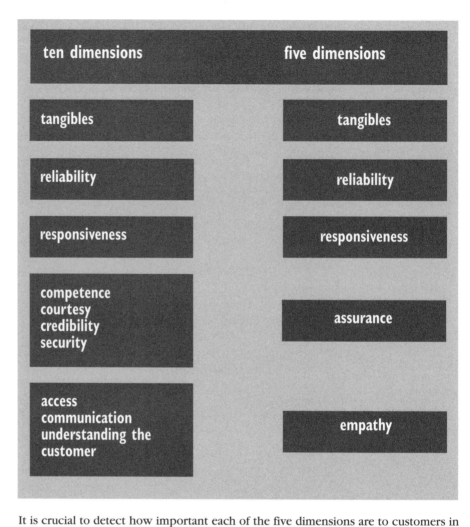

Figure 5-4
From ten to five dimensions

It is crucial to detect how important each of the five dimensions are to customers in general or to specific target groups. This affects the decision on which dimension(s) a service provider should concentrate its efforts in various market segments. Parasuraman (1995, p. 158) reports on three banking studies in Australia and the US.

the two most important dimensions

It appears that reliability and responsiveness are considered to be the two most important dimensions of these five in the two countries. We have seen similar findings in other studies. So, there seems to be a general finding that these two dimensions are the most important dimensions of service quality. It is also noteworthy to see that these two and many of the other dimensions hinge upon the service employees'

service employees' behavior

behavior and the way it is perceived by the customer.[60]

THREE TYPES OF SERVICE QUALITY

As stated in Chapter One it is possible to distinguish two dimensions of service quality: the technical quality of the outcome of the service delivery and the functional quality of the service-delivery process.[61] These two dimensions together determine the image of the service provider (see Figure 5-5). The service organization's image determines service quality, in turn, and thus whether a customer continues the relationship with the service provider or not. If the image is negative, there is little chance that new customers will actually be attracted. In fact, the technical quality concerns the outcome of a service (*what* is offered and received?). The functional quality concerns the way in which the service is delivered (*how* is it offered and received?). In Chapter One, we also added relational quality to these two (by *whom* is the service delivered?).

what is offered,
how is it offered,
by whom

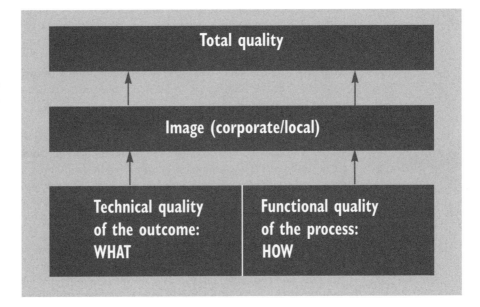

Figure 5-5
Grönroos' two service
quality dimensions

THREE TYPES OF ATTRIBUTES

If we take a closer look at the various criteria customers use to evaluate services, it appears these attributes of services and service delivery processes are not completely comparable. We can make a distinction between search attributes, experience attributes and credence attributes. Search attributes are characteristics customers can evaluate before an actual purchase. Experience attributes can only be evaluated during or after the service delivery. Credence attributes are characteristics customers cannot (or hardly can) evaluate, even after service delivery. Research shows customers evaluate the service quality mainly by experience attributes.[62]

search attributes,
experience attributes,
credence attributes

Now services have to be made – preferably objectively – measurable. The above classification can be useful to prepare, for instance, a questionnaire to map customers' experiences and evalutions of services. The emphasis will have to be different, depending on the nature of the service. For widely-known standard core services, search attributes will be very important in customers' judgements about quality. For unknown customized services, on the other hand, credence attributes will play a major role.

Now that we have discussed so many issues of service quality, we will present some models or frameworks which can be used to investigate service quality.[63]

5.7 THE SERVQUAL MODEL[64]

qualitative techniques

quantitative techniques

To gain a thorough insight into the many issues of service quality, two different methods can be applied: qualitative and quantitative methods. Examples of qualitative techniques are individual or group interviews with users, periodic interviews with the same group of users (panel), complaint analyses and mystery shopping (judgements of independent researchers acting as customers). Examples of quantitative techniques are the large-scale surveys with questionnaires, analyses of the number of complaints or the number of credit notes and the use of them as an indication for corrective action.

Zeithaml, Parasuraman and Berry's SERVQUAL model, which will be described in this section, can be operationalized by both qualitative and quantitative research. However, till now, the SERVQUAL model is mainly used in quantitative research (consisting of questionnaires).[65] Our own experience shows SERVQUAL can be applied via written questionnaires as well as by telephone interviews. In the SERVQUAL model, a distinction is made between the customers and the organization which consists of managers and (other) front office and back office employees working in various units and levels within the whole service organization (see Figure 5-6). The user-quality is measured as the differences between the expectations and perceptions of customers (Gap 5). The causes of (possible) poor quality are identified by four internal gaps in the organization (Gap 1-4). Here, we will discuss the SERVQUAL-model in detail.

CUSTOMER EXPECTATIONS[66]

opinion of other customers, personal needs

past experiences

external communications of the service provider

The SERVQUAL studies started with qualitative research in order to gain more insight into service quality. Focus-group interviews showed that a number of factors affected customers' expectations. First, the opinion of other customers is very important. Many customers said, for instance, that the high quality of a repair service was based on recommendations of friends and neighbors. Second, personal needs shape expectations. Customers of a credit-card organization, for instance, may want a maximum credit limit, where other organizations pursue more strict policies on this matter. Third, past experiences affect expectations. Customers, already experienced in private banking, expect more professional knowledge from banking consultants than customers with no experience. Finally, the external communications of the service provider play a key role with regard to what and how expectations are formed.

Consumer expectations about the service quality are affected by promises made by the service provider's indirect and direct messages. For example, a bank promises that customers will be served within three minutes or that phones will be answered within ten seconds. The SERVQUAL-model, with all its gaps, reflects a way of thinking that is applied frequently in present service-quality studies.

*Figure 5-6
The SERVQUAL
model*

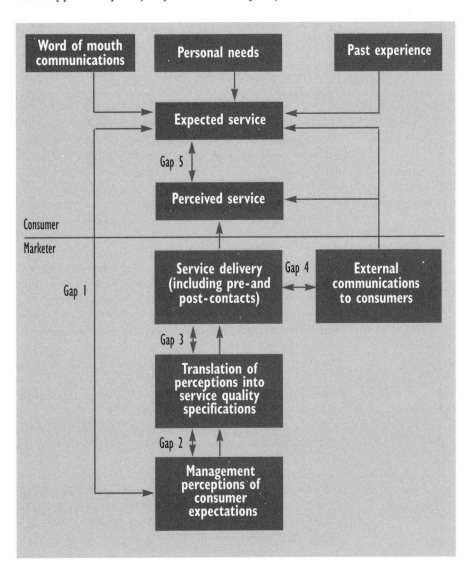

USER'S QUALITY

*quality as the
difference between
customers' expectations
and perceptions*

The SERVQUAL model defines quality as the difference between customers' expectations and perceptions of the service delivered. To measure quality, the respondents are asked to answer two sets of questions, dealing with the same subject. For example, customers of a bank are asked:

- employees in excellent banks will give prompt service to customers.
- employees in bank XYZ give you prompt service.

Customers complete these two questions on a 5, 7 or 9 point Likert-scale, indicating the degree to which they agree with the statement. For each subject and for the total service, a quality judgement can be computed according to the following formula:

Perception - Expectation = Quality
or P - E = Q

formula　　This formula implies the following in talking about service quality: if expectations exceed perceptions, quality obviously is poor and if perceptions exceed expectations, quality is excellent. This way of reasoning implies that two "curious" situations may exist:

- if consumers have low expectations which are met, quality exists; and
- if consumers receive more and better services than they need, excellent services are delivered. The quality level then may be too high for these customers.

All these situations indicate that excellent service delivery is a delicate matter. A service provider must have thorough knowledge of customer expectations. The provider must also be able to forecast competitors' behavior. In the latter situation, the service provider can hardly keep expectations low, if competitors deliver higher quality (which makes our second "curious" point rather unrealistic).

two kinds of questions　　The latest insights prompt two kinds of questions about expectations:
about expectations

desire　　1. the expectation with respect to what customers desire in a certain industry (already existing expectation question E)?;

minimum acceptable　　2. the expectation with respect to what customers will accept from this particular
level　　organization as a minimum acceptable level of the service offered?

zone of tolerance　　The difference between these two expectations is the "zone of tolerance".[67] This zone reflects what is tolerated from this specific service provider, when compared with the ideal situation in the branch or industry. Expectation question E is a "should do" question, whereas the second, newly added, expectation question refers to "acceptable" service, not "predicted" service.

The total service quality can now be measured, using the five dimensions mentioned before: tangibles, reliability, responsiveness, assurance and empathy. Service quality can be measured by these five dimensions via 22 questions. These 22 items are mentioned in Figure 5-7.[68] The expectation question (fill in: "excellent company") concerns the excellent company in the industry. The perception question (fill in: "company X") relates to the firm, of which the service quality is examined.[69]

higher performance　　Service quality can be influenced in two ways. Thus, not only a higher performance can affect service quality positively. The same effect can be achieved by lowering the

lowering the expectation level

managing expectations

expectation level. However, we should take into account competitors' behavior in this particular situation. Considering competitors' offerings, it might not be wise to lower quality expectations. In the long term, maintaining high expectations only makes sense if performance is equal to these expectations. So, managing expectations is crucial to service firms. Here, marketing management and all contact personnel have to play an important role although the whole internal organization (front and back office) contributes to accomplish a certain level of service quality (or not).

Figure 5-7
22 items of the SERVQUAL-questionnaire

DIMENSION	QUESTION

Tangibles
  1 The technical equipment of ... is totally up to date
  2 The office is attractive
  3 The employees are well dressed
  4 Tools to help perform the service are attractive

Reliability
  5 Promises to perform the sevice within a certain time are always kept
  6 Complaints or problems solved with great concern
  7 ... delivers the service correctly at one go
  8 ... delivers the service at the time agreed on
  9 The administration/order registration is never incorrect

Responsiveness
(–) 10 One cannot expect ... to inform customers about the exact time of delivery
(–) 11 It is not realistic to expect immediate service delivery from ...
(–) 12 Employees of ... are not always willing to help customers
(–) 13 It is acceptable that employees are too busy to help customers immediately

Assurance
 14 The behavior of the employees of ... impresses customers with the reliability of the service
 15 Customers feel confident when in contact with employees of ...
 16 Employees are always friendly and courteous
 17 Employees possess the knowledge to answer questions of customers

Empathy
 18 From employees of ... one cannot expect to pay attention to each customer individually
(–) 19 From employees of ... one cannot expect to pay personal attention to each customer
(–) 20 It is not realistic to expect from employees of ... to understand the specific needs
     of customers
(–) 21 It is not realistic to expect from employees of ... to only serve the interest of the customer
(–) 22 One cannot expect that opening hours are appropriate for all customers

INTERNAL GAPS IN THE SERVQUAL GAPS MODEL

causes for possible quality differences

answer the questionnaire from the customer point-of-view

It is now useful to consider the causes for possible quality differences. Therefore, not only users, customers, consumers and/or buyers are asked to answer the questionnaires, but employees and (top) managers as well. They are asked to answer the questionnaire from the customer point-of-view: imagine yourself in the customer's position and answer the questions. The model assumes that differences between the service desired by the customer and the service finally delivered by the service provider may be caused by the following four Gaps:

Gap 1:

Gap 1: consumer expectation – management perception gap.
> In formulating its service-delivery policy, management does not correctly perceive or interpret consumer expectations;

Gap 2:

Gap 2: management perception – service quality specification gap.
> Management does not correctly translate the service policy into rules and guidelines for employees;

Gap 3:

Gap 3: service quality specification – service delivery gap.
> Employees do not correctly translate rules and guidelines into actions; and

Gap 4:

Gap 4: service delivery – external communications gap.
> External communications - promises made to customers – do not match the actual service delivery.

The SERVQUAL-model (see Figure 5-6) shows the relationship between the external Gap 5 (perceived quality) and the internal gaps 1–4. Gap 5 depends on the size and direction of the four gaps associated with the delivery of service quality on the marketeer's side. If Gaps 1 to 4 are reduced, the service quality can be improved. It is, however, of major importance to examine whether the organization's opinions (employees individually or of groups of employees) are in line with customers' opinions about quality. If these opinions differ widely, the company will have opinions about service quality deviating from the consumers'. This is a severe managerial problem, to be solved immediately.

Such differences in the perceptions of quality affect the way in which the service is delivered. To be able to deliver excellent services, it is necessary to bring the customer's perception and the employee's perception together. After comparing the perceptions, it is clear that – besides the external (quality) Gap – a number of internal gaps can be identified.

relative importance of the internal gaps

Research into the relative importance of the internal Gaps 1 to 4 for the customer's quality perception shows that Gap 3 and Gap 4, especially, play a role in this matter. This means organizations should concentrate their efforts and tools on factors that influence primarily these Gaps: e.g. hiring qualified personnel, providing the right tools or equipment, giving employees more freedom of action, stimulating team work, introducing procedures for an optimal cooperation between, especially, the marketing department and the operational department and providing true, fair information.

CAUSES OF POOR SERVICE QUALITY

Using the four gaps identified in the SERVQUAL model, we will now discuss the factors explaining or contributing to a failure to deliver the expected service quality.[70]

Factors influencing Gap 1

management perception gap

Management perceptions of customer expectations with regard to the desired quality of a product or service may not be in line with real customer expectations. Three factors can cause this customer expectation – management perception gap (Gap 1).

First, managers may think that they understand their customers' needs and do not invest in marketing research. Neglecting research will lead to incorrect or incomplete manager perceptions. Especially for the growing number of markets where customer expectations are changing rapidly, it is absolutely necessary to conduct sound market research regularly.

Second, managers may spend too little time in gaining first-hand knowledge of their customers. Managers themselves may have too little contact with customers or collect too little information from employees who regularly interact directly with them. Figures, tables and analyses provide lots of information, but not a profound understanding of what customers really think and expect. Customer-contact personnel can also give their opinions about customer expectations. Thus, managers should listen carefully to these employees in particular, or try to gain an insight into customer expectations by being involved in in-depth research, or actually delivering services themselves. Some service organizations let their (top) managers perform as front office employees for a certain period per year. Managers of Hertz have to stand behind the desk to rent cars and bell boys in the Marriott Hotel are managers on a weekly "training" course. In this way, managers do have close contact with customers.

The third factor that may cause Gap 1, is the number of layers of management between top managers and customer-contact personnel: the organization's hierarchy. The larger the number of layers between management and contact personnel, the less objective the information will be that finally reaches management. On each level, the information will be interpreted differently and passed on to the next level.

Thus, the discrepancy between consumer expectations and management perceptions is influenced by:[71]

marketing research orientation

- marketing research orientation (–) which has to solve problems due to inaccurate information, inaccurately interpreted information about expectations and non-existent demand analysis;

upward communication

- upward communication (–), necessary to bring information from the firm's interface with its customers to management; and

levels of management

- levels of management (+).

Factors influencing Gap 2

management perception–service quality specification gap

Gap 2, the so called management perception–service quality specification gap, occurs when management correctly perceives customer expectations, but is unable to translate this information into clear quality specifications. Four factors may account for the discrepancy between managers' perceptions of customer expectations and the actual specifications established by managememement for a service. One explanation for the size of Gap 2 is management commitment to service quality (–). Management may focus more on cost reduction and short-term profit than on quality. These two objectives are more easily formulated and results are more easily measured. Other objectives may therefore receive less attention. Perhaps the department formulating (corporate) objectives hardly profits from designing quality specifications. Sometimes, the marketing department is the only one benefitting, or other departments think of improving quality only in terms of additional cost instead of additional revenues and profits. Another factor relating to the absence of management commitment to service quality is a lack of resources allocated to service quality; no internal quality programs exist; managers are hardly committed to quality and don't recognize its importance. A second factor that can play a role is the existence of goal setting (–). The absence of a formal quality program to define the quality of services will increase Gap 2. Some attention to quality at management level may be the case, but this has not (yet) resulted in clear guidelines and standards for delivering the required service quality by the employees. The third fator is related to the second factor: task standardization (–). Determining effective and accurate quality standards depends on the degree to which tasks can be standardized. Task standardization makes it easier to set and establish quality stadards. A fourth explanation of Gap 2 is the perception of feasibility (–). This is closely related to managers' perceptions of the extent to which meeting customer expectations is feasible. Management knows that customers have certain expectations, but employees have the impression that meeting these expectations is not feasible. Possibly, this impression is caused by the fact that employees do not really believe that they can meet the expectations. It can also be caused by a lack of organizational capabilities, skills or resources.

management commitment to service quality

existence of goal setting

task standardization

perception of feasibility

Factors influencing Gap 3

service quality specification–service delivery gap, internal organization

This service quality specification–service delivery gap occurs when employees are unable or unwilling to perform the service at the desired level. Factors accounting for the size of this gap are manyfold. They all have to do with the internal organization of the firm:

teamwork

1. *teamwork* (–)

   Inadequate or no teamwork at all is reflected here to the extent that employees do not respect colleagues or managers, and the extent to which employees do not feel personally involved or committed to the service role;

employee-job fit

2. *employee-job fit* (–)

   Lack of employee-job fit reflects the extent to which an employee is unable to perform the service adequately. Is the employee suited for his job?;

technology-job fit

3. *technology-job fit* (−)

The appropriateness and adequacy of the tools or technology employees use to perform their service roles;

perceived control

4. *perceived control* (−)

The extent to which employees perceive they are in control of their jobs and have the needed flexibility to serve their customers;

supervisory control systems

5. *supervisory control systems* (−)

Output control systems are often inappropriate for measuring employee performance relating to delivering quality service. In many cases, the performance of contact employees is measured by the number of transactions or end-of-the-day balancing (service output), but not by the way in which the service was delivered (process), customer satisfaction or other customer judgements;

role conflict

6. *role conflict* (+)

Organizations' interests are often in conflict with customers' interests. Customer-contact personnel must satify the needs of both groups simultaneously and may therefore experience stress. Role conflicts may, for example, occur when employees are expected to cross-sell services to the customer while the time to serve a customer is limited. Employees may be torn between the company's expectations and the desire to serve the customer; and

role ambiguity

7. *role ambiguity* (+)

Employees may be uncertain about what management expects from them with regard to their job and efforts, and how to satisfy those expectations. Employees should have an accurate understanding of what is expected from them.

Obviously, organizing a service company internally is a very complex matter, in which a variety of interests and relationships play a role. Despite this complexity, management tries to stimulate employees to function as a team to achieve high-quality service delivery. Management must therefore create conditions for a maximum job-performance. Role conflict and role ambiguity do not contribute to job satisfaction and thus lead to low quality performance.

Factors influencing Gap 4

external communications do not match the actual service delivery, propensity to overpromise

ineffective horizontal communication

Gap 4, where the external communications do not match the actual service delivery, mainly results from management's propensity to overpromise. Management is judged by its output. Therefore, management wants to show the services to be offered as the best possible. There is a risk that promises cannot be kept. Customer expectations are enhanced by external communications. Afterwards, the customer is disappointed because the promised service did not match the service expected: the service provider has not performed what he promised. In addition, ineffective horizontal communication between employees responsible for the company's external comunication and advertising, and operational personnel within an organization, may result in inaccurate instructions and procedures for front office employees. These employees should have a clear understanding of the promises made in the advertising campaign, to be able to deliver the service that matches the image presented (and know them before they are communicated to the customers).

5.8 SOME CRITICISMS OF SERVQUAL

In the past few years, several studies have been published examining critically the SERVQUAL model. The criticisms concern:

- the basic question whether it is necessary to measure expectations;
- the way expectations are measured;
- the reliability and validity of using difference scores;
- the number of antecedents (is this all or are more antecedents relevant?);
- the dimensionality of SERVQUAL; and
- the number of items in the SERVQUAL scale.[72]

SERVPERF-model

These criticisms led Joseph Cronin and Stephen Taylor (1992 and 1994) to conclude that it is much better to use questions about performance (=perception) only and delete all the questions on expectations. That is the essence of their SERVPERF-model. SERVPERF is, in fact, based on the perception items in SERVQUAL. One of their arguments is that the predictive validity of using only the perceptions component is higher than in using the perceptions-expectations difference scores. "However, SERVQUAL's developers have argued that measuring expectations has *diagnostic value* (i.e. generates information that would pinpoint *shortfalls* in service quality) and that basing service improvement decision on perceptions data might lead to suboptimal or erroneous resource allocations".[73] So, if managers want to maximize predictive validity, they can use the perception scores only (also those from the SERVQUAL-scale).

a starting point

also its importance

In our own studies applying SERVQUAL, we prefer to add two things to the SERVQUAL-model and questionnaire as presented in this section. First of all, the SERVQUAL dimensions and questions are a starting point for discussions with service organizations and their customers/clients to develop a unique questionnaire for that specific service organization and the problems they want to have solved. Second, for every issue questioned we propose to measure not only the expectation and the perception but also its importance to the customer.[74] We have started this procedure because we saw companies changing the wrong issues, e.g. those issues customers did not deem important. A disadvantage of this approach is that the questionnaire may become too lengthy. Then, we propose (and use) only the questions on perceptions and importance. So, in addition to the two SERVQUAL-questions presented in section 5.7 we add as a third one:

- Is it important for you that employees at bank XYZ give prompt service?[75]

5.9 MANAGEMENT'S USE OF QUALITY INFORMATION

Managers in service organizations can use the information from quality measurements to design and adjust strategic and operational strategies. Quality measurements may serve the following purposes: control; dissatisfaction management; market segmentation; strengths-weaknesses analysis; regular evaluations; analyzing competitors, and improvements with regard to the organization of the service delivery process and the service itself; strengthening the relationship between the buyer and the service provider.[76]

Control

Traditionally, commercial tools for control are revenues, profits, cross-selling and market share. In general, these tools are quantitative output indicators related to the production and selling of services. The quality of the service, as perceived by the customer, is also an important measure for control of services, which deserves more attention than up till now. Controlling service is difficult and different.

control Emphasis should be on the process of service delivery (throughput) instead of the outcome. Control is based on a number of characteristics. Basically, these characteristics are perception-based in service industries. Besides "hard" indicators, "softer" indicators (obtained from the SERVQUAL model, for instance) also play a role. They are used to evaluate or improve the organization at any moment, for example, to evaluate the service quality of the total organization or to assess the quality of its different branches, sales units, teams or regions.[77] In all cases, the subjective assessment of the quality characteristics, determinants, dimensions, or attributes (whether it be the aforementioned 18, 10 or 5) are important here.

Dissatisfaction management

In previous sections, we have shown that consumer dissatisfaction can be expressed in many ways. Voicing complaints is just one of those ways. We maintain that complaint management is not sufficient to tackle, solve, prevent or avoid consumer problems. This should be considered in the broader context of using all the information sources open to the company from which they can derive how customers assess the

dissatisfaction services rendered. This can be called dissatisfaction management: "the systematic man-
management agerial effort involved in collecting and processing consumer dissatisfaction data stemming from all internal as well as external sources with the purpose of communicating information to organizational decision-makers in order to enable them to detect, correct and prevent consumer dissatisfaction."[78]

Market segmentation

identify market If it is possible to identify market segments with different expectation levels, it can be
segments useful to make a distinction between these market segments in approaching the market. An example is the desired speed of repair service, in case of a break-down of a copying machine. Some people want it repaired more quickly than others and are therefore willing to pay a higher price for that service. These benefits, for instance, can be the basis for market segmentation.

Strengths-weaknesses analysis

Service-quality measurements may lead to immediate improvements in the service-delivery process. On a strategic level, structural adjustments – for instance creating better cooperation between different departments – may be necessary for a better control of the service-delivery.

strengths and weaknesses analysis

The strengths and weaknesses analysis cannot only be performed with respect to the position of the company and its services in the market. It may be applied to the internal services as well. For these will co-determine the strengths in the external market place. Research into the quality of internal services may be based on the same models and attributes of service quality as for the external quality in general. Six key needs were found in this respect: responsiveness, relevance, reliability, staying within budget, cost, and on time delivery. Reliability, responsiveness and on time delivery seem to be the most important areas.[79]

Service practice 5-17 Pizza Hut explores customer satisfaction[80]

Surveys always have been valuable tools for measuring customer satisfaction, but Pizza Hut believes their significance increases when they're linked to results.

Cynthia Riley, director of customer satisfaction for Pizza Hut, Dallas, discussed the chain's new customer satisfaction survey at the Eighth Annual Customer Satisfaction and Quality Measurement Conference in Washington, DC, sponsored by the AMA and the American Society for Quality Control.

Pizza Hut launched the customer satisfaction survey in January 1995, the culmination of the efforts of the newly created customer satisfaction department, which was established in 1993. The survey is used only at company-owned restaurants. The restaurant chain completed 2.5 million surveys in 1995 and currently conducts 50,000 interviews a week.

Data is collected through an outbound telephone survey of people in Pizza Hut's delivery and carryout data base and through an interactive 800-number survey of randomly selected dine-in customers.

The delivery and carryout customers are called within 24-hours of their purchase. Riley said the outbound interviews are limited to four minutes in length, and customers are given a 60-day breather before they are called again.

One of every 20 to 30 dine-in customers receives a coupon at the bottom of the receipt and a toll-free number to call to participate in the interactive survey, which lasts almost six minutes.

Tracking results showed that 67% of the surveys were completed within one day of the visit, fulfilling a desire by management that the inbound survey results be fresh.

Because half of the unit manager's quarterly bonus is linked to the survey results, Pizza Hut came up with several ways to manage data integrity. Calls from units and employees' homes are blocked, and multiple calls from the same phone number are deleted. Pizza Hut policy makes manipulation of the system grounds for dismissal.

The survey focuses only on issues that unit managers can control. Questions that deal in value, size of restaurant, and brand image aren't used since those factors are out of the control of the unit manager. The questions deal with service, food, and problems during the customer's latest visit. The company found a strong relationship between satisfaction and frequency among its Delco stores, carryout-and-delivery-only units located mostly in strip malls.

She said there was an inverse relationship between short-term sales growth and loyalty. Customers rushed to buy the new Stuffed Crust Pizza, but there was no subsequent rise in loyalty. Because of service problems, Riley said, new customers were not making return trips. The survey helped Pizza Hut identify the problems, and it now has a better understanding of how to handle the next major product launch.

Because customer satisfaction measurement like this had never been done at Pizza Hut, Riley said managers were given the first quarter of 1995 as practice, and the bonus plan started in the second quarter. She said Pizza Hut wanted to expand the bonuses based on survey results to front-line employees.

Regular evaluations

regular evaluations Through regular evaluations, the effect of earlier improvements can be analyzed. It is important to notice changes in performances as well as changes in customer expectations. For these will affect the behavioral consequences of poor service quality and consumer dissatisfaction.

Analyzing competitors

relative position of competitors By measuring customer satisfaction about competitor' services, further insight into the relative position of competitors can be gained. Also information about the expectations of own customers compared to expectations of competitors' customers can be gained. In its market expansion strategy individual prospects can be reached more effectively taking into account their specific expectations.

Improvements with regard to the organization of the service delivery process and the service itself

specific or structural improvements Several broad areas of the organization may need specific or structural improvements to accomplish a higher level of internal and external service quality. Examples are: human resource management, organizational structure, control, education and training. The latter issue, especially, is of major concern. The number of adjustments to be made can be numerous. Therefore, it can be useful to bring quality measurements and factors susceptible for improvement into a more structural connection.[81] These factors may need structural or specific improvement. Contact personnel may need training for answering the phone in a customer-oriented way. It may also be necessary to make changes in career-planning for the total organization. Quite often it appears that simple changes have a high renumeration.

impact of poor service quality

Probably the most important consequence of delivering service quality is seen when one realizes what the impact of poor service quality is. Figure 5-8 has been developed to that end.[82]

Figure 5-8
The effects of poor service quality

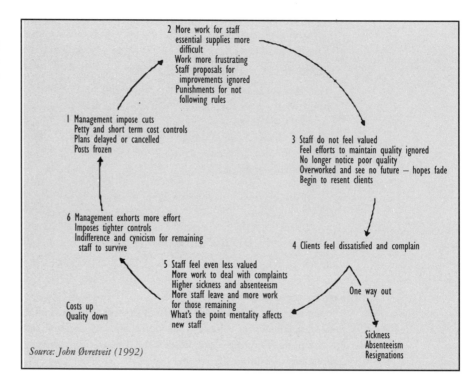

2 More work for staff
essential supplies more
difficult
Work more frustrating
Staff proposals for
improvements ignored
Punishments for not
following rules

1 Management impose cuts
Petty and short term cost controls
Plans delayed or cancelled
Posts frozen

3 Staff do not feel valued
Feel efforts to maintain quality ignored
No longer notice poor quality
Overworked and see no future — hopes fade
Begin to resent clients

6 Management exhorts more effort
Imposes tighter controls
Indifference and cynicism for remaining
staff to survive

4 Clients feel dissatisfied and complain

5 Staff feel even less valued
More work to deal with complaints
Higher sickness and absenteeism
More staff leave and more work
for those remaining
What's the point mentality affects
new staff

Costs up
Quality down

One way out

Sickness
Absenteeism
Resignations

Source: John Øvretveit (1992)

This figure makes clear how poor service quality affects not only the customer but also the employees. In this respect, the vicious circle leads to situations progressively becoming worse and worse. This may be avoided by delivering excellent service!

Strengthening the relationship between the buyer and the service provider

the relationship

With consistent quality of services, meeting the (perceived) expectations of the buyer, it is possible to enhance the relationship between the customer and the service provider. The client knows what they expect. Thus, by measuring regularly the quality of one's own services and the customers' (perceived) expectations, the service firm will create chances for "repeat" purchases and opportunities to utilize the word-of-mouth network, thus strengthening the relationship.

Putting it all together: the house of quality

house of quality

Another way of gathering information about quality and showing how it may affect or change the service organization's way of working, is found in using the idea of the "house of quality".[83] The "house of quality" idea is closely related to the management *quality function development* approach of "quality function development". The basic idea is "that products should be designed to reflect customers' desires and tastes – therefore marketing people, design engineers, and manufacturing staff must work closely together from the moment a product is first conceived".[84] Various scholars have elaborated on this idea and transferred it to the service sector.[85] The three key elements in the house of quality for services are:

1. the customer quality criteria, like the five SERVQUAL dimensions or other aspects deemed relevant by customers;
2. service company facets, like planning, procedures, routines, and personnel aspects of the service delivery system; and
3. a relationship grid, measuring the strength (or weakness) of the relationship between the customer and the service facet.

The resulting grid or map shows the links and provides the means for interfunctional planning and communication in a service organization. It starts with customers' evaluations of the issues they deemed relevant in service quality, and it shows if and to what extent the internal functioning of the service organization fits to that end in delivering such quality.

SUMMARY

The basics of quality management and marketing management are closely related. Both stress the consumer/buyer and their need satisfaction. Based on a summary of the developments, in thinking about product quality management, we have discussed service quality; especially the process of service delivery, customer expectations and perceptions play a key role in assessing service quality and – consequently – consumer satisfaction or dissatisfaction.

The SERVQUAL model provides a way of thinking and a method to measure service quality. Subjective quality judgements are determined by the size and direction of four gaps within an organization.

Each gap is caused by a number of factors, which can influence the size and direction of this gap. Together, these four internal gaps determine the quality of the service delivery, as perceived and evaluated by the customer.

Service quality can be measured via a large number of attributes or dimensions. It can be summarized by five dimensions:

1. tangibles;
2. reliability;
3. responsiveness;
4. assurance; and
5. empathy

of which reliability and responsiveness are the most important to customers assessing service quality.

Quality measurements like SERVQUAL and SERVPERF, which we have discussed in this chapter, can be used for a number of purposes, varying from defining market segments with equal quality expectations and control issues to strengthening the relationships between the client and the service organization. The house of quality shows the links between customer quality criteria, service company, procedures and customers' evaluation of quality items.

QUESTIONS

1 What is the value of using the "zone of tolerance"?
2 Define quality. Which definition of quality is used in the SERVQUAL model?
3 Service delivery is a process. Why does this make it difficult to control service quality?
4 Draw a parallel between the marketing concept and the notion of subjective quality.
5 Why is it important to pay so much attention to subjective quality in service delivery?
6 What should be done to improve internal service quality in companies?
7 Why can a consistent level of service quality enhance the relationship between the client and the service organization?
8 What factors will determine whether customers will express their dissatisfaction about services? How could this differ between dissatisfaction about "going to your local cinema" and a 14-day luxury holiday package tour to the Bahama's?
9 What kind of expectations do exist?
10 Which internal gaps are part of the SERVQUAL-model? Which factors give rise to the existence of these internal gaps?

ASSIGNMENTS

1 Prepare a list of questions to assess the service quality of your bank.
2 Do the same for your educational institution. In which subjects are the biggest differences between expectation and perception observed? What could be done to close the gap(s)?
3 Imagine yourself being a mystery shopper for a tour operator, specialized in youth vacations in Spain. What would you do to find out whether the hotel rooms meet expectations? And what would you do to find out whether customized augmented holiday services meet expectations?
4 Compare and synthesize Service practices 5-9, 5-10 and 5-11. What do you conclude?
5 What are the common denominators in the list of 18, 10 and 5 service quality dimensions?
6 CPA's are quite often mentioned in this chapter. Make a summary of what is said about them and their practices. What could CPA's do to improve their service quality and avoid customer dissatisfaction?

Case: AMERICANA DE AVIACIÓN. THE SECOND AIRLINE ON THE DOMESTIC FLIGHT MARKET IN PERU

Since 1990 air travel has grown faster in Latin America than anywhere else in the world outside Asia, and it showed no signs of slowing down in 1995. One of the countries involved with this enormous growth is Peru.

Notwithstanding the economic recovery and the general trend towards sustained economic development in most countries in South America during the early 1990s, airlines in this continent have not been immune to the overall crisis affecting commercial air transport companies worldwide.

In Peru air transport is very important given the country's difficult terrain. The liberalization of the Peruvian economy has ended the standstill of the commercial aviation sector. Structural measures are being taken by most Peruvian airline companies in their search for efficiency. Measures similar to those taken in the European and American air transport industry: operational rationalization, staff reductions, revision of fleet expansion plans and privatization. This led to, among other things, the privatization of the national flag carrier AeroPerú, and to the emergence of (until now) seven other airlines. AeroPerú and Faucett were the only two companies operating in the domestic market until 1990. Americana de Aviación and Aero Continente are the most

striking examples of new companies entering the Peruvian market. Because of this, competition is fierce, which entails an improvement of the service level and a reduction of airfares. A price war started in 1992, but has been terminated by an agreement signed in March 1995.

Commercial air transport is influenced by economic and socio-cultural factors, like a rise or fall in economic activity. In 1991, commercial air traffic of passengers decreased by 5% on a national level, according to the fall in production. Another possible factor that has affected air transport is the overvaluation of the Peruvian currency, which, in relative terms, made Peru become more expensive for foreign tourists.

Within the socio-cultural factors, the reduction of terrorism which afflicted the country for years entailed some structural changes in view of the modernization of the country. This is stimulating the tourism industry. In 1994 Perú received 390,000 tourists, for 1995 some 500,000 tourists were expected to visit the country. Also, people within the country became more mobile (both business and pleasure) because of the safer climate and the strengthening economy.

Americana de Aviación

Americana de Aviación is the first

Peruvian company to respond to the free market competition by focussing on customer satisfaction. It obtained its licence to operate regular air transport of passengers and freight in 1991 (only domestic). As from 1 July 1995, the company was operating with 350 employees and four aircraft flying 800 hours a month (before that date 600 hours). In 1993, the rate of occupancy of its aircraft was 78% during the high season and about 68% during the low season. Americana is the most efficient airline because they have the best rate of passenger occupation of all Peruvian airlines.

Americana's presence in the Peruvian market is characterized by two periods. Between 1990 and August 1993 the company entered the market with an aggressive strategy, resulting in a quick conquest of market share (12.25% of passengers in its first operating year, growing to second place in the domestic market the following year with 33.97%). However, since the low tariffs did not cover the costs incurred, Americana decided to change its strategy and to concentrate on their most important destinations mainly in the south of Peru.

Americana was the first company to have its airplanes stay overnight in Tacna (near Chile), Arequipa and Cuzco (both in the south), in order to be able to depart in the early hours for Lima. It also introduced fixed daily schedules to all destinations. Today Americana is the only airline that offers daily flights to all frontiers.

The fast conquest of the market share they have today, is owed to punctuality (in Latin-America the standards of what is punctual used to differ from those in Europe) and superior quality of service. This and the features mentioned above (early departures from the south, fixed daily schedules, etc.) attracted business people aged between 30 and 50 and a high socio-economic level.

Punctuality and superior quality of service determine Americana's image. Research conducted on travel agencies and frequent flyers said that more than 60% of the respondents associated Americana with "punctuality" and "good service". The other airlines were identified as "traditional" and "with experience". The agencies and travellers recognized the important role of Americana in the commercial Peruvian aviation business because of the superior service and efficiency. This creates the necessity for the traditional airlines to improve the quality of their transport.

Americana has branch offices in Cuzco, Arequipa and Chiclayo and general offices in most important cities. The company has its own office in Córdoba and Salta (Argentina) and is implementing offices in Iquique and Arica (Chile). Americana is also working with agents in the US, Germany, Australia, Italy, Spain, Chile, Bolivia, Ecuador and Columbia.

With all airlines focussing on service strategies as a result of the agreement to end the price war, it will become more difficult for Americana to maintain its strong position. It remains to be seen to what extent the companies will comply with their agreements: non-compliance has already been observed as regards air-passes.

The future: Americana goes international?

In line with overall economic policies, the watchword for the recent development of airlines in South America has been privatization. While foreign airlines (especially Spain's Iberia) have moved to create important alliances in the continent, it is noticeable that US airlines have preferred to tackle the emergence of increasing competition in South America with tariff wars rather than by forming alliances themselves (presumably because their own finances have been too weak to engage in investment-driven expansion).

The next challenge for Americana will probably be obtaining a position in the international aviation market. There are several foreign airlines which maintain frequent flights to and from Peru. The majority of foreign airlines operating flights to Peru are in this postion owing to bilateral and multilateral agreements between governments concerned. The most profitable routes are Lima-Miami-Lima and Lima-Buenos Aires. Competition on these routes is mainly between the national flat carriers of the respective countries, since they are subject to the above-mentioned bilateral and multilateral conventions. Among those companies, American Airlines, Iberia (from Spain) and Lan Chile can be considered the most important.

Factors that determine which airlines are preferred to serve international routes are: punctuality, security, quality of services on board, quality of services offered at the airport, tariff level, technology of the aircraft, technical preparation of the crew, schedules, frequencies, after-sales service and image.

Aeroperú, the former state-owned company, already has an international network: the company now flies to all South American capitals (except Montevideo), to Mexico City, Panama, Miami and Cuba; new flights are to be introduced shortly to New York, Los Angeles and perhaps a European city. Faucett started operating in 1928 and has been playing a major part in the country's commercial aviation market ever since. This competitor of Americana offers several flights a week to Miami.

It won't be easy to enter the international aviation market, however, the enormous expansion Americana showed in the past four years was not easy either.

Sources: La posicion de Americana en el mercado nacional. Americana, 1995. The Economist, October 21, 1995. Economist Outlook Report Peru, Martketing Association, Amsterdam, 1995. The Economist Intelligence Unit Ltd, 1995. EIU Country Profile 1994--1995. Informe de la publicacion mensual maximixe, dinamica competitiva de la aviacion comercial, Peruana, 1995.

QUESTIONS

1   Peru is an emerging market. How does that affect defining a marketing strategy and delivering excellent service quality?

2   Is it realistic to make a trade-off between quality and efficiency as Americana intends to do?

3   What do you think of the chances for success for Americana in the international market they want to enter?

ENDNOTES

1.   Pirsig, 1987, p. 186.

2.   Garvin, 1988, pp. 39-48.

3.   Abbott, 1955, in Garvin, 1988, p. 40.

4.   These are the cars larger than a normal car but smaller than a bus, used for "public transport" in French-speaking countries and Eastern Africa, the Philippines, Indonesia and Latin America.

5.   Garvin, 1988.

6.   Grönroos, 1990a,b.

7.   Grönroos, 1990a,b; Gummesson 1991.

8.   See also Kordupleski, Rust, and Zahorik, 1993; and, Neijzen and Trompetter, 1989.

9.   This is even further developed upon in Zeithaml and Bitner, 1996, pp. 126-127 (see also our section 5.4).

10 . Edvardsson, Thomasson and Øvretveit, 1994.

11.   In fact, this is also an objection to hiring specialized marketing personnel (and marketing departments) in an organization, in particular in an organization where almost everyone having contact with the customer, is involved in marketing. That is why it is sometimes said that every member of the contact personnel in a service organization is in fact a "part-time marketeer") (Berry and Parasuraman, 1991).

12.   Garvin, 1988, pp. 1-20.

13.   Ivancevich et al., 1994.

14.   Gummesson, 1993.

15.   Grönroos, 1990b, pp. 37-48.

16.   In Chapter Eleven we will discuss the issue of service recovery to elaborate on this point.

17.   In Chapter Ten, when discussing "blueprinting", we will examine the total process of service delivery in several steps.

18.   See, for more details on BPR, Chapter Ten.

19.   Rust, Zahorik and Keiningham, 1995, p. 59.

20.   Rust, Zahorik and Keiningham, 1995, p. 68.

21.   They will be discussed very briefly here. Later on they will be discussed extensively.

22.   In Chapter Eleven, we will discuss complaint management in detail; the next sections deal extensively with the concepts of (dis)satisfaction and quality and with expressing satisfaction and dissatisfaction.

23.   Fisk and Grove, 1995; Grove et al., 1992.

24.   Miller, 1977.

25. Berry and Parasuraman, 1991, pp. 58-59.

26. Zeithaml, Berry and Parasuraman, 1993, p.6.

27. Lewis, 1991, p. 60.

28. Schiffman and Kanuk, 1987,p.174.

29. Bolton and Drew (1991) proved in a longitudinal study how customer's perceptions of changes in service performance affected their global evaluations of service quality. See also Boulding et al., 1993.

30. Lewis, 1991, p. 60.

31. In this technique respondents are asked to report on their most favorite and least favorite service experiences. This qualitative technique will be elaborated upon in Chapter Six.

32. The Bitner, Booms and Tetreault, 1990, US study encompasses three industries: airline, restaurant and hotels. The Dutch 1995 Van der Ven-Verhulp et al. study is carried out in six industries: restaurants, job agencies, university, housing societies, public transportation and health care.

33. Multiple responses could be given for one incident. In this study, the critical incidents were also linked to the ten dimensions from the SERVQUAL-model (see section 5.6).

34. The second study indicates a small improvement in communication might lead to a disproportionately large increase in quality, while small shortcomings in reliability and competence will lead to disproportionately large decreases in service quality.

35. Johnston, 1995b, p. 57.

36. Bitner and Hubbert, 1994; Danaher and Mattsson, 1994; De Ruyter, Lemmink, Wetzels and Mattsson, 1997; De Ruyter, Wetzels, Lemmink and Mattsson, 1997.

37. Wakefield and Blodgett, 1994.

38. Hui and Bateson, 1991.

39. Swan and Trawick, 1994, pp. 37 and 40.

40. Oliver, 1997.

41. Johnston, 1995b.

42. Singh, 1990.

43. Feinberg et al., 1995.

44. Huang, 1994, pp. 264 - 265.

45. Murphy, 1997.

46. Bloemer, 1993.

47. Bloemer and Kasper, 1995.

48. Oliver, 1997, pp. 360-363. We slightly adapted the models Richard Oliver has developed.

49. Keaveney, 1995.

50. Dart and Freeman, 1994.

51. Van Wijngaarden and Van Thienen, 1994, provide these explanations in a Dutch study about CPA's.

52. Soons, 1995.

53. See the overview provided by Cronin and Taylor, 1992, 1994.

54. Oliver, 1993; Strandvik and Liljander, 1994a.

55. Bloemer, De Ruyter and Venetis, 1995.

56. Danaher and Rust, 1996, p. 70.

57. Zeithaml, Berry and Parasuraman, 1996.

58. Johnston, 1995b, pp. 53-71.

59. Zeithaml, Berry and Parasuraman, 1990, pp. 21-22 contains a summary of their 1985 findings.

60. That is one of the major reasons why we will start our discussion of the marketing mix with a chapter on personnel and the processes during the service delivery.

61. Grönroos, 1990b, pp. 37-48.

62. Zeithaml, 1981.

63. In Chapter Six we will look at the measurement instruments to be used. Here we only discuss the conceptual part of these models.

64. This section is mainly based on Parasuraman, Zeithaml and Berry (1985) and Zeithaml, Parasuraman and Berry (1990). An even more detailed discussion can be found in Zeithaml and Bitner (1996).

65. In developing the SERVQUAL-instrument small scale (and more qualitative) studies have been done as well.

66. Here we discuss the basic part of the SERVQUAL-model as it was developed originally. As we have seen in section 5.4 at this very moment more is known about the nature and determinants of expectations.

67. Berry and Parasuraman, 1991.

68. Parasuraman, Zeithaml and Berry, 1994.

69. Some questions are marked with (−). This means that the question is worded in negative terms. See also Chapter Six.

70. This section is heavily based upon the references listed in endnote 64 and Grönroos 1990b, p. 58-65.

71. In the presentation of this construct a minus sign indicates that a factor's presence should decrease the gap, a plus is increasing the gap.

72. We will discuss these methodological issues to a larger extent in Chapter Six on market research. Here we would like to add that Wetzels (1998) also holds that the SERVQUAL model seems quite hierarchical and top down, while nowadays flexibility and bottom up decision making processes are favored. Also, the instruments to measure the antecedents of each gap, need further improvement.

73. Parasuraman, 1995, p. 158.

74. Remember that we now propose to add the importance question to every item in the questionnaire and not only – globally – for each of the five dimensions. Now, one gets a better and more detailed insight per item.

75. We will continue this discussion on criticism on SERVQUAL in Chapter Six with respect to other methodological and measurement issues (see also Parasuraman, Zeithaml and Berry, 1994).

76. This section is largely based on Lemmink and Kasper, 1988.

77. The issue of control will be elaborated upon in Chapter Fifteen: Implementation and Control.

78. This topic developed in De Ruyter, 1993, p. 11 and De Ruyter and Kasper, 1997 will be elaborated upon in Chapter Eleven.

79. VanderMerwe and Gilbert, 1991.

80. Rubel, 1996.

81. Lemmink and Behara, 1992.

82. Øvretveit, 1992.

83. Hauser and Clausing, 1988.

84. Hauser and Clausing, 1988, p. 63.

85. Behara and Chase, 1993.

86. This figure from Zeithaml, Berry and Parasuraman (1996) has been adapted slightly for this Chapter.

87. Parasuraman (1995) even suggests a three dimensional structure wherein responsiveness, assurance and empathy mold into a single factor.

introduction to part three

STRATEGIC ISSUES

The first two parts of this book discussed some fundamental issues service firms have to take into account to survive.

First, the environment of service organizations was analyzed in Part I, while Part II contained essential topics about consumer behavior and service quality.

Once the basics from Parts I and II are known, more specific information is needed before the service provider can develop its strategy, let alone implement it. Therefore, information is needed as the basis for formulating strategies. These strategies may be formulated for the whole organization at corporate level or at (strategic) business unit level. Next to these generic strategies, the functional marketing strategy must be formulated. The ways in which this strategic information can be collected will be discussed here in Part III. All this information will be used by service organizations to actually formulate strategies in order to achieve goals set. These strategies can be applied at different levels, mainly depending on the size of an organization. The influence of the human factor on success in the service business will arise again in Part IV, when the marketing mix in service firms is discussed.

Part One: The Services Domain

FUNDAMENTALS OF SERVICES MARKETING (Chapter 1)	CLASSIFYING SERVICES (Chapter 2)	SERVICE ENVIRONMENT (Chapter 3)

Part Two: At The Heart

FROM BUYING BEHAVIOR TO RELATIONSHIPS (Chapter 4)	SERVICE QUALITY (Chapter 5)

Part Three: Strategic Issues

COLLECTING AND MANAGING MARKET INFORMATION
(Chapter 6)

- the specific market research problems of service organizations;
- to gather and manage information in order to take marketing decisions in service organizations;
- the outline of an international marketing information system for service firms;
- international implications of market research;
- the most obvious research techniques for service providers;
- the SERVQUAL and many other instruments to measure service quality;
- the criticisms on the SERVQUAL-instrument; and
- the critical issues in measuring service quality.

STRATEGIC PLANNING AT CORPORATE LEVEL
(Chapter 7)

- distinguish the different stages in the strategic marketing planning process of services;
- understand the need for relationship marketing in services;
- determine the position of a service provider;
- define several strategic options helpful to support the chosen position;
- set up a strategic plan for a service organization;
- recognize the key success factors in service firms;
- elaborate on the importance of relationships at strategic (corporate) level;
- argue why limited services providers (LSP's) are increasingly becoming a threat to General Services Providers (GSP's);
- what strategic activities GSP's should develop in order to defend their positions; and
- define the differences in strategies for core, augmented, standard and customized services.

SERVICES MARKETING PLANNING IN STRATEGIC BUSINESS UNITS
(Chapter 8)

- understand the many relevant issues in strategic marketing planning;
- explain the relevance of relationships in developing a marketing strategy;
- perform a service marketing audit;
- explain why a high quality service marketing audit is a prerequisite to high quality strategic marketing planning;
- develop a marketing strategy for service organizations within the framework of the generic strategy (as developed in the previous chapter);
- develop a strategic marketing plan for a service organization;
- develop an operational marketing xxxx
- be aware of the relevance of an internal marketing strategy and plan;
- understand the many relevant issues in strategic internal marketing planning; and
- argue why the external and internal marketing strategy and plans should coincide.

Part Three: Strategic Issues

INTERNATIONALIZATION
OF SERVICES
(Chapter 9)

- analyze the impact of services' intangibility on the internationalization or globalization in service industries;
- argue which reasons may lead a service firm to internationalize;
- understand why it could be difficult to export services;
- understand why it is (becoming more and more) feasible to export services;
- explain the reasons why service firms may start

operations abroad;
- analyze the different entry barriers or reasons why it is (or may be) difficult for service organizations to internationalize;
- discuss the various entry strategies service firms may apply in internationalizing their business;
- assess the various pro's and con's of different entry strategies;
- assess the various pro's and con's of

standardization versus adaptation of services within an international marketing strategy;
- decipher the uniqueness of relationship marketing in an international context; and
- understand the specific issues of controlling market orientation and service quality in international service industries.

Part Four: Services Marketing Mix

PEOPLE,
ORGANIZATION AND PROCESSES
(Chapter 10)

DEVELOPING AND PROVIDING
SERVICES
(Chapter 11)

COMMUNICATION
(Chapter 12)

DISTRIBUTION
(Chapter 13)

PRICING
(Chapter 14)

IMPLEMENTATION
AND CONTROL
(Chapter 15)

CHAPTER SIX

COLLECTING AND MANAGING MARKET INFORMATION

What you should learn from Chapter Six:

- *the specific market research problems of service organizations;*

- *to gather and manage information in order to take marketing decisions in service organizations;*

- *the outline of an international marketing information system for service firms;*

- *international implications of market research;*

- *the most obvious research techniques for service providers;*

- *the SERVQUAL and many other instruments to measure service quality;*

- *the criticisms on the SERVQUAL-instrument; and*

- *the critical issues in measuring service quality.*

LEFT: *All those people, all those stories, all those preferences, all those relationships!*

6.1   INTRODUCTION

Good client relations and professionalism are the two main characteristics marketeers want in a research firm, according to a recent survey.

More than 30 marketeers responded to the study by Market Directions, Kansas City, Mo. On average, they work with four different research firms on 11 projects a year. Nearly all those surveyed were told the research gathered is used in making business decisions, some of which will include customer retention, brand differentiation and new products.

The survey found that the 10 most important factors in selecting a research firm are:

1. maintains client confidentiality;
2. is honest with client;
3. is punctual with client;
4. is flexible with client;
5. delivers against project specifications;
6. provides high-quality output;
7. is responsive to client's needs;
8. has high quality-control standards;
9. is customer-oriented in interactions with clients; and
10. keeps client informed throughout project.

Because confidentiality was most important to respondents, Susan Spaulding, president and CEO of Market Directions, suggests that every step in the research process be handled with sensitivity, from masking the client's name on questionnaires to controlling distribution of final reports.

Protect your client's interests, she says, and "their success can also be yours".

"There is no room for 'nice to know' research and ... every question in every study must be actionable today. Research companies must aggressively pursue and deliver high quality. Additionally, they must gather and process the information at Mach speed without affecting its integrity."

To deliver quality work on time is especially necessary in a competitive and changing marketplace.

According to Spaulding, it is important for a research company to realize its own limitations. "It is crucial for research companies to know when they are not suited for a prospective assignment and to only take on what they can readily deliver." ... "If your company cannot be flexible with a client's changing needs or if a deadline is going to be missed, the client needs to be informed quickly with a resolution offered."

Results of the study also show that marketeerss are willing to hire research companies that are not full-service firms, but are national firms or speciality firms.

In order to take proper (marketing) decisions management need information. The collection and use of market information is part of the service firm's market orientation (see Chapter One). Decisions should be based on high quality information about developments in the relevant service environment in general and the behavior of customers and competitors in particular. Therefore, gathering information in a systematic and ongoing way is essential. The example in Service practice 6-1 shows two issues relevant for this chapter. First, it depicts relevant criteria market research agencies' clients use in their decision making about outsourcing market research. Second, it reveals how market research agencies have to care about their own service quality as well.

For service providers, it is important to "check" information for its objectivity. Service delivery is accompanied by a great deal of communication and interaction between individuals (the "soft side of the service delivery process" and service quality). In order to measure the underlying motives for actual behavior, proper research methods are needed. These research methods may differ per research question or service. However, the marketing research process itself does not differ much in structure between either services or physical goods for the different kinds of services we have classified in Chapter Two, or between local or international market research. This chapter will focus on the specific kind of information and market information service firms need: how it can be gathered and managed. Primary areas of concern are the service environment and its implications for the strategic decision making as well as the evaluation of the marketing mix, including its effects on the image of the firm. As maintaining and enhancing the quality of services is such a central theme in service marketing, various methods to measure service quality will be discussed. The SERVQUAL-model serves as an excellent framework to understand the origination of gaps between expectation, experience and perception of all parties involved in the service delivery. For that reason, this model merits special consideration as a way of measuring quality; other ways to measure service quality will also be discussed. One of the first sections will deal with some international aspects of managing information and research. This is because the international aspect of services marketing management is one of the themes of this book. Figure 6-1 serves as a brief overview of this chapter.

6.2 THE SPECIFIC KIND OF INFORMATION AND MARKET RESEARCH FOR SERVICES

market research

basic purposes of market research information

Marketing research is the systematic gathering, recording and analyzing of data to provide information useful to marketing decision making. Stated differently, market research is the means used by those providing services (and/or goods) to keep themselves in touch with the needs and wants of those who buy their goods and/or services. The two basic purposes of market research are: (1) to reduce uncertainty when plans are being made, (2) to gather information about the present service environment and future trends. This information is also needed before a marketing

Figure 6-1
Chapter outline

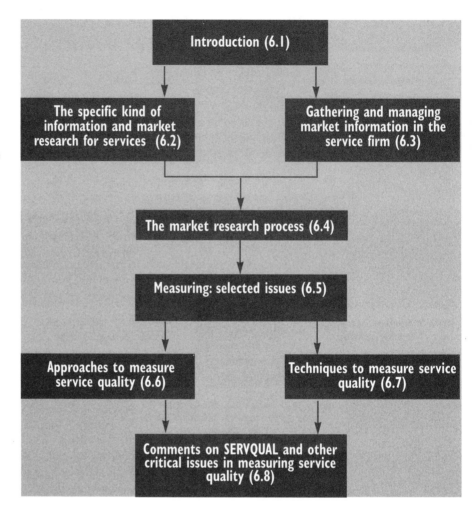

operation, -mix or -instrument will be implemented, to monitor performance after the plans have been set into motion and to evaluate the results of the marketing policy. The marketeers will have to find the most accurate and reliable data within the limits imposed by time, cost and the present state of the art. This research must be valuable and contribute to better decision making than if the research had not been done.

value of research   How to determine the value of research? This is the key issue for management if it faces the question whether or not to carry out research. Two approaches can be used to assess the value of research. One method analyzes the benefits the firm gets from the research carried out. The other identifies the downside risk the firm incurs if it does not carry out research.[2]

The value of research in making a particular decision may be determined by applying the following equation:

$$V(dr)\text{-}V(d)\text{>}C(r)$$

where

$V(dr)$ is the value of the decision with the benefit of research;

$V(d)$ is the value of the decision without the benefit of research;

and

$C(r)$ is the cost of research.

The value of the research should, of course, be greater than the cost of the research. However, the problem is that the value is often difficult to quantify up front. This applies both to the pure benefits and risks of not having the information. The second approach concentrates on the risks of inadequate research. The researcher can follow a "what if" decision procedure. For instance, what are the downside risks of launching a new hamburger, or establishing a subsidiary abroad without proper research.

four specific research areas
Given the organization's marketing strategy, its marketing mix instruments, the competitors and the relevant service environment, four specific research areas can be distinguished as typical topics for market research in services. They also hinge upon the specific characteristics of services. Therefore, these areas require special attention when service firms gather information and perform market research. These can be labelled as:

1. the present service environment;
2. future developments in the service environment;
3. ex-ante evaluation of the marketing mix as a whole or elements in the marketing mix; and
4. ex-post evaluation of the efficiency and effectiveness of the marketing policy.

All four areas apply for both standard and customized services as well as for core and augmented services. They are aimed at providing information for decision making about improving service quality, motivating people to improve service quality and accomplish the planned market orientation.

THE PRESENT SERVICE ENVIRONMENT

present service environment

customer

competitors

employees
The present service environment can be examined in the usual way by customer based research techniques with who/what/where/when/how and why questions. By examining and analyzing the service, the accent is upon using the service. However, buying and using the service is evaluated simultaneously and mostly by one and the same person. Quite often, more qualitative research techniques are needed due to the intangible nature of services, the process of service delivery, all the people and the machines involved. Researching competitors and your own position relative to the competitors' also fits to this area of research. Due to the participation of customers and employees in the service encounter, research amongst employees is important to increase service quality. Because of the intangibility of services and the perceived risk involved, much research focuses on customer perceptions. These subjective data should be combined with other and objective data in order to get the "full picture" (see also section 6.3).

FUTURE DEVELOPMENTS IN THE SERVICE ENVIRONMENT

new developments in the relevant service environment

In order to trace new developments by consumers, competitors and the other parties in the relevant service environment, research focussing on new trends should be as detailed as possible. Future research concerns, amongst others, tendencies in attitudes, patterns of behavior, economic and technological developments. All these developments have already been discussed in Chapter Three.

EX-ANTE EVALUATION OF THE MARKETING MIX

before the implementation

This type of research is aimed at gathering knowledge about (new) markets, market segmentation, services, and policies. Research projects in this domain can be related to the features or attributes of new services, studies about improving or changing existing services, in depth discussions with consumers (of the services) and pre-testing new ads. The word ex-ante indicates that research is carried out before the implementation of the proposed marketing mix. It also focusses on future consumer behavior, e.g. are customers willing to accept new ways of service delivery? When it focusses on how much more services will be sold when prices change, it hinges upon price elasticities. Research may focus on the whole marketing mix or on each of the mix instruments. It is important to position the results within the framework of the relationship between the service provider and the customer (the planned or actual relationship).

EX-POST EVALUATION OF THE EFFICIENCY AND EFFECTIVENESS OF THE MARKETING POLICY

during and after

compared with norms and standards

Examining the efficiency and effectiveness of the marketing policy and the specific mix instruments applied cannot be done without any measurements. Ex-post means that the evaluation takes place during and after applying each of the marketing instruments or any combination of them. Findings of ex-post studies have to be compared with previously established norms and standards. Examples are the testing of the "mix" in the field, computing actual price elasticities, sales, market shares, penetration, repeat purchase, image and financial results of introductions and comparing them to the goals set. It is in this ex-post stage that performance is monitored and the future predicted. Again, the results should be placed within the relationship framework. Trend data should be collected as they relate to the major components in the "mix" so that the "own" data may be compared with that of competitors on a continuous basis.

monitor the execution

control

The immediate goal of the evaluation is to monitor the execution of the operational plan. The evaluation of the service process itself gets too little attention during control of the marketing performance. Quite often, control is focussed only on the outcome of the service process (what is delivered, how many sales) and not on the service process itself (how is the service delivered). In terms of the control literature, one could say in service marketing management that throughput control should receive much more attention and the focus should not be on the – more traditional – output control. We will return to this issue in Chapter Fifteen. Here, it is important to stress that the company should conduct these kind of (market research) studies, depicting data about the servuction process, the process of service delivery itself, the key success factors involved and the related key control factors. The quality of the service delivery plays a crucial role in these evaluations. In addition, the quality of services, especially if it concerns personalized service, is by definition not at a constant level.

6.3 GATHERING AND MANAGING MARKET INFORMATION IN THE SERVICE FIRM

MARKETING INFORMATION SYSTEMS

information already available

Often, a great deal of the information needed to take decisions is already available within the service organization itself. The service provider and the client (frequently) come into contact with each other. Information can then easily be collected and stored. Therefore, it is possible that service providers already have a lot of information about their clients (very often without really knowing it).

Key questions are whether this information is recorded in a systematic way and whether it is accessible. In many instances, this information is only present in the minds of the contact personnel. In such situations, this information can hardly be used as management information in order to take decisions. So, the market information system (MIS)[3] should be designed to ensure that the data collected is relevant to management decisions. Particularly in service organizations, a service quality information system is needed. Such a system "uses multiple research approaches to systematically capture, organize, and disseminate service-quality information to support decision making".[4]

service quality information system

databases

Databases are becoming increasingly important to address customers directly, to communicate on a personal basis and to store the data collected on a continuous basis. Market-oriented service providers have organized their administration and database-management system in such a way that the essential information about their clients (individuals as well as target groups) can be retrieved from the system and delivered easily to the users. This is part of their systematic and ongoing activities to collect, store and disseminate market information (see also Chapter One). The information is stored in a usable form. A well documented data base is also advantageous to the clients: they do not have to repeat all the aspects from their "history" (their record) at each visit. For instance, clients of a bank, patients of medical doctors or dentists clearly benefit from such an approach. Examples of information about clients coming from their own administration are: the number and kind of policies per household at an insurance company, the household's "medicine consumption" in a pharmacy, the developments on personal accounts at banks, the development of clients' balances at a mail-order firm and also the family's doctor or hospital with all the medical data of a client.

technological developments

Technological developments offer many opportunities for getting better and faster information about clients from databases. All this data can be obtained from electronic databases for both standard and customized services as well as for core and augmented services.

International Marketing Information System

As in the domestic market, the challenge of an information system internationally is to define the relevant information needed, collect it, combine all the information gathered in an accessible way and disseminate it throughout the firm properly. As the number of foreign subsidiaries increases, the necessity of an International Marketing Information System (IMIS) will be felt within the organization. Employees in different countries are more aware that their organization knows much more than their own local subsidiary. However, the question for them is how to access that knowledge. An IMIS can assist here. It is a permanent system designed to generate, store, catalogue, and analyze information from sources within the firm and outside the firm. An IMIS can be used as the basis for world-wide and country-oriented decision making. In case the number of foreign outlets grows, the company has to determine which data has to be collected centrally or decentrally. The set-up of the data base has to be systematic. All parties involved need to be persistent in inserting data as the information system fails or succeeds with the individual contribution of all staff that should contribute to data gathering. Naturally, the process should be cost effective and the database should be accessible for all persons that are authorized.

easily accessible and understood

available in a usable form

Managing information internationally is a complex task. Secondary data, company data and primary data need to be stored in a form that is both easily accessible and understood by decision makers in various countries. It should not only be easily accessible and understood but also available in a usable form. In fact, is is often part of a global knowledge base in which other knowledge of the company is stored.

The IMIS based on such an internal data bank can be used to support strategic and operational/tactical decisions.

strategic decisions

Strategic decisions refer to areas like mergers and acquisitions, strategic alliances, core business and completely new business-lines, international expansion, etc. Information in various countries is typically gathered by scanning the macro-environment and meso-environment by means of secondary information. Once a target country or candidate firm has been selected, primary research should be carried out. A feasibility study or due-diligence study will be needed for the final decision.

other strategic decisions

Other strategic decisions, such as the developments of new services choice of channels, adding, closing or merging outlets, type of pricing policy, choice of information system to support the service delivery, etc. also need relevant information. Again, data from scanning the environment, such as technological developments and competitor analysis, should be available to marketing management in local subsidiaries to support these decisions. These decisions are often guided by company data and secondary data. In case there is not enough information available, this information is complemented with primary research.

operational decisions   *Operational decisions,* such as operational marketing mix decisions require company data, secondary data especially with respect to the local situation and primary research, i.e. to measure service quality, to manage supply and demand, and research employee satisfaction, etc.

INTERNATIONAL PROBLEMS

availability
reliability
comparability

Problems using marketing data internationally arise from: the availability of secondary data; and the reliability and comparability of data. This applies not only for secondary data but also to company data acquired through the subsidiaries or related companies and to market research with respect to newly collected, primary data.

These problems about data obtained from various countries often relate to the diversity of cultures, customs and languages encountered. In the development of an international marketing strategy, information is of crucial importance for effective marketing decisions.[5] Too often, decisions are made hastily, without any or with inadequate information. This in spite of the fact that – as said before – information has to be collected to solve specific decision problems. Furthermore, information is needed to monitor changing trends in the environment, strategies can then be adapted accordingly. Moreover, the effectiveness of these strategies can be evaluated and performance can be assessed.

international
marketing research

degree of
generalization

cultural differences

The growing need of companies for internationally oriented information necessitates the importance of performing international marketing research. The complexity of international markets, together with the (large) differences between countries, and the unfamiliarity with these new markets lead to an increasing need for international marketing research. However, in international marketing, and therefore in international marketing research, one major problem always emerges: the degree of generalization used in marketing research strategy and research instruments. In some markets, whether product or services markets, research results can easily be generalized from one country to another. This is especially true where more or less standardized services are involved, like postal services. With such services, cultural influence is limited, although national standards may differ on an acceptable delivery time. In other markets, cultural influences can be quite high. Also, in the services sector, differences can arise which can be attributed to cultural differences. In particular, the concept of service quality can be perceived quite differently in different countries with distinctive cultural backgrounds (see also Chapters Four and Five and the cultural map of the world). Perhaps in one country service quality is reflected by the speed with which a service provider solves certain problems. In the next country it could be the friendliness of the service personnel that determines service quality, whereas the technical quality might be crucial in some other country. It is obvious that clarification of this problem and correct use of the obtained information can pro-vide international marketeerss with enormous competitive advantages.

Cross-border generalization of measurement in market research gets easier if the nature of the object under study gets easier. Absolute measures like length and age, for example, can be generalized directly from one country to another. However, if more abstract objects like perceptions, different kinds of expectations, values or atti-tudes towards the quality of a certain service are being measured, direct generaliza-tion of research results becomes more difficult. So, factors having no direct relationship with the research problem, e.g. cultural traditions, familiarity with a

bias service or even the way in which the research is being done, may bias measurement in international marketing research.

Two aspects can cause differences in research results, especially in attitude research. First, there are the methodology related measurement effects. Second, real cross-cul-tural differences in attitudes or values may exist. These related differences are of great interest in international marketing research, because they indicate focal points of attention for the marketing of a service in foreign areas. Measurement differences are

response effects also referred to as response effects, which can have an immense influence on research
real cross-cultural results.[6] In order to obtain useful data in international marketing research it is there-
effects fore of great importance to separate response effects from real cross-cultural effects.

Until now, the problems associated with cross-cultural research did not receive much attention in applied cross-cultural marketing research on services. In contrast, cross-cultural studies and their problems have a long tradition in social sciences. In these disciplines, extensive literature exists in which specific methodological and conceptional problems in cross-cultural research are being addressed. Basically, these problems can be classified into two categories.[7] The first category represents very basic problems and causes of cross-cultural difficulties. These basic problems then lead to a variety of more detailed and specific problems, which represent the second category.

In general, two basic problems in cross-cultural research can be distinguished which
researcher's cause bias in cross-cultural research data. The first one is the researcher's self-
self-reference reference.[8] This phenomenon refers to the fact that researchers interpret reality from other cultures with beliefs, meanings and ideas originating from the researcher's home culture. This is the cultural bias of researchers which is caused by differenti-ating mental programming processes.[9] Self-reference affects each phase in the research process, but especially the conceptualization of research questions and con-structs, the development of measures, sampling, and the analysis and interpretation of results.

interaction between The second basic cause of methodological problems in cross-cultural research is the
cultural and research interaction between cultural and research specific aspects, like variables, for example.
specific aspects This interaction can lead to results which are quite difficult to interpret.[10] This problem addresses the issue of whether or not certain research designs and measures can be used in cross-cultural research and really identify cross-cultural differences.

Measurements in international research can be affected by very different socio-cultural reactions of respondents to measurement instruments, by the way in which the research is executed and by lacking adaptations of sampling procedures to different local environments.

phases in cross-cultural research

Both types of problem, cultural self-reference and methodological issues, create specific problems in the various areas of international marketing research projects. Especially, the following phases in cross-cultural research should be given careful attention: formulation of the research problem and objectives; operationalization of the cultural construct; development of the theoretical foundation; development of a model; establishment of cross-cultural equivalence in concepts; establishment of cross-cultural equivalence in research methods; establishment of cross-cultural equivalence in sampling; determination of the general research setting (field vs. laboratory) and analysis and interpretation of obtained data.

efficient procedures and rules for an international information system

This overview suggests difficulties in establishing efficient procedures and rules for an international information system. In particular, this might happen when the local participants do not see benefits arising from their own efforts to gather information. It may also occur when standardization in market research is lacking. Less standardized information often concerns market size, performance/effectiveness of the marketing-mix instruments, competitors, meetings between employees, meetings with clients and distributors, new services, type of transactions (deals), etc. Also, the information gathering about trends in the macro-environment (DRETS-factors) is often not standardized. As a consequence, management at headquarters has to establish procedures in which to guarantee the quality of the information, to make the data comparable between countries and to ensure that this data is brought quickly into the IMIS.

Data gathering by means of a uniform data-base is more efficient than allowing every branch or subsidiary abroad to develop their own data base. An integrated and centrally managed information system allows sound analysis across several countries or markets simultaneously. The marketing results from one country are then better tailored to the international comparison of market performance worldwide. As a positive side-effect, companies can prevent an overlap of market research activities or research undertaken on a particular topic already studied elsewhere.

centralized approach

In general, a centralized approach is preferred over local subsidiaries compiling data according to their own local rules. For, local information would not then have to be compiled at headquarters (with the accompanying chance of misinterpretation), even so much information still needs to be interpreted at head office. There, management has an overview of all information. Moreover, they are better able to recognize outcomes which are atypical. In this manner, they can request a foreign subsidiary for additional information.

Many international service firms have built their own databases and ways to analyze it. But, as the next Service practice shows, standardized software is becoming available precisely for this purpose.

*Service
practice
6-2
The
importance of
databases in
the financial
sector*

Mr Jeremy Bond[11] believes there has been a grand failure in collecting and storing the necessary details about one's clients. This, he feels, reflects upon the effectiveness of database marketing. He also stresses the fact that banks are failing to capitalize on opportunities opened up by the use of both "expert systems" and "networks" at the point of sale. The effective use of client information can prevent "hit or miss" cross-selling activities helping to maintain a more profitable long term relationship with customers. Bond cites the UK Advisa expert system as an illustration of a system which can be used by financial advisors as a sales tool while talking to customers about such things as mortgages, savings investments, etc. A full "fact-find" including knowledge of tax and legislation systems, and different companies charging bases and performance records, can aid the advisor in matching that client's specific needs. In this way, applications can be made directly over the network without having every time to punch in the same details. In addition, the information will be stored for database marketing and cross-selling purposes, and – when necessary – for government or regulatory inspections.

other issues

Besides the comparability, reliability and validity of data, other issues play an important role when using information effectively in an international service firm. These are: the dissemination and coordination of information; quality of the information system itself; the content of the information and the effectiveness of the information for decision making.

Dissemination and coordination of information

*information must
circulate*

Information may be present in the form of ideas and perceptions from both the foreign branches and the headquarters. This information must circulate through the organization, e.g. to those who are involved in the service development decision making process. Assessing client needs on a worldwide basis can help companies avoid falling into the trap of initially designing services for home markets, then looking to foreign markets and waiting for people's reaction.

Quality of the information system

*know exactly what is
happening*

Companies operating on a world wide basis and lacking an efficient information system are simply at a disadvantage. This is especially true when they implement a strategy involving certain degrees of adaptation, and simultaneously responding to market differences and similarities. Then, one needs to know exactly what is happening when and where in order to effectively forecast sales or customer satisfaction.

Content of information

quality and quantity

It appears to be a common belief that, in general, executives are dissatisfied with the quality and quantity of their marketing information. First, there is a lack of headquarter's involvement with regard to the collection and dissemination of marketing research information. Headquarters should be better informed in order to fulfill their responsibility of strategic planning. Marketing research, being an important source of information, should be closely monitored. From interviews within a major international bank, the overall consensus was that a more standardized structure of coordinating marketing information would be beneficial to all participants involved in international marketing and service development. In addition, it would help in answering questions regarding subsidiaries' and markets' performance. A systematic scanning of market-data includes, amongst others: collecting data, trends and judgements and values that will both directly and indirectly affect one's marketing operations. Issues might cover: measurement of markets, insight on competitor activities, environment, customer satisfaction and evaluating the efficiency of the different elements in the marketing mix. In practice, this could easily be done through the coordination of marketing information from foreign subsidiaries via exception reporting, monthly reports and the annual planning process (i.e. E-mail based).

interference
propositioning

If monthly reports were made by foreign branches, subsidiaries or franchisees, it might be helpful to require them to report on possible outcomes of proposed actions, e.g. report explanations made about their customers' response to certain marketing operations – this may be called interference. Propositioning might be a second requirement in this reporting procedure. It means encouraging foreign branches to make proposals in coordination with headquarters about product/service offerings in response to particular customer needs in their area. Possible testing might be suggested to assess customers' evaluation of particular new products or services.

Once a stage of standardized coordination of market information has been reached, management can begin to assess the different strategies and to govern and control the growth process of each particular service area.

Effectiveness of the information

effectiveness of
information

Finally, the effectiveness of information as a supportive tool in the management decision making process needs to be ensured. Both the value of the information and the data collecting process need to be evaluated periodically, for example once every three years. Crucial questions at such moments are: Who needs this information within our organization?[12] What will they do with it? Is the cost of collecting the data still worth the value? Are there alternative ways of collecting and distributing data? Should this type of report still be distributed periodically or be available on request only? Is there information available locally which merits being available centrally? What can other subsidiaries learn from the experiences in one country? Does the company miss any vital information from its decision making process? etc.

6.4 THE MARKET RESEARCH PROCESS

primary data

The service provider can, of course, obtain all kinds of secondary data about markets, consumers, competitors, future developments, and so on in addition to their own data. When all these sources appear to be inadequate for present decisions, one has to turn to gathering primary data by new market research. At this point, the value of research, cost and all the cross cultural problems again become relevant in the process of doing market research in an international service firm.

*phases of a research
process*

In the market research process we usually distinguish a number of phases. Whether it is in New York or in New Delhi, the process of market research follows the same pattern. Nevertheless, the challenges and pitfalls of doing international research discussed in the previous section should be recognized. So, in principle, no differences occur between international market research and (local) market research. These widely recognized phases of a research process are described in Figure 6-2.

Figure 6-2
*The market
research process*

> 1. **Problem recognition**
> 2. **Problem definition**
> 3. **Desk research (secondary data) and/or decision to collect primary data**
> 4. **Research design: descriptive study and/or causal study**
> 5. **Research method: questionnaire, observation or experiment**
> 6. **Sample design**
> 7. **Data collection: field work**
> 8. **Analysis and interpretation data**
> 9. **Research report: by word of mouth and/or written**

*recognition of the
problem*

*definition of the
problem*

The research process starts with recognition of the problem: what exactly is the problem? Does every manager perceive the same problem? After the problem is recognized and thoroughly discussed by all managers, it can be written down, and the content agreed. This is a time consuming phase, which is often overlooked. The problem should be formulated accurately so that it can be researched specifically. Not every problem can be circumscribed immediately in full detail. Exploratory research will often turn the initial problem statement into a problem that really can be investigated.[13] The further course of the research process depends on the exact definition of the problem. Defining the problem properly allows for a detailed description of the factors playing a role in solving the problem and the way it should be researched. It is important to establish clearly whether the research is focussing on the service itself or on the service delivery process or, whether it focusses on customer perceptions or objective data. At this stage, the hypotheses are formulated as well. A good way, at this stage, to indicate the value of research is to give possible answers to the questions or hypotheses.[14] Then, one can see if the outcome provides enough information to make the necessary decisions. This reveals whether the value of the research findings justifies the research costs. Next, the decision should be taken whether the researcher wants to obtain all or just a part of the information about the factors deemed relevant.

The third step in the marketing research process deals with the question whether secondary data can solve the problem. When this is true, these data should be analyzed. But when this is not the case, one should gather primary data and continue with the other phases of the process. Determining the sources of information to fulfil the research objectives is often more difficult in foreign markets, especially if the company is not (yet) represented in that country. The availability, validity, reliability and opportunities to use secondary data differ from country to country. One can not simply compare the United States with less developed markets, where the priorities and possibilities for accurate data gathering are less. Even if secondary data is available in a country, marketeerss are warned against using this information without verification: in many countries there is a large discrepancy between the real figures and the official ones. Screening the reliability and validity of secondary data is therefore essential. Also, market structures and institutional factors may differ, which cannot be compared without any modifications. As stated in section 6.3, service firms may already possess a lot of information about their customers. This is a kind of secondary data that can be used in analyzing consumer behavior, e.g. a bank's customers expenses over time.

the availability, validity, reliability and opportunities to use secondary data

Service practice 6-3 Solving validity and reliability problems

Marketeers should ask the following typical questions before validating data: For what purpose was the data collected? Who collected the data? Would there be any reason for purposely misrepresenting the facts? How was the data collected? (which methodology was used?). Is the data internally consistent and logical in light of known data sources or market factors? For example, by checking one data set with another.[15]

reliable sources

As a consequence of the scarcity of resources, service firms starting their international activities often need to use data that has already been collected. This data is available from reliable sources such as international organizations (i.e. The Statistical Yearbook, an annual publication of the United Nations; the reports of the World Bank and IMF), regional organizations such as the Organization for Economic Co-operation and Development (OECD), Asian Development Bank, Pan American Union, European Union, European Bank for Reconstruction and Development (EBRD - which is focussed on Eastern and Central European as well as Central Asian republics), governments and their various ministries, embassies, export agencies, directories, trade associations, Chambers of Commerce, industry organizations, national statistical offices, banks, specific literature, trade magazines, employee magazines and brochures of competitors, trade fairs and data bases.

gathering primary data

If all this secondary data is not available, or does not provide adequate or reliable information to build decisions on, then the gathering of primary data becomes a necessity. Decisions will have to be taken as to who will carry out the market research. Feasibility studies in large companies such as banks, international recruitment firms or accounting firms are often done by employees of the firm – including management trainees. Research with respect to the potential demand for existing services or new services is typically carried out by market research agencies – both local and internationally operating companies. In comparison with fifteen years ago, more and more, market research is outsourced instead of performed internally. The main reason behind this outsourcing trend is that this operational side of market research in many service enterprises is not viewed as their core business. Outside firms are normally more specialized and offer cheaper data collection methods than internal departments. As discussed in Chapter Three, the market research industry itself is becoming more internationalized. Thus, both head office and subsidiaries can increasingly rely on one firm (or an alliance of firms) and one account manager when it comes to do qualitative and quantitative international research.

way of organizing the field survey

While preparing field research it is important to realize that the way of organizing the field survey may have implications for the results of the process. In some countries, telephones are still only for the wealthy. This limits the scope for this research method. In Central and Eastern Europe, people are willing to cooperate in market research. At the same time, they are very anxious not to give market researchers an indication about their wealth as they never know who will use this information. The previous regimes have misused such information. Inadequate mailing lists and poor postal services are another problem that may limit the choice of a method.

research design
descriptive studies
causal studies

exploratory studies

In the fourth stage, the research design is specified: how the data is to be collected. Here, descriptive and causal studies can be distinguished. Descriptive studies hinge upon describing who, what, where, when and how. Causal studies examine the relation between two (or more) variables with a supposed causal relationship and show how variables affect one another. Exploratory studies have often already been done in earlier phases of the research process.

specific research method

Next, the specific research method is chosen. Do we send a written questionnaire to the respondents or do we use telephone interviews? Will there be an observation or an experiment carried out? Will it be a qualitative or a quantitative study? Do we use the Internet to collect data?[16]

sampling

Phase six deals with sampling issues. Is the sample appropriate? Will it be a selective or a random sample? In a random sample, each element in the population has an equal chance to be drawn: a representative cross-section of the population. In small scale, qualitative studies, it is relevant to have respondents who each represent a specific feature or life style in order to gather information on relevant service attributes. A representative picture is not needed when an inventory of various perceptions has to be made or a long-list of all the service attributes deemed relevant by the firm's customers.

data has to be gathered
data is processed, analyzed and interpreted

After establishing the research technique and the sample, data has to be gathered by a marketing research agency, preferably one specialized in research in service industries or by the service organization itself. Next, the data is processed, analyzed and interpreted. After this, conclusions and recommendations can be formulated.

cross check the information

triangulation

It is important for the market researcher and its client to realize that the quality, validity, reliability, and the usefulness of both secondary and primary data across borders may be limited. It is always necessary to cross check the information gathered with field personnel, resident managers and, if available, information obtained from other sources. Triangulation is necessary. In all cases, common sense is also a valuable asset to interpret the results of international research.

Service
practice
6-4
Some
misunder-
standings

In Japan, a respondent may have a different understanding of the word super-market than in Europe or North America. In Japan, a supermarket is typically a multi-story building that may sell clothing and durable hardware such as home appliances and audio. In North America, a supermarket sells mainly food and daily necessities, its average size is substantially larger than its equivalent in Europe (with the exception of France). In France, the term hypermarket is invented to label such a large retail operation.

Also, the understanding of a family is different in many countries. Where in some countries the family is limited to one household, in other countries all relatives such as uncles, aunts, cousins and nephews also belong to the family: the extended family or in-group.

With a proper a priori understanding of these issues, a lot of misunderstanding and useless market research can be avoided.

reporting the research
findings

Finally, reporting the research findings takes place. This can be achieved by means of a written report and/or by oral presentations to the client of the market research agency (even by teleconferencing).

An important issue is which market research agency will do the job, when it is not done by the market researchers within the company. This decision will depend on various issues like experience in a particular domain or with a particular technique. Of course, the object or area that needs to be measured will affect the final decision. Relationships with existing agencies in the home country or abroad may play a role. Sometimes, headquarters decide which agency should be "hired". The agency then follows the client on their international markets (see also Chapter Nine). The market research agency itself is also a service provider. As such, they should recognize that many of the key success factors for service firms in general will also apply to them. Service practice 6-1 shows what is deemed relevant in this business.

6.5 MEASURING: SELECTED ISSUES

The very nature of services has its consequences for the specific areas to be measured. Areas such as strategic decision making, image and service quality will be discussed briefly.

MEASURING FOR STRATEGIC DECISION MAKING

strategic context

In the strategic context, it is necessary to have data and information to take proper decisions. It will be useful to combine the strengths/weaknesses-analysis with an analysis of opportunities and threats. The first part consists of the analysis of the strong and weak points of the service. The firm as a whole, each of the separate services or the service delivery process are mapped out according to the perception of customers. This also can be done in bench marking the firm, each of the separate services or the service delivery process against the best practices of competitors. The second part consists of the analysis of opportunities and threats identified.

On the basis of such an analysis it is possible to give recommendations with regard to the marketing strategy (see further Chapters Seven and Eight on strategy). Also, much information about customers and clients is needed. All this information stored in the IMIS is needed to operationalize the service firm's market orientation, improve the service offering and motivate employees.

MEASURING THE IMAGE OF THE FIRM

images

Services are intangible. Services are evaluated on various aspects. Consequently, the image of a firm may encompass a large number of different characteristics. Such an image may vary for different market segments. Images may be based on well thought out evaluations of many aspects or on simple impressions. Many techniques can be applied in measuring images.

semantic differential

A popular technique to measure the image of a service firm is the semantic differential. Originally, this technique was developed in order to measure attitudes. The image of a service can be seen as an attitude, but more likely as the average of a number of different attitudes with regard to a particular service. Consequently, the scores of customers with regard to these items should be collected. Per item, a customer score is obtained, mostly on basis of a bipolar scale that exists from a pair of opposite adjectives, like "fast 1-2-3-4-5-6-7 slow".[17] Next a service profile can be drawn up in which different (competing) services can be projected. Figure 6-3 contains an example of the image of two banks: A and B.

Figure 6-3
Images based on a semantic differential scale

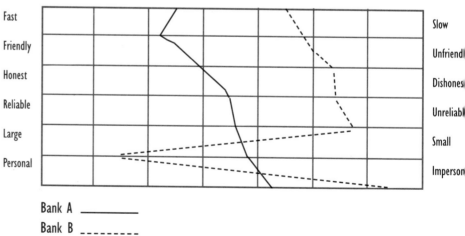

MEASURING SERVICE QUALITY

processes

Within the framework of market research for services, the process-oriented characteristics of services and service delivery should be emphasized. These processes make researching services very complex. Therefore, it is not only a matter of examining the service itself, but also the inseparable service delivery process. Consequently, several behavioral aspects in the service encounter, such as the interaction between contact personnel and clients, should then always be taken into

intangible nature

account. In addition, the intangible nature of services further complicates this research. For, subjective evaluations and perceptions of consumers are very often at

qualitative
pilot-studies

stake. For this reason, there always has to be considerable investment in qualitative pilot-studies, revealing these factors. One should always bear in mind "what process the client has to go through in the service encounter", as this is the important focus of researching service quality.[18]

Performing according to the desired level of quality is crucial to the entire organization. The quality issue is part of both ex-ante and ex-post evaluations of the marketing policy. Based on customer wishes, costs and expected returns, the quality of the service and the service delivery should be measured periodically. Service quality can be measured in many ways, for instance via the SERVQUAL-methodology. Monitoring, controlling and improving the quality of the service delivery is essential to the firm's market-orientation. Therefore, we will pay ample attention to measuring service quality and developing a service quality information system.

6.6   APPROACHES TO MEASURE SERVICE QUALITY

SOME GENERAL REMARKS

Measuring is knowing. This explains why various forms of market research for decision making should be done on a regular basis. In other words, one should measure periodically in order to know the variation in, for instance, the spontaneous brand awareness, image or brand loyalty, within a particular target group. Measuring quality may be even more crucial to the service provider as it heavily influences its image and (repeat) sales over a length of time. Managers and contact personnel often want to know whether the service actually corresponds with the objectives of the organization and the wishes of the customer. They want to know what the effect is of programs to improve the quality of the service. In order to answer these kinds of questions measurements are needed.

controlling,
evaluating and
improving
analyze the service
and the entire service
process

It may be self-evident, but it is worth emphasizing that researching service quality is necessary for three reasons. These are controlling, evaluating and improving services and the service delivery processes. In doing such research projects, it is necessary to analyze the service and the entire service process in all its distinct characteristics, properties or parts. Since the total service process consists of many other processes, it is necessary to gather as much information as possible about these processes, which can be used effectively for managerial purposes.

standards   The data has to meet certain standards. This seems self-evident, but the process- oriented character of service delivery and the customer's subjective evaluation of service quality are complicating factors. Although we have discussed some of those issues already in the section on cross-cultural research, we will recall such standards here:

completeness   **1.** *Completeness*: data should reflect the relevant aspects of service quality or activities;

validity   **2.** *Validity*: one should measure what one is supposed to measure;

timeliness   **3.** *Timeliness*: data should be sufficiently actual (and not out-dated);

accuracy   **4.** *Accuracy*: data should not differ from the real value;

reliability   **5.** *Reliability*: data should be consistent over time; and

costs   **6.** *Costs*: the (expected) value for the user of the data should outweigh the costs to get the data.

Finally some standards must be agreed upon in the presentation of the findings. The figures, tables, numbers, symbols or the text have to be understood without much effort by the users.[19]

VARIOUS APPROACHES

Various approaches to collect the relevant data about service quality can be used. Figure 6-4 depicts the approaches commonly used in measuring service quality.

Figure 6-4
Approaches for measuring service quality

Quality information can be collected on

• **a continuous basis; and on**
• **an ad hoc basis.**

Research may be directed at

1. **Employees; and**
2. **Customers.**

The nature of the research can be

1. **qualitative; and**
2. **quantitative.**

Due to services' intangibility and customer perceptions, one should try to find objective measures and not only rely on subjective indicators. The data can be collected via

1. **personal interviews;**
2. **focus group interviews;**
3. **mail surveys;**
4. **telephone surveys; and**
5. **internal databases.**

continuous, long
lasting research

ad hoc research

First of all, it is important to distinguish between continuous, long lasting research to build up and analyze trends, on the one hand, and *ad hoc* research with respect to one shot, specific questions. These approaches depict with what frequency the market researcher gathers the information: always or only when needed. Approaches may differ between employees and customers. This refers to the target group on which the research focusses for the group of respondents.

Employee research

(external and
internal) service
quality

Employees, especially in the front office, meet customers regularly. So, they should know a lot about their customers, their expectations and their perceptions. Moreover, employees in one department often deliver services to employees in other departments. Therefore, employees can be asked about their opinions on both kinds of (external and internal) service quality. In such research, the following questions can arise:

- are our markets (internal and external clients) satisfied about the service we deliver?
- which services would our customers appreciate in addition to our core service?
- what could we do ourselves (even without any additional costs) to improve the quality of the relationships with our clients, with whom we have frequent contact? This may even be targeted at individual employees.
- which activities are our competitors developing in, e.g. relationship building?

employee research

This employee research can be carried out on a continuous and *ad hoc* basis. It can be done in three ways: a mail survey (also used to measure job satisfaction), a personal interview, or a focus group interview with a number of fellow-workers (5 to 10). A positive side-effect of such projects is very often that it encourages people, enhances their motivation to deliver excellent service quality.

Customer research

customer research

Continuous customer research can be based on mail surveys, interviews with different groups of customers or interviews using the same group of customers (panels), and, customer cards (credit cards, loyalty programs, etc.). Data from customer service cards processed onto a database is often easy to apply. On the basis of the results generated via these cards, standards can be improved in the quality of the service delivery over the next period. The answers on these questions can establish how satisfied the client is with the service provided. An example is given in the next Service practice.

Service
practice
6-5
Measuring
service quality
simply

See how simply Délifrance collects data about the quality in their self service bars, brasseries and restaurants in Amsterdam Schiphol airport. You can pick up such a questionnaire yourself at the cashier.

New airlines in Central and Eastern Europe are seeking to improve their service level by following the example of western airlines in measuring quality. Estonian Air, flying with modern western aircraft, would like to improve their quality. Questionnaires in Estonian, Russian and English – all three in different colors for easy distribution and processing – are handed out to the passengers of Estonian Air.

Questionnaires investigating hotel guests' opinions are very popular. See what the New Zealand based Christchurch Park Royal hotel, the French Climat de France hotels, and the Holiday Inn hotels in The Netherlands ask their customers. These questionnaires are found on the desk in the hotel room.

Please note in what respects some of the questionnaires differ (see pp. 264-266).

monitor and control service quality over time

In this way, research provides data to monitor and control service quality over time. A disadvantage may be that the information obtained is not detailed enough to determine whether a client is really satisfied or not; then more qualitative information is needed. An innovative way of asking the questions is illustrated in the next Service practice.

Service practice 6-6 Proactive approach while checking out[20]

In some hotels, you find questionaires in your room or at the check-out asking you to give your opinion on service quality (see the previous Service practice). This is quite a reactive approach as the methods rely on the customer to take the initiative (and then the company reacts). Proactive methods are more effective to uncover service problems, as it involves the company making the initial contact.

Customers checking out of the Harvey Hotel in Plano, Texas, during the morning rush, may be approached by a "Lobby Lizard", a member of the management team who asks for feedback. This proactive approach prompts many more hotel guests to voice concerns or make suggestions than would be otherwise the case. General manager John Longstreet explains: "When we ask 'How was your stay?' the guest invariably says 'fine'. But when we ask 'Did you notice anything we could improve?' the response frequently is 'Well, now that you ask...'" If the situation warrants, the Lobby Lizard can implement immediate recovery service. The hotel has made numerous service improvements as a result of the guest feedback.

Ad hoc consumer research often takes place in the form of conversations with individual clients, focus group interviews or discussing a particular subject in a panel. Of course, questionnaires can be mailed to a particular sample.

Customer Case Research

The personal research methods are particularly suitable for research considering customized services and for researching the underlying motives of clients behaving in a certain way (this last point also counts for standard services), or for uncovering unexpected findings. Customer Case Research (CCR) is such a method:[21]

"CCR is a form of exploratory research that can discover critical purchase drivers that are outside the box of current thinking. It uses interviews and observation to trace the full stories of how real customers spend real money in a product category. Although it has a well-defined structure, CCR operates without preconceptions about buyers or purchase criteria. As customers relate their stories, CCR uncovers purchase drivers that might not be obvious, including hidden decision making, unintended product uses, and unanticipated decision criteria. More structured, quantitative research methods can then be used to understand and measure these newly discovered purchase drivers."

Service practice 6-7 presents an example of an unexpected opening.

Service practice 6-7 Unexpected openings	A bank wanted to enlarge its consumer business. Its previous market research examined customer perceptions of its performance along 30 dimensions, including service, friendliness, and price competitiveness. But it never clearly showed the bank how to attract new accounts.

At 8:30 a.m. one Monday morning in September 1990, a case researcher positioned himself at the bank's information desk. When people approached to open new accounts, he asked them, "What led you to open this account today?" Although he had interviewed only four new customers by 9:15 a.m., three of them said that they were moving their accounts from a nearby savings and loan bank that had just been closed due to insolvency.

By 9:30 a.m., the case researcher alerted bank management to this behavior. The bank management knew the S&L was closed and that a large bank had taken over its accounts. What they hadn't realized was how many of the S&L's depositors would be unaware that the facility was closed and would go there to do their banking as usual. If these depositors disliked either the location or the style of the large bank, they immediately sought an alternative – they were suddenly "in play".

By 10:00 a.m., the bank had an action plan. They immediately deployed staff to the shuttered S&L to distribute account opening kits and hastily-copied maps showing the route to their bank. Thousands of accounts resulted within two weeks.

This opening may seem obvious now, but it wasn't then. The S&L crisis created this opening for a limited period of time, but many such openings occur on an ongoing basis.

internal clients A special type of client research is research amongst the organization's own personnel. It is desirable to know whether internal clients (fellow-workers) are satisfied or not with the service delivered by colleagues (from another department). A service organization can check in many ways how clients evaluate the service and the service delivery process.

Third, it is important to make the well known distinction between qualitative and quantitative research. The first one is often small scale, while the latter one requires

30 seconds for your opinion *Holiday Inn*

Sukupuoli/Gender:	Mies/Male ◯	Nainen/Female ◯	

Vierailun tarkoitus/Purpose of visit:

Työmatka ◯ Business	Loma ◯ Pleasure	Kokous ◯ Conference	Ryhmämatka ◯ Group

Yöpymisen kesto/Length of stay?

1 yö/1 night ◯	2 - 4 yötä/2 to 4 nights ◯	5 tai useampi yö/5 or more nights ◯

Montako yötä olette viettäneet hotellissa viimeksi kuluneen vuoden aikana?

How many nights have you spent in a hotel over the past year?

1 - 10 ◯	11 - 25 ◯	26 - 50 ◯	Yli 50 + ◯

+   +

Tyytyväisyysaste: Level of Satisfaction	Heikko Low ☹	Tyydyttävä Average 😐		Hyvä High ☺	
Aulan yleisilme ja viihtyisyys **Attractiveness/overall appearance of the lobby**	◯	◯	◯	◯	◯
Henkilökunnan suhtautuminen pyyntöihinne **Staff responsiveness to your needs**	◯	◯	◯	◯	◯
Saamanne lähtöpalvelu (ystävällisyys, tehokkuus) **Service received at check-out (friendly, efficient)**	◯	◯	◯	◯	◯
Hotellin turvallisuus ja turvatoimet **Hotel safety and security**	◯	◯	◯	◯	◯
Hinta/laatusuhde **Value received for price paid**	◯	◯	◯	◯	◯
Suosittelisitteko tätä hotellia ystävälle/liikekumppanille **Would you recommend this hotel to a friend/ business associate**	◯ En No			◯ Kyllä Yes	

Lisäkommentteja?/Please share any additional comments:

_____

_____

_____

Päiväys/Date: _____   Huoneen numero/Room number: _____

office use only

+

264

CHRISTCHURCH PARKROYAL — GUEST COMMENT FORM

PLEASE TICK ☐

YOUR ROOM

How would you describe:	Excellent	Above Average	Average	Below Average
1. Room amenities?	☐	☐	☐	☐
2. The information in your room about the facilities and services?	☐	☐	☐	☐
3. The servicing of your room?	☐	☐	☐	☐
4. Was everything in working order?	Yes ☐	No ☐		

RESTAURANTS

How would you describe the service:

CANTERBURY TALES	☐	☐	☐	☐
VICTORIA STREET CAFE	☐	☐	☐	☐
YAMAGEN	☐	☐	☐	☐
IN ROOM DINING	☐	☐	☐	☐

The choice offered on the menu:

CANTERBURY TALES	☐	☐	☐	☐
VICTORIA STREET CAFE	☐	☐	☐	☐
YAMAGEN	☐	☐	☐	☐
IN ROOM DINING	☐	☐	☐	☐

The quality and presentation:

CANTERBURY TALES	☐	☐	☐	☐
VICTORIA STREET CAFE	☐	☐	☐	☐
YAMAGEN	☐	☐	☐	☐
IN ROOM DINING	☐	☐	☐	☐

The choice offered on the wine list:

CANTERBURY TALES	☐	☐	☐	☐
VICTORIA STREET CAFE	☐	☐	☐	☐
YAMAGEN	☐	☐	☐	☐
IN ROOM DINING	☐	☐	☐	☐

BARS

How would you describe the service:	Excellent	Above Average	Average	Below Average
ATRIUM LOUNGE	☐	☐	☐	☐
RUMPOLES	☐	☐	☐	☐
FIRST EDITION	☐	☐	☐	☐
YAMAGEN	☐	☐	☐	☐
HONOUR BAR	☐	☐	☐	☐

GENERAL

How would you describe:

Reception Desk Service	☐	☐	☐	☐
Concierge/Porter Service	☐	☐	☐	☐
Telephone Operator Service	☐	☐	☐	☐
Laundry & Valet Service	☐	☐	☐	☐
The overall standard of the Hotel	☐	☐	☐	☐
Was this your first stay with us?	Yes ☐	No ☐		

FURTHER COMMENTS/SUGGESTIONS:

What single point influenced you to stay with us? _____

Would you stay with us again?   Yes ☐   No ☐

If no, what do we need to change?

_____

_____

_____

To assist in utilising the information in these questionnaires we would like the following information:

Room No. _____   Arrival Date _____/_____/_____   Departure Date _____/_____/_____

Usual state and country of residence: _____

Male ☐   Female ☐

I am: on holiday ☐   attending a conference ☐   on business ☐   on a group tour ☐

Other (please specify) _____

Name (optional): _____

You are invited to make further comments on any aspect of your visit. Thank you for your co-operation.

qualitative research

large scale studies. Especially in service quality research, qualitative research should not be overlooked. It is especially important to hear from consumers themselves what they perceive as:

- their expectations;
- the relevant attributes of service quality;
- the importance of each attribute to the overall service quality;
- the causes of service failures;
- the competitors of a particular firm;

large scale quantitative research

and how they assess these issues. This can be the input for large scale quantitative research used to determine the exact magnitude of a particular opinion. When interviews or group sessions of the qualitative part are video taped, they can be shown to the firm's employees. This will help to convince them what they should do/change in order to satisfy the customer.[22]

The fourth type of approach deals with the way in which the data is collected. Figure 6-4 mentions five of them.

Personal interviews

in depth personal interviews

Whether services are standardized or customized, the individual consumers experience the service personally. And customers differ one from another. To investigate their personal feelings, perceptions, expectations, etc. thoroughly, in depth personal interviews are appropriate.[23]

Focus group interviews

group discussion

The group discussion technique – one may also speak of focus group interviews – can be applied for various problems. The method is based on the idea of group dynamics that always arise when people are interacting. The number of ideas, complaints, proposals, etc. a group puts forward, is greater than with individual interviews. Also, people can react to each other's opinions during a session. Frequently, deeper lying motives can be revealed. The group discussion produces no "hard" data, because the number of participants is rather limited (5 to 10). This can be met by working with a greater number of respondents or multiple groups. Often, this is not necessary since

generator of ideas

the method is especially suitable as a generator of ideas or as a first orientation about problems with fellow-workers or clients. Group discussions could be carried out by the company itself. The making and analyzing of conversation reports (protocols) is often a time-consuming occupation. Most of the time, one underestimates the requirements and skills of doing these interviews well. Therefore, specialized agencies should be preferred over own people.

Mail surveys

a mail survey

A mail survey can be achieved with many target groups. The following points are important when drawing up a questionnaire for assessing service quality (taking into consideration that the qualitative pilot-study has already taken place): defining the problem exactly; designing the questionnaire and processing the questionnaire.

*the customers'
perspective*

The problem has to be defined clearly, otherwise it is difficult to investigate (see also section 6.4). It is important to indicate clearly whether the research concerns the service itself, the service delivery process or both. In customer research, it is necessary to look at the service delivery process from the customers' perspective: which stages/phases are they going through, which steps should they perform during the service delivery process? etc. This perspective follows on logically from being market oriented.

In designing the questionnaire, all well known issues about questionnaire design are relevant. Three points are particularly important:

1. limit the number of questions. Do not submit to the challenge to ask more questions than are strictly needed;

2. ask simple questions. Do not use questions in technical terms belonging to the "language of the service provider" but in terms customers understand. While formulating the questions, it is important for the researcher to realize that the person who completes the questionaire has no help: nobody can explain questions; and

3. use so-called "closed" questions as much as possible. In closed questions, the answer categories are given already. Customers only have to tick the appropriate answer.

In order to process the questionnaire, one should use a statistical process package (like SPSS – Statistical Package for Social Sciences) on the computer. The analytical possibilities of such packages are large.

Telephone surveys

telephone surveys

Telephone surveys can be carried out quickly and at relatively low cost; also, in many countries it (still) has a high response. One important disadvantage is that only simple questions can be raised, and no visual aids, etc. can be shown. However, visualization is always a difficult point as services are intangible by nature. On the other hand, in some countries not all people have telephones.

Research based on internal data

There are all kinds of data that are registered in the administration of the service provider. We will mention some of the (already existing) types of data that may be recalled from the firm's own database:

firm's own database

- number of times (per week/month/year) clients call by telephone and ask for information or complain (about what);
- number of credit-notes sent, as an indication of the number of times mistakes in the original invoices or shipments have to be recovered;
- number of withdrawn accounts and policies, such as in banks or insurance companies;
- absence (due to sickness) per department; and
- number of passengers per flight.

An important advantage of this data is that it is very objective. A disadvantage is that the underlying motives for consumer or employee behavior are not known. This problem can be overcome; for example: by asking the clients who call why they complain about the organization or the provided services. Another disadvantage is the absence of norms in comparing the own figures with other organizations. Do the hundred complaints the organization receives per month represent a high proportion of customer transactions or just a low proportion? The accessibility of the organization when a customer wants to complain partly determines how many complaints will be received. Lowering such access barrieres via toll-free numbers is an often applied solution here. The number also depends on the degree of care with which complaints are actually registered and actions to solve them are taken.[24]

TOWARDS A SERVICE QUALITY INFORMATION SYSTEM

The preceding discussion revealed many different approaches which can be used in researching service quality. It is our firm belief that it is wise to always start such research projects with a qualitative pilot-study, whether it concerns customized or standard services as well as core- or augmented services. Research into customized services, to find out the causes of service failures, for instance, first requires individual conversations or group discussions and not large scale mailed questionnaires right away. Such large scale, quantitative studies are better suited for standard services known by the public at large that can be obtained easily and on a wide scale (or for customized services after the qualitative stage has been done).

feedback

With all the data gathered by means of market research, it is important that the results obtained are fed back to the personnel who are primarily responsible for the service delivery. Contact personnel and decision makers need this feedback in order to further improve the actual market-orientation and service quality. Therefore, it is necessary to combine all the relevant information collected by all the approaches used and make it available to (potential) users. In this respect, the concept of a Service-Quality Information System (SQIS) has been introduced.[25] This system stresses the need to flow continuously generated data "into databases that decision makers can use on both a regularly scheduled and as-needed basis".

Service-Quality Information System

(dis)satisfaction management

This SQIS should be an essential part of the firm's (international) marketing information system. It should contain all the information about the firm, its competitors and their service quality. It should also contain the data relevant to perform (dis)satisfaction management. Consequently, it will contain service quality data that may be obtained via various techniques.

6.7 TECHNIQUES TO MEASURE SERVICE QUALITY

Once the approach for measuring service quality has been decided upon, one (or more) particular technique(s) have to be chosen. For this purpose, various options are available. As the SERVQUAL model plays a central role in services marketing, the technique in following this model will be discussed extensively. Although SERVQUAL is a very popular and sound instrument to measure service quality, it is certainly not the only instrument to be used to that end. More simple and more complex methods exist, some of them being more qualitative oriented while others are much more quantitative. An example of a simpler method is applying grades like at school. An example of a more complex and quantitative technique is conjoint analysis. Other examples include techniques like the Critical Incidents Method, Problem Detection Study, Q-sort Methodology, protocol analysis and the Customer Satisfaction Index. These techniques will be dealt with first before turning to SERVQUAL.

SIMPLE GRADES

school grading system

The usual school grading system can be applied to assess service quality. Grades may range from excellent to very bad/poor. This looks very simple. Therefore, this way of assessing service quality can be used effectively in getting a first and global impression of service quality in a firm.

a first and global impression of service quality

The disadvantage is that no "anchor point" exists: what do people consider as adequate, bad or excellent? Do they all give the same content to these qualifications? That is why expectations should be introduced as a comparison standard for the perceptions. Another disadvantage of this approach is its use in international research projects. Different countries have different school grading systems, complicating the comparison between results from different countries, as the next Service practice shows.

Service practice 6-8 The international application of grading systems

The differences in traditional school grading systems per country may result in difficulties in comparing findings from different countries. For example, the grading scales ranging from excellent to very bad typically compose of:

- A (excellent) to D (very bad=fail) in the USA;
- 1 (very bad) to 10 (excellent) in The Netherlands;
- 1 (excellent) to 5 (very bad) in Germany;
- 1 (very bad) to 20 (excellent) in France; and
- 1 (very bad) to 30 (excellent) in Italy.

The market researcher will have to translate these national scales into one international scale.

MYSTERY SHOPPER

mystery shopper

In this case, a researcher acts as a customer who needs a service.[26] All the things the researcher experiences are recorded or written down afterwards. Such a mystery shopper can be a researcher from a research agency or an employee from another branch. They may have a particular assignment (e.g. to see what answers are given on a particular question about life insurance) or a broad one (e.g. check how we are dealing with customers).

The advantage is that detailed real life experiences and data are collected. One disadvantage is that the researcher may interpret the service encounter in a particular way, has to write it down afterwards, has to analyze all the stories afterwards, interpret them and formulate the conclusions. Proper training and experienced mystery shoppers may overcome these drawbacks and biases.

PROTOCOL ANALYSIS

protocol Within the services sector, a protocol can be defined as a record of a respondent's verbalized thought processes about a service or service provider.[27] This may hinge upon decisions in all three stages of the consumption process. Respondents have to "think out loud", talk and/or write down whatever comes to their mind when thinking about a service, service provider and the quality. All the protocols ("stories") have to be collected and analyzed: protocol analysis.

The analysis of these protocols may be time consuming. The data is collected in an unstructured way. Consequently, they are also very subjective.

This qualitative technique suits the starting phase of a research project. Safeguards have to be made in order to avoid research biases. It may be that different judges interpret the same data in different ways, or that customers do not give a full description of what they really feel, perceive and experience, etc. The big advantage is that all these real life examples provide great detail; they are formulated by customers in their own words. Consequently, they can be used to show employees how real life customers really think about them and the company.

CRITICAL INCIDENT TECHNIQUE

Critical Incident Technique The Critical Incident Technique (CIT) was originally developed by Flanagan (1954). CIT is a method to explore events and encounters where contact personnel and customers meet in delivering service quality.[28] It can be regarded as a particular type of protocol analysis. The technique assesses extremely positive and extremely negative service encounters from the customers' perspective. Via in-depth-interviews (or observation), the "bottlenecks" in the service delivery process are identified. Customers are asked to describe service events and experiences about which they are extremely satisfied or dissatisfied: the critical incidents. It is a qualitative research technique. Researchers have to find an order in all the answers given, and make some structure out of it that makes sense to managers. This will enable them to take decisions and improve service quality if necessary.[29]

Three aspects are especially relevant in the context of CIT-studies:

1. *timing of critical incidents*

timing of the incidents

Information about the timing of the incidents in the consumption process of the service and its delivery gives insight into the complexity and the importance of that specific stage to the customer. The service provider can use these insights to better fulfil the needs of the customer;

2. *locus of critical incidents*

initiator "locus" of the critical incident

This aspect means the initiator "locus" of the critical incident. In other words, the object or person that started the sequence of events or the person or object the incident refers to should be very clear; and

3. *content of critical incidents*

various aspects

CIT focuses on explicit behavior in specific service encounters. The result is the evaluation of the quality of the service in various aspects mentioned by the respondents themselves: there is no priority scheme of service attributes to be assessed. This is in contrast to, for example, SERVQUAL which focusses on the outcome of the service delivery process and measures quality ex-post on ten, five or three dimensions via 22 questions. Furthermore, the nature of the CIT survey instrument does allow deeper probing than the 10 SERVQUAL-dimensions. Therefore, SERVQUAL does not supply as much detailed insight into how service quality is obtained whereas CIT does.

In the tradition of CIT research, it is the responsibility of the researcher to uncover the meanings and themes in the experience of the consumer. Moreover, CIT research

depth and richness of detail

has depth and richness of detail which can only be achieved by such a qualitative technique. When many critical incidents have been collected they have to be structured in an ordered fashion. Then they can be analyzed by many quantitative techniques.[30]

MEANS-END CHAINS

means-end chain

A means-end chain is a simple knowledge structure containing interconnected meanings about attributes, consequences (benefits or perceived risks) and values.[31] When applied in the service sector, it is a qualitative technique aimed at uncovering deep, underlying arguments about service quality and service attributes.

Figure 6-5
A simple means-end chain model of consumers' service knowledge

ATTRIBUTES ⟶ CONSEQUENCES ⟶ VALUES

The service attribute is seen as a means to an end. The end could be either an immediate benefit (or risk) or a more abstract value. Because means-end knowledge structures contain the personally relevant meanings that consumers create for services, they are unique to each customer's own background and personal interests. Thus, we may expect different customers to have different means-end chains for the same service. Measuring means-end chains is accomplished by one-on-one, in-depth interviews that can probe deeper into the meanings of attributes and consequences and establish the "whys" of consumers' behavior.

We distinguish two main steps in measuring customers' means-end chains. These are:

1. *identify important service attributes*

identify the key service attributes

In the first step, the researcher has to identify the key service attributes customers consider important in choosing the service; and

2. *laddering*

laddering

The second step is to conduct a special type of interview, called laddering. In this interview, customers are encouraged to go through a series of "why" questions in order to reveal how the service attributes are connected to higher consequences and values.

A basic advantage of these means-end chain models is that they provide a deeper understanding of customers' service knowledge than methods focussing only on attributes or benefits. The strong point of this method is the acquisition of knowledge in terms of attributes, consequences and values.[32] Moreover, it reveals how customers "organize" these three levels of service knowledge and define them. It is assumed that from each means-end model consumers form meaningful associations that link service attributes with consequences and values (see Figure 6-5). An example is given in the next Service practice.

Service practice 6-9
Means to an end

In a qualitative study: why do customers participate in retailers' loyalty programs? special attention was paid to: Why do they buy in these particular stores? It is self-evident that concrete issues like number of coupons, bonus points or Air Miles, price, assortment and the like do play a role. But these are quite "superficial and concrete reasons". Via laddering, some other underlying arguments were also found. Three of the respondents revealed the following means-end chains:

Means-end chains of three customers indicating why they buy food in a particular store*

	customer 1	customer 2	customer 3
attribute(s)	shop is nearby/close by ↓	friendly employees ↓	receive coupons ↓
consequences (benefits)	time-saving ↓	feel treated as a person ↓	save money ↓
value(s)	happiness	respect	financial responsibility

*In reality, each respondent may mention more than one attribute, consequence or value. For reasons of simplicity we stick to one at each level.

PROBLEM DETECTION STUDY

Problem Detection Study

Research International, a well known international market research agency, has developed a technique called Problem Detection Study.[33] It is built on identifying what customers consider to be the greatest problem(s) in a service, service delivery process or service industry. This identification process follows two stages.

opinions on the problems

First, important (present and potential) customers and key employees are interviewed personally. They state their opinions on the problems, if any, customers might have with the service. These findings are combined with data from other sources collected via dissatisfaction management or stored in the service quality information system.

rank the problems

Second, the most important problems (according to the customer) are isolated. For this purpose, the market researchers interview 200–1,000 customers. They have to rank the problems mentioned in Stage 1 by answering the following question on a 4-point scale: "How serious is this problem to you?" The average scores over all items reveal the most serious problems from the customers' point of view. This list can be analyzed in various ways to get more insight into the data, for instance factor analysis or cluster analysis. It appeared that the highest ranking problems in many studies referred mostly to – what we call – functional and relational quality, and much less to technical quality.

Service practice 6-10 Esso Hotel guests weren't looking for lifts

The internal signal from the reception clerks and hotel hostesses was plain enough. "The problem is that people have to carry their luggage up and down stairs." But installing lifts in all the hotels having several storeys would have cost many millions.

At the same time, company management was thinking about something else: wasn't it true that guests found private hotels more pleasant, more service-oriented? A PDS study was done.

The problems that arose in the PDS research were entirely different ones from the content of the internal signals. Carrying luggage was not a problem, therefore investment in lifts was not necessary. Guests also didn't find personnel less service-minded than that at privately owned hotels. At this point, money had been saved by avoiding two unnecessary measures. But what were the big problems?

The first one came as a surprise and something of a shock. "It's boring to stay at hotels." This was shocking because "to give guests pleasant overnight stays" was apparently not sufficient as a business concept. It was therefore necessary to make guests' stay pleasant in other respects. Suddenly, it seemed necessary to look into the area of entertainment. In addition, the problem of "uninteresting food" came high on the problem list. Not that the food itself was not tasty. It was just that here was too little variation. The serving of breakfast was also considered to have its faults.

If you have stayed at Esso Hotels during the past few years you would surely have noticed many changes.

• A long-term environmental plan for both interior and exterior rebuilding has been started.

- An ad-sponsored TV channel, in addition to the ordinary TV programs, with the help of video. A 3-hour program shown twice each evening and including a good long film, is available in every room.
- At check-in, the video program is handed over to you together with your key.
- A special guest magazine – "Etapp" – is waiting in the room when guests arrive.
- Bulletins describing various activities available are posted in the lobby. Jogging paths, tennis courts, concerts, cinema and other entertainment.
- In some of the hotels, guest activities such as dancing, happy hour in the cocktail bar, wine testing, etc. have been introduced.
- In order to improve the variety of food, Esso Hotel's restaurants and inns have been working with various culinary drives, for instance providing more prepared meals. In addition, special weeks for special foods are held – French food week, USA week, Hawaii week, etc.
- In order to raise the general restaurant standards, several specific measures have been taken. Better coffee, greater variety of cheeses, better bread, etc.

Breakfast service has been radically changed. Generous buffet-style breakfasts at all hotels, and free morning papers with your coffee or tea are now available.

All these measures have been taken to meet specific customer problems that had been identified by PDS.

For Esso Hotels, these measures have resulted in successively increasing sales, leading to a greater market share. It is also possible to measure the effect of individual measures. An internal research indicated, for example, that 30% of the guests stated that the TV3 channel (video) was the main reason for their booking at Esso.

Q-SORT

sort through a number of statements

With this technique, respondents have to sort through a number of statements about, e.g. a service, service delivery process, company, industry.[34] These statements are usually written on separate cards. They can hinge upon various issues, for instance the many attributes of service quality. All these statements have to be sorted into a predetermined number of categories (usually 11) with a specified number having to be placed in each category/pile. Service practice 6-11 shows how this technique works.

CONJOINT ANALYSIS

conjoint analysis

attributes with varying quality levels

The technique of conjoint analysis uses different attributes in order to develop a number of existing or imaginary services. These services are described on cards and shown to the consumer. Customers then have to indicate their preference for a particular service package. First, attributes of the service with varying quality levels are

*Service
practice
6-11
Q-sorting in
practice*

In illustrating the Q-sort technique, assume that four subjects evaluate the test items dealing with travel and vacations. For purposes of illustration, only three piles will be used. The subjects are asked to sort items into:

MOST AGREED WITH (TWO ITEMS)	NEUTRAL ABOUT (THREE ITEMS)	LEAST AGREED WITH (TWO ITEMS)
+1	0	-1

The numbers above the horizontal line represent the number of items that the subject *must* place into piles 1, 2, and 3, respectively. That is, the subject may first select the two items that he or she *most* agrees with; these go in pile 1. Next, the subject selects the two statements that he or she least agrees with; these go in pile 3. The remaining three items are placed in pile 2. The numbers below the line represent scale values. Suppose that the responses of the four subjects, A, B, C, and D, result in the following scale values:

Quality Item	SUBJECT			
	A	B	C	D
1	+1	+1	-1	-1
2	0	0	0	0
3	+1	0	0	-1
4	-1	-1	+1	+1
5	0	0	0	0
6	-1	-1	+1	+1
7	0	+1	-1	-1

As can be seen, the subject pair A and B and the subject pair C and D seem "most alike" of the six distinct pairs that could be considered. We could, of course, actually correlate each subject's scores with every other subject and, similar to semantic differential applications, conduct factor and cluster analyses on the resultant intercorrelations. Typically, these additional steps are undertaken in Q-sort studies.

defined on the basis of (in-depth) interviews with clients. Each service is built up of a number of attributes with different quality levels. Next, for each attribute, quality levels are established in order to show a number of service packages to the customer.

benefits On the basis of consumers' evaluations of these packages, each service's benefits can be computed for an attribute's quality level. Because this is possible for each attribute and attribute quality level, the benefit-values between the attributes and attribute levels can be compared. In this way, it is possible to compute the importance that each respondent or group of respondents "attributes to each attribute". If the price is taken up as an attribute, is it also possible to express aspects of that service in terms of prices and differences in prices.

This technique can be used not only to evaluate existing services but also to develop and test new services. This will be explained in the following example about the repair and maintenance service of a manufacturer of copying machines.[35]

Service practice 6-12 Conjoint analysis

In conversations with managers, a few clients, the service manager and a few technicians, a service contract, in terms of attributes like weekend/overnight service, parts guarantees, maintenance and repair, price and the response time was defined. The response time is the time that expires between point of time of mentioning a malfunctioning of the copying machine and the arrival of the technician. These attributes and their respective levels are presented in Figure 6-6.

Figure 6-6
Attributes and attribute levels for service contracts

Attribute	Attribute levels
A. Weekend/overnight service	1. No week/overnight service 2. With weekend/overnight service
B. Spare parts included	1. Exclusive of spare parts 2. Inclusive of spare parts
C. Preventive maintenance	1. No preventive maintenance 2. One preventive visit 3. Two preventive visits 4. Three preventive visits
D. Price	1. $350 a year 2. $550 a year 3. $750 a year 4. $950 a year 5. $1,150 a year
E. Response time before a service technician arrives to do the repair	1. Response time 6 hours 2. Response time 8 hours 3. Response time 12 hours

A "typical conjoint" question may look like Figure 6-7.

Figure 6-7

An example of a "conjoint-question"

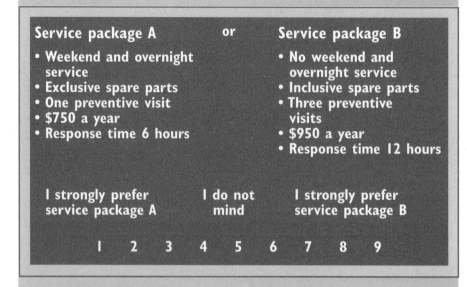

Customers are asked to make a choice between the left and the right service contract (the whole package) in Figure 6-7. Via computer analysis (ACA Software, 1985), the benefit values of the attribute levels ("utilities") are computed. The result of these computations are – as a fictional example – presented in Figure 6-8.

In this example, price appears to be of utmost importance. So, the copying machine manufacturer should price its service package very carefully.

As stated, price is the most important attribute here. The difference in benefits between a price of $350 and a price of $1,150 a year is 109 (27+28+32+22) benefit points. The difference in price between the highest and lowest level of the attribute price is $800. This means that – taken on average – a utility unit represents a value of $7.34 (800÷109=7.34).

In this way, it can be computed what customers are willing to pay on average for the weekend/overnight service, for example. The difference between getting the weekend/overnight service or not is 10 benefit points (18–8) and thus represents a value of $73.40. In other words, customers are willing to spend $73.40 on average for a weekend/overnight service.

The relative importance of the attributes based on the preceding figure can be computed (see Figure 6-9). This relative importance is computed by dividing the additional benefit that relates to each attribute by the total additional benefit of all attributes (the sum of all additional benefits in that third column). For the weekend/overnight service this is 10÷209=5%.

Figure 6-8

*Results of conjoint analysis: research service contracts**

Attribute levels	Average partial utility scores	Additional utility	Cost per incremental level
1. No weekend/overnight service	8		
2. With weekend/overnight service	18	10	$73.40
1. Exclusive of spare parts	2		
2. Inclusive of spare parts		20	$147.80
1. No preventive maintenance	6		
2. One preventive visit	24	18	$132.12
3. Two preventive visits	29	5	$36.70
4. Three preventive visits	33	4	$29.36
1. $350 a year	111	27	
2. $550 a year	84	28	
3. $750 a year	56	32	
4. $950 a year	24	22	
5. $1,150 a year	2		
1. Response time 6 hours	5		
2. Response time 8 hours	28	23	$168.82
3. Response time 12 hours	48	20	£147.80

*The data in this example are not real but fictional. They are only intended to show what kind of results can be obtained by applying conjoint analysis and how managers can interpret these findings.

Figure 6-9

Relative importance of attributes with service contracts

Attribute	Relative importance*
Weekend/overnight service	5%
Used materials	10%
Preventive maintenance	13%
Price	52%
Reaction time	21%

*Due to rounding up, this exceeds 100%

THE SMART-TECHNIQUE

Salient Multi-Attribute Research Technique

highest priority for improvement

SMART is another technique to measure service quality.[36] It is an instrument to diagnose the quality of services. The letters SMART stand for "Salient Multi-Attribute Research Technique". The strong point of this technique is that topics can be traced that should receive the highest priority for improvement according to the customer. It is assumed customers have a more or less hierarchical ordered preference for those service attributes that should be improved. It is not only assumed that customers know that order, but that they are also capable and willing to express that order.

most relevant attributes

From the qualitative pilot-study, preceding a large scale, quantitative SMART-study, a set of eight most relevant attributes of the particular service are defined. Next, the respondent is confronted with a situation in which all eight attributes find themselves at the lowest quality level. Then, respondents must indicate which attribute of this service they want to increase one quality level. This goes on till the highest level is reached. This process may also be terminated when the respondent indicates that a further increase of service level is not needed. On the basis of the answers given, both the (lack of) service quality as well as the ordering of priorities in attribute levels can be measured.

This technique is more or less comparable to conjoint analysis. However, the procedure of asking questions is different; now attributes are prioritized and not total packages. Here, customers indicate the highest priority for overnight copying services; in using conjoint analysis this would be the result of analyzing differences in total service packages.

CUSTOMER SATISFACTION INDEX

Customer Satisfaction Index

In the US as well as in Sweden, a Customer Satisfaction Index has been developed.[37] A large number of customers assess more than 3,900 goods and services quarterly in the US. The American Customer Satisfaction Index (ACSI) is based on the answers to 17 questions, rated on a scale 1-10. These questions hinge upon perceptions of service quality, the performance of the service compared to the expectations, etc. The results are combined and transformed into an overall score that may lie between zero and 100. The higher the score, the more satisfied customers are about a particular service, service company or service industry.

ACSI

The model to compute ACSI is shown in Service practice 6-13. Basically, it states that quality determines overall satisfaction which, in turn, determines how customers will express their satisfaction or dissatisfaction, e.g. via loyalty or complaints. The 15 questions used in measuring ACSI are shown as well.

Service practice 6-13 The American Customer Satisfaction Index: model and measurement

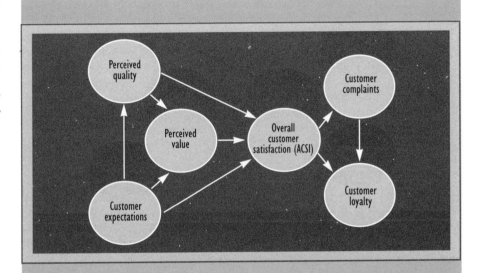

Measurement Variables Used in the ACSI Model

Measurement variable	Latent variable
1. Overall expectation of quality (prepurchase)	Customer expectations
2. Expectation regarding customization, or how well the product fits the customer's personal requirements (prepurchase)	Customer expectations
3. Expectation regarding reliability, or how often things would go wrong (prepurchase)	Customer expectations
4. Overall evaluation of quality experience (postpurchase)	Perceived quality
5. Evaluation of customization experience, or how well the product fits the customer's personal requirements (postpurchase)	Perceived quality
6. Evaluation of reliability experience, or how often things have gone wrong (postpurchase)	Perceived quality
7. Rating of quality given price	Perceived value
8. Rating of price given quality	Perceived value
9. Overall satisfaction	ACSI
10. Expectancy disconfirmation (performance that falls short of or exceeds expectations)	ACSI
11. Performance versus the customer's ideal product or service in the category	ACSI
12. Has the customer complained either formally or informally about the product or service?	Customer complaints
13. Repurchase likelihood rating	Customer loyalty
14. Price tolerance (increase) given repurchase	Customer loyalty
15. Price tolerance (decrease) to induce repurchase	Customer loyalty

Customer satisfaction is higher in industries with a significant level of competition and differentiation.[38] Customer satisfaction is also higher when involvement or experience with the service (or goods) is higher. And, customer satisfaction is high when switching costs, difficulty of standardization or ease of evaluating quality is low. It appears that satisfaction for goods is higher than for services and retailers. So, a higher degree of competition will lead to a higher degree of satisfaction (in the US). Nevertheless, it appears the ACSI gradually falls from the base line level of 74.5 in 1994 (when the ACSI was computed for the first time) to a 72.4 in the second quarter of 1996.[39]

SERVQUAL - METHODOLGY

SERVQUAL research methodology

In Chapter Five, the basics of the SERVQUAL-model have been discussed. This section contains the technicalities of the SERVQUAL research methodology in general. We maintain that the research questions should always be adjusted to the specific service and circumstances of service delivery.

The original SERVQUAL-model consisted of ten dimensions. Later, these were pooled into the five dimensions, as discussed in Chapter Five. It is our experience that when starting a research project about service quality, it is more attractive to start with ten dimensions instead of five.[40] This provides a more detailed starting point in developing the right questionnaire and in analyzing the service delivery process. The ten dimensions are defined in Chapter Five. Here, we give some examples on the operationalization of each dimension.

Service practice 6-14 SERVQUAL - examples

dimension	examples
reliability	accuracy in opening time; keeping clients' information correctly;
responsiveness	responding immediately to a telephone query; is the plumber willing to give me a specific time when he will show up to do the repair?
competence	knowledge and skills of the contact personnel; knowledge to refer quickly and effectively, if necessary;
access	not continuously overloaded telephone lines, short waiting times; convenient access to the organization (parking) or counter (entrance, waiting room);
courtesy	politeness when facing clients; how rude are cashiers when I cash my fifth travellers' cheque that day?

communication	explaining the procedure of service delivery in terms the customer understands; informing the client with regard to the procedure to be followed;
credibility	organization's reputation; personal characteristics of the contact personnel (attitudes);
security	physical safety of the customer when using the service; the client does not doubt when he is at the right address;
understanding/ knowing the customer	paying individual attention to a client by asking the right questions; providing precise service, also for instance during busy hours; and
tangibles	the offered facilities, to provide the service; furnishing of waiting rooms at counters.

check whether the actual service delivery matches customer expectations

the behavioral part of the service encounter

In these ten dimensions, customers' contact with front office personnel is central. This means that all these service encounters have to be performed and researched compared to the expectations held. Consequently, all these dimensions have to be made measurable in some way or another to check whether the actual service delivery matches customer expectations. The 22 questions of the SERVQUAL-questionnaire are a good point of departure for that purpose. The questionnaire is shown in Service practice 6-15. The dimensions refer to a very large extent to the behavioral part of the service encounter. In other words, they hinge more upon the functional and relational quality than the technical quality.

The SERVQUAL-instrument may reveal high quality data on service quality. It is based on an outweighing of good and bad experiences over time. Therefore, dramatic changes in such quality scores over time are not likely to occur.[41]

A new technique is always challenged by other academics. This holds for SERVQUAL as well. Therefore, the next section will deal with some of these comments and other critical issues in measuring service quality.

Service practice 6-15 SERVQUAL-questionnaire

CUSTOMER SATISFACTION SURVEY
APRIL 1992

PART 1

We would like your impressions about how well stores provide service relative to your expectations. Please think about the two different levels of expectations defined below:

> MINIMUM SERVICE LEVEL – the minimum level of service performance you consider adequate
>
> DESIRED SERVICE LEVEL – the level of service performance you desire

For each of the following statements, please indicate: (a) your minimum service level by circling one of the numbers in the first column; (b) your desired service level by circling one of the numbers in the second column, and (c) your perception of service by circling one of the numbers in the third column.

When it comes to . . .	My Minimum Service Level is: Low High	My Desired Service Level is: Low High	My Perception of Performance in the Store is: Low High	No Opin-ion
1 Prompt service to customers	1 2 3 4 5 6 7 8 9	1 2 3 4 5 6 7 8 9	1 2 3 4 5 6 7 8 9	N
2. Employees who are consistently courteous	1 2 3 4 5 6 7 8 9	1 2 3 4 5 6 7 8 9	1 2 3 4 5 6 7 8 9	N
3. Employees who deal with customers in a caring fashion	1 2 3 4 5 6 7 8 9	1 2 3 4 5 6 7 8 9	1 2 3 4 5 6 7 8 9	N
4. Providing services at the promised time	1 2 3 4 5 6 7 8 9	1 2 3 4 5 6 7 8 9	1 2 3 4 5 6 7 8 9	N
5. Employees who understand the needs of their customers	1 2 3 4 5 6 7 8 9	1 2 3 4 5 6 7 8 9	1 2 3 4 5 6 7 8 9	N
6. Visually appealing materials associated with the service (e.g., in-store signs)	1 2 3 4 5 6 7 8 9	1 2 3 4 5 6 7 8 9	1 2 3 4 5 6 7 8 9	N
7. Having the customer's best interest at heart	1 2 3 4 5 6 7 8 9	1 2 3 4 5 6 7 8 9	1 2 3 4 5 6 7 8 9	N
8. Willingness to help customers	1 2 3 4 5 6 7 8 9	1 2 3 4 5 6 7 8 9	1 2 3 4 5 6 7 8 9	N
9. Maintaining error-free records	1 2 3 4 5 6 7 8 9	1 2 3 4 5 6 7 8 9	1 2 3 4 5 6 7 8 9	N
10. Keeping customers informed about when services will be performed	1 2 3 4 5 6 7 8 9	1 2 3 4 5 6 7 8 9	1 2 3 4 5 6 7 8 9	N

When it comes to . . .	My <u>Minimum</u> Service Level is:		My <u>Desired</u> Service Level is:		My Perception of Performance in the Store is:		
	Low	High	Low	High	Low	High	No Opin-ion
11 Providing service as promised	1 2 3 4 5 6 7 8 9		1 2 3 4 5 6 7 8 9		1 2 3 4 5 6 7 8 9		N
12. Employees who instill confidence in customers	1 2 3 4 5 6 7 8 9		1 2 3 4 5 6 7 8 9		1 2 3 4 5 6 7 8 9		N
13. Employees who have the knowledge to answer customer questions	1 2 3 4 5 6 7 8 9		1 2 3 4 5 6 7 8 9		1 2 3 4 5 6 7 8 9		N
14. Dependability in handling customers' service problems	1 2 3 4 5 6 7 8 9		1 2 3 4 5 6 7 8 9		1 2 3 4 5 6 7 8 9		N
15. Readiness to respond to customers' requests	1 2 3 4 5 6 7 8 9		1 2 3 4 5 6 7 8 9		1 2 3 4 5 6 7 8 9		N
16. Performing services right the first time	1 2 3 4 5 6 7 8 9		1 2 3 4 5 6 7 8 9		1 2 3 4 5 6 7 8 9		N
17. Visually appealing stores	1 2 3 4 5 6 7 8 9		1 2 3 4 5 6 7 8 9		1 2 3 4 5 6 7 8 9		N
18. Giving customers individual attention	1 2 3 4 5 6 7 8 9		1 2 3 4 5 6 7 8 9		1 2 3 4 5 6 7 8 9		N
19. Employees who have a neat, professional appearance	1 2 3 4 5 6 7 8 9		1 2 3 4 5 6 7 8 9		1 2 3 4 5 6 7 8 9		N
20. Convenient business hours	1 2 3 4 5 6 7 8 9		1 2 3 4 5 6 7 8 9		1 2 3 4 5 6 7 8 9		N
21. Modern fixtures	1 2 3 4 5 6 7 8 9		1 2 3 4 5 6 7 8 9		1 2 3 4 5 6 7 8 9		N
22. Making customers feel safe in their transactions	1 2 3 4 5 6 7 8 9		1 2 3 4 5 6 7 8 9		1 2 3 4 5 6 7 8 9		N

PART II – RATING QUALITY, VALUE AND FEATURES

1. How would you rate the overall quality of service provided by _____ ? (Circle one number below.)

Extremely Poor							Extremely Good	
1	2	3	4	5	6	7	8	9

2. Thinking about service overall, please rate the value you feel you get for your money. (Circle one number below:

Poor Value							Excellent Value	
1	2	3	4	5	6	7	8	9

3. Listed below are five general features pertaining to retail stores and the services they offer. We would like to know how important each of these features is to *you* when you evaluate a retail store's quality of service.

   Please allocate a total of 100 points among the five features *according to how important each feature is to you* – the more important a feature is to you, the more points you should give it.

   Please be sure the points you give add up to 100.

   1. The appearance of the retail store's physical facilities, fixtures, personnel, and communications materials   _____ points

   2. The retail store's ability to perform the promised services dependably and accurately   _____ points

   3. The retail store's willingness to help customers and provide prompt service   _____ points

   4. The knowledge and courtesy of the retail store's employees and their ability to convey trust and confidence   _____ points

   5. The caring, individualized attention the retail store provides its customers   _____ points

   TOTAL POINTS ALLOCATED   100   points

PART III – RATING QUALITY, VALUE AND FEATURES

Based on your overall experience with service in the store, please indicate how likely you are to take the following actions. Circle the number that indicates your likelihood of taking each action.

How likely are you to . . .

	Not at all likely						Extremely likely
1. Say positive things about to other people	1	2	3	4	5	6	7
2. Recommend to someone who seeks your advice	1	2	3	4	5	6	7
3. Encourage friends and relatives to do business with	1	2	3	4	5	6	7
4. Consider your first choice to buy the types of products that stores sell	1	2	3	4	5	6	7
5. Do more business with in the next few years	1	2	3	4	5	6	7
6. Do less business with in the next few years	1	2	3	4	5	6	7
7. Take some of your business to a competitor that offers more attractive prices	1	2	3	4	5	6	7
8. Continue to do business with if its prices increase somewhat	1	2	3	4	5	6	7
9. Pay a higher price than other retail stores charge for the benefits you currently receive from	1	2	3	4	5	6	7
10. Switch to another retail store if you experience a problem with service	1	2	3	4	5	6	7
11. Complain to other consumers if you experience a problem with service	1	2	3	4	5	6	7
12. Complain to store employees if you experience a problem with service	1	2	3	4	5	6	7
13. Complain to external agencies, such as the Better Business Bureau, if you experience a problem with service	1	2	3	4	5	6	7

PART IV – FOR STATISTICAL PURPOSES ONLY

The following questions are for statistical purposes only. Your answers will be combined with others and will be kept strictly confidential.

For each question, please circle one number.

1. How long have you been a customer?
   Less than 1 year 1
   1 to less than 2 years 2
   2 to less than 5 years 3
   5 years or more 4

2. How frequently do you have face-to-face or telephone contact with employees?

   More than once a month 1
   About once a month 2
   About once every three months 3
   About once every six months 4
   About once a year 5
   Less than once a year 6

3. Have you recently had a problem with any of your transactions?

   Yes 1
   No 2

   (If "No", skip to question 5.)

4. If you did have a problem, was it resolved to your safisfaction?

   Yes 1
   No 2

5. Your sex is:

   Male 1
   Female 2

6. Your marital status is:

   Single 1
   Married 2

7. Your age is:

   Under 25 1
   25-34 2
   35-44 3
   45-54 4
   55-64 5
   65 or over .6

8. Your total annual family income is:

   Under $10,000 1
   $10,000-$19,999 2
   $20,000-$29,999 3
   $30,000-$49,999 4
   $50,000-$64,999 5
   $65,000 or over 6

9. The highest level of schooling you have completed is:

   High school or less 1
   Some college 2
   College graduate 3
   Graduate school 4

6.8   COMMENTS ON SERVQUAL AND OTHER CRITICAL ISSUES IN MEASURING SERVICE QUALITY

As it is such a central theme throughout the book, it is useful to examine the comments service marketing scholars have made about measuring service quality and the use of the SERVQUAL-methodology.[42] The comments are listed as eleven points of criticism and counter arguments. They are dealing with the following questions:

1. does SERVQUAL measure satisfaction or quality?
2. is it OK to use difference scores?
3. what about the effect of negatively worded statements?
4. how general are the dimensions applicable?
5. how static or dynamic is the model?
6. is it OK to use Likert scales?
7. what about different kinds of expectations?
8. what about raising expectations?
9. what about the length of the questionnaire if questions about (different kinds of) expectations, perceptions and importance are raised?
10. are hot items or general impressions reported by the respondents?
11. what is the best way to use and compute importance scores?

MEASURING QUALITY OR SATISFACTION

Here, the critics refer to the difference between satisfaction and quality.[43] Both the concepts can be defined as the difference between expectations and perceptions. In the literature, a debate is going on as to whether quality is an antecedent of satisfaction, or whether satisfaction is an antecedent of quality. Our position in that debate is given in Chapter Five: quality leads to satisfaction.

quality leads to satisfaction

USE OF DIFFERENCE SCORES

difference scores between expectations and perceptions

A second point of criticism concerns the method of using difference scores. Difference scores between expectations and perceptions are considered as the quality score. Consequently, this quality score can remain the same, while expectations and perceptions both change. In general, the critics on using difference scores holds. Though it has been shown that the factor structure of the answers given on the questions about expectations and perceptions and the resulting difference scores on all three are not always identical.[44] This makes interpreting the data complex.

perception scores alone

Recently, it has been shown that perception scores alone also give a good quality indication. Consequently, in order to overcome this point of criticism one could use perception scores instead of difference scores. Parasuraman (1995) reports on the findings of studies into comparing the psychometric properties of measuring service quality directly (=only by perceptions) and via difference scores. The difference scores are computed for the two-column format in their SERVQUAL-questionnaire (expectations versus perceptions) and the three-column format (expectations, minimum service level, desired service level) taking the zone of tolerance into account.

It can be concluded that:"In summary, the difference-score operationalisation of service quality appears to have psychometric properties that are as sound as that of the direct-measure operationalization. Therefore, the three-column format questionnaire yields richer, and perhaps more trustworthy, diagnostics than the two-column format questionnaire. Thus, operationalising service quality as difference scores seems appropriate."[45]

service quality as difference scores seems appropriate

NEGATIVELY WORDED QUESTIONS

In order to avoid tendency answers, researchers should use questions worded both positively and negatively. This is a general rule to be applied in much empirical research. However, questions about service quality formulated negatively are hard to ask and the results are hard to interpret when they are about expectations, perceptions and importance.

positively stated questions

In more recent research, negatively asked questions are no longer used. Only positively stated questions are used. In one of our studies, all negatively worded questions showed up in one factor in the factor analysis performed. This was probably an artificial result, as the questions did not show resemblance with respect to their content.[46]

GENERALIZATION OF THE DIMENSIONS

The division in 5 or 10 SERVQUAL dimensions suggests that they are the same for each type of service. This is not true, not all dimensions can be used in order to measure the quality of all services at all times and all places.

unique number of dimensions and attributes

In our view, each type of service has a unique number of dimensions and attributes. Therefore, additional (qualitative and quantitative) research is needed in order to establish the exact number of quality dimensions for a particular type of service. However, "At a *general* level, the five dimensional structure of SERVQUAL may still serve as a meaningful framework for summarising the criteria customers use in assessing service quality".[47]

STATIC SPECIFICATION

static fashion

A fifth comment concerns the static fashion of the SERVQUAL-model. It implies that changes over time in expectations and perceptions cannot be measured. We maintain that they can be measured over time. However, changes over time will not be that large.[48]

dynamic
SERVQUAL-model

The construction of a dynamic SERVQUAL-model is a possible solution to its static nature. Another approach would be to raise the questions regularly (for instance every year). Perhaps more important is the notion that the model can only be applied to the existing database of customers. In that respect, SERVQUAL as a strategic tool has its limitations.

USING LIKERT SCALES

Usually, the answers are given on 5, 7 or 9-point Likert scales ranging from "strongly disagree" (1) to "strongly agree" (9). One of the methodological points of criticism here can be that once respondents have marked the extreme point, and they want to express an even stronger opinion on a next item, this cannot be reflected any more in the answer (since the maximum score has already been given). However, this is more a general point of criticism of Likert scales and is not inherent to SERVQUAL as such. This problem could be overcome by using magnitude estimation scales. Then, respondents may express their opinion on scales without a fixed extreme. This may make analyses more complex. A suitable alternative can be to use two other types of scales. These may be based on:

general point of
criticism of Likert
scales

magnitude estimation

below or above what
the customer expects

- indicating whether the present service quality with respect to a particular service attribute is below or above what the customer expects; or

neutral point of what
customers expect

- creating a kind of neutral point of what customers expect, and stating that this equals, for instance, 50 points. Next, respondents have to indicate whether (and how much) the actual performance ranges between zero (poor) and 100 (excellent).

In practice, many researchers do not worry that much about these comments on the Likert-scale. Many researchers apply the usual scale to their questionnaires. Such scores can be used in further analyses, like many multi-dimensional scaling techniques such as factor analysis, cluster analysis and also in multiple regression analysis. Nevertheless, it should – in essence – always be checked whether the answers given contain a normal distribution.

normal distribution

EXPECTATIONS

forming expectations

Critics state that it is quite unclear how expectations are formed, how they change over time and what respondents will report when they are asked about their expectations. Therefore, the chapter on service quality addressed the issue of forming expectations at length. There, an overview of the different kinds of expectations was presented. Here, it suffices to state: the SERVQUAL instrument can be refined by distinguishing between the minimum service level expected and the desired service level. This leads to the zone of tolerance (see the questionnaire in Service practice 6-15); and, it is important to state clearly in a research project what kind of expectations should be taken into account when answering the questions.

what kind of
expectations should be
taken into account

the moment

Another problem to be discussed here refers to timing the moment of asking these questions. In many research projects, questions about expectations and perceptions are raised at the same moment when respondents have to complete the questionnaire. That will be done when the service experience is over. In assessing expectations at that very moment, a rationalization of the answers given may occur. Then, it is preferable to do a "two wave research project" and ask for expectations before the service encounter takes place and ask for perceptions afterwards. One of our colleagues at another university was confronted with this problem in evaluating his classes on service marketing management. He decided to give his students a questionnaire asking for their expectations about his class at the beginning of the course (at the first meeting they had to complete this questionnaire). When the course was over, he gave them a questionnaire asking for their evaluation of the course: their perception.

RAISING EXPECTATIONS

The eighth comment refers to the fact that the expectations of the persons interviewed are not static. They may change as a new competitor appears or change after using the same service frequently. The expectation levels will be adapted according to the service experienced. The state of mind, experiences, the moment the questions are asked and changes in circumstances also count for customers'opinions on the

expectations will change over time

service quality. Expectations will change over time, making it difficult to compare results from longitudinal studies on service quality. Therefore, this should be regarded as a fact of life. It demands repeat research projects of a qualitative and quantitative nature instead of doing just one study once using only one methodology.

LENGTH OF THE QUESTIONNAIRE

As discussed in Chapter Five, ideally, questions about expectations, perceptions and importance should be raised about each service quality attribute. We have also seen

questionnaire may become too long

that expectations should be split into the minimum level and the desired level. Then, the questionnaire may become too long, resulting in a huge non response. A solution to this problem is not to raise too many questions or topics in one questionnaire. As proposed in Chapter Five, one may also think of deleting the questions on expectations but keep the questions on perceptions and importance.[49]

BASIS OF IMPRESSION

In some of our own research projects, we found out that customers completing a

more than one service encounter

questionnaire about service quality build up their opinions on many occasions. So, it is a reflection of an "average impression" based on more than one service encounter. Therefore, one will not be able to detect significant changes over time. This happened to be the case when we applied written questionnaires or telephone interviews as research techniques. When we used personal interviews as a technique, when respondents had just left a bank or a public labor support office, it appeared that they based their opinion to a much larger degree on what they experienced during the service encounter in the last few minutes.

IMPORTANCE SCORES

measure the
importance

It is important to measure the importance scores. In SERVQUAL, this is usually done by allocating 100 points to the various dimensions. An alternative way to do this is to specify a multiple regression equation.[50] Then, the scores on "total (or overall) service quality" are the dependent variable and all scores on each of the "service dimensions" or all the "service attributes" are the independent variables. Such an equation may look like:[51]

$$TSQ = \alpha_0 + \alpha_1 TAN + \alpha_2 REL + \alpha_3 RES + \alpha_4 ASS + \alpha_5 EMP$$

in which

TSQ = total service quality
TAN = tangibles
REL = reliability
RES = responsiveness
ASS = assurance
EMP = empathy

Such an equation indicates, especially, the – great – importance of the soft side of the service process to overall service quality. This side is crucial to professional service quality, as was shown in the first Service practice in this chapter.

SUMMARY

Services are intangible. Consequently, researching services and service delivery processes is complex. Customers and employees interact in the service encounter. Therefore, research among customers and employees is extremely important in service organizations to collect data about service quality, customer satisfaction, job satisfaction, market orientation and the like. In this way, the company can be compared or even benchmarked against competitors and the impact of the DRETS-factors can be researched.

Management may apply market research for various decisions such as measuring the image of the firm, benchmarking the company on various service attributes, using the information collected for strategic decision making and for managing supply and demand. Researching service quality is a topic receiving much attention in this chapter. It can be measured in many ways, ranging from:

- very simple techniques to very sophisticated and complicated techniques;
- qualitative to quantitative techniques;
- on a continuous or *ad hoc* basis, and
- small scale to large scale studies.

Due to the nature of service, we made a plea to always start with qualitative, small scale studies to uncover the dimensions or attributes of services customers themselves deem relevant and use in their decision making.

Probably, customized augmented services will require more small scale, qualitative studies while firms offering standard core service will benefit more from large scale, quantitative studies (given the fact that qualitative pilot studies have been done before large scale studies are started).

The international dimension of market information focusses on the difficulties in collecting, analyzing, interpreting and comparing data from different countries. This applies for secondary and company data (both documentary sources), as well for primary data (market research). If a company shifts from decisions involving market entry to more standard marketing decisions in a growing number of countries, the need for an International Marketing Information System (IMIS) becomes more obvious.

The practical value of the systematic gathering of world wide marketing information is seen with firms providing excellent services, such as Singapore Airlines, CitiBank, DHL and EDS. Only management that frequently collects information about clients, competitors and other environmental factors is more aware of recent developments; they are also able to respond faster to change than their competitors. They can adopt their organizations earlier to changing conditions in the marketplace. No doubt, the use of centrally managed IMIS's enables international firms to bring their services faster to new markets.

It does not make a real difference whether service firms act in a small local market or in a large world wide market. Both need information

- to know how customers assess the company and whether its service offerings are considered as excellent or not; and
- to take (strategic, tactical or operational) decisions, if needed .

The intangible character of services and the process nature of the delivery of services makes conducting market research for service organizations complex. At the same time, another characteristic of services (the personal and individual interaction) will imply that much data about clients will be present in the administration of the service provider (at least, it should be, in essence).

While conducting market research, the expected benefits of the results should always outweigh the costs. Secondary research, research done by and among front office people as well as the application of information from internal data bases may serve this purpose on many occasions, consequently keeping costs down.

Many approaches and techniques have been discussed to research service quality. The Service Quality Information Systems needs to build on the findings from many studies: from small scale qualitative studies, from large scale quantitative studies, from internal and external data bases, from primary and secondary data. Data which is collected via the firm's dissatisfaction management system should also be part of it.

A wide variety of qualitative techniques has been presented, like mystery shopping, critical incidents or means-end-chains. Results from those studies reveal that the famous (5 or 10) SERVQUAL-dimensions can be detected in these studies.

In this chapter, the technical side of measuring service quality via the SERVQUAL-instrument has been discussed. The inventors of this model initially came up with ten dimensions, then reduced it to five and now it appears they can be condensed to three general dimensions. These dimensions build up the framework for summarizing the criteria customers use in assessing service quality. Eleven different critical points on SERVQUAL have been discussed. They range from the correctness of using difference scores and the negatively worded statements to issues about whether or not the SERVQUAL dimensions can be always applied and the definition of expectations. Many of these critical points do not only hold for SERVQUAL but also for many other techniques and models. They even apply when one relies on customer perceptions as the only way to measure service quality.

QUESTIONS

1 What qualitative and quantitative techniques exist to measure service quality?

2 What is the relevance of a qualitative pilot-study in market research for the service sector?

3 Why should the intangibility feature of services often imply that qualitative research techniques should be preferred over quantitative research techniques in services marketing?

4 In which respect are the SMART-technique and conjoint analysis the same?

5 What is the most important difference in outcome between the SERVQUAL-method and the Critical Incident Technique?

6 Why has this chapter on marketing research not only focussed on the outcome of the service delivery process, but also at the process itself?

7 Why is researching job satisfaction in service firms relevant? Does it have anything to say about customer satisfaction?

8 What makes cross-cultural research so difficult? Are there any additional problems or challenges in doing cross-cultural research for service firms operating on a global scale? Explain.

9 Is there any proof that service quality will improve when competition increases? Explain.

10 Summarize the criticisms of SERVQUAL.

ASSIGNMENTS

1 Relate the issues raised in Jack Honomichl's article at the beginning of this chapter to the ten SERVQUAL dimensions. What can you conclude from that overview?

2 Design on the basis of the questions of the ten dimensions of SERVQUAL a questionnaire in order to assess the service delivery by the railways in your own country.

3 Do the same for the disco or cinema you (regularly) visit.

4 Present your opinion about the relationship between market research for a service organization and their image.

5 Discuss the difficulties related with international market research for a multi-country retailer (i.e. Ikea or Toys R Us) and for a business-to-business service firm (i.e. a consulting firm or recruitment agency), both for entering a new country and after, once established on foreign soil.

6 Compare and assess the various questionnaires presented in Service practice 6-5. Are these questions formulated correctly? What is your opinion of the scales used? Are all the relevant topics represented in the questionnaire? What do you think of the sampling procedure used? Do they measure service quality, customer satisfaction? Are the six criteria mentioned in section 6.6 met?

7 In the first chapters much has been said about airlines. Summarize it and use this information as secondary data about airline service quality. What do you conclude from that?

Case: AIRLINE FOOD IS NO JOKE

Marketers improve menus to please passengers

By Karen Schwartz
and Ian Murphy

Karen Schwartz is a free-lance writer based in Elmwood Park, Ill., and Ian P. Murphy is Staff Writer at Marketing News.

Airlines are finding the way to the hearts – and pocket-books – of travelers may be through their stomachs.

Not long ago, the major US airlines – cash-poor from high jet-fuel prices, a lingering recession, and low passenger turnouts – were scrimping on culinary basics such as *lettuce* to save a few pennies. But now those same airlines, profiting from a strong economy and eager to please lucrative passenger segments, are piling on the vittles to attract more, or more loyal, passengers.

It's a new era for in-flight cuisine. The portions are larger; the selections are tastier and frequently more exotic.

These days, it isn't unusual for passengers to dine on cranberry brisket, Vermont maple carrots, and buttered noodles, followed by a steaming-hot cup of Starbucks coffee. Or they might be served a satisfying lunch made up of a full-sized sandwich, a Pepperidge Farm cookie, and bottled water. And that's just in coach.

What's behind the changes? "Airlines have gotten smart about what it is that draws people," said

Bob Dirkes, spokesman for BTI Americas, a Northbrook, Ill., travel-management firm that works with corporate accounts. "They all offer the same schedules, the same service, and the same fares, so they have to find a way to differentiate themselves for travelers through the service they offer."

He added that the major airlines are able to soak up the costs of better in-flight food service today for one reason: They're making more money. "The economy has improved, and there is a greater demand for travel," Dirkes said. "It used to be that if one airline had a fare sale, everyone else jumped on the bandwagon and ran at a deficit to compete. They don't do that anymore. Business fares are at their highest levels in history, and (the airlines) are doing extremely well."

Meal make-overs

Airlines traditionally have catered to the tastes of passengers with unique dietary needs mandated by religion, age, or health. With advance notice, passengers can order specially prepared diabetic, Hindu, Kosher, Muslim, low-fat, low-sodium, low-protein, vegetarian, toddler, or baby meals.

But only recently have the airlines begun to improve upon basic meal service and marketed the fact as one more reason to fly on their planes. On Delta Air Lines, for example, vegetarians dine on black-pepper pasta primavera, while the Muslims in the next row feast on grilled

scallops. And perhaps most significantly, even the average coach-class passenger is getting food that is, well, edible.

"For years, airlines were using pressed thigh-meat chicken, something many travelers referred to as 'mystery meat,'" said Danielle Gulli, food and beverage director for United Airlines' North American operations. "We wanted to get away from that."

The airline's Marketrak survey of passenger experiences already had told United that customers wanted food that was more varied and up-to-date. In May, the Chicago-based airline began serving Regional Classic meals, taken from the pages of Sheila Lukins' *USA Cookbook*, to passengers on long-range economy flights. The culinary expert signed with United as a consulting chef, and the airline touts her menu upgrades prominently in new print ads.

United also quietly increased the amount of food that's served to passengers. This means bigger bagels, larger desserts, and snacks such as Italian ice, finger sandwiches, bite-sized candy bars, carrot sticks, and Mrs Fields' brownies.

Brand-new bounty

Upgrading the eats to satisfy its customers was nothing new for United. When the airline surveyed business travelers and found they thought the coffee (their most-often-consumed beverage) could be improved, United listened. It had little choice: business travelers and others who fly at least 11 times a year account for 9% of United's passengers, but generate 44% of the company's revenue.

The airline began offering Starbucks coffee in all classes last year, and advertised the brand partnership in a TV spot starring a United ground crew worker who unwittingly leaves a trail of Starbucks coffee beans throughout an airport concourse.

The product pairing was so well-received that the airline soon began adding other brand names to the in-flight menu. First-class passengers can now enjoy everything from hoity-toity Godiva chocolates and Dom Perignon, while those in coach can get prole-posh Snapple beverages, Ben and Jerry's ice cream, and McDonald's Friendly Skies meals – a cobranded Happy Meal that can be ordered 24 hours in advance.

These amenities are promoted in mass-market print and TV ads and even in pre-movie factoid reels seen in theaters throughout the country. The airline also touts its partner brands in mailings to frequent fliers who belong to its Mileage Plus club as well as through in-flight commercials. Response to branded food options "has been good," Gulli said, noting that in focus groups, frequent fliers "related those brand names to United."

But the availability of food favorites may not translate directly to ticket sales, concedes Bob Sobczewski, manager of on-board service for the airline. "When

frequent fliers make a decision on what airline to fly, food is not at the top of the list," he said.

"It's safety, the price of the ticket, the frequent-flier program, and convenience of scheduling. Branding plays a key role when prices are close, schedules are close, and frequent-flier programs are similar," he added.

But what will happen if brands are lured away from their original meal-time marketing partners? "We're confident that the brand names are going to remain with United," Sobczewski said. "Some of our [partners'] products may be on different airlines, but in many cases, we're confident we'll keep the exclusivity."

Sampling taste trends

To keep up on what consumers might crave next, Atlanta-based Delta Air Lines consults its executive chefs who work for the company's catering units worldwide.

"They give us input as to what the latest trends are," said Hannelore Perez, Delta's manager of in-flight dining. In addition, she said, "we attend trade shows, research what restaurants are offering, and fly other airlines. [And] the marketing people let me know what the competition is doing."

Customer research, Perez noted, is also important in determining the menu offered. Before revamping its service in its overseas first and business classes, Delta asked customers what they liked and what needed improvement.

Half of Delta's customers said they wanted healthy choices at

mealtimes without needing to call ahead. About 50% wanted more exotic food choices, while the other 50% "went the other way," Perez said. "They want comfort, they want tried-and-true, they want to be able to recognize what it is we're putting in front of them.

"We took that into consideration when we developed our upgrades," she said. "We offer an entrée that might be considered a little avant-garde, we offer a tried-and-true entrée, and toward the end of the year, we're going to introduce spa-designed cuisine to respond to healthy requests."

Competitive cuisine

American Airlines also has a renewed emphasis on in-flight food, said Bill Dreslin, spokesman for the Dallas-based carrier. On domestic first- and business-class flights, "we redesigned more than half of the lunch and dinner entrées," he said, noting that many improvements were made with an eye toward cost.

"This is a very competitive business, and we always try to maintain a strong competitive position and be responsive to our customers within certain cost constraints," he said. "We're not saying, 'We're making money, we're going to spend as much as we can.' We've been able to do a lot of things in first class by working with our chefs, basically taking the same budget and looking at the menu design."

American did commit an extra $6 million to its coach-class meals, however. In surveys, passengers said they liked American's

"Bistro" meal service on short flights – pack-it-yourself bag lunches and breakfasts – but said portions were too small.

"We upgraded the sizes as well as the content of the meals," Dreslin said. "For lunch we used to serve half a deli sandwich, now we serve a full-sized sandwich. For breakfast, we serve eight ounces of orange juice, instead of the three ounces we used to serve."

"We were willing to make that investment because we felt the cutbacks [in the early 1990s] had been a bit severe", he said. "We're trying to find ground that satisfies the majority of people, while keeping in mind that this is a cost-competitive business."

American has not implemented a campaign focussing on its new menu; instead, the airline puts the word out with TV ads describing overall service improvements. Frequent fliers in American's AAdvantage program get updates on menu changes through the program's monthly newsletter.

Some airlines aren't convinced of the need to upgrade their grub. To keep ticket prices low, no-frills airlines such as Southwest offer minimal amounts of food service (often just peanuts and a soft drink). "Our customers are more interested in getting a low fare than paying for food," said spokeswoman Kristie Kerr. That, in itself, was a point of distinction for the "little airline that could" when it started 25 years ago.

But for larger airlines that want to be perceived as world-class and try to continually match or beat competitors on service, price, and convenience, food has renewed importance. There's just one question that major carriers can't yet answer about the improved menus they're rolling out, said United's Gulli.

"Are we bringing more people onto the plane or are we just better satisfying the people we already have?"

QUESTIONS

1   When airlines like Delta, United, American or Southwest want to research how their various target group passengers assess these changes in food, what would you recommend to them as the best research strategy? Take into account that such a research project has to be done on domestic as well as international flights.

2   Summarize briefly what is behind the changes in food and beverages offered by the airlines mentioned in each case. Make these summaries per airline. Do you see any differences between these airlines? Can you explain them?

3   What role does food play in the decision making process about selecting an airline?

ENDNOTES

1. Honomichl, 1995, p. H27.

2. Definition and equation are from Philip R. Cateora who gives an overview of marketing research in an international context, International Marketing, ninth edition, Irwin, 1996, p. 191 a.o.

3. For all details about and components of a MIS, we refer to Kotler (1997), Chapter Four; Dibb, Simkin, Pride and Ferrell (1997), Chapter Six; and, to Wierenga and Oude Ophuis (1997) for issues about Marketing Decision Support Systems.

4. Berry and Parasuraman, 1997, p. 65.

5. Douglas and Craig, 1983.

6. Van Herk and Verhallen, 1995.

7. Holzmüller, 1995.

8. Jahoda, 1980.

9. Adler, 1983b.

10. Adler, 1983a and 1983b.

11. Jeremy Bond, in his conference speech on "Financial Services in the Europe of 1992".

12. This could be considered as a kind of market segmentation within the company: who needs what when?

13. We have experienced that this "translation" of the problem into a problem that really can be researched is a very important step. Many times too few attention is paid to this step. Often this results in wasted money, since the real problem is not tackled i.e. the real question is not posed (and – thus – not answered). To us, this is one of the explanations for the fact that so many research projects have as one of their conclusions "more research is needed". Therefore, much effort should be "invested" in this stage of problem definition and also in small scale, qualitative projects before a large scale, quantitative study starts.

14. We mean the following: it is important that researchers say in advance e.g. "If 80% of the respondents agrees on this statement, what relevant management information do we get to make a decision and solve the problem". If this information is not relevant, then the item should be reformulated in order to provide relevant management information. (So, it is not a matter of manipulating the findings, but just a matter of posing the right questions.)

15. This suggestion is made by Philip Cateora (1996) in his standard work on International Marketing.

16. The basics of market research (types of research designs and research methods) should be well known to the reader. Therefore, we will not elaborate on them.

17. Another example of such a semantic differential scale has been given in Chapter Four. The first 12 items mentioned over there are tested and validated in cross-cultural research. This scale can also be used to decipher brand personalities, brand images, etc. (see Chapter Eleven).

18. We mean that this research should be done from a customer's perspective. It is our own experience that it is an eye-opener to management to analyze the service delivery process from the customer's perspective (which consecutive stages they have to pass) instead of merely researching each of the organizational entities separately (and assess their service quality).

19. This is an operationalization of the market/customer orientation of the researchers.

20. Berry, 1995, p. 103.

21. Berstell and Nitterhouse, 1997, p. 5.

22. In our own consultancy practices, this has proven to be a very successful technique to implement changes, overcome resistance to change and get them accepted.

23. Of course, this can be very costly. Such a cost-benefit trade-off should always be made. Today, some

advanced computer programs exist that can be used in large(r) scale qualitative research and which even allow for all kinds of multi dimensional scaling techniques (making large studies redundant).

24. See our discussion on the economic and behavioral model to express dissatisfaction in Chapter Five. Those models reveal factors also relevant in estimating the outcome of complaining.

25. This concept is already defined in section 6.3; see Berry and Parasuraman, 1997, p. 69.

26. By the way, this is also the way Consumer Unions often research the quality of service organizations, like shops, banks, brokers, real estate agents, travel agencies, public transport, doctors, etc.

27. This section is largely based on Green, Tull and Albaum (1988, p. 171) and Douglas and Craig (1983, p. 162-168).

28. De Ruyter and Scholl, 1995.

29. The first CIT-studies in the services area were done by Bitner, Booms and Tetreault, 1990; another study we refer to in this book is Van der Ven-Verhulp et al. 1995.

30. The Van der Ven-Verhulp et al. study shows that a detailed analysis of the many critical incidents in their study, reveals the SERVQUAL dimensions can be used to structure the findings.

31. Peter and Olson, 1993.

32. A more detailed discussion of these three concepts has been given in Chapter 4.

33. This section is largely based on the Research International brochure about PDS written by Robert Thams. PDS can be applied to products, services, industries, etc. Here we will apply it to services. Service practice 6-10 stems from this brochure.

34. This section is largely based on Green, Tull and Albaum (1988, pp. 308-309). Service practice 6-11 stems from that book.

35. This example is based on a research project our colleague Jos Lemmink recently performed.

36. Sikkel, 1993.

37. This section is largely based on Hoffman and Bateson (1997, pp. 267-269), Fornell (1992) and Fornell et al. (1996). In this section we will apply the ACSI model to services. Only 15 out of 17 measurement variables are used in the model estimation.

38. Fornell et al., 1996, p. 12.

39. See also Service practice 5-6.

40. It is also possible that in a specific research project one could start the discussion about the topics to be researched with the 18 items found by Johnston (see Chapter Five). Obviously, it is always best to base the proper list of quality topics upon qualitative studies performed among customers before a large scale quantitative study starts.

41. As said before in this chapter, the critical incidents technique will better fit such purposes.

42. For a more detailed explanation of points of criticism regarding the employed methodology we refer to Vogels, Lemmink and Kasper (1989), Hentschel (1990), Bolton and Drew (1991), Cronin and Taylor (1992), Lemmink (1992), Boerkamp and Vriens (1993), Grönroos (1993), Teas (1993), Strandvik and Liljander (1994a) and Parasuraman, Zeithaml and Berry (1994). Parasuraman (1995) provides a magnificent overview of the history of SERVQUAL and its critics. In that article Parasuraman presents excellent reply to all those critics.

43. See for instance Oliver, 1997 and Cronin and Taylor, 1992.

44. Vogels, Lemmink and Kasper, 1989.

45. Parasuraman, 1995, p. 167.

46. Vogels, Lemmink and Kasper, 1989.

47. Parasuraman, 1995, p. 160.

48. See section 6.7 and note 41.

49. Then also discussions about the methodological "pitfalls" of using difference scores are avoided. Unfortunately, the zone of tolerance cannot be computed any more.

50. Karin Venetis (1997) has applied both approaches in her PhD thesis and suggests that the regression analysis is to be favored over the 100 points allocation. For, when asked directly (= allocate 100 points) respondents "… are inclined to analyse the quality determinants more rationally than they actually do in real life". (p. 152). They then allocate especially less points to the soft side of service delivery processes (personal interaction, communication, etc.) than actually is the case (see also Taylor, 1995). One should – however – bear in mind that the specific industry (the advertising industry) may partly cause this effect.

51. This equation is given as an example. The number of dimensions may differ per service company and target group customers.

CHAPTER SEVEN

STRATEGIC PLANNING AT CORPORATE LEVEL

In this chapter, the planning cycle will be outlined and applied to service organizations. After studying this chapter you should be able to:

Are you making the most of all your strengths?

Today's marketplace is a sea of op- | Andersen Consulting can help you | working together, the reward may be
portunity. But to fully capitalize, | capture your potential. Instead of | greater than you ever imagined.
all components of an organization | isolated improvements, we'll work
need to be in optimal alignment. | to dramatically improve the perfor-
With vast experience in strategy, | mance of your entire organization.
technology, process and people, | And when all your strengths are

AC Andersen Consulting

Visit our web site at www.ac.com

ABOVE: *Strengths and opportunities: that is what it is all about*

- *distinguish the different stages in the strategic marketing planning process of services;*
- *understand the need for relationship marketing in services*
- *determine the position of a service provider;*
- *define several strategic options helpful to support the chosen position;*
- *set up a strategic plan for a service organization;*
- *recognize the key success factors in service firms;*
- *elaborate on the importance of relationships at strategic (corporate) level;*
- *argue why limited services providers (LSP's) are increasingly becoming a threat to General Services Providers (GSP's);*
- *define what strategic activities GSP's should develop in order to defend their positions;*
- *define the differences in strategies for core, augmented, standard and customized services.*

7.1 INTRODUCTION

Service practice 7-1 Alice in Wonderland

A presentation of the Dutch ABN-AMRO Bank concerning strategic planning for entrepreneurs in small and medium sized companies started with a scene from Alice in Wonderland. In this scene: Alice strolls along a path. She arrives at a crossroads and wonders which way to go. Then she sees a cat in a tree and asks him whether he could tell her which way to go. The cat first asks her where she intends to go to and Alice answers that she does not really mind where she arrives. The cat then says wisely: "Well, if that is so, it does not matter which way you choose".

The core of this story is the most important element for a company to know. You simply have to know what you want in order to be successful. A company should know therefore:

- what it wants and what it can achieve;
- which possibilities the market offers; and
- which direction to go to achieve the goals.

This chapter covers strategic planning. We will start with the premise that planning and plans are useful tools to make choices and anticipate future developments.

Section 7.2 discusses strategic planning at the general, corporate or business unit level in service organizations. This is the basic framework that has to be completed

Figure 7-1
Chapter outline

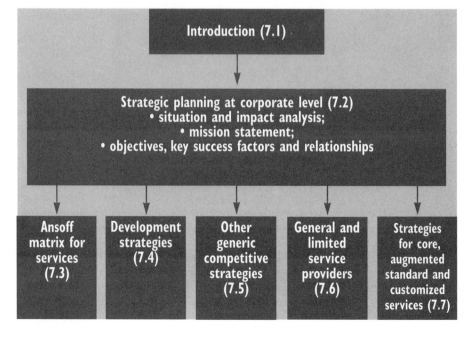

Introduction (7.1)

Strategic planning at corporate level (7.2)
- situation and impact analysis;
- mission statement;
- objectives, key success factors and relationships

| Ansoff matrix for services (7.3) | Development strategies (7.4) | Other generic competitive strategies (7.5) | General and limited service providers (7.6) | Strategies for core, augmented standard and customized services (7.7) |

with some other very relevant issues, like the key success factors in service organizations and the strategic view of relationship marketing. The well-known "Ansoff matrix" for strategy development can be applied to services as well; although it does need some minor adaptation, which will be shown in section 7.3. Some specific development strategies that can be used, for instance in situations of growth or stability, will be dealt with in section 7.4. At this corporate level, some more generic strategies related to low cost servuction processes or highly differentiated services are discussed in section 7.5. At present, a trend can be observed that general service providers (like banks) are challenged by more specialized service providers with limited resources (the topic of section 7.6). All these items are building blocks to elaborate on the strategic implications for our own typology of services: core, augmented, standard and customized services (section 7.7). This chapter sets the framework to be used for defining the specific, functional and marketing strategies for services (and that will be the topic of Chapter Eight). Figure 7-1 illustrates the connections between the main sections in this chapter.

7.2 STRATEGIC PLANNING AT CORPORATE LEVEL

organizational level

strategic services group

functional level

In large organizations, at least three levels of strategic planning can be distinguished: organizational level (holding); strategic service groups (SSG) and/or strategic business units (SBU) and the functional service level. These levels of planning are hierarchical. The strategic plan at the organizational level should be the starting point for planning on the level of strategic business units (SBU) or strategic services group (SSG), etc. Marketing planning, in turn, is at the functional level. This contains both tactical and strategic aspects. The strategic planning process should be market oriented. The "cascade" in Figure 7-2 illustrates this point of view. This emphasizes the important role marketing plays within the whole planning process.

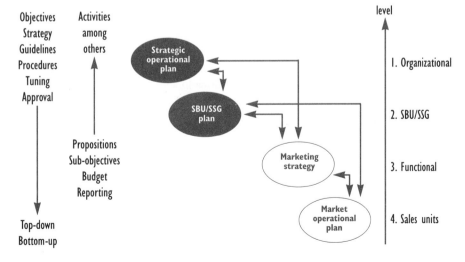

Figure 7-2
Strategic planning and marketing planning at different levels: strategic planning at corporate level

A large bank knows the strategic plan for the whole bank. This plan can be considered as the strategic plan at the organizational level, Level One. It contains the objectives and guidelines for plans in each of the business units being made at Level Two. At a universal bank, this concerns plans of the divisions for local and international affairs, investment banking or leasing and consumer credit. On both levels, the general strategies are defined. The strategic plans will be formulated into detail at the functional Level Three. The marketing unit prepares the strategic marketing plan. The information technology department prepares a strategic information plan. The human resources function develops a long term plan concerning the personnel and development of personnel in the organization. Of course, these plans must be finetuned to each other. In large organizations, the coordination of planning activities is done either by a staff manager or by a planning department.

Meetings concerning planning at top level (organizational level) make sure that the sub-objectives, the planned activities and the allocation of resources of the different parts of the company are being tuned to the overall objectives and resources of the highest (organizational) level.

Because of the similarity and overlap between the strategic planning at Level One (organizational) and Level Two (SBU/SSG), for the sake of simplicity, both are discussed in this chapter simultaneously. The reader should be aware, however, that this process takes place twice in large organizations, namely at the levels of the whole organization and the business unit. The functional marketing strategy will be dealt with in the next chapter.

As services differ fundamentally from physical goods this means that a number of techniques which stem from a physical-product-oriented-environment are not directly applicable to developing strategies for service organizations. One can think of the following differences:

- physical products are produced centrally, whereas services are produced at the point-of-sale;
- assessing product quality takes some time while the quality of services is usually accepted or rejected immediately;
- mostly, goods are not delivered personally while services are; and
- product innovation is sensitive to process technology and the material used for a new product. Innovations in services are more sensitive to cooperation between people and the proper use of innovation and communication concepts.

specific characteristics of services

For the specific characteristics of services we refer to Chapters One and Two. Each of these characteristics should be taken into consideration when developing a strategic planning process.

strategic planning process

In services, one can divide the whole strategic planning process leading to a marketing plan into eight phases:

1. situation and impact analysis of the whole organization, strategic service groups and strategic business units;
2. developing a mission statement;
3. determining organizational objectives;
4. making proposals of strategies to achieve organizational objectives;
5 (a) external and internal marketing planning processes;
   (b) services marketing audit;
6. appointing people to execute the proposed action plans;
7. determining deadlines for several action plans;
8. following, monitoring, evaluating and revising the planning components.

Phases one to four are being dealt with in this chapter. The other phases will be dealt with in other chapters.

SITUATION AND IMPACT ANALYSIS

SWOT-analysis

The first step in successfully selecting a strategy to be followed is analyzing the situation in which the organization currently acts. In this process, usually an analysis of strengths, weaknesses, opportunities and threats (SWOT-analysis) will be applied. The objective of such an analysis is to take advantage of the opportunities the environment offers, and to avoid or minimize threats. The information gathered during the structured external analysis of the service environment (Chapter Three) is valuable input for the SWOT-analysis. As will be shown later with developing services (Chapter Nine), the outcome of the following analysis will now be integrated. It concerns:

- the macro-environment (DRETS-factors);
- the service sector environment (marketing-related trends); and
- the competitive environment (forces in the industry).

benchmarking

The external environment has been extensively reviewed in Chapter Three. For that reason, the description of phase one can be brief. The SWOT analysis is useful in exploring strengths which are not yet used optimally. Furthermore, this technique affords the opportunity to reduce the company's weaknesses. Finally, the opportunities and threats from the environment are compared with one's own strengths and weaknesses, resources, etc. Benchmarking is a technique used. In services, benchmarking should focus particularly on the processes aimed at delivering excellent service quality and not only on the service as such. The key success factors of one's own firm and the competing firms are another relevant subject for benchmarking.

*Service
practice
7-2
Benchmarking
by Austrian
banks[1]*

The Kärntner Sparkasse is a major bank in Carinthia and belongs to an Austrian-wide banking group. During the last few years, the bank has worked extensively on strengthening its marketplace profile, strategic competencies and upgrading its capabilities with a view to expansion and intensification of sales within the existing customer base. This is due to the intensified competition in the Austrian market, anticipating changes that will facilitate the unification of Europe and Austria's integration into the European Community. The Kärntner Sparkasse has been a successful bank in recent years, with the Raiffeisenbank, the Bank für Kärnten und Steiermark and other regional banking institutions being the main competitors in Carinthia. During the last years, the Kärntner Sparkasse in Carinthia has been working on some strategic issues dealing with the assessment of corporate culture and customer satisfaction. A quality benchmark study should provide information and orientation for future strategic competencies and operational actions, i.e. internal marketing within the bank.

The measurement model developed (BDQU = Banken-Dienstleistungsqualität) compared the quality of delivered services of banks of the Sparkassensektor and the main competitors and the importance of several indices expected to be delivered by an excellent banking institution. In total, the developed items based on the qualitative study (which was carried out before this large scale study) amounted to 51, covering the 10 SERVQUAL dimensions. Some additional questions have been added, for example self-image of the interviewee, image of the main bank, future importance of the main bank, overall satisfaction with the main bank and demographic variables to relate the variables of service quality within them.

It appeared that the Raiffeisenbank is the main competitor of the Sparkasse. Both banks are positioned differently on service quality. They have, in common, a lack of understanding and knowledge about the customer. Credibility should also be improved. Sparkasse beats its competitor on dimensions like tangibles, security, access and competence while Raiffeisen has its relative strengths in dimensions like responsiveness, courtesy, credibility and reliability.

From a strategic point of view, Sparkasse should improve their weak points. These are variables under their own control since they are a kind of input variable.

The results of the SWOT analysis are not only important for their impact on strategic planning. We will see that these results are also useful during the development of the marketing strategy at functional level. For example, this information is used as input in the marketing audit. Of course, not all factors in the environment have the same impact on every organization. Some weak points, strong points, opportunities or threats are more relevant than others. For that reason, an impact analysis listing the most relevant issues of the SWOT-analysis and external analysis (Chapter Three) will complete Phase One.

impact analysis

MISSION STATEMENT

mission statements

Determining and describing a mission is a crucial step in the strategic plan. This second step determines the direction of the organization for a relatively long period. Mission statements inspire and motivate people to deliver excellent service quality and guide the resource allocation process.[2] They provide a sense of purpose and direction; ensure that the interests of key stakeholders are not ignored; sharpen a firm's focus; enable better control over employees (if needed) and promote shared values and behavioral standards.[3] In determining the mission, top management should answer the following central question, in other words: one should define the "playground or playing field for the company". Two factors in a service environment are present to make the determination of the mission for a service organization even more important than for a goods-oriented-organization, namely:

playground or playing field for the company

- the intangibility of a service; and
- the important role of people in achieving success in a service organization.

The description of a mission should make the service visible and should motivate the people working in the organization. This can be done literally by means of framed texts. An important function of the mission is to give direction to the growth of the organization. This applies especially in the service sector, where imitation (me-too-strategy) is part of everyday life. It is necessary to maintain focussed and remain different from your competitors, by means of positioning.

clear vision

The description of the mission gives a clear vision of the current and future business activities of the organization and the function that the organization fulfils in society. It indicates the intended degree of market-orientation and service level, including the quality of services. The values and norms (which the organization applies and upon which it stands) and the most important points in which one differs from the competitors are emphasised. In line with our discussion in Chapter One, it is necessary to give further content to the concept of market orientation. There, we discussed issues about the ways in which corporate culture is reflected in marketing practices. Here, in discussing the underlying norms and values giving meaning to the mission statement, it is necessary to have a deeper look at those norms and values.

market orientation

corporate culture

Hofstede (1991) defines corporate culture as "the collective programming of the mind which distinguishes the members of one organization from another".[4] This conceptual definition is operationalized by looking at culture via "the shared perceptions of daily practices".[5] His research depicted six dimensions to describe organizational cultures:

1. process orientation versus results orientation;
2. employee orientation versus job orientation;
3. parochial versus professional;
4. open system versus closed system;
5. loose control versus tight control; and
6. normative versus pragmatic.

A market-oriented corporate culture (also in service firms) appears to be results-oriented, employee-oriented, professional, open and pragmatic.[6] The kind of control in the culture of such an organization (dimension 5) should be balanced between loose (giving ample opportunity to empowerment) and tight (knowing the strategy as the formal frame of reference for – empowered – behavior). Significant attention to and care about people (customers as well as employees) is a dominant feature of a market oriented culture. These companies also possess high ethical standards and do business accordingly. Still, they are very results or goal orientated. Meeting customer preferences is much more important than applying the rules (for the sake of the rules only).[7] Market oriented firms prefer a long term orientation (over a short term orientation). Such an organization is open. Both management and employees accept risk taking. Employees are empowered and are able to accept the responsibility to act accordingly. To some extent, they can be seen as entrepreneurs within the enterprise.

foundation for the marketing strategy

These cultural characteristics are the foundation for the marketing strategy in these organizations. As stated in Chapter One, such a marketing strategy is dominated by a strong drive to be the best, thorough knowledge about present, and potential, customers and competitors (= the market), clear marketing goals and a positive attitude towards risk taking in developing new services. Moreover, such a culture is characterized by meeting the needs of the customers via target group specific marketing policies (customized offers) and setting marketing goals accordingly. These goals are clear and well communicated throughout the company in which (top) management provide an "example function" (role model) by showing how employees should work and treat customers. The company's offering is perceived to be of better quality than competitors'. Moreover, a market oriented company will be permeated with the marketing philosophy and aware of providing excellent after sales service. Within this company, the various departments cooperate quite well and exchange all the market information deemed relevant to other departments (almost) automatically.[8]

Service practice 7-3 Company mission defined: narrowly or broadly?[9]

By defining themselves as railways (internal orientation) instead of a company to help people solve their transportation problems (external orientation) the railways in the United States failed to make use of the possibilities they once had. Even worse, they got into the danger zone.

A railway company which reformulated their company mission in a broader sense, "transportation service" is Southern Railways Company. Profit per share for this company (an important criterium for stockholders) is one of the highest in the whole railway industry in the United States. Southern Railways Company achieved this position by means of a carefully integrated program, in which buying other railway companies is an important part. The developed and maintained mission of supplying useful and relevant transportation services for the clients is a broad but very well defined mission.

Currently, railways across the world are defining their business more accurately. Scaling-up by means of mergers, cooperation or unbundling (i.e. splitting of freight and passengers transport) is the order of the day.

The description of the mission shows the concern of the organization with survival (economic objectives), with personnel (internal image) and with the community (public image). In this description, a balance must be found between a mission that is defined too narrowly and one that is defined too broadly.

realistic character

the message is understood

The power of the mission stands or falls with its "realistic character" (can it be achieved) and the extent to which the message is understood inside the organization. The personnel must be able to identify with the unique mission. One should (so to speak) feel proud to work for the organization and to share its values, norms and ideas. Therefore, it is essential to let the mission LIVE within the organization and its culture. The market orientation should also be made very clear from the mission statement.

OBJECTIVES, KEY SUCCESS FACTORS AND RELATIONSHIPS

Phase three of the strategic planning process, as outlined in this chapter, embraces:

- establish and agree upon the objectives;
- indicate the (expected) key success factors; and
- formulate the vision of management on relationships (one of the possible success factors).

Mission and objectives

objectives

ratios

Organizations may strive for several objectives. Each company knows its own objectives. The formulation of these objectives should be precise (measurable), reasonable and indicate a target period (i.e. 10% growth of sales by the end of next year). General organizational goals like continuity, growth or profit objectives are also formulated in terms of ratios. In the banking industry, solvability ratios and efficiency ratios (operational costs divided by return from normal activities) are well known measures. Coach-work repair shops think in terms of an average number of damage hours per damage case and the period to have spare parts in stock (for the whole branch this is respectively 68 hours and 33 days on average). Some of these measures are stated in Figure 7-3.

Figure 7-3 shows that a number of ratios are industry specific. In various industries, results are gathered periodically to compare and assess/benchmark companies. The participating companies (which are often segmented on the basis of activities and sales) have the opportunity to lead by example and learn from other competitors. Such company comparisons take place in many service industries like retailing, hotels, restaurants, cafés, car-repair, real-estate agents, insurance brokers and airlines. In the airline-industry, companies are compared and assessed by their profits, sales or returns on investment. The disadvantage of such a financial approach is that the results may be affected by differences in tax systems or accounting methods (costs, depreciation, etc.). Moreover, the total outcome of all kinds of activities is measured and not the process of service delivery. These ratios are important for the financial

Figure 7-3

*Some ratios
for organizational
objectives of service
providing companies*

AREA	POSSIBLE RATIOS
Market	- Return and market shares per market segment, client, service - Occupation rate - Loading rate - Inflow and outflow of customers - Customer satisfaction
Service development	- Number and type of new services necessary to achieve market objectives
Financial	- Solvability ratio - Liquidity ratio - Return on equity - Return on investment - Retained earnings
Productivity	- Sales per year of labor, per company unit - Sales per square metre (per service) - Sales per square metre factory floor, sales floor - Sales turnover - Gross profit per year of labor - Gross profit per employee in money - Gross profit in percentage of sales - Sales per organizational unit, department, market segment, client, service or transaction
Costs	- Total costs per organizational unit, department, employee, etc. - Personnel cost per employee - Total personnel cost per organizational unit, department, etc. - Personnel cost as percentage of total costs - Total costs of automation as percentage of total costs
Personnel	- Ratio front office/back office employees in numbers and money - Money spent on training and development as percentage of total personnel costs - Personnel turnover, job satisfaction - Level of education divided over organization and functions - Sick-leave percentage
Technology	- Productivity of automated processes - Utilization of raw materials and components
Community	- Percentage re-use of waste material - Use of energy - Amount of non obligatory contribution to the community

output

input and throughput

analysts analyzing this industry. Thus, measuring is focussed on financial data (output) instead of service processes (input and throughput). The latter concentrates on availablity per ton per kilometre, occupancy rates, revenue per passenger per kilometre or customer satisfaction in addition to return on equity, gross margin or growth.

Service practice 7-4 Flying high on ratios

Michael Schefczyk (1992) applied a technique called Data Envelopment Analysis (DEA) to assess the operational performance of 15 airlines in 1990: Air Canada, All Nippon Airways, American Airlines, British Airways, Cathay Pacific, Delta, Federal Express, Iberia, Japan Airlines, KLM, Korean Air, Lufthansa, Quantas, Singapore Airlines, and UAL Corporation. DEA is a technique based on an holistic view, linking all factors of efficiency by evaluating the relationships between each input and output to arrive at a scaled measure of performance. Schefczyk concluded "the analysis indicates that high operational performance is a key factory of high profitablity. Other factors, of course, include efficient resource acquisition and marketing and sales activities. The 14 passenger airlines in the sample data display increasing performance with strong focus on the core business of passenger transportation. Obviously, high passenger load factors support high profitability, growth also stimulated profitability for the airlines in the sample.

A specific comparison showed that efficient, passenger-focussed airlines tend to have operating costs, excluding depreciation, amortization and aircraft rent, not exceeding 8 cents per revenue passenger km. Furthermore, the nonflight assets of such airlines do not exceed US $80 per 1,000 revenue passenger km."

---

occupancy rate and profit

The close link between occupancy rate and profit is crucial to airlines (and many other industries). A difference between 1% and 2% can make the difference between profit and loss. Given these findings, it is clear why airlines report regularly about their occupancy rates.[10] Most of them report three month figures which are highly valued by economists, bankers and investors.

business units

The mission statement and objectives (e.g. in terms of ratios) are not limited to top level in an organization. Business units can also state their own mission and objectives. Of course, management in these units should take into account the overall, generic organizational mission and goals.

management by objectives

Management by objectives is a technique to be applied to all possible levels in an organization. More specific objectives which are not described in the strategic plan will be put in the strategic and operational plans of divisions, business units and/or departments as subobjectives. Objectives are formulated for every year in the planning horizon. On average, the whole planning period is limited from three to five years. Preparing a plan for a longer term is difficult because of the fast changing environment of the service sector.

TABLE 7-1 *Key success factors at market leaders in services*		
Key success factors	Percentage of UK market leaders in services having a competitive advantage on that key success factor	Percentage of Dutch market leaders in services having a competitive advantage on that key success factor
Product/service quality	14.5%	52.2%
Close links with key customers	12.9	50.0
Company/brand reputation	12.9	54.3
Competitive pricing	6.5	28.3
Personal selling	17.7	26.1
Product/service performance	19.4	32.6
Speed of reaction to customer requirements	8.1	28.3
Distribution coverage and/or uniqueness	11.3	26.1
Product/service range offered	9.7	26.1
Advertising and promotion	9.7	19.6
A cost advantage in production	3.2	13.0
After sales service	17.7	21.7
Prior market research	6.5	19.6
Close links with industry suppliers	8.1	-
Superior marketing information systems	4.8	2.2
Finance and credit offered	3.2	2.2
Superior packaging	3.2	-
Product/service design	9.7	6.5
Number of responding firms (=100%)	62	46

Source: Hooley, (1992) Alsem and Hoekstra, (1994, 1995)

Key success factors

key success factors

competitive advantage

market leaders

In Chapter One, we concluded that quality, close links with key customers, the company or brand reputation, competitive pricing, performance and speed of reaction to customer requirements are considered as the key success factors by many European service organizations. The Dutch and UK studies cited in Chapter One also reveal in which key success factors these service organizations believe they have a competitive advantage. Table 7-1 depicts in which KSF's the market leaders in services actually claim to have a competitive advantage.[11] In the UK, these advantages are stated to be performance, after sales services, personal selling, quality, close links with key customers and reputation. The Dutch market leaders, in services, claim to have a competitive advantage especially in reputation, quality, close links with key customers and performance.

When the market leaders are compared to other service firms, it appears that, in the UK, the leaders differ from other service companies in only two respects. The leaders have significantly higher scores on performance and advertising/promotion than the other service firms. In Holland, quite a different picture emerges: there, the market leaders have more often a competitive advantage than the other service firms in: company/brand reputation, product/service quality, close links with key customers, distribution coverage, prior market research, advertising and promotion.

PIMS   The PIMS database (Profit Impact of Marketing Strategy) also contains data about service firms. Using this data base to search for the determinants of success in service industries revealed the utmost importance of a service company's image/reputation.

image/reputation   It reduces risk and increases market share (as long as it is a "positive" image, of course).[12]

Service practice 7-5 Only image and reputation count!

The main conclusions of the analysis of the PIMS data are:[13]

1. Forward integration increases market share and has a significant and positive impact on financial performance;
2. Alternatively, backward integration strategies do not seem to affect a firm's market or financial performance *per se*;
3. Service quality did not have a direct effect on service provider's financial or market results, but it did lower a firm's strategic or business risk;
4. A firm's reputation and service image not only increase market share but also lower business risk. Therefore, it appears that while managerial perceptions of service quality may impact on actual service quality, this study shows that it is the firm's reputation and perceptions of service image that ultimately drive performance;
5. Synergy of business operations and marketing activities increase market share, improve financial performance, and lower business risks;
6. High market shares appear to be double-edged swords according to the results of this study. On the one hand, high shares improve the financial position of a firm, but they also increase its risk levels;
7. In contrast to conventional wisdom, customizing services actually increases market share; and
8. Sales promotions appear to have a positive effect on firm's risk levels. In contrast, advertising has a negative effect on profitability but has a positive effect on relative market share as it lowers a firm's risk level.

image
quality

Obviously image, quality and close links with key customers are among the most important key success factors and competitive advantages of service companies.[14] Image has to do with actual behavior of (contact) personnel. Quality is what it is all

close links with key customers

about in services and the close links with key customers emphasize the issue of relationship marketing. All three are major topics throughout this book and hinge upon market orientation.

From a competitive analysis point of view, one should focus on the dynamics of competition in these issues: what competencies have service firms accumulated in order to perform so well and keep performing so well? This is an important issue next to competition for foresight, and the possibilities to shape industry evolution. Hamel and Prahalad discuss these new ways of thinking about competition and strategic planning in their book "Competing for the Future" (1994). They formulate, as one of their conclusions, that companies should "search for new functionalities or new ways of delivering traditional functionalities".[15] This is in line with our approach of services functions, benefits and consequences to consumers in Chapter Four. An example of this way of thinking differently is given in the health care research ADK-case at the end of this chapter. Here, it suffices to say that ADK had to change its thinking dramatically from promoting its functional attributes to its technology's benefits. It appeared that the technical capabilities will not create interest in ADK's service unless they are directly tied to benefits recognised by the client.[16]

competition for foresight

possibilities to shape industry evolution

benefits

clear company vision for the future

Hamel and Prahalad are convinced that a clear company vision for the future is the most important competitive advantage one can have. In their opinion, that vision should lead to a strategy of "getting in front" in the future instead of "catching up" with the present situation. Being an industry leader is not enough, shaping the future of an entire industry is what it should be all about.[17] And, that requires a clear vision. In other words, service organizations must be motivated, able, willing and have the opportunity to create such breakthroughs that are hard to follow or imitate by competitors in order to survive and find their own position in the market.[18] Other scholars in services management emphasize the need for creating close relationships with customers resulting in a high degree of customer loyalty because these firms really do deliver customer value. This should be operationalized in strategies using value for customers over costs, mostly achieving both low cost and significant differentiation.[19] This final point is in line with our previous statement about the strategy of market-oriented organizations, which is a combination of cost leadership and differentiation.

internal structuring of the servuction process

skills and knowledge of the employees

Service companies are interested in achieving above average profits by delivering superior value to their customers. Sometimes, this profit motive can be achieved via the lowest cost servuction process; at other times, it can be achieved via succesfully differentiating services that can be sold at a premium price. In both cases, it is important to realize that the internal structuring of the servuction process and the skills and knowledge of the employees are decisive factors that are hard to imitate and thus contribute to creating the competitive advantage. This is also true regarding the relationships established with customers.

Relationships

relationship marketing

In relationship marketing, the emphasis is on the continuous and long-term relationship between the customer and the firm, not merely on the sole transaction in the short term. This is a fundamental change of model in marketing.[20] We will elaborate on this relationship perspective and consider it as a framework for the strategies a service provider may perform (and the marketing mix elements that may be used to implement that strategy).

long term *relationships* The basic idea is that long term relationships are beneficial to both parties: the customer and the service provider. For both parties, transaction costs in (all stages of) the service encounter will be minimized. Or, "such relationships minimize transaction costs in several ways: they already understand each other; it reduces the time it takes to make a diagnosis; it reduces diagnosis error; it reduces the need to take defensive (i.e. protective) steps; it makes working together easier; it allows to integrate schedules and it provides greater comfort".[21]

Other experts add to it, from a suppliers' point of view, "relationship marketing would lead to greater marketing productivity by making it more effective and efficient. This in turn would lead to a greater willingness and ability among marketeers to engage in and maintain long-term relationships with customers. It is also our belief that this partnering relationship will be more favorably judged by public policy and social critics, as long as the marketeers or consumers do not abuse it."[22]

crucial issues

commitment

Relationship marketing emphasizes interaction, dependence, reciprocity, lack of opportunism, all kinds of bonds (social, investment, switching or "stuck" bonds), trust and commitment as crucial issues to be taken into account in establishing long term relationships in service businesses. Moreover, it appears that excellent service quality also contributes to establishing and continuing those relationships.[23] With respect to commitment, it has been shown that two kinds of commitment are important here:

- affective commitment, reflecting customers' affective motivations and positive willingness to continue a relationship; and
- calculative commitment, reflecting customers' calculative motivations, based on the incurred losses and costs of a switch to continue a relationship.[24]

cooperation *creating greater* *loyalty* So, affective commitment has to do with customers' desire to maintain the relationship, whereas calculative commitment refers to customers' need to maintain the relationship (often there is no way to "escape" from the relationship; for instance contractual bonding prohibits a customer from changing his or her life insurance). It all hinges upon clear and well thought out cooperation between the two parties in the service encounter. At the end, it is all aimed at creating greater loyalty to the brand or service provider, higher retention rates and more satisfaction amongst customers and employees. For example, a recent study about the advertising market shows that the quality of the work provided by the advertising agency, affective commitment, mutual trust, some bonds (to an extent) and calculative commitment are the most important factors determining the intentions of a firm to keep the relationship with the advertising agency (and not switch to another bureau).[25]

Phases one to three of the strategic planning process are closely related. Developing a mission statement, analyzing the environment in which the organization finds itself and setting goals are of enormous importance. When a mission statement is determined, it is fixed for a number of years. During the annual planning review, the mission is only evaluated for its relevance and passed over. Sometimes, it may be very valuable to analyze the mission for a little longer and see if everyone understands and agrees the importance of it. It is an opportunity to keep everyone in the organization focussed in the same direction.

In phase four of the planning process at the organizational and/or SBU-level, the different possible generic strategies to achieve these objectives are determined. As we have seen, in order to be able to develop these strategies properly, service organizations should know what their key success factors are and how one should look at them. In formulating a corporate and marketing strategy, service organizations should consider the issues discussed within phases one to three creatively when choosing one or more of the strategies discussed in the next sections and Chapter Eight. Here, we can distinguish some groups of basic strategies:

1. growth strategies with different service/ market combinations (section 7.3);
2. development strategies like growth, stability or withdrawal (section 7.4);
3. other generic competitive strategies (section 7.5);
4. strategies of general service providers versus limited service providers (7.6); and
5. strategies for core, augmented, standard and customized services (7.7).

groups of generic strategies
These are the groups of generic strategies used to achieve organizational objectives. Concerning these strategies for service organizations and their general applicability, we want to make the following remarks. The service sector consists of many industries. Also, the services provided can be very different. The sector varies from electricity companies and hospitals to airlines, who have high entry barriers for new competitors, to cafeterias, etc., where entry barriers are considerably lower. Therefore, it is dangerous to generalize too much. Differences in scale and the possession of electronic and physical networks like, for instance, credit card organizations, banks and hotel chains, enlarge the entry barriers. Service providers may also develop a strategy to make it expensive for a customer to change from one supplier to another (switching costs). For example, clauses in contracts may include redemption penalties on mortgages or lead to missing out on advantages like bonuses and discounts in case a client (partly) orders from another supplier.

7.3 THE ANSOFF MATRIX FOR SERVICES

To achieve the central goal of the organization it is essential to look at the strategic service/market combinations (step 4). A choice should be made from these combinations. In principle, organizations can grow in four ways.[26] Applied to services, this results in the following picture (Figure 7-4).

market penetration
A company will grow initially by reinforcing the current existing market position, by further penetrating the existing market (market penetration). This is achieved by persuading current customers to buy more, attracting non-users in the current market and/or getting competitors' customers to switch.

services development
A second option consists of developing new services for the existing market (services development). Accountants usually follow this strategy, by means of constantly introducing new services (which in service organizations often are called products) for their current clients. Tax consultants, company auditors and automation consultants also try to throw each other "the ball". By developing new policies

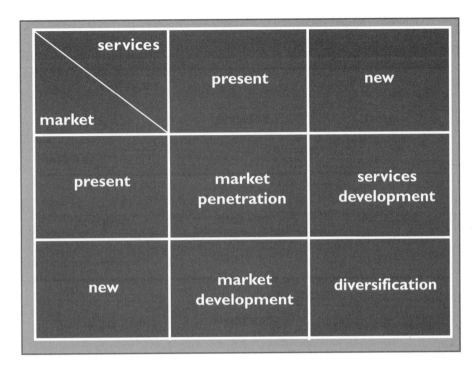

Figure 7-4
Services/market
combinations in the
Ansoff matrix

themselves, the offspring of the original accountant get more and more non-audit-clients. A third possibility is offering the present service to a new market combination.

market development

This means expanding the market with existing services (market development). This may mean new market segments within a marked geographical area, but it could also mean new geographical (international) market segments. A relatively small number of service providers, however, seem to be capable of successfully exporting their service

diversification

formula. The last option of the matrix is diversification. This means rendering new services for new markets. As in other sectors, this strategy can be dangerous since both services and markets are new to the company.

Next to the dimensions of service and market, technology can be added as a third dimension. This can be included when defining the business of a new service firm

technology

and consequently in developing its strategy. Changes in technology offer new opportunities for service firms. In Chapter Two, we pointed out the impact of IT and the substitution of labor by equipment, automation, and technology. Now that it can be used to create new services, and markets, technology enables one to serve customers better and distinguished it from competitors.

7.4 DEVELOPMENT STRATEGIES

The service/market combinations from the Ansoff matrix show the following strategies for a company to develop or to grow. These are called development strategies:[27] growth strategies; stability strategies; withdrawal strategies; combined strategies.

Every strategy has its specific advantages and disadvantages. The ultimate choice occurs according to the organizational objectives, the ambition of top management and the results of SWOT analysis especially with respect to (benchmarks on) the key success factors. The different strategies will be outlined in relation to service providers.

GROWTH STRATEGY

In this section, we will firstly outline a number of growth strategies, like internal growth; merger; horizontal integration; conglomerate diversification; vertical integration, and joint ventures.

Internal growth

expanding on one's own power

With this strategy, expanding on one's own power as an organization is essential. McDonald's never took over another fast-food chain. Many service organizations grow because of their own strength. Large firms of accountants, for example, grow by applying the concept of becoming a partner, when you have been a succesful employee for quite a long time.

Merger

merger

In most cases, a merger means a complete amalgamation of two comparable organizations. Chase Manhattan is the result of such a growth strategy in the USA.

Horizontal integration, conglomerate diversification and vertical integration

horizontal integration

Many organizations grow by means of acquiring another organization or setting up an organization with a similar line of activities (horizontal integration). Expanding market share is one of the primary objectives. This means that an organization may be able to diminish costs because of economies of scale. An example of this is ABN-AMRO, which took over a number of small banks in Illinois via its daughter La Salle Bank in Chicago. In a number of cases, horizontal integration will increase operational flexibility, e.g. by "instantly" expanding the network of branches, number of staff or the range of services on offer. This is important since flexibility and quick reactions to environmental changes are considered to be essential in today's competitive markets.

conglomerate diversification

If an organization takes over companies in other ("unrelated") industries, we call it conglomerate diversification. In recent years, the conglomerates are under fire. Their break-up value (sum of the parts) is sometimes higher than the present value of the whole. In 1997, for instance, ITT was the owner of unrelated companies like an insurance company and the Sheraton Corporation (an international hotel chain).

vertical integration

Vertical integration means that a company creates or buys other companies in the industry chain. Via backward or forward integration, the buyers attempt to gain more control over more or all companies in the channel/supply chain; a restaurant chain taking over a food processor, for example.

If the above mentioned strategies are followed by means of buying companies, it is called acquisition policy. Recently, this trend is clearly visible in industries like banking, insurance, catering, lodging, entertainment and the funeral business. In this latter case, the US based Service Corporation International (SCI) buys other firms in foreign countries. Since the funeral market is very fragmented (geographically spoken), they buy firms in areas where a large part of the population are over 60.[28]

Joint ventures and other possible cooperations

joint venture

Cooperation may exist between different organizations to achieve the goals of a specific project, cooperation on a specific topic or in a specific geographic area. All parties involved have a share in the newly founded company: the joint venture. In contrast with a merger, however, they do not merge all activities. The cooperation can be stopped after completing the project. One can also choose a long term agreement, or an agreement for an indefinite period of time. Joint ventures are set up for several reasons. In some countries, foreign companies, especially financial companies, are not allowed to operate any other way than in a joint venture with a local company. The choice is easy then, either a joint venture or no site at all. In several areas, for example in purchasing, developing new services, taking on large projects, breaking up markets and in the area of transferring knowledge, cooperation may be a solution to succeed in mutual growth. Strategic partnering with or without an equity stake in each other's capital is a common alternative to merging or a strength acquisition. Code-sharing in the airline industry is a form of strategic partnering.

Service practice 7-6 Airline alliances

Many airlines cooperate one way or another or even change existing partnerships.

The German based Lufthansa has a strategic alliance with SAS (in Europe), United Airlines and Air Canada (North America), Thai Airways and International (Asia/Pacific), South African (South Africa) and Varig (South America). In this way, the Star Alliance covers the "whole" world.[29]

Another example is KLM which has a strategic alliance, amongst others, with Northwest (US). This alliance started with a KLM stake in the Northwest shares. This was a unique situation when all the strategic partnering started in the 1990's. In 1997, KLM sold its shares again. Now, they have a "contractual alliance" with Northwest and, for instance, also with Alitalia.

twinning-contracts

Independent hotels may operate together in the area of promotion and reservation. And in former Eastern Europe, Western banks share their knowledge with established colleagues, via so called "twinning-contracts".

franchising

Franchising is another form of cooperation between service organizations. This is often used by retailers especially to succeed in growing over a short period of time. The combination of a standardized formula, central financial agreements and fast growth via a multi site strategy makes it difficult for competitors to imitate (see also Chapter Thirteen).

Figure 7-5
Different development
strategies at
organizational level and
their most important
advantages and
disadvantages

STRATEGY	ADVANTAGES
Internal growth	- Limited investment costs - Possibility for service/market diversification - Determine point of sales alone
Merger	- Critical mass in one step - Decreased chance for takeover - Possibility for synergy - Improving efficiency
Acquisition	- Build substantial market share in one step - Synergy (in the case of merging with existing unit) - Access to (new) technology, which otherwise would have to be invented/developed alone - Possibility of fast growth - Access to foreign markets
Joint venture and other kinds of cooperation	- Exactly fitting to needs, flexible - Useful tool in large, risky projects or completely new services (telecom) - Low investment costs per individual organization - Easy to end cooperation
Franchising	- Way to grow fast (divide financial cost and earn back investment quickly) - Access to motivated management - Access to new markets, which otherwise remain closed for a foreigner - Access to local (market) knowledge

	DISADVANTAGES
Internal growth	- Filling in the personnel (especially in specialized professions) - In the beginning marginal contribution, because of high start-up costs
Merger	- Problems because of integration - Cultural differences (especially when merger abroad) - Fiscal and legal problems
Acquisition	- High investment costs (goodwill) - Pressure on solvability - Profit per share under pressure - Integration problems - Cultural differences - Buy a pig in a poke
Joint venture and other kinds of cooperation	- Possibility of opposing interests - Possibility of no mutual philosophy in the commercial area - Possibility of not having a technical integration of administration - Assumptions about cooperation in contract or the way the two parents cooperate (commitment, trust, opportunistic behavior, etc.) do not come true
Franchising	- In comparison to a site of one's own, less guarantee for controlling the formula - Additional administrative and commercial costs for the organization rendering the franchise

Figure 7-5 gives a brief overview of the advantages and disadvantages of each of these different growth strategies.

STABILITY STRATEGY

stability strategy

A stability strategy is being followed by service organizations which, for example, have reached a point of saturation in their geographic area. They may also have other reasons why they cannot, or do not want to grow. Many smaller enterpreneurs in the service sector follow this strategy (unconsciously). They are satisfied with the way they run their business now.

WITHDRAWAL STRATEGY

withdrawal strategy

If a company's financial performance is constantly under pressure, a withdrawal strategy may be the only choice. Of course, there are other possible reasons. A turn around strategy occurs if the organization tries to change rigorously to be a more effective and efficient operation. A disinvestment strategy means that an enterprise sells a part of its business. Disinvestment, or sell-off, usually occurs when a company is in trouble or when it reorientates to its core business. Stated in a positive tone, we

harvesting

should say that rather than disinvesting or liquidation the entrepreneur is harvesting.

COMBINED STRATEGIES

combination

Very large service organizations like banks, insurance companies, accountants and government organizations often follow a combination of the above mentioned strategies. Their environment is so dynamic and they operate in so many markets at the same time that it forces them to follow this strategy. In the past 15 years, the financial world has been in a tremendous turmoil. The changes all occurred in an American, Asian, European and at a worldwide level most of the time, and not at the national level of a single country. The basis of these structural changes in the financial world are illustrated by four factors: clients becoming more demanding and more professional; more expensive funding and smaller returns on investments; improved technology; and changes in legislation.[30]

7.5 OTHER GENERIC COMPETITIVE STRATEGIES

Generic competitive strategies, which are developed at the organizational level, are based on competitive advantages an organization may possess. Then, one may think of the well known strategies of cost leadership, product differentiation and focus. Heskett (1986) elaborated on these generic strategies of Michael Porter for the service sector and defined the next three strategies:[31] strategies producing low-cost services; strategies producing highly differentiated services; and strategies producing highly differentiated low-cost services.

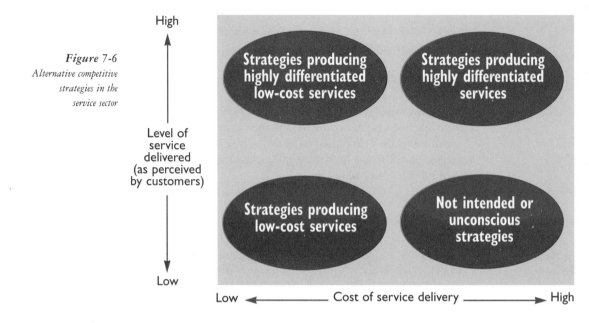

Figure 7-6
*Alternative competitive
strategies in the
service sector*

*low level of service
delivery*

Figure 7-7 shows that a fourth type of strategy can be developed next to the three mentioned by Heskett. We call this the strategy producing a low level of service delivery with high costs. This seems to be an unrealistic one although it may exist in real life. This strategy is only mentioned and not explained any further. This strategy is, hopefully, practised unintentionally or unconsciously. However, the outcome of such (often not formulated) strategies is still recognizable in many public services organizations around the world. Any service organization should avoid such a strategy. It is important to mention, when discussing service quality, that we focus on the perception of the client. It is conceivable that the service organization and all its personnel have a different opinion on the quality of a service than the client. Even in this quite unrealistic case it may be possible that customers perceive the quality of a service as too low with regard to the price of that service (too high). So, they do not get value for their money. This is a service problem to any service provider.

Standardized services typically occur more to the left side of the figure, where low cost is the major characteristic. Customized services usually are highly diversified and this implies higher costs in general, for both the client and the service organization. These customized services are positioned at the upper right side of the figure. For each of the three strategies, a number of characteristics will be formulated in order to accomplish them.

STRATEGIES PRODUCING LOW COST SERVICES

low cost services

A service organization can use several ways to accomplish the strategic goal of low cost services. Some of these options are: seeking out low cost clients; standardizing customized services; reducing human influence/the personal element and reducing a network's "tyranny".

Seeking out low cost clients

only the core service is left

Some service organizations try to "produce" services at lower costs by searching for low cost clients. A well known example is Southwest Airlines in the United States. The concept is simple: find out if there are enough passengers who fly from a certain point to another certain point regularly. If so, the service will be put in the flight-schedule. The company only flies one type of airplane to keep operational costs as low as possible. Passengers know that on board no additional service is delivered. The additional services are stripped and only the core service is left. Southwest, because of this strategy, is now one of the most profitable and fastest growing airlines in the world.

Standardizing customized services and reducing the personal element

standardizing services eliminating the personal contacts

Two more points contributing to lowering costs of a service are standardizing services and eliminating the personal contacts while rendering the service. Developing manuals for the service may reduce costs as well (see McDonalds and Taco Bell). Automated teller machines may also replace the cashier. The people-based character of a service is then reduced and the service becomes more technology and capital intensive. Alternatively, IT may supply a better service more suited to the customer once all data regarding the customer is stored in the database or service quality information system.

Reducing a network's "tyranny"

hub

When researching the function of a network of service providers, interesting results may be found. Federal Express does not fly the packages directly from place of departure to the final destination, but uses hubs. By sending everything to a central hub, which has the sorting and gathering function, and then flying it to the final destination, Federal Express reduced the "tyranny" of the network. Each time, it adds acity to its network, it simply adds one route to the hub. Instead of adding as many routes as there are cities, they apply this approach. Airlines and international suppliers of electronic data often follow this hub-principle. It is remarkable that two such dispersed logistic strategies like "hub and spoke" and "point-to-point" (in combination with the searching for low cost clients) can both be the basis for a low cost strategy.[32]

STRATEGIES PRODUCING HIGHLY DIFFERENTIATED SERVICES

improve and differentiate a service

value for money

Several options to improve and differentiate a service exist. The one thing that these competitive strategies have in common is that in generally improving the service it means costs are increasing as well. However, the question then is whether the customer's perception of value for money increases as well. It is important that customers perceive a positive trade off between actual cost and perceived value. Improving the service can be done by: making the intangible service (more) tangible; customizing standard services; quality control; give attention to training and the value-added per employee; and influencing customers' expectations of quality.

Making the intangible tangible

make their intangible service tangible as possible

Companies aiming at differentiating their services from competitors should make an effort to make their intangible service as tangible as possible. Why else should a client choose a customized standard service instead of an ordinary standard service? The richly coloured brochures of banks and insurance companies speak for themselves. The interior, decorations, etc. of banks with a counter and separate waiting rooms is an example of an effort to make a visible differentiation in services. The atmospherics of the servicescape are crucial in giving an indication of service quality.

Customizing standard services

customization

Another way to improve service to particular customer needs is customization. This sounds self evident. However, we feel (and have seen in our consultancy) that many service organizations forget the self evident. In essence, it hinges upon partly applying tailor made concepts without (too much) cost. A barkeeper addressing his clientèle by name creates confidence and a good atmosphere that "doesn't cost a dime".

Quality control

quality control

The importance of quality control in the service sector has been outlined in Chapter Five. Quality control can be exercised in many ways. If the service delivery takes place where the client can exercise visual control (supervision), the personnel will aim at more self control.

Attention for training and the value-added per employee

training and education

Both principles should be executed thoroughly in service organizations aiming simultaneously at diversifying the service and executing the service at a higher level. The costs for training and education will be higher in a company providing diversified, high level services than in a company providing simple and standardized services. But, it is simply part of the quality level of the services provided.

Managing customers' quality expectations

managing client expectations

As long as clients think that by improving services, even at higher costs, their satisfaction is at a higher level, one should follow the strategy of managing client expectations. Of course, market-oriented service organizations must look for the price elasticity of demand and must carefully watch their positioning relative to their competitors. The perception of management and employees may be different from client perceptions of the service and the way clients experience the service. Influencing the expectations of the client may be an interesting option to improve the image of a service in the eyes of a customer (upgrading). Influencing the expectations of a service may also be used to prepare the client for peaks in demand, which, due to limited capacity, may sometimes cause a lower level of service quality. Clients then take this into account and accept a lower service during peak-hours more easily. The quality of the service does not decrease then in the eyes of a client, because the level of expectations is lower. In Figure 7-7, this principle is presented graphically.[33]

Offering a highly specialized service almost always involves higher costs for the service organization. In practice, it should be researched as to whether a customer is actually willing to pay a higher price for this specialized service (value for money, price elasticity).

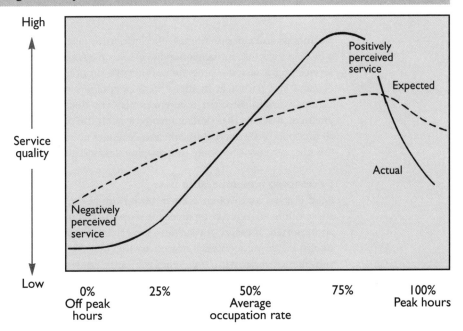

STRATEGIES PRODUCING HIGHLY DIFFERENTIATED LOW COST SERVICES

Competitive strategies often try to improve the level of the service and decrease the costs at the same time. (This theme will also be dealt with in Chapter Thirteen, in the framework of customer service and logistics.) The interesting combination of reducing costs and diversifying services can be accomplished via the following strategic options: do-it-yourself customized services; standardization; managing demand and supply; developing a membership base; control through ownership; leveraging of scarce talents/skills; substituting assets with information; managing the mix of people, systems/organizations and machines; managing the service triangle and focussing on providing one core service.

reducing costs and diversifying services

Do-it-yourself customized services and standardization

Companies combining these two options can be found in the financial and insurance industry. With help of an automated module approach, it is possible to develop a tailor made life-insurance. Just like service contracts for maintenance and cleaning, these are also standardized. Customers can do the customization themselves. For the service organization, it is important to standardize, to improve the control of the process and to keep the perceived service level high in the eyes of the beholder: the client.

standardized customization

Managing demand and supply

One cannot expect a waiter, on a hot summer's day in a peak time, to take your order as fast as he usually does on an off peak hour. On the other hand, it seems that service organizations have a hard time maintaining the service levels during periods when demand is low. We often come across this reverse demand curve in retail shops, hotels, restaurants and cafés or airlines. Too little work may cause boredom to the personnel which, in turn, may influence service quality in a negative way. Many companies in the service sector face the problem of optimally turning the available capacity to the real demand at a particular moment. This phenomenon is called capacity management. Various ways to solve the differences between demand and supply can be used. In practice, it seems that dealing creatively with the relationship with customers, using all the tools of the marketing mix and dealing with the strategic options mentioned in this chapter, may contribute to managing demand and supply effectively.

capacity management

Developing a membership base

membership relationship

Reed Elsevier and Wolters Kluwer have been at the top of the European list of most successfully managed companies for years. The annually increasing profits per share, an important measure for success, is very impressive. Part of the success of these publishers is undoubtedly related to the membership relationship several of the subsidiaries have with their clients. Both Elsevier Science Publishers (ESP) and Kluwer operate in niches. Even during economic recession, universities, etc. continue their subscription to this literature. Telecom companies also hold strong financial and strategic positions on the basis of their member relationship (telephone-calls), for developing new services at low costs. In Europe, many of them are now challenged in their national monopolies and want to strengthen relations with their customers to hinder new entrants.

All these companies have to realize is that customers will not continue these membership relations when, simply stated, they do not get the service quality they expect. We saw this phenomenon occur in a study in which members and non-members of a marketing club were compared.[34] Research among the members of an art museum revealed "the hazard of lapsing is lowered with increasing duration, participation in special interest groups whose goals are related to those of the focal organization, gift frequency, and increasing interrenewal times".[35] This implies that just being a member is not a guarantee for staying a member; ways must always be sought to increase customer commitment and involvement.

Control through ownership

cost control through ownership

Cost control through ownership is for established service firms (because of their reputation, private capital, and borrowing capacity) often more easy than for starting entrepreneurs. It applies to intangible assets such as brand name but also to tangible assets. For example, it is more easy for a company to reshape its building to optimally render services if it is owned, rather than if it is rented.

Leveraging of scarce talents and skills

leverage scarce talents

For many service organizations, it is advantageous to leverage scarce talents, just like the kind of leveraging in financial terms. Accountants and management consultants like to use this leveraging principle, by coupling seniors to less paid juniors. A senior executes selective supervision at strategic points in the relationship, project or process, using standardized procedures, developed to achieve a high quality result with minimal experience, or judgement. This facilitates the leveraging. Leveraging on such skills or competencies, especially when they are the key success factors, is often hard to imitate.

Substituting assets with information

substituting assets with information

Substituting assets with information can be seen in retail shops. Electronic information takes care of just-in-time delivery of stock and assets, in order to keep the lowest possible stock.

Managing the mix between people, systems/organizations and machines

right mix between people, systems and machines

By selectively using technology, and determining the right mix between people, systems and machines it is possible to lower costs and increase the level of services. In some industries, "high touch" (personal contact) will be more important than "high tech" (this is comparable to the distinction that was made in Chapter Two, between labour- and capital/or technology intensive). The challenge now is to balance people, machines, systems and organizations (procedures). A thorough analysis of the whole servuction process is very helpful here. Again, analyzing it creatively and thinking differently about what has been going on until now, can be very beneficial, to this end.

Managing the service triangle

the service triangle

The service triangle consists of: service company; contact personnel/the server, and customers. Managing this triangle carefully is essential. Personnel who leave the organization may take clients with them to another organization, or to their own new business. Loyalty is crucial here. For instance, which loyalty is the strongest: the loyalty between the customer and the company or between employee and client? This is mainly the question in professional services, where the relationship between personnel involved in the service delivery and the client is very strong. It counts heavily in the hairdressing, advertising and consultancy business.

Companies in this situation try to find a better balance between mutual relationships, like, for example, trying to explain the collective competencies of the organization to the client. Besides this, the organization may try to achieve an organizational culture, development programs, promotion structures, salary scales, stock options and bonuses, all in order to strengthen the relationship with their own personnel (in order to keep them).

Focussing on providing one core service

This last method is a well known strategy to establish low costs and from the point of view of the service organization it establishes a high service level. For the individual service organization this choice involves just limiting the number of services. The service organization may introduce all kinds of varieties to this core service. Customers and competitors in the same industry may perceive this as having to deal with specialized services. Examples of this strategy may be found in a wide range of companies, like in kindergartens, hamburger chains, etc.

varieties to this core service

FOCUS STRATEGY IN SERVICE ORGANIZATIONS

An organization cannot fulfil all functions for all people at all times. Service companies, for example, sometimes experience trouble working with different service levels for different market segments within a business unit or strategic service

focussing their service

group. Then, making a clear choice is needed. Organizations focussing their service on one type of client or providing one well executed service for more segments achieve both lower costs and higher service levels. The discipline of market leaders depends on their ability to choose a clear group of customers and narrow their focus to dominate the market.[36] In other words, a combination of low costs, high quality and strong focus may lead to higher productivity.[37] Productivity is defined in terms of substantial operating margins. The company achieves these margins on the basis of its normal activities. Operating margins, in this case, underly each competitive advantage. Profits and competitive advantages may contribute to the development of the assortment, operational strategy and people. This will be a useful starting point to formulate the strategic mix of a service organization.

low costs, high quality and strong focus

VARIETY STRATEGIES AND LOYALTY STRATEGIES

We have stressed the increasing interest in relationship marketing and the challenges it provides to establish long term relationships with customers. One of the reasons to do so is avoiding customer churn. However, customers also like variety. Consequently, a tension exists between loyalty and variety. This will affect strategies as well.

loyalty and variety

It is a common belief that loyalty is decreasing.[38] An overwhelming choice (created by companies themselves), the availability and easy application of information, individualism and commoditization (many products, even luxury ones, look almost the same) are amongst the causes of a declining loyalty.[39] The increasing opportunities to choose offered by the suppliers are, in fact, the outcome of strategies aimed at offering variety to customers and to perfectly fit to the needs of a particular market segment. A high-variety strategy ultimately leads to customization: a unique offer for (each individual) customer. On the other hand, customers have an instinct to seek variety. Curiosity, learning, internal needs due to satiation, natural survival instinct, changing needs over time (family life cycle, aspiration level) or just out-of-stock situations may cause this variety-seeking behavior.[40] Probably, the perceived variety by customers is the ultimate issue for companies to differentiate the offer. This will determine to a large extent whether customers do accept the (wide) variety or not.[41]

customized loyalty

Instead of customized variety, customized loyalty may be the purpose of relationship marketing. Here, five principles may apply:[42]

1. focus on specific types of customers (e.g. the most profitable ones);[43]
2. focus on creating value, not on reducing price;
3. focus on building loyalty, not just reducing churn;
4. systematically prioritize efforts based on ROI; and
5. create social and psychological bonds balanced with the financial requirements.

All kinds of relationship strategies and programs may help to decrease switching behavior and increase loyalty behavior. However, one should keep in mind that too much of loyalty or too much of variety may be too much for the customer (no freedom, too much choice) and the supplier (too much costs, too wide an assortment).

7.6 GENERAL SERVICE PROVIDERS (GSP's) VERSUS LIMITED SERVICE PROVIDERS (LSP's)

Established airlines like BA, Lufthansa and Delta Airlines are challenged by two types of newcomers in the market. First, companies like Virgin, Easy Jet and Southwest providing low costs ("no frills") services. Second, charter companies delivering customized airline services for business trips and incentive travel (i.e. rewarding personnel and dealers). The same applies to universal banks like CitiBank, Chase Manhattan and many Asian and European banks. Financial providers offering a very limited range of products are threatening these large institutions. For example, Schwab (a direct discount broker) offers a limited range of investment products mainly via telephone and the Internet to all investors (small and large). They are a serious rival for the established general banks. On the other hand, there are investment banks specializing in an industry such as high-tech or bio-technology offering very customized corporate finance advice (such as mergers, acquisitions, capital raising, financial engineering) to and about firms in this limited segment. It is expected that these LSP's will grow in number and market share in the near future (see Figure 7-8). We expect this process to happen in the airline and financial industry to a larger extent than at the moment, but also in other (unexpected) industries.

LSP's

Both types of newcomers are an extreme form of focussed strategy. The Limited Service Providers focus either on a specific range of services or a specific market segment. Their organizations are less complex than a GSP and more dedicated. Both

Figure 7-8
LSP's challenging
GSP's

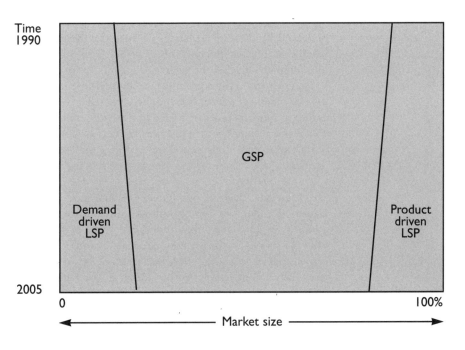

forms try to steal market share from the GSP. The product driven organization starts from a product focus. It seeks to define, from a technical point of view, a special product range by offering simple and/or standardized services. It concentrates on product features. Customer value is created by means of a low price and standardized

push concept

performance. Typically, these companies are cost-driven and apply a push concept to get their services on to the market. The demand driven incumbents focus on client needs. They provide a combination of customized and standardized services to meet the specific needs of their well-defined target group. This is the consequence of their

pull concept

market driven orientation resulting in a pull concept.

The established companies in various service industries, offering their broad spectrum of services to a wide range of customers (many segments), have to reconsider their strategic options. Either they can join the race, start such a specialized operation themselves or improve their existing activities in which costs, relationships (loyalty management), processes and multi-distribution channels are important aspects.

7.7 STRATEGIES FOR CORE, AUGMENTED, STANDARD AND CUSTOMIZED SERVICES

The James Heskett typology of basic competitive strategies in services can be adapted slightly and then fits our typology of services developed in Chapters One and Two. Both axes are labelled differently but represent, in essence, the same phenomenon in our's and Heskett's approach. Heskett's dimension of "level of service delivered" (as perceived by customers) has to do with the individual's assessment of the service whether it fits their personal needs or not. This is more or less equal to our concept

degree of customization

of customization, e.g. the degree of customization. Heskett's dimension of "cost of service delivery" ranges from low to high. These costs depend to a large extent on the complexity of the service and the service delivery process. This complexity varies as long as more features are added to the core service. In general, augmented services will be more complex than just the core service alone. This is reflected in the degree

degree of differentiation

of differentiation between core services and augmented services, the second dimension of our framework. This is shown in Figure 7-9.[44]

The main advantage of our framework in Figure 7-9 over Heskett's framework in Figure 7-6 is that the "strange" type of unintentional or unconscious generic strategies do not exist any longer. For, all the four types of strategies should aim at delivering value for money to the customers/clients. Another advantage is that this framework

wheel of servicing

can be applied to analyze the wheel of servicing (as an application of the well-known wheel of retailing developed by McNair in the fifties). The different stages of entry,

dynamics in services

trading-up and vulnerability can be applied here as well, showing the dynamics in services:

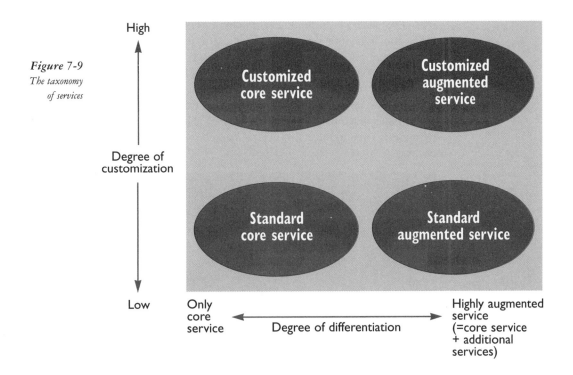

Figure 7-9
The taxonomy
of services

entry	1. entry	Most service providers probably start on a small scale and try to deliver services that are as tailored as possible. These services are targeted to a specific market segment with unique expectations. Quite often, services are not yet very complex.
trading-up	2. trading-up	As the life cycle of the service organization continues, the tailored core service delivery process becomes more efficient and/or new features are added. It will become more complex, on the one hand, and/or more efficient, on the other. So, two ways of development can be distinguished: one in the direction of more efficient core services (standard core services) and one in the direction of customized augmented services;
vulnerability	3. vulnerability	After a time, competition increases and competitive prices are of utmost importance. This may be the case for both situations described in the trading-up stage. The important task now is how to cope with this competition. A further trading-up may be the case leading to a higher and even more specialized level of tailor made augmented services. Another way is to harvest and leave the industry or try to survive in the cut throat competition by becoming more cost efficient. Quite often, this means that new low cost service providers may enter the industry and find more niches.

In this way, the wheel of servicing reflects the dynamics in service industries. The development that LSP's are eating away market share from GSP's, in particular when these established firms are not cost-conscious and do not adapt their marketing mix, fits in this "wheel of services" concept. The four generic service strategies can be compared to one another on many issues. We will elaborate on that in chapters to come. It will all be compiled in the chapter on implementation. Here, it is sufficient to start the comparison by just looking at each key success factor (quality, relationships, image, reputation, pricing and timeliness), offering and market focus. These issues have been mentioned before. Therefore, it can be put into one figure right away. Their implications for the marketing strategy will be discussed in the next chapter.

Figure 7-10
The four generic
service strategies

	Standard core service	Customized core service	Standard augmented service	Customized augmented service
Key success factors	Cost efficiency	Differentiation to unique client/segment relationships	Cost efficiency More complexity	Highly differentiated Complex
Offering	Standardized	Standardization +some differentiation (quite complex)	Standardization +some standard additional services (not so complex)	Specialization Unique services added to core (very complex)
Market focus	Broad No/hardly any segmentation	Narrow Very specific segments defined	Broad Some segments	Very narrow Individualized/ personalized

Up until now, we have gathered insights into the strategic planning process of a service organization at the top or corporate level or at the level of a strategic business unit. In the next chapter, we will deal with the planning for the functional level of strategic marketing planning.

SUMMARY

In this chapter, we have outlined the strategic planning process at corporate level in market-oriented service organizations. It is the framework in which strategic marketing planning should be developed. It is illustrated via the cascade in Figure 7-2. The positioning of an organization is outlined at the time in the mission statement. We have seen that the different strategies at the organizational level give direction towards the desired positioning. Key success factors in services appear to be quality, relationships, image, reputation, pricing and speed of reaction. That is why relationship marketing is also so important to service providers. Service/market combinations and development strategies are merely guidelines. To position a company which aims at a low cost strategy and/or highly differentiated services, several options are available. Influencing the expectations of clients, capacity management, self service, customizing standard services and quality control are only a few of these.

In total, we have discussed 20 different options. By means of combining these options, the positioning can be reinforced. It appeared that General Services Providers (GSP's) in mature markets such as airlines, banks, insurance companies and travel agencies have to take into account the actions of Limited Services Providers (LSP's). As a result of lower cost structure, the focussed LSP's are able to compete increasingly successfully in the "core business" of the established firms. Among others, by offering alternative distribution channels, setting up their own LSP's, cost reductions, strategic alliances and product innovations, the GSP's try to increase customer loyalty and to protect their market share. Devoting attention to the personnel and the organizational culture may make the chosen profile even more visible in the market and also harder to imitate by competitors. On top of that, we can support the desired positioning by making sure that marketing tools like the promotion mix, price and distribution policy are in line with the positioning.

This aspect, concerning the marketing planning process at functional level will be dealt with in detail in the next chapter.

QUESTIONS

1 Which stages can be found in the strategic planning process at corporate level in general and with respect to marketing planning?
2 What conclusion can you draw when you compare Tables 1-3 (on key success factors in services in general) and Table 7-1 (key success factors of market leaders in services)?
3 Why is it important to have a clear mission statement? Could that be related to the benefits customers are looking for when buying a service (see Chapter Four)?
4 What is the link between Heskett's framework and our typology of generic service strategies?
5 What do you conclude on the relevance of relationship marketing to services if you combine the ideas about relationship marketing from Chapters One, Four and Seven?
6 Caring about people appears to be an important part of a market oriented firm's corporate culture. Why?
7 What is the difference between a GSP and a LSP?
8 In what way can service providers offer differentiated services at low cost?
9 What growth strategies can be applied by service firms in the non-profit sector? Does that differ from the profit sector?
10 What is the wheel of servicing?

ASSIGNMENTS

1 Do the key success factors mentioned in this Chapter apply to the best (or worst) service firms you know? Give some examples and explain.
2 Give some examples of service firms producing highly differentiated low-cost services.
3 What options does a university have to respond to fluctuations in students' enrollment?
4 Compare the five principles of relationship marketing mentioned in section 7.5 to what has been said about the kind of bonds/relationships in Chapter Four. Does the content of the two chapters fit or not?
5 Four factors impacting on financial institutions are mentioned in section 7.4. Elaborate on this by means of the trends discussed in Chapter Three.
6 How can a bank stimulate variety seeking behavior? How can an airline encourage loyalty in its freight segment (so not the passenger part of their business)?
7 Search for the mission statement of the banks and one charity in your own town. Write them down. Are they clear to you? And to the companies' employees? Why or why not? Do they guide their daily behavior?

Case: Linking Core Competencies to Customer Needs: Strategic Marketing of Health Care Services[45]

ADK Research Corp. and Clinical Trial Services

The principals of ADK Research Corp. had, over a period of 10 years, developed expertise in data collection, database management, and networking technologies for large-scale, government-funded, clinical trial research projects. Unique, customized systems were developed that integrated leading-edge mini and micro-computing hardware with customized software applications. The systems reduced data-entry errors, enhanced data processing, and provided greater research efficiency (in data collection through report generation) while improving data accuracy. ADK's goal was to expand into the private sector. Market research was needed to determine if ADK's systems could be successfully marketed to the private sector. Target customers included pharmaceutical, biotechnology, and device manufacturers in need of clinical trial research services.

The clinical trial services required for developing a new drug or device are: clinical center review and selection; protocol development; clinical center management; data collection; statistical analysis; research report generation; and, FDA report generation.

Most manufacturers do not have the facilities or capabilities to manage all of their clinical trial work in-house. While some services may be conducted by the company developing the new product, others, however, are contracted to an outside clinical trial research supplier (CTRS).

Previous research in health care settings has shown that service quality, customer satisfaction, and subsequent market behavior are interrelated. ADK was concerned that its perceptions of consumer CTRS expectations might differ from actual expectations. Any expectation gaps would likely result in ADK developing and implementing ineffective marketing programs.

Of interest to ADK was the value firms would place on their hardware and software innovations. Specifically, information was desired regarding the (1) importance of CTRS technical capabilities relative to other criteria and (2) degree of satisfaction with current CTRS services, particularly dimensions related to the application of technology. Such information would help ADK determine if and how its core competencies could be translated into benefits sought in the marketplace.

Research Design

To provide ADK with insights into the CTRS market, a research study was developed that had three components. The first was information on the criteria firms use to select a research supplier. The second component included information on the evaluation of and satisfaction with prior CTRS use. These two components would provide insights into the CTRS selection and evaluation processes used by pharmaceutical firms. The third component entailed linking ADK's technological strengths with the selection and evaluation criteria. Establishing such links would identify the ways in which ADK could offer potential customers greater satisfaction while highlighting how ADK should market its services.

A questionnaire was designed to determine criteria used to select CTRS and satisfaction with CTRS use. Questionnaire items were developed following (1) a service quality literature review, (2) analysis of competitive CTRS marketing communication, and (3) exploratory indepth interviews with clinicians and/or researchers with clinical trial decision making responsibilities.

Survey participants were sought from pharmaceutical, biotechnology, and device manufacturers. The informants were typically vice presidents or directors of R&D, product development, or clinical research. Each informant was mailed a description of the study and a questionnaire. A reminder letter and questionnaire were mailed if the original had not been returned after three weeks. In total, 27 usable responses were collected for a 46% questionnaire return rate.

Of the 27 responses, 11 were from pharmaceutical companies, 8 each were from biotechnology and device firms. All of the firms in the sample had moderate to extensive experience using CTRS.

Results

CTRS Selection Criteria

Table 1 shows the attribute evaluations, ordered in terms of importance. The five more global benefits associated with each attribute (image, credentials, expertise, cost, and technology) also are listed.

ADK's chief concern was the relative importance of its core competencies – the attributes related to technological benefits. The three technological attributes – data management systems, telecommunications capabilities, and hardware and software configurations – were perceived to be relatively unimportant attributes.

Table 2 shows the relative importance of the six CTRS benefits, both overall and for each industry sector. CTRS' technological capability is one of the least important benefits when it comes to selecting a CTRS.

ADK's innovations, its technological competencies, were not highly sought by CTRS decision makers. Other benefits, particularly the CTRS' image, application expertise, cost, and certain of its credentials seemed to guide the selection process. Hence, ADK's core competencies are not perceived by customers as providing any differential advantage (tables 3 and 4).

Past CTRS Satisfaction

Table 3 shows respondents' satisfaction with past CTRS on six service dimensions. Four service dimensions were evaluated very similarly, yielding moderate satisfaction: data accuracy, staff responsiveness, and quality of reporting to clients and the FDA (the Federal Drug Administration). The remaining two dimensions – flow of communication and performing deliverables – only resulted in neutral levels of satisfaction.

Also, respondents assessed their overall satisfaction with CTRS services, and the resulting mean score was 4.64. From the service satisfaction measures shown in Table 3, the only dimensions with significantly lower satisfaction scores, compared to the overall satisfaction variable, were performing deliverables and flow of communications.

Given that satisfaction with CTRS seemed to be moderate at best, it should be explored why this might be the case. A useful way to understand relationships between attributes or dimensions is to explore intercorrelations. Table 4 shows correlation analysis results for the service satisfaction dimensions (including overall satisfaction). Table 4 shows four dimensions correlate very highly with overall satisfaction: performing deliverables, communication flows, staff responsiveness, and quality of reporting. The relatively low overall CTRS satisfaction is due in part to poor CTRS performance on meeting their deadlines and establishing good communications with their clients.

Communication flows appear to be highly correlated with performing deliverables, staff responsiveness, and reporting quality. Hence, communication flows may be a key dimension through which to facilitate quality service delivery.

QUESTIONS

1   In what way do ADK's own perceptions of customer satisfaction differ from customer's own perceptions?
2   How do you evaluate the market research study ADK performed?
3   What would you suggest that ADK do to become a market-oriented company (and loose its technology-orientation)?

TABLE 1 Attributes used to select CTRS

Selection factor	Benefit	Importance score*
Overall reputation	Image	6.33
Private sector/pharmaceutical industry experience	Credentials	5.73
Expertise in treatment/application area	Expertise	5.33
Price	Cost	5.13
FDA experience	Credentials	4.80
Prestige of clinical center(s) provided	Image	4.47
Prior NDA/PMA preparation experience	Credentials	4.43
Data management system	Technology	4.00
Telecommunications capabilities	Technology	3.36
Clinical research publication experience	Credentials	3.29
Hardware and software configurations	Technology	3.21
Location of supplier	Convenience	3.00
University affiliation	Credentials	2.93

Note: *Mean importance score across all respondents using CTRS. All attributes measured on seven-point scales, where 1 = not at all important, and 7 = very important

TABLE 2 Benefits sought from CTRS by industry sector

	Industry sector*			
	Total	Pharmaceuticals	Biotechnology	Device
Image	5.40	5.56	4.63	6.25
Expertise	5.33	5.33	4.50	6.70
Cost	5.13	5.00	5.25	5.50
Credentials	4.50	4.71	4.20	3.80
Technology	3.52	3.78	3.42	3.34
Convenience	3.00	3.22	2.50	3.00

Note: *Mean importance score across all respondents using CTRS. Importance score for each benefit represents average of all related attributes. Attributes measured on seven-point scales, where 1 = not at all important and 7 = very important.

TABLE 3 *Satisfaction with CTRS service dimensions*

Service dimension	Satisfaction score*
Data accuracy	4.93
Responsiveness of study staff	4.92
Quality of reporting to client firm	4.76
Quality of submission for NDA/PMA	4.75
Flow of communications	4.29
Performing deliverables/meeting deadlines	3.92

*Note: *Mean satisfaction score across all CTRS users. All dimensions measured on seven-point scale, where 1=not at all satisfied and 7=very satisfied.*

TABLE 4 *Relationship between CTRS service satisfaction dimensions*

Person correlation coefficients*

	Data accuracy	Meeting deadlines	Comm. flow	Staff responsiveness	Quality of reporting	Quality of submission
Meeting deadlines	.165					
Comm. flow	.590	.752**				
Staff responsiveness	.667**	.513	.776**			
Quality of reporting	.702**	.498	.866**	.645		
Quality of NDA/PMA submission	-.372	.567	.298	.365	.000	
Overall satisfaction	.389	.878**	.890**	.804**	.675**	.683

*Notes: * n=27. All dimensions measured on seven-point scales, where 1=not at all satisfied and 7=very satisfied.** Statistically significant relationship, one-tailed t-test, at p < .01.*

ENDNOTES

1. Wührer, 1995.
2. Bart, 1997, p.9.
3. The empirical research Bart has performed, however, shows these goals are hardly met in practice. Managers are quite negative about the content and usefulness of most mission statements in reality. Often, they are impossible to attain, partly because they are ambiguous.
4. Hofstede, 1991, p.180.
5. Hofstede, 1991, p.182-183.
6. Kasper, 1995, 1997, 1998; Kasper, Van Lit and De Ruyter, 1998.
7. Consequently, many governmental bodies and bureaucratic agencies have to make a big turnaround in this aspect when they want to become (more) market oriented. A mindshift for the employees and top management is needed then.
8. All these issues are mentioned here because the mission statement of a market oriented service firm should allow for and stimulate the accomplishment of these issues. The mission statement should not hinder its realization. Knowing the benefits customers are looking for is an important element of such a mission. Often, firms are more inclined to think in term of the technicalities of their services than these benefits (see also this chapter's case).
9. Payne, 1993.
10. In 1994, the 220 IATA members transported 8% more passengers and 14% more freight. Their average occupancy rate of passenger seats was 68% (being 65% in 1993). Seat capacity grew by 5% in 1994. All these members taken together did not make a profit in 1994. North West Airlines, however, accomplished almost a US $ 300 million profit in 1994. Their occupancy rate increased from 66.7% in 1993 to 68.1% in 1994. Mostly, it appears that higher occupancy rates lead to higher profits (or smaller losses). An occupancy rate of 66-70% seems to be the threshold for profits or losses.
11. The competitive advantages on KSF's seem to be almost the same in the UK and in Holland. However, note that the Dutch have much highers scores on these items than the UK.
12. The authors themselves maintain that study is still exploratory; data about consumer and industrial services are pooled by Bharadwaj and Menon, 1993. We would like to add that the reader should also be aware of the fact than many scholars have also critized the PIMS-database and analyses in some respects.
13. Bharadwaj and Menon, 1993, pp. 31-32.
14. In Chaper Eleven, we will elaborate on the key success factors in new service development. It appears many similarities exist with the finding reported here.
15. Hamel and Prahalad, 1994, Chapter Twelve.
16. Roth and Amoroso, 1993.
17. Remember this is more than just being a market leader with all its key success factors discussed in the previous pages. However, imposing such a vision on the whole industry is quite difficult. Firms realizing service breakthroughs are well on the way to shaping the future of an entire industry. Probably, this "stage" is easier to accomplish.
18. Heskett, Sasser and Hart, 1990.
19. Heskett, Sasser and Hart, 1990, p. 261.
20. Grönroos, 1990a; Sheth and Parvatiyar, 1995. A debate is going on as to whether relationship marketing is a new paradigm or just a restatement of the marketing concept. See, e.g. Petrof, 1997 and Gruen, 1997 for an overview. We believe that it is a shift in paradigm of the marketing concept taking "companies a quantum leap further into the realm of the customer" (Gruen, 1997, p. 37) just

as the strategic marketing concept (developed by Day and Wensley) was a new paradigm.

21. Davis and Manrodt, 1996, p. 332-335.

22. Sheth and Parvatiyar, 1995, p. 263.

23. Venetis, 1997.

24. Many authors have discussed the commitment concept in a marketing context, like Dwyer et al., 1987, Anderson and Weitz, 1992, Kumar et al., 1995, Morgan and Hunt, 1994, Geyskens and Steenkamp, 1995, Geyskens et al., 1996, Möller and Wilson, 1995, Venetis, 1997 and Schijns, 1998.

25. Venetis, 1997 in a study about the Dutch advertising market and the relationships between the ad agencies and their clients.

26. Ansoff, 1965. The technology dimensions in this section stems from Abel, 1980.

27. Here we refer to Johnson and Scholes, 1988. Many other books on corporate strategy can also be referred to.

28. This is their entry strategy in many foreign markets. Sometimes the firm's acquired keep their own name, sometimes their name is changed into SCI. More on entry strategies is discussed in Chapter Nine.

29. In Forum 97/3, a publication of the European Forum for Management Development (Brussels), it is shown that these alliances are one of the reasons why airlines become a kind of virtual company. The other reason is the outsourcing of many functions like check-in, catering, aircraft maintenance. Managing such a firm, means management of networks. This article indicates that to a large extent many of the outsourced services determine customer satisfaction. This has special implications in marketing and HRM policies to deliver excellent service quality and customer satisfaction.

30. These issues have been discussed in Chapter Three.

31. We use James Heskett's framework as a starting point for the discussion in this section, add some of our own insights to it, and, use our own terminology at certain points to avoid confusion.

32. This has to do with ways of organizing the (physical) distribution of goods and services as efficiently as posible (see also Chapter Thirteen on "organizing the distribution").

33. It should be pointed out that this observation is not based on a documented research, but on general experience. This figure is partly based on Heskett, 1986, p. 35.

34. Schijns, 1998.

35. Bhattacharya, 1998, p. 31. On the other hand, some other studies indicate that increasing duration has an insignificant effect on the probability to continue a subscription.

36. Treacy and Wiersema, 1995.

37. Heskett, 1986.

38. It not only occurs in consumer behavior but also in political behavior (e.g. floating votes) and the church.

39. These causes are mentioned in Schriver, 1997.

40. Kahn, 1998. In a commentary Lehmann, 1998 questions whether the basic assumption really holds that more variety is always better.

41. In the retail world, it appears the procurement department has an important say here. They decide what will be put on the shelves.

42. Duboff and Underhill Sherer, 1997 mention the first four; we have added the fifth.

43. We will challenge this common notion in Chapter Eight.

44. The reader will notice Figure 7-9 is exactly the same as Figures 1-7 and 2-1.

45. This case is based on the Roth and Amoroso, 1993 study about CTRS (see references).

CHAPTER EIGHT

SERVICES MARKETING PLANNING IN STRATEGIC BUSINESS UNITS

This chapter will enable you to:

- *understand the many relevant issues in strategic marketing planning;*
- *explain the relevance of relationships in developing a marketing strategy;*
- *perform a service marketing audit;*
- *explain why a high quality service marketing audit is a prerequisite to high quality strategic marketing planning;*
- *develop a marketing strategy for service organizations within the framework of the generic strategy (as developed in the previous chapter);*

- *develop a strategic marketing plan for a service organization;*
- *develop an operational marketing plan for a service organization;*
- *be aware of the relevance of an internal marketing strategy and plan;*
- *understand the many relevant issues in strategic internal marketing planning;*
- *argue why the external and internal marketing strategy and plans should coincide.*

BELOW: *Positioning and quality*

From the dynamic business capitals to the most exotic resort destinations in Asia Pacific

It must be Shangri-La

8.1 INTRODUCTION

Strategic marketing planning is an important tool for anticipating changes in the environment of an organization. However, some proof exists indicating it is not yet applied on a large scale basis in service organizations. So, to what extent have service organizations implemented (strategic) marketing planning?

In a 1992 study on strategic marketing planning in the Dutch business community, 13 companies from the service industry were represented.[1] The results produced, because of the limited number of these companies, no firm conclusions. Nevertheless, some interesting indications about strategic marketing planning in the service industry were provided. What do they do when they claim to apply strategic marketing planning? This is what turned out to be the case:

- more than 84% has put organizational objectives in the strategic marketing plan;
- almost 90% has put development strategies in the strategic marketing plan;
- 70% has put short term organizational goals in the operational marketing plan;
- almost 58% adjusts the marketing plan within one to six months (to changes in the external environment, for instance);
- a little more than 36% has defined how the sales force activities should be coordinated.

From these findings, we conclude that the link between some important issues in corporate strategic plans (objectives, development strategies) and the strategic marketing plans are clearly present. Plans are flexible and quickly adjusted when necessary. They provide direction to the activities but are not "set in concrete". The significance of its use should not be underestimated.

This chapter elaborates on the issues discussed in the previous chapter. In Chapter Seven, strategy development and planning were discussed at corporate level. Several generic strategies were formulated. They are the framework for the functional strategies of the organization. In this chapter, marketing strategies and strategic marketing planning will be discussed. Chapter Ten will deal with the human resource side of the functional strategies. Simply stated, in this chapter the final two boxes of Figure 7-2 will be explained.

For the sake of clarity, we have made a distinction between strategy and strategic planning at corporate level (Chapter Seven) and marketing strategy and planning at business unit level (Chapter Eight). To us, this distinction is especially relevant to (very) large service organizations structured in business units. For those service organizations structured differently or for (very) small service organizations it should be self evident that this distinction is not relevant. Still, the content of both chapters holds for them as well but should be applied to the one and only organization. In both types of organization the corporate strategy will be the input and framework (not the restrictions!) for the strategies at functional level such as the strategic information plan (STRIP), HRM plan, finance plan and, what is the focus of our study here, the marketing plan.

Since relationship marketing is such an important topic, we will elaborate on the relationship issues discussed in Chapter Seven and take an even more concrete marketing perspective that can be used in segmenting the market (section 8.2). We will then shift the focus towards the process of formulating a marketing strategy (sections 8.3 and 8.4). After this discussion on HOW it can be done, we will turn to WHAT has to be incorporated in this planning process. Eight stages are revealed in sections 8.5 and 8.6. Next to planning the marketing strategies directed at the (external) market, it is necessary to develop an internal marketing strategy. The way this can be developed and how it fits into the external marketing planning process is shown in section 8.7. Finally, making the planned strategies available to the branches or "sales" outlets service firms may have, some topics will be dealt with in sections 8.8 and 8.9. This is all shown in Figure 8-1.

8.2 RELATIONSHIP MARKETING

The shift towards relationship marketing and the implications for a firm's strategy have been discussed in Chapters One and Seven. Here, it is relevant to state that this shift not only implies a shift from short term to long(er) term orientation. It also implies a shift from offensive marketing to defensive marketing. This means a shift from attracting or conquering new customers to keeping and protecting the existing customers. The outcome of this mind shift will be the central theme throughout this section.

mind shift

Relationships appear to be defined in different ways. It is difficult to define them in a unique and unquestionable way. Therefore, it is better to look at the characteristics of a relationship that are mentioned in literature on relationship marketing to get an impression what it is all about.[2] The most relevant characteristics are:

characteristics of a relationship

interaction
- a certain (kind of) interaction between two or more parties (e.g. customer and supplier – as organization or as individuals);

period of time
- taking place over a (long) period of time;

goals
- aimed at achieving economic and/or non-economic goals;

continuity
- having a particular degree of continuity (the past impacts on the present situation and the present situation affects the future);

evaluation, formal and informal
- in which the evaluation of the interaction depends on factual and perceptual indicators; and

aspects
- which is characterized by formal and informal aspects.

behavioral side
Defining relationships in the literature on database marketing and direct marketing focusses on the behavioral side of a relationship: the way in which consumers behave

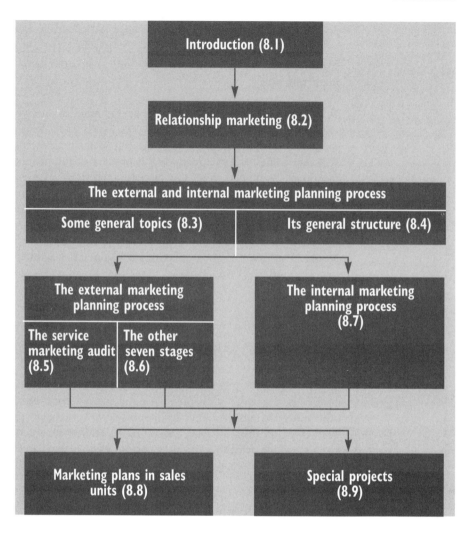

Figure 8-1
Chapter outline

*strength of a
relationship*

*how recently a service
was bought,
frequency,
monetary value*

is considered to be a valuable indicator of the strength of a relationship. What they buy, how much they buy and how often they buy appear to be important indicators of actual buying behavior. Then, variables like how recently a service was bought (R), the frequency with which services are bought (F) and the monetary value involved (M) are the main topics taken into account. However, these RFM- proxies for actual buying behavior may not be sufficient to define the strength of the relationship between a supplier and a customer properly.[3] Thinking in terms of the strength of a relationship is important because the stronger the relationship, the more difficult it will be to break it (e.g. the less likely it is that customers will switch). Researching the strength of a relationship also requires looking at the way in which customers perceive and evaluate the relationship: their attitude towards the relationship with the supplier based on, e.g. their commitment to the supplier. So, the (actual buying) behavioral dimension reflects the economic value of the relationship to the supplier, while the (attitudinal) perceptual dimension reflects the customer's

*attitude towards the
relationship*

relation perception and loyalty matrix

value of the relationship. To keep it simple, the values on both dimensions may vary between high and low. This can be depicted in the relation perception and loyalty (RLM-) matrix which is shown in Figure 8-2.[4]

Figure 8-2
The relation perception and loyalty matrix

		Actual loyalty in buying behavior (= behavioral RFM dimensions)	
		High (very valuable)	Low (= less valuable)
Perceptions/ attitude of relationship (= attitudinal dimension)	High (= strong)	Friends	Sympathetics
	Low (= weak)	Functionalists	Acquaintances

four segments

Service organizations can now use their database with actual data about consumer buying behavior and perceptual data on how customers perceive and evaluate the relationship, to segment their market into four segments, as shown in Figure 8-2.[5] These RFM-data on actual buying behavior may also be stated in terms of the customer(s) profitability to the service firm, e.g. as a return on investment (ROI). Then, customers with a high ROI are considered to be very valuable to the firm.

friends

sympathetics

functionalists

The customers in the four parts of the matrix have been labelled as friends, sympathetics, functionalists and acquaintances. Friends are customers who are very loyal to the organization and perceive themselves as having a strong relationship (commitment) with the organization. As these customers make above average contributions to the ROI and/or profit of the company, from the company's economic or financial point of view, these customers are very valuable. Sympathetics perceive themselves to have a strong relationship with their supplier. However, their sympathy is scarcely expressed in their behavior. So, in spite of the fact that they have good feelings towards the organization, they hardly contribute to the ROI and/or profit of the company. Functionalists perceive a weak relationship with their supplier but are of great economic or financial importance to the organization. These customers show a weak commitment towards the organization. Nevertheless, they might still buy repeatedly, e.g. because of bonds as a result of a contract (a matter of calculative

acquaintances

commitment). Acquaintances are customers neither perceiving a strong relationship, nor being of any economic or financial importance to the organization at a particular moment. However, these customers can be exploring a new relationship with this firm or consider ending the existing relationship.

Analyzing the actual distribution of customers over those four segments will reveal whether this is also the preferred distribution, whether all kinds of promotional activities have to be performed to let customers move from one segment to another in order to create a larger group of true loyal customers. The various strategies mentioned in Chapters Seven and Eight as well as the elements of the marketing mix can be used to that end.

customers move from one segment to another

long term customer relationship profitability

When data about individual customers are present, a service provider can check whether customers move from one segment to another. Banks and insurance companies can investigate these dynamics quite easily by looking at their clients' records. These shifts will affect long term customer relationship profitability.[6] For, customers do not provide the same profitability at every moment during their relationship with the service provider. In using this profitability perspective, the prime interest lies in understanding the cash flow effects on handling customer relationships in the long run; what are the revenues from and costs of serving a specific customer?[7] The key for effective relationship marketing management is an understanding of the customer's value creation process, which occurs at different levels of interaction during the relationship. The service encounter comes to the fore at various moments during this period. Therefore, a distinction can be made between the relationship, the episode and the actual action. A relationship consists of a number of episodes. Episodes are complete service events as seen from the customer(s) point of view, like an overnight stay at a hotel, a rafting holiday of two weeks, etc. Actions are service elements or activities within an episode, like checking out, making a reservation, etc. The quality of each action adds up to the total service quality of an entire episode, which in turn affects the quality of the relationship. This way of reasoning indicates that the relation between service quality and profitability is a complex one.[8]

the customer's value creation process

relationship episodes actions

As stated, it is important from a strategic point of view to define what kind of relationship a service provider wants to have and maintain with its customers, and, if and when they want to turn existing customers into clients for life. Such a relationship strategy aims at investing in customers and taking care of them (see Chapters Four and Seven). Mutual interest in cooperation is of utmost relevance. Strong relations are often exit barriers for customers and entry barriers for competitors, (when it is possible to enter the market or "steal market share" from the other suppliers). Therefore, it is very important to know why customers want to have a relationship with a service provider and why they want to maintain, strengthen or weaken the existing relationship. This may differ also for customers in each of the four segments of the RLM-matrix.

why customers want to have a relationship

Service practice 8-2 In search of continously stronger relationships

The Mitsubishi study cited in Chapter Four indicated that many customers wanted to have a stronger relationship with their car dealer than their existing one. This is the same for many suppliers in the car industry. It is self evident for such a high involvement product.

On the other hand, studies in the health insurance industry reveal that many insured do not have or want to have a strong relationship with their insurance company. Such a strong relationship is only required at the moment of truth when bills have to be paid or costs have to be met. Then, the low involvement service turns into a high involvement service. For each insurance company, it will be interesting to see how competitors deal with this phenomenon.

personal touch

As employees and customers are the actors in the relationship, episodes and actions, the personal touch will be much greater in customized augmented services than in standard core services. In the latter, much automation can replace the personal touch. Then, service employees can no longer be "used" to develop and maintain a strong relationship between the service firm and its clients. Other means have to be applied to that end. One can see that many banks, insurance companies, car manufacturers, car importers and car dealers all publish magazines to communicate to their present customers about new services, new types of service offers, etc. They also institute customer satisfaction programs to measure satisfaction levels. Just calling them customers often gives customers the feeling that the firm cares about them. Such an approach is often highly valued by customers, in consumer markets as well as in industrial service markets. The personal touch then is substituted by a printed (or telephone) touch due to changes in technology. All these activities are aimed at

retention rates

keeping customers; retention rates are important. This also happens to be the case in business-to-business service relationships. Then, the difference between the outcome of the process of delivering services and the process itself are important variables determining service quality and hence keeping the relationship.[9] Studies in the advertising industry reveal that the intentions of companies to keep the relationship

affective commitment

with their ad-agency mainly depend on the existing degree of affective commitment which, in turn, is largely determined by the professional business service quality, trust, and – negatively – by "stuck bonds". The professional business service quality is

outcome quality

mainly determined by three factors, namely the outcome quality (e.g. the advertising campaign, and the final outcome, e.g. the increase in sales due to the campaign), the

soft process quality
competence

soft process quality (clients' evaluation of the interactions with and the treatment of the customer during the service production process), and the competence (clients' evaluation of the competence and expertise displayed during the service production).[10] This demonstrates that the personal touch is important in keeping clients for a long time.

retention strategies

Retention strategies can be considered as a special case of strategies aimed at maintaining relationships with customers. More and more, it becomes clear that in mature markets keeping customers is much cheaper than attracting customers from competitors. When all companies are stealing customers from each other in a saturated market, it means that they all invest in stealing from one another and one may doubt whether this is a rational strategy from a macro perspective. For, the cost of winning customers (for instance, via advertising and other promotional campaigns) will result in higher consumer prices. Therefore, the goal of retention strategies is to keep customers and sell more services to existing customers (cross selling). Most of the time, this also implies investing in the knowledge of the customer. It is a way of

bonds

creating bonds with customers. The soft side of the process in delivering service quality contributes largely to increasing retention value, next to financial benefits. In terms of our service strategy typology, it means that the three types of bonds mentioned in Chapter Four must be mixed with the four generic strategies.[11] The

financial bonds

financial bonds are best suited to firms offering standard core services. "Cost leadership" is an important device for them. Probably, their customers are very price sensitive. Discounts and special offers will make them stay. These customers can be approached via these financial bonds. The greatest danger of this approach is that these customers have no real commitment to the service firm and may switch easily when another service firm has a cheaper offer. Many service firms start this type of bonding when they first apply the concept of relationship marketing and retention marketing. However, it is important to know whether their customers consider price that important. Fast food restaurants competing on price will induce switching behavior and will not win so much in the end (especially not in saturated local markets). At the other extreme are the customized augmented services. Here, the

structural bonds in addition to the financial and social bonds

service firm knows its clients very well and is dedicated to offering very personalized services. Then, structural bonds are created in addition to the financial and social bonds. For, the service is very valuable to the clients and not readily available in this way from other sources.

financial bonds and social bonds

The two other strategy types are in between these two extremes. Financial bonds and social bonds will be succesful in retention strategies for firms offering customized core services or standard augmented services. In both cases, services are more personalized than in the case of standard core services. Both parties start processes to get to know each other quite well. Contacts will be closer and customers will be transformed into clients. Developing the specific bonds is part of the changing positions in the wheel of services.[12] Figure 8-3 puts it all together.

Service practice 8-3 Retention in many ways

Many mail order houses send their specialized catalogues to well defined target groups. This is often based on prior buying behavior. The general (very thick) catalogues are being used to a lesser extent, while specialized catalogues, for instance on books, magazines, clothing or camping articles, are now sent to customers who have bought from these areas in the past. Publishers ask academics what their areas of interest are and send them their brochures on specific subjects. It is not only a matter of communicating directly with people interested in these areas, it is also a matter of avoiding waste and irritation about unwanted advertising.

Direct marketing is a booming business in the financial services industry. Many banks and insurance companies communicate to their clients in this way since technology has subsituted personal contact to machines, like the ATM's. Banks do not meet their customers at the counter anymore and need other ways to communicate with them, keep in touch with them and increase loyalty.

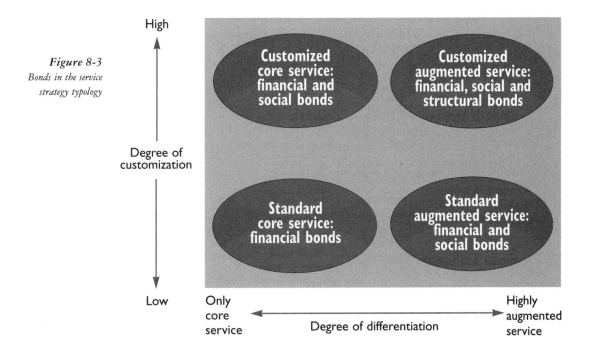

Figure 8-3
Bonds in the service
strategy typology

Until now, we have been discussing the relationship between the service provider and the customer. We did not mention competitors so much. That part of the market orientation concept will be highlighted now.

Many authors have focussed on competition at a functional service level. This means that the strategy has a more tactical and operational content. Ries and Trout state in their book "Marketing Warfare" that marketing needs a new philosophy.[13] Not the *competitor* customer, but the competitor should be the one to focus on: search for weak spots in the competitors' performance and focus marketing attacks on these weak spots. In many cases, the goal is not on keeping relationships but on inducing switching *searching for* behavior among competitors' customers.[14] Searching for weaknesses may be *weaknesses* succesful, as the following examples show. At the beginning of the eighties, Digital Equipment Corporation (DEC) was able to take advantage of IBM's weakness to produce and market small computers. Burger King was also succesful at that time in attacking McDonald's with its broiling, not frying concept.

Ries and Trout have defined four tactical ways to lead a marketing war: defensive tactics; offensive tactics; flanking tactics; and guerilla tactics. Each of these four tactics will be discussed briefly here.[15]

Defensive tactics

attack itself

This tactic is most appropriate for the market leader. The market leader must have the courage to attack itself. This attack sharpens the different business units and departments. It is known that if the market leader is not constantly innovative, the competitor will be.

The market leader always has to react to important movements of the (smaller) competitors. They may be niche players, to a larger extent than the market leader, thus satisfying specific customer needs to a greater extent than the market leader. Flexibility in adjusting strategies and tactics is needed here, as well as a proper understanding of customer needs and competitors' actions (present and planned ones).

Offensive tactics

offensive strategy

When one finds one's own organization number two or three in a specific service industry, one should use an offensive strategy to attack the market leader. Firstly, one must search for blind or weak spots in the strategy of the market leader. Then, one must concentrate the attack on this weak spot. Keep in mind that one should start the attack on a small front at first. Afterwards, the service company can challenge the market leader; in this way, it can broaden the battlefield.

Flanking tactics

flanking

Probably, flanking is the most innovative way to lead a marketing battle. The three principles of this tactic are:

1. a good flank attack should be made in an indisputable area. DEC applied a flanking technique in attacking IBM in the early eighties with small computer customers being positioned in the new category of "mini computers" against IBM's mainframe computers;
2. a tactical surprise must be a necessary part of the plan. For this reason, test marketing could be dangerous because it warns the competitors; and
3. continuing the action is as important as starting the attack itself. It takes time to develop a succesful new service, especially new services which are hard to imitate, being based on personal competencies in the firm. Once it shows that it pays off to be a winner, then keep it that way, continue and hold on.

Guerilla tactics

guerilla warfare

History has shown in many cases the success of guerilla warfare. The most important assumptions of such a tactic are:

- search for a segment in the market small enough to defend. This can be a geographic segment or a particular sales volume not vulnerable to attack by a big service firm. Local retailers often use this approach in attacking the larger national chains;

- no matter how succesful one becomes, never act as a market leader. Leaders are always the ones to challenge and attack. Often – when they are large – they are quite inflexible in responding to attacks by small competitors;
- stick close to the market and keep the overhead low; and
- be prepared to withdraw immediately if the situation requires such a change.

Before we go on, we would like to add something to this way of reasoning proposed by Al Ries and Jack Trout. Every service organization in the competitive market should be analyzed in full detail. Such an analysis will reveal a list of strengths and weaknesses and a plan could be actioned to exploit competitors' weaknesses, defend (and change) ones own weaknesses, cope with competitors' strengths and exploit one's own strengths. In practice, such an analysis would focus on the major group of *"peer group"* competitors or the "strategic group" the company belongs to.[16] This "peer group" of *major competitors* major competitors could be analyzed in several areas like marketing strategy, positioning, market share, financial ratios, marketing mix, operations, technology, available resources, relationship strengths with key customers, knowledge, skills, personnel and their position on the continua in the services matrices (see Chapter Two).

The need to know who the peer competitors of a service organization actually are is obvious. Moreover, benchmarking on all issues relevant to the peer competitors is even more important than those relevant to all competitors. When a service firm focusses to much on what they consider as their (peer) competitors, they may forget to view what customers and clients perceive as alternatives to this service firm. *defining peer* Defining peer competitors should also be based on customer perceptions of what *competitors* they actually perceive as competitors. In benchmarking, then, the comparison is aimed at finding out who scores best on particular issues of the service itself or the service delivery process. It may focus on front office as well as back office processes. For instance, Chase Manhattan Bank, as a conglomerate, can be compared to its peer American competitors like Nations Bank, Bank of New York, or EAB. In an international perspective, their peer competitors are banks like CitiBank, Hongkong Bank, Barclays, ABN AMRO, ING Barings, BNP and Deutsche Bank. In the worldwide competition to manage other people's money, the American, British, German, Spanish, Dutch and Swiss banks are becoming increasingly aggressive. Every bank worth its name, it seems, has bought, intends to buy or has linked up with a foreign asset management specialist. Everyone fights for a slice of the cake[17] that is called "savings and investments". Also, in other specialized areas such as brokerage, project finance, structured finance, mergers and acquisitions Chase Manhattan faces (partly) other competitors. For that reason, it is essential to define in what area the service firm operates in order to perform a competitor analysis that makes sense. Increasingly, the *potential rivals* analysis will have to focus on potential rivals. In the case of general banking, these may be found in software, supermarkets or direct writers (i.e. via the Internet). At this time, German banks, emulating successful examples in the USA, are opening up outlets in supermarkets, like Commerzbank in an Allkauf department store in Dortmund-Aplerbeck, and the Deutsche Bank in an Allkauf department store in Duisburg.[18] Similar actions take place in UK supermarkets.

too much emphasis on the competitor

We feel it might be questioned whether this Ries and Trout approach puts too much emphasis on the competitor. With this approach, a service firm may run the risk that the customer will be forgotten, because of the sole focus on the competitor, let alone the relationship with the customer. We think this attacking approach does not always fit well with the culture of a market oriented service firm. Relationship marketing and retention strategies emphasize the cooperation, trust, benevolence and commitment between service organizations and customers as well as networking. Such an approach is very different from the war-seeking and conflict approach. However, it appears to be very useful to know something about this "war approach" when a service organization is confronted with "war-minded" competitors or when the organization has become very unresponsive to developments in the market place. Then, it may be a suitable way to "wake them up".

8.3 THE EXTERNAL AND INTERNAL MARKETING PLANNING PROCESS

Now that we have described various kinds of marketing strategies, it is time to look at how one can arrive at such a strategy: what process can be applied to that end? In strategic planning at corporate level, it is important to define what one wants to accomplish and how this is going to happen. This process is part of the planning of a functional strategy, in this case the marketing strategy. The most important elements that contribute to this process are :

planning of functional strategy

- fine-tuning with other plans;
- customer expectations;
- competitor reactions;
- service characteristics; and
- the interaction between the internal organization, personnel and customers.

These five points partly coincide with the specific problems and features of strategic planning at corporate level within a market oriented service organization. However, some specific notes with regard to marketing in the service sector are relevant here. As a basis for our discussion, Figure 8-4 will be used, which is the same figure as Figure 7-2. Now, we will complete the two final boxes of the cascade.

FINE-TUNING WITH OTHER PLANS

optimally tuned with other plans

The marketing planning process in service organizations should be optimally tuned with other plans within the organization, as we saw in Chapter Seven. These other plans are the strategic plan at corporate level and the strategic business units, or strategic service groups' plans in different functional areas like personnel, automation, operations and finance. The internal and external marketing activities should also be coordinated. It is important not to forget the internal marketing of new plans developed for the "real", external market. The "internal side of the company" must be ready to execute the strategy externally (= on the market).[19]

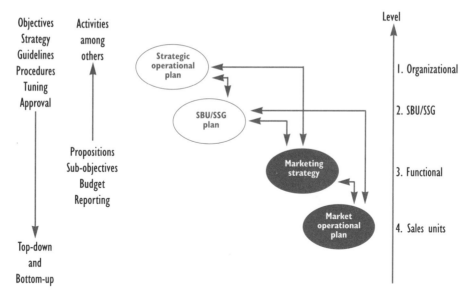

Figure 8-4
Strategic planning
and marketing planning
at different levels:
strategic marketing
planning in business
units

CUSTOMER EXPECTATIONS

customer expectations

Customer needs and wants are crucial. This applies to internal and external, present and potential customers. Customer expectations have to be fulfilled by delivering superior service quality. If not, this will lead to dissatisfaction and present customers will be lost and may not return. Then, every past investment in the customer will be gone and future revenues lost. These losses may be enormous if the "life time value of a customer" has been assessed.

ratchet-effect

It is very important that customers and employees know what they can expect from the organization and vice versa. This points to the market-oriented aspect of the organization to define both the service encounter and the role each party has to play. The impact of the ratchet-effect should be considered: the service is what is expected but to provide satisfaction, the service must meet or exceed expectations. Especially in the latter case, the service provider is constantly ratcheting up the service in the pursuit of satisfaction.

COMPETITOR REACTIONS

react to actions

The alternative side of the market orientation concept developed in this book maintains that a service company should strive at doing business more efficiently (= cheaper), quicker and generally better than competitors. It is self-evident to take into account what competitors are doing now and how they might react to actions initiated by one's own company. Especially, the market structure (monopoly, duopoly, monopolistic competition, etc.) will determine how tough competition will be. Concentration indexes will reveal how many competitors are really important. It is always important, though difficult, to find out exactly who the competitors are.

*Service
practice
8-4
Who is the
competitor?*

A technical engineering agency may find out who their competitors are by asking their clients how many firms were invited to tender for a specific assignment. One of the companies in this business, INTRON, does not compete for a specific assignment when more than three or four agencies are invited to tender. It is their firm belief that the client has made no proper analysis of the market if they ask so many bureaux to compete. Then, the short list is not carefully put together. From their experience, they know that most of the time they have to face three or four serious competitors whom they know very well. This is one of their ways of avoiding inefficient use of time devoted to tendering to assignments that probably will not succeed. It is part of their way of educating the customer.

SERVICE CHARACTERISTICS

*nature and types of
service*

The nature and types of service affect the operationalization and implementation of the chosen strategy, relationships with the customers and specific content of the marketing mix. In fact, the positions chosen on the continua developed in Chapter Two determine the specific content of the generic strategies developed in the previous chapter and, by definition, also the marketing strategies. For instance, we can think of:

control

- attention to perceived risk, as observed by the target group and individual customers. A service company should balance the efficiency of the delivery process with the customers' desired control in the service encounter. If customers have more control over the situation, their uncertainty will decline. On the other hand, it has also been shown that personnel's customer contact stress diminishes when they have greater control over the service encounter. Hence, it becomes very relevant to find an optimal service triangle;[20]

integral part

- consumers are an integral part of the servuction process. In services, one can not separate the production from the consumption. Different marketing instruments can be used only at the very moment of truth of actually producing the service. This requires thinking constantly about whether adjustments of the contact persons' behavior, the content of the relationship, the stage now in the relationship life cycle, or the change in circumstances, bring about alterations in order to deliver the quality desired;

*performances one
cannot grasp*

- a service company should see services as performances one cannot grasp. This intangible character of services should be made as tangible as possible, in the service delivery process as well as in the promotional activities; and

hard to standardize

- some services are hard to standardize. Personnel have to be flexible and take responsibility in order to satisfy the customer as much as possible and not be hindered by constraints due to strict and inflexible procedures. The creation of a market-oriented culture will contribute to high quality service offerings. Empowering contact personnel is another way to that end (see Chapter Ten).

Service practice 8-5 Standardiz- ation and flexibility

The international, Swedish-based Mercuri Urval recruitment and selection company has a standard format of seven steps to be taken in every assignment aimed at hiring the proper personnel for their clients. These seven steps are:

1. correct job definition;
2. describing the job demand profile;
3. recruitment;
4. selection;
5. decision reporting;
6. development reporting; and
7. follow-up.

The flexibility at Mercuri Urval (MU) is that one or more of these steps can be shortened if necessary in a particular recruitment assignment. Still, they all have to be performed. The steps are guidelines for structuring the procedure and showing the client what the Mercuri Urval way of working is. The specific assignment and the specific (market) circumstances the client faces will determine what should be done within each step.

It is remarkable to see that the actual recruiting and selecting activities are only two out of these seven steps. First, it is important to discover what the job is and what kind of profile of the candidate is needed. Reporting MU's decision about which candidate will be the best (step 5) and how this person should and could develop within the new job and company (step 6) are also very relevant. Finally, asking after a few months how the new person performs is a main part of the follow-up and feed back stage.

Here, it is also relevant to stress that a market oriented culture will contribute to guaranteeing that all customers will receive a similar level of service. One should avoid having different employees provide the same service in different ways. The service attitude of all contact personnel should be to avoid customers' feelings "being at the mercy of a particular clerk". Such a culture would then impact positively on the quality dimensions, e.g. on reliability and responsiveness.

THE INTERACTION BETWEEN THE INTERNAL ORGANIZATION, PERSONNEL AND CUSTOMERS

service triangle

The marketing planning process is based on the (unique) relationship between a supplier and a customer in the service triangle.[21] This relationship is the foundation for final profit. The strength of this relationship will depend on many different actions and episodes in the service delivery process and the interaction within the firm. This servuction process, as well as the scope and content of the interactions, being of utmost importance in starting, maintaining and ending relations, will be highly relevant to the organization to survive, deliver superior quality and create satisfied

the profit chain

customers. Here, the core competencies in terms of, for instance, controlling service processes or the typical employee skills and attitudes come to the fore. These should be investigated to see whether they are suited when delivering services to internal as well as external customers. Another way of looking at this interaction deals with the content of the profit chain.[22] The profit chain shows the interaction between the satisfaction and loyalty of both groups of people involved in the service encounter (customers and employees) to the company and its service, resulting in greater profits due to high(er) productivity (greater commitment and less role stress or ambiguity) and better service quality[23] (Figure 8-5).

8.4 THE EXTERNAL AND INTERNAL MARKETING PLANNING PROCESS: ITS GENERAL STRUCTURE

customers and competitors

people

Marketing planning in market oriented organizations requires focussing on customers and competitors by definition. However, yet another dimension has to be added to this statement. Since delivering services is generally people based, this "asset" of a company should be fully equipped to provide the service planned to external customers. Therefore, it is necessary to have performed all the "missionary and motivational work" within the company (the internal market of employees, departments and the like) about the new plans or new ways of working before it is communicated to the market. Commitment within all organizational layers has to be present. From Gap 4 in the SERVQUAL-model, the reader will remember how seriously service quality can be harmed when employees do not know what customers do

external and internal marketing planning processes

know or when promises cannot be met. Therefore, external and internal marketing planning processes are needed and should be well coordinated. The different components of both models should be integrated into the overall marketing planning process. Interactive planning, in which bottom up procedures are used effectively in combination with top down communicated frameworks, can be applied here. Other arguments for this integration are based on the idea that not only the quality of internal processes determines the final quality but also the power and control structure within the company. Or, as Jean-Paul Flipo puts it: "... internal marketing expresses the power marketers use to control internal participants in their external strategy. Conversely, the impact of these internal participants on the output of external marketing strategy expresses their power over the marketing function."[24]

The general structure of this overall marketing planning process is shown in Figure 8-6.[25]

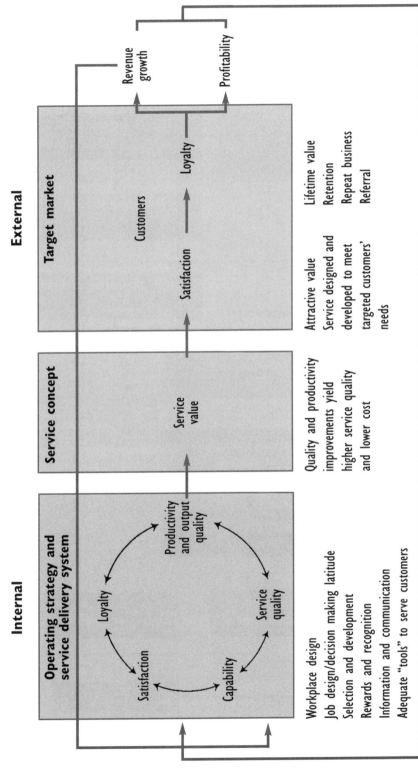

Figure 8-5
The service profit chain

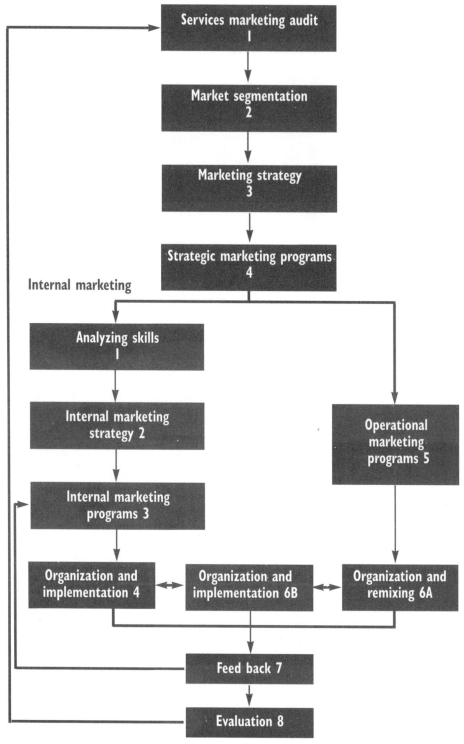

External marketing

Figure 8-6

The overall marketing planning process: linking the internal and external marketing planning process in service organizations

The main advantages of the picture sketched in Figure 8-6 are threefold. An internal marketing strategy is introduced explicitly in the whole marketing planning process; both the internal and the external marketing strategy have to be fine-tuned and in the implementation stage the two are combined (meaning both are completed).

process of planning the external marketing strategy

The process of planning the external marketing strategy consists of the next eight stages:

1. performing a service marketing audit;
2. defining the market segments to be served;
3. developing the marketing strategy;
4. defining the strategic marketing programs;
5. defining the tactical/operational marketing programs;
6. the organization and implementation of the plans;
7. providing feed back about the results obtained; and
8. evaluation of the results obtained and goals accomplished.

After the first four stages of the external marketing planning process, the internal marketing strategy becomes relevant to the whole process. Then, the next four stages of the internal marketing planning process should be followed:

the internal marketing planning process

1. analyzing the skills, talents and competencies needed to deliver superior service quality;
2. develop the internal marketing strategy;
3. defining the internal marketing programs; and
4. the organization and implementation of the plans.

The stages of organization and implementation in both the external and internal marketing planning should not be regarded as two separate things. They are very much interconnected. In fact, both should be coordinated simultaneously. Then, the feed back and evaluation stages can be taken again. This stage also includes the control to accomplish the goals set.

In the next sections, we will elaborate on each of these stages. The first one, about the service marketing audit, is the most comprehensive: it lays down the foundation for the whole planning process. (That is why we discuss it at length in a separate section). What goes wrong here or is done inadequately will affect the final outcome to a very large extent.[26]

8.5 THE SERVICE MARKETING AUDIT

The mission, corporate goals and corporate strategy have to be considered as given (as data) when a marketing planning process starts. Defining them is part of determining the strategic context of the organization (see Chapter Seven). A clear

clear strategic vision

strategic vision should be the basis for a strategy; that is one of the major lessons in the service sector.[27] The marketing planning process starts with a systematic analysis of the situation relevant in the marketing environment. Such an analysis is part of the service marketing audit. The audit is aimed at finding the relevant facts and data, the analysis of both internal and external aspects of the organization (amongst others, mission, goals, strategy, skills and knowledge), the analysis of services of the organization itself and the competitive external environment where the organization markets its services and faces the service offering of its competitors. That is the environment where the moments of truth have to come true: better, faster, cheaper or with a greater value for money ratio than offered by competitors; the data of the audit are being investigated for past, present and the future. For the service sector, we developed a service marketing audit consisting of five different analyses (see Figure 8-7). The components of the service marketing audit are analyzing:

1. the macro environment;
2. the specific service industry;
3. the market;
4. the competition and their strategies; and
5. one's own firm.

These five issues should not be regarded as separate items but should be taken together. They are not independent from one another.

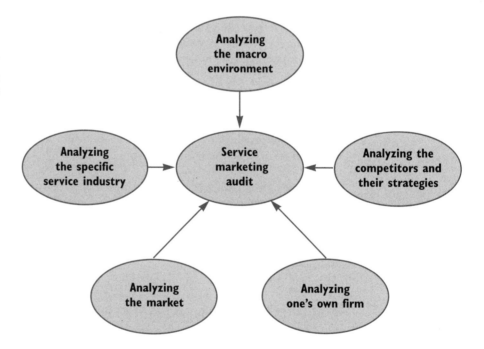

Figure 8-7
The service marketing audit

competitive analysis

Four out of these five components of the service marketing audit have been discussed in depth in previous chapters. So, in terms of systems, the organization should ensure that these components are stored in the central database of the service quality information system (or marketing information system) and are accessible to other departments. However, the competitive analysis has not been dealt with explicitly, therefore we will pay ample attention to that topic and competitive strategies.

ANALYZING THE MACRO-ENVIRONMENT

analysis of the macro environment

The analysis of the macro environment contains the present demographic, regulating, economic, technological and social (DRETS) factors and the expected changes in each of them. This analysis has been discussed in Chapter Three. One could use the framework developed in Chapter Three to analyze the impact of (changes in) the macro-factors for the service marketing audit. Trend extrapolation, expert opinions, scenario building, watching television, reading magazines and "just looking around" are means to decipher what is going on in the various environments that have to be analyzed in the marketing audit.

For instance, the ageing of the population can be used in many ways to develop particular services. Many publishers produce magazines for the 55+ generation. Railways have special tickets, prices and arrangements for the 60+ age group. In Arizona, new towns are built for the 55+ generation where the atmosphere is relaxed, nobody is in a hurry and where the service and merchandising in supermarkets is suited completely to the needs of this target market. This includes the medical infrastructure. Environmental concerns may offer opportunities for new products and services. In Switzerland, Coop Schweiz (the largest food retailer with a 13% market share) has developed the Coop NATURAplan. Animals (and their meat) are grown in an environmentally friendly way and consumers are educated to buy these products. These products are now generally accepted and no longer sold in a (small) market niche.[28]

ANALYZING THE SPECIFIC SERVICE INDUSTRY

trends and developments in the specific service industry

This analysis deals with the trends and developments in the specific service industry under consideration. These are, among other things, internationalization, buy outs, out sourcing, economies of scale, self-service, cooperation, franchising, vanishing differences between lease, rent and common property. For instance, in finance, banks merge within one country to become larger and subsequently internationalize. The same holds for many accounting firms and ad agencies. On the other hand, new niche-players see new opportunities in a particular industry because some segments cannot be served satisfactorily by large chains. In the hotel industry, the good quality, small family hotels and pensions are still succesful (and less expensive than many of the large hotel chains) as are small local ad agencies, being very familiar with local circumstances. In many industries, limited service providers are challenging general service providers.

ANALYZING THE MARKET

market segments and services benefits

The market segments and services defined by the service organization are the starting point of this analysis. It is of great importance to define market segments properly and understand the benefits this target segment is looking for and the extent to which these benefits are satisfied. The description of the organization's mission is crucial here. Positioning techniques are key tools to accomplish it.

ANALYZING THE COMPETITORS AND THEIR STRATEGIES

Michael Porter has dealt extensively with concepts of generic competition at the strategic corporate level. We have used those insights as well as the work done by James Heskett in Chapter Seven to develop our typology of four generic service strategies: standard core service; customized core service; standard augmented service; and customized augmented service.

what kind of services competitors are offering and how

peer competitors

This step in the whole process of the services marketing audit is aimed at analyzing what kind of services competitors are offering and how. It is important to see who those firms are that should be taken into account and who customers perceive or actually consider as alternatives for the firm under consideration. So, the firms customers do perceive as competing are not the ones that the firm itself considers as their competitors, but are, in fact, the peer competitors. For those firms, it should be analyzed what kind of strategy they apply (many of them are discussed in Chapter Seven and section 8.2), how it is implemented, how it is valued by their customers and how the firm under consideration scores on relevant benchmarks, like customer satisfaction, service quality, customer loyalty, sales, market share, distribution coverage, costs, profits, market orientation (the cultural side as well as the marketing topics deemed relevant), employee satisfaction and the like.

ANALYZING ONE'S OWN FIRM

aspirations and resources can be balanced

The marketing audit must reveal whether the firm's marketing aspirations and the available resources can be balanced. The analysis of the internal factors of the service process, the firms' capabilities, skills, routines, etc. that will be discussed in Chapter Ten, are crucial to that end. The corporate analysis then deals with the marketing instruments, the resources and capabilities of the service organization. It reveals what the content of the internal marketing strategy should be in order to actually execute all these skills.

THE FIVE ELEMENTS OF THE SERVICE MARKETING AUDIT TAKEN TOGETHER

The links between the analysis of the service firm itself and the four other elements of the service marketing audit can be established in many ways, for instance by such analytical techniques as: the analysis of strengths, weaknesses, opportunities and threats (SWOT); the service life cycle (SLC as counterpart to the well known product life cycle PLC); the service portfolio theory (as counterpart of the well known product portfolio and growth share matrix) developed by the Boston Consulting group; and multiple factor portfolio matrices as they are developed by the McKinsey company, General Electric and Shell (the directional policy matrix).

SWOT analysis

A SWOT analysis combines the main issues in the firm's external environment that can be regarded as opportunities and threats with its own strenghts and weaknesses. These issues are put together in a grid. When this is done properly, it is our firm belief and experience that the strategic (and operational) solutions easily follow from this overview.[29]

Service practice 8-6 A SWOT example

Recently, a market research agency conducted a SWOT analysis.[30] Amongst others, they found as their main strengths their large, very reliable database with much data about the economy of their home country, and, their knowledge and skills in research methodology. Their main weakness was their image: not market oriented, because of lack of personal relations with clients, responsiveness and reliability in delivery dates. The largest threat came from competitors trying to copy this database (which would cost a lot of investment-money and time) and their ability to deliver on time. The biggest opportunities involved the growing need of national and local public administration to underpin their policies with reliable data on economics and societal issues.

The research institute decided to broaden their database to include data on economic and social issues. Moreover, internal procedures were "sharpened" in such a way that on time delivery was guaranteed. The employees were trained intensively to act in this way and understand the customer. This strategy resulted from the SWOT-analysis that revealed this picture.

Strengths	Weaknesses
• large database	• image
• reliable database	not market oriented
• knowledge and skills of research methodology	• personal relations
	• responsiveness
	• delivery dates

Opportunities	Threats
• growing need for data to define public policy	• database copied
• data on economic and social issues	• competitors deliver on time

attractiveness and
success probability

The marketing opportunities can be defined in terms of their attractiveness and their success probability. Both can be high or low. The various combinations in this "opportunity matrix" that can be made now reveal what opportunities are amongst the most attractive and profitable ones. These should be nurtured especially.[31]

evaluate each of the
opportunities and
threats

Another way of looking at the environmental forces is to evaluate each of the opportunities and threats in terms of a major opportunity, minor opportunity, major threat or minor threat. When this is combined with the probability that they will actually occur, the seriousness of these opportunities and threats can be assessed.

portfolio planning

With respect to portfolio planning, service firms can offer more than one service to more than one target group of customers to spread risks or (seasonal) cycles in their activities. In the matrix of the Boston Consulting Group, relative market share and market growth rate are the two variables to be considered.[32] Four categories of services can then be detected: stars, problem children (sometimes called question marks), cash cows and dogs, as Figure 8-8 shows, each having their unique strategy.[33]

General Electric has developed a grid matching the internal strengths of the company with the opportunities in the environment (= attractiveness). This consists of a 3x3 matrix since each factor is divided into three components:

industry attractiveness
business strength

- industry attractiveness: low, medium, high; and
- business strength: weak, average, strong.

Again, companies, business units or services can be positioned in each of the nine cells of this matrix. Special development strategies apply for each of them.[34]

Index of Service
Marketing Excellence

Berry, Conant and Parasuraman (1991) have developed a framework for conducting a services marketing audit in which many of the items just discussed come to the fore. They propose to administer an "Index of Service Marketing Excellence" which is "a systematic, periodic, objective, and comprehensive examination of an organization's or organizational unit's preparedness for services marketing and its current effectiveness along the dimensions of marketing orientation, marketing organization, new customer marketing, existing customer marketing, internal marketing, and service quality." [35] It will be self-evident that, in our view, issues about relationship marketing (for instance, the composition of the Relation Perception and Loyalty Matrix) should be incorporated into this index as well.

assumptions

Before a service firm chooses one of the strategic alternatives, some assumptions have to be made. It is crucial that a service organization creates its plans under these assumptions, expectations of demand, changes in Gross National Product, inflation rate, changes in regulation, differences in national cultures and the like. The content of most of these assumptions will be depicted in the marketing audit. These assumptions have to be made for the whole market as well as for specific target groups. Moreover, a service firm should realize that planned and actual figures are compared to one another in the first stage of the marketing planning process. This takes place via the evaluation at the end of the planning cycle. Control is important

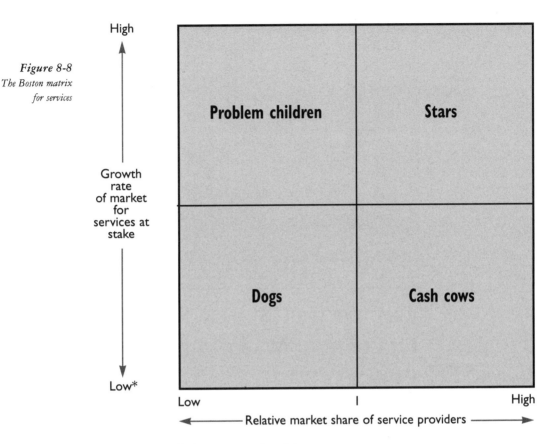

Figure 8-8
The Boston matrix
for services

low* may even mean "negative"

to that end. The results of the marketing audit, assumptions and comments on or explanations for the deviations between planned and actual figures are reported in the marketing report.[36]

Now that we have discussed the first stage of the marketing planning process thoroughly, we can turn to the other seven stages. This first stage of the marketing audit has been discussed that thoroughly because:

- a great many relevant topics should be analyzed at this stage. Information for the next stages should be collected here and the value of this information determines the quality of the rest of the planning process. Here, it is important to realize that "garbage in" means "garbage out"; a wrong analysis results in defaults in strategy; and
- it is important to set down these assumptions and starting points. This makes clear to everybody what assumptions are made. That is important to know, for instance, in controlling the marketing performance of the service firm.

Otherwise, it is difficult to structure and implement the strategy development process, which is very simple in its basic structure, as Figure 8-9 shows.[37]

Figure 8-9
The basics of marketing
planning

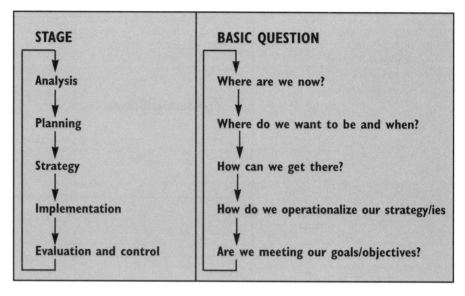

Figure 8-9
The basics of marketing
planning

STAGE	BASIC QUESTION
Analysis	Where are we now?
Planning	Where do we want to be and when?
Strategy	How can we get there?
Implementation	How do we operationalize our strategy/ies
Evaluation and control	Are we meeting our goals/objectives?

8.6 THE OTHER SEVEN STAGES IN THE EXTERNAL MARKETING PLANNING PROCESS

After having carried out the marketing audit, seven stages still have to be gone through in order to carry out the whole external marketing planning process, as shown in Figure 8-6. These seven stages are:

- market segmentation;
- defining the marketing strategy;
- developing the strategic marketing programs;
- developing the operational marketing programs;
- organization and implementation;
- feedback; and
- evaluation.

MARKET SEGMENTATION

target group of the organization

The target group of the organization is determined in this second stage of the external marketing planning process. The application of market segmentation brings the service organization closer to its target group. Hence, it is important to know what are the best criteria for segmentation. In Chapter Four, we discussed many of these variables, in particular the advantages of benefit segmentation and domain specific segmentation, as relevant ways of segmenting service markets. Also, the kind of relationships (and intensity) a service firm wants to have with their customers or clients can be a criterion for segmentation, next to the relationship the customer

benefit segmentation domain specific segmentation relationships

classification criteria

wants to be engaged in. In general, we maintain that the classification criteria mentioned in Chapter Two can be applied as ways to segment service markets. A few specific criteria will be dealt with now: they are closely linked to the specific features of services.

degree of participation

Since customers have to participate in the service encounter, the degree of participation can be a criterion to segment the market.[38] An obvious example is the difference between self service restaurants and restaurants where the guests are being served. As a consequence, customers must be willing, capable and motivated to participate. So, their ability to perform generic consumer tasks or to participate in specific servuction processes can be used as another criterion to segment the market. This customer competency can be defined as: "the goodness of fit between customer inputs (skills, knowledge and motivation) and customers' corresponding task roles in the service delivery system of the firm".[39]

organized around these market segments

A prerequisite to succesful implementation of market segmentation is that the service organization itself is organized around these market segments. The minimum requirement is that the information systems in the service firm (be it market intelligence or book keeping) are structured around these segments.

Service practice 8-7 Customer segmentation and corporate (re)structuring

The Belgian Kredietbank recently restructured its internal organization according to the defined market segments. Instead of being one large bank with an undifferentiated strategy, they have split up the bank into eight new banks each having its own target group of customers, for instance big companies or wealthy private customers. Each of these eight banks has its own network of branches and employees speaking the language of that particular group of customers. It appears that employees can now demonstrate their skills and capabilities more efficiently than before.[40]

DEFINING THE MARKETING STRATEGY

marketing goals strategy expected results identifying alternative mixes

This third stage contains the development of the marketing goals and strategy, estimating the expected results and identifying alternative mixes. This is all within the framework of the generic, corporate strategies developed and the (actual and intended) relationships with customers (see section 8.2).

STRATEGIC MARKETING PROGRAMS

marketing instruments are defined on the strategic level

In this fourth stage, the marketing instruments are defined on the strategic level. Long term activities (when, how, where, who) are planned in this stage and budgets are set. This program anticipates the actions of competitors. Scenarios may be developed to that end as well as estimates of the sensitivity of the company results to the expected actions of competitors.

OPERATIONAL MARKETING PROGRAMS

tactical or operational marketing programs

The elements of the strategic marketing programs are formulated more specifically in the tactical or operational marketing programs. Here, the planning horizon (mostly six to eighteen months) is shorter as compared to the planning horizon of strategic marketing programs (mostly a couple of years).

annual marketing plans

Many companies have operational marketing plans aimed at a one year period. These are typically called the annual marketing plans or commercial plans.

ORGANIZATION AND IMPLEMENTATION

external and internal marketing planning processes come together implementation

This sixth stage is a very important one. All the plans developed have to come true in the sense that they now have to be implemented into the organization. They must be carried out. The organization must be ready and capable to do the (new) things expected. This is also the stage where the external and internal marketing planning processes come together. We will return to the implementation topic in Chapter Fifteen. This stage contains two additional components:

marketing plan at the tactical level

fine tuning of the marketing plans with the other functional plans

- the organization and implementation of the marketing plan at the tactical level (stage 6a); and
- the implementation of the strategic framework (stage 6b). In this stage, fine tuning of the marketing plans with the other functional plans (purchase/procurement, R&D, automization/IT, production, finance, human resource management, etc.) takes place.

FEEDBACK

control system, customer feedback, "remixing"

The operational marketing program will be adjusted, if there is any reason to, on the basis of the company's control system and customer feedback. This process is called "remixing". It may mean that the internal marketing programs have to be adjusted as well.

It is self evident that other developments in or out of control of the company, will lead to adjustments in the strategic or operational marketing programs. So, the specifics of the control system are very relevant here. Control will be discussed in further detail in Chapter Fifteen.

EVALUATION

evaluation, internal and external perspective

In this final stage, all of the strategic marketing program, the operational marketing program and the internal marketing program, are evaluated. Such an evaluation can be done from an internal and external perspective. The internal perspective assesses whether the goals set are actually accomplished. The external perspective assesses whether the organization has been capable of really satisfying customer needs: are customers satisfied about the service quality delivered? It deals with the subjective evaluation by customers. It is investigated as to whether the organization has reached its service level more efficiently and more effectively than the competition (in particular the peer group of competitors). In that way, both major elements of the market orientation are being evaluated.

The outcome of the evaluation is written down in a report to top management. These results are the input for an adjustment procedure or change in the marketing strategy or marketing program and are of great importance to the next marketing plan.

8.7 THE INTERNAL MARKETING PLANNING PROCESS

internal marketing

Internal marketing can be defined briefly as getting the new way of working and new ideas accepted in the organization. It is a way of marketing these new issues in the organization. Therefore, it is important to check whether persons, procedures, routines, knowledge, structures, competencies, skills, capabilities and the like really fit into the new way of working or to the new requirements for the future (or need some adjustment). Moreover, internal marketing is a way of showing that the firm consists of individuals and departments that can be considered as each others' clients.[41] The principles of external marketing can also be applied within the organization.

internal marketing planning process

The organization can start developing the internal marketing planning process when the strategic goals for the external marketing strategy and plans are set. Defining the internal marketing plan consists of four stages:

- defining the required skills and knowledge;
- defining the internal marketing strategy;
- developing internal marketing programs; and
- organization and implementation.

DEFINING THE REQUIRED SKILLS AND KNOWLEDGE

resources

The internal marketing strategy can be defined properly from the point where it is clear what resources, what knowledge, which processes and which technical and social skills are needed for each member of the front and back office. Making such an overview should be done in close cooperation with those persons in charge of human resources management. New skills and resources are needed to accomplish the new goals and targets set, or to act according to the service attitude required (see

internal resistance

also Chapter Ten). The internal resistance that might occur when these new issues are introduced may block its implementation. Hence, the service organization fails to realize its plans and the promises communicated to its clients.

Such a resistance does not only apply with respect to customers in the external market. It may also apply to the way in which persons deal with their internal clients (their

segments within the service organization

colleagues from another department). Consequently, it is important to estimate how motivated, willing and capable the firm's employees are to act along the new lines. All these issues may differ between segments within the service organization. Hence, just as in the service marketing audit, it is wise to define here target segments as well, each having its own internal marketing strategy that must be easily communicated. Especially, when departments differ in their actual degree of market orientation, a tailor made training program may be needed for each of them to get to the desired level in the service firm. This can be used effectively to avoid role stress and role ambiguity amongst employees, which, in turn, will now not negatively affect service quality.

DEFINING THE INTERNAL MARKETING STRATEGY

In defining the internal marketing strategy, one should take into account the ways in which required skills will be "taught" to the employees (internal training, external training, or by other means of knowledge transfer) and the ways management could act in removing employees' resistance to the new "ideas" (e.g. by personal communication, motivation, increasing knowledge about why it is necessary to change, etc.). For each department, a focussed internal marketing strategy may be needed.

DEVELOPING INTERNAL MARKETING PROGRAMS

internal marketing programs

The internal marketing programs contain an overview of the planned activities in the areas of getting the (re)structuring of the organization and the new way of working accepted in the company by communication, education, training, increasing motivation, giving incentives, etc. Responsibilities and budgets are circumscribed and written down in these programs. They must be differentiated operationally to various segments of employees if deemed necessary.

As mentioned before, the internal marketing programs and the external marketing programs should coincide. A market-oriented service firm should give the highest priority to making its internal organization market-oriented before it can communicate its market orientation to the external market, let alone practise it in the external market.

Service practice 8-8 Segmenting the internal market for customized training programs

In one of our research projects within a health insurance company, we found four clusters of market orientation being present within that service company. Hence, all four clusters need a different approach in training and teaching to meet the standards the company has set with respect to its desired market orientation. The employees of departments belonging to the clusters that are already quite on track need only a few sessions to be able to act according to the goals set. The employees in departments belonging to the clusters that are defined as hardly market oriented or not market oriented have a long way to go. Nevertheless, the persons in the other clusters can be used as role models of how it should be.[42]

ORGANIZATION AND IMPLEMENTATION

coordination device

fine-tuning

One might say the internal marketing plan is meant to serve as a coordination device between the marketing department and the other departments of the service organization. The fine-tuning of the sales units and the functional (or line) organization is essential in implementing the marketing plans. The coordination of different sales units and large projects deserves special attention. That will be the subject of the next sections.

8.8 MARKETING PLANS IN SALES UNITS OF SERVICE FIRMS

sales unit, outlet, or branch

What has been said about internal and external marketing plans at corporate level in the service organization or at the business unit level applies equally to the level of the sales unit, outlet, or branch. This is the level in the service organization where it should all come true.

marketing plans for each of these local units

Sales units, like stores, offices of travel agencies, banks or hotels, being part of a large chain, have marketing plans for each of these local units. Such marketing plans exist at the strategic and operational level (annual plan). In essence, making these plans occurs at the same stages as in the marketing planning process described in this chapter. However, the scale of the activities is much smaller than at corporate or business unit level. The analysis and activities are much more focused on the direct, local environment of the sales units. Goals, about the kind of customer relationship desired and the content of the marketing mix, are more predetermined at higher levels in the organization. The freedom of action in such fields as service development, price policy and advertising policy is very limited at this sales unit level. Most of the time, adjustments to local circumstances are necessary and allowed by headquarters. Stores, local sales units of banks and travel agencies have to adjust their sponsoring and assortment to local circumstances, demographics and tastes. This is self evident if one thinks of the differences between Kensington Gardens and Tottenham Court Road in London, the "Village" and Fifth Avenue in New York. For, these plans end up as local plans for marketing in action. In many cases, local banks sponsor local events to increase consumers' brand awareness. It may go to an even

lower level

lower level in that account managers define their own year plan with commercial activities in their branch, for instance, by stating goals about the number of new accounts to visit and about the percentage of turning these prospects into new clients. Other goals with respect to activities of front office employees may be defined as well. The most important thing to realize at this sales unit level is that these plans are very concrete and operational by nature.

Such a local marketing-in-action plan is part of a local strategic marketing plan. It entails a time horizon of approximately three years. The first year plans are very concrete with respect to activities and marketing goals like sales volume, growth in number of clients, reconstructing the building (or parts of the servicescape), contribution to charities, local promotion, training of the front office employees, etc. The activities for the second and third year are more globally indicated in the plan. There is room for adjustments and improvements. Before the actual planning period starts, the sales unit's management receives guidelines and goals from the line and functional management. Line managers take the final decision, sometimes together with functional managers, and approve the plan.

8.9 SPECIAL PROJECTS

project management

Special projects important to the entire organization require a unique approach. For, many departments are always involved in implementing new plans initiated by marketing departments or R&D. Such plans as, for instance, the introduction of a new service or campaign on television, will be argued in the strategic and annual marketing plan. In approving these plans, managers have approved the preparations for these projects. Still, the actual start (or kick-off) of such a plan requires a careful planning of its expected costs, benefits, required skills, capabilities and other resources. This calls for a separate proposal of such a project. Sound project management and good internal marketing are needed here. This is to prevent the horizontal communication problems mentioned as one of the causes of Gap 4 in the SERVQUAL-model.[43]

SUMMARY

In Chapter Seven, we discussed strategic planning in service organizations at corporate level. That revealed the framework in which the planning of one of the functional activities of the firm, the marketing domain, must be accomplished. Here, we think of marketing planning at the business unit level and sales unit level of a large service firm or at the planning of the marketing activities in a small(er) service firm. Relationship marketing has been discussed as a new paradigm that can be used as the basis for many marketing strategies. Bonds, trust, commitment and loyalty are especially important topics in that framework.

The marketing planning process consists of an external and an internal part. Both have a strategic part for the long term and an operational part for the short term. The general structure of these plans is given in Figures 8-4, 8-6 and 8-9, showing the interdependence between the many concepts involved and revealing that the strategic and the operational parts of both the external and internal marketing plans should coincide. It is important to realize that decisions made about the characteristics of services discussed in Chapter Two now show their impact on the service firm's strategic room for manoeuvre. This also determines what skills the front and back office employees should possess (or should learn if not available right now).

The external marketing planning process starts (given the constraints and opportunities of the firm's strategic plan) with the service marketing audit. It consists of an analysis of the service firm's macro environment, its industry, its market, its competitors and the firm itself. In the competitive analysis, an investigation is undertaken into what strategies competitors use and what the firm could do. Many analytical tools can be applied, like the Boston matrix, the GE-matrix and the SWOT-analysis. Some authors state that marketing is war and have developed a strategic terminology accordingly in order to "steal" customers from other suppliers; others are in favour of cooperation and

relationships and have developed different strategies to maintain relationships and focus on retention (instead of investing heavily in attacking competitors and "stealing" customers away from a competitor). With respect to these warfare strategies, defensive, offensive, flanking and guerilla techniques can be used.

The other seven stages of the external marketing planning process refer to market segmentation, marketing strategy, strategic marketing programs, operational marketing programs, organization and implementation, feed back and evaluation. The stage of "organization and implementation" is where the external and internal marketing strategy come together. The three stages of the internal marketing planning process preceding the implementation stage refer to the required skills and knowledge, the internal marketing strategy and the internal marketing programs.

Since employees are so important in service encounters, much attention should be given to their skills, capabilities, knowledge and behavior needed to perform according to the goals set and the service attitude required. That also explains why ample attention should be given to control, implementation and organization. If the employees cannot do what they are expected to do, the service firm can never accomplish its goals or its promises communicated to the market. Therefore, the firm should be fully prepared internally and ready to do what it is expected to do externally. Otherwise, customer expectations cannot be met and dissatisfaction about poor quality will occur. This idea goes back to the notion that everyone within the organization should understand and work towards, the mission. The idea of the profit chain stresses that customer satisfaction and loyalty and employee satisfaction and loyalty are very interrelated and all determine the actual profit by contributing to achieving excellent service quality.

Many service organizations are so large that they

have a large number of sales units in their distribution network. All those sites will have their own strategic and operational marketing plans for the local market, being part of the sales unit's strategy. Due to operating on such a large scale, special projects should be defined when service firms introduce new services or new communication campaigns. Then, all employees are aware of what is going to happen. Moreover, they will know what is going on before the customer or client knows it. It is also important to have such special projects in order to close Gap 4 of the SERVQUAL-model in which quality problems are explained via, e.g. inadequate horizontal communication.

QUESTIONS

1 Which stages can be found in the external and internal strategic marketing planning process?

2 Why is it necessary that the external and internal marketing planning process should coincide?

3 What arguments are in favor of a relationship focus instead of a warfare focus in developing competitive marketing strategies in service organizations? Which are in favor of warfare strategies?

4 What are the five elements of the service marketing audit? Why should they be taken together carefully?

5 Why is the implementation and organization stage so important in marketing planning in service organizations?

6 Describe the SWOT analysis, the Boston matrix and the GE matrix briefly. In what way are they linked together? In what way are they different?

7 Argue why consumer competencies to participate in the service encounter could be used as a criterion for market segmentation.

8 What is the essence of the service profit chain?

9 What is the relation perception and loyalty matrix all about?

10 What factors are relevant in determining why firms want to retain their relationship with a business-to-business service provider (like an ad agency or accounting firm)?

ASSIGNMENTS

1 Do you know some examples where the execution of the marketing strategy in service firms is not in accordance with what they claim in, for instance, advertising campaigns? Elaborate on these examples and try to find an explanation.

2 Perform a service marketing audit for the university or school where you study now. What kind of strategies do competing schools apply?

3 Perform a service marketing audit for any other service firm you like (dentist, hospital, accountant, food store (or chain), bank, insurance company, travel agent, hotel, bar, airline, building society, etc.) Compare it with one which you do not like. What are the main differences?

4 Write a two page note on the relevance of relationship marketing to non-profit service organizations like charities, based on what has been said about relationship marketing in this chapter and the previous ones.

5 Complete a Boston matrix or GE matrix for the (service) company where you work. What should be changed in their strategy, if any?

6 If you had to develop an internal marketing strategy for the student union you are a member of, or, for the company you work for, what would it look like?

7 Have a critical look at the marketing planning process at your local bank or travel agency (or another service firm). Check whether Figures 8-4, 8-6 or 8-9 apply. Explain.

Case: RETENTION STRATEGIES AND ORGANIZATIONAL CHANGE AT THE KREDIETBANK[44]

In 1990, the Belgian Kredietbank changed its policy dramatically. Increasing competition forced them to make a clear strategic choice. They had to choose between two strategic options:

1. becoming a price leader by being the cheapest bank; or
2. creating a clear added value for its clients.

The strategic option

The Kredietbank chose to create a clear added value for its clients rather than becoming a price leader, for more than one reason. First of all, there is the wish and the strategic option of Kredietbank to remain a leading general bank in Flanders (the Dutch speaking part of Belgium) that can as such cover all types of customers. A second reason is the enormous customer base: more than 1.3 million retail customers bring about a huge volume in deposits and loans so a tough price war instigated or followed by Kredietbank could endanger Kredietbank's profitability. The third reason is the strong competition of some niche-banks concentrating on specific segments and specific services. These niche players can severely compete on prices due to their segmentation strategy.

Since price competition was clearly out of the question, Kredietbank decided not to be the "cheapest" bank but to offer the customers a clear added value. In this strategy, relationship banking is the core theme. It means that the bank wants to meet all of the customer's financial needs in order to increase customer satisfaction and profitability. It has been known for a long time that it is much "cheaper" to retain a customer and deepen the relationship with that customer, than it is to attract new customers by means of competitive pricing, especially in mature or saturated markets like the banking industry. Next to relationship banking, customer loyalty and improved service quality (e.g. via new branch design, extended opening hours, innovative products, discounts for best customers in some cases) are crucial parts of the new strategy.

The Kredietbank implemented this option strategically by

- shifting from low profit and normal financial services to more profitable advisory services;
- a far reaching market segmentation; and
- developing and building intensive relationships with the client.

From low profit and normal financial services to more profitable advisory services

In the Belgian retail banking business for private customers, low profit and routine bank services will be provided via machines, like ATMs. Next to these ATMs to withdraw money, machines will be introduced to pay bills, put one's money into one's bank account, or cash cheques. Also, many simple deals will be done by telephone, fax or PC in the near future (home banking).

In the business to business banking industry, the Kredietbank is experimenting in the Antwerp region with paid advice and consultancy services to small and medium sized businesses. These customers appear to be willing to pay for these services, especially when the bank helps in executing these advices. The Kredietbank is also experimenting with services like being a broker in between firms wanting to buy and sell firms. Research showed that many owners/directors of SME-sized firms have problems in finding successors or selling the firm when they want to retire.

Far reaching market segmentation

The Kredietbank used to follow an undifferentiated strategy towards its wide spectrum of customers. These ranged from simple households to large enterprises, from well-to-do clients to multinationals, etc. Delivering added value to their clients could not be accomplished by such an undifferentiated strategy.

In the new strategy, Krediet-bank concentrates on four segments in the domestic Belgian market: the corporates, the large companies, the private banking segment and the retail segment. Within this retail segment of private customers and local enterprises, Kredietbank defines eight sub-segments:

1. Youth (under the age of 25);
2. Families (parents between 25 and 55);
3. Seniors (older than 55);
4. Starting businesses;
5. Self employed;
6. Professional service providers (doctors, lawyers, etc.);
7. Small and medium sized enterprises; and
8. Non profit organizations (schools, hospitals, etc.).

Now, each segment can be approached by target group specific, tailored service offerings.

This segmentation strategy has far reaching consequences for the whole organization of the Kredietbank. Segments like the big multinationals or the well-to-do private clients are serviced via a unique network of branches with employees talking the language of the client. This results in higher customer and employee satisfaction. Moreover, it leads to a much more efficient use of employee skills and capabilities.

Another consequence of this approach is that each segment is serviced by a special business unit within the Kredietbank, having its own board of directors, staff, network of branches and employees. Cyriel van Tilborgh,

one of the Kredietbank's CEO's and expert in the field of services marketing, explains why this is done this way: "Top management should think of only one target group, devote all its attention to it and should not split itself over to many groups of clients."

Intensive relationships

Traditionally, most banks concentrate on attracting new customers and clients. Hardly any attention is paid to keeping customers, says Cyriel van Tilborgh. A great deal of effort is put into all kinds of instruments in the marketing mix, but they all are aimed at making new clients. Marketing communication is usually aimed at creating a positive image, not at stimulating interaction. Generally, the only real communication with customers occurs when the account shows a deficit. The Kredietbank wants to get rid of this way of thinking and working.

Interaction at the Kredietbank will come now via;

- a customer service department where complaints are handled or information is given;
- info service for quick answers to simple questions; and
- very personalized direct marketing.

The three zones concept

Another important change at the Kredietbank can be found in the servicescape, the area where the service encounter actually takes place. The physical facilities at the local branches have to be restructured/rebuilt/reconstructed.

This is the consequence of introducing the three zone concept.

The first zone consists of the area where all automatic machines are situated. These are the machines aimed at handling all the routine (and simple) service encounters. In the second zone, the "quick-service" counters are present for those clients having businesses that are a little more complex than the routine which can be dealt with in the first zone. This zone is also meant for those clients in need of a little help. In the near future, the Kredietbank expects this zone to vanish and be replaced by staff guiding clients to proper help desk specialists. The third zone is exclusively reserved for advice. Using computers with the file of the customer, the bank specialist will give advice to the clients as to what is the best for them. The computer will instantly provide opportunities and offers that the Kredietbank has to solve the clients' problems or questions asked. This is also one of the ways to strengthen the relationship between the clients and the Kredietbank.

Performance

The new segmentation in the retail area has already shown a succesful increase. In most sub-segments market share has grown, be it gradually and slowly. Moreover, Kredietbank noticed a raise of the gross income that is brought about by each of these eight sub-segments. But, as Cyriel van Tilborgh says: "the customer profitability is one of the major concerns for the next years: since we are able to determine for each customer what income, costs and profit (s)he brings about for each service, we are laying more emphasis on how to improve our customers' profitability." So, the new strategy urges for defining and using financial as well as non-financial indicators to assess Kredietbank's performance.

QUESTIONS

1   What do you think of these changes at the Kredietbank to build and strengthen the relationship with their clients?

2   What other means can you imagine to strengthen the relationship between a bank and its clients?

3   How does the idea of re-structuring the organization of the Kredietbank fits into the concept of market orientation elaborated upon in this book?

4   Do you know similar examples from your own country?

5   Do you have any idea what kind of shifts take place in

- the three types of bonds developed by Berry and Parasuraman as cited in Chapter Four and shown in Figure 8-3; and
- the six types of relationships developed by Kotler, and Schijns et al as cited in Chapter Four at the Kredietbank?

ENDNOTES

1. Leeflang et al., 1992.
2. See for instance Dwyer et al., 1987, Diller and Kusterer, 1988, Peelen, 1989, Poiesz and Van Raaij, 1993, Bruhn and Bunge, 1994, Diller, 1994 and Schijns, 1998.
3. Schijns, 1996, 1998. This view is the challenge we talked about in note 43, Chapter Seven.
4. The discussion of this RLM-matrix heavily depends on Schijns, 1996. As Schijns (p.28) states, the framework for this model is not new, as it is rooted in models of Hoekstra, 1993, Krapfel et al., 1991, and Strandvik and Liljander, 1994b, and is analogous to the relative attitude-behavior relationship of Dick and Basu, 1994. However, measuring relationship strength by relationship commitment (Wilson, 1990, 1995), and using relationship strength as the attitudinal dimension are non-traditional.
5. For the sake of simplicity only 4 segments are mentioned. It is self evident that more segments can be found when each dimension is subdivided in more than two.
6. Storbacka, 1994.
7. Storbacka, 1994. The following remarks stem from Strandvik and Storbacka, 1996 and Liljander and Strandvik, 1995.
8. See also section 8.3 on the Service Profit Chain.
9. See e.g. Halinen, 1994, Holmlund, 1997 and Venetis, 1997.
10. Venetis, 1997, pp. 154-175.
11. See the bonds as defined by Berry and Parasuraman, 1991.
12. This classification of the three types of bonds to the specific features of our four strategies is used here as a model to think about this configuration. Nevertheless exceptions will be found in daily life. Moreover, this model has not yet been tested, but fits to our consultancy experience.
13. Ries and Trout, 1986.
14. We do discuss these 'switching issues' in this section on relationship marketing because competitors may always try to break existing relationships and 'steal customers'. This danger should not be overlooked by firms focussing (too much?) on relationship marketing.
15. Quite often the proposals of Ries and Trout are stated very normative and it looks as if it is very simple. Reality is far from that.
16. Porter, 1980; Daems and Douma, 1989.
17. Adopted from: Andrew Fisher about German Banking and Finance, Financial Times, May 1996, VI, p.6.
18. Stefanie Bergmaier reports these stories and also a number of misfits in Germany in Wirtschaftswoche, April 24, 1997. This phenomenon of bank shops in department stores or supermarkets exists already in, e.g. France and the USA. It is now tested again in Germany.
19. That is why we have positioned them at the same level in Figure 8-1.
20. Wetzels, 1998.
21. See section 7.5.
22. Quinlan, 1991; Heskett, Sasser and Schlesinger, 1997.
23. Wetzels (1998) depicts the relationships in the service profit chain as more complex than this Figure 8-5 shows.
24. Flipo, 1986, p. 13.
25. The basis for this figure has been laid by Alain Loosveld in his MBA thesis on marketing planning for industrial services.

26. However, the different lengths of the sections do *not* imply that length equals importance of the stages in the whole planning process.

27. See Heskett, 1987.

28. Because of this success, Coop Schweiz won the GFM-Marketing Preis (=Award) in 1997. See Marketing Journal, 1997, no. 6, pp. 400-402.

29. Such an analysis also can be done at corporate level. Then the result will be a (new) corporate and marketing strategy. We discuss it here in order to incorporate all the relevant marketing-issues to deliver excellent service quality.

30. This example is largely based on an actual past situation at the research institute where one of the authors is director. Fictional issues are added.

31. The discussion of these issues about SWOT, Opportunity matrix etc. is largely based on Palmer, 1997, Chapter Three.

32. Of course, more factors are deemed relevant to assess markets and services than just these two. One should remember that in completing this matrix. One of the authors, once applied this matrix succesfully in positioning on the one hand all Dutch universities to decipher the positions of Maastricht University and all schools at Maastricht University on the other hand. The well known strategies for each of the four segments could be developed easily for our University and the various schools.

33. These strategies are well known and can be found in each textbook on marketing management. Since they belong to the basics, we will not elaborate on them.

34. The same as in note 33 applies.

35. Berry, Conant and Parasuraman, 1991, p. 261.

36. In fact, the marketing audit can be part of the corporate audit, containing for instance also a financial, production, personnel and IT audit. See Palmer, 1997, p. 50.

37. This figure is a slight adaptation from Palmer's Figure 3-1, p. 47. This simple structure is the foundation of the more complex Figure 8-6: the overall marketing planning process.

38. Faes and Van Tilborgh, 1984, pp. 107-112.

39. Canziani, 1997, p. 8. In this paper, an interesting classification of new customers has been developed: Virgin Newcomers, Virtual Newcomers, Value Switchers and Vagabond Switchers. It would go to far here to elaborate on it in detail.

40. See also this chapter's case.

41. Definitions of internal marketing and a comprehensive discussion of the concept will be given in Chapter Fifteen. See also Stauss, 1991.

42. Kasper, 1995.

43. Zeithaml, Parasuraman and Berry, 1990.

44. This case is based on Andriesse and Holzhauer, 1994 and additional information provided by Cyriel Van Tilborgh, one of the Kredietbank's CEO's.

CHAPTER NINE

INTERNATIONALIZATION OF SERVICES

After studying this chapter, you should be able to:

BELOW: *"Glocal" services: think global, act local within a network*

- *analyze the impact of services' intangibility on the internationalization or globalization in service industries;*
- *argue which reasons may lead a service firm to internationalize;*
- *understand why it could be difficult to export services;*
- *understand why it is (becoming more and more) feasible to export services;*
- *explain the reasons why service firms may start operations abroad;*
- *analyze the different entry barriers or reasons why it is (or may be) difficult for service organizations to internationalize;*
- *discuss the various entry strategies service firms may apply in internationalizing their business;*
- *assess the various pro's and con's of different entry strategies;*
- *assess the various pro's and con's of standardization versus adaptation of services within an international marketing strategy;*
- *decipher the uniqueness of relationship marketing in an international context;*
- *understand the specific issues of controlling market orientation and service quality in international service industries.*

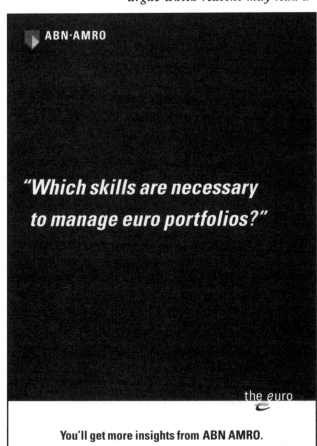

ABN·AMRO

"Which skills are necessary to manage euro portfolios?"

the euro

You'll get more insights from ABN AMRO.

9.1 INTRODUCTION

*Service
practice
9-1
Another look
at entering a
foreign market*

The German Customer Barometer 1995 measures quality and satisfaction in a great many German industries. Also, in a number of German service industries prof. Anton Meyer asked thousands of German customers about their satisfaction with the services of their most used (= main) supplier. It is their firm belief that a main criterion for customer orientation is the overall satisfaction of a customer. This is measured by means of the following question

"How satisfied are you with the services of your main supplier altogether?" (1 = completely satisfied; 5 = completely dissatisfied).

For 1995, the ranking of German service industries was – based on the average scores per service industry – as follows:

• holiday destinations	1.97
• pharmacies	2.16
• credit card companies	2.21
• gas stations	2.27
• car repair shops	2.29
• radio stations	2.29
• travel/tour operators	2.29
• automobile associations	2.30
• health insurance companies	2.30
• automobile insurance companies	2.32
• frozen food suppliers (retailers)	2.32
• airlines	2.35
• consumer electronic and appliance stores	2.42
• banks and savings and loans	2.43
• household appliance repair service	2.45
• supermarkets/grocery stores	2.45
• mail order companies	2.46
• furniture stores	2.47
• drug/variety stores	2.52
• building societies	2.58
• mobile communication service providers	2.58
• power supply companies (utilities)	2.58
• home improvement stores	2.59
• department stores	2.64
• parcel delivery services (consumers)	2.73
• Deutsche Post AG	2.81
• telephone company	2.84
• public transportation in the city	2.91
• Deutsche Bahnen (railway)	2.93
• churches and religious organizations	3.03
• public administration	3.07

- police (public security)   3.09
- broadcasting/TV networks   3.27

In most German service industries, improvements should be made in terms of "friendliness to the customer" and "quality to price ratio" (= value for money). Here, the focus should be on the core services and service providing processes (no frills). German customers appear to have high expectations of the following quality attributes:

- reliability (e.g. keeping promises and being notified of delivery problems);
- comprehensibility of invoices;
- cleanliness and tidiness of business premises;
- acting on customers' individual wishes;
- friendliness of the staff; and
- prompt reactions to complaints.

Overall, one should realize that staff friendliness (apart from some retail industries) actually achieved the highest ratings.

Source: Anton Meyer and Frank Dornach, The German Customer Barometer 1995 – Quality and Satisfaction, 1996.

Usually, market opportunities are defined in terms of, e.g. purchasing power for products and services, margins, lack of competition and competitive advantage. Putting a great emphasis on service quality and customer satisfaction, we believe these issues can also be applied in analyzing foreign market opportunities, as Service practice 9-1 shows. The human side of the service encounter needs much improvement in Germany. That is *the* service quality attribute for incumbent firms to achieve in Germany.

In the previous chapters, a globalization trend on the supply side became evident. Academic debate as to what extent demand is global, local, regional or inter-regional (e.g. countries in the European Alps where consumers have strong regional preferences), still continues. It is clear, however, that in some industries demand may trigger the internationalization of services. For, business travellers and companies may expect the same high quality services from hotels, airlines, etc. all over the world. It may also be that service providers are forced to internationalize and deliver greater service quality world wide when their national clients internationalize. Business to business customers may want to deal with their local agency world wide and expect the same service everywhere. There are even examples of service firms that could loose their local clients if they cannot service them worldwide.

These findings force the individual service provider to decide whether the firm will join this race or invest on a local, regional or domestic basis only. The answer lies mainly in factors like available resources, management's ambition, type of activities, present scale of operation, competitive advantages, expectations about sustainability in the foreign market in the long run and entry mode. Nevertheless, it is important to realize that service firms may start foreign activities because they want to themselves.

internationalization, globalization

Globalization and internationalization are often used as synonyms. Indeed, both terms indicate that national boundaries are becoming of less importance across the world, even in service industries. The scope may differ, however. Internationalization mainly refers to organizations going abroad whereas globalization encompasses a broader scope of converging demand and supply in many areas around the world.[1] But even then, we may see different opinions. For "... any service firm doing business across national frontiers can claim to be international" whereas "... a truly global company is one that not only does business in both the eastern and western hemispheres, but also in both the northern and southern ones. In the process, geographic distances and time zone variations are maximized."[2] In essence, the difference between globalization and internationalization is not that important here, since we intend to focus on service organizations starting their international activities (and no one will know where it will end up: in some, many or all the countries of the world). So, both concepts will be used interchangeably here.

With respect to the international marketing strategy of a service organization, we will discuss the following issues: the internationalization of intangibles; internationalization versus other growth strategies; reasons to internationalization; barriers to entry; the choice of a particular entry mode; standardization or adaptation; and service quality.[3] Many of these issues apply to all kinds of firms. However, we will adjust it to the services sector. The outline of this chapter is given in Figure 9-1.

9.2 INTERNATIONALIZING INTANGIBLES?

intangibility

One may wonder whether it is really possible to internationalize in the service industry. Typically, the specific characteristics of services are considered to determine the predominantly "local" structure of service firms. These well known features stem from services' intangibility. This basic feature, in turn, leads to services' perishability, simultaneity of production and consumption, and close buyer/supplier interaction. The "service encounter argument" refers to the need for physical presence of both parties during the service encounter. This would complicate the internationalization process in services; it could even make it impossible.

But, if so many authors argue that it is so difficult to internationalize in services, then

- why do we see that such a large proportion of many countries' exports consist of services (see Table 9-1)?; and
- why do we see that so many service organizations operate internationally now?

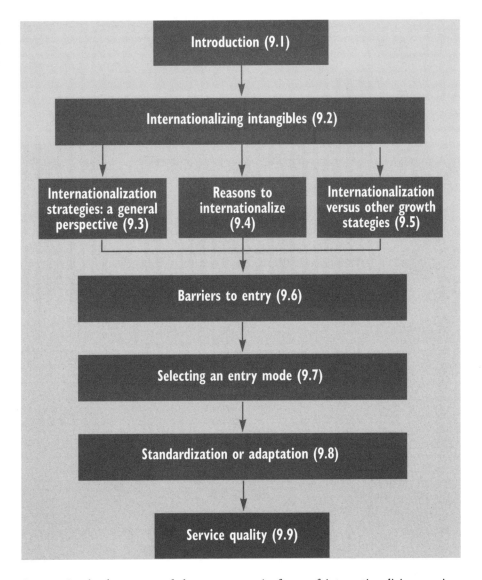

Figure 9-1
Chapter outline

Introduction (9.1)

Internationalizing intangibles (9.2)

Internationalization strategies: a general perspective (9.3)

Reasons to internationalize (9.4)

Internationalization versus other growth stategies (9.5)

Barriers to entry (9.6)

Selecting an entry mode (9.7)

Standardization or adaptation (9.8)

Service quality (9.9)

It must imply that many of the arguments in favor of internationalizing services outweigh the risks and problems of going abroad. Or, it must imply that some changes have taken place in the service encounter allowing for new opportunities. The answer is given by various service scholars who argue that, at present, those risks are much lower than in the past. The arguments given refer to some of the issues we mentioned in Chapter Two on classifying services. In general, we could say, different positions on several of the continua developed in Chapter Two offer the opportunities to *changes in* actually export services. Changes in information technology appear to be a major *information technology* driving force in this respect.[4] Recent changes in technology make it possible to export services and organize the accompanying international marketing activities in a different way than one or two decades ago. In this respect, it is important to stipulate the differences between knowledge/information-based services and resource-based

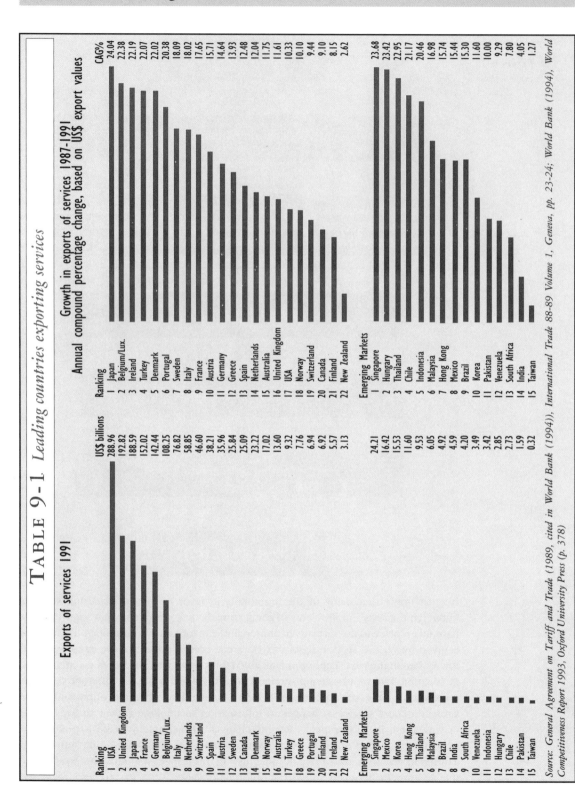

TABLE 9-1. *Leading countries exporting services*

Exports of services 1991

Ranking		US$ billions
1	USA	288.96
2	United Kingdom	192.82
3	Japan	188.59
4	France	152.02
5	Germany	142.44
6	Belgium/Lux.	108.25
7	Italy	76.82
8	Netherlands	58.85
9	Switzerland	46.60
10	Spain	38.21
11	Austria	35.96
12	Sweden	25.84
13	Canada	25.09
14	Denmark	23.22
15	Norway	17.02
16	Australia	13.60
17	Turkey	9.32
18	Greece	7.76
19	Portugal	6.94
20	Finland	6.92
21	Ireland	5.57
22	New Zealand	3.13

Emerging Markets

Ranking		US$ billions
1	Singapore	24.21
2	Mexico	16.42
3	Korea	15.53
4	Hong Kong	11.60
5	Thailand	9.53
6	Malaysia	6.05
7	Brazil	4.92
8	India	4.59
9	South Africa	4.20
10	Venezuela	3.49
11	Indonesia	3.42
12	Hungary	2.85
13	Chile	2.73
14	Pakistan	1.59
15	Taiwan	0.32

Growth in exports of services 1987-1991

Annual compound percentage change, based on US$ export values

Ranking		CAG%
1	Japan	24.04
2	Belgium/Lux.	22.38
3	Ireland	22.19
4	Turkey	22.07
5	Denmark	22.02
6	Portugal	20.38
7	Sweden	18.09
8	Italy	18.02
9	France	17.65
10	Austria	15.71
11	Germany	14.64
12	Greece	13.93
13	Spain	12.48
14	Netherlands	12.04
15	Australia	11.75
16	United Kingdom	11.61
17	USA	10.33
18	Norway	10.10
19	Switzerland	9.44
20	Canada	9.10
21	Finland	8.15
22	New Zealand	2.62

Emerging Markets

Ranking		CAG%
1	Singapore	23.68
2	Hungary	23.42
3	Thailand	22.95
4	Chile	21.17
5	Indonesia	20.46
6	Malaysia	16.98
7	Hong Kong	15.74
8	Mexico	15.44
9	Brazil	15.30
10	Korea	11.60
11	Pakistan	10.00
12	Venezuela	9.29
13	South Africa	7.80
14	India	4.05
15	Taiwan	1.27

Source: General Agreement on Tariff and Trade (1989, cited in World Bank (1994)), International Trade 88-89 Volume 1, Geneva, pp. 23-24; World Bank (1994), World Competitiveness Report 1993, Oxford University Press (p. 378)

services.[5] Knowledge and information-based services are easier to export than resource-based services. For, these services contain a large technology component.

We will elaborate on these issues in the next sections, proving that services can indeed be internationalized. Changes in technology are very relevant in this development. That is why we will discuss that "trend" at first.

TECHNOLOGICAL COMPONENT WITHIN SERVICES

The increasing technological component within services not only has a tremendous impact on the opportunities to internationalize in services but also on the choice of entry-mode. Technological advances may avoid the necessity of the physical presence or physical proximity during the service encounter. In turn, this will make it easier to cope with the risks connected with servicing foreign markets.

opportunities to
internationalize
choice of entry-mode

A classification scheme for internationalizing services can be based on a six-sector matrix (see Figure 9-2).[6] It originates from the idea that modes of service internationalization are based on decisions about the next two issues:

nature of the service

1. the nature of the service (mainly the degree of interaction between service provider and customer during the service encounter); and

way in which the
service is delivered

2. the way in which the service is delivered (for instance, the degree to which the services are embodied in or delivered through tangible goods).

relative involvement of
goods in a service,
degree of
consumer/producer
interaction

The vertical axis in Figure 9-2 represents the relative involvement of goods in a service. The horizontal axis depicts the degree of consumer/producer interaction (which is low in sectors 1, 2 and 3 and high in sectors 4, 5 and 6). Services in sector 1 are limited in international potential in their present form. Services such as retailing, couriers, fast food, and hotels have promising opportunities for internationalization because goods form quite a substantial part of these services. Software, CDs, movies on videocassettes (sector 3 services), are easy to export from the country of origin, because these services are (almost) fully embodied in goods. Sector 4 encompasses labor intensive and almost completely intangible customer and business to business services like consulting, advertising, medical services and insurances. Many of these services are famous for their experience and credence attributes. In this sector, the interaction between clients and staff is essential, making it relatively difficult to export this kind of services. For, internationalization of services almost automatically involves the internationalization of people one way or another. Sector 5 services involves both people and goods and a balance between the two should be searched for in the internationalization of this kind of service. The services in sector 6 both have a high rate as far as goods and interaction are concerned. Interaction is always (at least) a two-way phenomenon. However, here it often takes place through machines rather than people, for example electronic diagnostics, teleshopping, and so on. With the development of new information technologies in-house and to customize services, this sector is likely to become more globally significant in the future. The European television watcher, for example, can order Pan-European advertised goods and services by telephone.

Degree of consumer/producer interaction

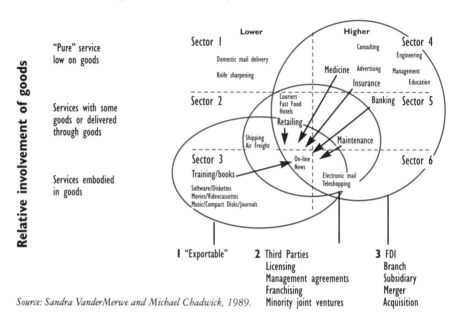

Source: *Sandra VanderMerwe and Michael Chadwick, 1989.*

matrix

This matrix is a useful conceptual tool, because the relative involvement of goods and the measure of interface between the staff and the customer provide a framework for a good understanding of the clustering of services. It is even thinkable that some services from sectors 1 to 5 will change in due course and resemble sector 6 services. In addition to the wish or need to invest in a country, these six sectors give an impression of which entry mode is recommendable for entering foreign markets. For example, consulting, advertising and insurance services (sector 4) are more difficult to export as they require staff in addition to services embodied in goods (cluster 3).

KNOWLEDGE-BASED SERVICES

Knowledge-based or
information-based
services

information component

Knowledge-based or information-based services can be distinguished from resource-based services. Here, it is relevant to consider that the rapid changes in information technology make such services easily accessible in a wide geographic area and not only in the direct local environment. Moreover, the information component of some services is growing, in the sense that customers may retrieve information themselves from the service system or add to it. Electronic banking is such a service. Customers now perform some activities that the bank used to do. Moreover, they receive more and faster information on their bank accounts, giving them more opportunities for, e.g. cash management.

information society

The "information society" is also growing. Scientific knowledge is increasing and is more accessible to a wide variety of people and organizations. In Chapter Three, for instance, we saw that – on average – the world population's level of education is increasing. This will stimulate the search for more information. We also saw the trend to more self service activities in many industries. Here, we have combined those trends and expect it to stimulate the internationalization of services.

In fact, breakthroughs in information or communication technology, the growing competition among such service providers which reduces their prices and the world wide deregulation in this sector (especially in public utilities for telecommunication) made this possible. In countries such as Ireland, India and The Philippines, for example, companies could easily develop administrative (back office) services replacing the expensive labor-intensive handling for banks and airlines in other Western countries, because of new information and telecommunication technologies. If we think about it, we can easily imagine that many services which required a local

physical presence

presence in the past, can be exported tomorrow. Therefore, the physical presence of both service provider and customer in the service encounter should not be taken for

location bound services

granted. Usually, one agrees that such location bound services should be distributed abroad in the same way as in one's own country. So, this will change.

The way companies are delivering services in the home market will also change in the course of time. Certain services contain a degree of information gathering and/or utilization of knowledge (notably legal, consulting, design and architectural services, and some banking services) that does not need that physical presence in the future as much as in the past.[7] When the "production" of the service can take place domestically by customers themselves, the interaction between supplier and customer must be facilitated by telecommunications. Sometimes, a (face-to-face) visit by the service provider's account manager is still necessary. That account manager can use the information technology installed at the customer's to ease the communication with the bank. Clever market-oriented employees and marketeers will detect changes in technology, demand, competition and other factors, offering opportunities for alternative service delivery modes.

local presence

For many service providers though, a local presence in any form is often necessary and unavoidable to operate successfully in foreign markets (to cope with cultural and foreign language barriers). Even for professional knowledge/information-based services a local representative, or at least a regional representative, often guarantees more success abroad. For instance, many foreign management consulting firms now offering services in Central and Eastern Europe from regional centers sooner or later will find themselves confronted with the dilemma to either withdraw or establish a permanent branch or office in these countries. Local firms which have a natural advantage of native speaking employees and relationships in the country will now become more competitive in knowledge and pricing.

investment costs

Finally, the investment costs of establishing information/ knowledge-based services abroad are often substantially lower than in resource-based services such as retail outlets, hotels, etc.

ECONOMIES OF SCALE AND SCOPE

sources of competitive advantage

The sources of competitive advantage in service industries are changing.[8] A combination of structural, market, regulatory, and technological changes have provided a shift in the existing balance of activities within service firms. In the past, the strong emphasis on "front office" activities and the perceived closeness to the customer, direct interaction between service provider and client as well as limited economies of scale or scope in services, did not result into internationalization as the most obvious growth option for service firms. Information technology now offers the opportunity to separate front office and back office activities, thus leading to an increasing number of service firms operating in many countries. A stronger emphasis on "back-office" activities may decrease the level of perceived risk, and enhance potential benefits attached to international expansion.[9] If cost advantages of scale and/or scope are feasible, service firms are likely to internationalize. Table 9-2 gives an overview of several of these potential sources of economies of scale and scope in services in the first two columns. (The third column will be elaborated upon in the next pages.)

separate front office and back office activities

sources of economies of scale and scope

Service practice 9-2 The impact of technology on scale and scope

American Express Information Technology has a positive effect on, i.e. response times, new products, distribution channels and add-in on services.

Through scale and scope in information technology, Benneton has reaped the benefit of responsive merchandising, inventory elimination, customized production and credit management.

British Airways has developed sophisticated software to maximize yield from higher-revenue seats on all flights. This is a major contribution to profitability in a cost-intensive service business. Its reservation system automatically gives preference to flights with British Airways or associated airlines, creating exclusion effects for competitors.[10]

asset structure

Besides scale and scope activities in services, the asset structure of service firms has also changed. Knowledge of assessing, analyzing and managing information is becoming essential for success in many service industries (e.g. finance, software, information, brokerage, library services). The internal processes, routines, skills, capabilities important in linking information management, human resources management, operational research and marketing in the company have become more vital for survival. The new way of looking at the traditional paradigm that services are not perishable, has led to the conclusion that in many sectors services can be stored. Knowledge is an asset that can be stored on the shelf. Knowledge or information can be retrieved from the shelf for a certain span of time at little or no cost (e.g. an advertisement, a software programme). Many services offer a firm-specific pool of tacit knowledge. Service firms, e.g. management consultants, are investing heavily in human capital. The knowledge of how to combine the three factors, human capital, physical capital and information technology, is becoming more important.

services can be stored

<table>
<tr><td colspan="3">

TABLE 9-2 *Potential sources for economies of scale and scope, and experience effects in services*

</td></tr>
</table>

Economies of Scale	Economies of Scope	Experience Effects
Geographic networks Physical facilities	IT/IS shared information networks Shared learning and doing	Ownership structures Organization structure centralization/ decentralization
Purchasing/supply Marketing Logistics and Distribution Technology/IT/IS Production resources	Product or process innovation suppliers Shared R&D Shared channels for multiple offerings Shared investments and costs Reproduction formula for service system	Overcome entry barrier Optimal entry strategy Personnel (hiring/firing/training/appraisal/ remuneration) Reproduction formula for service system
Management Organization	Range of services and service development Complementary services	Coping with environmental factors (DRETS) abroad
Operations support Knowledge	Branding International franchising Training Goodwill and corporate identity Culture Internal exploitation of economies Reduced transaction costs Common governance Privileged access to parent services	Adjusting market policies and marketing-mix Funding/finance Finding (the right) clients To fasten start-up and break-even Real-estate contracts Local organization Processes, procedures and information technology Reduced transaction costs Negotiations with local parties Culture

Source: Economies of scale/scope, Segal-Horn's judgement and compilation from Normann (1984), Bartlett and Ghoshal (1986), Endewick (1989) in The Internationalization of Service Firms, Advances in Strategic Management, Volume 9, p.34, (1993), JAI Press Inc and authors' compilation of experience effects.

experience in some foreign markets

A few other factors also contribute to decreasing the risks for service firms with foreign market aspirations. Companies with experience in some foreign markets are better prepared for the risks of entering new markets. Learning from past successes and failures will be beneficial to these organizations. For example, an international bank with a minor stake in a joint venture bank may easily conclude next time to acquire a major stake including a management say, or not to invest at all when they are faced with outstanding loans as a result of third-party lending or bad judgements by local management. An international audit firm that is profitable one year after starting up in Poland probably perceives the risk of entering the market in Kazakhstan as lower than colleagues lacking such an experience.

first-mover   Often, the strategy to become the first foreign firm in a country, the so called "first-mover", pays off. As the service firm gains experience in the foreign market, it learns to perform better in the new environment. The result is that the average cost of producing and delivering a service in foreign markets tends to fall with the experience accumulated.

reducing the risks   Market factors substantially reducing the risks are: a fair estimate of the potential market share within the market segments focused on (e.g. by following existing clients abroad) and the combination of a strong brand name/concept with fragmented or (almost) monopolized markets abroad. As a result, foreign market participation while concentrating on certain market segments can accelerate the accumulation of learning and experience, creating additional advantages viz-à-viz the competition. Here again, it turns out to be a combination of customer orientation and competitor orientation, being two of the important elements of the service organization's market orientation.[11]

9.3 INTERNATIONALIZATION STRATEGIES IN SERVICES: A GENERAL PERSPECTIVE

It is possible to export intangibles to other countries. Therefore, an issue of growing importance to service firms is "how to select a country which is interesting to enter?" Many criteria for this selection process can be found.[12]

joint corporate goals   First of all, joint corporate goals should be investigated: what benefits can be offered to potential customers in other countries, and how does it impact on the company's goals? What quality levels do exist in the foreign countries under investigation, and what quality levels do customers expect or desire in those countries? What contribution can the company make in increasing the desired quality level in that

characteristics of internationalizing firms   country (or for a specific segment in that country)? With respect to characteristics of internationalizing firms, their size is also noteworthy here. In general, larger firms are inclined to find internationalization "easier" than smaller firms. Service firms are often quite small; only a few service firms are large and thus have the resources, attitude and guts to go abroad. Existing experience in the international business scene is an asset with regard to extending the activities in foreign countries. Often, this is the consequence of having been forced to follow clients from the home country in their own international activities. It may also have been caused by the fact that the market leader in the home country started foreign operations and that other firms had to follow.

market related factors   Another group of criteria hinges upon market related factors, like how large is the host country market, what growth rates are present or can be expected and what kind of economies of scale or scope can be achieved? It appears that companies are more likely to invest, for instance, in larger and growing overseas markets than in smaller and shrinking ones. The intensity of competition and the degree of fragmentation in the market are variables also belonging to this group; it has been shown that highly competitive markets are not attractive to enter. The degree of similarity between the home market and the host country market is also important to check. This is related to another argument dealing with the geographical proximity and cultural distance of the host country: the more they are both alike, the easier it will be to internationalize, as indicated in Chapter Four with our cultural map of the world.

infrastructure   The third group of criteria can be labeled under the heading of infrastructure. It encompasses, for instance, the economic and physical infrastructure: when a country is poorly developed, it will be difficult to use cars or IT to produce services that need this kind of support which is necessary to actually meet customers. Trade barriers and governmental regulations may hinder entering a foreign country; sometimes governmental decisions may be favoring contracts (e.g. contracts to develop harbors, dykes or a mobile telephone system, etc.). Country risk, be it political or economic, may also affect the decision to invest. Service firms critically evaluate issues like ownership, control, convertibility of currency, transfer of profits, etc. The riskier the country, the riskier the international activities will be.

interaction of the service supplier and the client   Finally, the interaction of the service supplier and the client may affect the market choices: can the service encounter in the home country be transferred to another country? In what way should it be adapted to fit local norms, values and culture? In what way can long term relationships be built, if any? Or, when the complexity of the information supplied by the client is low, the probability of entering countries which are culturally distinct from the home country may be high. More complex information implies that customers and suppliers have to interact more closely during the servuction process. The formal and informal structural arrangements that have been made at home should be reviewed to check whether they need adaptation when going abroad. Due to the characteristics of the service encounter, the service organization intending to internationalize has to check whether the service should be delivered personally or not (whether face-to-face interaction between supplier and customers is needed). Second, they have to ask themselves whether a physical outlet is needed to perform the service. If the answer to both questions is negative, principally there is no reason why they should not export the service, provided there is a market and no other major obstacles exist, such as legislation prohibiting exports or imports. However, before starting an internationalization strategy it pays to prepare an analysis focusing on the strengths and weaknesses of the firm, opportunities in the selected market(s), including internal and external barriers. Moreover, it is necessary that all costs and benefits of obtaining and retaining control in a specific situation must be carefully weighed against each other. The most efficient (entry) mode is the

benefit-to-cost ratio   one with the highest benefit-to-cost ratio.[13]

The service characteristics relevant to the stages in the decision making process of service globalization can be listed in hierarchical order (see Figure 9-3).[14]

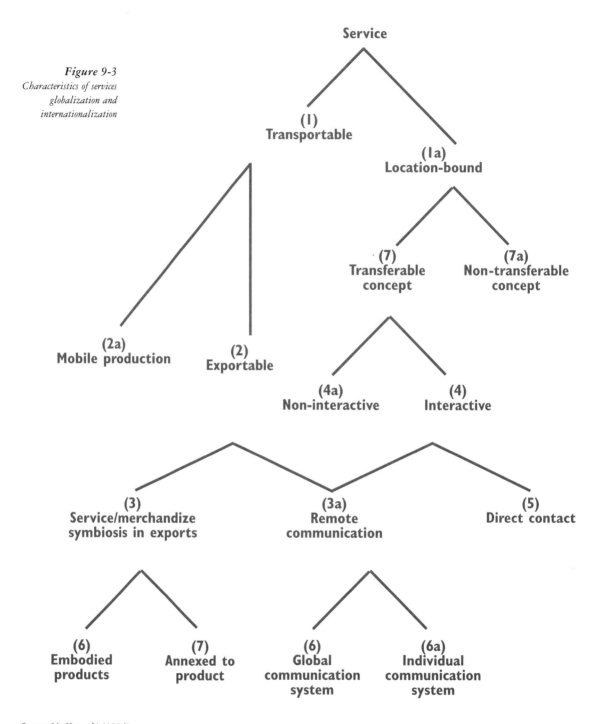

Figure 9-3
Characteristics of services
globalization and
internationalization

Source: M. Koestecki (1994).

This scheme basically rests on three service characteristics:

1. transportable services versus location-bound services;
2. transportable services which are exportable versus services delivered through mobile production units; and
3. services traded through their symbiosis with the merchandise trade versus services exportable through remote communications.

Next to these three basic distinctions, it is relevant to take the following issues into account as well in understanding and developing a globalization or internationalization strategy in services:

- client/producer relations can be divided in interactive and non-interactive ones;
- interaction can be direct or remote;
- the client can be reached through a global or an individual network;
- the service may be transferable or non-transferable;
- the flexibility or rigidity in responding to national needs; and
- the extent as to divide or not the service bundle while internationalizing.

transportable and location-bound services

transferability of the service concept

The first variable at the top of the figure depicts a dichotomy between "transportable" and "location-bound" services, i.e. services which have to be consumed at the place of production. Globalization of the latter category of services (e.g. supermarket retailing) calls for the location of a service provider abroad. Also, the transferability of the service concept is an essential variable in assessing the attractiveness of globalization by means of franchising, establishing an agency, direct investments or other forms of participation in another country. Service and process innovation encouraged by technological change renders a large number of services transportable, especially in financial services and back office services.

transportable services which are exportable through mobile production units

The second variable distinguishes between transportable services which are exportable and those which are delivered through mobile production units (e.g. airlines or an orchestra on tour). The latter form of service delivery is encouraged by improvements in travel services. The increased tradeability of numerous new financial products (e.g. securitized loans) was made possible because of information technology.

services which are exportable through remote communication and traded because of their symbiosis with the merchandise trade

The third variable differentiates between services which are exportable through remote communication (e.g. data processing or TV shows) and those which are traded because of their symbiosis with the merchandise trade (e.g. a filmed art show that is exported together with the supporting video tape). Obviously, all merchandise trade relies on a range of annexed services – in most cases marketing services. Sometimes, the service component is limited to the "shipment" of a product or to "port services" which are linked to the transport of cargo and people in foreign ports. These additional services may also include a wide range of distributing services, after-sale services and the like.

remote communication

Remote communication is the central variable in the current globalization process, and many service firms emphasize the management of technology and information as a strategic resource in their international expansion. To banks, insurance companies or travel agents, the telecommunications network provides a "lifeline" to the customers and constitutes the key delivery mechanism in both domestic and foreign operations. In tourist or air transportation, access to a global network is a sine-qua-non condition of successful marketing.

So, the service industry is in transition from a traditionally local one to an international or global industry.[15] Various causes can be found. First, the deregulation in key industries like telecommunications and banking has spurred international competition in those industries. Second, as manufacturers go international, so have their service providers (they are forced to follow). Finally, technology is making national boundaries borderless. These trends counter argue the risk of being distant from the customer in the service encounter and the problems of maintaining effective quality control at the point of service delivery. Being a world wide market oriented service provider might overcome these problems. It means, for instance, that such a service firm must be willing to take the risk of going abroad and consider this risk as an acceptable one inherent in normal company behavior (so, comparable to the risk taking behavior of market-oriented firms in general).

Service practice 9-3 Factors impacting on the decision of Australian firms to export services [16]

Especially, the perceptions of the company of barriers, benefits and risk to export determine whether a service firm will go international or not. These were the most important areas among the five factors found influencing the decision to internationalize or not:

1. barriers to internationalization (know how limitations, restrictions in target country, investment required, country-of-origin bias, intensity of competition in foreign markets, difficulties imposed by the nature of the service);
2. perceptions of benefits and risks (attitudes to benefits of exporting, attitudes to risks of exporting, attitudes to relative profitability);
3. competitive environment in home market (intensity of domestic competition, rate of new service obsolence);
4. the organization's capabilities and characteristics (development of differentiated services, effective communication, service quality, service cost advantage, size, research and development); and
5. managerial capabilities (percentage of managers with university degree, who worked abroad, who speak a foreign language).

9.4 REASONS TO INTERNATIONALIZE

Next, we will present an overview of five different categories of reasons found relevant.[17] These five driving forces are:

- ambition and commitment;
- knowledge and skills;

- market threats at home;
- market opportunities elsewhere; and
- finance, risks, costs and profits.

AMBITION AND COMMITMENT

ambition of top management

The ambition of top management counts as the single most powerful driving force behind internationalization. Such a personal spirit or entrepreneurial vision may encourage the whole firm to think and act international. Meeting other cultures, acquiring new ideas and technologies that may be implemented in the home operations, are arguments underlying this ambition.[18] A strong international flavor will then be part of the corporate culture. To a certain extent, this may be detrimental to the firm if they have to withdraw from the international scene. Then, such an amputation and change in what everyone in the organization considers as the foundation of the organization would have major negative effects on its customers, employees and the rest of the stakeholders. However, it can be the best decision. Some American banks followed this strategy in the early eighties. They withdrew from overseas markets in Europe and Asia due to outstanding loans to countries in the Third World and problems in real estate financing back home.

top management commitment

However, it is not only ambition that counts. Particularly "when things go wrong abroad", top management commitment towards the international activities and investment becomes extremely important. Here, top management has to show that it is important to continue and solve the (un)expected problems. In a learning organization, the whole firm will learn from these experiences.

KNOWLEDGE AND SKILLS

managerial superiority and/or organizational superiority

Managerial superiority and/or organizational superiority of the international service firm over the local firms in the market about to be entered are the next category of factors driving globalization or internationalization. Existing knowledge about such issues as back office procedures, service quality, implementing customer friendliness, market orientation, shelf space allocation, in-store marketing, electronic data interchange, may be applied in foreign markets to get a competitive advantage over there. Stated differently, internationalization can be caused by looking for ways to

synergy, especially in terms of the core competencies

accomplish synergy, especially in terms of the core competencies of the firm (so, not on all issues where some kind of synergy could always be found, but only on the core competencies). So, further exploiting internal strengths may be a reason to go abroad.

MARKET THREATS AT HOME

market threats at home

More and more companies experience market threats at home which drive them abroad. As demand reaches its peak or competition is heating up, companies start looking for alternatives to survive and/or grow. The development of new services, adding additional services to existing services, providing distinctive service quality, diversification and market development, are then viable options. Market development will bring the organization to the point where foreign plains lure. This "domestic push" to internationalization can thus be caused by intense local competition, small home markets, saturated home markets, declining purchasing power or diminishing consumer sentiment in one country (while not, at present, in other countries). In the retail world, it can also be the answer to the concentration and internationalization among manufacturers. Then, internationalizing retailers can be a countervailing power against these large manufacturers.

In many service industries, the competition of a few truly global companies is putting the heat on the other firms. Typically then, the strategic choice is becoming a simple one: either "join the race", internationalize, get a top position in the market (or even become market leader), or become a niche player specialized in a particular "region". Many service industries are becoming dominated by a few large global players. These oligopolies seem to result in fiercer instead of less competition. So, international competiton in the home market may be at stake. Whether it is in waste management, auditing or urban transportation, oligopolistic market structures seem to take over the former full competition or monopolies.

oligopolistic market structures

Service practice 9-4 Eye witnesses to globalization

Travelling around the world, we can witness the "globalization of the supply side" with our own eyes. Whether it is in New York, London, Kuala Lumpur or in far flung places like Zandvoort or Palanga, you may find service firms like Hertz, Avis or DHL. International hotel chains such as Marriott, Sheraton, Holiday Inn, Ibis, Bastion offer a consistent level of service throughout the world. McDonald's, Burger King and other fast food chains are nowadays found all over the world, even in the (former) communist world. In the centre of Budapest, one sees so many McDonald's restaurants that it looks as if you are in the US.

A growing number of retailers are now proving great flexibility in their strategies for entering new geographic markets.[19] Some are already world powers (like Benetton) whereas others are pursuing aggressive growth (like Toys R Us). Also noteworthy are cross-border retail alliances. This applies for selling as well as for procurement/purchasing. The Swiss based Associated Marketing Services (AMS) is a strategic alliance in the European food retail industry between Ahold (Holland), Allkauf (Germany), Argyll (UK), Casino (France), Kesko (Finland), ICA (Sweden), La Rinascente (Italy), Mercadona (Spain) and Migros (Switzerland) aimed at improving conditions to buy one way or another. Another example is the French DIFRA group consisting of many French retailers (Arlaud, Casino, Catteau, Coop Normandie-Picardie, Montlaur, Rallye, SCA Monoprix), the Belgian Delhaize group and the Italian retailer Zanin.[20]

MARKET OPPORTUNITIES ELSEWHERE

demand pull

Multinationals and other firms operating internationally may ask their service providers to serve them abroad once they enter foreign markets. This client following motive is a kind of international "demand pull"[21]. The advantages for the buyer are obvious: a more homogeneous quality of service, established/well known relationships decreasing transaction costs and central purchasing of these world wide services will lead to lower costs and headquarters know what kind of service is received elsewhere. This applies not only to business to business services but also to consumer services. Consumers also can rely on similar quality levels with international hotels, car rentals and credit cards, for instance. These services provide some safety and security during their trips, with so many new experiences in other cultures. For service firms, even small requests may open doors for large international activities.

Service practice 9-5 Large consequences of seemingly small requests

> In the 1930s, one of the ancestors of the Dutch ABN AMRO Bank was confronted with a demand from its Moslem clients in the then "Nederlands Indië" (nowadays Indonesia) to change money in Saudi Arabia on their pilgrimage to Mecca. As the expected demand was solid enough, the bank established itself as the first foreign bank in the country. The entry mode was prescribed by local regulators: a joint venture.

Successful service organizations may draw attention from local authorities, individuals, firms or other organizations in an unsolicited way. Their mere presence and way of working may lead these bodies to invite them to do business. This demand pull motive is initiated by these bodies in that foreign country.

universal values

the attraction of the global market place

According to Ted Levitt (1983), customer needs, values and customs are converging all over the world. Human nature is becoming more uniform in its needs for universal values such as the need for security, the need to experience self worth, materialism, etc. This argument can be labelled as the attraction of the global market place. Thus, segmentation should no longer be based on geographics, culture or language as such, but global segmentation should be based on the convergence patterns occurring.[22]

niches

The existence of unexploited markets attracts entrepreneurs with an open mind, a prerequisite to being market-oriented. Service firms exploiting niches at home may well try to apply their capabilities to similar niches abroad. In some of these very specialized industries, customized services are not only needed, but self evident and international by nature, like industrial software or financing the diamond trade.

large margins

Within this group of drivers to internationalization, one can also position the opportunities fragmented or monopolized markets offer. In both instances, large margins may attract more efficient competitors. The only prerequisite then is that these markets are not protected by local governments. This would prohibit firms to enter.

portfolio of countries

Entering a new country can also be explained by the fact that this is a strategic addition to the portfolio of countries the service provider is doing business with already. This offers new opportunities for cross selling. It may also upgrade the firm's image and reputation, to be present in a particular country. In turn, this may affect the firm's network of clients in a positive way (clients feel they are upgraded too; they may belong to a service firm's network doing business in so many well known countries).

convert existing good will and image into money

National "service champions" and international service firms with a well established name and reputation may find it lucrative to convert their existing good will and image into money in other countries. This driver of internationalization is backed by international travel and communication. The expansion of the UK retailer Marks and Spencer is an example here. They can even export their private label.

removal of entry barriers

Finally, the removal of entry barriers can be mentioned as a driver of internationalization. This argument is used in the following way. Once a service provider has entered a foreign country on a small scale, it may start to grow and expand. Once the customers in that country have largely accepted this firm's offerings, demand pull cannot be ignored and entry barriers will no longer play any role.

FINANCE, RISKS, COSTS AND PROFITS

risks

This group of drivers of internationalization hinges upon the financial side of doing business. First of all, risks may be spread when a firm is doing business in different countries with different economic climates. But, differences in time may also spread the risk of doing business. Brokers, financial consultants and other firms may benefit from selling and buying stocks and shares at the many stock exchanges all over the world. Via IT, it can be done 24 hours a day.

cost of capital, ease of access to capital

The cost of capital and the related ease of access to capital may differ in various local financial markets. Interest rates may differ, depending partly upon differences in exchange rates. In some instances, financial institutions may prefer to finance international service firms than local ones. At present, local and foreign banks in Central and Eastern Europe are eager to finance McDonald's whereas the local "pop and mom" restaurant will have great difficulties finding money outside the close circle of friends and family to invest in their own restaurant.

The growing rate of technology in services will require more financial investment. Therefore, it will become relevant for service firms to spot financial markets and see where the cost of capital is the lowest. In other words, in which markets supply of capital is redundant. This capital can then be invested in the development of new services (software, telecommunications, etc.) which require a lot of investment and – sometimes – large pay back periods. On the other hand, it is also conceivable that

surplus capital

international service providers invest surplus capital from one country to another. This brings us to the next globalization driver in this section.

*higher profits in new
foreign markets*

After analyzing foreign markets, management may decide to start in the most promising market in terms of profits. The lure of higher profits in new foreign markets may well be a serious reason to internationalize. As a final consequence of such a strategy, the activities in the home market may even be stopped.

Although we ended this section with financial reasons to internationalize, one should not forget that the service business is a people's business. Therefore, the cultural closeness between the foreign markets will partly determine how well customers, personnel and companies may interact and cooperate. The analysis in Chapter Four

*cultural closeness and
geographic closeness*

has indicated that cultural closeness and geographic closeness do not necessarily mix. Still, this is an important issue to consider when the decision to internationalize has to be made (especially when it must be outweighed by the decision to grow in the home market).

To conclude, the benefits of internationalization can, however, be considerable to the service firm. A "positive circle" can result from successful internationalization.[23] For, internationalization may enable the firm to serve its clients better. Efforts to reproduce this success formula abroad can sometimes help to reveal its basic character and the basic issues determining great service quality. Consequently, it may streamline the service management system in the home market even more. Tackling new markets may raise the general quality level. The image may be enhanced, not only in the eyes of the customer, but also in the eyes of the staff and the markets for potential employees. An international structure with a richer network also opens up opportunities for attracting new types of financial and human resources and for the further development of knowledge and ideas.

9.5 INTERNATIONALIZATION VERSUS OTHER GROWTH STRATEGIES

After discussing the reasons for internationalization, it is now time to pay attention to the question: should a service provider really internationalize in order to grow? This topic will also be discussed within the framework of relationship marketing.

STARTING TO INTERNATIONALIZE

Having said so much about the benefits, risks, opportunities and pitfalls of internationalization in services, it will be no surprise that service providers should not start their activities abroad prematurely. The sequence according to which a firm develops a – growth – strategy, usually is a function of:[24]

1. the expected value of profitability, measured by the return on investment of each strategy; and
2. the risk or expected variation in profitability.

It is particularly the downside risk of a strategy that is indicated here. It is linked to three different growth strategies. The impact of five risk areas (finance, market and competition, compatibility of marketing programs, technical requirements and government regulations) should be estimated for each of three possible growth strategies. These strategies are:

1. developing new services;
2. entering out-of-country markets; and
3. concentric diversification.

Concentric diversification and service development bear approximately the same risk. Out-of-country market expansion is risky.

financial considerations

Service providers run a lot of risks regarding their financial considerations. First, the risk that the reimbursement period for foreign service operations is long. The service provider must go abroad personally in most cases and face the customer (the "moments of truth" in the service encounter in a foreign country). Second, the exposure to currency fluctuations is great for service marketeers because of price inflexibility and the inability to transfer easily the site of production. As they have to face the customer from day one, the service firm has high personnel requirements. Expatriate management and, particularly in the start-up phase, specialists from abroad will be needed to succeed in the foreign market place. Freshly hired local staff need to be trained in procedures, systems and become acquainted with the corporate culture of their new firm. Quality control is also a tricky affair. In internationalization, the main message is always: think before you start and think again. Alternative ways approaching growth strategies probably involve less risks. Therefore, it may be wise to have a look at relationship marketing from an international perspective as well.

INTERNATIONALIZATION AND RELATIONSHIP MARKETING

Relationship marketing is not a universal model suited for uniform global application: "Formulations of relationship marketing based on contemporary western interpretations may fail if transplanted to overseas countries, where the cultural and economic environments differ significantly from the country for which a relationship marketing policy was originally formulated." [25] Therefore, the first requirement is to look at the cultural distances as revealed in Figure 4-1: which countries are culturally close to one another and which not? Next, it is necessary to consider the state of economic and social development of a country as factors impacting on the relationship between buyers and sellers.

social aspects of exchange

In some cultures, social aspects of exchange form a relatively important part of the whole exchange process. Service providers trying to attract new business on the basis of stressing the tangible benefits of services or creating financial (and not social) bonds may therefore fail in such cultures. Then, relationship marketing strategies should emphasize the honor of maintaining long term relationships with a trusted supplier.

relational exchange

Relational exchange occurs within a framework of rules and norms. National governance systems can be placed, for instance, on a continuum ranging from predominantly legally based to predominantly morally based. A service firm developing international relations should understand very well the basis of buyer-seller governance in overseas markets. In many societies (especially in what westerners call the Far East) shared ethical values form the dominant governance mechanism for relational exchange. There is, for example, an assumption in many Far East cultures that business partners will be faithful in delivering their part of the bargain.

governance mechanism for relational exchange

In less developed countries, the infrastructure and technology may present a constraint on the extent to which relationship marketing can be developed. This applies especially when computer technology is involved in keeping track of customers. Moreover, in many countries in the so-called "developed world" loyalty programs may be regarded with suspicion by regulatory authorities as a device for limiting competition.

importance of relationship marketing

The importance of relationship marketing in the international busines to business service industry could be explained by a number of factors. First of all, clients of these professional service firms are becoming more knowledgeable, sophisticated and discriminating in their choice of supplier firms. Second, such professional service firms are facing increased competition from peer professionals, "para-professionals" and "do-it-yourself" "professionals". Both factors explain partly why it is getting more difficult to keep current customers. Developing excellent relationships with current customers and providing them with excellent service will give a service provider added value over competitors. Third, international business customers will increasingly expect their service suppliers to be able to follow them internationally

stable quality all over the world

and provide stable quality all over the world. If the service firm chooses to follow them (thereby adopting a client follower strategy), a relationship with the client develops more or less automatically. Still, maintaining the relationship will require considerable investments in, and adaptations of, resources and efforts. Showing real

commitment

commitment to the customers and to the development of relationships are important factors for success. Although relationship marketing adds value to the service, it is not a substitute for having a strong up-to-date core service.[26]

If the service firm chooses not to follow their present clients internationally, this may even be detrimental to keeping the relationship locally when the client wishes to be served everywhere by the same service provider. This is a trend that can be seen, for instance, in the advertising industry, the auditing industry and in the insurance brokerage industry these days.

So, in developing international relationships in general and applying relationship marketing in particular, the social, economic, political, cultural, and technological environment of the host country must be considered, and the exchange values of foreign markets should be examined carefully. It is dangerous to apply a strategy of

management by assumption

"management by assumption" implying that one presumes to know what will be normal practice in other countries (without proper verification).[27] The attitude and willingness towards creating and the acceptance of financial, social or structural bonds may therefore differ in various societies. These will be established quite automatically in the more collectivistic societies, while a lot of effort must be put in creating loyalty programs, as is done in Western Europe and North America these days (the more individualistic societies). Personal relationships between front office personnel or account managers and the clients will be very important here. All this will co-determine the challenges to develop, maintain and terminate relationships between customers and service providers.[28]

SOME OTHER INTERNATIONALIZATION STRATEGIES

beating the clock

The concept of relationship marketing may set the framework for other strategies to be defined. Service firms can also create relationships with their clients in various countries when they apply a multi country strategy or follow their customers to those countries. Beating the clock can also be used to that end. This is a strategy in which competitive advantages can be gained owing to the fact that one can bypass the constraints of the clock and the constraints of domestic time zones, including time-based domestic work rules and regulations. Then, a 24 hour service can be provided.

client following

The most simple distinction that can be made is between "client following" and "market seeking".[29] The "client following" motive means that the service firm enters foreign markets primarily to serve the foreign subsidiaries of their domestic clients. Most international brokers and auditing firms use such a strategy. Sometimes, they are forced to follow these clients, not only because of new business in a foreign country but also because of not losing the existing business in the home country.[30] The "market seeking" motive refers to the case where a service firm enters foreign markets primarily to serve new foreign customers.

market seeking

soft service firms

Next, two kinds of service firms can be distinguished. Soft service firms are those service providers for which it is impossible to decouple production and consumption. Then, the physical presence of both parties during the service encounter is necessary. In hard service firms, it is indeed possible to separate production and consumption. Soft service firms cannot export, whereas hard service firms can. This again is based on the location bound character of services.[31]

hard service firms

client following motive fits into the ideas of relationship marketing

We would like to add that a client following motive fits into the ideas of relationship marketing; building and maintaining the relationship in the home market as well as abroad. Of course, one can also build relationships with foreign firms in a market seeking strategy.

9.6 BARRIERS TO ENTRY

Any organization that intends to start activities in a foreign country (also in the service industry) has to beat the obstacles that might hinder them to easily enter that market. Thus, part of the decision "to go international" is to investigate these obstacles and see how these can be met in a creative way.[32]

*Service
practice
9-6
Overcoming
barriers to
entry in the
past*

When, centuries ago, the Spanish, Portugese, English and Dutch set up their international trade routes, they had many barriers to overcome. These hindrances included:

* access to capital to finance the sailing ships;
* scurvy amongst the crew during their long trips;
* hostility of foreign nations;
* cultural differences;
* access to buyers and sellers of a sufficient size, etc.

In those times, solutions were found to overcome these barriers.

The Portugese married into foreign communities to overcome cultural barriers and to forge long lasting relationships.

The Dutch merchants, in close harmony with their monarchy, founded the "Vereenigde Oost Indische Compagnie" (VOC). Via this corporation, traders obtained economies of scale and scope. The trade corporation promised access to capital and safeguarding of the distribution channels, something that was difficult for individual merchants to acquire. Even in inland oriented and places almost inaccessible to foreigners, like Japan, the VOC was allowed to operate.

The English had their own ways of levelling the barriers of entry. A famous one was to export their sports. By doing so, they were able to export part of their values and customs as well. As a result, cultural barriers between the two parties decreased.

barriers to entry

The barriers to entry, or the challenges to be met in internationalizing the business, are many and well known from the literature on international management or international marketing. Therefore, we will mention them briefly and elaborate on only a few of them. These include at the industry level: economies of scale; economies of scope; experience effects; service differentiation; capital requirements; technological requirements; switching cost; access to distribution channels; cost disadvantages independent of scale; and competitive intensity. Some general international barriers include issues like: tariff barriers; cultural hindrances; other non-tariff barriers; and internal company resistance to go abroad.

decreasing unit costs

Many of these barriers are indeed barriers when a firm does not possess opportunities to exploit them. Decreasing unit costs per service is very important in the international hotel business, for instance. Having no experience in doing business in other countries means that knowledge about this way of operating is lacking. This may even come to the fore when lacking knowledge about which technologies can be used. Moreover, issues like paying expatriates and well skilled locals higher salaries to attract them, investing in language training programs, high rents for offices and

cost disadvantages

apartments, etc. may be other cost disadvantages to be met.

service differentiation

Service differentiation (whether perceived or actual) is an important means local firms can use to build relationships with their customers and clients. Then, new

switching costs

entrants have to spend a lot of resources to overcome this obstacle. This argument is in line with the issue of switching cost already mentioned. Buyers of the service of the new entrant, have to face switching costs when they leave their "old service provider". Changing from an established supplier to a new one may require the buyer to train staff, purchase new equipment, hire technical help, change procedures and ways of working, etc. Seemingly unimportant issues may have large consequences here. Think of changing banks, leading business clients to printing new letters and invoices with the new bank account. In essence, it means the new customer must be convinced that the established service provider cannot deliver the service (now or in the near future) as promised by the new service provider.

distribution channels

Being excluded from established distribution channels may be a major threat to foreign companies. Here again, creativity may solve the problem. A large insurance company operating in many countries around the world had problems in building a traditional network of intermediaries in Japan. To overcome this barrier, the company decided to use gas stations as its distribution channel to sell standard policies. In Japan, gas stations offer an extensive range of products and services. That is why this distribution channel was appropriate. Moreover, gas stations in Japan are typically known for their high level of personal service, which fits the insurance business.

cultural hindrances

Cultural hindrances are usually mentioned as one of the important barriers to entry. We certainly will not underestimate the relevance of this argument. In Chapter Four, we showed which cultures look alike which are very different and in what way. Still, the impact of cultural differences should not be overestimated. The adaptation of marketing strategies to national or local cultures is also possible.[33] The country-of-origin bias may work out in a positive as well as in a negative way (see also Chapter Four).

tariff barriers, non-tariff barriers

Tariff barriers are widespread and effective ways to block newcomers. Also, non-tariff barriers like licences, legislation, taxation, no access to public procurement and not being allowed to bid for public contracts and competition from the public sector, may exist for protecting home industries.

internal resistance to go international

Finally, we would like to mention the internal resistance to go international as a barrier to entry. It may be that some stakeholders in the company show resistance to go international and are not willing to invest time and/or money in foreign activities. For instance, shareholders may find internationalization not an attractive option for growth as it would require long term commitment, low short term revenues and decreasing return on equity. Such a "negative" way of thinking, combined with a corporate culture of avoiding risks as much as possible, is not really in line with the essence of a market oriented firm and, it may block internationalization efforts.

After discussing these barriers to entry (Service practice 9-7), they may be taken into account when selecting the proper entry mode.

In many professional service firms, like lawyers, one finds professionals somewhat individualistic and even ecclectic in their work. Accordingly, managing these often large, professional bureaucracies is difficult. Organizing and managing these individual lawyers is exacerbated by geographical spread and cultural differences. Furthermore, many clients, even large institutional clients, still relate to their individual lawyers and the service rendered is still very personally bound.

Nicolas Ulmer, former partner in Jones, Day and Reaves & Pogue, a leading international legal firm, found this particularly true in Europe. Based on his experience, he argues some client resistance to internationalize is also present when this means specialization will take place (when you have to deal with different people). However, this resistance seems to diminish nowadays.[34]

9.7 SELECTING AN ENTRY MODE

how to enter foreign markets

The previous sections indicated a wide variety of topics to be taken into account when a service organization intends to internationalize its activities. When the analysis of all these topics has indicated the company really should go international, it is necessary to decide on how to enter foreign markets. These entry modes will be discussed in this section. Since many of them are well known from the literature on international management and international marketing, we will discuss the basics here. More attention will be given to its application to services as well as to the process of selecting an entry mode.

ENTRY MODES

getting physical access

Firms planning to serve and actually servicing foreign markets may develop and implement three generic strategies to do so. They all are aimed at getting physical access to the new territory and to serve customers. They are exporting licensing of (pure) franchising and foreign direct investment.

exporting

The entry mode of exporting implies exporting services through own or independent intermediaries. One may think of using the export department (direct exports) versus agents, distributors, trading companies, etc. (indirect exports).

licensing and franchising, foreign direct investment

Licensing and franchising are contractual modes to enter another country; other service providers are allowed to offer the service in that country in ways as described in the contract. Foreign direct investment includes many options like: a representative (office); a sales office; capital investment (only); joint-venture(s); starting a company owned distribution channel with own branches, shops or stores (typically used by banks and retailers). These are often subsidiaries (majority stake or fully owned); mergers; and acquisitions.

integrated entry modes, non-integrated entry modes

Entry modes, such as direct-to-customer channels, "overseas" sales subsidiaries, foreign production modes such as branches, offices and fully owned subsidiaries, represent integrated entry modes. Non-integrated entry modes are exporting through intermediaries, contractual transfers and joint ventures. Generally speaking, integrated modes of entry require a greater commitment of resources and carry larger risk, but are also characterized by larger degrees of control, physical presence, physical intimacy and, hopefully, higher returns.[35] So, in terms of service quality, the integrated modes of entry offer more and better opportunities for quality control and assuring clients excellent quality at all times (i.e. the reliability dimension). The same advantage holds for assuring the implementation of the company's desired market orientation.

dynamics

However, since we have seen that the physical presence is not always necessary during the service encounter, the arguments given may change in particular service circumstances. The dynamics in service industries may affect the internationalization mode. What had been a proper entry mode at one time, may be out-dated by another.

THE PROCESS OF SELECTING AN ENTRY MODE

location of the servuction process

In the process of developing foreign market servicing strategies and in making a decision about the appropriate entry mode, or changing in between, several variables are relevant.[36] These variables refer to the basic location of the servuction process. So:

1. distinguishing between entry modes where the production is location bound to the home country (exporting, licensing and franchising) versus the other entry modes where production takes place in the host country;

and, next, assessing these entry modes in terms of:

2. degree of experience, knowledge, desired control and perceived risk;
3. situational influences, both internal and external, impacting the entry mode at the start and the switch in operations later; and
4. availability of resources.

This all influences the:

5. choice of operation mode as a process.

servicescape

resource based industries

As indicated before, the actual physical surroundings, the servicescape, is an important issue to take into account when internationalizing services. Some service providers have little choice. They have to establish themselves in the foreign market right from the start. In particular resource based industries, such as hotels, restaurants and hospitals, belong to this category. Also, many professional services should be based on foreign soil. They include auditing, generic law firms and advertising. In this respect, an important distinction between three kinds of services can be made: people-processing services, possession-processing services and information-based services.[37]

people-processing services

People-processing services involve tangible actions to customers and require that customers themselves are present during the service encounter. For, they themselves are part of the servuction process and a high degree of contact with front office personnel is needed. Consequently, the service provider has to maintain a local geographic presence in order to deliver the service. Possession-processing services involve tangible actions to physical objects to improve their value to the customer.

possession-processing services

Consequently, the object is part of the servuction process, customers are not necessarily (unless they want to be present to see whether it is all done the right way, that service providers are not cheating the customer, etc.). Information-based services encompass collecting, manipulating, interpreting and transmitting data to create value. Customer participation in the servuction process is often reduced to a minimum. Consequently, the local requirements of the service provider will be very limited, often only a computer terminal, telephone or fax is enough when such service firms start foreign operations.

information-based services

knowledge/ information-based services

Another relevant classification influencing the mode of entry is the knowledge/ information-based services opposed to resource-based services. Again, the technology component will play an important role in answering the question – which entry-mode should a service firm choose overseas? We can easily imagine that services with a mixture of tangibles and non-tangibles (such as software and professional information services, i.e. Reuters, Bloomberg, Dunn & Bradstreet, Moody's and compact disks containing easily accessible information on publications) may be exported.

Exporting, licensing and franchising also differ from the various forms of foreign direct investment in that the necessary degree of experience, knowledge and risk are generally lower than with foreign direct investment. In its most simple form, exporting can be distinguished from the other two groups of entry modes by the "location" effect.[38] For, with exports, the bulk of value adding activities takes place in the home country, whilst in the other two modes all, or a high proportion of, the value adding activities are transferred to the host country markets by the internationalizing firm. Similarly, both in licensing, franchising and in the various forms of foreign direct investment, the activities are performed by firms external to the firm internationalizing. As a result, these entry modes can also be distinguished from exporting by the internalization effect. In exporting, such activities are "internalized" and remain with the initiating firm. However, depending on the juridical forms employed, one could also say that in some forms of foreign direct investment (like strategic alliances or majority stakes in joint-ventures), the activities still take place within the (holding) company. Broadly speaking then, the location and internalization effects separate the four generic forms of market servicing (see Figure 9-4).

internalization effect

The greater the knowledge of and experience in a foreign market, the more confident a firm tends to be when making real commitments to the activities abroad. It also appears that such firms are more confident about the risks they take in starting this "adventure". Relevant knowledge and experience should provide important feedback in the process. One of the key issues in the process of selecting the optimal entry-mode, then, is how to obtain management control. As many services are dependent

management control

Figure 9-4
The location and
internationalization
effect

Internationalization effect

Market servicing=f(X,L,F,FDI)

Location effect

where X =exporting

L =licensing

F =franchising

FDI=foreign direct investment

Source: based on Buckley, Pass and Prescott, 1992a, with adaptation from the present authors.

full ownership

on the quality of people rendering the service, the most obvious way to control this process is by full ownership. Also, full ownership will facilitate the control of many of the risks inherent in servicing foreign markets. Though full ownership is often attractive from many points of view, not the least being that rendering services is still a "people's business", in many instances local circumstances, entry barriers or even the perception of country risk, will lead to a different approach of exercising management control. For example, regulation may require the participation of local partners, as majority or minority owners. Although management control may be high on the list of requirements of the foreign firm, the market may seem so promising that a joint-venture is the only solution. In these cases, "management contracts" and an option of "first refusal" (if one of the other partners wants to sell their stake in the

effective control

venture) may serve to obtain effective control. Sometimes unexpected situations occur like, a sudden request to become a partner in an international service activity or the opening up of borders. Then, service firms have to act quickly, but should still go through the issues and steps mentioned here. The opening-up of Central and Eastern Europe was such an unexpected event. Service firms wanting to benefit from this one-off opportunity had to move quickly with limited resources and to choose practical entry routes such as joint-ventures even if they were not fully agreeable to the company's internationalization policy. Others are left with a choice to either opt for small-scale subsidiaries which will be sometimes of lower quality level at the start than under normal foreign market conditions, or to leave the "first mover" advantages to the competition.

availability of
resources

One of the eminent influencers in the selection of an entry strategy is the availability of resources. Suppose a firm has the ambition to conquer the whole world with its unique service concept, there is a great management commitment and a focussed internationalization strategy preferring full control, there are even clear market opportunities and the competition intensity is small; even then the availability of

financial and human
resources

resources will determine largely how far the company can jump. Financial and human resources are among the most quoted constraints to establish a fully owned subsidiary. Concessions to the most ideal way of operation may then lead to practical choices such as exporting, licensing, franchising or joint-ventures. Licensing or, to a lesser extent, franchising may be attractive as it enables a firm (particularly the ones constrained by a shortage of management and capital resources) to gain rapid market penetration. Because it does not involve direct entry into the market, it avoids head-on competition with local suppliers. On the other hand, the royalties obtained may represent a poor result on an innovative process or service, with the ultimate danger that the technology, concept or service may be "captured" and developed further by competitors, leading to the elimination of the firm's initial competitive advantage.[39] In the case of franchising, this danger is less present but the successful expansion of the franchise formula in a foreign market may still need a lot of management attention as well as finance. Both licensing and franchising require that the company possesses an identifiable technology, a rather unique service delivering process, special knowledge or a service formula which can be packaged in such a way that it becomes saleable.

(top) management commitment

Talking about resources means real (top) management commitment to the internationalization activities and the allocation of financial and other resources. This may differ between firms implementing a market seeking and a client follower strategy.

Service practice 9-10 Commitment to existing and new clients differs!

A sample of US international service firms was used to test the hypotheses that, on average, client following strategies are associated with higher levels of involvement in that market than market seeking entries.[40] The level of involvement is defined as the amount of managerial and financial resources specifically committed to a certain market. The researchers expected that a firm following its current domestic clients abroad is more knowledgeable regarding its market than a firm entering a foreign market to serve foreign customers.

The study showed that service firms exhibit greater involvement in choosing entry modes when following their existing clients than when serving new customers. Market seeking entries showed a far stronger inclination to team up with external entities than firms who were client following. The study finally showed that these variations between client followers and market seekers could be attributed, with reasonable confidence, to differences in market knowledge (an important issue which we discussed earlier).

process oriented approach

One way of deciding about the specific market entry mode and the shifts between modes is the process oriented approach. The choice of operation is reasoned as a process rather than as the outcome of separate factors or a combination of these. Behavioral factors are here the main explanation of the internationalization. In analyzing many patterns of internationalization in services, the most consistent pattern found, is one of "evolution" rather than "revolution" – i.e. from low commitment to high-commitment gradually over time[41]. However, recent evidence shows that firms are not only leapfrogging some steps in such an evolutionary process, but also speeding up the whole process.

SOME ADDITIONAL REMARKS

Once a company has decided to start its own operations abroad, it is self evident that it has to cope with far more issues than just marketing. To give the reader an idea about which topics a bank has to deal with, while establishing itself in one foreign market, we have produced a "basis" for a more detailed checklist in Table 9-3.

consistency in strategy

Consistency in strategy is always an important issue. However, this does not mean that the service firm has always to adopt the same entry strategy in every country. This will depend on all the topics discussed before leading to different contingencies for entry into every country.

Service practice 9-11 Different entry modes within one firm

A UK study revealed how banks, building societies and insurance companies go abroad. It appeared a wide variety of reasons for going abroad were at stake. Moreover, it appeared that one of the UK insurance companies had a wholly-owned subsidiary in France, a joint-venture and a branch in Germany, a wholly owned subsidiary for general insurances plus a joint-venture for life insurances in Italy and a branch in Spain.[42]

Analyzing the entry modes IKEA used, it appears that wholly-owned stores are present in culturally and geographically proximate countries, whereas franchising is quite dominant in culturally and geographically distant countries.[43]

Recent research among small and medium sized service firms in Australia shows that the selection of an appropriate operation mode designed to enhance and protect the competitiveness of the firm is dependent on an amalgam of specific factors (e.g. the nature and "uniqueness" of the firm's competitive advantage and resource availability), industry-specific factors in target markets (e.g. the level of market concentration and the extent of barriers to entry, or effective entry) and location/country-specific factors (e.g. the extent to which products/services need to be adapted to meet local requirements, host governments policies on tariffs, subsidies, etc.).

success of internationalization

The success of internationalization is attributed greatly to the commitment and vision of one or more executives. So, managers considering internationalization must realize that this seems to be a pre-requisite for successful foreign market entry. Furthermore, it is abundantly clear that services in their international context are far from being homogeneous.[44]

four different types of service firms in international markets

Four different types of service firms in international markets can be found. This classification is based on whether the service provision is location bound or not, and whether standard or customized service packages are delivered. The findings are presented in Figure 9-5. Each cell provides an overview of the organizational profile, the behavioral profile, the attitudes towards internationalization, the entry mode and the international operations profile. The findings are as follows.

TABLE 9-3 *A basis for a bank branch development checklist in a foreign market**

1. Identify:
   - demographic, regulatory, economical, technological, social (DRETS) factors in general view of the potential establishment
   - potential customers/target group
   - range of products offered (in line with local regulations/license restrictions)
   - competitors

   Based on market research (total market, market % to be obtained, present performance of comparable units) an estimate/target can be made with respect to volume and kinds of transactions/products.

2. Based on the outcome of 1. a pessimistic and an optimistic scenario could be made with respect to the projected development. The scenario selected finally (pessimistic, realistic or optimistic) should be the starting point for commercial, organizational, operational and logistical requirements.

   All commercial risks should be covered (as much as possible) by means of structural, precedural and risk control measures. The maximum investment risk can be estimated by means of a worst case scenario.

3. Commercial aspects
   - product descriptions (purpose and nature), marketing strategy, pricing, etc.
   - authorizations/segregation of duties
   - install limits (credits to customers, credits to banks, positions in foreign country, etc.)
   - identify credit authorities
   - guidelines with respect to selecting correspondent banks
   - identify corporate responsibility guidelines (+ influence on forms and contracts)
   - codes of conduct (money laundering, private business restrictions, etc.)

4. Organizational aspects
   - identify number of commercial staff, management, back-office functions and support functions. Develop structure taking into consideration: optional support of business functions, segregation of duties, no conflicts of interest, efficiency aspects, etc.
   - signing authorities (+ recording of delegated authorities)
   - staff recruitment procedures/aspects (local staff/expatriates)
   - job descriptions
   - training of staff (incl. risk management)
   - segregation of responsibilities between branch(es) and Head Office
   - communication of address, etc.

5. Operational aspects
   - tax rules/responsibilities
   - local rules/regulations regarding commercial activities/reporting requirements
   - audit rules/regulations
   - reporting requirements (lay out/frequency/subject) to Head Office/Local Central Bank/Central Bank in home country
   - accounting system/procedures (incl. accounting structure/reconciliation rules, etc.)
   - capital requirements
   - remittance of profits/dividends
   - registration guidelines for swift/telex/fax/messages

6. Logistical aspects
   - premises (office purchase/rent, location, conditions of the contract)
   - office lay out
   - staff housing/remuneration
   - safety aspects
   - office equipment (incl. communication equipment)
   - EDP systems
   - office supplies

The above-mentioned items are the basis for a more comprehensive checklist

*The authors gratefully acknowledge W.F. Hogewoning (ABN/Amro Bank) for providing the first draft of this check-list

value added customized services

Value added customized services, such as executive search, market research, transportation, finance, insurance and IT, have the most international profile. Their clients often urge them to follow them in foreign markets or are tempted by unsolicited orders from abroad. They perceive high risks and high profitability in the foreign markets.

location-free professional services and location bound customized services

Low management commitment to internationalization was found in companies offering location-free professional services and location bound customized services such as engineering. Government regulation in Asia often still prevents these companies establishing their own subsidiaries. Joint ventures are difficult to arrange since local partners are hard to find.

direct representation

Direct representation via own sales representatives is the leading mode in cells 1, 3 and 4. As one architectural and property development firm with offices in Auckland (New Zealand), Jakarta (Indonesia), Hong Kong and Port Moresby (Papua New Guinea) said: "Personal contact with the client is crucial in this business."

services bundled with goods

Both categories of service providers where services are typically bundled with goods (Hilton Hotels and recording companies) choose mainly a franchise, licensing or management arrangement for delivery and distribution of their services overseas. Their main motivation to internationalize was market seeking and the vision and commitment of top management.

Well-established service firms, such as international banks, often have a preference for wholly or majority owned subsidiaries. They want to exercise management control, e.g. in order to steer the credit process. In markets with a high political or country risk, these institutions may begin by choosing a lower investment, e.g. by means of a majority owned joint-venture bank. Many professional firms, including lawyers and auditors, seem to have a preference for partnerships with established colleagues in mature markets. In fast developing countries, besides partnerships, greenfields are often a logical choice. For, then the professional firm would only require market share of local firms and has to invest heavily in people by means of hiring, remuneration, training and development. In any case, it has to introduce its own procedures and service standards in the foreign market.

Foreign direct investment may be expensive and risky in the long term. For technology-based or highly specialized business-to-business services it is often the only way to penetrate successfully in the foreign market on the long term.

Reality seems even more complex than existing theory as many entry strategies and shifts between modes seem to be situation and firm specific.

Figure 9-5
A typology of service firms in international markets

High

Low

Degree of Tangibility

Pure Services

Services Bundled with Goods

Cell 1
Location-Free Professional Services

Typical Firms: Executive recruitment, Market research, Environmental science consulting, Transportation, Finance and Insurance, Information technology, Product design services.

Organizational Profile:
• Degree of customization: Firm Size: Small (median size = 25 employees). Foreign ownership 14%

Behavioral Profile:
• Moderate risk perceptions regarding internationalization (3.7); Preparedness to invest in foreign market (3.6) and competitive intensity in foreign market (3.6) is not as much of a hindrance to internationalization: Modest managerial commitment to internationalization (3.2); Client "chasing" (3.1) and unsolicited orders (2.6) are only moderate motivators to internationalize.

Attitudes to Internationalization:
• Perceives moderate benefits to internationalization (3.6); Perceive low costs (3.0) or internationalizing; Considers profitability in internationalizing equivalent to domestic market (3.0)

Entry Mode Profiles:
• Direct representation 61%; Agency relationships 21%

International Operations Profile:
• Low international business intensity: International business as % of sales =21%; High international performance (4.3): Moderate satisfaction with international performance (3.9): High propensity to continue in international markets (4.5)

Cell 2
Location-Bound Customized Projects

Typical Firms: Project management, Engineering consulting, Management consulting, Human Resource Development consulting, larger Market Research firms, Legal Services.

Organizational Profile:
• Degree of customization: High: Firm size Largest in sample (median size = 160 employees): Foreign ownership 9%.

Behavioral Profile:
• High risk perceptions regarding internationalization (4.1): Preparedness to invest (3.1) and competitive intensity in foreign markets (3.2) hindering internationalization: Modest managerial commitment to internationalization (3.4): Client "chasing" is moderate motivation to internationalize (2.9): Unsolicited orders are low motivator (2.3).

Attitudes to Internationalization:
• Perceives moderate benefits to internationalization (3.8): Perceive moderate costs (3.5): Profitability equivalent to domestic market (3.1).

Entry Mode Profiles:
• Direct representation 35%; Local presence (branch) 38%

International Operations Profile:
• Moderate international business intensity: International business as % of sales-25%: High international performance (4.2): Moderate satisfaction with international performance (3.9): Very high propensity to continue in international markets (4.6).

Cell 3
Standardized Service Packages

Typical Firms: Software development, Installation/testing of new hardware/equipment. Development of distance education courses. Compact disks

Organizational Profile:
• Degree of customization: Low, Firm size: Small (median = 40 employees). Foreign ownership 13%

Behavioral Profile:
• Moderate risk perceptions regarding internationalization (3.4): Preparedness to invest (3.5) and competitive intensity in foreign markets (3.7) is not as much of a hindrance: Modest managerial commitment to internationalization (3.2): Client "chasing" provides only low motivation (2.3): Unsolicited orders provide moderate motivation (2.8)

Attitudes to Internationalization:
• Perceive moderate benefits to internationalization (3.6); Perceive low costs (3.0): Profitability equivalent to domestic market (3.0).

Entry Mode Profiles:
• Direct representation 46%; Local presence 13%: Agency relationship 21%: Franchising, Licensing, Management Agreements 13%

International Operations Profile:
• Low international business intensity: International business as % of sales = 22%: Moderate international performance (3.9): Moderate satisfaction with international performance (3.9): High propensity to continue in international markets (4.3)

Cell 4
Value-Added Customized Services

Typical Firms: On-site training, Computer hardware consulting, Facilities management, Accommodation services, Catering, Software training and support.

Organizational Profile:
• Degree of customization: High (3.9): Firm size: Medium (median = 55 employees): Highest incidence of foreign ownership 21%.

Behavioral Profile:
• High risk perceptions regarding internationalization (3.9): Preparedness to invest (3.1) and competitive intensity in overseas markets (3.3) are barriers to internationalization. High management commitment to internationalization (3.9): Client "chasing" (2.8) and unsolicited orders (2.9) are moderate motivators to internationalization

Attitudes to Internationalization:
• Very high perceived benefits in internationalization (4.3): Perceive moderate costs (3.5): High profitability relative to domestic markets (3.6).

Entry Mode Profiles:
• Direct representation 37%; Local presence (branch) 26%: Agency relationship 22%: Franchising, Licensing, Management Agreements 12%

International Operations Profile:
• Moderate international business intensity: International business as % of sales = 36%: Very high international performance (4.6): High satisfaction with international performance (4.1): Very high propensity to continue in international markets (4.8).

Sources: (See table in text) Note: Adapted from VanderMerwe and Chadwick (1989)

9.8 STANDARDIZATION OR ADAPTATION?

standardization

The standardization-adaptation issue is a critical topic in the whole literature on international marketing and international management. It is not yet resolved. The major pro's of standardization are: cost savings; consistency for customers (if they so wish); improved planning and control; and exploiting good ideas on a world wide basis.

differentiation
adaptation

However, approaches found to be effective in one market need not be effective in other markets, by definition. Differentiation per country is the basic idea behind the adaptation argument. The major pro's of adaptation are related to overcoming barriers to entry: consumption patterns; physical environment (e.g. climate); stage of economic development; industry conditions; competitive practices; marketing institutions and distribution channels; legal restrictions; technical requirements; and cultural factors.

The obstacles to standardization are summarized in Table 9-4.

converging trend

From this discussion, the reader may get the impression that it is hard to standardize in international service businesses and that the only thing that counts is customization. However, we think there is a converging trend.[45] Customization, traditionally achieved through interaction with people, and especially vis-à-vis interaction, can now also be achieved with remote communication. For instance, in service industries like computer services, software and shopping, telephone and electronic links are rapidly growing as an addition to or replacement of more conventional ways of delivering services. Call-centers, home-shopping, electronic banking and direct-banking are forms which are all quite new and growing. It also implies that international service firms are now able to operate parallel with various modes in different countries, and even within one particular country. The growing knowledge of combining the three relevant production factors in services, namely human capital, physical capital and information technology, offers many opportunities to combine standardization and customization.

combine
standardization and
customization

9.9 SERVICE QUALITY IN AN INTERNATIONAL CONTEXT

service quality in
different cultures

When service firms are internationalizing, they will be confronted with different beliefs about the meaning of service quality in different cultures which depend on the servuction processes in different cultures.[46] Such a process consists of three sets of resources:

- customer resources and their style of participation in the service encounter;
- contact resources (contact persons of the service provider and their style of delivering the service); and
- physical resources.

TABLE 9-4 Obstacles to standardization in international marketing strategies

Factors limiting standardization	Elements of marketing program				
	Product design	Pricing	Distribution	Sales force	Advertising & promotion: branding & packaging
Market characteristics Physical environment	Climate Product use conditions		Customer mobility	Dispersion of customers	Access to media Climate
Stage of economic and industrial development	Income levels Labor costs in relation to capital costs	Income levels	Consumer shopping patterns	Wage levels, availability of manpower	Needs for convenience rather than economy Purchase quantities
Cultural factors	"Custom and tradition" Attitudes toward foreign goods	Attitudes toward bargaining	Consumer shopping patterns	Attitudes toward selling	Language, literacy Symbolism
Industry conditions Stage of product life cycle in each market	Extent of product differentiation	Elasticity of demand	Availability of outlets Desirability of private brands	Need for missionary sales effort	Awareness, experience with products
Competition	Quality levels	Local costs Prices of substitutes	Competitors' control of outlets	Competitors' sales forces	Competitive expenditures, messages
Marketing institutions Distributive system	Availability of outlets	Prevailing margins	Number and variety of outlets available Ability to "force" distribution	Number size, dispersion of outlets	Extent of self-service
Advertising media and agencies				Effectiveness of advertising, need for substitutes	Media availability, costs, overlaps
Legal restrictions	Product standards Patent laws Tariffs and taxes	Tariffs and taxes Antitrust laws Resale price maintenance	Restrictions on product lines Resale price maintenance	General employment restrictions Specific restrictions on selling	Specific restrictions on messages, costs Trademark laws

Source: Robert Buzzel, "Can you standardize multinational marketing?", HBR. Nov. 1968. pp102-113.

participation style of the customer, service style of the company employees

The interaction between the first two sets of resources is at stake here. So, it hinges upon the participation style of the customer and the service style of the company employees. There should be a link between these two styles, within the framework of the physical resources. Four dimensions can be used in describing and explaining differences in these service styles. These are:

1. empathetic versus non-empathetic deals with the degree of empathy shown by service providers in their approach to the customer;
2. efficient versus non-efficient refers to the efficiency of the service production process as seen from the customer's point of view;
3. remote versus close indicates how customers perceive and assess service employees; and
4. attentive versus non-attentive refers to the speed with which contact employees react to the customer's needs.

Oriental Service Style

American Service Style
European Service Style

These dimensions can be used to explain three different and one basic service styles (= the styles performed by the employees). The Oriental Service Style (OSS) will be practised in the Far East, Japan and India; its nature is empathetic and remote. The American Service Style (ASS) is extremely close and friendly; contact persons try to be attentive and friendly toward customers. The European Service Style (ESS) is made up of many sub-styles because Europe does not have a common culture. In general, the European style is not as efficient as the American one and not as attentive as the Oriental one. In the Nordic countries, for instance, remoteness is more clearly present than in the south. Service firms going abroad should take these cultural differences into account and might change their strategies and scripts in the service encounter.

These service styles can be related to the cultural maps of the world as presented in Chapter Four. Countries in the Far East score, in general, quite high on masculinity, power distance and collectivism which has some resemblance to being empathetic but remote. North America belongs to a cluster of countries scoring high on individualism, masculinity, uncertainty avoidance and short term orientation; this is reflected in being attentive and friendly, but one always questions whether all attention is really meant and whether one really wants to build relationships. Chapter Four indicated Europe consists of various sub-cultures; the Anglo-German cluster, the Roman-Southern European cluster and the Dutch-Scandinavian cluster; therefore each will have their own service style (see also Service practice 9-1).

Due to the differences in expectations about service quality, benchmarking studies should be carried out in various countries to get a better idea about how the service should be provided for each country and culture.

SUMMARY

An integrated global marketplace has been rapidly unfolding where cultural, political, legal and technological gaps are diminishing, and competition and service development costs are accelerating. Naturally, this puts pressure on international operating service organizations to redefine their marketing approaches by integrating trends, facts and markets into one overall global framework to allow managers to enter markets simultaneously rather than on a country by country basis.

According to Levitt, the global corporation operates with resolute constant, at low relative cost, as if the entire world (or major regions of it) were a single entity; it sells the same things in the same way everywhere. In his view, the global corporation and the multinational are not the same as the latter operates in a number of countries, and adjusts its goods, services and practices in each, at high relative costs. The impact of global competition factors to large service suppliers is immense. If the latter have not yet developed an international marketing strategy, or at least a strategy to counter global competitors in their homeland, the greater is the chance that the competition will simply force them out the market. "Companies that do not adapt to the new global realities will become victims of those that do" wrote Levitt in 1983. The ultimate challenge for enterprises and countries is to keep up with the internationalization. For both companies and governments, the question is how to capitalize on the opportunities that internationalization offers.

Of course, there are still service industries where the competition is dominated by local players but the trend seems to be competing with an inter-national dimension. In many countries and in numerous service industries, local entrepreneurs will meet ever increasing competition from inter-nationals, foreign franchise formats, multinationals and globals during the coming years. In fact, the more fragmented or (state) monopolized a service industry is, the more attractive such a market may become for a service provider with a clear formula plus sufficient scale, scope, experience and resources.

Technical progress in information technology, communications, production and logistics have made it possible to accommodate clients better. International service suppliers are nowadays able to customize services more to local needs and even to individual tastes. This is more evident in most service industries where personal touch, voice-driven information or sophisticated delivery systems can be easily tailored to the needs of the customer. Services, once seen as typically local, labor intensive and low cost activities are now often exportable as a result of changes in technology, deregulation, asset-structure and ambition of managers. Saturated home markets and more intensified competition in many industries force thriving companies to look for new frontiers.

With the changes in the nature of service delivery systems, firms may find themselves changing the existing entry mode, or operating in more than one mode. For managers, it is no longer enough to think of their service business as one business. Around the world, each part of the service may be delivered differently. Combinations of mode can be used by banks or insurance companies, offering highly added value services as merchant banking or captive insurance from a regional service by exporting the advisors, instant insurance from self-dispensing machines and direct banking/insurance or branch-banking through a local subsidiary. As information technology services are, in all three clusters, a new "all-in-one" internationalization mode seems to have emerged. Other authors also stress the influence of the changing technology in the internationalization process of service firms. This new mode will require a new thought process, more flexible organizations and more flexible managers. The role and the control or coordinating functions at head office will change. Linkages between the two and between all branches will become increasingly important. The transfer of knowledge will take place face-to-face and via technology. New managerial formats will be needed to manage a new hybrid-type of global operation in which a geographical separation between front office and back office will become more and more prevailing.

Regarding the issue of standardization or adaptation of the marketing strategy it appears that high cost savings are possible by somehow standardizing, while other arguments are in favor of adaptation to local needs. However, in most cases "glocalization", a certain degree of adoption to local conditions, will be necessary to be successful in the global market.

QUESTIONS

1 What are the globalization and internationalization drivers at macro-level?
2 Which five categories explain the internationalization of service firms at individual business level?
3 How important are, according to you, the ambition and commitment of the top managers to the internationalization process of a service company? Under which circumstances will the commitment show up?
4 Explain why incumbent firms can benefit from a competitive advantage in terms of the human side of the service encounter when entering the German market, as stated in Service practice 9-1? How is this related to the dimensions of service quality discussed in Chapters Five and Six?
5 In this chapter, various entry modes are described. Give a summary of all the characteristics of these entry modes and summarize them into one overall figure or scheme. You should, at a minimum, pay attention to risk; control; physical presence or intimacy; experience, knowledge; and the location of the servuction process. But you will probably find more topics to study.
6 How might information technology affect the internationalization process and entry mode of service firms?
7 Is physical proximity always necessary in service firms acting in various countries?
8 Does excellent service quality mean exactly the same in different countries?
9 In Chapter One, we stated that "caring about people" is an important aspect of a market oriented service firm. Caring about other persons is also an important issue in describing national cultures via the masculinity/femininity dimension. In which countries, then, would market oriented firms probably be over represented given our cultural map of the world? Explain.
10 What is the difference between a client following and a market seeking strategy?

ASSIGNMENTS

1   Describe the barriers of entry an insurance company and bank will experience if they want to establish themselves in a foreign country. Which entry barrier will be of crucial importance in these industries? Are there other modes of operation which you can suggest to these companies?

2   Give your opinion about the suitability of internationalization of (a) a middle sized company in industrial cleaning services into a nearby European country, (b) an American large waste management company into a large European country, and (c) a successful Japanese department store in Malaysia.

   How do you judge, in these cases, the option internationalization versus other strategic alternatives?

3   Write a short essay about the possibilities of standardization or adaptation of marketing approaches for a large international corporate bank.

4   Search for the Christopher Lovelock and George Yip article in your library and analyze it thoroughly and apply the eight globalization drivers to the various types of services distinguished in Chapter Two.

5   In Chapter Two, we mentioned a wide variety of issues to be used in classifying services. Have a thorough look at them and discuss how these distinctions might affect their potential to internationalize. Take into account the location problem and the proper entry mode.

6   Add the insights about relationship marketing discussed in this chapter to what you have learned about relationship marketing in the previous chapters. What can you conclude now in addition to what you already know about this paradigm?

Case: THE INTERNATIONALIZATION OF FINNISH FINANCIAL SERVICE COMPANIES[47]

Banks and insurance companies in Finland

The banking and insurance industries have traditionally been quite oligopolistic in Finland. Both sectors have, however, during the last few years, experienced major rearrangements in the domestic field. As a consequence, in the beginning of 1995, the banking industry consisted of four major players: the commercial banks Kansallis-Osake-Pankki (KOP) and the Union Bank of Finland (SYP) (KOP and SYP merged in 1995), the state-owned Postipankki (PSP) and the cooperative Okobank (OKO). The internationalization process of the Finnish Banking sector has been dominated by the two commercial banks, KOP and SYP. PSP and OKO have also established themselves in a small number of international centers.

In the insurance industry, in turn, five major company groupings have traditionally controlled over 90% of the total market. After the major rearrangements in the industry in Finland, which took place in 1993-94, the market has been dominated by three major company groupings: the Pohjola Insurance Group (POH), the Sampo Insurance Group (SAM), and the Tapiola Insurance Company. Of these three, Pohjola and Sampo are clearly bigger than Tapiola. The two have also been

the major companies in the internationalization process of the Finnish insurance sector.

We will look at the processes of internationalization in terms of "first entries" into various countries by these four Finnish banks and two major insurance companies during the period from 1964 to 1990.[48]

The types of operation taken into consideration were non-majority or majority ownerships, wholly-owned subsidiaries, and the establishing of representative offices.[49]

Data collection and analysis

The data was gathered mainly from the annual reports of the companies and from articles published in business magazines and newspapers. On some occasions, the material was backed up by interviews with managers responsible for the foreign operations of the particular company. This was done in cases in which the information provided by printed material was not felt to be either adequate or reliable (for example, in order to check the correct year of entry to a particular market). The interviews also provided insights into the actual planning and implementation of international operations in the banking and insurance sectors. The number of managers contacted in different companies during the research process totalled 13. All in all, the

study can be argued to have benefited from a multi-method approach.

The analysis is based on rank correlations between the internationalization patterns (i.e. the year of first entry to each country) of each company and the various indicators of customer following and market seeking. Rank correlations will be indicated as Kendall's tau-*b* correlation coefficients.

The internationalization of the domestic customers of Finnish financial service sector companies – that is, Finnish manufacturing companies – will be operationalized with the help of three indicators. The following indicators will be compared to the internationalization patterns of banks and insurance companies in order to measure the customer-following aspect:

- the total amount of Finnish net investments (no portfolio investments included) in various countries in 1965-1990 (foreign direct investments, FDI);
- the total amount of Finnish exports of manufactured goods into various countries in 1964-1990; and
- the indicator of cultural distance between Finland and the target country (see Hofstede in our Chapter Four).

The market-seeking aspect is measured by comparing the internationalization patterns of Finnish banks and insurance companies to one of the following indicators of the situation in the industry:

- the leading international banking countries, in terms of foreign banking activities; or
- the leading international insurance countries, in terms of insurance premiums (instead of "turnover").

Findings

The pattern of internationalization of the Finnish financial-sector companies is presented in Table 1. It shows the historical and geographical side of the internationalization patterns of the four banks and the two insurance companies: when they did enter and what country. In this context, no attention is paid to the mode of operation. Only first entries by the six companies into various markets are reported.

Prior to the 1970s, the international activities of Finnish financial-sector companies were few. In the 1970s, there was a significant increase in the international activities of the two major banks (KOP and SYP) and the two major insurance companies. In the 1980s, the companies continued their international expansion, but the pace of internationalization slowed down slightly.

The high number and the relatively early appearance on the list of certain "exotic" countries (from the Finnish perspective) is an interesting point. Countries such as Singapore, the Cayman Islands, Bahrain, Lebanon,

Bermuda, the Bahamas or the Ivory Coast have not been among the most important countries from the perspective of Finnish Exports of FDI's. Rather, being important international financial centres, they have been targets of Finnish financial sector companies because of their taxation and/or financial incentives and benefits, etc.[50]

Table 2 provides the rankings of the countries entered by Finnish financial service companies in terms of various indicators for customer following and market seeking. As explained earlier, FDI's, exports and cultural distance will be used as indicators for customer following, whereas the rankings of international banking centres and insurance countries will be used as indicators for market seeking.[51]

The internationalization of the two banks (KOP and SYP) can be described as being dominated by market-seeking considerations. The internationalization pattern of the most internationalized insurance company (POH), in turn, is highly correlated with the indicators for customer following (see Table 3).

As regards the other companies, namely PSP, OKO and SAM, it is more difficult to determine which aspect has been dominant in their international activities. PSP and OKO seem to have been slightly more oriented towards customer following, which also distinguishes them from the other two major banks. In the case of SAM, no correlation can be found either with market seeking or customer-following indicators.

In general, it can be observed that the more foreign market entries the company has made, the more clearly its activities have been dominated by either the customer-following aspect (as in the case of POH) or the market-seeking aspect (as in the case of KOP and SYP). The companies with a smaller number of entries (PSP, OKO and SAM) cannot be definitely described either as customer followers or market seekers. Instead, their internationalization can be said to have elements of both customer following and market seeking. Consequently, the results for the most internationalized Finnish financial service companies indicate as strategies in their internationalization customer following for insurance companies and market seeking for banks.

However, it is obvious that all the companies have, to some extent, elements of both customer following and market seeking as regards their internationalization. Moreover, the dominance of either customer following or market seeking may have changed over time.

As to the relationship between the cultural distance and the internationalization pattern of the different companies, an interesting fact may be pointed out. It would appear that cultural distance has not played a significant role in the internationalization of Finnish banks. As regards the insurance companies, on the other hand, the correlation between cultural distance and the pattern of internationalization is significantly higher. This implies that insurance companies have limited their international operations to countries which are culturally closer to Finland than the target countries of Finnish banks.

The high correlations between the internationalization patterns of the four banks on the one hand, and the two insurance companies on the other, indicate quite a strong phenomenon of a company following the internationalization of its competitors. Banks have followed other banks as far as their international operations are concerned, and insurance companies, in turn, have followed each other. The low overall number of unique entries by the companies is also an indication of competitor following.

Despite the evident phenomenon of competitor-following, we cannot find high rank correlations when the internationalization patterns of banks are compared with those of the insurance companies.

As regards the internationalization of insurance companies, it ought to be kept in mind that international reinsurance has long traditions in the industry. International reinsurance activities are, in fact, a form of exporting and importing insurance services and are thus very important from the perspective of the international operations of insurance companies. Consequently, as the exporting of services was not included in our empirical analysis, this may influence the results we get, and thus prove a limitation on our study.

Overall conclusion

The most dominant feature in the internationalization of the Finnish financial-service companies has been the fact that both banks and insurance companies have tended to follow their competitors (banks have followed banks, insurance companies have followed insurance companies) in the process of internationalization. This game of tit for tat means, essentially, that the companies have reacted more strongly to the actions of their competitors than to any other changes in their environment.

QUESTIONS

1 What are the main differences in the internationalization process of Finnish banks and Finnish insurance companies? Explain.

2 What can you conclude, in general, about the characteristics of the countries in which these Finnish firms invested when you analyze the data in Table 2?

3 Explain the following statement: the two commercial banks started their internationalization slightly earlier and also had more entries to various markets than the remaining banks and insurance companies.

4 One of the conclusions from this study is that the most internationalized Finnish insurance companies have applied a strategy of customer following and the most internationalized Finnish banks have applied a strategy of market seeking. Summarize the arguments found for this conclusion and provide an explanation for the differences between these two groups of companies.

5 Cultural closeness seems to play a different role in the internationalization process of Finnish banks and Finnish insurance companies. Elaborate on this conclusion with the data from this case and the cultural maps and data on national cultures, as presented in Chapter Four.

6 From a methodological perspective, what is the impact of the issues discussed in endnotes 47, 48, 49 and 50? How could this affect the conclusions from this study?

TABLE 1 *Internationalization patterns of Finnish Banks and insurance companies 1964-1990*

Year of first entry (includes wholly-owned subsidiaries, majority and non-majority ownerships and representative offices) by

Country	KOP	SYP	PSP	OKO	POH	SAM
Switzerland	_1964_	_1964_	-	1976	1976	-
Brazil	_1966_	1974	-	-	-	-
France	_1967_	1985	1982	-	1975	-
Denmark	-	1985	-	-	1973	_1968_
Great Britain	1971	_1969_	1979	1973	1974	1972
Singapore	_1970_	1978	-	-	1978	1986
Soviet Union	_1972_	1975	1985	1986	-	-
Germany	_1972_	1974	-	-	1976	-
Japan	1981	_1972_	1985	1986	-	-
Netherlands	1976	-	-	-	_1973_	1978
Cayman Islands	1986	_1974_	-	1986	-	-
Hong Kong	1976	_1975_	-	-	1982	-
Bahrain	-	_1975_	-	-	1982	-
Lebanon	-	_1975_	-	-	-	-
Norway	-	1985	-	-	_1975_	-
Canada	-	-	-	-	1978	_1976_
Luxemburg	1977	_1976_	-	1979	1985	-
USA	1979	_1977_	1988	1986	_1977_	_1977_
Mexico	-	1985	-	-	-	_1978_
Australia	_1979_	1984	-	-	-	-
Bermuda	-	-	-	-	_1979_	1980
Italy	-	1984	-	-	_1980_	-
Ivory Coast	_1980_	-	-	-	-	-
Austria	-	-	-	_1981_	-	-
Bahamas	_1983_	1987	-	-	-	-
Sweden	1985	_1984_	1986	1986	1988	-
Spain	1989	_1985_	-	-	-	-
Ireland	-	-	-	-	_1989_	-
Poland	-	_1990_	-	-	-	-
Hungary	-	_1990_	-	-	-	-
Czechoslovakia	-	_1990_	-	-	-	-

Note: First year of entry to each country underlined

TABLE 2 *Rankings of countries in terms of various indicators*

Ranking of the country in terms of

Country	(a) Finnish FDI's	(b) Finnish exports	(c) Cultural distance	(d) Int'l banking	(e) Insurance premiums
Switzerland	11	12	5=	5	11
Brazil	20+	32	28=	10	33
France	6	6	34=	6	5
Denmark	10	9	1=	40+	19
Great Britain	3	3	9=	2	4
Singapore	20+	39	17=	7	38
Soviet Union	20+	1	40+	40+	6
Germany	5	4	5=	4	3
Japan	20+	13	36=	9	2
Netherlands	4	8	1=	19	12
Cayman Islands	20+	53	40+	15	60+
Hong Kong	20+	34	17=	3	60+
Bahrain	20+	56	40+	27	60+
Lebanon	20+	49	40+	30	60+
Norway	9	7	1=	40+	20
Canada	7	16	9=	11	7
Luxemburg	8	11	40+	12	54
USA	2	5	9=	1	1
Mexico	20+	42	37=	40+	28
Australia	20+	15	9=	16	9
Bermuda	20+	48	40+	40+	60+
Italy	13	10	5=	13	8
Ivory Coast	20+	54	40+	40+	60
Austria	16	17	15	40+	17
Bahamas	20+	55	40+	14	60+
Sweden	1	2	1=	40+	14
Spain	12	14	28=	17	13
Ireland	14	19	9=	34	25
Poland	20+	25	40+	40+	44
Hungary	20+	26	40+	40+	48
Czechoslovakia	20+	27	40+	40+	23

Notes: '+' sign indicates a ranking above the figure (i.e. a ranking above the highest one provided by the data). '=' sign indicates a tie ranking.

TABLE 3 *Rank correlation between internationalization patterns (in terms of first entries) and various indicators*

	KOP	SYP	PSP	OKO	POH	SAM
Customer following correlation with						
FDI's	0.15	0.01	0.30	0.27	0.57**	0.27
Exports	0.25	0.14	0.48**	0.32*	0.37**	0.12
Cultural indicator	0.12	0.04	0.08	0.05	0.54**	0.27
Market seeking correlation with an indicator of the industry						
Int'l banking centers	0.52**	0.45**	0.22	0.20		
insurance premiums by country					0.25	0.18
Correlation with competitors						
with KOP		0.44**	0.35*	0.30	0.20	-0.03
with SYP			0.29	0.40**	0.06	-0.13
with PSP				0.49**	0.14	0.11
with OKO					0.04	0.00
with POH						0.47**

*Notes: 2-tailed significance *P< 0.05** P< 0.01.*

ENDNOTES

1. Kostecki, 1994, pp. 220-221.
2. Lovelock and Yip, 1996, p. 65.
3. To a great extent this chapter is based on the masters thesis of two of our students. Saskia Veendorp's thesis "Globalization of Marketing Approaches: A Literature Study, Analaysis of Globalization Activities in Seven Companies, and Interviews with Employees Within the ABN" was prepared during her internship with ABN Bank in 1989. Ringo Janssen's thesis "The Internationalisation of Business Services, Satisfying Clients Through Relationship Marketing and Service Quality" (1996) is based upon his internship at ABN AMRO Insurances and their planned international activities.
4. VanderMerwe and Chadwick, 1989.
5. Buckley, Pass and Prescott, 1992a.
6. See VanderMerwe and Chadwick, 1989 and Bradley, 1995.
7. Buckley, Pass and Prescott, 1992a, p. 89.
8. Segal-Horn, 1993.
9. In the previous section we saw an example of the internationalization of back offices activities in India, Ireland and the Philippines.
10. Segal-Horn, 1993.
11. In the first two columns of Table 9-2, we have listed the potential sources for economies of scale and scope according to Susan Segal-Horn. The third column represents our own view on potential experience effects. We regard these effects as a separate category of company advantages when the company is going international or global.
12. This section is based on Douglas and Craig, 1995, O'Farrell and Wood, 1994 and Lovelock and Yip, 1996.
13. Erramilli and Rao, 1993.
14. Kostecki, 1994, pp. 204-208.
15. Patterson and Cicic, 1996.
16. Patterson and Cicic, 1995.
17. The previous section has indicated that technological changes may make the internationalization of services possible. These dynamics may transform traditional soft services into hard services. See also note 31.
18. On the other hand, the danger of ego-boasting may also occur. Then irrational arguments dominate the internationalization process, while the real arguments, advantages and disadvantages are woven/swept away.
19. Czinkota and Ronkainen, 1994, pp. 494-495.
20. On should realize that this kind of cooperation is tied to the rules on competition set by the European Union. The EU is constantly watching whether such cooperation is not leading to economic powers so large that they can set prices themselves and exclude competition.
21. Sometimes such a strategy is called "client chasing". We do not think this is the proper wording when a service organization wants to be a market oriented one. Following the client expresses a better attitude towards the market. Still, one should not regard that as a meek followers strategy. It is good that the service firm takes a pro active role in following the client.
22. See also Chapter Four on Consumer Behavior and the sections on culture and segmentation.
23. Normann, 1984.
24. Carman and Langeard, 1980. We have analyzed those strategies in Chapter Seven and Eight. Moreover they will be dealt with in our chapter on Distribution when amongst others single site

and multi-site strategies are analyzed.

25. Palmer, 1995, p. 471.
26. Crosby and Stevens, 1987.
27. Bonoma, 1985.
28. In studies in international marketing based on the relationship marketing paradigm of the Industrial Marketing and Purchasing Group, it appeared that a company's ability to break down cultural barriers and establish close social and business relationships with clients, is a major factor for success in international industrial marketing (David Ford, 1984, 1997).
29. Erramilli, 1992; Erramilli and Rao, 1990, 1993.
30. This section is based to a large extent on Jean Pierre Schreurs MBA thesis on International Retailing. The arguments given for the retail sector will also apply to the services sector in general. See also Kasper, 1994.
31. This argument was found in Ringo Janssens's (1996) MBA thesis about the international insurance brokerage industry.
32. Peter Wright, Charles Pringle and Mark Kroll, 1992 say that many of the factors mentioned as barriers to entry in internationalizing the business, count also when entering a new business or industry in the home country. Then, it is a matter of creativity and corporate culture to deal with these issues and challenges (and not call them problems or barriers right away).
33. Usunier, 1993.
34. See Ulmer in Kostecki, 1994, p. 171.
35. See also Miles, 1993.
36. Kostecki, 1994 and Benito and Welch, 1994. This section is based on the ideas of M. Kostecki c.s. We have added some new points to it.
37. This distinction is based on Lovelock and Yip, 1996 and is also presented in Chapter Two, when we classified services.
38. Buckley, Pass and Prescott, 1992a, p. 3.
39. Buckley, Pass and Prescott, 1992a, p. 3-4.
40. Erramilli and Rao, 1990, 1993.
41. Benito and Welch, 1994.
42. Buckley, Pass and Prescott, 1992a.
43. Laulajainen, 1991 and Kasper and Bloemer, 1997.
44. Patterson and Cicic, 1995.
45. VanderMerwe and Chadwick, 1989 and Segal-Horn, 1993.
46. A similar idea about the capabilities and skills of customers and front and back office personnel in order to participate in the service encounter and accomplish the market orientation of the service firm, will be developed and applied in Chapter Fifteen. The terminology used here was originally developed by Uolevi Lehtinen.
47. This case is based to a large extent on the 1994 Pasi Hellman study "The Internationalization of Finnish Financial Service Companies".
48. The periods ends in 1990, because soon after, several new areas of expansion (e.g. Estonia, Latvia) opened up for Finnish banks and insurance companies. No information about Finnish investments or exports to these countries prior to their independence has been available, thus making is impossible to include them.
49. Other options banks and insurance companies have of engaging in international operations such as the formation of correspondent companies are not taken into account here, due to their often quite informal status, which would also have made the obtaining of information difficult. Only first entries into each country were considered. In several cases a company had first established a

representative office, which was later turned into a subsidiary.

50. There are two further comments that need to be made with regard to Table 1. In several cases a representative office was the first mode of operation in the particular market, after which the commitment was increased by establishing a minority or majority ownership or by setting up a wholly-owned subsidiary. Exits from markets are not included in the table.

51. There were some differences in the availability of data for the chosen indicators. The Bank of Finland provided only the twenty most important recipient countries for Finnish FDI's. In order to avoid missing values in the analysis, other countries were given a ranking of 20 (indicated in the table by 20+). For the indicator of cultural distance, data were available only for the culturally closest 40 countries. Some of these countries received a tie ranking (indicated by =), and the countries not on list of the top 40 were given a ranking of 40+. In the case of international banking centres data were also available for the top 40 countries, and in the case of insurance premiums for each country, the list contained the top 60 countries. In a similar manner as with other indicators, countries not on the list (i.e. ranking above 60) were given a ranking of 60+.

introduction to part four

SERVICES MARKETING MIX

Now that we have discussed the strategic side of service companies' behavior, it is time to see how it can be operationalized. There are two important aspects:

1. the elaboration of the marketing mix as such; and

2. making sure the plans about strategy and marketing mix really work.

In both cases, the implementation is aimed at actually accomplishing the goals set, the competitive advantage(s) given the relationship the firm and the customer want to attain and the success they are looking for.

At this stage, the important task is not only to define strategies but to develop the conditions and mechanisms under which they can be implemented effectively and efficiently. This part of the book hinges upon that implementation. The four strategies developed in our service typology at the beginning of this book imply that a different content must be given to the marketing mix in those four cases. This was revealed at the end of each of the chapters on the marketing mix. In the final chapter, it will all be integrated into a coherent overall picture. This will ease the implementation of these strategies and the way they are operationalized via the marketing mix within the framework of establishing long term relationships.

Providing services is a people's business. Therefore, the interaction between the customer and the service provider is crucial in the actual service encounter. The employees are the most valuable asset in a service organization. Rendering excellent quality services depends very much on the way employees behave. They have to execute the strategy formulated. That is why we pay special attention to the knowledge and skills of the employees, their service attitude, internal marketing and the culture and structure of that organization. Moreover, these skills are quite often the only assets a service organization can use in its internationalization policy to accomplish a competitive advantage.

The interaction between customers and service provider sets special standards for the service encounter. The service provider must be motivated, willing and able to act according to the required market orientation and service quality. Customers must be motivated, willing and able to participate in the service encounter according to the role they have to play. This puts special requirements on the implementation of the marketing strategy. That is the reason why "internal marketing" is an important topic in our chapter on personnel and in the chapter on marketing strategy.

As employees are that crucial to a service business, the opening part of this chapter will be on People and the accompanying Organization (structure) and Processes: POP. Then we will turn to the next P: the Product, here called the Service. Consequently, Chapter Eleven is on developing and producing services. As the public sector is one of the largest services sectors in many countries, this sector deserves special attention. That is why we discuss what public bodies have to offer (and the way in which they do or could do their marketing). Communication with customers has proven to be an essential element in services marketing. External communication or Promotion will be dealt with in Chapter Twelve. Internal communication has already been discussed in the chapter on POP, as services delivery is usually closely linked to the physical proximity of the service provider and the actual presence of the customer is needed to participate in the service encounter. The chapter on Distribution deals with those issues. Finally, services have to be sold at a certain price. As the physical evidence in services is closely linked to different mix instruments, this feature will be discussed, amongst others, in the "mix-chapters" on Processes, Services, Distribution and especially on Communication. Price is the final P to be discussed before we put it all together in the chapter on Implementation and Control (Chapter Fifteen).

The next scheme reveals the benefits of this part, e.g. what the reader should learn from this part's chapters.

Part One: The Services Domain

FUNDAMENTALS OF SERVICES
MARKETING
(Chapter 1)

CLASSIFYING
SERVICES
(Chapter 2)

SERVICE
ENVIRONMENT
(Chapter 3)

Part Two: At The Heart

FROM BUYING BEHAVIOR TO RELATIONSHIPS
(Chapter 4)

SERVICE QUALITY
(Chapter 5)

Part Three: Strategic Issues

COLLECTING AND
MANAGING MARKET
INFORMATION
(Chapter 6)

STRATEGIC PLANNING AT
CORPORATE LEVEL
(Chapter 7)

INTERNATIONALIZATION
OF SERVICES
(Chapter 9)

SERVICES MARKETING
PLANNING IN STRATEGIC
BUSINESS UNITS
(Chapter 8)

Part Four: Services Marketing Mix

PEOPLE, ORGANIZATION AND PROCESSES (Chapter 10)	DEVELOPING AND PROVIDING SERVICES (Chapter 11)	COMMUNICATION (Chapter 12)

PEOPLE, ORGANIZATION AND PROCESSES
(Chapter 10)

- indicate what are the consequences of the fact that delivering services is something done by people and not by machines;
- define the characteristics of a "service attitude";
- be aware of the consequences of being a market oriented service organization for its personnel policy, human resources management, organizational culture, structure, leadership style and for controlling the service encounter and back office processes;
- break down the process of providing services into roles, scripts and routines of the front and the back office;
- analyze the types of queueing and waiting lines in services and possible solutions;
- explain the necessary external and internal orientation of a market oriented service organization;
- define the internal strengths of a service organization; and
- recognize the link of this chapter with the previous chapters on strategic planning and marketing planning.

DEVELOPING AND PROVIDING SERVICES
(Chapter 11)

- apply the insights you have acquired into the relationship between planning, creating, providing and evaluating services when strategic and operational service policies have to work;
- translate theories on the hierarchy and life-cycle of services into a service strategy;
- use the concept of strategic and tactical services effectively when marketing services;
- become aware of how to develop and implement new services;
- know the basics of breakthrough services;
- reproduce the basics of dissatisfaction management and complaints management;
- apply the basics of service recovery to get a competitive advantage;
- detect the main differences of the service features in the four different types of service firms.

COMMUNICATION
(Chapter 12)

- be able to explain the key features of communication in services;
- understand why and how communication contributes to creating the desired image of the service organization;
- understand why and how communication can reduce the perceived risk inherent to services;
- understand how communication adds to strengthening the relationship between service organization and customer;
- know the link between service quality and communication;
- be able to explain the relevance of internal and external communication;
- know why branding is so important in services;
- understand the communication mix in services, especially the role of the staff in personal selling;
- be able to determine the objectives of communication;
- know the basics of developing a communication plan;

Part Four: Services Marketing Mix

COMMUNICATION
(Chapter 12, continued)

- see the importance of the determinants of service quality for different services; and
- know how to use the different elements of the communication mix for core and augmented services, and for standard and customized services.

DISTRIBUTION
(Chapter 13)

- indicate which issues must be taken into consideration when formulating distribution goals;
- formulate the relationship between these goals and some distribution strategies;
- recognize the links between corporate goals and distribution goals;
- argue the merits of the location opted for;
- name a few innovations and trends in the field of distribution;
- detect why such innovations are not always accepted;
- be aware of the impact of new information technologies on the distribution of services; and
- understand the consequences of our service typology on the distribution of services.

PRICING
(Chapter 14)

- understand the relationship between an organization and pricing objectives;
- formulate a number of pricing objectives according to the type of organization;
- explain terms like demand fluctuations, level-capacity strategy, price bundling and segmented pricing;
- understand the essence of costs made by the company and consumer;
- interpret the relationship between price, quality and type of service;
- comprehend why the value of a service is linked to quality and price;
- apply value strategies (satisfaction based, relationship and efficiency pricing);
- price profitably for different services;
- recognize the more intuitive pricing tactics which are used in practice and be able to explain how these fit within the underlying theoretical principles of this chapter; and
- improve intuitive pricing by applying the theory as outlined in this chapter.

IMPLEMENTATION AND CONTROL
(Chapter 15)

- discern the unique problems on implementation and control of the marketing strategy in a market-oriented service firm;
- formulate ways to avoid these problems and/or solve them;
- position the problems on implementation and control within the framework of the SERVQUAL-model;
- discern the importance of accurately formulated corporate and marketing objectives at corporate level as well as in the strategic business units;
- realize that these goals set the framework for the financial and non-financial criteria for evaluating actual service performance;
- fine tune the various elements of the marketing mix in services given the chosen strategy of the service firm and relationship marketing;
- determine how demand and supply can be matched;

Part Four: Services Marketing Mix

IMPLEMENTATION AND CONTROL
(Chapter 15, continued)

- define the role of the consumer, the contact personnel and the rest of the personnel in the service encounter to achieve excellent quality in service delivery by cooperating between these three partners in the service encounter;

- see the need to apply the concept of internal marketing in easing the implementation of high quality service strategies and tactics;

- define and measure performance in service industries;

- control strategies and activities in market oriented service organizations; and

- take notice of a stepwise plan to introduce strategies which can increase quality and/or market orientation in a service organization.

CHAPTER TEN

PEOPLE, ORGANIZATION AND PROCESSES

After studying this chapter you should be able to:

- *indicate what are the consequences of the fact that delivering services is something usually done by people and not by machines;*

BELOW: *Who should be served the most?*

- *define the characteristics of a "service attitude";*

- *be aware of the consequences of being a market oriented service organization for its personnel policy, human resources management, organizational culture, structure, leadership style and for controlling the service encounter and back office processes;*

- *break down the process of providing services into roles, scripts and routines of the front and the back office;*

- *analyze the types of queueing and waiting lines in services and possible solutions;*

- *explain the necessary external and internal orientation of a market oriented service organization;*

- *define the internal strengths of a service organization; and*

- *recognize the link of this chapter with the previous chapters on strategic planning and marketing planning.*

PRICEWATERHOUSE COOPERS

Success requires a meeting of the minds. Which is why we just brought 140,000 of them together.

www.pwcglobal.com

© 1998 PricewaterhouseCoopers   PricewaterhouseCoopers refers to the member firms of the worldwide PricewaterhouseCoopers organization.

10.1 INTRODUCTION

Jan Carlzon, the former CEO of the Scandinavian SAS Airline company, stresses the importance of service encounters and the moments of truth that take place. The first encounter between a customer and a service company is such a moment of truth. Here, the first impression about the service company is formed.

Bill Fromm and Len Schlesinger provide many examples of people who have decisive roles in the first impressions generated by service encounters in their 1994 book: *The Real Heroes of Business... and Not a CEO Among Them*. One of them is Phil Adelman, a doorman, "... who has turned what many could perceive as a relatively minor job at the front door of a Marriott hotel into a franchise from which he virtually creates the entire personality of the hotel. Phil Adelman works the door at the Marriott Hotel in Cambridge, Massachusetts, and he could not be a more persuasive embodiment of the power of first impressions in the service industry. Many customers treat jobs like Phil's – doorman, greeter, security guard – as if those rules and those people didn't exist. But the real problem is that many companies treat them that way as well. Jobs that involve constant customer contact are by their very definition highly visible. Companies that make the most of the service opportunities these jobs present gain great competitive advantage.

Phil has taken just such a job and turned it into a position from which he sets the tone and personality of his hotel. He leaves a first impression of extraordinary helpfulness, knowledge, hospitality, and security. He knows how to make customers welcome. And, as a bonus, he is also often the last person guests encounter at the hotel, sending them off with a lasting *last* impression."

Conclusions with a similar impact can be drawn with respect to the importance of jobs like room maid, cashier, waitress (like Paula Dorrichi, so good that customers wait in line up to an hour to eat at one of her tables – passing up empty tables elsewhere in the restaurant so they can be served by her in the Ruby Tuesday restaurant in Greenville, South Carolina), ticket-inspector and dustman. They all have one thing in common, that their jobs are important in delivering first and last impressions of service quality, while earning low salaries.[1] That is the reason why some people suggest that those people who act closest to the customer should receive the highest salaries in the company. Consequently, CEO's and other managers, often up on the highest floor of corporate head quarters and hardly meeting any customers, should have the lowest pay for their activities.

the first impression   In many instances, the first impression is the one that really influences consumers decision to enter a store, restaurant, bank or university. These are the first impressions they use to form an opinion of the business, the people working there and their expectations about the quality delivered. The initial impressions shape the image of the business immediately. And, it should be noted "one does not get a second chance to form a first impression". In services, employees play a decisive role in shaping *employees* these first impressions – people will make or break the service. It also appears that defaults in services can be attributed quite often to behavioral defaults.[2] So, people *customers* are decisive in service quality. This holds not only for front office as well as back *servuction process* office staff, but also for the customers participating in the servuction process

This chapter elaborates on subjects traditionally dealt with in general management, as well as in the personnel policy, or human resources management literature and operations research (OR). These insights will be applied to service organizations within the framework of our marketing perspective. The link between those two different sciences will be more obvious if the reader understands the existing inter-relationship between "job satisfaction" and "consumer satisfaction", as mentioned in discussing the service profit chain.

We will not elaborate on all details about personnel policy, HRM, organizational culture, structure, leadership style, control systems and OR. The intention is to concentrate on some of the subjects separately, thereby indicating the elements which are especially relevant to service organizations.

The orientation of the service firm and the employees is important in delivering service quality and being market oriented. Therefore, the external and internal orientation of the employees should be investigated. In turn, this affects their service attitude. The style of leadership is also decisive here. All these issues co-determine the way the process of service delivery should be structured. Hopefully this is done in such a way that clients will be served quite quickly. However, "waiting" seems to be a basic feature in many service delivery processes. Since waiting is a phenomenon often occurring in service encounters due to its specific nature (non storable), we will pay special attention to that topic. Waiting often occurs because of the way the service process and the service encounter are organized. Waiting may also be caused by the way in which customers come to the service provider (all at once, spread over time, etc.). The discipline of operations research provides some insights to solve those problems.

Controlling processes and people to attain the goals set is a basic element of company management. This topic will be tackled briefly in this chapter; here we will only focus on the human resource side of it (it will be discussed to a greater extent in Chapter Fifteen).

Lastly, the personnel implications to our service typology will be revealed. The outline of this chapter is summarized in Figure 10-1.

Figure 10-1
Chapter outline

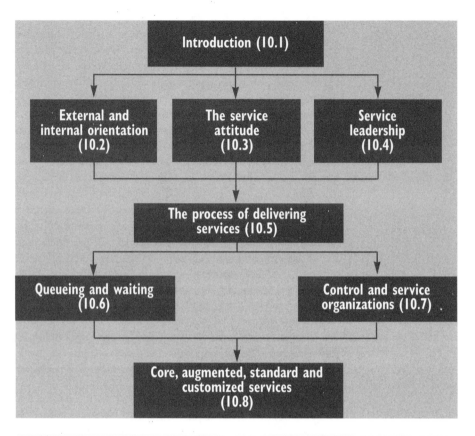

*Service
practice
10-2
Does
nationality
matter?*

From an international perspective, it is not only important to understand what people in different countries and cultures expect service employees to do (and how) but also what they themselves are willing to do (and how). Chapter Four gave some examples about this issue in discussing national cultures. Different weights may be given to the technical, functional and relational quality in different cultures as the pillars of total quality. The same holds for the relative importance of the dimensions underlying service quality.

This will also affect decisions on "whether and how many expatriates will run an office in a foreign country", "who is dealing with the foreign branch of the client in our home country", "whether and how many locals are employed at our foreign office", etc. To us, the answer is simple: just employ those persons best fitting to the whole configuration (or Gestalt) of the national culture, the corporate culture and the clients. Then, nationality does not matter.

10.2 EXTERNAL AND INTERNAL ORIENTATION

contact-personnel
"part-time marketeer"

In previous chapters, we have already highlighted the very important role of the employees, especially the contact-personnel, in service organizations. Everyone who belongs to the contact personnel is in fact a "part-time marketeer".[3] So, the organizations these employees work for should encourage them to perform this role. The culture, structure, leadership style and delegation of responsibilities and competencies should all support the employees and their part-time marketeer role. Just having a marketing manager or a marketing department is no guarantee for the market orientation in a service organization. The employees' mentality is more important to that than formal positions, functions and departments.[4]

We have stated repeatedly that delivering services in many industries is still something mainly done by humans and not by machines. This means that the personnel are able to make or break the service.[5] The question is then how many tasks and competencies the personnel have and on which supporting activities they can count. The distinction between front office personnel and back office personnel in the servuction process is a well known one in services management. Four types of employees can be distinguished, each having an increasingly greater commitment to marketing and contact with customers.[6] These four types are:

isolates

1. *isolates*   –   back office functions having hardly any commitment to marketing and marketing planning, e.g. purchasing, procurement and other supporting functions such as accounting;

influencers

2. *influencers* –   marketeers, R&D people who are committed to marketing, determining the marketing strategy, knowing the market and thus having contact with the market;

modifiers

3. *modifiers*   –   people like receptionists and telefonists, often having personal contact with the customers in daily activities, must know customer expectations and be aware of procedures and rules in the company; are not so much or not at all involved in marketing planning; and

contactors

4. *contactors* –   people regularly meeting customers (sales, customer service, etc.) involved in marketing or sales jobs and in marketing planning.

So, contactors and modifiers are two types of front office personnel. Isolates clearly are the typical back office employees. Influencers may belong to both types, but should at least have an external orientation toward the market.

external as well as an
internal orientation

It is generally accepted that "successful marketing" requires an external as well as an internal orientation of the organization's employees. This, of course, also applies to the service sector. The need for such an internal and external orientation was taken into account in the previous chapters on the organization's corporate and marketing strategy.

internal strengths and weaknesses

In developing strategies, most of the time more attention is paid to the external, than to the internal elements of the service organization. A thorough analysis of the internal strengths and weaknesses can be very useful though. It will indicate which and how many employees are able and motivated to perform according to goals stemming from the market orientation desired. Taking advantage of its internal and external strengths and orientations is important when the organization wants to be market oriented. The link between the subject of this chapter and the previous chapters is shown in Figure 10-2. It depicts the importance of the internal and external orientation and the relationship between them within the framework of the organization's corporate strategy, marketing strategy and human resource strategy.

Figure 10-2
Internal and external orientation in a service organization

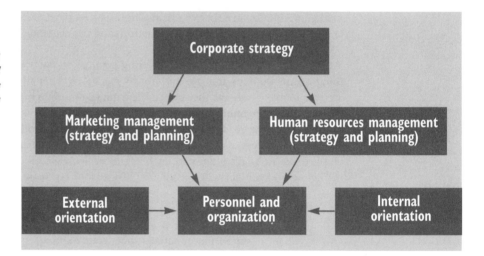

The strategies and activities in the fields of marketing management, OR and human resources management contain, as functional strategies, a further specification of corporate strategy. These activities, together with the goals of the organization, will dictate not only the desired behavior of the employees, the whole organization as such in the market place, but also the customers' behavior in the service encounter. Managers hoping to increase the customer orientation of their personnel should strive to develop an understanding among their employees of what is expected of them and increase employee identification and involvement with the organization

organizational socialization

through the process of organizational socialization.[7] Implementing this does not only involve the persons but also the processes necessary to perform the service on the appropriate quality level. Next to that, a balance is needed between the external and internal orientation of the organization.

EXTERNAL ORIENTATION

external orientation

One of the skills contact personnel and marketeers in a service organization need to have and to be able to perform well, is an external orientation. This requirement applies to the part time as well as the full time marketeers. Such an external orientation implies an orientation focused on knowing, exploring and recognizing the developments, situations, plans, opinions, wishes and needs of the market players. The role of the customers, clients and competitors is important. However, the role of the government (national or local) should not be forgotten. This external orientation is important when an organization wants to be market oriented, have a sustainable competitive advantage and when it wants to accomplish its function in society (its mission). On this view, contact personnel should be externally oriented in order to

"boundary spanning role"

give full content to their "boundary spanning role", on the edge of the organization and its environment. Employees performing a boundary spanning role should be focused on observing the latest developments in the environment (see Chapter Three). Through these observations, they should collect this information and com-

dissemination of the market information

municate it through the organization (see Chapter One). The dissemination of the market information must be executed quickly and correctly in order that the information arrives wherever it is needed. This is only possible though, when a good information exchange between the different departments and persons takes place.[8] Formal systems and procedures should enable this; the informal structure may encourage it. In order to make this information exchange successful, the atmosphere and culture in the organization should encourage this and make the employees be capable and willing to perform their part-time marketeer role (see section 10.2).

INTERNAL ORIENTATION

An organization should be structured in such a way that accomplishing a sustainable competitive advantage is possible. The internal resources and capabilities of the

internal resources and capabilities

organization can be used to that end.[9] In highly dynamic external markets, own resources and capabilities can form a more stable base for sustaining the identity and strategy of the organization than the needs of the market the organization wants to fulfil because these markets change that much. This implies that in developing

internal strengths as a very valuable asset

strategies, plans and operational activities, the internal strengths of the organization should be considered as a very valuable asset. This viewpoint is in line with our firm belief that the employees, the internal production processes of the services provider's back office, and the way the service encounter is structured are crucial in delivering service quality (under the assumption that the company knows what the customer wants, what the firm may mean to the customer, what problems can be solved, which funtional contribution the firm can make to the customers' well being, etc.). This internal orientation, therefore, has nothing to do with an inward looking orientation, failing to see what is going on in the external world.

The resources are the input for the production process, like the financial, physical, human, technological, organizational resources and the reputation/image of the organization itself.[10] Resources thus include intangibles like knowledge, experience

resources and capabilities

and skills. Having defined the firm's resources and capabilities, it is of the utmost importance that the service organization is able to coordinate, integrate and fine tune each of the separate resources and capabilities.[11] This should lead to a number of

routines

behavioral routines which will help accomplish a sustainable competitive advantage. Such routines will guide the behavior of the service organization and its employees. Most of the time, the behavioral routines in a service organization are complex because of some of the basic characteristics of services: intangibility, labor-intensiveness, simultaneous production and consumption and the partial participation of the consumer in the service delivery process. The more complex the behavioral routines and the better the organization is able to control these behaviors, the stronger will be the sustainable competitive advantage. This means that the complexity of the routines depends, amongst others, on: the type of service firm the organization wants to be in terms of core and augmented services; and, in terms of standard and customized services. In these routines, the human factor for example, is reduced considerably if delivering the service becomes more capital, or technology, intensive. This human factor is reduced also when greater participation from the client is demanded (self-service). The resources and capabilities, most of the time, are intangible – and invisible – elements. Examples are the organization's image and brand image, knowledge, skills and behavior of the personnel, and the degree of market orientation in the organization and in the organization's culture. This, in turn, leads to the features of the service attitude, in which the internal and external orientations should be balanced. That will be discussed in the next section.

sustainable competitive advantage

THE EMPLOYEES' TRIAD

To be market-oriented, the internal organization of a service company must not create a barrier to being externally oriented. Therefore, it is necessary that both these orientations are present and balanced; that all employees are able and willing to be market oriented; and that employees have the resources and capabilities to be market oriented. The motivation of the employees is essential. The organization cannot be market oriented where employees are not committed to the company, and not involved in the organization, goals and the market. Exchange of information is crucial to that end.

motivation

Service practice 10-3 Collecting information – sharing information [12]

Do employees in service organizations really collect and disseminate market information? And if so, in what way? Both roles can be performed in "a good or bad way". "Good collectors" have a long-term relationship with their customers, a positive attitude towards collecting and disseminating market information. Collecting this information is an integral part of their job, and they have a very small resistance to performing new tasks. "Good disseminators" have a positive attitude towards collecting market information and a very small resistance to collecting and disseminating this information.

Many service employees still do not belong to one of these categories, leaving ample opportunities to increase a firm's market orientation by way of changing their boundary spanning role and use of market information:

- good collector, good disseminator 30%
- good collector, bad disseminator 28%
- bad collector, good disseminator 6%
- bad collector, bad disseminator 36%

"commitment to the organization"

The existing HRM-literature on "commitment to the organization" stresses above all, the relationship of an employee with the organization.[13] This is sometimes phrased in terms of the bond with the organization, the membership of the organization or the loyalty to the organization. It then becomes an important issue whether individual employees can identify themselves with the goals of the organization: the individual goals of the employee should be, at best, identifiable with the goals the organization pursues. Research has shown that job satisfaction is higher when the individuals commitment is higher. This means, for a service organization, that there is a positive relationship between job satisfaction and customer satisfaction. A higher commitment to the organization results, normally, in a better provision of the service. A consequence of commitment is, then, that both the employee and the customer are

stay loyal to the organization

likely to stay loyal to the organization. Both will not switch to another service firm for their job or for buying their service." Increasing job satisfaction among service personnel has the potential of generating higher customer satisfaction, repeat purchases by current customers and positive word-of-mouth recommendations to potential customers. This indicates that job satisfaction of service personnel can be increased by hiring individuals who tend to be highly empathetic, training current employees how to be empathetic, providing employees with clear job descriptions, empowering employees within the customer/employee area to make decisions that will result in higher customer satisfaction with the service and in establishing a clear unity of command for each employee."[14] Avoiding role stress and role ambiguity contributes to increasing job satisfaction and thus loyalty.[15]

More factors than just motivation or commitment play a role in becoming market-oriented and satisfied as an employee. Therefore, we like to differentiate between the motivation, the capacity and the opportunity of employees in a service organization to be market-oriented.

motivation

capacity

Motivation deals with the intensity as well as the direction of the market-oriented behavior of the employees and the whole service organization. Here, the mentality comes in, as well as the willingness to think and act in a market oriented way. Capacity entails whether the employees and the whole organization are physically and mentally able to behave in the desired market-oriented way. Are the physical resources and capabilities present to do so?

The opportunities have to do with whether the employees and the whole organization have got enough time to accomplish the intended market orientation. In other words, is there enough time and enough support of the organization to make the interaction successful in the service encounter? Again, the resources and capabilities are important, as well as the existing routines with respect to the implementation of the service process.

a proper implementation

block the implementation

These three factors have to be present in order to guarantee a proper implementation of the firm's market orientation, marketing strategy and marketing policy. Different factors can block the implementation of (marketing) strategies, e.g. a lack of identity and direction of management to be(come) market oriented, little commitment at the top when plans have to be realized, a short term vision instead of a long term vision, little teamwork, a mismatch between the job demands and the knowledge and skills of the personnel, unclear roles and tasks, insufficient time available and little and/or poor internal communication about present or future situations and developments inside the organization and on the market.[16] Lack of proper internal communication appears also to be a crucial problem when trying to attain excellent service quality in the market place, as Service practice 10-4 reveals.

Service practice 10-4 Bad internal service quality causes bad external service quality

Service interfaces are services provided by distinctive organizational units or the people working within these departments on behalf of other units or employees/groups of employees within the organization.[17] In a study, researchers applied the critical incidents technique to the after sales organization of a large multinational.[18] This Malcolm Baldridge Quality Award Winner manufacturer of office equipment let them study the internal support service of the field desk. In total, 144 interviews were conducted with internal customers of the field desk, resulting in the analysis of 126 satisfactory and 195 unsatisfactory incidents.

The unsatisfactory incidents mainly focussed on two topics belonging to the "communication infrastructure" (namely accessibility of the field desk, and accessibility of the individuals working at the field desk) and one feature of the information itself (usefulness). Incidents with respect to the "recognition of the importance and responsibility of the job of the internal customer" were mentioned as the most satisfactory ones.

It was concluded that an "important source of poor internal service quality appears to be accessibility, both at the level of the department and individual employees".[19]

How then, can external service quality exist when internal service quality is blocked by poor information, poor communication and poor communicator behavior?

10.3   THE SERVICE ATTITUDE

"service attitude"

The employees (and especially the contact personnel) in a service organization need to have a particular "service attitude" to accomplish the goal of delivering excellent service quality and a market-oriented service. This does not necessarily mean that the employees have to be servile and accept everything customers want, however strange. What is important though, is that customers know what they can expect from the service provider and what they are expected to do themselves. This relates to the issue of managing customer expectations, as discussed in previous chapters, a major marketing responsibility.

managing customer expectations

The importance of a person's service attitude has to be taken into account when selecting new employees. After that, training is necessary to generate and encourage the attitude. The question can be raised – What exactly is a service attitude? Which resources and capabilities (skills, knowledge, equipment, procedures, etc.) are needed? A distinction can be made into three different groups of resources and capabilities:

- technical know how about the business;
- ability to serve customers well and maintain the quality of the service; and
- ability to work in a team.

corporate culture of service providers "taking care"

The underlying factor in all three points refers to the corporate culture of service providers. It is a cultural factor linked with elements of "taking care" (the feminine part of national cultures!) and skills to deliver services. It reveals how thing are done (to be done) in this service company. Recruiting new employees with these skills, etc. (or training present employees in this way) implies that "the input" to the service delivery process is directed towards what the firm actually wants to achieve within the organization. Management and long term employed staff are expected to behave as role models.

TECHNICAL KNOW HOW ABOUT THE BUSINESS

thorough knowledge

apply this know how technical quality

functional or relational quality

Thorough knowledge of the latest developments in the business is a prerequisite when one wants to deliver a good service, let alone when one intends to deliver an excellent or breakthrough service. The employees need to have the skills and routines to apply this know how in an appropirate way so that customers are satisfied. These skills are necessary to meet the standards set for the technical quality. There are, of course, other prerequisites which are linked to the functional and relational quality; then, the personal touch comes to the fore. In the many studies carried out about service quality, it appears that technical quality is not decisive to the customers but the functional or relational quality is. The technical quality has to meet a certain minimum quality level, but the other two are decisive in the customers' final assessment of service quality.

ABILITY TO SERVE CUSTOMERS WELL AND MAINTAIN SERVICE QUALITY

really serve customers

Contact personnel, when delivering a service, should be able to really serve customers.[20] What does this general and obvious statement imply? It has to do with many dimensions of the SERVQUAL-model (amongst others, responsiveness) determining the functional and relational quality to a large extent. That is why it is important that each member of the contact personnel is sensitive to the situation of the customer in that moment of the service encounter; can understand the customer; can communicate with the customer; can ask the right questions, find out what the customer really wants and needs; and show customers some alternatives from which they can choose and what fits them best.

These general statements can be applied in many cultures. It will require a particular adaptation to fit each specific culture. Each culture may look in different ways to sensitivity, understanding, communication, asking questions or the customers' choice. We have seen, for instance, what retail customers in three different cultures expect: Taiwan, the USA and The Netherlands. Respect and politeness prevail in all three cultures. Differences occur as well. Such differences should be taken into account. Also, the traits of excellent service providers, as shown in Service practice 10-5, may need adaptation to the local situation. In general, they hold for every culture.

Service practice 10-5 Do something and don't try to avoid it!

Bill Fromm and Len Schlesinger concluded from their small scale qualitative research project that the fourteen people in their sample had some common traits that might explain their being excellent service providers.[21]

It appeared that all of them had a remarkable childhood in which their parents showed an unconditional commitment to their own customers: they were important mentors or role models to them (and they still talk eloquently about the values these people passed on to them). All fourteen people adhere to the work ethic of being there for their customers. They all work many hours (and sometimes receive modest financial rewards), are wonderfully good-natured and love their work. They are charming, easy to like, come to work enthusiastic (even cheerful), manage to leave their own problems at home when they come to work and are consistently good-humored. Every one of these persons sees his or her world, and job, from the customers' point of view, and thus apply their market orientation in this way. They trust their customers, a trust that infuses each encounter they have with customers, and creates an atmosphere that makes customers feel welcomed and respected.

Bill and Len found that "a key element in the way these service performers related to customers is that they almost all take a very long-term view of their relationships – they aren't worried about the immediate payoff. ... For almost all of these world-class performers, financial rewards are a by-product of good performance, not the goal of good performance. They have confidence that investing in secure relationships ultimately pays off. ... This kind of patience may be the hardest thing to nurture in employees."

One of the most remarkable traits of these people is that they always have time to do anything right the first time. They all want to find ways to do the job, not excuses to avoid it. They have a talent for seeing what is missing and hastening to supply it. They have put themselves and their companies on a miniature continuous-improvement program. They always want to improve their own performance.

Contact personnel also need an attitude enabling them to deliver an intangible service to the customer and make the customer feel at ease so they can then deal with any uncertainty. An employee with the right attitude is able to deliver excellent service to the individual customer who asks for a customized service, as well as to a *quality of services*

group of customers satisfied with a standard service. Here, the different dimensions which play a role in the quality of services intervene (see Chapters Four, Five and Six). For example, this means that the contact employee should be trustworthy, responsive, accessible, courteous, honest and fair, while delivering safety/security, and speaking the language of the customer. It also means that contact personnel should be able to make their own decisions and take responsibility so that "the boss" is not bothered by every little problem which is not in the formal instructions.[22] This is only possible though, when an adequate delegation of competencies and responsibilities occurs and when contact personnel are capable and motivated enough to have this independent decision making come true. Communication turns out to be a crucial item in serving customers during the service encounter. Consequently, communication skills are very important to employees. However, not everybody communicates in the same way, or has to.

communication

Different communication functions of employees interacting with customers can be found.[23] A typology based on the communication demands placed on service sector employees by customers creates three types of persons:

Type 1

Type 1: answers questions; provides brief, standardized information to numerous kinds of customers; establishes relationships between customer and firm; gives direction; and processes restricted customer instructions;

Type 2

Type 2: listens effectively; answers questions; persuades customers; explains moderately complex information; and establishes ongoing but limited interpersonal relationships with customers;

Type 3

Type 3: asks questions; explains complex information; persuades individuals and groups of customers and firm personnel; interacts creatively with customers to solve problems (brainstorms) and establishes an interpersonal relationship consisting of repeated interactions with customers over time.[24]

Some examples of these types of communication and specific jobs in some service industries are given in Service practice 10-6.

Service practice 10-6 Type of service organization and employee

Type of service organization	Type 1 "answers questions"	Type 2 "listens effectively"	Type 3 "asks questions"
Bank	teller	individual loan officer	commercial loan officer
Physician	receptionist	nurse	doctor
Schools	secretary	administrator	teacher

WORKING IN A TEAM

team work

The third kind of skills and knowledge relevant to a real service attitude is called team work or working in a team. It refers to one of the ways to close gap 3 of the SERVQUAL-model. Especially in large service organizations like banks and insurance companies, the customer is likely to be served by different employees. The employees together, then, should be able to deliver excellent service. This makes it necessary for each employee to know the arrangements made with the customers by each of their colleagues. Therefore, it is important that the internal communication and administrative work is efficient, effective and well known to all colleagues. If the communication does not occur in the proper way, the quality of the service will be negatively influenced.[25] For this reason, some organizations have installed special contact employees or account-managers for specific clients or groups of clients. But working in a team means also getting along with colleagues.[26]

account-managers

Working in a team, cooperation and the dissemination of the collected market information are characteristics of the culture of a market-oriented organization. The importance of teamwork is thus not only inherent to service organizations, but is a general necessity for organizations wanting to be market-oriented. What else can be said about such a culture?

THE UNDERLYING CULTURAL DIMENSIONS

Geert Hofstede's (1991) research into the cultures of organizations and countries provides more insights into the subject of this section. National cultures may differ on five dimensions. One of these dimensions hinges upon the distinction between masculinity and femininity.[27] The femininity part of that dimension stands for the "caring" character of a country's culture. Here, the importance of caring for relationships and for persons (customers, colleagues, family) becomes clear. In feminine cultures, for example, teachers at universities or other schools, are evaluated more on friendliness and social skills, than on criteria such as intelligence and academic achievement (the latter criteria are more important in masculine societies). So, service firms in feminine cultures may have a competitive advantage over service firms from masculine societies because their employees may have already a natural background for the "right service attitude". A similar conclusion can be drawn for firms from collectivistic societies (as indicated in Chapter Four).

The culture of a country can, to a certain degree, be masculine and feminine at the same time. Each country can have subcultures which are more masculine than other existing subcultures. What is important is the degree to which service organizations care about people (customers and employees) and these employees care about their customers and colleagues. It is a matter of being attentive or obliging, not a matter of being servile. And, customers really value these efforts positively.[28]

10.4 SERVICE LEADERSHIP

style of leadership

caring about people

female style of leadership

The results of our discussion on service attitudes has a great impact on the style of leadership in a service organization. The focus point of this style can be summarized very briefly in "caring about people", both the customer and the employee. It also implies that interest in the customer cannot be seen separately from the interest in the employee. This logic can be explained from another point of view: customer satisfaction and job satisfaction both affect each other. Caring is an essential part of the feminine side of a national culture. That may mean that a "feminine way of leadership" is important to service industries. In other words, the norms and practices highly valued in feminine societies (or by women in general) might be important to successfully manage service organizations: a "female style of leadership" may be needed to run a service firm and gain a competitive advantage.

Service practice 10-7 The female advantage: women's way of leadership

A qualitative study of the way a number of women manage the organization where they work involved analyzing their diaries and watching their way of working. These women shared a number of values.[29]

In interpreting these findings, the following should be taken into account. "This is not to say that men do not share these values; some share many, others a few. But these values may be defined as female because they have been nurtured in the private, domestic sphere to which women have been restricted for so long." It appeared that these women "...usually referred to themselves as being in the middle of things. Not at the top, but in the center; not reaching down, but reaching out. It is the middle position in the web, not a hierarchical position in the organization. Authority is expressed in a subtle way. It encompasses a way of working in which emphasizing relationships and an orientation towards processes are central. These women appeared to have an ability to model and persuade others in this web structure instead of leading their organization via an hierarchical position. "In a web structure, where talent is nurtured and encouraged rather than commanded, and a variety of interconnections exist, influence and persuasion take the place of giving order. Compassion, empathy, inspiration, and direction – all aspects of nurturance – are connective values..." being of utmost importance here. Empowerment and human development are stressed over subordination to the chain of command.

These are characteristics of this women's way of leadership that can be succesfully applied in "... bridging the gap between the demands of efficiency and the need to nurture the human spirit. Reconciling these values is particularly important in today's competitive economic landscape, where the intelligence, commitment, and enthusiasm of employees are more crucial to the success of an enterprise than they have been in the past."

Managers in service organizations should delegate as many tasks, responsibilities and competencies as possible to contact personnel and other employees. In the *"empowerment"* management literature, this is called "empowerment".[30] A central theme in the many descriptions of this phenomenon is "granting employees the decision-making authority they need, to deal with the issues and problems that arise on their jobs without first seeking supervisory approval".[31] This implies that employees must be motivated themselves, and should be able to understand and solve the problems they encounter during work. They should not bother their boss, or someone from a higher hierarchical level, by asking permission for a certain decision. This emphasis on *bottom-up* empowerment also means that: much attention should be devoted to bottom-up *communication* communication in the organization, not only top-down. The result of bottom-up communication will be a higher motivation and commitment of the employees. The organization's structure should be as flat as possible and the organization should be as informal as possible; the leadership style should be as feminine as possible because service delivery requires a feminine culture-trait of caring. Probably, the masculine trait of competition will be more prevalent in organizations producing standard services acting in a very competitive market, or in organizations implementing the "war-tactics", instead of a cooperative strategy or relationship marketing with the communication in the organization being as open as possible.

Different levels of empowerment can be distinguished. All of these levels differ in their degree as to what extent "production line processes in services" are at stake, versus services at which contact personnel possess more information and power *production line* and authority.[32] In a production line situation, no empowerment is at stake and *situation* control is exercised via direct supervision or technical control in the production process or output control (see also section 10.7). In another situation, employees may formally voice some suggestions and control is a bit looser. In this situation of *suggestion involvement* suggestion involvement, no real empowerment is at stake. In a situation of "job *"job involvement"* involvement", employees will use more of their skills and talents and gain insight into the added value they provide. Team work increases back office personnel's commitment. Management will get a more supporting role than a controlling one. *high involvement* Finally, in case of high involvement, employee commitment is increased by providing them with information about the results of the whole organization and allowing them a high degree of decision making.

Cost leaders in services with low personal contact services, operating in a stable and quite simple environment, can effectively apply a management style similar to a production line approach without any form of empowerment. At the other extreme, in a very differentiated service firm offering customized augmented services, very qualified employees are needed, being prepared and willing to make a lot of decisions themselves (high degree of empowerment).

Another way of looking at the features of excellent leadership in service organizations is given by Len Berry (1995).[33] "Service leaders exhibit most if not all of the qualities often ascribed to leaders in general – vision, persistence, high expectations, expertise, empathy, persuasiveness, integrity. Yet, the focus on service achievement makes four qualities essential". These four qualities are service vision, belief in others, love of the business and integrity.

vision

"Service leaders view excellent service as the driving force of the business. ... Service leaders focus on the details and nuances of service. ... Service leaders define the service vision for their organization. They not only articulate it in words, they model it daily in their behavior. ... Vision empowers. ... The stronger the vision – the greater its clarity and emotional buy-in – the thinner the company service policies and procedures manual."

believe in people

"Service leaders believe in the fundamental capacity of people to achieve and view their own role as setting a standard of excellence, providing the tools needed for success, and encouraging leadership behavior throughout the organization." They make communication with their employees a priority. Service leaders are coaches. "Their most fundamental service is to serve the server."

love the business

"The best service leaders love the business they lead; they love their immersion in the intricacies of the business, the problems that test them, the sense of accomplishment after a good day; they love the action."

integrity

"Service leaders do the right thing – even when inconvenient or expensive. They place a premium on being fair, consistent, and truthful with customers, employees, suppliers, and other stakeholders. ... "They 'earn trust.' ... "Personal integrity is an essential service leadership characteristic. ... Integrity is the source of a leader's commitment to fair play and truthfullness. Integrity propels the leader's vision of what the organization must be. Integrity assures consistency, which evokes trust. ... Great service requires extraordinary effort; integrity generates such effort. Integrity inspires." Four ways to nurture this kind of service leadership are: promote the right people; stress personal involvement; emphasize the trust factor; and encourage leadership learning.

role model

direct contact with customers

In our opinion, the leaders and their style of working, as described in this section, not only say what should be done and how. They do more than that. They also are able and willing to actually deliver the operational service themselves. In doing this, they perform two basic functions. They are a role model for the rest of the organization or, stated differently, they function as an example for the rest of the personnel (and use that as a way of exercising informal control in the organization, see section 10.7). Next to that, they also get into direct contact with customers. And that is one of the ways to meet the people whom you care about. In many companies, this is the way to give (top)managers a feeling of what is going on in the market and on the shop floor.

Service practice 10-8 Threatening marketeers

One of the authors of this book often asks in seminars with representatives from the business world "when did you last really meet and speak with a customer?"

This question is often seen as a very threatening one, since many managers hardly speak to customers or only know them from large market research reports as anonymous customers transformed into average figures.

How then can one ever be market-oriented, care about people, motivate co-workers and be a role model?[34]

10.5 THE PROCESS OF DELIVERING SERVICES

process

At various places throughout this book, it has been indicated that delivering services is a process: a process not only with a front office and a back office but also consisting of interaction in actions, episodes and relationships. This process is not static but dynamic, as can be seen, for instance, in the transfer of many back office activities, in the financial services area, from many countries to Dublin, Ireland. It is therefore important to find out what are the important elements in such a process approach of the service delivery and how it affects the moments of truth. The notion of the moments of truth in service encounters can be differentiated now into three new concepts.[35] These are the temporal duration (varying from brief to extended), the affective or emotional content (the emotional arousal associated with the encounter, which may be high or low), and, the spatial proximity of service provider and customer. These three concepts can be applied to give real content to the relationship between customers and service providers. To explain the dynamics in more detail, we will focus in this section on the following topics: roles and scripts; and flow charts, blue-printing, and service-maps. Other relevant issues about these service delivery processes, like waiting lines, avoiding waiting lines and controlling the service delivery process, will be discussed in subsequent sections.

temporal duration
affective or emotional
content,
spatial proximity

ROLES AND SCRIPTS IN THE SERVICE ENCOUNTER

The interaction between the customer and service deliverer occurs in the "service encounter", this is where the moments of truth appear. During this service encounter, both customer and service employee should be able to perform a certain number of activities, often according to some procedure or guideline, given the company's mission and strategy.[36]

role

Customers should know what is expected from them in this respect, that is, what role they are expected to play. This role is partly defined by the strategic positions the service organization has chosen, in the services matrices developed in Chapter Two, and the relationship they want to establish with the customer. A role can be defined here as a set of behavioral patterns learned through experience and communication, to be performed by an individual in a certain social interaction (e.g. the service encounter) in order to attain a maximum effectiveness in goal accomplishment. The principal idea proposed is that in a service encounter customers perform roles, and their satisfaction is a function of, amongst others, role congruence (whether or not the enacted behaviors by customers and staff are consistent with the expected roles). Therefore, it is important that roles are clear and that one understands what is expected to be done (or not to be done).[37] This all implies role-expectations but also role-conflicts and role-ambiguity will or can exist. Conflicts and ambiguity typically occur in cases of a lack of clarity of the resources, capabilities and routines. This then, will hinder an adequate implementation of the service delivery. Role conflicts often occur when contact personnel serve different customers simultaneously, but are not

role congruence

role-expectations

role conflicts

role ambiguity

able to answer all the questions in that particular time span. Sometimes, rather than perceiving a role conflict, employees may not understand their role at all. Role ambiguity results, amongst others, when employees do not understand the processes their job is part of, or what the job is intended to accomplish. This may be caused by incompatibility or inadequate training and/or recruitment.

script

A script not only contains information about the own role to be played but defines the information about the roles and behavior of the other participants in the process. The script describes how the service employee and the customer should behave during the service encounter. Customers can learn the content of the script in advance (before the actual service encounter takes place), or find out by experience and communication what the script is. Problems about knowing the exact terms of the script can be avoided or reduced by standardizing the activities in the service encounter to a certain extent or by providing clear information about the roles each party is supposed to play (see also Chapter Twelve on communication). Probably, role conflict and role ambiguity will occur to a lesser extent with standard services, already on the market for a long time, than with newly developed, customized augmented services not tested extensively. Service employees can tell customers

educating the customer

personally what the exact script is and what they are expected to do. Educating the customer in this respect can also be done by TV commercials, showing what actually takes place. McDonald's shows their restaurants' interior and the counter. Dutch Postal services shows how postmen can behave. These ads not only educate customers but also the service provider's employees.

proper match

It is of utmost importance to have a proper match between the knowledge, skills and competencies of the service employee, the job, the internal processes, the supporting equipment and the respective characteristics of the customer. Only when these elements are matched is it possible to deliver services according to the expectations, created, amongst others, by the external communications of the service organization. Good, clear roles and scripts can belong to the previously stated routines which are

employee-job fit and the technology-job fit

difficult to imitate (see section 10.2). These issues refer to what has been mentioned in Chapters Five and Six as the employee-job fit and the technology-job fit.

Service organizations may use experienced and less experienced employees in organizing their work; especially consultancy firms who use junior and senior consultants on projects. Particularly when the work is quite standardized, the leverage effect of juniors doing the work and being less expensive may be notable (especially when they take over the senior's budgeted time).

FLOW CHARTS, BLUEPRINTS AND SERVICE MAPS

thorough description and analysis of the service delivery process

The concepts discussed above deal with a thorough description and analysis of the service delivery process. In this section, our analysis is seen more from an operation research perspective than from a marketing perspective. Here, essentially, the whole service delivery process is broken down into different elements. The elements should then be placed according to the sequence followed by the customer, in the whole

direct contact

service delivery process. This means that the sequence need not be the same as the functions in the organizational structure. It is important to find out during which moments of the service delivery process, the customer has direct contact with the organization or with the person in charge of the service organization. Again, this refers to the previously discussed service encounters with their many moments of truth occurring during the actions and episodes in the relationship with the customer.

from the customers'
perspective
part time employees

During the service encounter, everything should be focussed at delivering excellent service quality and thereby satisfying and keeping customers. Using the above mentioned tools to analyze the service process, the well-known division between two parts of the organization must be recalled: the one part being visible to the customer (the front office) and the invisible part (the back office) of the servuction process. Flow charts, blueprints or service maps are applicable in describing and analyzing the whole process of delivering standard and customized services, as well as core and augmented services in detail. In all services, the analysis is made from the customers' perspective: where do they interact with the service organization, at what stages in the service delivery process can consumers be regarded as the part time employees who have to perform some activities themselves? Figure 10-3 shows the general structure of a service map, that is, it shows the different elements of the service delivery process and the points of interaction.[38]

sequence the customer
follows

different steps

total chain of
activities aimed at
delivering service
quality

Figure 10-3 can be understood as follows: the sequence the customer follows coincides with the different steps or phases the customer passes through in the service delivery process. Each step or phase includes visible and invisible aspects of the service delivery and of the internal organization of the service provider. These visible and invisible aspects are again seen from the customer's perspective. The degree of visibility (and thus tangibility) can vary among the different steps of the whole process. It is possible that after a number of relatively invisible steps, suddenly a strong contact with the service organization appears. An example is an actual visit to a medical specialist after different research/check ups in different rooms and after having done analyses in laboratories. In such a scheme, it also becomes clear where the front office activities are depending strongly on back office activities. This may indicate where the weaknesses lie in the whole process to deliver excellent service quality. It thus shows where the weaknesses are in the total chain of activities aimed at delivering service quality. It also indicates which poor internal service quality affects external quality.

flow charts
blueprinting
service mapping

The difference between flow charts, blueprints and service maps is not always obvious. More or less, they can be used as synonyms, although blueprinting has a more technical perspective, and service mapping a more psychological perspective. The central purpose of all three tools is to get more detailed knowledge about the whole service delivery process, including the resources, capabilities and routines needed. They show which elements of the servuction process are visible to the customer and which not (the front and the back office). Next to that, one can indicate the time needed to pass through the different stages. Consequently, these techniques can be used in developing and designing new services and new service delivery

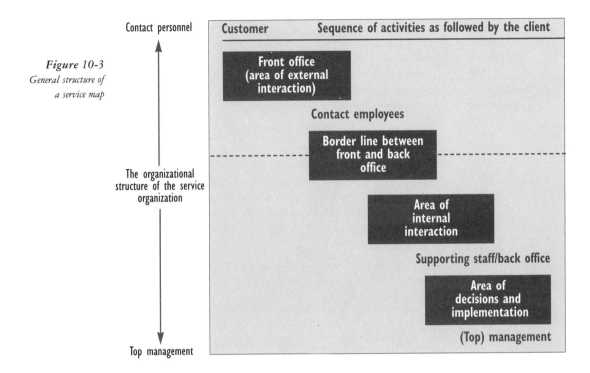

Figure 10-3
General structure of
a service map

processes as well. Innovations in services often have to do with changes in the process and customer participation/presence based on the new opportunities provided by information technology (see also Chapter Eleven).

The techniques can also be helpful in analyzing the services and service delivery processes of competing organizations (benchmarking). In this way, differences in, e.g. processes, resources, possibilities and routines, will be highlighted. Breaking down the service process into different elements is a valuable way of looking at the process, for the organization as well as for the customers. The complexity of the process is identified, as well as possible interactions which can be simplified, for example by a greater input of machinery. Flowcharting allows the manager to understand which parts of the operations are visible to the customer and hence are part of the servuction process. This will speed up managerial decision making processes because one can see whether the same information is shared at the same levels and the same functions. Moreover, a market oriented service firm has to look at the whole process of service delivery from the customers' perspective as well. This will show how customers perceive and assess the whole process. Such an approach may lead to a completely different picture of the internal structure and the way the process is organized than the official organizational chart (organogram) of the company might indicate. Customers do not look at a service company from the formal structure side, but perceive the organization by the logical order they have to go through in getting the service delivered. They don't mind the formal structure. Taking this perspective offers new insights to improve the organization, enhance customer satisfaction and service quality, as Service practice 10-9 shows.

*Service
practice
10-9
The Maasland
hospital*

A couple of years ago, The Maasland hospital in Sittard located in the "deep south" of The Netherlands, asked us to search for ways to improve its service quality. As a research methodology, we followed an approach leaving the formal organizational structure aside. We took the "patient-approach" in a qualitative study among 20 patients.

We described and analyzed the whole process from making an appointment with a doctor, going to the hospital, finding a parking place, entering the hospital, to going to the reception desk, finding one's way to the proper waiting room, waiting, being served, making a next appointment, doing tests, hospitalization (waiting, being called for exact date, going there, "finding" the right room, tests, surgery, recovery, dismissal) and next visits. Of course, the description can be more detailed than given here. Nevertheless, it is important to note two things:

1. all service encounters were described, for all these and many more steps in the whole process of delivering service by the hospital, as perceived by patients; and

2. it was an eye-opener to the hospital's management, looking at their internal processes this way. They eventually linked the invisible, back office processes to patients' flowcharts of the service process.

This way of looking at their organizational structure and putting the patients' perspective first provided means to avoid discussions about demarcation lines and authorities of medical doctors while improving service quality.

Figure 10-4 shows the model of a service map describing the process persons travelling by train and buying their ticket might go through. Depending on the characteristics of the traveller (e.g. travelling frequently or not), the map can be adjusted.[39] This is, in general, the visible process. Every phase of the service map can be further elaborated, as well as the possible support of the back office (stock of tickets, machinery at the desk, maintenance expertise of the dispenser). From a

servicescape

customer's point of view, it is also important to take the servicescape into account: the number of other travellers around you, the noises in the hall, the atmosphere, the accessibility of the machines, but also the number of pickpockets, etc.

Business process redesign is another important instrument to analyze the service delivery process. Here again, the scope is to map the whole service delivery process. However, a different perspective than in the three former techniques is used. Business

*Business Process
Redesign*

Process Redesign aims at a thorough analysis of the processes in the service organization and between the organization and its external environment (especially customers). While analyzing the entire process, the question is asked: "Which

information technology

possibilities does information technology (IT) provide to improve the process?" An improvement, in this case, aims especially at increasing the efficiency of the service delivery to the consumer. This affects the competitive position in a positive way. This analysis focusses on the front and back office; the way the customer participates in the

Figure 10-4
Service map for buying
a train ticket

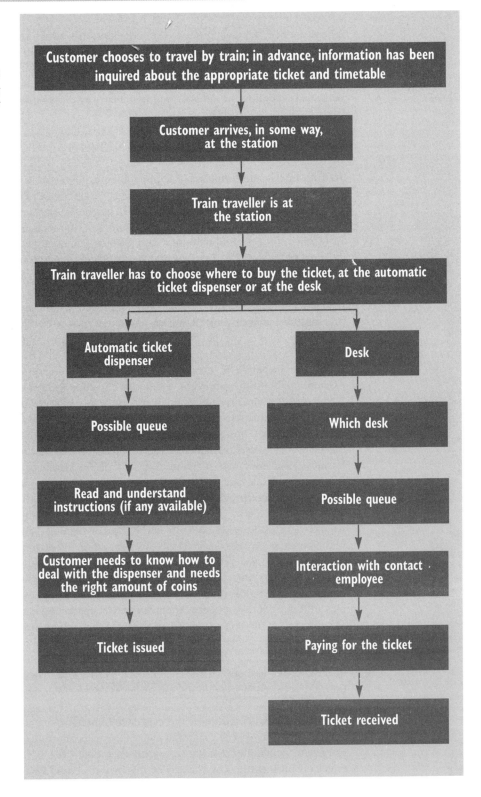

whole service delivery process; the organizational structure; and the information systems and accessibility. Taking into account the classification of services made in Chapter Two, this topic hinges upon the degree of labor or capital intensity in a ervice firm. This is a strategically important issue, especially when the organization wants to realize a competitive advantage by a particular way of (re)-structuring the firm.

BUSINESS PROCESS REENGINEERING

business process reengineering

Starting in the early nineties, the phenomenon of business process reengineering (sometimes called business process redesign) has emerged. The concept of business process reengineering (BPR) was induced by the unsatisfactory levels of business performance improvement that resulted from process rationalization and automation. In essence, process rationalization and automation were mainly used to speed up existing processes. The fundamental performance deficiencies, however, were not addressed by process rationalization and automation. Business process reengineering is a concept that uses two new starting principles in attacking business process deficiencies: enablers and the clean slate approach. These can be applied in service organizations as well. In BPR, it is assumed that processes might provide companies with a new kind of competitive advantage instead of goods or services.

enabler

Firstly, the principle of enabler can be defined as something that facilitates the execution of a business process. Examples of enablers are IT-enablers, organizational enablers and human resources enablers. In the pre-BPR era, information technology (IT), organizational structure and human resources were considered as constraints for the definition of business processes. An organization would normally formulate business objectives. Consequently, these objectives were operationalized by defining business processes that were in line with these business objectives. The use of information technology was in most cases derived from the information requirements of those business processes. When business process reengineering is applied, the enabling influence of IT, ways of organizing and the availability of specific human resources, are considered explicitly in the stage of creating the business objectives and in the business process design stage. IT, organizational structure and human resources

inputs

are no longer considered as constraints but have become major inputs in challenging existing business objectives and processes. Given the capabilities, routines, skills and knowledge of employees in service businesses, this is crucial to these kind of companies. BPR does fit to our central theme of service marketing management in this book, as expressed in the Preface and Chapter One. For, reengineering can be defined as the fundamental rethinking and radical redesign of business processes to achieve dramatic improvements in critical, contemporary measures of performance, such as cost, quality, service and speed and IT is crucial to that end. Therefore, a "recursive relationship between IT capabilities and business process redesign exists."[40]

An example of an IT-enabler is the existence of network technology, e.g. the Internet and the world wide web that allows service organizations to penetrate markets with respect to geographical distance, which they could not have entered before. The effect on business process design of this enabler could be downsizing the service

case team

"stove pipes" functions

organization into a smaller number of regional offices. An example of an organizational enabler is the emerging concept of a case team. In these BPR-projects the elimination of middle-management levels in organizations will be made possible by creating case teams of flexible professionals that will make the former "stove pipes" functions redundant. This means that the emergence of new organizational structures can have an enabling influence on how business processes are executed.

Service practice
10-10
IT works!

A classic example of using case management as an enabler for business process reengineering is the Mutual Benefit Life Insurance Company from Newark, New Jersey. They transformed the business process Underwriting and Issuing from having an average lead time of 22 days involving 40 steps, into a case management process with a lead time of two to six days, thereby cutting (mainly personnel) costs by 40%.

An example of an human resources enabler is the existence of educational qualifications and capabilities of individuals. For example, the existence of people having knowledge and experience that cuts across functional stove pipes can lead to the creation of new job descriptions. At Dell Computer, a recently designed function comprises dealing with the customer taking customer orders, as well as providing technical support.

In Figure 10-5, the business process for tax collection at the Internal Revenue Service Centers in the United States is shown in the pre-BPR situation (left) and the reengineered situation (right).[41]

starting with a clean
slate

what value does this
step add

Secondly, the "starting with a clean slate" principle has become a major characteristic of many business process reengineering projects. By applying this principle, BPR projects focus explicitly on the way in which processes are designed. The breakdown of business processes into steps, the sequence of these steps and the waiting times between consecutive steps are part of the analysis as well. The crucial question is: what value does this step add to our customer service or product? In many cases, old steps will be eliminated from the process or a number of old steps will be regrouped into a new process. An example of a successful BPR effort that led to the creation of an entirely new business process was the accounts payable process at Ford. Ford changed their accounts payable policy from; "we pay when we get the invoice" to "we pay when we get the goods". As a result of this BPR project, the headcount in the accounts payable department was reduced by 75%.

Business process reengineering can be considered as an organizational activity in which business processes are analyzed and redefined using the latest development in (information) technology, human resource issues and organizational structures. BPR, therefore, should not be considered a "one-time only" event, but should be part of the organizational planning cycle in which the service organization will scan its environment on the emergence of new enablers. The possible impact of these enablers on corporate objectives, business processes and information requirements should be

Figure 10-5
Internal revenue service automated collections system

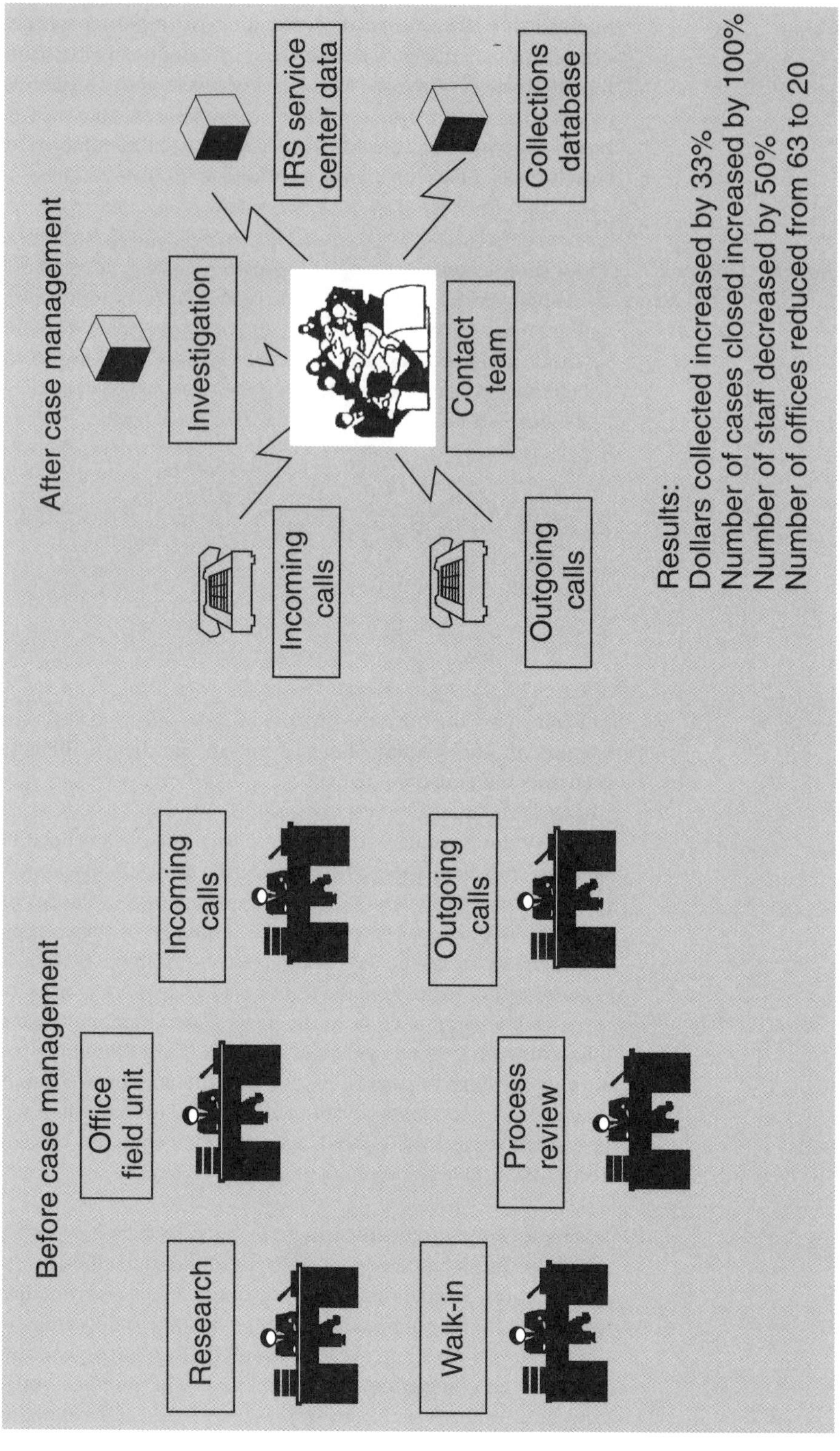

After case management

IRS service center data

Collections database

Investigation

Contact team

Incoming calls

Outgoing calls

Results:
Dollars collected increased by 33%
Number of cases closed increased by 100%
Number of staff decreased by 50%
Number of offices reduced from 63 to 20

Before case management

Incoming calls

Outgoing calls

Office field unit

Process review

Research

Walk-in

assessed in this planning cycle.[42] So, when airlines start using electronic ticketing instead of using the paper tickets because processing them electronic is much cheaper ($1-2 instead of $8 per ticket), they have to look for its impact on other parts of the service delivery process, as the *Financial Times* (October 23, 1996) indicates. This (re)-structuring of activities will also determine to what extent customers will be helped immediately or have to wait. The intangibility characteristic of services implies that storing services is difficult if not impossible. Therefore, waiting will often occur in service. Perhaps it is unavoidable in service delivery processess (or not?).

10.6 QUEUEING AND WAITING

waiting time and queueing

In service organizations, waiting time and queueing are receiving more and more attention. Effective organizing of waiting lines and minimizing waiting times have a profound impact on the customer"s quality perception of the whole service. This is because waiting quickly causes irritation and dissatisfaction. Waiting is related to, amongst other things, the service provider's capacity, the predictability and forecasting of consumer behavior (demand) and the planning within the service organization (processes).

Waiting problems can be studied from a perspective focussing on the organization of the service delivery process. We will follow that perspective below. Then, an operations research approach to waiting problems will also be elucidated. First, we will look at this phenomenon from a customer's perspective.

Waiting is a very complex phenomenon that encompasses a number of aspects, related to the capacity of the service organization to meet customer needs and organizational goals. Social and psychological aspects of waiting impact on the subjective experiences and perceptions of waiting by customers. A few examples of these factors are the fairness of the sequence in which customers are served, the feeling of being "in-process", the attractiveness of the waiting environment and the amount of information that is given about the cause and duration of the waiting.[43].

Service practice 10-11 Wait a minute!

Most of the time, waiting is perceived as a negative experience. This need not be the case, as in the famous words of Al Jolson (1927) in The Jazz Singer indicate: 'wait a minute, wait a minute, you ain't heard nothing yet.'

These words were the first ones spoken on the silver screen.

However, quite often service employees respond by saying "wait a minute" and then show up after a long wait.

WAIT FOR SERVICE

waiting is inherent to services

Sometimes you get the feeling waiting is inherent to services. This is probably due to the fact that services are perishable and intangible and therefore cannot be stored.

However, this argument can be questioned. Imagine how often you have to wait at a counter or during a service delivery process. Sometimes, you feel hospitals, public transportation and other service providers (especially monopolies and public service providers like utilities) are "famous" for the waiting times they create. When they eventually help you, it feels like "mercy". Waiting time is a big problem for customers in shops, supermarkets, airports, etc.

"pre-process waits"

As this introduction shows, waiting times and delays are crucial in determining service quality. In order to get a good insight into these issues, it is necessary to make a distinction between various kinds of waiting and delays.[44] Customers may have to wait before, during or after a transaction between service encounter or servuction process. There are even various kinds of "pre-process waits": pre-schedule waits (the customer arrived too early), delays (post-schedule waits when the dentist's treatment starts 15 minutes after the time agreed upon) and queue waits (lining up due to being served on a first-come-first-served basis). In general, we can conclude that longer delays result in lower evaluations of service. Overall service evaluations are directly affected by evaluations of punctuality, the uncertainty and anger created by delay. Anger and uncertainty were affected directly by the length of the delay and degree to which time was filled during the delay. Anger was also related to the degree of control the service provider had over the delay.[45]

punctuality, uncertainty and anger

reliability in performance
perceived risk

The subjective evaluations of punctuality are in line with many things we discussed before about reliability in performance. This is an important service quality dimension. Subjective feelings of uncertainty and anger are partly related to perceived risk: uneasiness, unsettledness, anxiety, annoyance, irritation and frustration play a crucial role here. This also indicates that the subjective evaluation of the time of waiting or delay is important, next to the actual waiting time.

THE OBJECTIVE AND SUBJECTIVE SIDE OF WAITING

Time perception, psychological cost, economic cost contextual characteristics

The previous section revealed, in researching and analyzing waiting problems, that one should not only pay attention to the objective (actual) waiting time (as measured in minutes, for example), but also to the subjectively perceived waiting time. Time perception, the psychological cost and the economic cost of waiting co-determine the effective response to and the acceptability of waiting.[46] However, the value of consumer's time is not constant but depends on contextual characteristics of the decision situation.[47] For instance, Swiss clients are less tolerant while waiting at the Post Office than while shopping at Migros, a large Swiss retailer.[48] This implies to service organizations that irritation and dissatisfaction, which arise from waiting, may and can be solved not only by reducing the objective waiting time. The reduction or sweetening of the subjective waiting time is often an important issue in increasing customer satisfaction and the quality of the service delivery. Issues stemming from architecture, environmental psychology, operations research, sociology, marketing, etc. may also impact on affect and thus waiting time perception and evaluation.[49]

Service practice 10-12 What to do while waiting?

This is what airline passengers do while they have to wait at Geneva airport[50]

reading a newspaper	80%
shopping	79%
going to a restaurant/bar	63%
reading a book	60%
working	52%
phoning	50%
staying in a lounge	47%
doing nothing	32%

irritation about waiting

A review of the international literature about this topic shows irritation about waiting is extremely high if one: has to wait for a long time whilst in a hurry oneself; has nothing to do during the time one is waiting and consequently gets bored and gets the feeling that waiting is unfair (especially when a person coming in later is being served sooner).[51] Contrary to this, if somebody has to wait while not being in a hurry and in pleasant surroundings, then the subjective waiting period is considered as being shorter and less irritation will arise.

An important question which can be raised is:"which kind of waiting time correlates best with the irritation about waiting": is this the subjective or objective waiting time? The answer is clear: the subjective waiting time shows a higher correlation with irritation about waiting compared to the objective waiting time.[52]

side-effects of waiting

Therefore, as in so many instances in service industries, the role of perception is evident in the customer's evaluation of this aspect of service delivery processes. This affects the total quality judgement. Some other side-effects of waiting on the overall quality perception may occur as well. It has been found, for example, that if one has to wait for a longer period, one has the idea that the personnel are working less efficiently and are more unfriendly. Such side-effects may occur, which can increase the total quality evaluation in a negative direction. Service delivery organizations will have to realize this. For, even in the first contact between the customer and the service organization waiting often occurs. For customers, the feeling of unpleasantness then arises.

satisfaction with waiting

A model can be developed to study the impact of waiting on customer (dis)satisfaction about the service delivery, in which, e.g. the satisfaction with the service delivery is also determined by the satisfaction with waiting.[53] The satisfaction with waiting, then, is determined by three factors, e.g. the expectations customers have at entering the waiting situation; the tolerance the customer has with waiting at that time; and the evaluation of and judgement about the waiting situation itself. We will expand upon these factors now.

expectations customers have when entering the waiting situation

The expectations customers have when entering the waiting situation, in fact, consist of an estimated waiting time. This estimated waiting time can be adjusted during waiting. The expectation depends on the probable estimated waiting time (which again is determined by, for example, previous experiences from similar situations, the expectations originating from the communication policy of the service organization, what one has heard from friends and acquaintances and the suggestion made by the service provider). The expectation also depends on what one sees and expects, as soon as one enters the waiting room (what is said at the counter about waiting, how many people are already there and how long it takes to help a new customer, etc.).

tolerance of how long one finds acceptable to wait

Here, we can also define a zone of tolerance. That is, the tolerance of how long one finds acceptable to wait. It can be compared with the "zone of tolerance", which was introduced in the SERVQUAL-model. This acceptable waiting period depends, on the one hand, on the estimated waiting period during the actual waiting and on: the number of alternatives when the customer has to use different service organizations (at the registry office of our local town you really have to wait, because nowhere else you can declare the birth of your child); the switching costs when any alternative service organizations might exist; and the circumstances out of control of the service provider (such as force majeure; emergency cases; the break down of electricity).

evaluation and judgement of the waiting situation itself

The third factor determining the satisfaction with waiting is the evaluation and judgement of the waiting situation itself. This subjective evaluation not only depends on the objective waiting period, but also, for example, on the extent to which the waiting environment is appealing or pleasant; the distraction during waiting; the justice and fairness one is experiencing in queueing; and the extent to which the customer knows how long it will take. Therefore, in parks like Disneyland, Phantasialand, Futuroscope or De Efteling, signs are placed with information about the expected waiting time. This information reduces the uncertainty and anxiety of waiting. Travellers by train or plane appreciate information about the cause of waiting and delay. To hear nothing while the train is standing is very annoying, especially if one uses public transport instead of the car for long distance business appointments.

Banning waiting periods and queues is too much to ask from the service provider. However, regulation and attention designed to make waiting more pleasant certainly belongs amongst the tasks of every market-oriented service organization. Queueing models can be used to optimize processes and provide information to, hopefully, abolish waiting times to a large extent.

THE STRUCTURE OF QUEUEING MODELS

queueing model

In management science or operations research, a waiting line is called a queue. A queueing model (or queueing theory) describes the quantitative factors of queueing in order to give insight to the causes of waiting. In combination with mathematical or statistical analyses and simulations, these models can help to improve the efficiency of a waiting system.[54]

customer arrivals at a service facility

All queueing situations involve customer arrivals at a service facility, for example a hairdresser, a theater, an airport or a post office. At all these places, customers may have to spend some time waiting for and then receiving the desired service. As one can imagine, every queueing situation is different: customers may arrive all at the same time or there may be some (random) time between arrivals; there may be one server or many; customers may have to stand in a single waiting line or may have the choice between more than one line, etc. Queueing models can be used to describe and (hopefully) improve queueing behavior. Therefore, the situation is translated into a queueing system which consists of one or more servers, an arrival process, and a service process, along with some additional assumptions about how the system works.[55] The number of customers in the queueing system at any given time is the number of customers in the queue plus the number of customers in service.

queueing system

number of customers in the queueing system

Many mathematical models of queueing systems exist. Most of these queueing models use equations that are built up around eight factors: the type of arrival process; the type of service process; the number of servers; the number of stages in the whole service process; the number of queues; the capacity of the system; the size of the population from which the customers come; and, the queue discipline. Each of these factors will now be elaborated upon.

Type of arrival process

arrival process, customers arrive singly

The arrival process describes how the customers appear for serving. Three aspects are relevant. Firstly, queueing models usually assume that customers arrive singly, although some models do allow for the batching of arrivals. The first type of model might apply when customers arrive in a supermarket, the latter when a touring car/bus arrives at a roadside restaurant or customers pick up their luggage after a flight. Secondly, several probability distributions can be used to represent the time between arrivals. Most models assume that customers arrive totally at random, that the arrivals are not scheduled at regular intervals and are independent of each other. Customers will sometimes arrive close to each other, sometimes far apart. This assumption leads to a so-called Poisson process, in which the times between arrivals have an exponential distribution. The great advantage of assuming an exponentially distributed interarrival time is that just one single parameter, called the mean arrival rate, is enough to describe the entire process. Thirdly, most models assume that the same interarrival time distribution applies to all customers throughout the period under investigation. In case of random arrivals, this means the average time between two arrivals does not vary over time. If this average interarrival time does vary considerably over time, it might be appropriate to develop two models instead of one: one model suited for peak hours and another one for slack periods (overcapacity).

customers arrive totally at random

mean arrival rate

same interarrival time distribution

Type of service process

service process

The service process can be described in almost the same way as the arrival process. The following aspects are relevant to a sound analysis of the service process in which the service encounters actually take place. First of all, most models assume that the service time has an exponential distribution. This means, in this context, that the likelihood for the service to be completed within a next time-interval does not depend on the time that the service has already been ongoing. Because the service process now can be fully characterized by a single parameter, the so-called mean service rate, this is the easiest distribution to work with. Next, the service process is usually assumed to be independent of the arrival process. So, most models assume

service time

mean service rate

independent of the arrival process

that a server does not work faster when several persons are waiting in line then when no one is. Moreover, all models assume the mean service rate must exceed the mean arrival rate, so that the queueing system must have more than enough capacity to service all customers. Without this restriction, the waiting line would grow indefinitely.

Number of servers

single-server queueing system

multiple-server queueing system

In a single-server queueing system, all customers are served by the same server. This one and only server can be one single person, for example a dentist, but it can also be a machine, for example a ticket vending machine, or a complex entity, such as an airport runway. In a multiple-server queueing system, more than one server performs all the desired services, for example a toll station on a highway.

Number of stages

number of service points or stages

single-stage system

multiple-stage system

Another way of analyzing queues refers the number of service points or stages customers must pass through before they can or may leave the system. A single-stage system involves just one service facility; in a multiple-stage system each customer must receive two or more kinds of service and therefore has to wait in multiple queues. Examples of multiple-stage systems are manufacturing processes, the process described in the Service practice 10-9 on the Maasland hospital, or a situation in a retail outlet, where a customer wants to buy a washing-machine and first has to wait at the pay-desk and then at the loading dock.

Number of queues

single queue

separate queues

When customers form a single queue, the leading customer proceeds to the first free server, as is done usually in US banks and recently introduced in Dutch post offices (as an innovation to improve processes and decrease waiting times). The situation is slightly different when arriving customers must select one server and wait in separate queues, as is usually the case when checking out at a supermarket (and many people always have the feeling of having chosen the longest line).

Capacity of the system

capacity of the waiting system is infinite

In most situations, it is assumed the capacity of the waiting system is infinite. This means that an infinite number of customers can join the waiting line(s). This seems to be a quite realistic assumption. If there is a limited amount of waiting room, for example in the emergency room of a hospital, or for any other reason customers are prohibited from joining a queue once it reaches a certain length, we say that the queue or the system has finite capacity.

Size of the population

source population is infinite

The population of customers from which the arrivals come is called the source population. Usually, this population is assumed to be infinite. Sometimes, though, it is useful to create a model that is able to limit the number of potential arrivals to some finite number. For example, when a maintenance facility may service only ten machines in a fleet, the source population is finite: if they are all being repaired (in maintenance), no arrivals are possible.

Queue discipline

queue discipline
FIFO

LIFO
RSS

Queue discipline refers to the rule by which the next customer to be served is selected. The most common queue discipline is first in first out (FIFO), where customers receive service in order of their arrival. The FIFO principle is almost a general rule, although there are cases when other principles make more sense. Last in first out (LIFO) can be of use in some situations, for example when using elevators, and random service selection (RSS) is for example usually applied at a theater refreshment counter during intermissions or breaks. A wide variety of other queue disciplines, each involving various kinds of priorities or classifications, exist as well. These are routines determining the fairness of the waiting time and the organization of the whole process (like the discipline at UK bus stops).

Different combinations of each of the eight topics discussed will provide the exact description of a service delivery process. All topics can be applied in classifying the service delivery process, analyze them in terms of, e.g. blue prints, compare them with competitors' processes, and use them in benchmarking studies. Then, it is important to know how these models can be applied in practice.

QUEUEING MODELS IN PRACTICE

capacity, variability
in arrival and service
times

The number of possible combinations in queueing models based on the many issues mentioned in each of the eight topics, is enormous.[56] Although not every assumption underlying these models is 100% realistic, these models still work surprisingly well in many practical situations.[57] Of all the eight factors listed, capacity and variability in arrival and service times are the most important ones. An awareness and understanding of just these two factors for the occurrence of waiting could be of considerable practical interest. Substantial reductions in waiting times might be obtained by a more careful allocation of capacity or by reduction of variations in arrival and service times. Some important results are derived from empirical studies; practical examples will be given to show how this can be done. Then, one quite comprehensive example follows.

Queueing models have already provided some interesting results with valuable implications for the structuring of the service delivery process.[58] Knowing the probability distribution of the number of customers in the system (so knowing the likelihood that one, two or three, etc. customers are in the waiting system), can be useful in designing the capacity of the waiting facility. Another example is that of a call center, where the probability that a calling customer cannot be helped directly can be an important measure of service quality.

The mean number of customers in the waiting line or in the whole system accounts for the number of customers waiting in line or receiving service. Knowing the average number of customers waiting in line or in the system can help to establish the size of the waiting facilities. The mean customer time spent in the waiting line/in the system represents the total time spent by a customer waiting in line and/or receiving service. When costs can be allocated to these averages, it can be used in

server utilization factor

economic analysis. It is also part of the costs clients have to incur to get the service. So, it will be used in the client's trade off between cost and benefits of a particular service experience.[59] The server utilization factor is the proportion of time that the server actually spends with the customer. Knowing this, it is easy to estimate the time that the server has to do secondary tasks not directly involved with the customers.

"explosion phenomenon"

Knowledge about this "explosion phenomenon" can be used in practical situations, for instance in hospitals. Doctors often plan their appointments with patients near to full capacity (server utilization rate is high), so the doctors do not have to wait. The consequence is that any minor complication will lead directly to a long waiting line of patients. One may doubt whether this really is an example of market oriented health care. On the other hand, some people may argue that waiting lines in health care indicate that a full usage of capacity is present and no over capacity exists (which could be an interesting feature looking at the health care industry from a macro economic perspective). However, by planning at a slightly lower occupancy rate, this can lead to significant improvements for doctors and patients. Even when the doctor would have to wait for a patient, there will be various little things to fill his time usefully. The customer will feel much more satisfied for having been helped right away than after a long waiting period. Again, managing customer expectations, about these waiting times, will improve service quality performance.[61]

In this way, we sketch the almost unavoidable dilemma between the desire to obtain full utilization of a server and the desire to keep the mean queue length short. The intuitive sense that the system is "in balance" when the arrival rate is equal to the service rate is clearly wrong.[62] This dilemma also shows it is important to monitor and control the whole process of service delivery. That is the topic for the next section.

10.7 CONTROL AND SERVICE ORGANIZATIONS

control and control systems

indicators

In the management literature and in the accounting and auditing literature, a lot has been written about control and control systems.[63] In essence, control and control systems are means to find out whether the stated goals are indeed accomplished. Many performance indicators can be used to that end and help to increase the probability that the goals set will indeed be accomplished. It is of utmost importance that these indicators do fit the goals formulated in corporate strategy and in the strategies for the various functions in the company as such and at the business unit level (what we called the strategic service groups) or at the sales outlet level. We will now focus on some elements which are of great importance in controlling the marketing performance in service firms focusing on the human resource aspects.[64]

*Service
practice
10-13
The explosion
phenomenon* [60]

One of the most easy to use mathematical queueing models is the model with the following characteristics: exponentially distributed inter-arrival and service times; single-server; single-queue; single-stage; infinite capacity; infinite population and FIFO as a queue discipline.

In this model, the expected time a customer spends waiting in the system can be easily calculated by

$W = 1 / (C - A)$

where
- W = mean customer time spent in the system;
- A = arrival rate (number of customers) per minute;
- C = service rate (number of customers that can be handled) per minute.

For example, suppose the server can serve one customer per minute and on average four customers arrive in 10 minutes.

Then $C = 1$ and $A = 0.4$ so that $W = 1 / [1 - 0.4] = 1.67$ minutes. If we keep the service rate constant at 1 minute, this calculation can be repeated for different arrival rates as shown in the next table.

A (number of arrivals per 10 minutes)	W (mean time in system in minutes)
4	1.67
5	2
8	5
9	10
9.5	20
9.9	100

Should the number of arrivals per 10 minutes grow from four to five, it would only lead to a minor increase of the mean time in the system to 2 minutes. But with eight customers per 10 minutes, the time in the system would already be 5 minutes and this will double to 10 minutes by just adding one more customer per 10 minutes. As one can see in the table, the time spent in the system grows explosively when adding still more customers. If, for example, on average 9.99 customers per 10 minutes arrive (so almost every minute a customer arrives), the waiting time will have grown nearly to 17 hours!

Source: Nico van Dijk, *To Wait or Not to Wait*

CONTROLLING THE MARKETING PERFORMANCE

Because the service delivery process is the vital element in the service organization, there should be a control system to monitor this particular process carefully. Not only *output, throughput* the output, but also the throughput should be controlled, like the length of waiting times and queues (objective as well as subjective), duration of the treatment, friendliness during service encounter, ability to build trust, etc. All these elements deal with the objective characteristics of the service process (facts) and the subjective perception of this process. They are also linked to the question as to whether the goals set for the services attitude are met.

input control

Next to output and throughput control, "input control" is also important in service organizations. This means that sufficient attention should be paid to recruiting and selecting contact personnel and management with the right services attitude. Training these people constantly is also important (e.g. via institutions like the McDonald's Hamburger University). Input control becomes more and more important in market oriented, informally organized service organizations, where the empowered people are given the appropriate responsibilities and competencies to execute their tasks at the operational level of day to day activities. Examples of service organizations where input control plays a crucial role are professional organizations such as hospitals, universities, higher vocational schools, etc. Another important instrument

role model

for controlling the service delivery process is the "role model" of management; who should make the contact personnel understand what is expected from them. This can be supported by service leaders themselves behaving in the desired way.

technical, functional and relational quality

satisfaction

Next to input, throughput and output dimensions of control and control systems, the technical, functional and relational quality of the service delivery and the satisfaction of the customer will be important control instruments in market oriented service organizations. We have indicated, in many instances, that technical quality will no longer be decisive in service quality. Of course, technical quality is important. However, the other two services are more decisive in the customers' final assessment of service quality. Control of the functional and relational quality can be called a

behavioral control approach

behavioral control approach. Our own research into the culture of market oriented organizations shows that these organizations highly value behavioral control. In fact, they consider customer satisfaction as the crucial factor in control, which influences all other financial, output related criteria.

One of the dimensions of service quality is the tangible element of the service delivery. Examples are not only the logo and the letters of a bank, but also the decoration and interior of the bank (servicescape), the clothes of the front desk personnel, the clarity of an account-sheet and the appearance of the equipment used. A disorganized service environment does not stimulate any interaction and will negatively influence the quality of the service delivery. In designing the service delivery process, one

physical environment

should take into account the physical environment in which the service delivery takes place.[65]

PERCEIVED CONTROL IN THE SERVICE ENCOUNTER

Employees in a service organization, having competencies and responsibilities, need the feeling that they can guide and control the interaction with customers.[66] This applies also to the customer, being the "opposite party" during the service encounter.

perceived control and autonomy

Many research projects reveal that both contact employees and customers need a certain degree of perceived control and autonomy during the service encounter. When necessary, this perceived control will help both parties control the process of the intangible service delivery. The satisfaction with the job or with the purchase will be influenced in a negative way if the relationship is unbalanced or undesired.[67] Increased perceived control will result in more consumer satisfaction for the customer and more job satisfaction for the contact personnel. This then, will increase the loyalty towards the organization and the service for both parties. To avoid the problem that one or both parties do not feel in control, it is necessary to construct clear roles and scripts. These should be based on a detailed blueprint of the service delivery process. Giving more control is also a basic characteristic of empowering people. And if it is not given, employees will search for it. For instance, contact employees in convenience stores may use different kinds of tactics to get more control over these service encounters. Service practice 10-14 shows four groups of tactics used: effort ("a tactic which seeks to satisfy the demands placed on the service worker"); negotiating ("tactics which attempt to alter the demands placed on the customer-contact worker"); pre-empting ("tactics which attempt to prevent the role senders from placing demands on the customer-contact worker"); and, avoiding ("tactics which allow the customer-contact worker to manipulate and alter the demands received from role senders"). It will be clear that these tactics to a large extent conflict with being market-oriented and do not fit into what we have circumscribed as the service attitude. Obviously, such actions occur when role stress is at stake and service employees feel themselves out of control over the customer and the service encounter.

clear roles and scripts

empowering people

effort, negotiating, pre-empting,

avoiding

The negotiating tactics tend to be used when there is role ambiguity. The link between customer satisfaction and job satisfaction in the service industry is very clear: "While customer-contact workers' use of negotiating tactics was not related to job satisfaction, the use of effort was. Job satisfaction was also negatively related to the use of avoidance tactics. This suggests that satisfied customer-contact workers may exhibit more effort to satisfy customer demands, and that dissatisfied workers may use avoidance tactics such as "playing dumb" and implying an unawareness of customers' role demands".[69]

10.8   CORE, AUGMENTED, STANDARD AND CUSTOMIZED SERVICES

At various places in this chapter, we have made references to the typology of service firms developed in Chapters One and Two. The requirements in terms of skills, knowledge, empowerment, control and the like may differ to the type of service strategy chosen. In Figure 10-6 we summarize some of the main issues discussed in this chapter.[70]

It sounds plausible that delivering standard and core services requires "less and other skills" from employees and service leaders than processes aimed at delivering augmented and customized services. Another kind of contact with the customer is

*Service
practice
10-14
Tactics of
customer-
contact
workers*

Effort: tactics to satisfy role demands

Attempting to perform various tasks efficiently enough to please organizational and customer demands (e.g. becoming so familiar with routine facets of the job that they can be done simultaneously with other tasks; such as putting merchandise on a shelf while answering a customer's question).

Negotiating: tactics to alter role demands

Delegating. Getting other organizational members (including supervisors) and/or customers to perform some of the aspects of the service (e.g. asking another waiter to "refill the iced tea at table four"; asking the customer to put the laces in a shoe while the employee measures another child's foot).

Explaining. Giving reasons why certain expectations cannot be fulfilled (e.g. "company policy only allows us to give refunds under these circumstances..."; "the manufacturer is out of this item and we don't know when to expect any more";"if we do what you are suggesting, we won't have time to complete this other project").

Rewarding. Doing extra favors or providing unusually good service to customers or other organizational members in return for their requests not creating role stress for the employee (e.g. telling favored customers of special deals; calling other stores to find out where the customer can find a certain product; doing tasks normally outside the scope of the employee's position).

Punishing. Penalizing supervisors or customers who add to the worker's role conflict (e.g. sabotage in extreme cases; making a customer wait while finishing another task).

Pre-empting: tactics to avoid the sent role

Ingratiating. Seeking to put the customer or supervisor in a good mood or in a state of mind in which they think favorably of the employee so that they will not want to overload the employee with expectations (e.g. complimenting a customer's sense of fashion; talking with the supervisor about his/her favourite sports team).

Distracting. Engaging customers or supervisors to prevent them from having the opportunity to express expectations (e.g. talk about the weather, the "big game", the latest fashions; asking the customer or supervisor to do something which keeps them too busy to ask the employee to do something).

Avoiding: tactics to avoid the received role

Reinterpreting. Pretending to comprehend the customer's or organization's expectations in a way which minimizes role stress (e.g. the customer asks a retail sales clerk to find a certain product, and the sales clerk acts as if s/he believes the customer is asking for general directions and tells the customer that "the item should be on the left side of aisle 6").

Ignoring. Providing no feedback to customers who try to get the employee's attention (e.g. a bank teller keeping his or her eyes focused on paperwork and acting as if the customer or supervisor is speaking to someone else; a waiter pretending not to see a patron motioning for service).

Figure 10-6
Personnel and the
service typology

HRM policy	Standard core services	Customized core services	Standard augmented services	Customized augmented services
Kind of contact personnel	contactors	contactors modifiers	modifiers contactors	modifiers
Role (top) management	direct control	direct control supporting	supporting initiating	initiating coaching
Standardization in work procedures	high	high	moderate	low
Type of empowerment	production line	production line suggestion involvement	job involvement	high involvement

required, different scripts and roles might be at stake. Probably, empowerment and qualification must be higher in the latter group of services. This will also require another (less directive) kind of control and leadership. Direct control, a high degree of standardization of work procedures and a production line type of empowerment might best suit firms delivering (simple?) standard core services in which contact employees often have the role of contactors.

SUMMARY

A book about services marketing management would be contradictory in essence, if discussions on the marketing mix did not start with a chapter about employees, personnel, the organizational structure and the processes involved in excellent service quality. The employees (the full timers and part timers being paid by the service firm and the customers as part time employees) are the most valuable asset a service organization possesses. In fact, that is the main reason why we started this part of our book with this chapter and not with a chapter on services (the "product"; this will be the subject of the next chapter).

The employees, and their way of operating in service delivery processes, play a crucial role in actually delivering these services, especially when these services are labor intensive (from their point of view). The "quality chain" in a service organization will be as strong as the weakest link in the whole service delivery process. Hopefully, that will not be the human factor, nor caused by poor internal service quality. To accomplish the service attitude and the strategy of the organization, the employees need to have an external and internal orientation. The employees should be motivated and capable and should have the opportunities to perform, as desired by the customers and the organization's goals. Therefore, an empowered, informal organization is needed, with a feminine style of leadership in which care and attention for people (consumers and employees) is a focal point. These issues come to the fore as the essentials of the service attitude and service leadership.

The whole service delivery process can be broken down into roles, scripts, contact moments, etc. crucial in the service encounter. Also, the temporal duration, emotional and affective components and, the spatial proximity of the service provider and the customer play a role in the moments of truth and thus in assessing service quality. In that respect, the functional and relational quality (both related to the personal touch of servicing), seem to be more decisive in customers' evaluations of service quality than the technical quality.

Flow-charts, blueprints and service maps are useful in describing, structuring and analyzing the process, as well as in developing new services. In this context, business process re-engineering highlights the role of information technology in the delivery process.

The control a service organization exercises should be in line with the above mentioned characteristics of market oriented service organizations. It does not only hinge upon the output of the service delivery process, but should focus more on the process itself (throughput as well as input control). From a marketing management perspective then, quality and satisfaction indicators could be of more importance than financial indicators such as turnover, profit and return on investment.

Many issues discussed in this chapter apply for all kinds of service organizations. Finally, we attempted to indicate how some issues may differ for delivering core services, augmented services, standard services or customized services.

A common theme throughout this chapter has been the notion that customer satisfaction and job satisfaction are merging in the service industry: satisfied employees will give better service resulting in increased customer satisfaction which, in turn, makes employees feel (and be) more satisfied, etc. Consequently, rumours about lay-offs may affect customer satisfaction and service quality in a negative way.

QUESTIONS

1 Why, next to an external orientation, is an internal orientation important for service organizations to gain and maintain a sustainable competitive advantage?
2 Which similarities and differences exist between the Triad-model in Chapter Four (customers) and Chapter Ten (employees)?
3 In this chapter, it is stated that contact personnel can be regarded as part-time marketeers and customers as part-time employees. If a service organization applied those two concepts, would that be a guarantee for a market oriented service delivery during the service encounter (that is, during the interaction process of the service delivery)?
4 When the goal of the service organization is to deliver excellent service quality, why then should more attention be paid to input and throughput control, than to output control?
5 How would you relate the findings of the Rogers, Clow and Kash study to the issues raised in closing Gap 3 of the SERVQUAL-model?
6 Why is getting along with the customer and getting along with colleagues important for market oriented service organizations to deliver excellent service quality?
7 What is the difference between subjective and objective waiting time?
8 Is it always necessary to reduce objective and subjective waiting times to increase service quality?
9 What types of queueing and waiting lines exist?
10 Can role conflicts and role ambiguity of service employees and customers affect service quality? Why or why not? And if so, how can it be solved?

ASSIGNMENTS

1 Try to design a blueprint or service map of the service delivery of your school. You may select a particular service delivery process.
2 Design a script for an ideal lesson, ideal lecture or seminar at your school. Compare your design with that of fellow students and prepare together a proposition for the ideal lesson, lecture or seminar.
3 Summarize the different characteristics of market oriented organizational cultures (as stated in previous chapters) and indicate which characteristics can be added after having studied this chapter about personnel, organization and processes.
4 What are the characteristics of a services attitude? What characteristics do you notice in deaily life when dealing with service organizations? Make a table stating the good and bad points of service deliverers; try to group them according to certain elements, for example the SERVQUAL dimensions or the steps involved in the service delivery process. How do your findings relate to the characteristics of service leaders (Berry, Helgesen) and service employees (Fromm and Schlesinger)?

5 Make the calculation in the Service practice 10-13 showing that the waiting time will have grown to nearly 17 hours when, on average, 9.99 customers arrive per 10 minutes in this model.

6 Discuss and explain Figure 10-6. What do you think of this classification and the way it is elaborated?

7 Describe and analyze the waiting lines at your local post office and bank. What do these companies do to make waiting time as short or attractive as possible?

Case: RECRUITING EMPLOYEES IN THE AIRLINE INDUSTRY

Christopher Lovelock (1995), pp. 218–219) wrote the following case history about the way in which new software redefines skill needs at Singapore Airlines:

"Normally, it takes three weeks to train a check-in agent for an international airline. Much of the training centres on correct use of the computer terminals employed to confirm (or make) reservations and assign seats. Older reservations systems need to be literally programmed by the agents, who require a certain amount of technical skill to perform this time-consuming task.

Recently, Singapore Airlines (SIA) was having trouble in recruiting and retaining check-in agents for its home base at Singapore's Changi Airport. With wages rising in this island nation, it was getting harder to recruit people with the necessary skills for the wages SIA was willing to offer. And, once they were working, many agents found it rather unchallenging. The predictable result: relatively high turnover and constant repetition of the expensive recruitment and training process.

As part of a major programme to update its departure control systems, SIA computer specialists worked to create new software for check-in procedures, featuring screen formats with pull-down windows, menu-driven commands, and other innovations on the video terminal displays – all designed to speed and simplify usage. The net result is that SIA has been able to lower the educational criteria for the check-in position. The job is now open to people who would not previously have qualified and who consider the work and the wages fairly attractive. Because the new system is so much easier to use, only one week's training is needed – a significant saving to SIA. Employee satisfaction with this job is up, and turnover is down. Finally, agents are able to process passengers faster, making the former more productive and the latter happier."

Another story about recruiting service employees was published in the February-March 1995 issue of *The Flying Dutchman*, the magazine of KLM's frequent flyer programme. It says Northwest Airlines (an important KLM partner) recruited and selected eighteen Japanese stewardesses for the KLM flights to Osaka, Japan. KLM asked Northwest to do this because Northwest has much experience in recruiting and selecting Asian cabin crew. The Japanese stewardesses have been sought especially because of their knowledge about the importance of style in Japan. Japanese passengers obviously prefer their own way of service during a flight. KLM, of course, will meet these expectations. Northwest tested the applicants with respect to their skills in meeting Japanese standards, while KLM eventually tested them with respect to their skills in meeting European standards. After being trained for several weeks in which special attention was given to high service quality, flight safety and a training flight, they are now on normal duty.

Scott Kelley cites in his paper Mark Maremont and his 1990 *Business Week* article on British Airways ("How British Airways Butters up the Passenger") to show that appropriate values and expected behaviors are conveyed through socialization, resulting in a more customer-oriented work force. In (p 34) "an effort to enhance the customer orientation of its employees, British Airways has instituted an extensive training program in order to socialize its workforce toward customer-oriented values and role expectations. The enhancement of employee motivation and commitment levels through training programs and extensive preaching of customer-oriented values has given British Airways one of the best service reputations in the airline industry."

QUESTIONS

1   What is the relevance of training service employees to deliver high service quality? What can you report on the actions Singapore Airlines, British Airlines and KLM took in that respect? Do you think it is wise what they did? How is this related to Jan Carlzon's moments of truth and the Service practice on the airline industry at the beginning of Chapter One?

2   What does this case say about the link between job satisfaction and customer satisfaction? How does that fit into what is said about that relationship in this chapter?

3   Do you know yourself of examples of service firms in which training the employees results in new ways of working valued by customers, improving efficiency, etc.?

4   Do you know of examples of service firms where the employees definitely need training programs in order to deliver a better service quality? What should be improved in their way of working? Why? How would you organize such a training program if you were the consultant hired to do that training program? Would you just lecture or have, for instance, role playing as well?

ENDNOTES

1. Fromm and Schlesinger, 1994, pp. xx, 4, 5.
2. Lehmann, 1993.
3. Gummesson, 1991.
4. Perhaps, the consequence of a market oriented service organization is that there is no marketing manager or department present at all. Such a point of view would be in line with the recent discussions about the status of marketing in the firm. See, for instance, Webster, 1992, 1994.
5. Traditionally, the human side of servicing is stressed. In Chapter Two, we have seen that service firms may shift their position on the continuum of labor intensive – capital intensive. Services become more "unpersonal" and more technological. Hence, the role of the human factor diminishes.
6. Judd, 1987.
7. Kelley, 1992, p. 34.
8. Remember that this issue of cooperation and information exchange is one of the features of Narver and Slater's definition of market orientation. We have incorporated that issue in our definition of market orientation. We found such a cooperation and information exchange to be one of the basic elements of a market oriented corporate culture.
9. Grant, 1991.
10. In Chapters Two, Seven and Eight, we have shown that image or reputation is one of the key success factors of market leaders in services.
11. All the resources form the capabilities of the organization, that is, "the capacity for a team of resources to perform some task or activity" as Grant, 1991, p. 119 states.
12. Langerak, Peelen and Commandeur (1995) interviewed 112 service employees and detected the four types of service employees mentioned in this Service practice.
13. The Organizational Commitment scale, developed by Porter et al., 1974, Mowday et al., 1979 and Mowday et al., 1982, is well known in this respect.
14. Rogers, Clow and Kash, 1994, p. 23 concluded this after a study among service personnel working in retail outlets.
15. Wetzels, 1998.
16. See for instance our discussion about the causes of the gaps in the SERVQUAL model and Thom Bonoma's work on implementing marketing strategies. In Chapter Fifteen we will continue the discussion on implementation and control issues in services organizations.
17. Strauss, 1994, p. 29.
18. De Ruyter, Kasper and Wetzels, 1995.
19. De Ruyter, Kasper and Wetzels, 1995, p. 77.
20. See also Tettero and Viehoff, 1990.
21. Fromm and Schlesinger, 1994, pp. 307–315.
22. In the next section, this will be further elaborated on in the discussion of "empowerment".
23. Booms and Nyquist, 1981.
24. A further description of these types and the role in the service organization's communication policy, is given in Chapter Twelve.
25. See, for example, the problems with Gap 3 of the SERVQUAL-model in Chapter Five of the Service practice 10-4 on internal service quality.
26. Working in a team means you may never blame your colleague or the computer for things that have gone wrong: you are the one the customer wants to solve the problem! So, getting along with the customer and getting along with colleagues is relevant to delivering excellent service quality.

27. See Chapter Four the definition of each dimension and the cultural clustering of countries.
28. Mohr and Bitner, 1995.
29. Helgesen, 1990, pp. xxi, 45, 46, 53, 58, 225, 227, 234.
30. Bowen and Lawler, 1992.
31. Swartz, Bowen and Brown, 1992, p. 6.
32. Bowen and Lawler, 1992.
33. Berry, 1995. The citations given stem from pp. 9-30.
34. This will also hold for full professors only paying attention to graduate students or Ph.D students. When they do not teach in first year classes, how can they expect their assistants to be motivated to do so?
35. Price, Arnould and Tierney, 1995.
36. Working according to global guidelines (and not according to detailed instructions of the boss), is a characteristic of market-oriented organization cultures. Employees in organizations with such cultures know the mission and strategy, because these are communicated well within the company.
37. Specific roles are required to perform the actions that belong to the episodes and relationships customers and company want to establish.
38. This very simplified structure is essentially based on Gummesson and Kingman-Brundage, 1992.
39. In practice, of course, a more detailed map can be made. Especially, analyzing the "automatic ticket dispenser" path may help in researching why some people have problems in accepting this new way of selling tickets (see also Chapter Twelve).
40. Davenport and Short, 1990; Hammer and Champy, 1993. (See also *Business Week*, May 24, 1993, p. 5.)
41. This figure is adapted from Davenport and Nohria, 1994, p. 12
42. See also Hammer, 1990; Klein, 1994 or Venkatraman, 1994.
43. Larson, 1987.
44. Taylor, 1994.
45. Taylor, 1994, p. 65.
46. Hui and Tse, 1996.
47. LeClerc et al., 1995; Kostecki, 1996, mentions a lot of these contextual characteristics.
48. Kostecki, 1996.
49. Baker and Cameron, 1996.
50. Kostecki, 1996, p. 301. Multiple answers could be given.
51. Pruyn and Smidts, 1993.
52. Pruyn and Smidts, 1993.
53. Pruyn and Smidts, 1993.
54. We will discuss the basics of queueing theory here; more detailed approaches can be found in the references (see e.g. Van Dijk, 1990; Van Dijk, undated; Lapin, 1988; Larson, 1987, and Ravindran et al., 1987.
55. Ravindran et al., 1987.
56. For a more elaborate discussion of these models and their equations, the reader may consult almost every textbook on quantitative methods, operation research, or management science, for instance Ravindran et al., 1987, or Lapin, 1988.
57. Ravindran et al., 1987.
58. Lapin, 1988.
59. We will further analyze these customer monetary and non-monetary costs in Chapter Fourteen, where a great number of issues dealing with costs and prices from the customer's and service provider's point of view will be discussed.
60. Van Dijk, *To Wait or Not to Wait*, undated.

61. See, e.g. Haynes, 1990.

62. Ravindran et al., 1987.

63. For an overview, see Suchanek, 1998.

64. More on control will be revealed in Chapter Fifteen: Implementation and Control. In general it can be concluded that controlling the marketing performance, when discussed in the marketing literature, mainly deals with verifying whether the stated goals with respect to turnover, sales, market share, profit or return on investment, are accomplished. Those goals are output focussed and based on financial figures. Next to these goals, attention is paid to the effectiveness of communication campaigns, price changes and the (team of) sales representatives.

65. This will be elaborated upon in Chapter Thirteen on distribution.

66. Bateson, 1985.

67. In Chapters Five and Six, many more factors were mentioned as causes and solutions to Gap 3 of the SERVQUAL model.

68. Weatherly and Tansik, 1993.

69. Weatherly and Tansik, 1993, p. 13.

70. In this scheme, we have put some issues together to structure the many issues discussed. Every classification is arbitrary to a certain extent. So, the reader should critically look at this figure, and adapt it whenever deemed relevant.

CHAPTER ELEVEN

DEVELOPING AND PROVIDING SERVICES

This chapter on services is the second in a series covering the marketing mix.
After studying this chapter you should be able to:

BELOW: *Service innovations: pensions by phone*

- *apply the insights you have acquired into the relationship between planning, creating, providing and evaluating services when strategic and operational service policies have to work;*

- *translate theories on the hierarchy and life-cycle of services into a service strategy;*

- *use the concept of strategic and tactical services effectively when marketing services;*

- *become aware of how to develop and implement new services;*

- *know the basics of breakthrough services;*

- *reproduce the basics of dissatisfaction management and complaints management*

- *apply the basics of service recovery to get a competitive advantage; and*

- *detect the main differences of the service features in the four different types of service firms.*

Scottish Widows, Direct Sales, PO Box 17037, 69 Morrison Street, Edinburgh EH3 8YD. The value of units can go down as well as up. Future bonus rates are not guaranteed. Further details of our Pension Plans are included in the product literature, available from us on request. For your protection, your calls to Scottish Widows may be recorded or monitored and information or advice will only be provided on Scottish Widows' products. Issued by Scottish Widows' Fund and Life Assurance Society. Regulated by the Personal Investment Authority.

11.1 INTRODUCTION

*Service
practice
11-1
To train or not
to train: core
services and
additional
services at
Deutsche
Bahnen*

The German railways, Deutsche Bahnen, are constantly seeking opportunities to improve their service quality and to increase the efficiency of their operations. As a result, several research projects are being carried out to investigate how their customers will react to changes in the present way of servicing.

One of those studies concerned long distance trains in Germany (InterCity Express, ICE). Given the large distances and the various train schedules, people travelling from the North to the South may have to change trains once or twice during their trip. It was investigated, amongst others, whether customers would accept one or two additional changes on the track from Hannover, via Dortmund and Cologne, to Karlsruhe – combined with a time period to change trains of zero – 5 or 10 minutes. Many travellers indicated that they were not happy with these "new forms of service". Only the alternative of one additional change without any waiting time (a direct connection) was acceptable. The changes were going to affect customer satisfaction in a negative way. However, only a very few travellers would choose another mode of transportation. The other ways tested to improve the schedule would affect customer satisfaction in a very negative way. Then, indeed, an increasing number of train travellers would stop travelling by train and switch to another transportation mode (airplane or car).

Another study concerned the provision of food and beverages in the long distance trains (ICE) of Deutsche Bahnen. The main question was what kind of food and beverages train passengers would like and to what extent this would affect their decision to travel by train or not. The service offered consists of beverages, snacks and full meals. These can be obtained via self service in the train's restaurant, via personal service at one's seat or via a vending machine (food and small snacks only).

It appeared that only about 10% of the travellers actually used one of these means of obtaining drinks or food. Moreover, the availability of food and beverages hardly affected the choice to travel by train. Offering a smaller assortment of food and beverages did not appear to have a significant effect on the number of Deutsche Bahnen customers.

In sum, more changes in the train service will decrease the number of Deutsche Bahnen travellers seriously, while a smaller assortment of food and beverages hardly affects their decision to travel. Stated differently, a change in the core service (the process of transportation by train) will be a dramatic one, while a change in an additional service will not show any effect on "the consumption of these railway services".[1]

To develop the organization's service strategy, we will apply many elements from previous chapters. First of all, some international aspects will be sketched in this introduction. The link between the previous chapters and the service policy will be clarified in section 11.2: we will illustrate how a service is applied as an instrument of the marketing mix within the framework of the relationship approach mentioned before. It will also be shown how marketing, operational activities and human skills interrelate when a service is provided. This relates particularly to the process of the provision of services, with its know-how, routines, capabilities, etc. Ultimately, this comes down to the technical, functional and relational quality of services. The discussion of the service hierarchy and the concept of a life-cycle for services – found in section 11.3 and 11.4 – provides a second corner stone for a more in-depth study of the service (11.5) and the development of new services (11.6). After-sales services (11.7) and solving consumer problems in other ways (e.g. via dissatisfaction management, complaint management and service recovery) will be discussed before we turn to the topics of managing capacity (demand and supply). Finally, our own service typology will be elaborated upon, regarding this part of the marketing mix, in section 11.10 as a kind of summary of this chapter.

Figure 11-1
Chapter outline

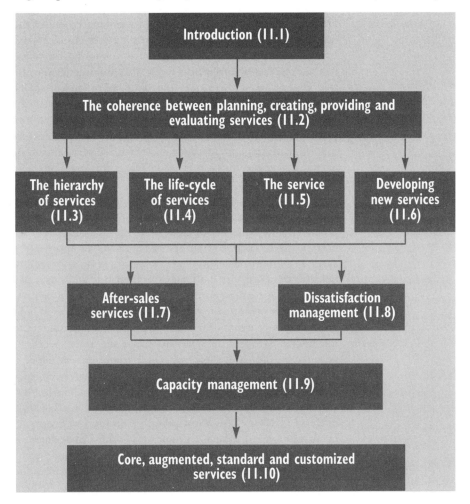

In our opinion, all four types of service strategies can be applied in internationalizing a service company. It will depend on the market segment to be served. The service of hotel chains like Campanille and Formule I (a rather simple core service) or Marriott and Hilton (a core plus augmented service including many opportunities for customized offerings) are both exported. International advertising agencies have to fully meet the needs of their local clients. The same applies to international management consultants and lawyers offering tailor made services.

international standardization

The features of a service encounter many limitations as to the extent to which they can reach international standardization.[2] Despite the benefits of economies of scale, there are very few companies that can fully standardize their services for the markets they serve. Instead, the challenge is to be able to bridge the gap between the various local adaptations and the need to standardize some components. Multinational companies are now focussing on developing this new breed of global services which builds on that essential ingredient of flexibility to tailor the end "product" to the needs of individual markets. In most cases, only a portion of the final design can be standardized. A modular approach can be used to that end.[3] In the service sector, the

modular approach

modular approach is utilized in automation and lay-out of the back office and front office. It enables companies to export their services and adapt them to local circumstances. Regular visitors of international hotels and car rental companies recognize this standardization of services easily. Paraphrasing Jeannet and Hennessey, we could state that global services offer the potential to answer similar needs among similar market segments, and as transnational services they also allow for adaptations to cope with national differences.[4] In general, however, companies without the ability to develop such a line of ideal global services follow the next two development strategies when moving into foreign markets with services already developed in their home markets, an extension strategy or an adaptation strategy.

extension strategy

An extension strategy for service development requires more care and accumulation of background information on the different situations marketeers find themselves in. This will include, e.g. information covering opportunity costs and entry costs of each service. A "one size fits all approach" must be handled with care.[5] Too often, managers fall back on a generic approach to service development

demands and costs

because they are torn between the demands and costs of missing a fast moving market, and the risk of entering a market with the wrong service. If the risk of devel-

risk

oping a new service, for example, is high and the cost is low, then the goal is to create a service that is 100% right at market launch time rather than miss a fast moving market window. In order to make the right decisions, extensive testing is required in the early stages of research and development, allowing customers to review concepts and make sure that the design concept meets the individual preferences being addressed.[6] If opportunity costs matter, but less than entry risk, there may be advantages in testing that service in a market niche outside the normal range of activities. This allows the organization to keep mature technology in the profitable larger markets, without delay whilst experimenting with new products. Others, fighting high opportunity costs without much entry risk, may see a competitive advantage for services which can be quickly introduced without delay. And if entry risk matters, but less than the opportunity costs, then there may be pressure to enter the market directly with a new service, thereby cutting the development costs and reducing opportunity costs.

adaptation strategy   An adaptation strategy is applied when some changes are required to fit the new market requirements. Due to the nature of many services (i.e. financial, professional) it seems more plausible that service features and elements will have to be adapted to some degree in the different legal and cultural environments. Those changes could be minor or quite major. Certain basic financial services such as credit cards, personal loans and current accounts can be promoted in almost every market. However, the more sophisticated financial services, particularly in the investment and insurance areas, will require a thorough re-examination of the marketing approach. For that reason, the marketeer should look not at what services they would like to sell, but at what services the public would like to buy.[7,8]

In all instances, whether services are provided on a national or international basis, it is important to decipher how closely the planning, creation, delivering, evaluation assessment of services are linked. Feedback and forward planning are indispensable to the delivery of excellent service quality by market-oriented providers.

11.2   THE COHERENCE BETWEEN PLANNING, CREATING, DELIVERING AND EVALUATING SERVICES

The marketing mix has to be implemented in the same way as the corporate and marketing strategy with respect to targets, planning, the organization's market orientation, desired quality of the service provided, choice of positions in the various matrices as developed for the classification of services, choice between core services and augmented services, choice between customized services and standard services, and target groups, market segments and market position. National and international external opportunities and risks have been taken into account at corporate and marketing planning, as well as the organization's internal strengths and weaknesses. The people, routines, resources and possibilities the organization needs to actually realize its plans were discussed before; now we turn to the "service" itself. For the sake of brevity, the preceding matters will be referred to as "the results of Chapters Seven,
the framework of the   Eight, Nine and Ten", which sets the framework of the service concept (the first box
service concept   in Figure 11-2). The strategic targets and plans, together with the (limited) resources, determine the contents of the service concept from a strategic point of view, in the same way as they determine the service concept in a more tactical or operational sense. Both concepts will be reflected in the way the services will be delivered. Finally, the performance of the service and the process of providing it needs to be evaluated. This process is summarized in Figure 11-2. In it, we primarily intend to show the coherence between and the need to coordinate all these components from an organizational and process-oriented viewpoint.[9]

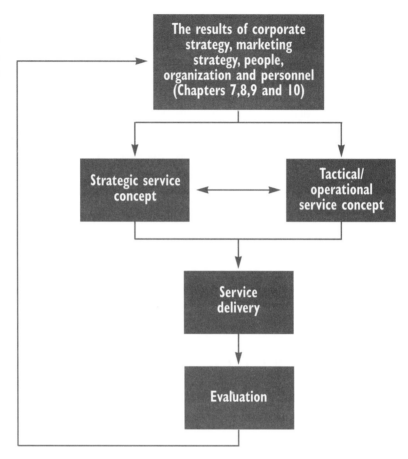

Figure 11-2
To plan, create, deliver
and evaluate services

The results of corporate strategy, marketing strategy, people, organization and personnel (Chapters 7,8,9 and 10)

Strategic service concept

Tactical/ operational service concept

Service delivery

Evaluation

strategic service
concept

tactical or operational
service concept

process of delivering
the services

The strategic service concept is very much based on the market orientation the organization has opted for: the needs and desires of the customer with regard to service and provision. In other words, the focus has to be on the desired benefits of the service, its function and its position relative to the competitors. In giving actual content to the tactical or operational service concept, the geographical range and organization of the activities, is, amongst other things, determined. It indicates when the consecutive components of the service providing system must be ready to fulfill their specific tasks. The strategic service concept as well as the operational service concept influence the decision shaping the process of delivering the services. Now, the service provider must find practical answers to operational questions such as: the order of the various steps taken during the delivery process: where, when and at what speed should these steps be taken; the actual division between front and back office activities; the level of delegation (are tasks like information and reservation left to others or contracted out, or do we handle things ourselves?); the nature of the contact and the process between client and service provider; and the instructions for handling the scarce capacity (reservations, waiting and such), atmosphere and ambience (scripts for personnel, variation in the setting, lights, music and such).

performance assessment

When the service has actually been delivered, the performance can be determined and evaluated. This performance assessment, mainly, covers to what extent the quality experienced matches the expectations, as far as the clients are concerned. It goes without saying that other interested parties apply different standards. Staff will pay attention to the working atmosphere, opportunities for career development and renumeration. Shareholders will measure the performance of the service company by means of its profits, increase in value and/or dividend per share or other index numbers.[10]

All the strategic, procedural and organizational components in an organization need to be coordinated to actually fulfil the expectations of its clients and other interested parties. This is based on the ideas that internal service quality will co-determine external service quality, and that strategy and operations should not be separated.

11.3   THE HIERARCHY OF SERVICES

seven levels of services

Just as with goods, services may be defined at different levels. This hierarchy is important to give meaning to services at different strategic and operational levels. We distinguish seven levels of services: need family, services family, service class, service form, service type, brand, and service variation.[11] With the exception of level 6 (brand), every hierarchic level constitutes the sum of the parts of the consecutive level. Thus, together, the service variations constitute one service type. All different service types that are strongly interrelated combine into one service form, just as all service forms combine into one service class, and services may have a different life-cycle at each of these levels. The strategic choices refer mainly to levels 1–4, while the tactical choices mainly refer to levels 4–7. So, level 4 may possess characteristics of both levels. One should be aware of the fact that a brand name has great strategic value. A brand can have strategic value for the firm in terms of its brand equity[12] or for the customers in terms of visibility and image, thereby reducing perceived risk. Moreover, it has been mentioned before that brand name, image and reputation are among the key success factors of service providers.

11.4   THE LIFE-CYCLE OF SERVICES

life-cycle of a service

The life-cycle of a service can be developed at any level. This will differ for any given level. The introduction of new services or service variants may also give new impetus to the turn-over (profits) and/or extend the life-cycle. The service hierarchy and the life-cycle concept imply that the organization must make several choices as to its service policy. This is sometimes called managing services by means of their life-cycles.

managing services by means of their life-cycles

<table>
<tr><td rowspan="8">*Service
practice
11-2
The hierarchy
of life
insurances*</td><td colspan="3"></td></tr>
</table>

	Level	*Definition*	*Example*
	Need family (type of need)	The core need forming the basics of the service	Old-age security
	Services family	All service classes which are more or less effective in satisfying the core needs	Savings and income
	Service class	A group of services within the family of services which can be recognized as belonging to one class. It concerns essential basic services which cater to clearly outlined generic needs	Financial services
	Service form	A group of services (comparable to the "product line") within the service class that are closely related to each other, either because they function in the same way, or because they are being sold to the same group of clients or are distributed through the same channel or come into the same price-range (the "service line")	Life insurance
	Service type	All parts of a service form that have one or more characteristics of the service in common	Capital insurance or endowment life insurance policies
	Brand	The name connected to one or more objects within the service form, used to determine the origin or character of these segments	American Express, AIX insurance, Swiss Life, Aegon insurance or Citibank
	Service variation	A distinct unit within a brand or service line that can be distinguished by way of size, price, or other common attributes/characteristics	The male/female insurance policy of Nationale Nederlanden, the American Express Life Insurance, etc.

introduction phase

During the introduction phase at the beginning of the life-cycle, emphasis will be put mainly on developing the primary demand for the service (class). Different pricing strategies may then be pursued. When a new restaurant has been established, one can see that, initially, prices are kept low to attract a sufficient number of curious visitors. Prices will go up once a regular group of people begin to visit the new establishment frequently.

growth phase

The growth phase is characterized by a rapid increase in sales. Opinion leaders and early-adopters are prepared quickly to use the service. Competitors are attracted by the new offering because prices and margins are high and/or because some services can be imitated relatively easily, trying to lure clients by offering additional services. The pioneers will now have to aim at perfecting their service concept, check whether the service lives up to the clients' expectations, make improvements if necessary, develop additional services along with the core service, and so forth. New target groups and distribution channels may now become more important. Advertising, once focussed on an overall service (single-premium assurance policy, supplementary pension schemes, cash dispensers and debit cards, for example) can now be aimed at one's own specific service. All this is as done since the first mover advantages seem to erode.

*adulthood,
saturation, or
maturity*

During the early phases of the service's adulthood, saturation, or maturity, the efficiency of the internal and external service delivery process becomes more important. Often, there is still the ability to add additional services. At the same time, room becomes available at the bottom of the market for consumers who, for price techni-

wheel of servicing

calities or other reasons, prefer to use the core service only (for example, flights with no on-board service). Similar to the "wheel of retailing" we talk about the "wheel of servicing" here. Firms that only concentrate on up-grading their services, which often entails increasing costs, complexity and divergence, are gradually ignoring a still growing share of the market. This creates opportunities for new entrants (who offer little service) at the bottom of the market. Besides this, there are other well-known strategies to survive during the saturation phase: modification of the many elements of the services marketing mix; market modification. The service organization can try to enlarge the market for its brands and services by influencing the two factors that determine the turnover (volume = number of users∗ quantity used per client) and service innovation.

decline phase

Finally, at the end of the life-cycle, during the decline phase of a service, a maximum effort will be made to limit all marketing mix expenses. This is sometimes called the passive sale of a service. It means that the service will only be provided if the client explicitly asks for it. Often, the service is deleted from brochures or price-lists. In the end, it will be removed from the assortment completely. As in retail firms, every service organization may apply its assortment policy to detect each brand's market share, contribution margin, quality, customer satisfaction, etc. This is an essential part of the service policy. Another possibility is to modify the service in such a way that a new life-cycle starts. Of course, entering new foreign markets is a way to cope with the decline in a particular country's service market.

11.5 THE SERVICE

A market-oriented service policy must be directed at putting into practice all the benefits a service provider is able to offer to its clients. These are the general benefits of doing business with the organization as a whole, but include also the brand name, the assortment of services available and the actual range of services. This addition makes the general formulation somewhat more operational, but before a tangible service can be offered it must be given a more concrete form. In fact, this is about the "translation" of the matrix positions, opted for in Chapter Two, into a concrete service and actual service delivery process. Here, we again distinguish between choices of a strategic, tactical or operational level. This will give meaning to the function of the

benefits or utility

service to the customer and will serve to provide consumers with the benefits or utility they seek.

As far as the tactical/operational level is concerned, choices will relate mainly to brands and the actual offering and delivery of all sorts of services. The composition of this offering is based on the assortment. The difference between strategic and tactical cannot be taken in the absolute sense here: sometimes there is only a difference of degree. Figure 11-3 depicts the major elements of the service to be discussed in this section.

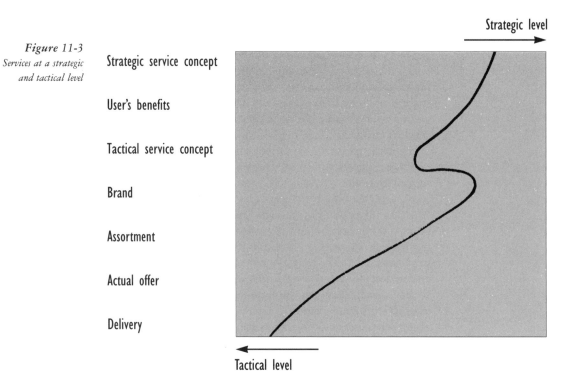

Figure 11-3
Services at a strategic
and tactical level

Strategic service concept

User's benefits

Tactical service concept

Brand

Assortment

Actual offer

Delivery

Strategic level

Tactical level

THE STRATEGIC SERVICE CONCEPT

strategic service concept

The decision taken by an insurance company, not to limit themselves to issuing only life insurance policies but instead to extend their services to property insurance and savings, is an example of a strategic decision. Within the limits of the strategic service concept the organization intends to develop for one or more specific market segments, it is possible to develop a positioning strategy. This strategy encompasses, amongst other things, on which issues one's own strategic service concept can be distinguished from those of the major competitors (peer group).

Decisions on the core service(s) of an organization will be taken at company or SBU level. If one knows what the client considers to be the core (and therefore the basic benefits), the service can be expanded by adding additional services, or limited by deleting them. This distinction also serves as an aid for improving current services or developing new services and service delivery processes.

Important make or buy decisions, too, should be taken at company or SBU level. Here, the focus is mainly on the internal service processes, in the sense that the organization always has a choice: do we produce it ourselves or do we buy it elsewhere? In this context, a distinction is made between three functions of a service: a function of production; a function of direction; and a function of distribution.

function of production
function of direction

function of distribution

The function of production refers to the actual "producing" of the service. Do we produce the service ourselves or do we buy it on the market? The function of direction refers to the assessment of the needs of the internal clients and translates these into a list of requirements. The function of distribution facilitates the maximum convergence of supply and demand. The question to be asked is whether this should be realized through internal service providing processes or by ordering the services from an external supplier. At present, more and more service providers ask themselves whether they are able to upgrade their (internal) services, should privatize them (hive them off), or buy them in as external services from third parties. This means that the production function may sometimes be contracted out; the function of direction and distribution, however, cannot. In the computer industry especially, but also in the airline industry, we see an increasing number of third party maintenance organizations.

USER'S BENEFITS

bundle of benefits

"What's in it for me?" Irrespective of the fact whether a marketing class or a cinema ticket is concerned, the (personal) benefit to the prospective user must be clear. For this reason, John Bateson (1995, p. 25) alleges that a service can only be defined from the point of view of the user's benefit: "It is perceived service which matters, not the actual service". The key issue of a service's raison d'être is: "what benefits does the service offer to the prospective user?" Services can be defined as a bundle of benefits, these benefits are mostly a combination of functional, efficiency and psychological qualities. These benefits can only occur when the service is available to the consumer, i.e. when the service can be provided actually at a particular spot/place. That is why design and operation of the service delivery system is a key element in defining a specific service. It is the user's benefits which determine what elements within this service delivery system have to be considered as crucial in quality control. Particularly, those elements in the process that are paramount to the user's final assessment (key success factors) will need checking and control to see that they come up to the desired quality level. This is a consequence of the company's market orientation.

To transform expected or desired "benefits" into profitable services may prove difficult. For example: the needs of and benefits to the user cannot always be clearly investigated. The user's benefits change in the course of time, due to, amongst other things, good or bad experiences and the creation of new expectations influenced by environment and so on. Even if the client's needs and the benefits a service offers to the user have been listed, it may still be difficult to measure these benefits; and customers may focus more on the perceived risks than on the perceived benefits. These issues require a great deal of attention from both the marketing department and the operations staff of a company. Defining and analyzing the user's benefits in time is of vital importance to all decisions concerning design and delivery of a service.[13]

attributes and benefits

When applying the idea of enhancing user benefits for the service strategy, it is also important to draw a distinction between attributes and benefits of a service. A (potential) user will associate a service with its attributes. As for the benefits, the advantages of the service to the user are what counts as well as its simplicity of use. To illustrate this, we have summed up various attributes (or features) and (possible) benefits of credit cards in Table 11-1.

TABLE 11-1 *Distinction between features of a credit card and its possible benefits to credit card users*

Attributes/Features	Benefits
1. Small	1. Easy to carry
2. Plastic	2. Durable
3. Legal tender	3. Buy now, pay later. Less money in one's pockets, leading to better cash management
4. Can be used abroad	4. Less need for traveller's cheques and less need for cash money on a journey
5. Distinctive color	5. Prestige: color is linked to income and credit-worthiness of customer
6. Monthly debit notices	6. Proper administration of expenses and spending facilities
7. Credit facilities	7. More spending facilities, self-regulation of the extent of cash position
8. Can be used to pay with in many places	8. Increases usability
9. Insured against loss. Money-limited liability in case of abuse	9. More security as compared to cash theft
10. Receipt of copy of a each liability	10. Better management of all transactions

---

The difference between attributes/features and benefits is significant because a supplier will try to adapt the benefits of a service to correspond with the user's needs. Its further objective is to make a central presentation of these benefits in the sales promotion phase. It is important to acknowledge that what is useful to one person does not automatically become advantageous to another. The measure of benefits – considering its subjective nature – is difficult to assess by all involved; service providers try to get a better understanding of this by carrying out market research. Market segmentation and targetted promotions, by way of recommending certain advantages to individual customers or target groups, may help service providers to emphasize the benefits that can be reaped by the customer.

Service practice 11-3 Different needs on cash and credit cards

Some customers see a high quality credit card firm as one that offers an unlimited amount of money to spend. Other customers perceive such a company as one that sets a maximum on this amount and warns the customer when the credit limit is exceeded.[14]

THE TACTICAL SERVICE CONCEPT

tactical or operational
service concept

The tactical, or operational, service concept contains a description of the service package sold to the customer, as well as of the relative value of this package to the user. This definition enables the marketer to take into account the influence exercised by non-tangible aspects which are difficult to measure and often implicitly influence the consumer's decision to purchase a concrete service.

package of services

The relative importance of the package of services to the customer also includes the actual, generic benefits an organization can offer. A service organization with an excellent market reputation is able to charge a large fee compared to unknown service providers in the same industry.[15] In other words: when determining the tactical service concept the service provider must answer the question: taking our organization as a whole, how do we cater to the demands of the market? Again, this issue is closely related to the position the service provider intends to create and maintain in the market and thus to the strategic service concept. Now, it is made more "concrete".

BRANDS

Service
practice
11-4
What
difference does
a brand make?

It might be a good thing for service providers to assess one of the functions of their brands by means of a simple question: are clients prepared to wait until the service provider has enough capacity (barbershop, restaurant, architect, repairs and such) available to them or to give them some assistance? The answer will say a thing or two about the brand's impact: will customers wait or switch? So, will the brand facilitate loyalty?

Customers can reduce the risks associated with services in several ways. A popular method of risk reduction is going straight for a well-known brand or the positive image of a respected supplier. And, in the case of a repeat purchase, visiting the same supplier again: brand loyalty. The familiarity with the brand name and its dependability will diminish the risk.

key success factors
stabilize the
relationship
power of manufacturer
brands

private labels

Brand awareness, brand loyalty, brand personality, brand name and image have become important (non-tangible) company assets. In Chapters One and Seven, we have already pointed out the importance of the service company's name, brand or image as key success factors. Brands help to stabilize the relationship between customers and service provider; however, recently, things seem to have subsided. On the one hand, a declining economic climate, more price-sensitive and well-informed consumers and the rise of retailer brands causing a decline in power of manufacturer brands in a number of industries; on the other hand, well-known service companies in the retail sector such as Walmart, Marks and Spencer and Ikea create an aura of security with their own brand (private labels) which was previously only attributed to manufacturers' brands. We can assume that in the financial and travel sector the *brand strategy*

image of the distributor (a reputable bank or a chain of travel agencies), is replacing the labels of an insurance company or a tour operator. The service sector only recently discovered the value of developing a brand strategy in connection with improving its market position, offering security and creating a good relationship with the customers and employees.

function of reduction
function of
facilitation
symbols

Brands may perform different functions for the consumer and supplier of services. In general, they perform a function of reduction to customers: reducing search costs, risks, etc. To service providers, they perform a function of facilitation: facilitating new service introductions, promotions, segmentation, premium pricing, etc. They can be regarded as symbols around which relationships are built. This applies also for the consumer market as well as the business to business market.[16] The reason for this is quite simple. Since services are intangible, customers have difficulties in assessing services and service quality. Consequently, it is important for service providers to add extrinsic value like a brand, image or company name to the service. These images play an important role in services in general. This role may even be more important in the first phases of the life cycle of the service or in the first stages of the relationship life cycle. For, then, services have to be bought for the first time and consumers have to go through all phases of their decision making process. In many instances emotional factors play a decisive role in buying services. This activity is often associated with a high degree of perceived risk. Then, the brand names of firms with an excellent reputation provide trust and security about quality, consistency and reliability and contribute to the perceived benefits.[17] Brands not only have such a security function but also an associative function for customers. Then, the combination of various signals and symbols results in association in the customer's mind. These associations may have a positive or negative meaning to the customer about the services intended to buy. Brands have an economic function as well. This hinges upon the efficiency improving character of brands as perceived by customers. Now, they have to remember only a small number of services/brands. This makes the decision making process much easier, as alternatives do not have to be assessed every time one wants to buy a service. Brand loyalty is a very relevant concept here. Brands may also have an expressive function, in the sense that by using such a brand the customer expresses a particular life style or status. Additionally, there is the social-adaptive function of brands.[18] Customers of a particular service may want to imitate a particular life style or want to identify themselves with a particular sub-group in society.

add extrinsic value

security function
associative function

economic function

brand loyalty
expressive function
social-adaptive
function

In business to business services, brands also perform several functions for the industrial customer. In these markets, the industrial buyer is not always the very rational, well informed customer often assumed. Here, emotions also play a role. Brands also have a security function as well as an expressive function. Moreover, in these markets brands have a continuity function. The brand name, reputation and image of the service provider guarantees the delivery of these services in the future and hence the continuity of one's own firm.[19]

continuity function

Brands have also a particular meaning and function for the suppliers of services in consumer and business-to-business markets. Now, branding may change services from commodity services into identifiable and well-recognizable services. Branding then *differentiation function*   has a differentiation function for the service provider. This is a way to avoid price competition and sometimes even charge higher prices in particular market niches. A higher prestige credit card company can also charge higher membership fees; then branding facilitates the cash-generator function. The security function of brands leads *cash-generator function* to brand loyalty and hence a more stable market share for the service provider arises.[20] Brands have a communication function for the service provider: an umbrella *communication function* featured in the logo of insurance companies strengthens the impression of security. Many service firms have only one brand name for all their services. Strong brand *brand and line extensions* names then offer opportunities for succesful "brand and line extensions". This relates to the life-cycle and differentiation functions of brands. In the retail sector, brand names are also associated with a particular amount of power in the distribution channel.

Brands are important in the relationship between customers and service providers. *relationship partners* They can even act as "relationship partners", often helping to resolve or address important personal issues.[21] Seven attributes are essential to creating and maintaining *high-quality, enduring bonds* high-quality, enduring bonds. These are love and passion (consumers feel affection and passion for the service or are obsessed by it, and may experience separation anxiety if the service is not available); self-concept connection (using this service brand helps consumers address a life issue on level one or two of the services hierarchy); interdependence (the service brand is inextricably woven into the consumers' daily lives and routines); commitment (consumers stick with the service through good and bad times); intimacy (consumers describe a sense of deep familiarity with the service and an understanding of its attributes); partner quality (consumers seek certain positive traits in the brand as if it were a best friend, such as dependability, trustworthiness, accountability; and nostalgic attachment (the service brand brings back positive memories).

brand name   The brand name can contribute heavily to operationalize these seven attributes. It is also an essential part of brand management, nationally as well as internationally. In services, the brand name often equals the company name (Marriott, Avis, Marks and Spencer, Ikea, etc.): and even indicates the specific services industry (Air France, Deutsche Bank, etc.). In services, "the 'branding' effect of a good corporate name is a potent marketing tool".[22] So what are the features of strong service brands?

Service practice 11-5 Strong brands

A "strong service brand should posses some, if not all, of these characteristics:

1. *distinctiveness*. It immediately identifies the supplier and distinguishes it from competitors;
2. *relevance*. It conveys the nature of the service or the service benefit;
3. *memorability*. It can be understood, used and recalled with ease; and
4. *flexibility*. It is broad enough to cover not just the organization's current business but foreseeable expansion."

"In short, a cohesive branding program requires effective blending of *all* communication elements and use of them consistently and imaginatively across services and media. The bottom line is still that the quality of the service determines the success of the image. If you don't satisfy customers, the name won't help. But of course, if you combine good performance with a good name, you will generate the most powerful branding effect for your services."[23]

brand parity

Nevertheless, brand management is a hard job, especially, since it has been found that brand parity is high in some service industries. This means customers perceive no or hardly any difference between service brands. The advertising agency BBDO, for instance, has found that in Europe brand parity for credit cards is about 80-90%.[24] This means that only 10-20% of Europeans perceive (and are aware of) differences between the well known credit cards like Visa, MasterCard, American Express, Diners, etc. Clearly, in these cases, brand management has not resulted in a distinctive positioning of these companies. It seems to be quite difficult to create global brands in retail financial services, not so much in the wholesale and professional financial services. Probably, only American Express and the French insurance company Axa have a global brand in their retail financial services (CitiBank attempts to). Such a brand can be built relatively quickly only "... if the company is committed to the task, and has a simple story to tell".[25]

separate brand policy

For a greater part, choosing a specific brand name is a strategic matter too, just as the choice between a family brand or individual brands. A separate brand policy is followed particularly if major differences in market segment, price, quality and envisaged image exist; the distribution strategy necessitates this. A large market share, for example, makes the brand too dominant within a distribution channel or market area. By introducing a second brand, it becomes possible to implement more intensive distribution of the service in the same market area. Examples of this are the consumer financing and leasing that are offered by general banks as well as subsidiary companies which carry a different label (and different conditions); sufficient means are available (advertising budget, operational and management budgets); and there is a good chance that dissatisfaction with one particular service will adversely affect the sale of the remaining services.

Service practice 11-6 Brand managers with airlines

In the mid-eighties, British Airways introduced the position of brand manager for its (sub) brands. Under the guidance of these marketeers, British Airways tried to develop its brand strategy. These brand managers were expected to initiate service innovations. Furthermore, they operated as "change agents" within the organization in order to have an overview of all changes necessary to innovate products, services, or quality improvements. They had to make a precise inventory of the consequences their proposals would have for the organization. A management team was formed for every brand. In those days, British Airways carried seven different brands: Concorde, First Class, Club World, Club Europe, Long-haul Economy, Short-haul Economy, Super Shuttle. Is it wise to have so many brands in one company?

family brand

The choice of a family brand, on the one hand, opens the way to a more consistent handling of all services and, on the other hand, necessitates this. From a customers' perspective, it helps in reducing risk. It also facilitates the efficiency of operational activities and advertising efforts. The generic investment funds of Fidelity, Templeton and Invesco are examples of company policies to develop a family or umbrella brand. However, a family brand policy is not a static one. For instance, the investment banking activities of Deutsche Bank and ABN AMRO have recently changed their names. Where the brand names of the banks were once carefully associated with the old merchant banks they had acquired (like Deutsche Bank, Morgan Grenfell or ABN AMRO Hoare Govett), these names have been dropped, e.g. ABN AMRO Securities. The new name reflects the business they are in. It all has to do with ways of accomplish-

brand extension ing brand extentions. Brand extension occurs when service providers try to use the goodwill of the existing (family) brand for the benefit of the new service. In this respect, KLM has renamed their regional partners Cityhopper, Air UK and Air Excel: e.g. Air UK is now called KLM UK.[26] However, if consumers think that the new service is broadly different from the existing assortment, this may bring about a negative attitude towards the newcomer to the business. This side effect must be taken into account in branding and positioning services. Our way of dealing with the topic of market orientation may be helpful here. The market-oriented strategy, based on the combination of low costs and specific target groups, can be the foundation upon which the assortment of services and brands is based. This can be expressed in a kubic as in Figure 11-4.[27]

Figure 11-4
The market-oriented
brands kubic

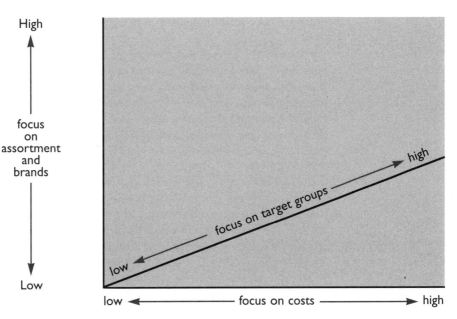

Such kubics can be used to position present competitors, develop new services and brands based on the niches found in the picture. Customized augmented services will be provided by firms scoring high both two dimensions (not on costs), while core standard service will probably be provided by firms scoring high only on the dimension of cost (but low on target group and number of brands).

name of the retailer In the retail business (food and non-food), the name of the retailer is often used as the name of their brand (private label). Many of them are very successful like The Limited, JC Penney, or Sears using the company name. Marks and Spencer, or C&A use a particular name for their private label: St Michael resp. Canda.[28] One step further is *"branding the store"*

"branding the store".[29] Then, the combination of specific merchandise (goods, services, brands) *and* attributes of the retailer (image, personality) build up the store (or chain) as a brand. Marketeer of the year 1997, The Gap, remakes itself as a brand by integrating marketing into the merchandise formula. The Gap made its name into a brand expressing value, family, fashion and fun, and recognizes that everyone in the stores is a marketing agent for the company.[30] Also, a country's tourism services can be branded. For a country like New Zealand, this could be based on three parameters: New Zealand's culture's values and behavior, the generic attributes of New Zealand's natural resources, and thirdly, tourists' perceptions or images of New Zealand as a country and holiday destination.[31]

brand personality

As we have said, in services, images, reputation and brands play a crucial role. Another issue, brand personality, should not be overlooked. This opens another way of analyzing the functions of brands in service industries.[32] Brand personality is usually defined as the set of human characteristics associated with a brand, or in other words "the set of meanings which describe the 'inner' characteristics, or human features of a brand".[33] Probably, the content given to the relationship between a service provider and customers, will also depend on liking the brand personality or not.

personality of the actual service provider

The brand of a service is largely based on the personality of the actual service provider. So, the personality of front office employees is very important in giving actual meaning to a brand. Their behavior and outlook will affect the service firm's image and brand. With respect to brand personalities, Steven Carr (1996) even talks about the "cult of brand personality". A cult brand arouses passion in the customer. Most of the time, such cult brands belong to niche products and services "... that attract a loyal following few mainstream brands enjoy". These brands not only have a personality, but – more important – have a passionate following. Moreover, they "... have charisma that is off the charts. The customer and the brand have a relationship, an affinity without a rationale; an emotional rather than an intellectual response."[34] Next to this conceptual part of brand personality, the operational part is relevant: how can it be measured? The semantic differential scale can be used to determine whether service brands are associated with positive or negative personality traits, while the Likert-scales can be used to determine which personality traits are associated with a brand (without an assessment of it in positive or negative terms). With respect to the latter kind of research, it appeared that five dimensions of brand personality could be found out of a list of more than 100 personality traits.[35] These five dimensions were

sincerity, excitement, competence, sophistication, ruggedness

sincerity (down to earth, honest, wholesome, cheerful); excitement (daring, spirited, imaginative, up-to-date); competence (reliable, intelligent, successful); sophistication (upper class, charming); and, ruggedness (outdoorsy, tough). Different target group customers may perceive the same service provider as having a different personality.

All these factors may affect brand loyalty in a positive way: the relationship is strengthened. In previous chapters, we have recalled that loyalty is decreasing in many industries. Several typologies of customers have developed, revealing differences in loyalty (= switching).[37] Loyalty programs can be used to increase loyalty.[38] Here, we will have a further look at the relation between brand loyalty and brand equity.

*Service
practice
11-7
Different
brand
personalities*

Passengers of Air France, British Airways, Lufthansa, Iberia and KLM were interviewed at Schiphol airport about the personality of the airline they had just
flown with.[36] It appeared that there were hardly any differences between males
and females, or younger and older passengers. However, a country-of-origin
effect was present: their own airline was rated more positively than foreign
ones. All five airlines had quite a positive personality; BA, Lufthansa and KLM
had a more positive personality than Air France and Iberia in terms of the
following factors: pleasing and strength; cultivated; safe and sound; modern;
ease and action. However, experienced and frequent flyers associate a more
positive personality to the airlines than non-experienced flyers. Also, business
passengers see airlines as having a different personality than private (= non-
business) passengers.

Finally, it turned out that in the decision making process of buying an airline
ticket and choosing an airline, brand personality actually plays a role only
among non-frequent flyers, non-business flyers and non-experienced flyers.
Price, reliability and service are more decisive in this process than personality.

brand equity
Brand Asset Valuator

Brand loyalty is one of the important issues in calculating brand equity.[39] Young and
Rubicam, a well-known advertising agency, have developed their Brand Asset Valuator
to calculate brand value. This instrument was applied world wide for the first time in
the beginning of the 1990s. They claim that brands develop via different stages based
on how consumers perceive the brand.[40] First of all, it is important to decipher to

differentiation.
relevant to consumers

what extent a brand is different from all other brands: differentiation. Next, brands
have to be relevant to consumers: to what extent are they convinced that a brand
meets their personal needs. Both steps differentiation and relevance determine a

vitality, esteem

brand's future growth potential: its vitality. The third stage can be labelled as esteem:
the extent to which consumers value the brand, i.e. how they regard the brand.

knowledge, awareness
and familiarity

Finally, knowledge, awareness and familiarity are important. This reflects the degree to
which knowledge about the brand has permeated into household life. This refers not
only to "... being aware of the brand but also a consumer belief that there is an understanding of what the brand stands for"[41]. Both esteem and knowledge determine the

stature of a brand

stature of a brand. Vitality and stature can be used to develop a power grid of brands.
This is a graphical representation of a brand's power: the position of a brand in such
a grid will determine what strategy and actions should be taken. For each of the two
dimensions a score can be computed for each brand, ranging from zero (low) to 100

leaders, unrealized
potential, declining
potential, unfocussed

(high). The four cells in the grid are labelled as leaders, unrealized potential, declining
potential, and, unfocussed (or not yet on the market in that country). All four can be
applied to each of the four service strategies from our typology. That will help to
define what strategies can be applied to have brands change to a preferred position
in the grid.

Figure 11-5
The brand asset
valuator power grid

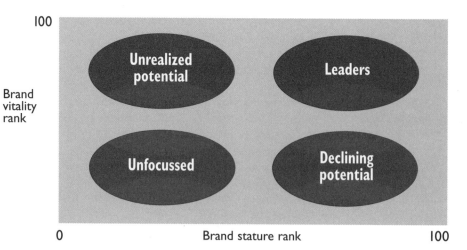

Jim Williams, a vice president of Young and Rubicam, once said that service brands had low vitality because they were poorly differentiated.[42] Service brands that have succeeded in differentiating themselves are, e.g. American Express, Virgin Atlantic, Southwest Airlines, First Direct, Ikea, Marks and Spencer, Aldi, DHL, KLM and Albert Heyn. They redefined the business in which they compete and offer a new vision of how they can improve people's lives.

Young and Rubicam did the study in many countries. It appears that the grid differs per country. Nevertheless, airlines, car rental, credit cards and financial services appear to be quite weak brands. With respect to airlines, the own airline has a very high brand value in the home country, but usually not abroad: there is still a lot of work to be done to build those brands in a foreign country, or to develop them as real global brands.[43] Figure 11-6 reveals the grid for service firms in Germany in 1993.[44]

protection of service
brand names
The internationalization in services also generates attention for the protection of service brand names. Practice has shown that it is difficult and costly to come up with a decent international title and, subsequently, to have it registered in many countries. Often a chosen title is already copyrighted elsewhere. The service provider then faces new choices: to try and register the second best title; consult with the owners of the registered title in the various countries; decide not to advertise in certain countries; or just to start operations and take the risk, if it concerns small businesses in those countries that do not operate in the same line of services. A significant development is the change in trade-mark laws in the "new" countries (specifically in Eastern Europe). Because of the disintegration of the Soviet Union, Czechoslovakia and Yugoslavia, new trade mark registers were formed in the Baltic, Czech Republic and Slovakia. Other political events may also affect brand policy.

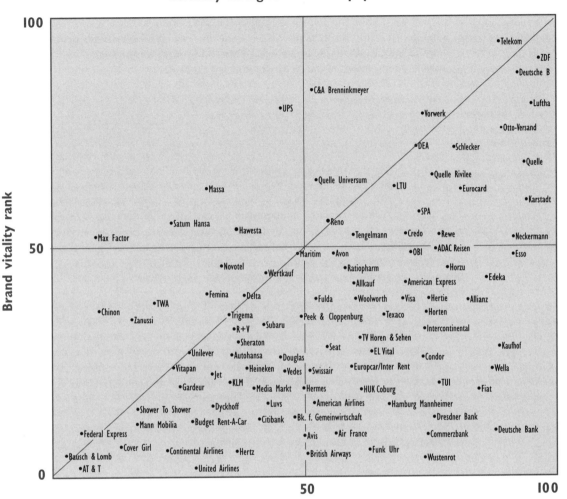

Germany-caring/service-total population

Figure 11-6
The brand asset
valuator for services in
Germany

Brands can play a decisive role in services marketing. This role will even increase. The big question is, however, do customers/clients only experience brands once they have actually bought them? Some people believe that brands are not yet used in creating a preference for a particular service provider.[45] That is one of the biggest challenges for the near future, especially in the business to business services sector.

ASSORTMENT

assortment policy width and depth

When we discuss the assortment policy, it is self evident to pay attention to the width and depth of the assortment. As the following examples will show, this can also be applied to the service sector. Then, a portfolio of services and brands can be accomplished and offered to different target group customers.

Service practice 11-8 Width and depth in the service sector

The hospitality industry. When comparing the Marriott with the McDonald's formula, it turns out that both corporations are interested in the family segment. Only the focus is different. Recently, although McDonald's has given teenagers and business people (breakfasts) more attention around the globe, it's main focus is still on families. Marriott's prime target in most countries is the business clientèle. In doing so, the latter enterprise opts for a wide range of facilities. In the same building, people can often have meetings, telephones, breakfast, lunch or dinner. Considering the extensive range of services from lodging to different menus, often offered through various in-house restaurants and room service, and the ample choice of alcoholic and non-alcoholic beverages, we can speak of a relatively wide assortment of facilities.

The mortgage business. In the financial sector, every supplier has a different approach to the mortgage market. The commercial banks have adopted a service policy that offers a broad assortment directed at both private and business markets. By further extending their offers of mortgage variants, supplemented with personal advice by means of PC-software, these banks are trying to combine customized services and standardization. Building societies in the United Kingdom offer a smaller range of services to mainly the consumer market. Specialized mortgage advisors (whether or not franchised) apply a formula based on an even smaller range directed at combining services on mortgages and objective personal advice (so, a combination of a strong focus, depth, customized services and standardization).

Within the limits of their restricted service assortments, firms like McDonald's carry a rather wide range of service variations. In the case of McDonald's, these are the kinds of hamburgers and in case of a building society, the various types of mortgages. Therefore, we can label this assortment as small but deep.

portfolio of services brands

In service organizations, assortment strategy plays a major role. The answer to the question as to what a portfolio of services brands should be composed of in an actual situation depends on the strategic and tactical service concept. The portfolio's build-up of services can also be linked to the relationship or familiarity with the organization; the service delivery process; and/or the sales.[46] As to relationship with the organization, one can think of the deployment of one organization or distribution channel for various forms or types of services (offering various kinds of package tours, for example). Relating services is usually aimed at increasing efficiency during the consecutive phases of providing services. Bundling services is a way of making this more concrete.[47] The transportation sector offers a number of examples. From this point of view, shipping, transportation and logistic services can be combined. For a transportation firm, it is paramount to cater to the needs of the clients by way of various logistics and distribution concepts instead of thinking from a procedural and organizational angle.

A service provider may complete the renowned Boston Consulting Group matrix (with the axes constituting the relative market share and market growth) for service brands that are available in the service provider's assortment. A similar matrix can also be composed for other levels of the service hierarchy, such as the service class, the service form, the service type and also, naturally, the service variation. This depends on the level at which one wishes to make these analyses. Brands can also be positioned in the graphs of Figures 11-4 and 11-5.

THE ACTUAL SERVICE OFFER

actual service offer

The last part of the service concept is the actual service offer and the supporting service delivery processes (its provision in particular). The actual offer of services is a specific and detailed form of the service concept and assortment. The service offering is determined at an operational company level and can be regarded as the answer to many management questions, such as what services will be offered; what will be their definite form; when will these services be offered; how will they be offered; where are they offered; who is going to offer the services; and what costs do these services entail to the organization? Those responsible in an organization for defining the final service offer should at all times take into account three supply aspects when making decisions. These are the service elements; the final design of a service; and the level of service provision.

service elements

The service elements are the ingredients of the total supply of core services and additional services. Together, these elements form the one-off package of tangible and non-tangible matters that actually constitute the augmented service offer. However, the success of a service or the consumer's judgment on the quality of the service, naturally, depend on many other matters. The success of a holiday is not only determined by the elements the tour operator is responsible for, but also by group interaction, the people you meet, the amount of snow or sunshine, one's mood and unexpected events.

Managers in the service sector have to deal with a number of challenges when defining their offer to the client. Often, it is difficult to give a detailed summing-up of all tangible and non-tangible elements which constitute the service offer. Usually, the tangible elements are easier to point out than the non-tangible ones. In addition, calculating the cost will be difficult in both cases (just as the expected revenues); an offer not only consists of the service assortment (such as current accounts, mortgages, etc. by a bank) but also includes matters such as opening hours, the location of the branch and the like. The servuction process hinges upon the interaction between the clients. This will also affect service offerings and the quality of services as perceived by the consumer. So,

design

a broad and integrative perspective is needed to design the "perfect offer".

service delivery process

The process of looking for the final form in which a service will be presented is aimed at a minute examination of the various options that exist for every service element. The decision on the precise structure of every service element (and so of its final design and the service delivery process) is based on factors such as market demands, competitors' policies, the need to balance the various elements within each service and all the competing services in the same branch. Service providers can make this as complex or as simple as they like. Naturally, the paramount question is what does the client desire and what the competition (already) does. Here, in a very concrete manner, substance is given to the firm's market orientation and the positions opted for. Low cost and differentiation now have to become a reality in service offers and brands. Upon determining the service offers, it is also necessary for every service, service variation and service providing process, to decide at what level of service provision one should operate. Just as is the case with the other elements of the service provided, here too the service level, level of reliability, and operational feasibilities have to harmonize with the positioning and competitive strategy opted for. If a company feels strongly about cost reduction it will, for example, limit the possibilities to provide customized services by means of human interaction. In addition to the available means, routines and capacity, naturally, play a role in this

11.6 DEVELOPING NEW SERVICES

Up to this point, existing services and present service providing processes were at stake. In this section, some major policies for developing new services and new service providing processes will be discussed.

innovations

"new"

These innovations are possible at levels 3–7 of the service hierarchy. For our purpose, "new" will include all services that are totally new to the organization and the market; new service classes or services additional to the existing service class; principal changes in the service form, type of service, new brands, and service variations developed by a firm; repositioning existing services; existing services for new market segments; or new services that produce the same results at a lower cost to the service organization. The service providing processes required to match these adaptations are also considered to be a part of the new service policy. This will often mean a change in the internal processes, flow charts, or organizational structure. One could say that "new" is a result of every change in position the firm has adopted in the matrices of Chapter Two. There are several reasons to innovate services, such as the client desires something else/new; differentiation is adding value for the customer; the yield for the organization is lower costs and/or higher profit margins; to reach out for new segments; the sales of existing services are decreasing; the competition launches a new service; strategic considerations.

market-driven innovations

This overview of reasons shows that new services can be market-driven or technology driven.[48] This may also be labelled as a market pull versus a technology push. Market-driven innovations may result from a customer request for better service quality, meeting the needs of specific customer segments (like McDonald's introducing Businessman's McDonald's in the US), or matching new needs (like tour

technology-driven innovations

operators developing more active holiday packages). Technology-driven innovations in services may hinge upon introducing more technology in the service delivery process (like the standardization of work flows at McDonald's or the new kitchen equipment at Taco Bells which leads to "smaller kitchens" and larger floor space in the restaurant), using more information technology (computer help desk by phone), extending the service delivery process (market research agencies provide more advice nowadays in addition to only the data), shortening the service delivery process (more low budget hotels like Campanille and Formule I in France and other European countries) and service bundling (grouping several services together at a lower price than for each separate service).

An organization can develop new services and/or service providing processes by itself, buy and sell them (in part) to third parties, acquire them by means of a company take-over or develop them in close cooperation with other parties.[49] In principle, each firm could develop new services, if there is a market segment and the desired positioning and competitive strategy have been determined. But even then, successful services in one country cannot always be exported automatically to another. McDonald's do not offer hamburgers in India; instead they offer the "Maharaja Mac" made from Indian mutton. The spicy-sweet flavors of Jollibee's local hamburgers are more popular than McDonald's hamburgers in the Philippines. In most cases, plans for new services and new service providing processes are part of the marketing plan.

INNOVATIONS OF SERVICES AND SERVICE PROCESSES IN GENERAL

ideas for new services and service providing processes

company staff

Service organizations have many sources from which to generate ideas for new services and service providing processes, such as one's staff in general, especially front office employees; research and development; distribution channels, public relations staff; present clients; colleagues, competition; trends in the service sector and developments in the macro-environment (DRETS factors). The company staff can be a valuable source of ideas: for the development of new services and service providing processes and for the purpose of better fulfillment of customers' needs. It will also depend on the organization's market orientation and the employee's service attitude: hopefully, the firm uses all information every staff member can provide when it is constantly assessing the present positions in the various service matrices developed in Chapter Two analyzes consumer behaviors and reads (trade) journals and magazines. Particularly, any information on possible improvements and new services that may develop when (somewhat) different positions are taken up in these matrices is useful here. The frequently present quality programs and suggestion boxes stimulate staff in developing new ideas. During the sales process and through direct contacts with customers, many new ideas may spring up to improve a service or to add a new service to the assortment. In other words, the distribution channel and the staff who are directly in touch with the customers play a major role in this process.

present buyers

Another prominent source of service innovation and information are the present buyers of a service. For that reason, it is important that an organization handles adequately any suggestions or complaints. New services can emerge by means of better anticipation to principal buying motives in the market. In this way, the service provider can look for segments (niches) which have common needs, are accessible to and defendable by the service provider. Particularly, the present heavy users form an important category as they often account for a considerable share in profits. Moreover, they often have clear ideas on how the service provision can be improved as they use it so often. When they also belong to the group perceiving a strong relationship with the company, this would be an excellent group for generating new services.[50] In industrial marketing, for example, a great deal of attention is paid to clients who are lead-users. By keeping close contact with these businesses, who are often front-runners in their field, the service organization is able to develop new ideas which may take years for competitors to catch up with.

imitation

In many service providing industries, the association principle is applied. We regularly see that the successful services of colleagues or competitors are imitated. Imitation in the service business ("me too") is rife. This imitation, in turn, leads to market uniformity; it also leads to transparency as many services look the same but still retain minor differences. It may also cause a high degree of brand parity. Consumers are sometimes troubled by these forms of unclear service differentiation. At the same, this is *the* challenge for innovations.

BREAKTHROUGH SERVICES

breakthrough services

A new category, on its own, is service breakthroughs.[51] Breakthrough services are so new, so different from the existing services that they have caused a revolution in this particular industry. Completely different standards are set to exceed customer expectations and needs (or meet them). This is all done in a very systematic way. Sometimes, there are high quality services having high prices, sometimes such high quality is delivered at very low prices.[52] Breakthrough services change the "rules of the game" fundamentally: the development of a whole industry is changed.[53] Breakthrough services are "... significantly differentiated from competition both on matters important to customers and the manner in which it achieves its results, whether that be through a well-defined, focussed, and positioned service concept; a high-commitment organization; a comprehensive data-base; a hard-to-duplicate network or technology; clever financing arrangements; or other methods."[54]

customer loyalty and employee loyalty

Customer loyalty and employee loyalty are at the heart of all service breakthroughs: they are mutually dependent. To accomplish loyalty of both groups, it is of utmost importance to take advantage of the service encounter and the "moments of truth" every time the two meet. In line with this way of reasoning, Heskett, Sasser and Hart

service encounter as a self-reinforcing process

developed a model that focusses on the service encounter as a self-reinforcing process rather than looking purely at the service encounter in terms of a set of trade-offs.[55] Such trade-offs would draw the attention to merely managing the outcome of the value of a service to the customer and the profitability to its provider (the two rectangle boxes in the figure). On the contrary, however, the self-reinforcing process focusses on the leverage of value over cost to achieve profit (the outer line in Figure 11-7).

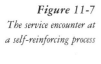

Figure 11-7
The service encounter at
a self-reinforcing process

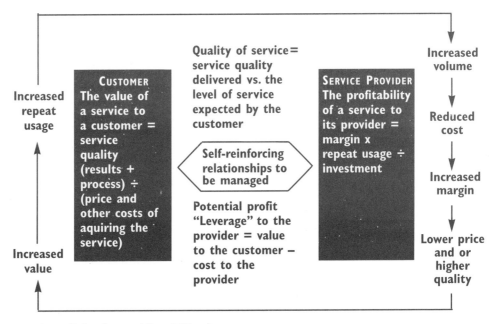

Source: Heskett, Sasser and Hart, 1990, p.4

Figure 11-7 shows the process leading to excellent service, which "is built first around an understanding that:

1. the value associated with the results a service provides and the quality of the way it is delivered depends on the extent to which a provider can reduce a customer's perceived risks;
2. increased value in relation to the costs of acquiring a service leads to a higher probability that a customer will become a repeater;
3. repeat customers, because they have established expectations, growing respect for the provider, and greater knowledge of what is expected of them in the service delivery process, are less expensive, and therefore more profitable to serve, than new customers; and
4. the value of service to a repeat customer grows with the reliability of the way it is delivered and the results it achieves."[56]

information   Proper information about the market (customers and competitors) is crucial. Therefore, monitoring customer satisfaction, loyalty, complaints and other ways of expressing dissatisfaction, service quality, service quality costs and the cost of losing customers is essential in this process of creating breakthrough services. As a result of this knowledge, these service companies improve their services; take actions to develop loyalty programs, trainings or seminars for both employees and clients; develop procedures to take a better advantage of the service encounter, etc. Other insights from successful breakthrough service providers include, amongst others: produce results/benefits for customers; growth in restrictions in order to discourage unwanted clients (often based on market segmentation and undesired relationships as revealed in the relationship portfolio); seeking "contrary positions" in service and operation as, i.e. Hamburger King did in differentiating itself from McDonald's (but let it always be based on marketing research of customer and competitor needs); using (unconditional) service guarantees and giving high priority to service recovery initiatives; motivating, empowering, informing and training servers.

Service practice 11-9 The Maastricht University service breakthrough

The Dutch government founded Maastricht University in 1976. It had to be distinctive from the other universities in The Netherlands. Its distinctive feature is its "technology applied in teaching": problem based learning. This student-centered approach is completely different from the traditional teacher centered approach. Students work in small groups and not only learn scientific knowledge, but have to apply it in many practical situations. Self-reliance and self-discipline are important skills needed to succeed during all the group work. At the same time, students learn many social and analytical skills in solving problems. They have to work in teams, chair meetings, give presentations, solve cases and tasks, perform empirical studies with companies, etc.

While, at first, the other Dutch universities were very sceptical about problem based learning, they have now started imitating it. Maastricht graduates are highly valued in the job market and the Maastricht market share is increasing in the Dutch "first year enrolment market", which is declining. At this time, Maastricht University is even exporting this service breaktrough via their own consultancy agency.

benchmarking

Benchmarking can be done by comparing "merely good" service providers and "breakthrough" service providers. The advantage of this approach is that it tries to analyze what many successful companies such as Citicorp, UPS, Marriott, Federal Express and American Airlines have in common in order to be leaders in their fields. Small firms can also be very succesful, as shown by Mark Twain Bancshares in the United States, a small but successful bank. This bank is full of eager young managers working on the basis of delegated responsibility within a set of well-defined limits. The bank amazed the world in 1995 by becoming one of the first banks offering payment transfers via the Internet.

To illustrate the practical use of such a benchmarking approach, Table 11-2 shows some of the most basic issues in creating breakthrough services.

INNOVATION AS A PROCESS

We just indicated which sources can be tapped to come up with ideas for new services and service providing processes. This section will deal with the same matter, but now from a processing or organizational perspective. Any shift in the continuum of the Chapter Two matrices depicted for service providing processes, supply, service providers, or consumers may lead to a new service or new service providing a process for the organization and for its clients. However, the line of approach to improve efficiency and the effectiveness of the process is particularly relevant. This

TABLE 11-2 *Creating breakthrough services*		
Dimension	"Merely good" service providers	Breakthrough service providers
Approach to the design of the service encounter	Regard the relationships in a service encounter as a series of trade-offs (higher quality *vs.* higher productivity, lower cost *vs.* lost customer loyalty, etc.)	Regard the relationships in a service encounter as a series of mutually reinforcing concepts (higher quality *and* higher productivity, lower costs *and* higher customer loyalty, etc.)
Emphasis on quality and value	Concentrate on producing services of the highest quality	Concentrate on producing services of the highest value to customers, taking into account quality in relation to price and other customer costs of service acquisition
Emphasis on sales — building efforts	Design marketing and service efforts for sales growth	Focus marketing and service delivery efforts on building the loyalty of existing customers while also attracting new ones
Approach to building customer satisfaction	Measure customer expectations and meet or exceed them	Measure both customer and server expectations and meet or exceed both, recognizing the self-reinforcing relationship between server and customer satisfaction

can take place, among other things, by applying techniques such as flow charting, blueprinting, service mapping, or by describing the "play" of the service encounter, the service providing process and the internal organization by way of roles and scripts. Developing circuit diagrams is a technique that is also used to chart the new service providing process which will be needed at a later stage, when the service innovation is provided.

reducing divergence

reducing complexity

In the course of developing services, two crucial choices are implied, namely by manipulating its complexity and its divergence.[57] Reducing divergence will lead to uniformity at the same time. This may not only have the effect of a cost reduction but flexibility will be diminished also. On the other hand, an up-scaling of divergence will stimulate flexibility and allow for more customized services. This, in turn, will usually bring about higher costs, however. Reducing complexity is a specialization strategy and often implies that the service provider unbundles various services.

If we use such analytical techniques for every step in the service delivery process, if we are aware of the desired positioning and if we have proper insight into the dimensions of classifying services, a powerful innovation source will be the result. Ultimately, positioning can take place, in each step of the process of delivering a service. Such an approach requires much creativity in the service firm. This is part of the skills service providers must possess. Figure 11-8 shows the application of this approach to producing and delivering a restaurant meal in other ways than currently practised. Starting with the first step, the restaurant owner may choose between taking table reservations (more complex/divergent) or free sitting (less complex/divergent). Similar choices are available all the way through the "meal-consuming" process. It is the task of the management to make sure that the individual choices of each step are in line with each other and with the desired positioning of the restaurant. Of course, potential clients should know beforehand what to expect from the restaurant and the levels they expect in order to have an excellent service encounter. Physical evidence such as menus, interior photos and table settings visible through the window will help in this process.

Service practice 11-10 Complexity, divergence and the expert

IBM, Océ, Rank Xerox and numerous software houses have their own experts in certain market segments, types of products, variety of activities (designer, systems analyst, programmer) or, apart from the nature of the services rendered, have their own pre- and after-sales service, for example. This growing multitude of experts is an organizational response to the expanding assortment of service prodivers, the increasing complexity of the nature of its activities and also, the increased independence of the client compared to a decade ago.

An alternative and frequently followed route in response to the increasing complexity and divergence in these service organizations is to make use (in part) of technological solutions (the telephone computer help desk for instance). It may change such industries dramatically.

SUCCESSFUL DEVELOPMENT AND IMPLEMENTATION

systematic approach

success or failure of new business to business financial services

Service providing organizations who try to develop new services and service providing processes by "hit and miss" and "trial and error" are taking great risks. A systematic approach is needed. Many factors determine the success of the process of, e.g. developing new financial services. They appear to be essential to many service providing businesses. The success or failure of new business to business financial services is strongly associated with eleven factors: synergy, service/market fit, quality of execution of the launch, unique/superior product, quality of execution of marketing activities, market growth and size, service expertise, quality of execution of technical activities, quality of the service delivery, quality of the execution of pre-development and the presence of tangible elements of the service.[58] These are listed in the first column of Table 11-3.

Figure 11-8
Structural alternatives
in positioning a
restaurant service

LOWER COMPLEXITY/DIVERGENCE   CURRENT PROCESS   HIGHER COMPLEXITY

LOWER COMPLEXITY/DIVERGENCE	CURRENT PROCESS	HIGHER COMPLEXITY
No reservations	Take reservation	Specific table selection
Self-seating. Menu on blackboard	Seat guests, give menu	Recite menu: describe entrees and specials
Eliminate	Serve water and bread	Assortment of hot breads and hors d'oeuvres
Customer fills out form	Take orders prepare orders	At table, taken personally by maitre
Pre-prepared: no choice	Salad (4 choices)	Individually prepared at table
Limit to four choices	Entree (15 choices)	Expand to 20 choices: add flaming dishes; bone fish at table. Prepare sauces at table
Sundae bar: self-service	Dessert (6 choices)	Expand to 12 choices
Coffee, tea, milk only	Beverage (6 choices)	Add exotic coffees, wine list, liqueurs
Serve salad and entree together Bill and beverage together	Serve orders	Separate course service; sherbet between courses; hand grind pepper
Cash only: pay when leaving	Collect payment	Choice of payment, including house accounts; serve mints

Source: G. Lynn Shostack, "Service positioning through structural change", Journal of Marketing, January 1987, pp. 34-41. Reprinted from Journal of Marketing.

TABLE 11-3 *Success factors in new financial service development*

	Business to business services	Consumer services (financial)
Marketplace	Market attractiveness	
Corporate environment	Overall corporate synergy Product/market fit	Overall company/product fit Compatibility importance
Development	Quality of execution of: pre-development activities, launch activities, technical activities Effective management	
Marketing support	Service expertise	Staff: skills and support Distribution strength Effective communications
Product offering	Unique superior product Service quality evidence Quality of service experience (service complexity)	Product/tangible quality Quality of service delivery

business synergy   The number one factor separating successes from failures is business synergy. It is defined as the degree of fit between the needs of the project and the resources, skills and experiences of the company. Successful services are more synergistic than failures. Synergistic services featured a strong service/company fit in a number of key areas such as fitting in the company's delivery system; with the firm's expertise and human resource capabilities; with existing management skills and preferences; within the scope of the financial resources of the organization; and the firm's sales and promotional capabilities and resources. Moreover, they used existing, behind-the-scenes production or operation facilities to a larger degree; and they relied more on the firm's marketing research capabilities and resources. Such synergistic new services were over four times as successful as services that were low on synergy.

service/company fit

service/market fit   The number two factor in service success is service/market fit – the degree to which the service meets customer needs and wants. Services strong on this dimension satisfy clearly identified customer needs; respond to important changes in customer needs and wants; and are consistent with existing customer values and operating systems. New services with a good service/market fit were in 80% of the cases successful, whereas services that lacked such a service/market fit were only 14% successful.

quality of execution of launch, unique/-superior service quality of execution of marketing activities

The quality of execution of launch, unique/superior service and quality of execution of marketing activities are strongly linked with the success rate of new services. The other factors mentioned in Table 11-3 score significantly lower in explaining success. Research also shows that organizations implementing successful new services have an internal culture/environment in the firm that is supporting service innovations and offers a strong sense of involvement; an official and extensive introduction program; formal up-front processes (design and evaluation) or "state-gate systems"; and technical and professional expertise.

success factors of new financial consumer services total service offering marketing support

The second column of Table 11-3 reveals the findings of a study about the determinants of success factors of new financial consumer services.[59] The core of a new service is only of secondary importance to its success factor; it "... is the quality of the total service offering, and also the marketing support that goes with this, that are of key importance." For, the key success factors in introducing new financial consumer services are: effective communications; overall company/service fit; effective distribution; compatibility/importance; service/tangible quality; quality of service delivery and skills and support staff (= front office personnel).[60]

new service development team development and launch resources developed carefully and deliberately better upfront work

market is well-known and properly targeted

objectives

front office employees' acceptance of the new service

integrate the launch stage into their development process

Successful new services are characterized by several features in many internal and external activities and disciplines within a service organization.[61] At the organizational level, it appeared "... a highly motivated, highly qualified, highly visible and well-supported new service development team is required". With respect to the allocation of resources, successful new services are "... those which receive the development and launch resources they need". In terms of the formalization of the new service development process (NSDP), successful new services "... have been developed carefully and deliberately so that, to the extent possible, guesswork is removed from the process". Within this NSDP, the better upfront work like preliminary assessment and design testing, "... the higher the probability that the new offering will be a success in the market place". With respect to the use and content of market research, successful new services "... are those for which the market is well-known and properly targeted". Looking at the financial or business analysis carried out during the NSDP, it became clear that successful projects are characterized by a clear understanding of the desired objectives before this analysis takes place; a realistic analysis as such; and a review which is conducted after the numbers become available to determine the probability of the project actually achieving its objectives. Here, market synergy is examined also in terms of front office employees' acceptance of the new service: "... time and effort must be spent getting the 'front lines' excited about the new service, rather than allowing an all-too-common, 'not another new service', feeling to take over". Finally, with respect to the launching stage of the NSDP, successful new services "... tend to integrate the launch stage into their development process".[62] A "lousy" organization of this stage, is a guarantee of a failing new service. The managerial implications of these findings are several. First, successful outcomes are managed, not left to chance. Succesful new services are put through comprehensive development programs. Second, a systematic approach and process to developing new services enhances the probability of success. Third, successful new services also include the launch stage as an integrative and important part of the whole development process. Last, successful development of a new service is a controllable event.

strong strategic
orientation
analytical attitude

A French survey covering the hotel and catering businesses, retail credit card organizations and life insurance companies revealed that a strong strategic orientation and an analytical attitude of an organization had a positive effect on phasing the service innovation.[63] By this we mean dividing the innovation process into well-known steps, such as generating ideas, testing or screening ideas, business analysis, testing, introduction and commercialization. In addition, this factor appears to have a positive effect on the financial results of the surveyed companies. A strong organizational commitment to and involvement in new service development seems to be a pre-requisite for success.

organizational
commitment
involvement

innovators

The following can be said about the strong involvement of the internal environment: dead fish float along with the stream, fish that are alive swim upstream. Service firms need innovators: people who are prepared to stick their necks out to launch new ideas; people's creativity should be used effectively. Employees must be encouraged to voice ideas. In many firms, however, we see a cultivation of behavior intended to avoid individual risk taking, particularly in large service organizations where innovators are not yet rated at their true value. This explains why there is ample room for new initiatives in the service sector in the form of new firms which discover their own niches and exploit them successfully. An organization should breed a culture that does justice to innovators. Market-oriented organizations are not afraid of taking risks. Even if the service champion (a translation of "product champion") had no decisive role in the development of the new service, the organization will have to reward initiatives and pro-active actions. The development process can be given strong stimulus when, at all levels, employees have their minds on innovation and the organization uses certain reward and control systems supporting the innovation process. Open communication lines between all parts of the organization and a strongly commited top management, combined with the aforementioned issues, set the conditions for success or failure of innovations in service organizations.

service champion

cooperation and
interface

In sum, it is essential in NSDP to have a great cooperation and interface between the marketing department and the research and development department, backed up by a truly committed company management.[64] A second factor that seems to have a decisive influence on the successful development of a service is to have an official, well-documented and detailed program of introduction during the new service's development and launch phase. This information and good internal and external communication about the new service is referred to in one of the Gaps of the SERVQUAL model. The introduction program includes a well prepared launch and an extensive training course for personnel participating in the service providing process, an official promotion program developed for front office employees as well as for the customers themselves (the script!), and the testing of the new service in an early phase of its development. A formal up-front design and evaluation clearly is a prerequisite to success.

program of
introduction

technical and
professional expertise

Technical and professional expertise is a major driving force in the developing process aimed at distinguishing between successful and unsuccessful services, especially in business to business services. For, companies can often opt for developing a service themselves, or to buy it as a business service. Usually, if there is a more complex situation, it is a more natural thing for clients to look for external suppliers. Appointing highly specialized services that really solve a client's need, will have a better chance of success. Another reason is that over the past few years the application of complex technologies (computer and informatics sciences in particular) have been responsible for the emergence of many new services.

11.7 AFTER-SALES SERVICES

The relevance of after-sales support can be formulated as follows: "After-sales support is a litmus test of a firm's intention towards its customers. In effect, the customer judges the company by its willingness to stand behind its products and provide satisfaction to even the most unreasonable buyer."[65]

services added to the core service

After-sales service will be among the additional services added to the core service. To some companies, this service provision will consist of a standard service, to others it will be customized. Consumers will tend to use after-sales services when core services or goods are not up to standard. The supplier must realize that the consumer's perception and state of mind will have a strong influence on the per ceived quality of the after-sales service. The same techniques and line of approach used to measure the quality of services that were previously mentioned are applicable when measuring the quality of after-sales services.

after-sales service

After-sales service can be described as the philosophy and all accompanying activities that can help to maximize consumer satisfaction following the purchase or the use of a good or a service by the consumer. After-sales services receive a lot of attention these days. Both consumers and firms consider them very relevant to developing and

relationships

maintaining relationships. It is important to consumers because it is a means to gather information from the supplier; a means to solve problems; makes it possible to settle complaints; is an essential part of the overall offer/proposition; and is an additional service. For service providers, it is an essential part of their strategy because it creates competitive advantages; forges or consolidates a bond with the clients; creates or consolidates brand loyalty and leads to repeat purchases; generates feed-back from clients (particularly in case of complaints); provides more precise standards for the design of goods and services; provides services when a problem arises (service recovery); forces the organization to focus on the client and his/her needs and desires; and emphasizes the image of a market-oriented organization.

MANY KINDS OF AFTER-SALES SERVICES

It is important to know whether after-sales services are based on people or machinery, how the client and the organization meet (who goes to whom?) and whether goods or services are concerned. In addition, there is another distinction between support services, on the one hand, and feed-back and restitution services, on the other.[67] Guarranties, repairs, maintenance, availability of spare parts, replacements, delivery, installation, instruction, directions for use, user's help (help-desk of computer

support services
feedback and
restitutions

suppliers and software houses), training, help in replacing spares, information, advice, etc. can be counted as support services. The feedback and restitutions category, for example, includes handling complaints, solving problems, refunds, 1-800 telephone numbers for information, reactions to service staff's undesirable behavior, dispute resolution, service recovery, returning products, etc. For both groups of after-sales services, the quality will be determined by the perceptions and expectations of the

after-sales service
quality

client. Here, too, the well-known what, how and by whom determines after-sales service quality.

With respect to after sales services, it is for service providers necessary to identify what causes the problems (if any): is it the service around the product or the product itself? That answer gives management information as to what should be done to solve the problem and avoid the problem in the future (prevention). Four types of situation might occur:

- the unbeatables: product is good and after sales is good;
- walking wounded: product is good and after sales is poor;
- time bombs: product is poor and after sales is good; and
- dead on arrival (DOA): product is poor and after sales is poor.[68]

unbeatables

It will be self evident that only unbeatables will deliver excellent total service. On the other hand, great after sales services may sometimes be accepted in the short term as a remedy for imperfect goods. In the long run, however, no firm can survive with such a strategy. Then the time bomb will go off. Also, poor after-sales services and good products will not be a viable situation in the long run; not to mention the DOA situation.

INVESTIGATING AFTER-SALES SERVICES

creating excellent
after-sales services
a way to solve customer
dissatisfaction

Just as with any services discussed in this book, the quality of after-sales service can be investigated in many ways. All the ways mentioned in the Chapters Five and Six can be applied. It all hinges upon creating excellent after-sales services. A special issue here, however, is that in many cases after-sales services have to be used to solve consumer problems because something has gone wrong. So, after-sales services are important as a way to solve customer dissatisfaction.

satisfaction with the
after-sales services

Also, in general, when customers do not have any problems, after-sales services are essential. For instance, in the automobile industry, satisfaction with the after-sales services of the dealer (check ups, "normal" repair and maintenance, etc.) often appear to have a larger impact on dealer loyalty and brand loyalty than satisfaction with the car itself. This has turned out to be the case for many European, American and Japanese

service employees

brands.[69] Since this service is also a people business, the way these service employees behave is often decisive in the perceived after-sales service quality. The business to business world is no exception to this rule. Many people working in the business to business sector have a technical background and often pay less attention to social skills and social interactions in the customer-supplier relationships. However, it turns out that

"soft skills"

the "soft skills" are most important in this industry. No one should forget that – even in this often technical world – issues like responsiveness, credibility and trust are crucial in the assessment of service quality. How technicians behave and interact with the customer is crucial from a marketing point of view. These part time marketeers are often decisive in repeat buying decisions. This is one of the reasons why it may be so difficult to manage business to business services.[70] In the industrial world too, it is important to know whether customers have the same idea, opinion and expectations about excellent after-sales quality as the company offering this service. If this is not the case, the first cause for a lack of quality can be found, according to the SERVQUAL-model.

Service practice 11-11 After-sales services in the industrial world [71]

A large European manufacturer of copying machines had its after-sales service researched among its Dutch customers. The data from 525 customers (out of 775) and from 25 service - top and middle - managers (out of 35) were obtained and analyzed. They had to rate questions on the quality of the copying machines, the quality of the after-sales services and how important each of those items were in the total service quality.

Analysis of the customer data revealed that three factors are important to customers in assessing the firm's after-sales service quality:

1. the hard core elements of the augmented copying machine (like quality of machine, spare parts, paper, ink, instruction sessions; quality of delivery of the machine; service contract options; availability of spare parts during service calls; price performance ratio);
2. the general attitude about the relationships with the copying manufacturer (relations with vendor in general; relations with vendor's sales staff; administrative services; complaint handling); and
3. the relationships with the technical services staff who have to perform the after-sales service and their way of working (this relation in general; dispatchment of break down calls, availability of the technical services staff; repair time; general attitude and behavior of technician; response time).

Comparing the opinions of the customers with the answers given by the service managers on how they think the customers would answer provided some interesting differences. In general, managers thought customers would rate the service quality lower than they actually did. The study also revealed service managers think industrial customers will give a higher importance score but a lower quality score than they actually do to those after-sales items that can be labelled as the more tangible service items. Service managers think customers will give a lower quality score and a lower importance score than customers actually do to those after-sales items labelled as the more intangible and more personal service items.

These contradictory opinions may be a source of new problems when managers only use their own frame of reference in developing service improvements.

Both service managers and customers considered the response time as the most important item of the after-sales services. Unfortunately for the firm, all respondents gave the lowest quality score to this item. So, customers had to wait longer than expected.

Significant differences of perceived after-sales service quality exist between different segments of industrial customers. Differences in importance score for various items occurred among these segments as well.[72]

11.8   DISSATISFACTION MANAGEMENT

Traditionally, dealing with customer complaints is an important part of after-sales services and service recovery. Although complaining is just one of the many ways to express customer dissatisfaction (see Chapter Four), it has received much attention while the other ways of expressing dissatisfaction have received little. Therefore, we will discuss dissatisfaction management here as the overall framework in which complaints management, service recovery and unconditional service guarantees can be placed. Dissatisfaction management is "... the systematic managerial effort involved in collecting and processing consumer dissatisfaction data stemming from all internal as well as external sources with the purpose of communicating information to organizational decision-makers in order to enable them to detect, correct and prevent consumer dissatisfaction."[73] This way of looking at consumer dissatisfaction and the way it is expressed, offers the opportunity to the service organization to integrate all the data from the many ways dissatisfaction is expressed: complaints, asking for refunds, contacting Better Business Bureaux or consumer unions, telling friends about the bad experience, switching store, doctor or bank, etc. The service organization should collect, file and analyze these consumer-initiated communications and even encourage customers to voice their discontent in order to improve the future service quality. The basic assumption here is that it is better knowing about the problems than not knowing about them. In the latter situation, the service firm can do nothing to solve or prevent problems due to a lack of information. The combination of data from various sources reduces the disadvantages of just having to rely on one source. For instance, in terms of complaints, it is common wisdom that the complaints actually received are just the tip of the iceberg. These various information sources, taken together, will improve the quality of information for organizational decision making. Information from market research studies on consumer behavior, image, positioning of the firm, employees' behavior, how many credit-notes are sent, how many products are returned, repairs offered, how many premiums were miscalculated, how strong is brand loyalty, etc. can be added to the Service Quality Information System.

*dissatisfaction
management*

*consumer-initiated
communications*

*Service Quality
Information System*

*Service
practice
11-12
Dissatisfaction
management
at two US
service
providers* [74]

An American service firm providing health insurance and medical care (1,700 employees; $1.8 billion sales in 1990) had about 200,000 registered consumer-initiated contacts a year. About 20% of them related specifically to consumer dissatisfaction (the remaining 80% related to requests for information). They register complaints, problems, appeals, grievances, (dis)satisfaction rates and (dis)loyalty rates. 28 people work in the Consumer Affairs department and use a pc network with standard software to file and analyze this data. This department's manager reports to the Vice President of Consumer Affairs.

A US firm providing services on leasing and renting cars, vans and buses (40,000 employees; $5.2 billion sales in 1990) had about 500,000 consumer-initiated communications in 1990, 25% of them being related to consumer dissatisfaction. They register complaints, (dis)satisfaction rates and (dis)loyalty rates. 80 part-time employees work in their Consumer Affairs department and use a mainframe computer with customized software to file and analyze this data. The CAD-manager reports to the Group Director of Rental Operations.

Both firms value this system highly over just having only data on complaints. It gives a much richer database, better information and leads to better decision making.

COMPLAINTS MANAGEMENT

complaints management

Complaints management is not simply a matter of "just settling the complaint", but is, supposedly, a serious activity on the part of an organization. It covers all activities in the organization from the very moment that a complaint is received up to the moment that the client who complained receives a reaction from the organization, and, finally, knowing whether the complainant is satisfied with the solution offered.

free market information

Complaints should be considered as free market information: consumers take the initiative personally to tell the organization that something is wrong with the service. In the service sector, we find that many complaints are linked to staff behavior and to the agreements made (the how of service quality). Many companies, do not yet fully grasp all the opportunities to benefit from complaints.[75] Almost a quarter of the surveyed (Dutch) companies have no guidelines for handling complaints; almost 40% of the surveyed companies have no special provisions or official bodies where consumers or clients can send their complaints; almost one quarter of the surveyed companies do not register the incoming complaints, not even at minimum level whereby name, address, and residence of the complainant is registered; and only about one half of the surveyed companies have some form of complaint registration (varying from very simple to extremely advanced, automated and detailed systems) including periodical reviews/reports. Only this latter group of companies have a systematic approach to complaints management.

Chapter Four revealed what service consumers can do to express their discontent. One option was to take no action at all. Within the framework of complaints management it is crucial to prevent this from happening. In other words, and perhaps something of a paradox: within the framework of complaints management a firm must make a serious effort to receive the maximum number of complaints. For an organization can do something about such a complaint (and with it – try to – keep the client). It may also result in generating new ideas for services. Therefore, it is essen-

easily accessible

tial that the organization is easily accessible to dissatisfied consumers. This is the first step in complaints management, consisting of four steps altogether (see Figure 11-9).

developing guidelines

The second step consists of developing guidelines for staff members who will

staff members

actually be in touch with those who voiced complaints in order to give them guidelines on how to handle complainants and their complaints. The third step concerns the employment of one or more staff members who will be responsible for the complaints registration, the internal coordination of complaints and the follow-up of complaints for the organization's strategy (particularly to prepare preventive and structural measures to avoid any future complaints). The fourth and last step is the

correct and swift handling of the complaint

correct and swift handling of the complaint, from the point of view of the individual complainant. This may include a survey on whether the complainants were satisfied with the way the complaint was settled, or a survey on the quality of complaints settlements.

Figure 11-9
The four steps in complaints management

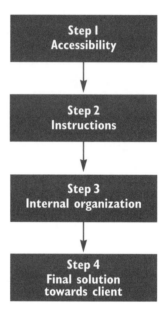

Step 1
Accessibility

Step 2
Instructions

Step 3
Internal organization

Step 4
Final solution
towards client

SERVICE RECOVERY AND UNCONDITIONAL SERVICE GUARANTEES

"service recovery"

Simply stated, the firm's response to a service problem can be called "service recovery": "two broad purposes should influence the development of a recovery service strategy: to resolve the problem and restore the customer's confidence in the firm; to improve the service system so that the problem occurs less frequently in the future."[76]

preventive action
service recovery strategy

Such preventive action should be taken in order that the problem does not occur in the future. Then the essential steps in a service recovery strategy are: teach the importance of recovery service – an attitude that should be taught throughout the whole organization (and be part of the service attitude); and identify the service problems. Encouraging customers to complain is important in this step. It provides the necessary information to make analyses and take decisions in order to improve service quality. Resolve problems effectively in a personalized way, quickly, at the first point of contact whenever possible; empower people, keep the customer informed, emphasize a fair solution and finally improve the service system – analysis will offer possibilities for corrective action.

empowered service
employees

Employees have to be trained to respond in a proper way to dissatisfied customers. The essence of service recovery, though, is that "canned responses" are not appropriate.[77] Empowered service employees must be able to not only perform the standard response but add something unexpected to it: the spontaneous art of service recovery[78].

Service
practice
11-13
Service
recovery in
reality

An American critical incidents based study on service failures in retailing revealed that three large groups of retail failures exist:[79]

1. employee responses to service delivery system failures (out of stock, bad information, etc.) and/or product failures (product defects, etc.);
2. employee responses to customer needs and requests; and
3. unprompted and unsolicited employee actions (like mischarging, embarrassments, attention failures, and, accusations of shop lifting).

Recovery strategies included, amongst others replacement, refunds, correction, apologies, discounts, but also manager/employee intervention. In some cases, the failures escalated or unsatisfactory correction was provided.

A critical incidents based UK-study about service recovery in industries like distribution, hotels, catering, transport, communication, banking, finance, insurance, public administration, education and health care revealed "four main types of failure: the service system, the physical goods, a customer's body failure (i.e. medical) and customers making a mistake." The "key attributes of staff affecting a recovery are to appear pleasant, helpful and attentive, show concern for the customer, act quickly and be flexible. The key activities in the recovery process are to provide information about the problem, take action and that staff should appear to put themselves out to solve the problem and if possible involve the customer in the decision making."[80]

service breakthroughs

The service employee's role is important to the quality of the service recovery. Measuring this service quality is useful since it affects store loyalty, brand loyalty and the like. Therefore, service breakthroughs can also be found in this area: "Recovery is a different management philosophy, one that embraces customer satisfaction as a primary goal of business. This mind-set can change the rules of the game for service companies. It shifts the emphasis from the cost of pleasing a customer to the value of doing so, and it entrusts frontline employees with using their judgement ... But recovery is fundamental to service excellence and should therefore be regarded as an integral part of a service company's strategy.... In service businesses, the old adage must be revised: To err is human; to recover, divine."[81]

unconditional
guarantee

A special topic to be discussed within these ideas about service recovery, is the unconditional guarantee.[82] Such a guarantee is characterized as unconditional (it

promises customer satisfaction unconditionally, without exception); easy to understand and communicate (simply written, concise); meaningful (it guarantees those
aspects important to the customers and it is financially meaningful in the sense that
it calls for a significant payout when the promise is not kept that is easy and painless
to invoke; dissatisfaction can be expressed quite easily); and easy and quick to collect
on (customers should not have to work hard to collect a payout).

Service practice 11-14 Who is right?	Many companies use this slogan nowadays to show who is unconditionally right in the market place. Their employees should always have in mind as rule 1: The customer is always right. And if the customer is not right, rule 1 applies.

Similar to what we stated in the section on after sales services, unconditional service
guarantees set clear standards, generate feedback, force the company to understand
why they fail, and build marketing muscle (it enables one to boost marketing).

11.9 CAPACITY MANAGEMENT

Capacity plays an important role in the service providing process. For that reason, it
is discussed in several sections of this book. Capacity is one of the options open to
the management to reduce costs and to improve service standards. The level-capacity
strategy is an attractive pricing method to affect any demand fluctuations.[83] The better
a service provider is able to make reliable demand forecasts, the better it will enable
it to optimize demand and supply management. It pays, therefore, to gather information on this subject by several means, such as performance statistics, own
administrative systems, and the literature about the trade and industrial sector. Before
finding a solution to demand fluctuations, it is important to trace the cause of these
fluctuations. Perhaps, only certain groups of clients or even a small number of large
clients may prove to be responsible for the (largest part of the) fluctuations in
demand.

optimize demand and supply management

A service provider can try to adapt to changes in demand by several means. It goes
without saying that it must be certain whether these changes are of a temporary or a
permanent nature. A temporary solution for a peak in demand can consist of a more
efficient use of the undercapacity. Also, one could try and shift the prevalent peak in
demand to periods with a low occupancy rate.[84] Structural changes in demand can
also occur and require a company to adapt strategically.

*Service
practice
11-15
There goes
Royal Class!*

Due to external circumstances which were considered to be of a structural nature, KLM bade farewell to its first class (Royal Class). Because of the limited clientèle and high operating costs, the Royal Class became completely inefficient. To many, saying goodbye to all this exclusivity, was a heavy blow. "Tourists and business travellers have different expectations. Still, one should try to please both groups as much as possible. Luxury is not a must at all costs", says former KLM chairman of the board Pieter Bouw.[85]

*disequilibrium
situations*

Capacity management can be directed at controlling demand as well as controlling supply. In both instances, it hinges upon disequilibrium situations. These may hold for the long or short term. Moreover, they may be foreseen or unforeseen.[86] The imbalance may be due to two kinds of situations:

1. excess demand/slack supply; and
2. slack demand/excess supply.

CONTROLLING DEMAND

control demand

Several methods can be used to control demand, such as pricing, promotion, service differentiation, segmentation, adding additional services and reservation systems. Prices, for example, are based on the expected rush. This solution is common in the travel industry during the high, low, and intermediate season, or on the railways by way of an off-peak railcard. It is also possible to persuade present clients to buy the service in times or periods that are off-peak or off-season by means of promotion, lower prices and service differentiation. Approaching customer segments with differ-

customer segments

ent demand patterns will also lead to better capacity deployment. Business hotels that offer family arrangements on weekends and in holiday periods follow this line of reasoning. Often, this solution (necessarily) comes with lower prices and/or adjustments in service. Certain high season facilities, for example, are not available to tourists or those avoiding the winter cold during the low season. In order to attract (additional) clientèle, extra services can be added to the core service. In this way, the service provider is still able to cover (part of) his capacity costs/fixed costs. The introduction

booking systems

of booking systems is also frequently used to steer demand. Chains of hotels, dentists, hospitals, travel bureaux, airline companies, and theatre booking offices apply this technique. Sometimes, consumers make reservations while not showing up. This is particularly so when the making of reservations is free of charge. Service providers try to counter this by charging the no-shows, or by demanding immediate payment when the reservation is made, for example by checking the customer's credit card number by telephone.

CONTROLLING SUPPLY

control supply   The following subjects can be used to control supply: adapting provision systems to demand, hiring of part-time personnel, increasing efficiency, increasing clients' participation, building up extra capacity, or sharing capacity with others.

The service providing system can be influenced, for example, by providing standing room during a pop concert (instead of seating arrangements) or by establishing a self-service buffet during breakfast hours in hotels (instead of staffed service).[87] A service provider is able to relieve the capacity during peak hours by offering additional services while having to wait for the core service. In this way, a golf player can practice at the golfing range before teeing off. A popular method, particularly applied in shops, the hotel and catering business is to react to demand by employing part-time staff (contract labor, seasonal workers, temporary employees, employees on call).

Maximizing the efficiency of the service providing process can be effected by various means, amongst which are analyzing the service process by using flow charts, blueprints and service maps. In addition to this, at specific times, a certain degree of specialization can be introduced or preliminary work can be done (investing for peak periods). For example, employees who put aside their own work in order to assist others during peak periods. Other employees can carry out preparatory duties during the low season or when business is slow. The preparations can be, for instance, restocking, resulting in more efficiency during peak hours. This is what happens in restaurant kitchens. These activities can also take place in order to make the most of the capacity, for example, having the outdoor swimming pool painted by the pool staff during the low season instead of contracting out the job. Other possibilities are aimed at a more efficient working method during peak periods, at improving the productivity of the service providers, and at cross-training. Cross-training is a means of giving personnel from the less busy sections the coaching they require to assist during peak hours wherever necessary.

Introducing self-service is one of the methods to increase customer participation. It means that certain costs are no longer made by the service provider but, in part, are relegated to the consumer.[88]

Prior investments in future expansion programs are known to have positive results. One can think of hiring property that was first considered to be oversized. A minor additional investment in the beginning is often more economic than making all sorts of adjustments at a later stage.[89] Another solution to be applied is sharing capacity. Hospitals, with their mutual agreements on bedding capacities, or on sharing the use (and costs) of expensive medical equipment; airline companies that make their ground handling facilities available to one another in their homeland, or exchange crews, according to capacity; doctors who take care of each others' practice, are examples of sharing capacity.

11.10 CORE, AUGMENTED, STANDARD AND CUSTOMIZED SERVICES

The typology of services developed in Chapter Two can be elaborated upon with respect to some specific features of services, as discussed in this chapter (see also Figure 11-10). Not so many topics will be discussed here, since most of the issues from this chapter apply to all four types of services.

Many of the standard services will consist of the core service plus, perhaps, some facilitating services, while the opposite (customized augmented services) will be broader by definition and will consist of core, facilitating and supporting services. The assortment of standard services probably will not be so wide, while the assortment of customized services will be quite broad. Augmented services will go along with deep assortments, while core services will be characterized by shallow assortments. The interpersonal relationship will consist of low contact in the case of standard core services (much labor substituted by technology) and high contact in case of both types of customized services. Finally, capacity management may be characterized by chase demand when both types of standard services are at stake, while customized services might opt relatively often for level capacity.

Figure 11-10
Service typology and
services policy

Service policy	Standard core services	Customized core services	Standard augmented services	Customized augmented services
Strategic services concept	core + facilitating services	core + facilitating services	core + facilitating + supporting services	core + facilitating + supporting services
Assortment	not wide, shallow	broad, shallow	not wide, deep	broad, deep
Services process: - personal interaction - capacity management	low contact chase demand	high level capacity	low/middle contact chase demand	high contact level capacity

SUMMARY

The management of services during their life cycles is necessary to survival. Amongst other things, it means a service provider must be able to introduce new services and/or new service providing processes at the right time. We used a broad meaning of the definition of "new". In the international context, service providers, as we have seen, can opt for either an extension or adaptation strategy if they want to sell their services in foreign markets. As we already saw in previous chapters, the capacity problem of service organizations calls for management's continuous attention. Solutions to this problem can be found in the control of demand and of supply. Developing new services and service providing processes and the adaptation of the existing ones are vital in order to survive in this sector. If a company fails to adapt to the continuously changing environment and does not have a keen eye of the benefits for its clients, it will not only price itself out of the market but it will vanish altogether. The reason for its existence (to provide benefits for the client) is than no longer present. Moreover, the position of the settled companies will be affected by the initiatives that are taken by competitors and new entrants. There are several sources and methods to generate ideas. Brands perform a crucial function for service customers in reducing perceived risk;

they have a facilitating function to service providers. In the service sector clients, competitors and staff are important to create breakthrough services. The service innovation challenge can be tackled from a processing and organizational line of approach. The many factors found crucial to the success of new service development closely resemble the key success factors of service firms in general.

Every change of position made in one of the matrices in Chapter Two actually implies a new service or a new service providing process. This needs to be elaborated upon within the selected goals about market-orientation, strategy and desired quality.

We ended this chapter with the after-sales services (definition, necessity, classification, links with our division into core and additional services) and the basic elements of dissatisfaction management as part of the service strategy. This latter topic was discussed as the framework for complaints management, service recovery and unconditional service guarantees. They all hinge upon the service firm's strategy and policy to avoid customer problems, take successful corrective actions and solve customer problems quickly, fairly and properly in order to accomplish excellent service quality.

QUESTIONS

1   What difference is there between features and benefits? Why is it important to make this distinction in service strategy?

2   Describe the relationship between planning, creating, providing and evaluating a catering service.

3   Give an explanation of the thesis why every change of position in one of the matrices on service classification found in Chapter Two actually implies a new service or service providing process. Illustrate this by describing the phrase "new" used in this chapter.

4   What is the relationship between the service hierarchy and the differences between the strategic and the tactical service concept?

5   What is the use of branding in services? What functions do brands perform?

6   On many occasions in this book, examples of airlines have been given. Summarize those findings. Then, develop a brand strategy for airlines to increase loyalty among the different segments of passengers. (You yourself may define what segments you deem relevant.)

7   How can service firms impact on demand and supply? What strategies can be used to that end?

8   What is dissatisfaction management? How is it related to a Service Quality Information System?

9   Why could it be relevant to avoid standard or canned responses in service recovery or complaints management?

10 What are breakthrough services?

ASSIGNMENTS

1   Make a diagram that depicts how the family of services, classes, and forms, the type of services and the service variations interrelate in the transportation sector.

2   Provide some examples of how service firms that you know actually manage their capacity.

3   What (positive and/or negative) reactions did you get when you once complained at a service firm? What was the problem? How was it solved? How satisfied were you with this solution? What should have been altered in your opinion?

4   Over the past few years, the hotel and catering business has put in an effort to innovate services by introducing new hotel formulas. Describe one of these and indicate the main starting-points for service innovation by means of the theory from this chapter.

5   Give a few examples of service innovations which, for the greater part, have emerged under the influence of the DRETS factors discussed in Chapter Three. Give an example for each of the five factors.

6   Make an overview of:

a. the key success factors of service firms (Chapter One and Seven);

b. the factors that distinguish exporting from non-exporting service firms (Chapter Nine); and

c. the key success factors in new service development (this chapter). What can you conclude when you analyze those findings (look especially for similarities and differences)?

7 What kind of service recovery do you know in the retail business? How does that fit to Service practice 11-12?

Case: CLUBMED: TREND-SETTER OR TREND-FOLLOWER?

Serge Trigano will take control of the company from his father Gilbert, one of the founding-fathers of the ClubMed formula. Young Trigano will be responsible for once again making his father's derelict goldmine pay. For this purpose, the new managing director focuses his attention on individual holiday makers and elderly people. Young French holiday makers, in particular, made ClubMed into a large firm during the seventies.

ClubMed stood for organized entertainment for the well-off youngsters who often spoke no foreign language and who had no idea of the local poverty.

For years on end, the social aspects were the main feature of the French holiday paradise. One was obliged to be on a first-name basis and plastic beads were the only means of payment. Naturally, the beads could not be bought with shells. Every year, managing director Gilbert Trigano would open new clubs in destinations that were yet unknown.

Foreigners – Americans in particular – and other travelling organizations discovered Club-Med's concept. Imitations like Club Adiane, Club Robinson and Club Marco Polo emerged. Until the eighties, ClubMed held on to its luck. The fad was over then and the fear of aids affected the other aspect of holiday romance. The crisis brought about by the Gulf War made an impact on

many holiday budgets. This, in turn, led to a tariff-war against low-cost travelling organizations. In 1993, problems were accumulating. In politically unstable countries like Egypt and Turkey, ClubMed had to contend with cancellations. In Europe and Africa, 13 out of the 77 holiday villages closed down.

There is hardly any money to renovate the older holiday villages. ClubMed has its own distribution channel.

Trigano: "In those days the success of ClubMed ran parallel to the growth of the economy. In times of crisis you must find a different formula. Success is not guaranteed by offering an abundance of food and sports activities."

Between 1991 and 1992, the tourist industry made an almost full recovery to pre-Gulf War levels. The following developments are evident in Europe:
- the EU – member states have a high level of vacation participation;
- a high number of holidays in comparison with Asia and North and South America;
- in 1992, there was a rise in the total holiday expenditure in many countries in Europe, whereas the number of holidays were decreasing;
- the decrease in holidays linked up with the lowered index for consumer confidence in most EU-countries. Extended holi-

days participation, in particular, appears to be sensitive to the conjuncture (just like at the beginning of the eighties and in 1990);
- there is a growing interest in camping, adventure travel and active holidays;
- the impression is that the number of extended holidays by air are influenced, among other things, by the economic barometer, the kind of summer weather people had in their home country last year, and the pricing;
- the cultural interest is growing;
- the number of senior travellers is increasing;
- consumers lay greater emphasis on health, environment, tranquility, open space and anti-stress surroundings;
- the travelling industry has to deal with an ever-increasing number of clients.

How does ClubMed prepare themselves for present-day demands? Several changes took place.

The individual holiday is no longer presented in uniformity. More attention is paid to quality and luxury: matters that are important to senior holiday makers.

The new ClubMed formulae 1 and 2 have been developed by applying service innovation. Both formulas are composed of a sports holiday on a sail-equipped cruise ship and are aimed at a broad audience (elderly people not necessarily included). The brochures now contain phrases like "long live the bride", "in future we welcome children of ten or over", "especially for bachelors"... "passionate golf players". This new service is a cross-breed between the old club formula and the cruise formula. All basic sports facilities like water-skiing, surfing, sailing and scuba-diving can be practised from the boat. The sporting character of the holidays is further accentuated by the presence of a fitness center and/or a golf simulator.

The business-to-business segment is stimulated by offering ClubMed incentives to personnel, dealers and business relationships. The travelling organization is able to accommodate groups of 50 up to 1,300 people.

The existing French travelling organization Club Aquarius has been taken over. This means that ClubMed, by way of a simpler formula, is able to offer a lower price to dormant members, among others, who bade farewell to the club for pricing reasons. There are hardly any restrictions on new memberships. ClubMed, subsequently, aims to attract these consumers for other formulas. The age-group of Club Aquarius lies between 25 and 45 years (many families). This low-cost company division saw a rise of 45% in its occupation rate this year.

QUESTIONS

1 What assortment strategy did ClubMed adhere to during the last few years? Please give your comments.
2 Make a comparison between the aforementioned service innovations and ClubMed's position and image and give your opinion on whether things are well coordinated.
3 Give your opinion on ClubMed's target group strategy.
4 Which are the main service elements of the organization's service offer?
5 Which growth strategy(ies) was (were) followed by ClubMed with regard to its service innovation?
6 In your opinion, which critical success factors are essential for each of ClubMed's service innovations previously mentioned? Give a reason for your answer.
7 Describe a service innovation for ClubMed as proposed by yourself and based on ClubMed's position. Indicate your target groups and the overall service providing process in the form that you think this service should take.

ENDNOTES

1. This Service practice is based on the studies two of our students, Karin Zinken and Tatiana Zinken, carried out for Deutsche Bahnen while they studied at the University of Hannover via the Erasmus program. We gratefully acknowledge professor Ursula Hansen's supervision of these two MBA theses.

2. This section on internationalization has been written to a large extent by Saskia Veendorp. We acknowledge her contribution greatly.

3. Such a modular approach has become popular in the auto industry. In the US, manufacturers, in part, have moved toward the creation of world components to combat, among other things, Japanese competitiveness.

4. Jeannet and Hennessy, 1988, p. 340.

5. Krubasik, 1988.

6. See also the Deutsche Bahnen case at the beginning of this chapter and the section on (the key success factors in) new service development.

7. Jeannet and Hennessy, 1988, p. 8.

8. In both (extension and adaptation) strategies of services in the international context, communications will play a major role in making the public aware of these services and reducing perceived risk. As soon as either a service or its communications needs to be adapted, qualitative research must be available which focuses on groups in order to generate ideas for the essential features of new services and their acceptance. They, for example, can throw light on new service ideas. Such surveys should include testing of benefits, attitudes, and promotional appeals (advertising, sales or personal selling) toward that particular service.

9. The diagram is based on one of Lovelock's models, 1991, which we have adapted to our own ideas.

10. A large number of (financial) performance indicators were already mentioned in Chapter Seven, others will be mentioned in subsequent chapters.

11. Based on Kotler, 1991, p. 431.

12. Aaker, 1991.

13. Next to "perceived benefits", "perceived risks" are a major factor in the process of buying services. Literature on marketing of professional services, for example, shows that the purchase of many professional services actually comes down to a purchase intended to reduce the risks.

14. This example was given by prof. A. Parasuraman during some lectures in Maastricht, Spring 1996.

15. See Service practice 4-8 in a previous chapter revealing the surcharge accountant firms could attain in New Zealand.

16. Overviews of the many functions of brands are given by Berthon, Hulbert and Pitt, 1997; Chernatony and McDonald, 1992; Dobree and Page, 1990; Al, 1997; Hattink, 1995; Kapferer, 1995; and Aaker, 1991. A great part of this section on branding and services is based on the MBA theses of two of our students, Robin Hattink and Monique Peters.

17. Onkvisit and Shaw, 1989.

18. Assael, 1987.

19. Bouts, 1989; Koopmans and Versteeg, 1989. The December 1989 issue of the Dutch journal of marketing was a special issue on industrial brands.

20. Onkvisit and Shaw, 1989.

21. See Dan Grifford, jr. 1997, about Susan Fournier's research on brand-relationship-quality. We have adapted the text slightly to the service arena.

22. Berry, Lefkowith and Clark, 1988.

23. Berry, Lefkowith and Clark, 1988, p.2-4.

24. As told by Andy Mosmans at a 1996 conference on International Service Management, Maastricht, The Netherlands.

25. Martin, 1998, says American Express, Axa and Citibank have a global brand in retail financial services. To us, at present, this only holds for the first two companies, Citibank still attempts to.

26. As said by Rosa Zeegers, head of KLM Brand Management in Adformatie, no. 6, February 5, 1998, p.5. Also the other partners in the strategic alliances with KLM (e.g. Northwest and Alitalia) have to be positioned clearly within this alliance.

27. This figure is based on Besig et al., 1996. Some minor adaptations have been made by the present authors.

28. This does not mean that every own brand is successful. This differs per product category even if the store itself has a very high brand equity (Steenkamp and De Kimpe, 1997).

29. Berry, 1997.

30. Cuneo, 1997.

31. Gnoth, undated.

32. This section on brand personality is largely based on Monique Peter's MBA-thesis. See also Gotta, 1989; Meyer and Tostmann, 1995; Aaker, 1997; Blackston, 1992; Durgee, 1988; Plummer, 1985; and, Triplett, 1994.

33. Aaker, 1997, p.347; Aaker and Fournier, 1995, p.393. Other definitions are given by Upshaw (1993, p.152): the element that makes the brand come alive, that bestows it with human features, that makes it more accessible and more touchable.

34. Carr, 1996, p.2.

35. Jennifer Aaker, 1997, did this study among 37 goods and services in the USA.

36. Peters, 1997,

37. Mitchell, 1997, distinguishes between two kinds of users: committed and convertible (that is wavering in their loyalty) and two kinds of non-users: available and non-available (that is, potentially convertible to your brand). Lazarus, 1997, distinguishes between:

— Switchers have a high purchasing repertoire but low involvement with an individual brand. They purchase the type of product frequently but are not loyal to any particular brand and are generally highly influenced by price.

— Habituals have low involvement and a narrow purchasing repertoire. They purchase a particular product or brand out of habit and may switch if their interest is aroused.

— Variety seekers love the product and probably buy a lot of it, but are not committed to only one particular brand, preferring to vary their choice.

— The truly loyal consumers have a narrow purchasing repertoire from a particular category and a high involvement with that individual brand.

Whereas Berstell and Nitterhouse, 1997, see these five groups:

— Switchers: customers who frequently change vendors, even without price incentives, might have needs that have not yet been fully satisfied. They are often more likely to point the way to tomorrow's products than are customers content with current offerings.

— Polygamists. Customers who use multiple vendors for the same product might have several different ways of buying the same product. These "embedded segments" can reveal strategies for opening doors to the most entrenched accounts.

— Newbies. New customers, or those who have recently increased purchases significantly, might indicate new segments or customers whose needs have recently changed.

— Quitters. Lost customers can quickly reveal changes in market or competitive structures, or help a company zero in on small problems when they get out of hand.

— Persisters. Customers who go out of their way to do business with you can often articulate your competitive strengths better than those who buy from you merely because it's convenient. For example, retail stores sometimes attract regular customers from far outside their normal trading range.

38. Loyalty programs have been and will be discussed at other places in this book.

39. Aaker, 1991.

40. Agres and Dubitsky, 1996; Kuin, 1998, discusses the results of the not yet publicly available 1997 BAV study.

41. Agres and Dubitsky, 1996.

42. To us, it is unknown when that speech was held. The argument is in line with previous statements that service firms just recently started thinking about brands and branding.

43. See also Chapter Twelve on Communication policy and branding.

44. We gratefully acknowledge Jos Ahlers, Young and Rubicam's Consult, for providing these data.

45. Capps, 1997.

46. A more detailed overview of these factors is given by Hurts and Van Mechelen, 1997.

47. See Chapter Fourteen on bundling.

48. Heuvel, 1993.

49. We will no longer discuss the well-know step-by-step process consisting of generating ideas up to and including the launch of a new service. This is assumed to be known by the reader.

50. This group are the "friends" from Chapter Eight.

51. Heskett, Sasser and Hart, 1990.

52. See also Chapter Seven for a service strategy typology based on differentiation (high, low) and cost (high, low).

53. Such changes are more or less in line with the new strategic thinking and competitive strategies developed by Hamel and Prahalad in their 1994 bestseller "Competing for the Future", as discussed in Chapters Seven and Eight.

54. Heskett, Sasser and Hart, 1990, p. VII.

55. This model largely resembles the already discussed model of the service profit chain, later developed in Heskett, Sasser and Schlesinger (1997) and discussed in previous chapters. Sears has recently implemented such a model: see Rucci, Kirn and Quinn, 1998.

56. Heskett, Sasser and Hart, 1990 p. 11.

57. Shostack, 1987.

58. Cooper and de Brentani (1991) did a study on firms in the Canadian financial industry (banks, near-banks, insurance companies and investment brokers) and analyzed data on 50 successful and 50 failed service products.

59. Storey and Easingwood, 1996, did this study in the UK.

60. Storey and Easingwood, 1996, p. 47-48.

61. Edgett (1994) examined successful and unsuccessful new service activities of some British banks and some building societies. He analyzed 78 successes and 70 failures stemming from 88 financial institutions.

62. Edget, 1994, pp. 45-48.

63. Jallat, 1993 and 1994.

64. Kasper and Peters, 1993.

65. Lele and Sheth, 1987, p. 98.

66. Kasper originally made this overview in a 1992 lecture at IOCU, the International Organization of Consumer Unions.

67. The various criteria for classification used in Chapter Two can be applied to after-sales services as well.

68. Lele and Sheth, 1987. They have developed four kinds of remedies as after sales policies. These are labelled disposables, repairables, rapid responses, and, never fail.

69. This has been shown e.g. by Bloemer and Lemmink (1992) for a Japanese brand and by Bloemer and Kasper (1996) for two German brands. See also Bloemer and Kasper, 1998.

70. See for instance Homburg and Garbe, 1996; Venetis, 1997.

71. Kasper and Lemmink, 1989.

72. Kasper and Lemmink 1988, 1989 also found that the segmentation criteria applied in segmenting the market for the copying equipment itself (the apparatus) is not necessarily the same as the segmentation of the aftersales service market for this equipment. Both segmentations may lead to different groups of customers. The most important managerial implication of this finding is that the firm should not offer one type of after-sales service to each copying machine but have the customer choose out of a variety of after-sales service options (at a particular price of course). That will enhance perceived service quality and customer satisfaction.

73. De Ruyter, 1993, p. 11; De Ruyter and Kasper, 1997.

74. De Ruyter, 1993.

75. Lemmink, 1988.

76. Berry, 1995, pp. 94, 98-108.

77. Clemmer and Schneider, 1993, p. 227. They advised this solution with respect to solving waiting problems, we think it can be generalized.

78. Berry, 1995, pp. 94-108.

79. Kelley, Hoffman and Davis, 1993.

80. Johnston, 1995a.

81. Hart, Heskett and Sasser, 1990, p. 156.

82. Hart, 1988

83. See Chapter Fourteen.

84. When the pricing instrument is used to maximize occupancy rates, this is called yield management. Price differentiation and price discrimination can be used also; see Chapter Fourteen.

85. Pieter Bouw, Elsevier, December 25, 1993.

86. Shemwell and Cronin, 1994.

87. This also stresses the point that different positions are opted for in the service matrices from Chapter Two.

88. These issues are discussed in Chapter Four and will be elaborated upon in Chapter Fourteen. Then we will pay special attention to some more of these monetary and non-monetary costs.

89. However, this does carry the risk that the service provider will set himself up as a sort of real estate developing company (with all the risks associated to that business).

CHAPTER TWELVE

COMMUNICATION

This third chapter in our series about the marketing mix deals with communication. When you finish this chapter, you should:

- *be able to explain the key features of communication in services;*
- *understand why and how communication contributes to creating the desired image of the service organization;*
- *understand why and how communication can reduce the perceived risk inherent to services;*
- *understand how communication adds to strengthening the relationship between service organization and customer;*
- *know the link between service quality and communication;*
- *be able to explain the relevance of internal and external communication;*
- *know why branding is so important in services;*
- *understand the communication mix in services, especially the role of the staff in personal selling;*
- *be able to determine the objectives of communication;*

- *know the basics of developing a communication plan;*
- *see the importance of the determinants of service quality for different services; and*
- *know how to use the different elements of the communication mix for core and augmented services, and for standard and customized services.*

BELOW: *Listening always listening*

12.1 INTRODUCTION

Perhaps this is the most important guideline in the communication of services: do not promise too much and do not create greater expectations than you can realize or satisfy.

Holiday Inn once promised their guests "No surprises". This hotel chain had to take this slogan back because it was causing too much irritation in the cases when something went wrong in the service delivery process.

Swiss Telecom is advertising itself as "your best connection" to the USA with the promises: direct, perfect, private and cost-effective. They explain: "Of course we love the USA. But when the issue is your best connection to the Bahamas, we prefer the direct access route, without detours." Despite the good relationships between the USA and Switzerland, the Swiss stimulate competition in telecommunication. Therefore, the headline in one ad. is: "For once, we're turning our backs on the USA."

Randstad, a temporary employment agency in many European countries and the USA, is promising future employees and employers the following: "You are searching for a job, we find the job." The claim is clear.

IBM claim about the client/server: "It is good for your people because it gives them easier access to more information. It is good for your business because it removes barriers, giving you new flexibility to reorganise and to reengineer."

IBM positions itself as: there is a difference between knowing what needs to be done and knowing how to do it.

Every organization communicates with a multitude of target groups – consumers and other buyers, suppliers, employees, shareholders, journalists, schools, universities, local and state government bodies, neighbors, etc. Communication with these target groups aims at influencing knowledge, attitude and/or behavior. However, what has been promised, has to come true. That is one of the basics of creating service quality. Nowadays, marketing calls for more than just developing a good service; pricing it attractively and making it accessible to target customers is also important. A modern marketeer needs to actively support a good service and is cast into the role of communicator and promoter. This applies to all front office employees.

The interaction that occurs in the service encounter, be it personal or impersonal, calls for a thorough understanding of communication processes and how they affect human behavior within the framework of the script and roles to be performed. In services, the various phases used in the process of buying and consuming services sets specific requirements for this process. Consequently, communication affects the way in which relationships are developed and maintained. It all impacts on the quality of the services. Therefore, this chapter starts with a section on communication in general: some of the basics that apply uniquely to services will also be discussed. The link between communication and service quality will be investigated. Then, it is time to turn to the mix of various communication instruments that can be used. Branding is a topic deserving special attention, especially when it is considered in the framework of establishing global brands in services. Before we discuss the differences in communication policy for various types of services, we will give an overview of some guidelines for the effective communication of services. This is all presented in Figure 12-1.

Figure 12-1
Chapter outline

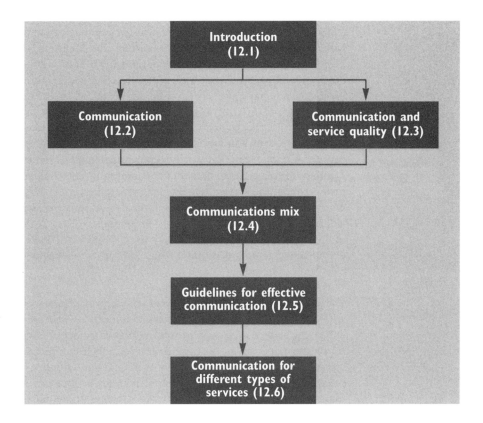

12.2 COMMUNICATION PROCESSES

SOME BASIC ISSUES IN COMMUNICATION

inter-personal communication

non-personal communication

verbal and non-verbal communication

indirect communication

direct communication

instrumental and expressive communication

Much communication in the service sector is personal: the front office employee and the customer interact. The inter-personal communication, with all its advantages and eventual drawbacks may impact directly on the short term service action, episode or long term relationship. Customers may indicate a personal preference for a particular employee to serve them. However, non-personal communication may also occur, for instance, in a written form to support the personal communication or to make people aware of particular services (advertising, etc.). Another distinction is that between verbal and non-verbal communication. Employees and customers can tell verbally what they can offer and what they want and conclude if and how the two match. In the service encounter, non-verbal communication like body language and facial expressions can contribute to creating trust and thus reducing perceived risk. The servicescape and the way it is designed will impact also on the overall quality impression. This is not only a type of non-verbal communication but also a kind of indirect communication: for it can be considered as one of the tangibles customers use as a cue or search attribute to form their service quality impression. Direct communication in services may take place in various ways as long as it occurs between the service provider and the customer in a personal or non-personal way (direct marketing). A final distinction is between instrumental and expressive communication. The first one often has to do with communicating facts (cognitive – objective – information) about the service (e.g interest rates, tariffs, prices, etc.). The latter has to do more with the emotional, affective information creating the image of the firm and providing security to customers. These distinctions are very relevant, in the first stages of the relationship life-cycle, to create trust. In previous chapters, we have indicated that affective commitment has a larger impact on maintaining the relationship than calculative commitment, e.g in the advertising industry.

local adaptations

These four distinctions are relevant to service providers, since they all are associated with various challenges in communicating services and creating, maintaining and enhancing service quality. However, cultural differences between countries may call for different accents in the communication policies of international service companies: are local adaptations needed or is a standardized policy possible? For example, reducing perceived risk will be more relevant in societies with a high degree of uncertainty avoidance than in societies showing a low uncertainty avoidance (= a higher willingness to take risks).

THE COMMUNICATION PROCESS

communication process

Figure 12-2 shows the communication process.[2] In this process, the sender or the source sends a message to the receiver through a medium. Of course, an organization sends a message with a particular intention. A message can aim at informing

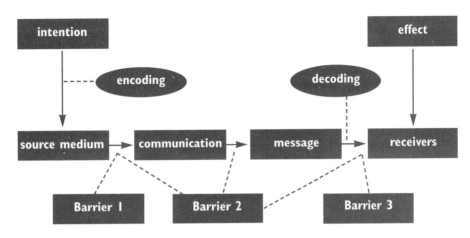

Figure 12-2
The communication
process

consumers. It can also aim at influencing consumers' attitudes (e.g., "Our services protect the environment") or at eliciting action (e.g. "Buy our service now!"). To get the message through to a receiver, it is necessary to effectively communicate the right signal at the right moment. Services are already intangible, which makes it even harder to design the right message. It is even more difficult to communicate services internationally. Different languages and cultures put a burden on the communicator. In addition, perceived risk and consumers' expectations may be different per country, for instance with respect to the mail delivery time. If we take a look at the consumers' wants and expectations about the speed of delivery, some clear differences are observed. Italians are satisfied if they receive a letter three days after sending. In The Netherlands, people are more demanding. They want to have a letter the day after sending. So, a swift delivery will have different connotations in these two countries.

encoding

The first step in the communication process is encoding. That is the process of putting ideas and thoughts into words and symbols. In designing a message, it is important to keep in mind that the sender's field of experience must overlap with that of the receiver. Cultural or aesthetic differences between different countries, for instance, may play an important role. A particular color communicates a particular atmosphere or event. This may vary from country to country. For example, internationally, different colors represent mourning: in some countries, black represents mourning, in other countries yellow or purple.

communication
channels
decoding

Once formulated, a message is transmitted through communication channels, called media. After the target audience has received the message, it is decoded. Decoding is the process by which the receiver assigns meaning to the symbols transmitted by the sender. In other words, the receiver interprets the message.

reliability and
credibility

noise

Whether the intended message reaches its audience (and the extent to which the receiver responds to it) depends, amongst others, on the reliability and credibility of the sender and the extent to which sender and receiver "speak the same language". Another factor that must be taken into account is noise – disturbances in the links of the communication channels. Noise may cause distortion in encoding and/or decoding the message. There is a growing risk of noise as the distance between source and receiver is growing. Especially, cultural barriers may lead to ineffective communication or unintended effects. A few of the potential cultural barriers are:

- Barrier 1: head office outside target country: message devised in target country.
- Barrier 2: message created by company outside target country and disseminated by local channels.
- Barrier 3: company, message creation, and channel outside target country, directed at local consumers.[3]

These are but a few of the problems one may face in communicating services internationally: consequently, it is important to check for the existence and meanings of different values in different cultures. The figure showing the cultural map in Chapter Four can help with that.

Communication is an important topic in marketing services in many ways. In previous chapters, we have come across many of these issues. Communication is a means to reduce perceived risk and subjective waiting times. Communication is needed to make clear to all employees exactly what the market orientation of the service organization is and how it should be practised in the service encounter. Communication is needed to get information from customers in the external and internal market. Many gaps in the SERVQUAL-model can be closed by more and better communication. Over-promising is one of the major causes of communication problems and also raising expectations, as shown in Gap 4 of the SERVQUAL-model. So, communi-

image   cation will help to create the desired image of the service organization.

COMMUNICATION AND BUYING SERVICES

In Chapter Four, the process of buying services is broken down into three stages: pre-purchase phase, consumption phase and post-purchase phase. The communication objectives in all three phases will differ. This is illustrated in Figure 12-3.[4]

pre-purchase phase   In the pre-purchase phase, consumers are not (yet) aware of the service provider as such or of one or more of its services, especially the new one(s). Therefore, first of

awareness   all, awareness has to be created before some actions can be taken or even before the first steps in building a relationship can be made. The image of the company as such,

reducing the perceived   its reputation and its quality image, may help in reducing the perceived risk associat-

risk   ed with buying particular services for the first time. Besides the intrinsic image of the service itself, the corporate image of a service organization and the service industry can play an important role in "tangibilizing" quality. Positive word-of-mouth communications is an excellent method of influencing the consumer's attitude here. As it may be unknown to consumers what is expected from them when they start buying

script   a (new) service, communicating the script of the service encounter and the roles to

roles   be played by each "party", is a crucial event in securing (ex-ante) service quality. Increasing customer awareness about a particular service is a prerequisite to increasing the probability that a purchase will take place.

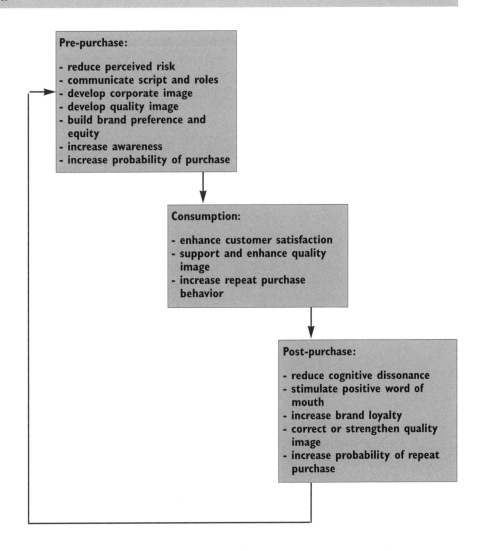

Figure 12-3
Communication
objectives and buying
services

consumption phase

functional and
relational quality
satisfaction

service profit chain

overpromising

During the consumption phase, front-office employees usually communicate with customers about the service to be provided and about the actions customers have to take. It may clarify the script and the roles to be performed. Their way of communicating will affect the functional and relational quality. In the end, it will impact on customer satisfaction in a positive (or even in a negative) way. Communication can contribute to enhancing the firm's quality image, repeat purchase behavior, loyalty and the relationship. In this stage of the buying process, wrong communication does not only have negative consequences for consumers but also for employees. Customers can show their dissatisfaction during the consumption stage, which may directly affect employees' motivation and satisfaction. The basics of the service profit chain come immediately to the fore: the circular relationship between employee satisfaction and customer satisfaction. Overpromising then, can cause serious problems, resulting in poor service quality leading to customer dissatisfaction which in turn may lead to switching behavior (of customers and employees).

post-purchase phase
reducing cognitive
dissonance

In the post-purchase phase, communication can, if necessary, help in reducing cognitive dissonance or dissatisfaction by reassuring customers that they have still bought the right service. During and after the consumption stage, consumers evaluate the performances of the service provider. These (past) experiences affect expectations and impact on decisions to continue the relationship or not. It may stimulate positive word-of-mouth communication, increase brand loyalty, repeat purchases and correct (if necessary) and strengthen the firm's quality image. It will add to deepening the relationship by giving rewards or incentives (such as Air Miles, coupons or discounts for loyal customers), or by enhancing commitment.

continue the
relationship

communication about
service quality

In essence, in services, communication with customers hinges on communication about service quality: all the issues deemed relevant in determining service quality are potential sources to be communicated. Image and reputation appear to be very relevant here. Probably, the best guideline for service providers is to recognize what customers perceive as relevant in their way of evaluating service quality. So, communication is about what people do or should do in the service encounter, ending up with the firm's perceived service quality and image. From the service provider's point of view, the promises made should be kept.[5]

COMMUNICATION AND RELATIONSHIPS

trust
confidence

In the first stages of the relationship life cycle, trust has to be created in order to start a relationship between the customer and the service provider. Personal communication will help in establishing this trust and confidence. Most of the determinants or dimensions of service quality hinge upon social interaction. These are often hard to grasp; they can still be used in communications to create an atmosphere in which customers – especially newcomers – feel at ease and safe. On the other hand, focussing on tangibles and evidence will also help create confidence and reliability; it is looked at as a kind of testimonial about quality.

reliability

The advertising industry illustrates that communication about the process in creating adverts (time schedules, delays, ideas, etc.) is important in keeping the relationship and adds to the overall service quality. The personal communication and interaction on the soft side of the process is essential. In the business-to-business services world especially, personal relations between buyer and seller appear to be crucial.

personal
communication

relationship loyalty
perception

Our discussion on the relationship loyalty perception model (RLM-model) revealed that four types of customers exist: friends, acquaintances, sympathetics and functionalists. Communication can help to move customers from one segment to another, if deemed relevant. However, increasing the loyalty or commitment to the firm will require different communications than, for instance, increasing the number of tickets bought. According to the RLM-model and under the condition that it is a company's goal to get as much friends as possible, sympathetics have to be encouraged to buy more or buy more frequently, in order to increase the sales. In this strategy, functionalists have to become more committed to the service provider. It remains to be seen whether the company should invest in communication with acquaintances at all.

financial bonds
social bonds

Enhancing commitment can be done via social and emotional factors, while increasing sales can be accomplished via discounts and sales promotions. The latter, however, will strengthen the financial bonds. Enhancing commitment will lead to more intense social bonds (which, as we have seen before, are more difficult to break than the financial ones). Branding is another way to strengthen relationships, especially when it can be used to create brand loyalty.[6]

servuction process

servicescape
physical evidence

The communication of services takes place mainly just before, during and right after the production of services.[7] Not only personal communication during the servuction process, but also such tangibles as the exterior and interior of the building, name and logo play a role in the communication of a service to customers. Neglecting these servicescape factors results in passing up an important opportunity to communicate. In other words, this is related to the P of physical evidence which is important in the marketing and communication mix of service organizations.

It will be no surprise that the role of communication in services marketing will be discussed in this chapter not only as such, but also within the framework of delivering service quality.[8] This latter issue will be illustrated by using two models: the well known SERVQUAL-model (focussing on external and internal communication) and a model developed by Martin (focussing on internal communication).

12.3 COMMUNICATION AND SERVICE QUALITY

external
communication

service employees
behavior

Throughout this text, service quality and its dimensions are a main issue. As shown, quality can be influenced by the external communication of the service organization thus stimulating or persuading customers to buy services. Communication can be used to manage expectations as well as perceptions. Since the service employees' behavior is essential too, communication cannot be the responsibility of the marketing (or communication) department only, but also of operations.[9]

SERVQUAL

The SERVQUAL-model maintains that four internal gaps determine the external gap of – lack of – service quality. This external gap arises when the expected service quality differs from the perceived service quality of a customer. The model assumes that expectations are strongly affected by four factors: word-of-mouth communications, personal needs, past experience and external communications to consumers.

Two of these four factors directly relate to communication. However, only one factor (the external communications) is under the direct control of the service provider, the other three are not (see Figure 12-4).

Figure 12-4
Communication affecting
expectations

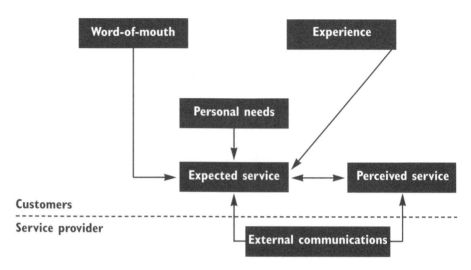

word-of-mouth
communication

The first factor, word-of-mouth communication, is a strong influence in the service sector. Some authors even argue that this factor is a major influence on customer expectations of service quality.[10] We should add a critical note here. The influence of the four factors varies according to the type of service. A dentist benefits from word-of-mouth communications, whereas past experience determines quality expectations of airlines. Positive word-of-mouth communications is often regarded as a factor of major importance. This seems to be based mainly on the subjective way in which quality is defined. Since a service is often intangible, it is hard to define its quality by way of search attributes. A receiver of word-of-mouth communications sees the sender of the message as a person who has experiences with that particular service organization. Experiences often make the sender an authority. Thus, his/her judgement carries great weight. When word-of-mouth communications do not conform to the advertisement of a service organization, the consumer relies more on word-of-mouth communications. Those people are more trusted than the non personal adverts.

experiences
authority

Gap 4 of the
SERVQUAL-model

The lower part of Figure 12-4 relates to Gap 4 of the SERVQUAL-model: the gap between the perception of the actual service delivery and the external communications to customers.[11] Problems in the horizontal communications and "overpromising" have been called the major causes for this gap, in Chapters Five and Six. Here, we will elaborate on these issues and increase the number of causes. In fact, five key reasons can be found.[12] These are: inadequate management of service promises; overpromising in advertising and personal selling; insufficient customer education; inadequate horizontal communication; and differences in policies and procedures across branches or units.

inadequate
management of service
promises

The inadequate management of service promises stems from the fact that the company lacks the information and integration needed to make fulfillable promises.[13] Often, services are not yet available while promises about their availability have been made already. This gap can also occur when services providers do not inform customers (on time) of special offers, novelties, improvements in quality or new rules of the game. Overpromising in advertising and personal selling may be due to miscommunication between marketing and operations: operations have to make true what marketing promises: the moments of truth. Increasing competition and deregulation bear the danger of overpromising in order to win customers. This is a tricky approach since poor quality and dissatisfaction will easily occur when perceptions stay under expectations. Inadequate customer education originates from ambiguous roles and unclear scripts in the service encounter: customers do not know completely what they are expected to do. And, inexperienced customers will, by definition, not know what they are expected to do. So, it is self evident that customers really need training to participate correctly in the servuction process; however, that may hold for the service provider as well, even in universities.

overpromising in advertising and personal selling

inadequate customer education

Service practice 12-2 Training students and professors

As Maastricht University is now using the system of problem based learning, it needs to train its students in how this way of learning and studying works. In the first three weeks of the first year of their studies, the freshmen learn what the pedagogical justification for this new way of studying is, how students have to behave in group meetings, how they have to study in between the group meetings, how they have to prepare for special kinds of tests that are made, how to use the library, etc. Otherwise, they will not succeed.

Problem based learning is a student centered approach and not a teacher centered approach. Students have to solve the problems by means of thorough discussions and self-studying. The professor does not give lectures and tell students what they should know. On the contrary, professors have to play a role of tutor, mediator or facilitator during the group meetings. Knowledge of their field is necessary in preparing excellent teaching material before the group meetings start. If this is developed well, they do not have to interfere during the group meetings and only watch the process of discussion that is going on and the content: a quality check. Professors are trained to perform their task this way; they may not tutor a group if they are not fully trained. If the group works well, professors keep their "big mouth shut" during meetings. (That is an unusual task for teachers, but it really works!) Perhaps, training students and professors alike is one of the reasons why this service breakthrough works and why it is hard to imitate this new "technology in teaching".

inadequate horizontal communications

Inadequate horizontal communications may be caused by insufficient coordination between marketing and operations: contact personnel cannot deliver the promised service because they are not aware of what promises were made. When this is related to insufficiently motivated personnel, human resource management (HRM) has an

differences in policies and procedures across distribution outlets

important job to do to correct it. Differences in policies and procedures across distribution outlets in performing the actual service will lead to inconsistencies and confused patterns of service performance to customers. While branches belong to the same bank, customers may experience differences in output or in the way they have to participate in the servuction process.

Because of these five reasons, four strategies to match service promises with service delivery or exceed the service delivery have been developed. These are: manage service promises; reset customer expectations; improve customer education and manage horizontal communications.[14]

service promises can be managed
resetting customer expectations

Service promises can be managed by making realistic promises, offering service guarantees, keeping customers informed about changes, negotiating unrealistic expectations or setting prices to match quality levels. Resetting customer expectations can be accomplished by offering different choices or options in (quality of the) service, creating tiered-value offerings, communicating the criteria for service effectiveness or communicating the realities of the specific service industry. As long as it is typical in hospitals or airports that patients and travellers have to wait and queue in areas with many people around them, this is a reality inherent to those businesses. The company that can really solve this issue will change the rules of the

improving customer education

game in that specific industry and create a service breakthrough. Improving customer education can be done via preparing customers for the service process, confirming performance to standards, clarifying the expectations about what might happen after the sale, and teaching customers to avoid peak demand periods and seek slow periods. Especially in the latter case, informing customers about these time slots and offering them different (=lower) prices at particular moments, may encourage them to use the service facilities at off-peak hours. Horizontal communications can be managed or improved via the creation of cross-functional teams (from various disciplines or at least from front and back office), opening channels between sales and operations, opening channels between advertising and operations and by aligning back

horizontal communications can be managed

office employees with external customers. In the latter case, they meet real-life customers and experience how the people they have to serve but never actually meet, feel, think, act, and the like.

These causes and solutions to Gap 4 of the SERVQUAL-model reveal that inadequate communication can be "killing" an otherwise excellent service quality. However, communication should not only be interpreted here in terms of what is said in advertising, brochures, leaflets, or said by sales persons, account managers, or by front office

servicescape

employees, waiters or even a porter at the entrance to a hotel. The servicescape or the physical surroundings where the service encounter takes place also communicates in a particular way the image of the service provider. The same applies for the

price

price of the services. Often, consumers use the price as a proxy for quality, implicitly assuming that a higher price will imply a higher quality. This way of reasoning often applies to customers who start using a service for the first time, and use this tactic as one of the ways to form an impression of the quality to be expected. Finally, mistar-

mistargeted communication

geted communication may be a problem unique in services, since it may result in the presence of various groups of customers who do not match.[15] For instance, a hotel or restaurant may suddenly realize that price-conscious groups have come in because they have read an advert about special prices without noticing the actual amount still to be paid. Neither the usual clientele or the newcomers will enjoy this service experience and will feel dissatisfied (but for different reasons).

INTERNAL COMMUNICATION

internal
communication
procedural dimension

Another quality model in which communication plays a very important role is Martin's model.[16] This model focusses on the internal communication in the service firm. Service quality is assumed to be a combination of two dimensions: the procedural dimension and the service attitude level. The first dimension, the qualilty of the procedure determines the quality of the production process of a service. This process includes external communication – communication between customer and front office personnel, as well as internal communication. Internal communication is

departments

essential to link the several departments within an organization, as indicated in the previous section. If several departments are not linked properly, failures are bound to

time

occur. Time, anticipation, feedback and a particular management role determine the procedural dimension. Time is part of the service: long waiting times, for instance, may result in a negatively perceived quality. Anticipation means responding to the

anticipation

specific wants of customers before they have expressed them. Quick response is considered to be positive by a customer. The question to what extent the feedback

feedback

of customers reaches the organization refers to the market orientation of an organization: is the organization able to translate customer orientation and competitor orientation into the action desired? Finally, management has to create the conditions for excellent service quality.

service attitude level

The second dimension, the service attitude level, consists of nine indicators. When we mention its major indicators (attitude, non-verbal communication, tact, and name),

convivial dimension

it is understandable why this dimension can also be called the convivial dimension: it hinges upon the service attitude. For every service, a negative service attitude of employees is fatal. A negative attitude is immediately sensed and experienced as unpleasant. Nonverbal communication implies, for instance, that eye contact and a warm smile can perform wonders. Saying the right words in different situations requires tactful, experienced and skilled personnel, such as calling a customer by name, when arriving and leaving – a hearty welcome must always go hand in hand with a warm goodbye.

need for proper
communication
between front office
personnel and back
office personnel

In this model, internal communication is valued very highly. Contact personnel must not only know what consumers want, they also must be able to comply with it. In fact, the need for proper communication between front office personnel and back office personnel is emphasized. When the internal communication between these groups fails, there is a growing risk of customers not getting what they are entitled to. Front office personnel may not know what customers want or may not be sufficiently

"freezer"
"friendly zoo"

supported. Martin calls this "freezer" and "friendly zoo" organizations (see Figure 12-5). But there are also clearly communicative components. The quality of a service quickly decreases when tact and non-verbal communication fail. The customer is treated

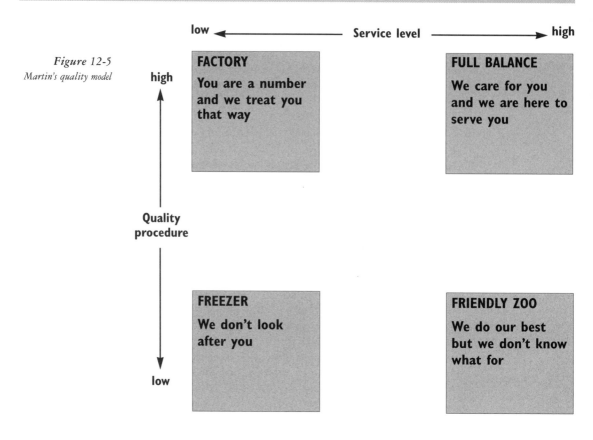

Figure 12-5
Martin's quality model

high

FACTORY
You are a number and we treat you that way

FULL BALANCE
We care for you and we are here to serve you

Quality procedure

FREEZER
We don't look after you

FRIENDLY ZOO
We do our best but we don't know what for

low

"factory"

"full balance"

like a number and Martin therefore calls it "factory". An optimum quality level only arises when the quality of the procedure and the service attitude level are high, or, as described in the matrix, when they are in "full balance".

EXTERNAL COMMUNICATION TO EMPLOYEES

staff

role model

This heading may sound a little bit strange, but it is deliberately formulated this way. Staff frequently form a secondary audience (next to customers) for any service provider's external communication, especially for its advertising.[17] It may be shown in commercials, for instance, how the service provider should perform and wants customers to be treated. Then, a kind of role model is shown intended to motivate their own staff to perform this way. Companies like IBM or the Dutch postal services have used this way of communication to show the public a more positive image of the organization and at the same time showing employees how they should behave. It should be recognized, though, that employees can only perform this way once they have received the proper information and training to do so. Commercials can then be supportive to accomplish that way of working and to remind service employees what customers expect them to do in order to keep promises made. The discussion of the horizontal communication problems shows that employees should be informed properly before such commercials are broadcast (or pictures are shown in

brochures or leaflets).[18] If the promises made in the commercials on TV cannot be
met, customers will be disappointed and strengthen their belief that advertising

clear messages   depicts an unrealistic world. Using clear messages in this external communication is
not only necessary for customers to understand, but also for employees. When Delta
Airlines introduced the slogan "You never hear a Delta professional say : 'That is not
my job'", the message to their employees is clear. Delta employees are expected to
solve a consumer's problem instead of transferring it to someone else. And since this
is communicated to the customer, Delta employees are not supposed to be able to
escape from it. In this way, employees are the owners of a problem they have to solve
(a crucial item in quality management these days).

sponsoring   Sponsoring has appeared to be another effective means of communicating to employees (and to customers). An association with a particular event (like the Last Night of
the Proms, world championship football or the Olympics), sportsman, sportswoman
or team is used to create a particular image in an indirect way. These sports teams are
also considered to be a kind of role model for the employees. ABN AMRO bank is
sponsoring Ajax Amsterdam as a football team, not only to communicate to their customers but also to their employees. The danger then is, of course, when a sportsman
does not behave in "the right way" that it may be detrimental to the company (this
applies, in general, when using celebrities in communications.)

BUILDING SERVICE BRANDS

positioning a brand   In Chapter Eleven, service brands have been discussed. Positioning a brand in the
minds of the customers is a task typically performed by communication about the
brand, e.g. by advertising.

brand loyalty   Communication is an important means of creating brand loyalty and thus creating
relationships   relationships with customers. When service providers act globally, customers will
consistent image   know everywhere what the service will be about, when a consistent image of the firm
and its service has been created. Creating a consistent brand perception internationally is necessary for customers to know what can be expected from the service
provider, how they have to behave in the service encounter, what risks similar to
those at home can be run, etc. It is also in line with one of the most important dimen-
reliability in   sions of service quality: reliability in performance. Communication about the brand
performance   has to be the ultimate means of keeping promises.

Company image, company reputation, brand image and brand personality will depend
on the communications made, not only in the home country but also internationally.
differentiation   This will determine, in turn, the differentiation of one brand from another and the
relevance of the brand relevance of the brand to the customer in various countries. These two items are the
brand vitality   two determinants of brand vitality, as defined in Young & Rubicam's Brand Asset
Valuator.[19] It will be clear that this brand vitality may differ per country, as shown in
Chapter Eleven.

*consistency in brands
(inter)nationally*

The service itself, its visual identity, its positioning, the idea or message to be communicated and the final execution of the message in a particular form of communication (e.g. advertising, point of sales, etc.) build up the framework for achieving consistency in brands (inter)nationally. While the differentiation in services is very low in the car rental business, Avis has a clear visual identity via its logo and its red color. Their message "we try harder" is a unifying theme all over the world. It also expresses a kind of personality. Despite its product being a unifying factor and a consistent worldwide product identity in terms of product, packaging and storefront, Kentucky Fried Chicken (KFC) has a variable brand image. This is partly due to local advertising autonomy.

*centralized
organizational
structure in
communications*

So, next to a consistent conceptual framework, building worldwide consistent brands probably requires a centralized organizational structure in communications (either by the company itself or by the agency taking care of the integrated communications strategy). Lufthansa, for instance, creates its brand advertising centrally: a very strict format is prepared, also for local and tactical, short term and action oriented advertising. It appears that this strategy does indeed preserve consistent brand identity, but allows insufficient flexibility to adequately meet local needs. The same holds for the Holiday Inn hotel chain and British Airways. However, British Airways allows some tactical flexibility when needed, realizing that this may imply some inconsistency in image which has to be sacrificed temporarily. McDonald's is able to have a consistent brand image world wide combined with a considerable local autonomy for local advertising and sales promotions. Their vision is clear; it sets the framework for local communication policies and excellent internal communications procedures. This way of organizing the world wide communications combines centralization and decentralization; rigid frameworks plus local autonomy can be combined to create consistent brands worldwide. If the vision is lacking, centralization is necessary.[20]

In terms of the internationalization strategy of advertising agencies, this implies that it is not always necessary to have a branch in every country where the client is present. Many advertising agencies still believe that it is necessary to be close to the market. However, Bartle Bogle Hegarty, a London-based advertising agency has shown that it can operate successfully for their international clients from one single office in London.[21]

*Service
practice
12-3
Winning
abroad by
staying at
home*

Bartle Bogle Hegarty believe that its international service is best offered from London. Its campaigns for international clients are created in a single London office. They believe that a network of agencies all over the world is a barrier to creating good international campaigns. They do have an office in Singapore, but this will not be the start of a network. BBH maintains that overseas offices in large networks become too close to their local markets. This would make it difficult for them to concentrate on the regional similarities essential to creating effective international campaigns for clients who want to portray a consistent brand image across various countries. For its clients, says BBH, "the size of an agency's ideas has become more important than the size of its network".

Many of the BBH campaigns have been award winners. BBH itself received the Queen's Award for Export and thus became the first advertising agency to achieve this honour in the UK.

12.4 THE COMMUNICATIONS MIX

The exact content and implementation of a communication plan depends strongly on the type of service and the goals set, but in general a communication plan involves the steps presented in Figure 12-6.

Figure 12-6
Steps in developing a
communication plan

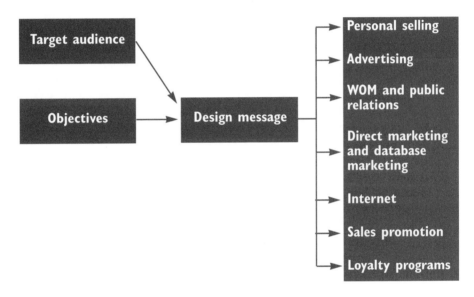

Although most tools are already known, we think that it is useful to pay attention to a number of components of the communications mix, because services are intangible. We will not only focus on the tools themselves but also stress the clarity of the message, and the effectiveness of the tools being used in the service sector. First of all, it is always necessary to define the target audience and objectives as precisely as possible. These should be in line with the general objectives of the corporate and marketing strategy.

define the target
audience and
objectives

PERSONAL SELLING

personal selling
front office personnel

For personalized services, personal selling is considered as the backbone of communication in services marketing. The importance of front office personnel becomes clear if we take into account the next points: buying services goes along with a perception of relatively high risk, especially in the first stages of a new service buying process; selling a service mostly requires personal contact between seller and buyer (compulsory attendance in the service encounter: presence and participation is required); the front office employee as a part time marketeer; and the customer as a part time employee. These points make personal selling an indispensable tool for a large part of the service industry. A useful application of this expensive tool requires a limited number of customers; a small market; a high purchase price; a long-term obligation; an adjustment to individual needs; an explanation required by the customer; negotiations about the price; and a strong relationship with the existing supplier.[22] If we regard all these points with a critical eye, they all are more or less relevant to core and augmented services. Especially for providers of customized services in a small regional market, personal selling is a frequently used tool. In the end, this may result in a high degree of loyalty of the customer to the service provider. Very often, customers want personal, face-to-face contact with service provider's employees. Many simple core services can be performed without personal contacts. However, when personal selling is involved, the employees should have the right service attitude, as discussed in Chapter Ten. Moreover, the lists of dimensions deemed relevant in excellent service quality reveal that empathy, assurance, responsiveness and reliability (plus all the items of which these dimensions are composed)

traits   are traits the sales force should possess to be market-oriented and to deliver excellent service quality. Industrial service representatives, for instance, should be, in general, "people-oriented, responsive, knowledgeable, and hard to ruffle".[23] In particular, in market-oriented companies these service representatives should be good listeners, know where to get data, handle stress well, respond quickly, be problem solvers, and be polite.[24] Then, the foundation has been laid to start and maintain profitable, long-term relationships with customers. Now, in one-on-one relationships, expectations can be managed before, during and after the service encounter.

personal touch   The personal touch is important to provide security, confidence and credibility in services. Personal contact also offers the opportunity for a dialogue with customers. Empowered employees can give improved service surprises, exceeding expectations, when needed or apologize for things that may go wrong despite all the existing quality checks.

ADVERTISING

Advertising   Advertising can be defined as "any paid form of non personal presentation". Like the other tools, advertising can be used to influence or manage customer expectations.

distinguish themselves   Furthermore, service providers can try to distinguish themselves from their
from competitors   competitors. It may seem attractive to create high expectations, but it is obvious that promises must be kept. This implies honesty and fairness. A service provider must surely meet the minimum level of expectations created in the advertisement. Service surprises are often valuable in exceeding these minimum levels at moments unexpected to the client.[25]

changing the actual behavior
employees

Furthermore, we must take into account that there is a second target audience. Employees are the ones who determine quality and therefore have to be motivated and willing to deliver the service on an adequate level. Showing in adverts how service personnel behave, can contribute to changing the actual behavior of these employees.

clear messages

It is essential to design clear messages in adverts, because a message must meet several expectations. Not only the customer, but also the employee has to be reached and stimulated. To minimize the danger of wrong expectations of a message (selective distortion), a message must be clear. In standard core services, advertising, in particular, is the tool to inform the customer and the service provider about the service and about the role they are both expected to play in the service delivery process.

affect customer
participation
achieve positive word-of-mouth

An advertising campaign will have to attract the customer to a particular service after awareness has been created. Basically, this can be done in two ways. The first is trying to affect customer participation in the process of service production: increase or decrease the participation-intensity. The second way is to encourage customers to show their satisfaction. In principle, this means trying to achieve positive word-of-mouth communications.

Printed adverts in the form of brochures, images and/or persons are often meant to make a service tangible and understandable. For many households, vacations start with glancing through piles of travellers' guides. The insurance industry, more and more, uses TV commercials. Humorous situations are designed to show the importance of being insured (and not the dangerous situations of not being insured). Fear does not always seem to be an effective item in creating trust and confidence in service industries altering the target group's behavior.

WORD-OF-MOUTH COMMUNICATIONS AND PUBLIC RELATIONS

positive word-of-mouth communications

Positive word-of-mouth communications are the major influence on the perception of quality, but are hard to control. The main reason for this is the independence of the word-of-mouth communicator. A word-of-mouth communicator is not paid, nor is he necessarily an employee of an organization. Reactions of a word-of-mouth communicator are purely based on their own, although subjective, experiences. Nevertheless, word-of-mouth can often still be managed, to a certain degree, by service providers. Members of a health club get discounts if they introduce friends. The same goes for Weight Watchers. Testimonials are used a great deal in promotion for many kinds of services, especially domestic services, holiday companies, etc.

*Service
practice
12-4
The great
trains*

The July/August 1995 issue of the Dutch glossy magazine Elegance contained an article on great train rides of the world. Issues like nostalgia, style, comfort and adventure were discussed with respect to luxury train ride holidays in many countries, like:

- the Amtrak Superliner or California Zephyr (USA);
- the Rocky Mountaineer (Canada);
- the Ghan and the Indian Pacific (Australia);
- the Royal Scotsman (a roundtrip in Scotland);
- the Eastern and Oriental Express (Singapore, Kuala Lumpur, Bangkok);
- the Venice Simplon-Orient Express (from London to Venice);
- the Al Andalus Expresso (a five day round trip in Andalusia, Spain).

Here, trains are not used anymore for transportation from A to B, but as a "vehicle to make a cruise in a country or region". This free publicity makes potential train passengers eager to find out more.

*public relations
publicity*

Publicity has a strong impact, making public relations an important component in the communications mix of a service provider. To a certain extent, publicity can be influenced by the effective use of public relations. The following can be applied to a PR department of a service organization: provide brochures and newsletters; keep good contacts with the press; give talks, presentations and seminars; write or contribute to articles in professional magazines or columns and build strong community relations. Many glossy magazines contain reports or articles on specific industries. Quite often, they hinge upon touristic events. The service providers in that industry will benefit from that free publicity.

DIRECT MARKETING AND DATABASE MARKETING

direct marketing

Direct marketing can be defined as a specialized form of marketing that aims at building and maintaining a relationship between a seller and a selected buyer. An action in writing is called direct mail, an action by telephone is called telemarketing.

*direct channels of
distribution*

Direct marketing can also be applied in the channel of distribution as a promotional tool. Direct writing and relationship marketing are, in fact, direct channels of distribution. In this section, we subscribe to one of the views on direct marketing, which is about special operational activities within the framework of the marketing mix.

*quality and
availability of the
data base and
mailing list*

Related to the service sector, a great advantage of this tool is the personal way in which a first contact is established and the following contact can be maintained. Therefore, this tool can be used by any service provider. However, its success depends mainly on the quality and availability of the database and mailing list. For providers of customized services, this is quite simple. As a platform, they use their own existing customer database or target their mailing on the district in which they are established. The quality of the database and database management systems are crucial here. Since many service organizations have large databases with information on clients, they can be used for direct marketing activities or doing research among their clients. We have experienced recently in some studies that doing research among clients gives them the feeling that the service firm really cares about them. To a certain extent, that strengthens the relationship between firm and client.

Recency, Frequency and Monetary value RLM matrix

database marketing

Database driven direct marketing will certainly enhance the effectiveness and efficiency of communications and contribute to the service provider's profitability. In its ultimate form, direct marketing is a concept in which the buying behavior of the target group of customers is measured and registered via, for instance, the Recency, Frequency and Monetary value. Now, direct marketing is part of a deliberate policy to develop the RLM matrix, deemed so relevant in relationship marketing.[26] Direct marketing is part of a continuous process that strives to build a solid personal relationship between the supplier and buyer. The database is an indispensable asset. Therefore, it is better to talk about database marketing than direct marketing. Often, service firms invest heavily in increasing sales, supported by advertising, but never really know whether it pays off. Take, for example, a bank. Many banks are not able to calculate the contribution in profits or loss, per service, per client or per responsibility center. Mostly, it is believed to be more important to serve a global corporate client than a local medium sized company. The global client may receive first class service in every country at rock bottom prices with each country manager thinking that although the client is not very profitable in their country, other countries would make probably more profits from that client. This kind of "management by assumption" could be dangerous to the bank's overall profitability since these managers' assumptions may be wrong. Moreover, it may be underestimated how the client perceives the relationship with the banks. It could be the case that the local firm is a "friend" while the large international firm is positioned in one of the other quadrants of the RLM-model. Therefore, the two dimensions of the RLM-model should be investigated to position the bank's clients and to give direction to the firm's communication policy by using the database.

THE INTERNET

Internet

storage, accessability and diffusion of information

Internet technology now opens new ways of communicating and distributing services.[27] Here, we will discuss the impact of the Internet on communication. The basic idea is that it revolutionizes the storage, accessability (and thus) diffusion of information. Much information becomes easily available to many customers via a computer network. This computer-based communication system is no longer a one way communication, but an interactive (two way) communication. In that way, it is an important tool in relationship marketing. So, marketing communication via the Internet is more customer driven than company driven.

Many service providers and other companies advertise their services on the World

middle men

Wide Web and tell (prospective) customers what they can offer. Consequently, one of the main reasons for the existence of middle men in a distribution channel (the function of providing information and making markets more transparent) is becoming obsolete. Customers do not need an insurance broker anymore, but search themselves for the best policy. In turn, the traditional insurance companies can compete via this computer technology directly with the direct writers, and add another communication channel to the existing ones. The large majority of Internet users indeed use the Internet for searching for information (and as electronic-mail).

searching for
information

Once customers are motivated, able, willing and have the time to use the Internet, they can search for all the information they need. Especially in the first stage of the consumption process, the Internet may function as the medium to search for information and reduce perceived risk. Customers themselves can determine what information they will need and use in their decision making process. Consequently, customized information can be extracted from the enormous (and often redundant) amount of information available in our present society. All the different service providers can be compared to one another on specific items: a kind of comparative testing usually done by Consumers Unions, which can now be performed by customers themselves. In the US, the used car market is a big item on the Internet. But also, employees may browse the Internet or Intranet for information. At Morgan Stanley, for instance, every employee's computer is already fitted with a Web browser. Logging on brings up an internal home page containing internal news that is updated daily.[28] Internet banking and thus communication about bank services via the Internet is growing rapidly, as is the case in Canada, for instance.[29] All of Canada's financial institutions plan to have on-line banking by 1999. On-line banking transactions cost less than if it were done by teller machines, telephone or in-branch services, they deepen the relationship with the customer and thus strengthen bank customer loyalty. Major Canadian banks on-line services, which makes for a competitive sector of marketeers stressing convenience, simplicity and brand nuances.[30]

As stated, customers must know the rules of the game in using the Internet and be able to use them. It may be costly to get them learn to do so. Some estimated this cost at about $12.5 million in Canada in 1997.[31] But it does not always need to cost that much to teach customers the new service encounter, as the case of Canada Trust illustrates.

Service
practice
12-5
Canada Trust
stresses ease[32]

In contrast, Canada Trust spent just $355,000 on a nine-month print and radio campaign to introduce its EasyWeb Internet service (www.canadatrust.com). The simple and humorous creative phrase from Cormark Communications of London, Ontario, and Harrod & Mirlin, Toronto, stressed easy access and 24-hour convenience.

Introducing listeners to EasyWeb was a quirky fellow named Simon, who went to extremes to test the service. In one radio spot, he checks his account at 4:25 a.m. In another, he puts EasyWeb's anywhere-in-Canada access through its paces. "That would explain the suitcase," the advert's announcer quips. Simon replies: "I'm off to Chibougamou. Then Moose Jaw. Then it's off to Wawa."

A year after its December 1996 launch, EasyWeb had drawn about 125,000 users, having met its first year's target after only nine months.

extensive testing

In general, the many opportunities information technology offers these days, provides ample opportunities for telecommunication services, as the next Irish example shows.[33] It also reveals that extensive testing is necessary in order to introduce new ways of offering services and educating customers.

Service practice 12-6 Irish firms forge stronger links between technology and services

In September 1997, the Irish national telecommunication network service provider, Telecom Eireann, announced that it was spending IRL£15 million on funding Ireland's first "Information Age Town". Several towns competed for this job-creating investment and Ennis was eventually chosen as the most likely location to benefit from a huge investment in the latest information age technologies for homes and businesses. The Ennis presentation convinced the competition adjudicators that its residents were most open to new technological developments.

Ireland's Information Age Town is the first project of its kind in the world that will have all the available communications technologies and tools deployed at one time and in one place. The project features:

- a telephone with digital voicemail in every home;
- an ISDN connection and high speed access to the Internet for every business;
- a personal computer linked to the Internet for the majority of homes;
- a full range of public services provided on-line; and
- the latest smart card technology.

Other service providers are also backing the initiative in partnership with Telecom Eireann. Ireland's two leading banking corporations, Bank of Ireland and AIB Bank, are partnering the telephone company to launch an electronic purse trial in Ennis. The electronic purse is a plastic card which stores credit on a chip. It is different from a Callcard in that it is reusable. The card can be replenished from the customer's bank account via advanced telephones or bank self-service machines. From September 1998, the townspeople were able to pay for public telephone calls, car parking, newspapers and other small value purchases using the new electronic purse rather than cash. The electronic purse will be acceptable in retail outlets in town which will be equipped with machines to accept the card as a payment device. The card itself will be supplied by Visa Cash.

The banks and the telephone company will run the year long trial to assess customer attitudes, commercial viability and retailer reaction.

SALES PROMOTION

sales promotion

Sales promotion refers to a magnitude of activities aimed at stimulating consumer buying behavior, especially in the short term. Quite often, it just focusses on stimulating impulsive purchases and brand switching. It is generally assumed that sales promotion can be used effectively in the case of services having a low perceived risk, which are bought frequently, which are familiar to the customer and which differentiate themselves from competing services by price.[34] In other words, sales promotion is mainly used for quite standard and/or core services. It is seen as adding something to the service: either tangible products or more intangible services. Customized services and/or augmented customized services use sales promotion only to a very limited extent.

stimulating impulsive purchases and brand switching

attract and keep customers

Sales promotion is becoming more and more popular among services firms to attract and keep customers. The main reasons are that competition is increasing in many industries, brand parity is growing (especially among standard and core services) and the need for brand proliferation is thus increasing as well. It is an effective means of creating first trials (consumers using the service for the first time) and thus starting the first stage of a relationship life cycle. This short term effect, hopefully, leads to a long(er) term relationship. Quite often, existing customers ask for something extra; this can be offered via a premium or coupon. But many more actions belong to the category of sales promotions, like club promotions, celebrity promotions, self-liquidating premiums, events, patronage awards, contests/sweepstakes, tie-ins, rebates/refunds, price-offs, sampling and frequency or loyalty programs.[35] Premiums are additional merchandise offered free when purchasing a particular service. For example, a customer receives a compact-disc when opening a bank account. In some countries, the law forbids adding premiums stemming from another industry than the service they are added to. Coupons are certificates entitling the bearer to a discount on the purchase of a service or product. An example is spending two nights in a luxury hotel at a special rate when buying a credit card. Another example is discounts on admission fees for amusement parks when staying overnight in a hotel. When this becomes a permanent and all-season activity, we call it a form of price-bundling. Celebrity promotion is creating a promotion centered on a fictitious character or a celebrity. The clearest examples are the cartoon characters of Walt Disney supporting the promotion of Euro Disney in Paris or the opening of new shops by a famous actor or sportsman. Of course, this form of sales promotion must be used together with advertising. Self-liquidating premiums differ from premiums in that they are not offered for free but at a price that covers the costs. This technique is often used additionally to support or reinforce the brand image. Events are activities that aim at stimulating "rumour around the brand". For a service, this is expected to result in positive word-of-mouth communications. The tobacco industry tries to realize this by organizing large-scale sporting events like motor racing (Marlboro/Lucky Strike) or surfing (Pall Mall). The Whitbread around the world yacht race is another example, with many boats sponsored by service firms.

creating first trials

premiums

coupons

celebrity promotion

self-liquidating premiums

events

patronage awards

Patronage awards can also be found in the service sector. They focus mainly on loyal customers. Here, loyalty is rewarded by merchandise or cash. For example, a Chinese restaurant provides gift stamps to collect towards a meal or a sauna provides credits for visits that can be redeemed for a free bath towel. If a patronage award is a long-term action, it becomes an integrated part of a service. In that situation, a patronage award can no longer be considered a sales-promotion tool. Because of the permanent character, the Frequent-Flyer Program of airlines is no longer a sales promotion but *contests and* remains so as to strengthen customer relationships. With contests and sweepstakes *sweepstakes* consumers can win prizes. Both are effective means in building custom, e.g. when opening a restaurant or shop. People who like excitement and stimulation are especially vulnerable to this type of sales promotion activity.

tie-ins Tie-ins are especially suitable to promote low-demand services in combination with a high-demand service or cross-selling (new) services. "Promotional tie-ins include two or more goods or services within the same promotional offer. The tie-ins can be either intracompany or intercompany. Intracompany tie-ins are those involving two or more distinct services within the same company. For example, Pepsico, which owns Kentucky Fried Chicken, could place a 20% discount coupon for KFC on their six-pack soft drink package. Intercompany tie-ins involve two different companies offering complementary-type services. For example, the St Louis Cardinals baseball team could provide a 50% coupon to the nearby Gateway Arch with the purchase of an adult ticket to a Cardinals game".[36]

rebates and refunds Rebates and refunds imply cash reimbursements to consumers paid with a proof of purchase. They are very suitable to price-sensitive consumers and brand loyal customers. In establishing long-term relationships, these are not the best ways forward; only financial bonds are created and these are easy to break by competitors offering even lower prices. Therefore, they should be applied in close connection with the creation of other bonds. For branded services, this kind of sales promotion is to be preferred over real discounts since it will not harm the brand image (that much). Price *price discounts or* discounts or price-offs are used to attract new customers or shift demand to off-peak *price-offs* hours. Unfortunately, these services will also be bought by current customers, who would have been willing to pay the full price. In some industries, like the travel business, this sales promotion tool is used so often that travellers wait until the discounts *sampling* occur and only a few people pay the full fare or room price. Sampling is offering a free delivery of an actual service. The first visit to a dentist, attorney or a free visit to a museum belong to this kind of sales promotion. Hopefully, more visits will result and a relationship be established.

Since frequency or loyalty programs are so popular today, we will discuss them in a separate section.

LOYALTY PROGRAMS

Many of the sales promotion tools are aimed at stimulating short run sales and *frequency programs* inducing brand switching. Frequency programs, on the other hand, are designed to enhance repeat purchases among current customers. Sometimes, the relationship *loyalty programs* with the customers is becoming that strong that we speak of loyalty programs.[37] What has been started as a frequency program, as part of a sales promotion activity, is used more and more as a strategic device to create loyalty within the framework of a relationship marketing strategy.

American Airlines was the first airline which started a frequent-flyer program, in 1981: the AAdvantage. Today, almost all airlines have such a program. Consequently, the competitive advantage that American Airlines once had, has disappeared. Obviously, such a program was easy to imitate.

commitment

If customer commitment to the brand is high, real brand loyalty will occur. So, loyalty programs should add to increasing this commitment. Then it will be hard for competitors to get customers to switch. Otherwise, customers use a frequency program just out of inertia and are easy to manipulate and will switch. This will be the case for instance, when frequent flyers just collect Air Miles to get a free ticket to an exotic destination and are not interested in the airline as such.

relationship marketing programs

Relationship marketing programs occur in many forms. Various criteria can be used to describe them. Some programs do require a kind of subscription rate or entrance fee, others are free. Some programs only apply for the short term (one sales promotion activity during 1 or 2 months) or can last longer. Sometimes, personal data about the "members" are recorded in a (simple or advanced) database, sometimes it is anonymous. The means used are very different; they range from stamps, coupons, premiums, newsletters, catalogues, membership cards, bonus miles or magazines sent to the members of the club. Often, many of these means are used simultaneously. The advantages to the customer vary from goods and services for free, discounts, information, special treatment at special events (concerts, sports), special credit facilities and privileges (e.g. entrance to the business class lounge) and the use of help desks. It may be one or more companies running such a program, like American Airlines, Lufthansa or KLM. It may also be a group of service providers in the same industry, like the Alliance Gastronomique, the Unique Corporation's restaurants or the Star Alliance of selected airlines. It may even be run by a special organization like Air Miles, in which several retailers participate to offer air miles while completely different service providers like holiday resorts (Center Parcs), zoos and airlines accept the miles as payment for their services. Sometimes, the programs are very simple to administer: the restaurant that puts a stamp on an unpersonalized card every time customers visit them. Sometimes, the programs are very sophisticated due to the use of new computer technologies. Then, the service company (like the airlines) knows the name and address of the passengers, the trips they make (distances, frequency, business class or economy class, purpose of the trip, connecting airlines), the hotels where they stay, the money they spend, etc. Consequently, customized offers can be made to these frequent flyers. The database created can also be used for various

direct marketing campaigns

direct marketing campaigns: large service providers can get to know their customers personally and communicate on a one-on-one basis with them. This is crucial in highly competitive industries and in the later stages of the relationship life cycle. It also requires an effective back office organization to run such a program.[38]

12.5 GUIDELINES FOR THE EFFECTIVE COMMUNICATION OF SERVICES

As we have said, communication about services will impact on the perceived quality of the service in the eyes of the beholder (= consumer). So, communication will affect the various dimensions of service quality as well as the overall service quality. In this section, two issues hinging upon the effective communication of services will be discussed as new items, in addition to the ones already discussed. For, it is self evident that clear marketing goals have to be present to set up the framework within which the communication goals can be implemented. We will not discuss issues like the clarity of the message, the proper target audience, the financial means and the cooperation with an advertising agency to create excellent quality adverts during a long term relationship between service provider and advertising agency. However, we will pay attention to three effective styles of interpersonal communication and six well-known guidelines for effective communication in services.

THREE STYLES OF INTERPERSONAL COMMUNICATION

front office employees

The quality of a service depends strongly on the performance of the service organization's employees, especially the front office employees. Internal and external communications directed to this target audience are crucial, next to a thorough recruitment and selection process and (on the job) training. In general terms, employees must be motivated, able and willing to perform different communication activities in particular situations or to particular clients. How to communicate to a particular customer is part of the company's market orientation. When employees know their customers well, this will be rather easy to accomplish. Three communication styles, depending on the demands customers place on the employees, can be distinguished.[39] In turn, this makes clear what kind of jobs are required in the service industry. Employees must have these skills to communicate and do their work effectively. The three types of jobs presented below show an increasing complexity in communication. These service staff types are:

demands customers place on the employees

Type 1
frequent, brief, 'once only' type interactions with countless customers

Type 1: "Persons holding this type of position must deal effectively with frequent, brief, 'once only' type interactions with countless customers. The exchanges usually handle simple information and often require limited responses to customer requests. Effective communicators in this job category must be able to process short, rapid messages very quickly, provide a limited number of appropriate responses to consumer inquiries, avoid objectifying (i.e., treating persons as objects) and being objectified themselves, provide clear concise instructions, listen effectively, diffuse anger and establish customer relationships very quickly. Such employees are generally interchangeable. Examples of jobs requiring these kinds of communication skills are bank tellers, receptionists, and ushers." This type of employee behavior probably fits well into (simple) core services.

Type 2
restricted interactions
of somewhat longer
duration between
employees and
numerous, often repeat
customers

Type 2: "The communication aspects of jobs of this type can be characterized by restricted interactions of somewhat longer duration between employees and numerous, often repeat customers. The information is mixed – partially simple and partially more complex – and requires some independent decision making. An effective communicator in this category exhibits skills in listening effectively, establishing trust, giving clear instructions, interpreting information, making decisions and persuasion in the one-to-one encounter. The relationship between the customers and employee is usually ongoing over time and the flow of information more intense. Generally, little substitutability of employees in the interaction takes place. Examples of jobs requiring these kinds of communications skills are individual loan officers, school administrators, hotel managers, and nurses in physicians' offices." Probably, this kind of employee behavior is required when offering customized core services or standard augmented services.

Type 3
repeated interactions
with a consumer over
time and an extensive
flow of information

Type 3: "Positions in this category require more complex communication skills. The communication consists of repeated interactions with a consumer over time and an extensive flow of information. The employee is not interchangeable in the interaction. The communication tasks in this category are complicated and often non-repeatable. Effective communicators in this category must be able to listen effectively, process complicated information efficiently, ask questions, brainstorm ideas, express feelings, make decisions quickly, and think creatively in face-to-face interactions. Typically, these people also must be able to communciate effectively with groups. Ex amples of jobs include commercial loan officers of banks, physicians, insurance sales people, and teachers." This kind of employee behavior best fits customized, augmented services.

It is important to note that a service organization may have employees in one, two or all three of these categories in order to meet the specific requirements of the service encounter with their customers. Also, customers may expect different kinds of response from the employee depending on the kind of questions they have or the situation the customer is in (contingencies). So, it is important for service employees to have a service attitude in which they can easily detect what role they have to perform in this particular contingency. In visiting a restaurant, regular guests may expect different treatments should they come with their family for a quick lunch or with business partners for a five course dinner (or vice versa). Communication will be the more effective, once the right tone is used, despite these different situations.

OTHER GUIDELINES FOR EFFECTIVE COMMUNICATION

guidelines for
successful and effective
communication

Given the importance of external and internal communications about services, sound deliberation about the tools used is most desirable. Some guidelines for successful and effective communication in services are: having external communication directed to employees; stimulating word-of-mouth communications; providing tangibles; making services understandable; continuity in communication; performing what has

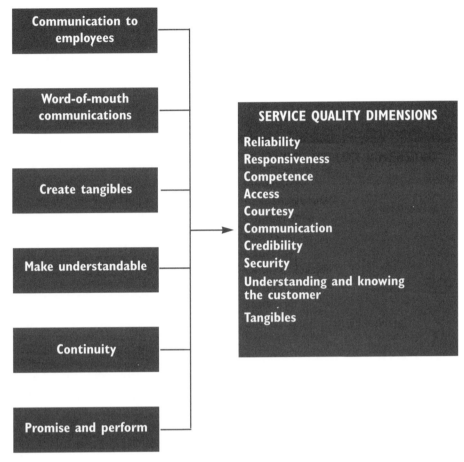

been promised and integrating communication with the other elements of the marketing mix.[40] Each of these six points can be linked to one or more of the service quality dimensions, for instance to the ten SERVQUAL-dimensions (see Figure 12-7). The content and relevance of some of these issues has been discussed already and will not be repeated here. A few additional items will be brought forward.

*external
communications for
one's own employees*

The relevance of external communications for one's own employees has been demonstrated clearly. The acceptance of the role models portrayed in the adverts can be increased by involving employees in the advertising campaign. In this way, employees will identify with the message more quickly than when professional models are used. As a result, personnel will convey competence to a certain extent.

competence

The famous American Ritz-Carlton hotel promises to deliver to guests service of the highest level. This includes a welcome (if possible) by name and a warm goodbye when the guests are leaving. The promotion is therefore not only external but also internally oriented. The slogan is: "We are ladies and gentlemen serving ladies and gentlemen."

stimulation of word-of-mouth communications

The stimulation of word-of-mouth communications has been discussed before. Its importance will increase as consumers become more aware of the complexity and heterogeneity of services. Especially in labor-intensive services, where it is difficult to establish some sort of standardization, the judgements of others may be decisive in

judgements of others

the selection process. For services with a greater perceived risk and/or services with little search attributes, this is of major importance. To find the right doctor, hair-dresser or school for the children, consumers will rely on the opinion of others who already have had experience with these service providers. In general, two communication techniques can be used for the purpose of stimulating word-of-mouth communication: the use of satisfied consumers (so-called testimonials); or the use of celebrities to affect the trend setters or opinion leaders and later on the innovators, early adaptors and early majority, etc. Both forms aim mainly at increasing (i.e. through

credibility

endorsement) credibility.

creation of tangibles

The next guideline is the creation of tangibles. Because intangibility is the key feature of services, the risk that goes with the purchase of a service is estimated to be quite high. Although the service itself stays intangible, adding tangibles may help to decrease the risk perception of the consumer. The use of figures (for example: 45% of our pupils pass the driving test in one try!) or the "personification" of a service by

confidence

using celebrities in promotions may be effective in creating confidence.

making the service understandable

Furthermore, in decreasing the perceived risk, the service provider will also have to focus on making the service understandable. The protection offered by an insurance company can be made visible by using an umbrella in its promotion or logo. In building information systems, the software industry frequently uses schemes and flow charts, designed to make the invisible system understandable to the customer.

continuity

Continuity forms the fifth guideline. For tangible products, packaging is a permanent and recognizable aspect. A service provider has to create this by the frequent use of the same slogans, themes and symbols in advertising. Continuous repetition of the

packaging

symbols and slogans should, as it were, form the packaging of the service. Therefore, the ideal situation for a service provider is that a consumer is able to associate the advertisement with the service organization without mentioning the name of the

corporate personality

organization in the advert. This continuous repetition finally results in a "corporate personality".[41] In the long run, a customer will see the organization as a person he or

knows well and trusts

she knows well and trusts. We discussed brands, brand image and brand personality in Chapter Eleven. It is why many retailers look carefully for a "store personality".

do as promised

Last but not least: do as promised. In its communications, a service organization must only promise what can be accomplished. Realistic expectations of customers are proven to be better than high expectations, which cannot be accomplished. To

reliability, competence and credibility

promise only the possible closely relates to the quality determinants of reliability, competence and credibility. This links on to what we have mentioned before as an essential part of market orientation: managing customer expectations. A customer will be dissatisfied when promises and the raised expectations that go with it, are not realized. Overpromising – it has been said before – is "killing in services".

dimensions of service quality
communication objectives embedded within company goals, the marketing objectives and the chosen target group

All of these guidelines are more or less linked to the dimensions of service quality. These guidelines and dimensions can be extremely appropriate in formulating the communication objectives of the service provider aimed at creating the desired image, and the way to accomplish them effectively. But, one more theme should be added. Internal and external communications of services should be embedded within the company goals, the marketing objectives and the chosen target group. Moreover, communication should not be isolated from the other elements of the marketing mix but should create a coherent image of the service company and its offering. Communicating new service issues requires perfect planning and organization of all other elements, as can be seen from the next Service practice on flying business class.

Service practice 12-7 Air carriers step up business class marketing efforts[42]

Domestic airlines are stepping up their marketing efforts to promote the benefits of flying business class. Long known, by international carriers, as being a substantial market segment, business class flyers are finally beginning to be embraced by US carriers. Since business class was first introduced to the US market in the late 1980s, it has grown gradually to the point that it now accounts for approximately 16% of the entire domestic flight market, according to a recent Advertising Age report. The price range for business class air travel falls between the cost of a full-fare coach ticket and a first-class seat. Since corporations have cut back substantially on travel budgets, the air carriers have begun to take advantage of the increasing amount of business travelers who can no longer afford first-class but are willing to pay a little more for some of the perks that are not associated with flying coach. By concentrating their marketing efforts on this segment, airlines are reaching out to high-frequency fliers and eliminating many costs associated with first-class services, from which most airlines derive only about 3% of their revenue. At the same time, they are allowing business travellers to be separated from those travelling coach and making them feel that they are receiving the treatment that the ticket price warrants.

The battle for this market segment is quite heated. Here are a few of the perks which some carriers have begun to offer:

- Continental Airlines has instituted a "Business First" program in which they offer 55-inch-wide sleeper seats. These seats were once only offered to international business class travellers.
- US Air started its "Business Select" program in which seating on many of its flights can be adjusted, transforming three-across into two-across seating. The amount of business class seats can be increased from four to 45, designed to accommodate business travellers on high-use, short-haul runs between major cities in the Midwest and Northeast.
- American Airlines has an "Executive Coach" program that rewards passengers with pre-boarding, reserved overhead bins, meals served and picked up first and, whenever possible, middle seats left open.

measure the
effectiveness of
communication
goals were
accomplished
marketing
communication
intensity

In many fields of marketing, efforts are made to measure the effectiveness of communication. The first attempts in services marketing have been made recently. Once goals have been formulated, for instance in terms of brand awareness or image, it can be researched afterwards whether the intended goals were accomplished. Another way of doing this is by relating annual marketing communication expenditure to annual sales and considering this as a kind of marketing communication intensity. Similarly, advertising intensity is defined as the ratio of advertising expenditures to sales.[43] It appeared that the assumption that services' intangibility will make their communications or advertising less effective (than communications or advertising in non-service businesses) is not supported. This year's communications and advertising expenditures not only affect this year's sales but also future sales; significant carry-over effects exist for consumer service firms as well as for business-to-business firms.

However, it always remains a difficult question to answer as to how much advertising is enough? Or, what amount of money is the most effective? United Parcel Service, for instance, was a closed company; for the past few years they have opened up to the public. They still wonder what the effect of their investments in advertising is on their position, especially as against Federal Express in the US.

Service practice 12-8 UPS in packaging[44]

United Parcel Service and Federal Express are the major players in the US air express market. In 1996, UPS had a 42.5% market share in overnight deliveries (packages of 3–70 pounds) and Federal Express 40.0%. In the market for letters and envelopes (two pounds or less), Federal Express had a 59.0% market share and United Parcel Service 12.8%. UPS is pushing to keep its lead in express delivery of larger shipments and to catch up with Fedex in overnight letters.

United Parcel Service developed advertising campaigns in 1996 at a cost of $80 million to $100 million, including its sponsorship of the Olympic Games in Atlanta, where it is based. It wants to look public without going public. "These efforts are driven in large measure by the bruised ego of a company that until the early 1980s saw itself as an unassailable American institution. Then, Federal Express came along." UPS re-engineered its operations and corporate philosophy to cope with Fedex and invested heavily in computer technology. Now, they communicate these plans and actions widely to show that they can compete with Fedex.

However, "there is a growing awareness at UPS that customers don't fully realize how much of it has changed. 'We spent millions and millions of dollars on advertising, and if you still ask a lot of people they think we're a great reliable company, sound and steady,' Mr Nelson, the UPS CEO said. 'But they don't realize what our technological capabilities are, the systems we've built, some things that no one else can do.'"

12.6 COMMUNICATION FOR DIFFERENT KINDS OF SERVICES

Depending on the company goals, the communication objectives, and the target group of customers, service providers can ask themselves two fundamental questions:

1. can services differ among themselves to such an extent that the communication mix for one service will not fit another service?; and
2. are there other aspects which deserve extra attention in deciding on advertising, promotion and other means of communication?

Although the existing literature offers little help in finding the definite answer to these questions, we assume that we have to answer them positively. There are, for instance, some specific differences in advertising for various services.[45]

CONVENIENCE, SHOPPING AND SPECIALITY SERVICES

The following three types of private services (services of the public and nonprofit sector are not considered here) can be found: convenience services; shopping services or services whose buying needs a great deal of information search; and, speciality services which are often professional services and may for the greater part overlap business services.

convenience services   Convenience services mainly distinguish themselves by the quality determinant of accessibility. In external communication, organizations offering convenience services should – compared with competitors – put emphasis on having: more branches/outlets/sites; more favourable opening hours; outlets which are more convenient in terms of accessibility. A characteristic of this type of service is that communication *access* mainly focusses on access.

shopping services   Many shopping services seem to depend on experience and reliability. Examples of shopping services are barber shops, brokers, etc. Through communication, these organizations may position themselves in two ways. First, this can be done on the *specialism* basis of specialism. Their advertisements must then contain terms like:

- We are specialists in...
- We mainly aim at...
- For all your repairs to...

credibility   If a new service organization positions itself as a specialist, then credibility will be affect-
speciality services   ed positively. A provider of speciality services may also position itself on a particular quality level in general or for specific dimensions. If this aspect is desired, the possible differentiating advantages will have to be communicated to the buyers via claims like:

- long experience (established since...)
- reliability or size (the biggest in...)

creating tangibles

Listing these kind of advantages falls within communication techniques aimed at creating tangibles.

professional services

Professional services need to be elaborated upon a little more. Into this category come lawyers, architects, marketing consulting firms, etc. Professional services will have to convey quality, professionalism and reliability. Access and favourable opening hours, which are very important for convenience services, clearly come second. Professional service providers, in their advertisements, could center on the less risk-sensitive services, because there is a clear negative relationship between the degree

risk

of risk and the willingness to buy.[46] As the risk increases, the buying intention will decrease. Considering all these points, the professional service provider will have to

corporate image

use a strong character to communicate the corporate image.

Service practice 12-9 World champion 1986

In 1986, the Royal Dutch Airlines (KLM) won the title **"airline of the year"**. To celebrate this honorable event, they tried to make their corporate image even better by the following advertisement slogan:

"Some airlines think good service is the smile on the face of the stewardess. For KLM it's the smile on the face of the passenger."

CORE, AUGMENTED, STANDARD AND CUSTOMIZED SERVICES

augmented services

Often, augmented services are more intangible than many standard or core services. This means that experience and credence attributes probably play a more important role in their perceived quality than search attributes. In general, augmented services involve a bigger perceived risk than standard and core services. Therefore, the communication strategy must focus on "tangibilizing" the intangible (or: visualizing the service delivery process) and influencing customer's attitudes/expectations to reduce perceived risk.

standard core services

In trying to antipicate customer expectations effectively, we can assume that standard core services usually are less complex than customized and augmented services. Therefore, the participation intensity of the consumer is higher than in the first group of services. Communication strategies of standard core services could therefore focus especially, on informing consumers about the "quite simple" role they are expected to play in the service delivery process.

customized and augmented services

The participation intensity in customized and augmented services is lower most of the time; the employee (lawyer, consultant) does do most of the work. The consumer contributes less to the production process of the service and depends more on the skills and capabilities of the service provider. However, the perceived risk may increase, as the perceived control in this process decreases. This may make the consumer feel insecure. Therefore, informing, supervizing and reassuring a customer is of major importance during the delivery process of these services. Physical evidence, brochures, videotapes and PR activities can be used to instruct the consumer about the contents of the process, in order that the perceived risk and perceived control are still acceptable to the consumer.

The various instruments of the communication mix can be applied to all four kinds of services. However, the degree to which they can be applied will differ per type of service, and will depend, of course, on the goals set. In general, we think that Figure 12-8 reveals these differences quite clearly.

Figure 12-8
The communications
mix per type of service

	Standard core services	Customized core services	Standard augmented services	Customized augmented services
Service staff	Type 1	Type 2	Type 3	Type 4
Advertising	appropriate. Communicate message internally and externally	very appropriate for big organizations. Aim internally and externally at differentiation by additional service delivery	appropriate, but relatively expensive, especially for new organizations	appropriate. Mainly aimed at quality and image
Personal selling	mostly inappropriate. Only used when explanation is required	mostly inappropriate. Only used when explanation is required	crucial. Service delivery process often is personal selling	service delivery process is initiated by personal selling
Sales promotion	can be used in several forms	can be used in several forms	can be used in several forms	only as image support
Word-of-mouth and public relations	important	important	essential	essential
Direct marketing and database marketing	effective when big (general) database and mailing lists (of the organization) are used	effective when big database and mailing lists (of the organization itself) are used	effective when small – mostly local mailing list is used	effective when small specific mailing list is used

*Service
practice
12-10
Which role do I
play?*

McDonald's provides an excellent example of communicating a customized core service. It is necessary to inform the customer about the role he or she is expected to play. McDonald's is a self-service restaurant, but customers don't know that, they may be waiting for a waiter to come to their table for hours. McDonald's advertisements show customers who order at the counter – the customer plays the leading part.

Our two types of augmented services are aimed at informing, supervizing and reassuring customers. Health care services are directed especially at these objectives. Patients who need radiotherapy face a lot of uncertainties and are hardly able to participate. Participation is limited to lying on their bed and doing nothing. To take away uncertainties, it is necessary to inform patients before therapy, to supervize and reassure them during the process. Professional employees therefore play a major role in communications.

SUMMARY

This chapter is on communication of services. Different types of communication are relevant in service industries. Communication can play a major role in reducing perceived risk, in providing clarity about the roles to be played by customers and employees in service encounters, in getting the necessary information from customers about their needs, in creating the desired image, in attracting the right employees, etc. Many topics about information are closely linked to quality issues. That is why we made explicit links between communication and the dimensions of service quality. Not only is external communication to customers relevant but also the internal communication within the service organization (to motivate employees). Often, the external communication is also aimed at influencing employees.

Many factors impact on customer expectations. Corporate image and brands are very relevant to service industries in this respect. Here, we have focussed on those factors related to communication in the various stages of the consumption process of services. In order of importance to services, we have discussed:

- personal selling;
- advertising;
- word-of-mouth communication and public relations;
- direct marketing and data base marketing;
- the Internet;
- sales promotion; and
- loyalty programs.

These means have been applied to different types of services, such as:

- convenience, shopping and speciality services; and
- core, augmented, standard and customized services.

The chapter contains several guidelines for the effective communication of services. These are:

- direct communication to employees;
- stimulate word-of-mouth communications;
- provide tangibles;
- make a service understandable;
- aim at continuity; and
- do as you promised.

In the discussion of these guidelines, three types of communication styles were mentioned which service organization's employees must have to meet the demands placed on them by their specific customers in particular contingencies effectively.

QUESTIONS

1 Which four basic issues in communication can be distinguished? Provide examples of each in the service industry.
2 How can the communication goals differ per stage in the process of buying services?
3 In what way can communication contribute to creating and maintaining long term relationships between a service provider and a customer?
4 What is the function of an image in services?
5 Why is it relevant to create brands and brand personalities in service industries?
6 What are the essentials of the various elements of the communication mix in services?
7 How do loyalty and frequency programs fit into relationship marketing strategies?
8 What three types of service staff behavior can be found?
9 What is important in determining the effectiveness of communication in services?
10 What are the main differences in communication policy for standard core services and customized augmented services?

ASSIGNMENTS

1 Recall the 18, 10 or 5 dimensions of service quality discussed in previous chapters and discuss how they are related to a service firm's communication policy.
2 What service quality dimensions are referred to in sections 12.5 and 12.6? Explain.
3 Select a few airlines, universities or major banks. Analyze their communication mix. Which elements do they use and why? How different are their activities? Is the communication in line with their strategy and other elements of the marketing mix? How does this fit to their positioning?
4 Develop a communications plan for a local insurance agent, specializing in life insurances for the upper class, to enhance the company's awareness among its target group from 25% to 70% in one year.
5 Discuss the following hypothesis: The increasing use of computer technology in services will diminish the personal communication in services. This will have a negative effect on service quality since the personal interaction is crucial.
6 Provide examples of firms (service and non-service firms) using their external communications to motivate their employees. Analyze these examples. What do they have in common? How does this fit to what has been said in section 12.3?
7 Assume the portfolio of clients of a well-respected restaurant consists of 25% friends, 50% acquaintances, 15% functionalists and 10% sympathetics. The restaurant, once in a while, advertises in a regional newspaper. Word-of-mouth communication appears to be very important to them. What communication policy would you recommend them to increase the percentage of friends to 55%?

Case: RANDSTAD AUTOMATISERINGSDIENSTEN: DIFFERENT CLIENTS REQUIRING DIFFERENT COMMUNICATION[47]

Randstad Automatiseringsdiensten (RAD), which was founded in 1989, is an independent company within the Randstad Holding nv.

Randstad Holding nv

Randstad Holding nv is an international group of staffing services companies active in the field of temporary staffing, cleaning, security, technical automation and training services. In 1994, revenues were NLG 3.8 billion and net income was NLG 112 million.

The essence of all Randstad's services is to provide staff and expertise to organizations in order to operate flexibly. A daily average of 90,000 people work through the Randstad Group, which employs more than 500,000 individuals in the course of a year.

The Randstad group ranks among the world's largest temporary staffing organizations, and is market leader in temporary staffing in the Benelux countries. Currently, the group has companies operating in The Netherlands, Belgium, Luxemburg, Germany, France, Great Britain, Spain, Switzerland and the United States. Activities are conducted through approximately 900 offices, of which 350 are situated outside The Netherlands. The headquarters are in Amsterdam.

Randstad's activities have an intensely local character. The group's flat, decentralized organizational structure assures that the staff in its offices are in optimal positions to be alert and respond rapidly to circumstances in the local labor markets.

Randstad's primary goal is continuity of the enterprise. Growth and profits are viewed as the means to assure continuity. This is, likewise, crucial with regard to the concern for maintaining the job satisfaction of the staff.

Randstad history

Randstad Holding nv was founded in 1960 by means of a thesis that the current chairman and chief executive Frits Goldschmeding, then a student of economics at the Free University Amsterdam, wrote on temporary work. Together with his fellow student Gerrit Daleboudt, he decided that it was worthwhile to give the thesis a chance and started Amstelveen Uitzendbureau (in 1963, this was renamed into Randstad Uitzendbureau). Soon, the first appointment became a reality, a few seconds after, the company needed a multilingual secretary and a Miss Honhoff called to register as a multilingual secretary.

Randstad Automatiseringsdiensten bv

Randstad Automatiseringsdiensten is part of the division Randstad Dienstengroep, which is divided into Randstand Uitzendbureau and Randstad Speciale Producten (nicheplayers).

Randstad Speciale Producten is a group of companies that are active in different disciplines of temporary employment in technical, staffing services, automation, health care and training.

Randstad Automatiseringsdiensten works regionally and has divided The Netherlands into five regions in which its five branches, Amsterdam, Rotterdam, Eindhoven, Zeist and Zwolle, are situated strategically. Through these branches, approximately 600 (direct) employees who are specialists on automation, are put to work in different areas of systems development, computer operations, control and development. The employees are kept up-to-date and educated through their own training centre. An average of approximately 25 direct employees are being managed by one account manager (the so-called indirect employee) who also deals with the orders. This job combines commercial and people management.

Market situation

Randstad Automatiseringsdiensten is active in the Information Technology market, which can be divided into total solution providers and "workfield oriented" suppliers (=specialists in IT for a particular job or problem).

Total solution providers offer a complete package of services and in most cases take responsibility for the complete offer.

Workfield-oriented suppliers aim at a specific set of services in the IT market. The workfields of these companies are very diverse, one can be a hardware or software supplier; or a supplier of (network) services. Randstad Automatiseringsdiensten belongs to the latter group.

The market in which Randstad Automatiseringsdiensten acts, can be divided into:

1. companies that analyze the problem and define the solution;
2. companies that supply the specific professional "expertise" that is needed for the solution (e.g. Randstad Automatiseringsdiensten);
3. flex companies that meet the demand to support the job (e.g. Randstad Uitzendbureau).

Randstad Automatiseringsdiensten does not merely see the analyzing companies as competitors; these companies also make use of the professional skills of the employees of Randstad Automatiseringsdiensten in their projects. Their Unique Selling Point and core business is to work out complex problems, not employ professionals who can specialize in the problem.

The other players in the market, flex companies, are not expected to give a thorough contribution to the development of the employees.

The unique position of Randstad Automatiseringsdiensten compared with other companies that do secondment is that they do more than just find the right person the fastest way. Randstad Automatiseringsdiensten combines this with know-how. More and more companies are drifting towards analyzing companies (groups), Randstad Automatiseringsdiensten doesn't, they want to remain where they are at their best!

Communication

Randstad Automatiseringsdiensten, as a Randstad company, has to work with the advantages and disadvantages of the brand-association that a big sister like Randstad Uitzendbureau has established over the years. Where flexibility is concerned, the advantage is enormous, where expertise on automation is concerned, it sometimes is not recognized. But overall, the link with Randstad stands for quality and therefore if there is a barrier, its priority is to explain misunderstandings and turn them into an advantage.

Communication goals

As far as the communication goals of Randstad Automatiseringsdiensten are concerned, most effort is put into improving the image of the company. Randstad Automatiseringsdiensten has to put more emphasis on its expertise in finding, managing and coaching the right professionals by an account manager combined with job expertise and flexibility of the automation professional. This is equally as important for obtaining and keeping clients as well as applicants. Especially the last group which must not be underestimated, since it is essential to find the best in their field.

The main communication goals of Randstad Automatiseringsdiensten are:

- stressing expertise;
- stressing the unique proposition of Randstad Automatiseringsdiensten within the Randstad group;
- communicating its employee conditions to clients/prospects and applicants (continuity, training, courses and coaching);
- continuing to stress its flexibilty;
- communicating the position in the market (same price level and healthy profit goals); and
- paying attention to internal communication and cooperation with sister companies.

Communication target groups
External
Clients
Especially with larger companies, the people who decide on buying are no longer the automation experts (head of automation, EDP managers) but more and more it is the personnel managers who decide. This change gives the combination of Randstand Automatiseringdiensten and Randstad Uitzendbureau an opportunity. Large accounts prefer to make package deals for the long term.

Clients: solution providers

As we mentioned before, Randstad Automatiseringsdiensten has competitors as its clients. This means that it is very important to be on the shortlist of these companies when they need the people to solve their problems.

Influentials

Accountants, industry organizations, IT-suppliers (software and hardware suppliers), educational institutions, schools, universities and business press, they all form a group of influentials determining Randstad Automatiseringsdiensten's sales and images.

Internal

Direct employees

In view of the targets that the firm sets itself, a constant recruitment campaign to fulfill the demand for personnel is created. Both the newly graduated and the experienced specialist form an equally important group to reach. If people who have just graduated have potential, but not the necessary knowledge through experience, Randstad Automatiseringsdiensten offers them a tailormade training programme.

Indirect employees

This is the group that consists of account managers and staffing personnel. The account manager maintains the contacts with the clients, they are commercial and not technical speicalists and work with approximately 25 direct employees.

Randstad Uitzendbureau/ Randstad group

Intercedents and account managers are a very important target group for Randstad Automatiseringsdiensten. Because Randstad Uitzendbureau has this wide-spread network of outlets throughout a country, Randstad Automatiseringsdiensten has a unique steppingstone in the labor market. The condition being that the Randstad Uitzendbureau employees know and realize the extra value and specialism of Randstad Automatiseringsdiensten. This is a project that needs constant attention and also applies to the other Randstand companies.

Means of communication
External

Corporate campaign

To enhance the corporate identity and increase name recognition (top of mind awareness), Randstad Automatiseringdiensten, in cooperation with the other Randstad Special Products companies that carry the name Randstad, created a corporate campaign with a double page advertisement. The campaign was placed in both management and business magazines and was used for the second half of 1995 and for the whole of 1996.

The target group in these advertisements was both the clients/ prospects and automation specialists. The campaign put the emphasis on expertise of the employees ("analytic minds" and "winners"). In order to communicate this, the visuals in the advertisements were of two famous dutchmen, Jan Timman, a famous chessplayer and Ronald Naar, Hollands' best mountaineer. These two seemed to match with the perfect profile of Randstad Automatiseringsdiensten.

The campaign was supported by a radio commercial broadcast twice a year for a minimum of two weeks per period. The commercial has the same ingredients as the advertisement.

Besides this campaign, Randstad Automatiseringsdiensten made its presence felt in the (business) media through its recruitment advertisements.

Recruiting personnel

In 1995, a new layout was chosen for the recruitment advertisements. The new aim was to show high quality, stress expertise, emphasize the unique proposition of Randstad Automatiseringsdiensten within the Randstad group and communicate the employee conditions when working in secondment. The advertisements were created to show the human element of Randstad Automatiseringsdiensten. In the end, that is the essence of the company. The structure of the jobs that are vacant is clear and always the same.

A target group for the coming period are graduates in disciplines which are interesting for Randstad Automatiseringsdiensten. A special version of the corporate campaign was created to attract this group. Other actions, like visiting schools, universities and special seminars have to support this. The firm also uses the Internet for its recruitment initiatives.

Brochures

To support different actions, several brochures are available to explain all the different areas where Randstad Automatiseringsdiensten are capable of supplying the right personnel. This applies to clients, prospects, applicants, and also other Randstad companies.

(For applicants a special brochure has been developed to explain the work that Randstad Automatiseringsdiensten does and the procedures for applicants).

Direct Mail

Direct Mail actions are conducted and initiated at the branches. Most of the time, they follow a theme that is real-life or is actually used within the Randstad company. The Direct Mail actions are supported by the communications departments who control the uniformity and are able to help with supporting material (e.g. leaflets).

Seminars

For clients and prospects, several meetings are arranged. The conference facilities at the Randstad Holding headquarters are often used for these meetings. For these seminars, topics are chosen that are real and have an application with "work" and automation.

Furthermore, several meetings are arranged per regional office for its clients by Randstad Automatiseringsdiensten. Often, it is possible to be invited to join the actions and events that Randstad Holding participates in (e.g. golf and tennis tournaments or business dinners with international prominent people e.g. Gorbatsjow).

Internal

For the internal information Randstad Automatiseringsdiensten has a journal that is solely for the employees and deals with all aspects that concern them.

The best communication, however, is personal. Therefore, the account manager visits the clients as often as possible per period (e.g. month), to pay every employee a visit and discuss the business.

Equally important is to invite the employees to the Randstad-outlets/offices. The importance here lies in the fact that these employees work "outhouse" at different locations with clients, though they are employed by Randstad Automatiseringsdiensten. Therefore, different meetings are organized. Every few weeks, a regional office arranges an evening where several matters, formal and informal, are dealt with.

Other internal communication actions are programmes that arise when Randstad Automatiseringsdiensten, the Randstad Holding or a sister company participates in projects, e.g. sponsoring The Olympic Games or the annual company party.

The Communications department of Randstad Automatiseringsdiensten deals with all the communication actions and is supported by the Corporate Communication department of Randstad.

QUESTIONS

1 Compare the main communication goals of Randstad Automatiseringsdiensten with the six guidelines of George and Berry: what can you conclude?

2 What role does communication play in Randstad Automatiseringsdiensten's own HRM-policy?

3 Is there anything you would advise Randstad to add to their external or internal communication policy?

ENDNOTES

1. This Service practice is based on various advertisments.
2. This figure is based upon Semenik and Bamossy, 1993, p. 307 and Jeannet and Hennessey, 1995, p. 468.
3. Jeannet and Hennessey, 1995, pp. 467-498.
4. This figure is based on Kurtz and Clow, 1998, p. 417. The present authors have adapted the figure slightly.
5. Zeithaml, 1990; Zeithaml, Parasuraman and Berry, 1990.
6. See previous chapters, especially Four, Five and Six.
7. This view is amongst others held by Booms and Bitner, 1983 and Cowell, 1984. Although the same may apply to communicating goods, it is important to recognize that during the production of goods the producer does not communicate to the customer at that very moment about those particular goods.
8. Zeithaml, Berry and Parasuraman, 1988.
9. Zeithaml, 1988.
10. Webster, 1989.
11. See our discussion of the SERVQUAL-model in Chapter Five.
12. This section heavily relies on Zeithaml and Bitner, 1996, Chapter Sixteen.
13. Zeithaml and Bitner, 1996, p. 452.
14. Zeithaml and Bitner, 1996, pp. 456-472.
15. Hoffman and Bateson, 1997, pp. 193-194.
16. This section heavily relies upon Martin, 1986 in: Neijzen and Trompetter, 1989.
17. This idea has been put forward by George and Berry, 1981. It has been elaborated upon by e.g. Zeithaml, 1988 and Hoffman and Bateson, 1997. Then, however, the focus is on advertising only, while we broaden the perspective to communications in general.
18. Internal marketing has been discussed to a certain extent in Chapter Ten; it will receive further atttention in Chapter Fifteen.
19. See Chapter Eleven. In this section we will rely on a speech given by Jim Williams, one of the Young & Rubicam's vice presidents. See also Killough, 1978.
20. We have seen in many instances in this book that a clear vision and goals are necessary as the framework within which employees and business units are entitled to work and be empowered. This is typical for market-oriented firms.
21. This statement and Service practice 12-3 stem from a Patrick Harverson Financial Times Exporter article about BBH.
22. Floor and Van Raaij, 1989.
23. Oliva and Lancioni, 1996, pp. 44-45.
24. Oliva and Lancioni, 1996, p. 49.
25. Berry, 1995.
26. See our discussion of the RLM-model in Chapter Eight.
27. Hoffman and Novak, 1994; newspaper article in NRC Handelsblad, March, 21, 1998.
28. See an article in Euromoney, June 1996, pp. 231-234.
29. Bowes, 1998; Barrington, 1998.
30. Barrington, 1998, p. 30.
31. Barrington, 1998, p. 30.
32. This example is taken from Barrington, 1998, p. 30.

33. This example was provided by Dr William J. Glynn. In The Netherlands, the electronic purse was not a success because two groups of banks have introduced a competing system of electronic purses.

34. Lovelock, 1991.

35. See Kurtz and Clow, 1998, Chapter Thirteen for a detailed discussion.

36. Kurtz and Clow, 1998, pp. 431-432.

37. The shift is not only gradual. Often, the terms are used interchangeably, however. See also, Riezebos, De Vries jr. and Waarts, 1996.

38. Kurtz and Clow, 1998, pp. 432-435 pinpoint on the many (internal conditions that have to be fulfilled in order to run such a program smoothly and make it difficult to imitate. See also Barlow, 1992 and Schijns, 1998.

39. Booms and Nyquist, 1981.

40. George and Berry, 1981, have developed the first six points of this overview. They have focussed on the guidelines for succesful and effective advertising in services. We have broadened the scope to communication in general.

41. Firestone, 1983.

42. Adapted from Services Marketing Today, vol. 11, no. 5, October 1995.

43. Herrington, Lollar, Cotter and Henley Jr., 1996.

44. Blackmon, 1996.

45. Nillesen, 1992.

46. Hite, Fraser and Bellizi, 1990.

47. We gratefully acknowledge M. Beck of Randstad Automatiseringsdiensten who prepared this case, which was finally edited by Hans Kasper.

CHAPTER THIRTEEN

DISTRIBUTION

This chapter on the fourth marketing mix instrument "distribution" deals with the delivery of services. After studying this chapter, you should be able to:

BELOW: *UPS*

- *indicate which issues must be taken into consideration when formulating distribution goals;*

- *formulate the relationship between these goals and some distribution strategies;*

- *recognize the links between corporate goals and distribution goals;*

- *argue the merits of the location opted for;*

- *name a few innovations and trends in the field of distribution;*

- *detect why such innovations are not always accepted;*

- *be aware of the impact of new information technologies on the distribution of services; and*

- *understand the consequences of our service typology on the distribution of services.*

UNTIL OTHER DELIVERY COMPANIES HAVE A TRACKING SYSTEM AS SOPHISTICATED AS OURS, YOU'LL JUST HAVE TO TRUST THEM.

Once an important package leaves your hands, about all you can do is keep your fingers crossed. Unless of course you've made the exceedingly wise decision of sending your package UPS.

You see, only UPS offers you the security of Total Track®, a highly-sophisticated computerised package tracking system that monitors the progress of your package from its point of origin all the way to its destination. Here's how it works. Your UPS driver now carries a hand-held computer to electronically record critical information about the status of your package. Throughout the day the information is automatically downloaded from his

vehicle to the UPS mainframe.

Using UPS OnLine™ Tracking software (or the Internet), you can access that information on your PC within minutes. You can determine the whereabouts of your package at any point along the delivery route or confirm delivery including the exact time and the name of the person who signed for it. This unique technology is so advanced, it even allows you to view the

actual signature of the recipient. So why hand your next important package to just any delivery company and hope it gets where it's going? When you can trust it to the one that knows where it is every step of the way. UPS.

Consider it done.

For more information on the technological advances that make shipping with UPS so easy and so reliable, visit our website at: www.ups.com or call your local UPS office.

13.1 INTRODUCTION

*Service
practice
13-1
The adoption
of mobile
telephones*[1]

Traditionally, telephone services are provided by means of physical equipment present (mostly standing or hanging at fixed places) in houses, offices or telephone boxes. The introduction of mobile telephones has changed this service dramatically. Now, one can call from almost anywhere and receive messages. The development of new information technology offers these opportunities. A new way of distributing telephone services has thus occurred. This is partly due to the fact that in many countries the monopolies on telecommunication have been abandoned. The new entrants in the market have concentrated in many cases on these new (mobile) services and consider this to be an interesting market (niche).

Mobile telephone services have started a new wave of communication in the business-to-business sector in many western countries. People are now not dependent on the physical spot where the telephone is located, but can be reached wherever they do business. We see, in many countries, that mobile telephone services are being introduced and accepted in the consumer market to a greater and greater degree. Reasons why consumers buy these services have to do primarily with status, ease, accessibility, social needs and security.

This change in market segment also requires a different way of distributing the devices: from – often industry zone located, lean and efficient – outlets, where firms buy their equipment, to stores in malls and city centers, in order to sell as a convenience service.

The introduction of these telephone services is rapidly taking place in the former Eastern Europe. Traditional telephone services were not extensive in those countries. The traditional cable system was not widespread and will no longer be widespread in the future. This phase in the life cycle of telephone services will be skipped, since it has been taken over right away by mobile telephone services. Investment in the traditional physical place of communication is now not needed.

Service practice 13-1 illustrates that technological developments may change the distribution system of services dramatically. So, technological changes, especially those in information technology, may change the way the distribution of services is organized and structured. This trend will be a central theme throughout this chapter because it has so many consequences for the distribution of services. Different positions in the service delivery matrices developed in Chapter Two become reality because of these developments. It will be no surprise that new technologies may affect the distribution of services and their contribution to creating value or excellent service quality to a large extent in the near future. In turn, this will impact on the kind of service encounter required to provide the service:

- where will the service be provided?
- what kind of behavior is the customer expected to perform?
- how much participation is required from the customer?
- what and how many outlets are needed to perform the service?, etc.

In essence, the discussion about the distribution of services hinges upon the (physical) location of where the service is to be provided. The basic characteristics of services usually imply that they have to be delivered with direct and immediate contact between service provider and customer. The development of new technologies will challenge this conventional wisdom. This applies to internal service delivery as well as to the service delivery to external clients. It is a big challenge to marketeers to respond properly to these opportunities in a creative, market-oriented way.

The issues discussed in developing the service delivery matrix are the starting-point for the distribution objectives. Subsequently, we will focus on the three potential distribution strategies, namely multisite, multisegment, and multiservice strategies. In addition to the explanation of each of these three strategies, we will pay attention to the relationship between the organizational objectives and the distribution objectives, as these cannot be considered individually. The distribution strategy chosen will also impact on the service provider's capacity to meet demand.

The choice of a particular location is another important aspect in the decisions about the actual place of service delivery. Section 13.5 first shows the importance of the actual location chosen, and its influence on the client as well as on the service provider. Section 13.6 will initially discuss the links between marketing and logistics in the form of customer service in logistics. That section will be concluded with a number of well-known distribution innovations: franchising, JIT, Internet, call centers, co-makership and relationship marketing. A brief explanation of each of these innovations will follow. Their applicability within the delivery of services will be discussed. This chapter will be rounded off by indicating what implications our - typology of services has for the distribution of services (see section 13.7).

new information technologies

Throughout the whole chapter, the international dimension of distributing services will come to the fore. As stated previously, in both cases, when a market seeking or client following strategy has been developed, the actual presence in the international scene is very important. This is a matter of distributing services at a physical place in a foreign country. Nevertheless, technological changes may challenge this common notion. Especially, the introduction of the Internet will play a crucial role here, for it will result in fundamental changes in the domestic and international delivery of services. Such technological changes will ease the communication processes between headquarters and foreign branches. Consequently, the whole service company will become more decentralized than is the case without these new information technologies.

Figure 13-1
Chapter outline

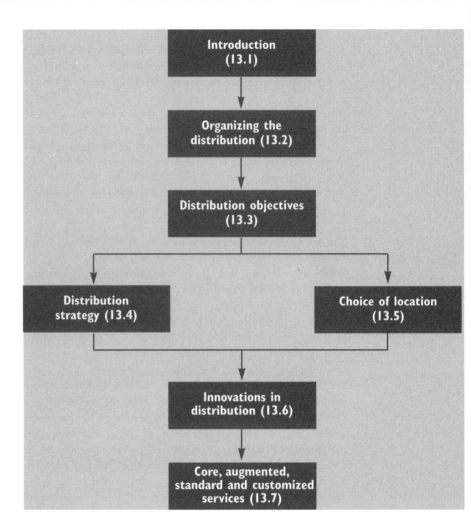

13.2 ORGANIZING THE DISTRIBUTION

In services, distribution has to do with the way the actual delivery of the service is organized. Is it only possible to distribute services at the spot where they are produced? Are there still some possibilites to store services? Does the internationalization of service firms add extra complications to distributing excellent quality services in various countries? Does the distribution of services differ for different kinds of services? These are a few of the questions relevant in distributing services stemming from a) the intangible nature of services and b) the intention to be market-oriented.

client's presence   The client's presence will not always be necessary when delivering the service. This phenomenon will increase in the future. Travel insurances, home shopping, and the services of the tax counsellor do not now always require actual presence during the service encounter. Mail order shopping is another, long standing, example here, also indicating that the service provider does not need to be visible during the service encounter.

degree of visibility
degree of flexibility

servicescape

This degree of visibility in the servuction process is marked by a certain degree of flexibility. Whether certain activities should be executed by the back or front office is not a matter that has been determined in advance and forever. A service provider will have to make a strategic choice on whether or not these services will be executed in a visible way and how the servicescape will look. This has to do with, among other things, the positioning desired. A restaurant owner, for example, could install an open kitchen instead of a kitchen behind closed doors. A security firm could opt for dressing its staff in customized outfits or instead operate with silent alarms and staff who cannot be identified as belonging to a security firm.

market-oriented
distribution system

In addition to these matters which tend primarily to refer to the internal organizational structure of the firm and its distribution system, it goes without saying that the external market requires attention too. Both issues are essential in having a market-oriented distribution system. Relevant questions regarding the external environment are, for example, "What system of distribution does the competition have?", "How cost-effective are those systems?", "How can we differentiate ourselves from our competitors in distributing services", and "Which technological changes affect their distribution?"

position

distribution objectives

Taking into account the market opportunities and risks resulting from the external analysis, the service provider will have to position its service clearly, prior to the actual process of delivering services. Such strategic choices cannot be made seperately from other decisions. For this reason, the distribution goals follow from the organization's (corporate) objectives and strategic decisions. Distribution objectives should indicate what the organization strives for, while taking the following four aspects into account:

- what degree of coverage in service distribution is the service provider aiming for?
- who travels to whom?
- are any booking possibilities being created? and
- does the service delivery take place individually or collectively?

fine tune decisions

In principle, all the issues discussed in classifying services, with respect to the kind of service delivery, could be taken into account at this stage of developing the marketing mix. As always, it is important to fine tune decisions about the distribution part of the marketing mix with all the other mix instruments. The marketing strategy and the corporate strategy which contain, amongst others, the firm's goals with respect to market orientation and service quality, are the framework within which these distribution decisions must be taken. The strategic choices made determine the options for the relevant distribution strategies and the location(s) opted for (see Figure 13-2).

Internal and external factors play a decisive role in making these decisions. It takes a thorough inventory of all assets (means of production, know-how, routines, skills,

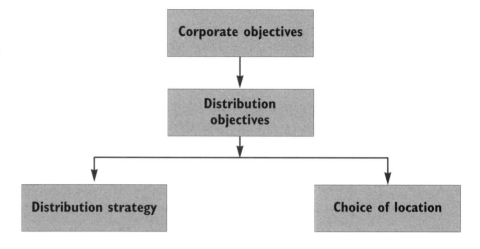

capabilities, core competences and such) linked to the internal strength, to determine the possibilities the service provider has in effectively and efficiently allocating his resources. The number of staff members and their skills, the financial situation and the information available are crucial factors, co-determining the size of the area where the firm will distribute its services. The size of this area, which is known as the sales area, is closely related to the means available. Obviously, a pharmacist with a single shop and a few shop-assistants can only operate locally. A commercial bank, on the other hand, has so much personnel and means at its disposal, that it may have branches operating on a national, or even an international scale. Even if the pharmacist wished otherwise, he would still lack the resources necessary to set up a larger network in most cases. A pharmacist who really wants to expand could probably tackle this problem by mobilizing other links in the distribution channel (intermediate chains or franchising).

sales area — marginal note

Service
practice
13-2
International
brokerage in
insurances

The Bureau International des Producteurs d'Assurances et Reassurances (BIPAR) is the international association of insurance brokers and middlemen. BIPAR has a large database for cross border insurance brokerage. The local middlemen can contact this database when one of their own clients moves to another country or buys a second house in another country that has to be insured and needs advice about the best policy in that country. Contacts with local brokers in a foreign country can be established quite easily this way. Moreover, many incidental contacts have resulted in long-term cooperative relationships between brokers in various countries, thus establishing an international network aimed at servicing clients going abroad.

distribution function — marginal note

Usually, the distribution function emerges as the way to solve imbalances between demand and supply. Since both occur simultaneously in services, distribution is not the only way to meet this problem. Many classical ways to solve this imbalance have been discussed in previous sections.[2] Here we will discuss all the other issues related to distribution.

The most simple distinctions in this respect are twofold. First it depends on whether the distribution channel is direct or indirect. Second, the ownership of the distribution channel is an issue.

direct distribution channel

indirect channel

A direct distribution channel is, characterized by the absence of middlemen or intermediaries, just between the producer of the service and the customer. A lawyer having one office in a city serves that community with his advice directly. Direct writers in the insurance industry communicate and deal directly with their customers without any brokers. In an indirect channel, one or more middlemen are present in bridging the distance between the service producer and the customers in order to deliver excellent service quality. These distances may be geographical, but they can also be of a social or psychological nature. This is especially the case when middlemen are needed to lower thresholds to meet a service provider. Geographical distances have to be bridged especially when a service provider acts in various countries. It is often important to be in the direct neighborhood of the customer abroad. An "importer of services" may be needed in some cases when the service firm is not working with local or company owned outlets. This will also depend on the entry strategy chosen. In many countries, ticket offices are selling tickets for theater performances in other countries. A central office distributes this service to, for instance, local tourist offices. Direct distribution implies that the "original" service supplier delivers directly to the "end-user". A short distribution channel is characterized by having one middleman, a long channel by various middlemen. The decision on what kind of distribution channel a service provider should choose depends on many

costs versus benefits

desired market orientation of the service provider

things. In general, it is accepted that it is a matter of costs versus benefits. In our view, at least two other criteria should be taken into account. The first one is the desired market orientation of the service provider and the way in which the partners in the distribution channel can perform accordingly. If this performance is not in accordance with those goals, the service provider cannot accomplish what it intends to do. Bad quality, dissatisfaction, complaints, customer switching, etc. will occur, eventually leading to unintended images and loss of sales. The second argument refers to the

partners' capability, motivation and attitude

distribution partners' capability, motivation and attitude to be market-oriented and towards creating and delivering excellent service quality. Then, managing service quality throughout the whole distribution channel becomes a crucial item.

ownership

In our opinion, the ownership issue in the distribution channel has to do with the opportunities and means to manage the distribution channel according to the goals set by the service provider. The control of a fully owned distribution channel will be different from controlling a distribution channel with many, independent middlemen all seeking to pursue their own interest.[3] For that reason, some service providers state explicitly in their marketing strategy that their objective is "to control the end-user". It means that all strategies are subject to this objective. For example, if such a service firm wants to form a strategic alliance with another company it will never give up this control.

multi channel strategy

Figure 13-3 illustrates the various forms of distribution channels that may occur. It is important to note that the service supplier may use various forms of distribution channels simultaneously. A multi channel strategy fits a differentiated marketing strategy aimed at reaching different market segments and target groups. It might also be that the various channels compete with one another. They may also "quarrel" when margins, prices, conditions and the way of dealing with the customer differs per channel. The risk of channel conflicts is then a reality. In the insurance business, in some countries, brokers and middlemen have a long standing position in the distribution channel of insurances. In Sweden, for instance, this has not been the case. Now, it is considered as a kind of innovation in the Swedish insurance business to start working with independent agents to a larger extent than before when the insurance companies only had their own, company paid agents.

Figure 13-3
Typical distribution
channels

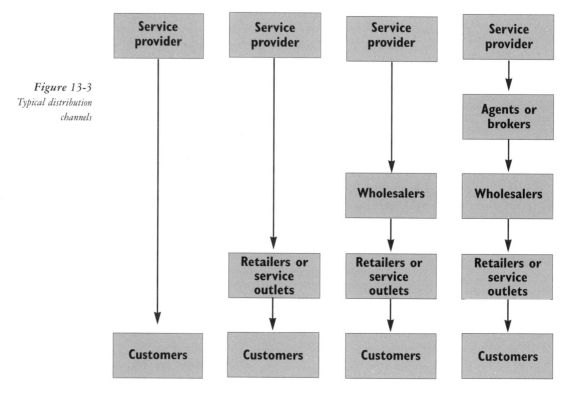

direct marketing

One of the ways to look at direct marketing is to regard it as a particular form of distribution where the service provider approaches the customer directly in a non-physical way. Information technology and data base marketing offer many opportunities for this new way of distributing services and communicating to the customer. Direct writing is a popular way of distributing insurances in many countries. Experiences in this field reveal that this way of selling insurances was easier for simple insurances to the majority of the population, or to the higher educated segment of the market capable of dealing with more complicated insurances.

Information technology and especially the Internet could easily change the whole traditional way of distributing services in many industries, not only banking or travelling.[4] Traditionally, airline tickets were sold via travel agencies. They made the bookings and sent the tickets to the traveller (most of the time a few days before the stressed traveller would depart). Now, many airlines are selling tickets on line. The world wide web is then used as the airlines' front office. South East Airlines (USA) and KLM (Netherlands) are already working this way, and are not using travel agencies as intensely as before. Easy Jet (a European "no frills" airline) accepts only direct bookings from the (business) customer.

channel conflicts   The enthusiasm for running many distribution channels simultaneously may be tempered by the risk of channel conflicts, especially when services are the same, but prices (and conditions) are different. Then it will be easier to use different brand names in different channels, which would also avoid cannibalization.[5]

13.3   THE DISTRIBUTION OBJECTIVES

distribution objectives   One way to formulate the distribution objectives that have been set by the service provider is by means of the service delivery matrix (Chapter Two). Naturally, there are other methods and indicators which may be used to formulate the distribution objectives of the service provider, but irrespective of the method, the following aspects need to be looked into: distribution coverage; who travels to whom; booking possibilities; and actual delivery: individually as compared to collectively.

COVERAGE

distribution coverage   First of all, the purpose of the intended distribution coverage has to be determined. Therefore, the initial question that needs to be answered here, is whether a large coverage in distribution is desirable. If the answer is negative, the number of locations will be limited to one or a few. If the answer is positive, it is most likely that new outlets will have to be founded. It goes without saying that an organization that seeks increased distribution, instead of limiting itself to one place of business, must opt for other strategies to reach this goal. It is of paramount importance to make a principal choice of the desired coverage of the distribution network (outlets) first, before fur-
intensity of   ther dealing with the question "how to reach this goal". The intensity of distribution
distribution   (exclusive or intensive) is at stake here. Intensive distribution is often necessary when convenience in services is deemed relevant by customers (banks, fast food).

WHO TRAVELS TO WHOM?

Generally speaking, when a service is provided the customer and the producer may get in touch with each other in three ways: the client goes to the producer; the producer visits the client; or no physical contact is involved.

client travels to the producer

The first and most prevalent way is for clients to physically make their way to the service provider. Thus, the client travels to the producer. In Chapter Fourteen, we will see that clients are already incurring expenses before they can consume the service because they have to travel and go there themselves. With this form of contact it is important that the producer is accessible. So, the initial costs will remain acceptable to the consumer. The social environment in which the service provider has established itself will also play a significant role in this situation. Large banks, law offices or consultancies prefer to set up their offices at A-locations: surroundings that are classified as prime locations.[6]

producer of the service comes to the client

materially-oriented service providers
people-oriented services

The second form of contact is the one where the producer of the service comes to the client. Two types of services can be distinguished here. Mostly, it concerns a type of service aimed at maintaining real estate. The plumber, the house-painter, the gardener, the window cleaner, all of them travel many kilometres each year to visit various clients at home. The reason for their visit is obvious as the wash basin, the front of the house or the back garden could not possibly be transported to the service provider. In addition to these materially-oriented service providers, there are other organizations which visit their clients at home. The services of doctors visiting their patients at home is an example of these more people-oriented services. One can also think of pizzas delivered and merchandise brought home by a subsidiary of the supermarket. These services are sometimes called convenience services or comfort services. The service provider feels very strongly about convenience and comfort, which is why it is the service provider which makes an effort and invests its time, instead of the client. Obviously, the exact location of a home delivery company is of less importance than the location of one of the ordinary supermarkets. In contrast to an ordinary supermarket, a home delivery company can, in principle, be found in practically any industrial zone in a country.

delivery without any physical personal contact

As extraordinary as it may sound, the last form of contact involves a delivery without any physical personal contact (arm's length services). Actually, partially or entirely, the service is supplied through the back office by using hardware. A call center or help desk of an IT supplier are examples of this type of distribution. Telecom providers offer round-the-clock fax and telephone services by way of telephone and fax to millions of consumers without ever contacting the consumer in the process. Except for repairing possible malfunctions and giving advice on the purchasing of equipment, the only contact made is the bill being delivered by mail (and even that bill may not be seen when the money is automatically transferred from the customer's bank account). The electricity company is another supplier who makes impersonal daily deliveries to millions of households. In our present society, the availability of gas and electricity is considered as a given fact, but it is the power stations which bear the responsibility for the day-to-day functioning of gas and light. Smooth operation of these services is possible only when the service is able to absorb any peaks in capacity demand and the delivery process. Here, proper distribution and good yield management go hand in hand.

BOOKING FACILITIES

booking system

As the decentralization of distribution diminishes, the potential client, when travelling to the service provider, will probably have to invest more time and effort in order to acquire the service. The service probably won't be available around the corner. Assuming there is a specific and well-known demand, a possibly higher degree of coverage in distribution may make a booking system non-essential, or even superfluous. When new technologies offer opportunities to do business at times other than usual opening hours of the service provider, systems which take up time of the service providers will be unnecessary. Home banking via the computer does not require the physical presence of bank employees during the service encounter. The individual and business customer can communicate with the bank's computer any time they like. Information technology has already made a dramatic influence on this kind of

virtual stores

service delivery and this will increase in the near future. Virtual stores are now on the Internet, providing many opportunities for home shopping. Wal-Mart launched on line shopping in 1996.[7] In The Netherlands, Macropolis is a virtual shopping center.[8]

Service practice 13-3 IT and insurances

The integration of financial markets, particularly strategic alliances between banking and insurances or even mergers, are appearing in a large number of countries. In many countries, the result causes an upset in the insurance business. In an industry that adheres to strict separation of the various distribution channels, insurers mount the attack by using all distribution channels at the same time. Nowadays, insurance companies have the following distribution forms available, which are frequently used side by side: direct writing; distribution through the bank's branch-offices; and through insurance intermediaries, advisors or brokers or possibly through one's own sales personnel. They are still searching for possible ways to have an even more efficient administrative process when accepting new policies and dealing with claims.

It seems that insurance companies will use any strategy to market their services. The increasing role that technology plays here is proven by the founding of networking systems. Industry systems networks (ISN) typically have insurance companies as shareholders. ISN oversees the electronic communications between insurance companies and their agents. The principle is simple. Both the company and the agent have an on-line connection to the ISN network, a so-called electronic mailbox. Each party drops his messages here, which are then distributed automatically by ISN.

Among other things, this yields returns, in the form of increased speed and cost-reductions. The insurance broker needs a PC and possibly, a so-called decentralized data system to dispatch the policy applications. If the application is approved by the decentralized data system situated in the agent's office (80% of applications are confirmed), the policy can be printed out immediately.

The insurance company receives the new entry and all relevant information.

> Should the application not be accepted at first, the agent will forward the information (NO) to the insurance company which will subsequently send off the policy three days later when it is accepted after all.
>
> Meanwhile, the importance of the data systems has been recognized and several insurance companies are now offering their own acceptance software to insurance brokers. The insurance companies put their programs at the disposal of the agents provided the latter have an on-line connection with ISN. Other program options include the use of the software by the insurance company to send the application by modem in the form of E-mail, Lotus-Notes or Internet directly to the insurer instead of by mail.

ACTUAL DELIVERY: PERSONAL VERSUS COLLECTIVE

An individual delivery of a service often requires perfect accessibility. If the actual delivery of a standard service is also the wish to provide the service on a personal basis, then, if the client has to travel, a high number of outlets in the distribution network is necessary. Customized service and personal delivery can remain "exclusively" established, provided that the sales area remains local or regional. The situation with respect to collective deliveries constitutes more of a problem. On the one hand, it is logical that more outlets are opened when collective delivery is aimed for, on the other hand collective delivery (in practice) is usually a result of the choice made to set up a limited distribution system. This, in turn, depends on the specific service: tourism, pop concerts, etc.

13.4   DISTRIBUTION STRATEGY

market segment

geographically concentrated servuction system

With regard to the choice of location, the KISS-principle (or Keep It Simple Stupid) has been introduced. A service provider must be easily accessible and recognizable. For that reason, a precisely defined market segment should be taken as a basis on which the service provider can direct his services. This segment needs to be served by means of a geographically concentrated servuction system in such a way that a clear image is portrayed. Actually, the KISS-principle clearly indicates the relationship between strategy and the location of the outlet.

STRATEGIC ALTERNATIVES

intensive distribution

Usually, distribution strategies can be labelled as intensive, selective or exclusive. Intensive distribution is a strategy directed at developing as many outlets as possible. This strategy is the result of an objective directed at a high coverage rate in the distribution network. If the distribution is limited to a few branches or even only one,

selective and exclusive distribution

then the selective and the exclusive methods of distribution form strategic alternatives. These strategies apply respectively to convenience, shopping and speciality services. However, considering the specific features of services, we can also distinguish between the following three distribution strategies: multi-site strategy; multi-service strategy; and multi-segment strategy.[9]

Multi-site

multi-site strategy

The multi-site strategy consists of repeating one particularly succesful basic formula at several other outlets or locations. Possible differences in environmental factors are hardly significant here. The formula is and remains standard and there is no, or hardly any, reason for adaptations. This can actually be defined as a standard service and holds for both core and augmented standard services. Franchising is an example of a multi-site strategy. The only question that needs to be solved in the field of marketing is: "Will it catch on here?". This strategy closely resembles the well-known selective or intensive distribution strategy, depending on the number of outlets where the standardized service will be provided. In the hotel and catering business, this strategy has been applied many times over. The fast-food chains excel in the degree of standardization. McDonald's hamburgers in San Francisco have almost the same taste as those in Moscow.

selective or intensive distribution strategy

Multi-service

multi-service strategy

The multi-service strategy is designed particularly to provide various services: service differentiation. Relying on the existing goodwill of the consumers and the firm's thorough knowledge of them in one particular area, the service provider begins offering new and different services to the existing assortment. It is a kind of new service development and service innovation. Essentially, a pure multi-service strategy would consist of one outlet, which targets its various services in a particular market segment. This is an example of an exclusive distribution strategy. The multi-service strategy is applied by many software houses. In particular, software suppliers that focus on a specific target group frequently offer three core activities: innovation, developing new programmes; maintenance of existing application programmes or machine software; and technical management.

exclusive distribution strategy

Multi-segment

multi-segment strategy

The last of the three strategies, as seen in its purest form, is the multi-segment strategy. From one particular location, a particular service is targeted at several market segments. This strategy is often applied in situations in which part of the capacity remains unused and the fixed costs in providing the service are relatively high. If this unused capacity is structural, the service provider will be inclined to use it, and usually a different target group is opted for. In a pure multi-segment strategy this is, once again, an instance of exclusive distribution as the number of establishments could be limited to one. An amusement park targets several segments from one location with one service (entertainment). Crowd-pullers like Disneyworld, Disneyland, or EuroDisney have to make considerable investments each year to maintain their appeal for various target groups. The investments are necessary to maintain, or increase the number of visitors. Thus, more traditional tourist destinations such as easily accessible cities in the USA, Europe or Japan must compete with these

exclusive distribution

parks attracting millions of visitors every year in spite of their being in more remote locations. But, how much do these cities invest in creating "suspense and sensation"? In extending their assortment of services, these amusement parks also offer hotel facilities. Hotels with different offerings, services and prices then attract different market segments.

In sum, the multi-segment and the multi-service strategies are exclusive distribution strategies, as delivery takes place from one or very few outlets. The multiservice strategy can be compared to selective or intensive distribution. In theory there is a clear distinction, but in practice the distinction is less so, as actual strategies are usually a mixture of the two. In such a hybrid variety, elements of two, or possibly three distribution strategies can be applied at the same time.

HYBRID STRATEGIES AND SITUATIONS

hybrid variety   Naturally, a hybrid variety has its advantages and disadvantages. We speak of a hybrid variety between multi-site and multi-service if a service provider directs his activities at different market segments and has various outlets at his disposal. The great advantage of this hybrid variety is, of course, the extended market coverage. If a service provider has more than one branch, it is only natural that it, and its service can cover a larger sales area. The possible disadvantage of this hybrid variety is the risk to the organization of losing part of its identity. Part of its recognizability or its profile may be lost. Being well known for offering a wide variety of financial services to a large number of market segments via many branches may be a strong feature of a bank's image and service quality. On the other hand, this way of operationalizing the bank's market orientation may create quite a diffuse image as well, since it is not focussing on anything in particular. Many banks have to find the balance between these two options, or reorganize, as the case on the Belgian Kredietbank illustrated.

Quite often, service providers who have chosen a particular positioning via their multi-site or multi-service strategy are further tempted to develop their business. Adding new sites or services to the existing ones may be detrimental to the existing image. For service providers with a clear cut position in the mind of their target group (e.g. McDonald's), this may end in a much vaguer and consequently less recognizable formula by increasing the number of services ("product line") for a multi-site company. Starting from the other side of the spectrum, a company that is recognized in the market as a multi-service company wants to increase its outlets in an attempt to increase profits. By doing so it has to make hefty investments because these companies are typically "resource" or "information" based. The question now will be can these investments be covered by the additional outlets? In the case of EuroDisney, we have seen that the start-up period, in terms of number of visitors (paying an attractive entrance fee for the company and spending reasonably during their visit) was extremely long in comparison with the Disney's in America and Japan. It means that in both these instances developments may cause problems to the multisite company, because of its natural tendency to add services (and therefore to create a diffused image) and to the multi-service as it is tempted to invest in new locations (by doing so it invests too heavily and offers lower than expected returns). As a final consequence, both companies may eventually disappear if they are not really aware of what is happening/might happen. Sasser has called this the danger of the Bermuda Triangle.[10] In Figure 13-4, we have shown this process towards an imaginary Bermuda Triangle for McDonald's and Disney.

danger of the Bermuda Triangle

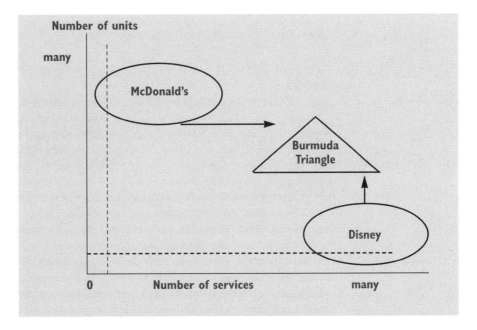

Figure 13-4
Multisite
multiservice

The hybrid variety between multi-site and multi-service can be observed also in the general banks. These offer a broad assortment of services at hundreds of locations all over the country for many of their clients. On the other hand, a specific clientèle, namely the affluent citizens in many of the rich countries, threatens to opt for small, specialized private banks, where people are still treated as individuals instead of simply becoming account numbers. A relatively small bank meeting this challenge is the Chicago based Northern Trust bank. They have followed their "snowbird-customers", and now have 22 branches operating in Florida. "We're not a big retail bank", says chairman William Osborne, 49. "We're not into credit cards; we're not a big investment banking operation." ... We have a very focussed business strategy compared to most financial situations, it focusses on two main businesses: personal and private banking, and providing investment services to retirement plans and institutions."

Service practice 13-4 The bank as a hybrid, or focussed animal[11]

Northern Trust went to Florida simply "...by following its clients as they sought to escape frigid winters. Starting in the 1970s it moved into Florida and

Arizona, home-away-from-home for many of the bank's wealthy Chicago customers. In the late 1980s the bank rolled into Texas and California, where it started trust operations, acquired banks and set up branches downtown in Dallas and Los Angeles and in wealthy suburbs like Park Cities and Newport Beach. Now Northern plans to try its luck in the Northeast in pursuit of the Forbes Four Hundred crowd."

Networks

The servuction process differs per service industry. Therefore, some services require a physical outlet to be produced, while others do not (e.g. providing information via computer networks or telephone), consequently offering the possibility of remote *network based service* service delivery. In this respect, we can think of network based service businesses as *businesses* "those that deliver a significant portion of their value to their customers by transporting people, goods, or information from any entry point on a network to any exit point."[12] The weakest network businesses are those where most of the value to customers arises from physical outlets, like many retail chains; the strongest network businesses are those where the links between the outlets are crucial to deliver the service, like telecommunications and Internet businesses. Consumers may use a *use a network* network in different ways. Some may use just one branch of a bank or food retailer (in their neighborhood) while others use many branches of the same bank or retailer in various cities (or even countries). Information technology now makes it possible to trace consumer behavior and see which branches they use and when. This can be used as research into decisions about the proper number and coverage of outlets, and types of multiple channels used.

In essence, three usage patterns can be distinguished: zero concentration; zone *zero concentration* concentration; and lane concentration. Zero concentration is when in the aggregate customers use a network truly at random. Even if they do not use all the links in the system, what consumers really value is the general connectivity of the entire network. *separate zones of* It makes strategic sense to think of the network as separate zones of concentrated use *concentrated use (zone* (zone concentration) when large numbers of customers concentrate their usage in *concentration)* some portion or portions of the network. For instance, customers in a given area tend to concentrate the use of ATMs according to a common pattern. This may be the case in a suburban area or in a particular shopping mall, where – as in Gothenburg, Sweden, for instance – many ATMs are located in one shopping centre. The use of these machines may be even increased when they do not only dole out 100 Kroner notes or $20 dollar bills, but also sell stamps, print up checks, or even watch your back (increasing the feeling of safety).[13] In lane concentration, customers use or value greatly individual links in a network, as in telephone services. Although customers need and value universal connectivity, they make certain calls with notable frequency.

In assessing the relevance and performance of an outlet it is important to define the outlet's function in the network precisely: what pattern of concentration holds for this particular outlet in attracting and keeping customers.

MORE ON THE RELATIONSHIP BETWEEN CORPORATE STRATEGY AND DISTRIBUTION STRATEGY

Figure 13-2 shows that the objectives of an organization form the input for the distribution goals, whereas these are determining the distribution strategy and the choice of location. In Chapter Seven, we discussed, among other things, the organization's objective of expansion and the ensuing growth strategies of Ansoff, containing the combinations of new and existing services/markets as a direction for growth. The penetration strategy (existing market, existing service) often demands an increased coverage of the distribution network. This increase can be accomplished through selective or intensive distribution. The multi-site strategy, which should lead to improved distribution due to opening several outlets, is the logical option for strategic distribution. The development of services need not, *per se*, have consequences for the number of establishments. This strategy may well be executed from one location only. It will then lead to the offering of more services, or to a multi-service strategy.

When Bateson's three distribution strategies are coupled to Ansoff's well-known growth matrix, then the relationship as depicted in Figure 13-5 emerges. This also shows the link between the distribution strategy and the opted for location. The multi-site strategy demands new choices of location, whereas multi-segment and multi-service do not. In the latter case, a new location is only required if the strategy is applied in a hybrid form with multi-site. Market innovation in the form of internationalization, with a new branch being opened abroad, is therefore a hybrid form of multi-site and multi-segment. If there is any element of the forms being hybrid, then diversification may occur.

link between the distribution strategy and the opted for location

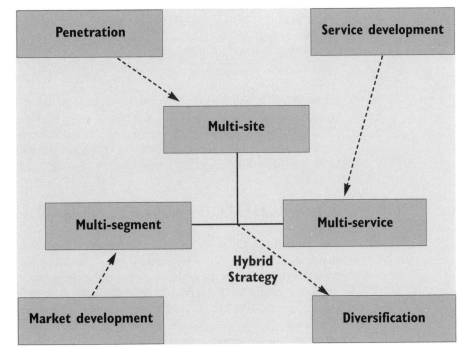

Figure 13-5
Distribution strategy

New distribution strategies can be planned by a company. Whether they are implemented is a completely different story. This not only depends on the skills, knowledge, experience, financial resources and laws/restrictions, but also on what competitors do or allow one to do. For instance, American Express wanted to use more and other distribution channels (banks) than the existing one (direct mail). MasterCard and Visa blocked this plan, as the next Service practice shows.

Service practice 13-5 Let the credit cards compete [14]

If you called your bank (in America in 1996) and asked for an American Express or Discover credit card, you'd be told to go elsewhere. Virtually all the 6,500 banks nationwide that issued credit cards belong to the Visa or MasterCard associations, and the handful of big banks that controlled these groups had collaborated to eliminate unwanted competition (by issueing a bylaw forbidding members to offer American Express or Discover cards to their customers in the USA; thus creating a limit on customer choice for financial services).

American Express, Discover and other potential credit card companies wanted to have the opportunity to offer their services through banks. These restrictions in the credit card arena contradicted the principle of open markets and price competition.

Consumers see banks as providers of financial services, and banks are delighted to encourage one-stop shopping. However, today's constricted choice of credit cards, which are arguably the average American's most important retail credit tool, is hardly consistent with the image of a "financial supermarket" brimming over with a broad selection of competing products. And as consumers take advantage of the increasing conveniences available through their bank accounts – from debit cards to home banking on the Internet – the ultimate scope of this non-competitive arrangement could be astonishing.

A completely different example refers to CitiBank in Japan in the early nineties.[15] CitiBank started a "mini-revolution" in Japanese retail banking in 1994 by having 60 ATMs available and operating 24 hours a day. This has contributed to a huge increase in their customer base, since Japanese banks did not offer that service. (These 60 ATMs were the only ones in the whole country offering this service at that time.)

13.5 THE CHOICE OF LOCATION

If clients come to the service provider, the physical surroundings in which they will then find themselves plays a role in their (subjective) assessment of the service. But the impact of a location goes further. Not only the client, but also the service provider can benefit from a healthy service environment. Just imagine what will happen when airports get crowded because of the large number of passengers and airplanes, in the near future. Delays will increase and overall travel satisfaction will decrease.[16] The

service environment

importance of the service environment, therefore, depends on:

- who is present in this environment; and
- how complex is the environment.[17]

impact of the physical environment

In choosing a location, one should also look at the impact of the physical environment on the client and the service provider. All this and more should be taken into account when selecting a particular spot/location.

WHO IS PRESENT IN THE ENVIRONMENT?

Three categories of presence can be considered here: clients travelling, personal interaction and distance services. In fact, this corresponds to the question of who goes to whom, except for the fact that here the presence in the service environment is taken into account.

clients travel

personal interaction

interpersonal services
distance services

If clients travel to the service provider there are two possibilities. One of these is that they may end up in an environment with mainly clients being present. Participation in the servuction process is probably high and will create a self-service facility. The other possibility looks at the personal interaction. If there are direct contacts between client and service provider and they are both present in the environment, then we speak of interpersonal services. A particular kind of services can be labelled as distance services: services where, prior to delivery, a certain distance must be travelled. The service is delivered at the client's home, or there is no contact between the provider and the client.

HOW COMPLEX IS THE PHYSICAL ENVIRONMENT?

complexity

Here, the criterion is formed by the question to what extent an environment has to possess any specific features or requirements. As more demands are put into an environment, its complexity increases. Examples of complex service environments are hospitals, airports, head offices of several professional services, or specific outside facilities where a service is provided (golf course, surf beach). For that reason, a golf course has a high degree of complexity. For, not every site is suitable for a golf course because playing the game of golf requires specific features of the environment. A rubbish-dump, on the other hand, is much less complex. Here, possible social inconvenience plays a role, although the site itself will always meet requirements. Nowadays, environmental provisions will have to be taken into account. Other non-complex environments are the barber or the dry-cleaner.

THE INFLUENCE ON THE CLIENT AND THE SERVICE PROVIDER

Figure 13-6 can help in clarifying the influence of both the physical environment and the location of the client and the service provider. It hardly needs any explanation that the environment of a self-service facility must be fine-tuned to the client, whereas the environment where the client is not present should be fine-tuned to the staff. Tensions will rise where client and staff meet. When furnishing a sick-room in a hospital one should take into account the patient's comfort and satisfaction and also the productivity and job satisfaction of the staff.

Figure 13-6
Service environments
with respect to
distribution

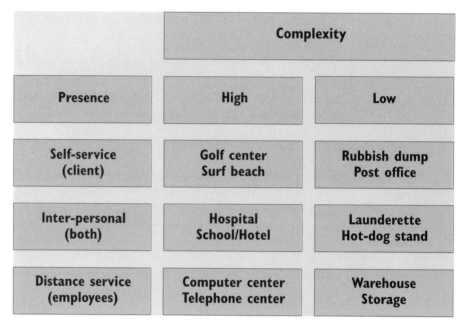

	Complexity	
Presence	**High**	**Low**
Self-service (client)	**Golf center Surf beach**	**Rubbish dump Post office**
Inter-personal (both)	**Hospital School/Hotel**	**Launderette Hot-dog stand**
Distance service (employees)	**Computer center Telephone center**	**Warehouse Storage**

servicescape

Physical environments (servicescape) can evoke extreme positive or negative reactions from clients and service providers.[18] Service providers work harder and have longer hours and also become more involved when the environment is right. Naturally, the opposite is also possible. Similar extremes of behavior can be observed with clients. They can spend more/less, be more/less loyal or even positive/negative in their comments when the environment or the location is pleasing/disappointing. Therefore, the service environment obviously plays a decisive role. This is taken to such lengths that customers even consider people who work in a top location to be more skilful than colleagues who are working elsewhere in more modest locations.

functional quality

This can be partly explained by the technical, functional and relational quality. The "how" or the functional quality is also determined by the environment. The "how" is not only then reflected on the client, but the service provider's confidence may also increase because of the top location. This will be one of the main reasons why professional service providers like to establish themselves at top locations that are owned or rented. For instance, Regus offers fully furnished, staffed and equipped offices worldwide at top locations. On the other hand, it may also be necessary to switch to simple locations or even mobile locations to serve certain target groups best. This will depend on the strategy chosen, the target group of clients selected and their mobility. An example is given in Service practice 13-6.

Service practice 13-6 Banks go mobile to service low-income areas [19]

Some banks have hit the road to serve low-income residents and improve customer relationships. Huntington National Bank opened the Mobile Banking Center, a custom-built 38-foot-long vehicle, to serve low-to-middle income neighborhoods in Cincinnati (USA). The branch helps customers open deposit accounts and apply for loans and mortgages. It also has two enhanced automated teller machines, including one that can cash a check. The branch needs only two full-time personal bankers. The unit covers a different neighborhood each day, Tuesday through to Thursday, hitting the same locations at the same time each week to establish consistency. On weekends the branch is used as a promotional vehicle at special events throughout Ohio. The unit has already helped more than 600 people open new accounts.

Carl McCrary, mobile banking office manager for Huntington, said the mobile branch is part of the community center banking (CCB) program, which works through churches to offer services to the community. While many middle-class people are accustomed to traditional banking, a segment of low to middle-income people are more likely to use a currency exchange to cash a check. "These are communities that have been underserved by banks in general. Some [residents] have never been to banks," said McCrary. "The biggest part of the education is getting them comfortable with banking."

Mobile branches started as a way for banks to meet some of the requirements of the federal Community Reinvestment Act (CRA). The CRA was enacted in 1977 to make sure banks served the needs of all of their communities and not to intentionally exclude low-income areas. Banks are graded based on the service they provide, and the amount of loans given to low- middle-income families and this plays a significant role in determining the grade.

SITE SELECTION

The literature on retail management pays a great deal of attention to developing a retail location strategy. The basics of selecting a store site can also be applied to selecting the location of a travel agency, a bank, a hospital, a university, etc. The marketing strategy chosen is the starting point for the decisions about three issues relevant to the spatial environment where the services will be delivered/distributed. These are the regional analysis, the areal analysis and the site evaluation itself. [20]

regional analysis

The regional analysis refers to "the identification of regional markets such as cities, towns, and metropolitan areas in which to locate new" service outlets. Regional variations in demand are considered here. Since the competitive environment may differ spatially, the

areal analysis

evaluating the site

areal analysis "focusses on the immediate area surrounding potential sites". The emphasis should be on the characteristics of the target group of clients or customers. Finally, evaluating the site "focusses on the characteristics of the sites at which a new store may be located. The characteristics of each site are analyzed in detail with respect to traffic flow, access patterns, compatibility, and terms of occupancy." Indexes of buying power or saturation (e.g. how many outlets already exist) may be applied here, next to the potential of the market and the competitive situation, in order to forecast the sales of a particular outlet.

trade area

trade area estimation
primary trading area
secondary area

Trade areas determine potential sales. A trade area can be defined here as the geographic area from which the service provider draws its customers and clients. So, the first step in forecasting sales for any outlet or branch is the trade area estimation. Here, we can distinguish between the primary trading area (the area closest to the service outlet accounting for the majority of the customers) and the secondary area (the rest). The trade area size depends to a large extent on the willingness of customers and clients to travel to the service outlet (if any). Information about this aspect of consumer behavior must be present, for instance, via analyzing where clients live, how easily they can travel to the outlet, the outlet's accessibility, etc.

analog method

regression analysis

Several techniques can be applied to forecast sales of new service outlets. We will mention three of them: the analog method; regression analysis; and the spatial interaction models. The analog method forecasts sales by studying sales, profits, consumer behavior, service quality and the like in a similar outlet in a similar environment. The results are then transferred to this new outlet and used as a basis for forecasting the sales, etc. of the new outlet. A second method is based on regression analysis. Here, regression methods quantify the relationship between an outlet's sales and the factors determining these sales. Data of quite a large number of outlets are needed to count for reliable outcomes. Sales or other indicators of an outlet's performance are considered to be the dependent variable in these equations, while all the other variables are labelled as the explanatory variables. Service practice 13-7 lists some of the store, site, and trade area characteristics commonly found to be related to sales.

spatial interaction models

attraction of the service outlet

The attractiveness of a store or a service unit as such is another important issue in the image of a service provider, determining whether customers will enter this branch or another one. This is especially true in situations where customers can choose from a number of branches within a small neighborhood (like a shopping mall with various supermarkets). Third, spatial interaction models can be used. These models are also known as gravity models. These models forecast the sales the service outlet is expected to generate from different parts of the trade area. They view trade areas to be probabilistic rather than deterministic. This means these models assume customers may visit several service outlets, but with different probabilities. Here, the attraction of the service outlet (e.g. a supermarket) to the customers relative to all other relevant service outlets (e.g. supermarkets in the evoked set of the customer) is a crucial variable to be measured in order to forecast sales of the trade area. Service practice 13-8 contains an example of how the mathematical formula of such a relative attractiveness may look like when applied to retail stores.

Service practice 13-7 Some store, site, and trade area characteristics used in regression models [21]

> *Store characteristics*
> > Store size
> > Size of frontage
> > Number of employees
> > Level of advertising and promotion
>
> *Site characteristics*
> The site characteristics used in regression models vary depending on whether the store is located in a mall or is freestanding.

Mall location
        Size of mall
        Number and type of anchor of the mall
        Sales of the mall
        Number of direct competitors within the mall
        Proximity to main entrance, food court, or center court of mall
Freestanding site
        Visibility
        Traffic flow
        Proximity to major roadway/intersection

Trade area characteristics
        Total population and age composition
        Household or per-capita income
        Employment characteristics
        Percent who own (rent) home
        Average property value
        Life-style characteristics

*Service
practice
13-8
Relative
attractiveness
of a store*[22]

The probability of a consumer visiting a particular store equals the ratio of the consumer's attraction for that store to the sum of the attraction of all competing stores of that type in the area. In other words:

$$P_{ij} = \frac{Attraction\ of\ store\ j}{\Sigma\ attraction\ of\ all\ stores\ in\ the\ area}$$

where P_{ij} is the probability of consumer i shopping at Store j. Since the attraction of a store is given by S^a_j / D^b_{ij}, the probability of shopping at a particular store can be formally expressed as:

$$P_{ij} = \frac{\left(\dfrac{S^a_j}{D^b_{ij}}\right)}{\sum\limits_{j=1}^{n}\left(\dfrac{S^a_j}{D^b_{ij}}\right)}$$

where
    S = the size of store j
    D_{ij} = the distance or travel time between consumer i and store j
    n = the number of competing stores in the area

    a = a parameter reflecting the consumer's sensitivity to store size
    b = a parameter reflecting the consumer's sensitivity to distance or travel time

The symbol Σ indicates summation. The denominator of the formula sums the attraction of all competing stores in the area.

ATMOSPHERICS

atmospherics

The attractiveness of servicescapes contributes to service quality, not only with its physical outlook but also with the atmospherics created.[23] Atmospherics are the psychological effects or feelings created by any service outlet's design and its physical surroundings.[24] Especially in services with a high degree of experience and credence attributes, the atmospherics can be used as a proxy for service quality. Atmospherics can also be used as a way to differentiate from competitors. Since it has to do with the how and why of service quality, it may be decisive in service quality, for the tangibles (clothes, cars, etc.) may be clear and more or less comparable between competitors. Atmospherics may help to convert behavioral intentions into actual buying behavior and serve as an attention- and message-creating medium in which a service provider expresses various core values to potential and actual customers as a basis for service outlet and/or brand choice decisions. The brand name of the service provider, for instance a store or bank, may also contribute to creating atmospherics and atmospherics affect store patronage behavior to a large extent.[25] Effects or emotional responses induced by the servicescapes are primary determinants of the extent to which individual consumers may spend beyond their original plans.[26] A feeling of contentment and arousal of the senses, created by atmospherics are especially decisive factors in this respect. Levi Strauss used this knowledge when redesigning its shops and creating the new Original Levi's Stores.

Service practice 13-9 The Original Levi's Store

The plans for redesigning each Levi's store state: each Original Levi's Store will be individually designed to maximize the potential of its location and to ensure the right mix of contemporary and heritage expressions of the brand. The European design is flexible yet focussed, creating contrasts in product presentation, colour, materials, mood and lighting. The stores will be zoned, each zone is designed to give the consumer a mix of visual and emotional experience.

The atmospherics add to the service outlet's image. This can be defined as "the way the service outlet is defined in the customer's mind, partly by technical, functional and relational qualities and partly by an aura of psychological attributes".[27]

The image of service outlets are shaped by many factors above and beyond brand images. This is especially true in retailing where atmospherics play an important role. Some outlets like the Rainforest Café apply a new concept like retail entertainment in creating a positive atmosphere.

13.6 INNOVATIONS IN DISTRIBUTION

The ultimate goal of choosing a location and determining a distribution strategy is a simple one, namely to be able to actually deliver the service effectively and efficiently. Strategy and the choice of location become irrelevant if the organization is not able to translate this into action. A service does not have any value until it reaches the client at the right time. In view of this interest and the increasing competition, for example, several new distribution forms and tendencies have emerged over the past decennium. We will now discuss some of them: customer service; franchising; the Internet; call centers; JIT in the service industry; co-makership; and relationship marketing.

CUSTOMER SERVICE

interface between marketing and logistics, customer service

The interface between marketing and logistics arouses a great deal of interest from the business world.[28] Within this context, customer service relates to all factors and elements influencing the process of making the service available. As far as goods are concerned, customer service can be considered as an additional service attached to the core product. Within the service world, customer service is part of the delivery, transportation and distribution issue and may be regarded as the logistical side of the process.

Customer service not only involves the timely delivery of a service. Flexibility (in the case of rush orders), swiftness and reliability play an equally significant role. Customer service aspires to satisfy the clients' wishes as far as the availability of goods is concerned. Within the service provision, so it seems, this is easier said than done. Clients' wishes may differ greatly. Wishes, and the quality of the service, are not only measured on the basis of the actual performance but more on how the performance was perceived. In a particular industry, a short term delivery is an important aspect, whereas in another reliability is paramount, with a less significant role attributed to the term of delivery. It is essential, therefore, to regard customer service in terms of "various service/market combinations, each with their own specific requirements". Thus, every service/market combination will need to be analyzed individually in order to be able to execute a customized

effective customer service policy

service policy. The three starting-points for an effective customer service policy are: as a firm, define an overall philosophy on customer service in terms of desired attitude, organization and responsibilities; develop internal customer-service standards, which must be quantifiable and thus provide measurable costs and revenues. In this way, it is possible to develop the most cost-effective policy for every service/market segment and inform the clients about the customer-service level they are bound to expect.

quality and availability

pre-transaction transaction bound

Quality, availability and price appear to be the essentials that lead to a transaction agreement. Quality and availability are the most important issues determining customer service. Here, a distinction between pre-transaction, transaction and post-transaction elements can be made. Pre-transaction elements have to do with the suppliers' image, terms of delivery, problem solving capacity, accessibility, etc. Transaction bound elements can be, for instance, freshness of the product, reliability in delivery, assistance when installing the product for the customer and training the customer. Post-

post-transaction

transaction elements are, for instance, complaint handling, repairing defects, delivery of spare parts and installing the spare parts.

performance in customer service

Performance in customer service can be measured via such criteria as level of stocks, flexibility, tracking and tracing orders, time needed between ordering and actual delivery, quality of this type of service, etc.

Many firms that have been performing their logistics themselves are now outsourcing this kind of activity to transportation firms who specialize in this business. Some of them even take over the whole wharehousing function. Therefore, this part of the business to business services sector is growing. New developments in information technology resulting in electronic data interchange (EDI) and efficient consumer response (ECR) now offer these possibilities to manufacturers (especially those of fast moving consumer goods), retailers and transportation firms.

FRANCHISING

franchising

The multi-site strategy can be implemented, amongst others, via franchising. Franchising is a form of commercial cooperation laid down by contract, in which one party, the franchisor or the franchise provider, confers a number of rights on one or more other parties (the franchisee or franchise holder). The franchisee, for example, can obtain the right to use the franchisor's trade name, brand and/or other means of distinction during the sale of services (or goods). The franchise provider, however, does determine the marketing concept in advance, including any additional conditions the delivery must comply with. In exchange for the rights, the franchisee pays a certain fee. It is important to note that in this form of cooperation the franchise provider controls the way the rights are used, in order to guarantee a uniform presentation towards the public as well as an equivalent service quality. In brief, frachising boils down to selling a succesful basic formula to someone else who, subsequently, starts his own establishment. In fact, it is a multi-site strategy in which another person is liable for a part of the investment and risk.

strategic flexibility

The success of franchising is brought about by the strategic flexibility of this form of distribution. The formula can be applied both ways, i.e. when opting for an offensive strategy or for a defensive strategy.

offensive strategy

An offensive strategy can be aimed at economies of scale, growth in new or existing domestic market segments or internationalization. On an international level, franchising is regarded as (one of) the most succesful strategie(s) enabling a service provider to enter a new country. For this reason, this entry strategy is applied frequently by the international service provider. The international consumer is prepared to make a quicker choice when confronted with a known brand which guarantees a certain quality level. The motives which can lead to a defensive strategy and the application of the franchise concept must be attributed particularly to protection of the market share and more control of the distribution channel. In many countries, we see a growth in well-known service providers who are succesful franchise operators, like McDonald's, Domino Pizza, Benetton and Holiday Inn. A franchise strategy is also often used when service providers enter foreign markets that are geographically or culturally distant. The risks of entering such a country can then be diminished by applying a franchising strategy, especially when local management is hired.

THE INTERNET

Internet

The Internet has a communication and a distribution function; hence it may change communication and distribution patterns in a fundamental way. The opportunities the electronic highway offers are supposed to be enormous. The future will tell whether this really is the case.

new way to communicate

two-way-communication

Companies having their offer and other information on the Internet, World Wide Web and the like, can use this as a new way to communicate with their present and prospective customers. The shop, service outlet or traditional media like TV, newspapers, flyers or magazines are no longer the only vehicles that have to be used to that end. Now, computer systems open up the way to two-way-communication (when customers have all the necessary equipment at home and are able, willing and motivated to use it).

distribution

In terms of distribution, it means that customers do not have to come to the shop or service outlet anymore. It may even mean that intermediary institutions like brokers, importers, wholesalers, agencies and retailers become obsolete. The whole issue will become even more contentious when virtual shopping becomes a greater reality. Then, shopping and being served at a distance will become true for most if not all products. Today, many examples exist for teleshopping in the food business and the – what we use to call – mail order houses. Amazon.com is, at present, the world's largest book store, not via outlets but via the Internet. The Internet provides more and new opportunities here. To some extent, the Internet encourages disintermediation.

As indicated in our chapter on consumer behavior, in the context of the Internet, consumers must be motivated, willing and capable of using the Internet for their information gathering and buying decisions. They will also make a comparison between the benefits and costs of their traditional activities to collect information and make buying decisions as against the Internet.

Service practice 13-10 Trade-offs in using the Internet [29]

In an experimental study about the perceptions of new banking services (e.g. home banking, for instance via the Internet), new distribution methods (the delivery vehicle) and the relationship between the two in Australia, it appeared that "consumer consideration of home shopping (and in particular home banking) and other high technology telecommunications products depends on three factors:

- relative advantages or benefits of the delivery vehicle;
- relative advantage of the banking service; and
- compatibility (the congruence between the two)."

It seemed that "the relative advantage of innovative telecommunications media (i.e distribution methods) is yet to be established" and "that home banking services have to spend more effort in explaining the link between PCs and operating savings accounts relative to that put into getting the PC as a distribution vehicle" in Australia.

The link between the service and the distribution method and their respective benefits or utilities to the customer seems to be decisive in accepting these innovations in distribution.

CALL CENTERS

call centers

Call centers are a means to make interactive marketing more concrete. In general, call centers are independent companies or departments of a company taking care of the incoming and outgoing telephone contacts and direct contacts between a firm and its customers in a well-structured way.

These contacts may hinge upon providing information, solving complaints, or serve as a means of maintaining relations with customers. Sometimes, they work for a company in a particular country, sometimes they take care of all these contacts for several (or many) companies working internationally. In essence, firms outsource these activities to call centers. The international form of a call center, providing these telephone services to many firms in many countries, calls for highly educated and well-trained people performing these jobs. It appears that the number of languages spoken in a particular country is a competitive advantage of such a country to attract call centers. Mercedes Benz founded a call center as part of their Customer Assistance Center in Maastricht, The Netherlands. Within two years, 500 employees worked there, serving customers in 70 countries and speaking 12 languages. Service practice 13-11 shows what is going on in a call center in the airline industry.

Service practice 13-11 Call center of excellence [30]

The Sabena inflight magazine contains an article about a new call center operating for several airlines. It says:

"As the telecommunications business gears up for the 21st century, call centers have become increasingly important to the European travel industry. A call center is the focal point where all calls – local and long-distance – are received. We at Sabena and our partners are using this technology in Germany in a way that is unique in the airline industry.

With Swissair and Austrian Airlines, we have set up a company in Frankfurt to handle all calls, whether straight from the customer or the travel industry, for reservations and information. Called Service Line, the center became operational on July 1, 1996.

> Why is the center unique? Because it is one-third owned by each of the partners and because the specially recruited staff are trained by each of the three airlines. This means that each employee is familiar with all the products of Sabena, Swissair and Austrian Airlines and can answer your questions no matter which of the three you call. Being employed by an independent company also means that employees feel impartial and not obliged to sell more of one airline's seats than another."

> Service Line is open longer than the usual reservation offices and it frees the staff at regional offices to make more sales visits. The call center also operates for daughter companies like Crossair and Tyrolean Airways. Plans exist to make the services available to other carriers as well and to operate on a 24-hour basis.

> "Service Line is managed by Margit Reimann, who joined the company from Swissair, and is operated by a staff of 20, shortly expected to rise to 25."

JIT IN THE SERVICE SECTOR

Just-In-Time principle supplier

In the beginning of the eighties, a new management philosophy became popular on both sides of the Atlantic, inspired by the success of Japanese industry. The principle was to minimize stock costs by decreasing regular stocks and by imposing more stringent terms of delivery. This philosophy became successful in the manufacturing industry and proved to be advantageous to service providers also. The service provider is able to apply the Just-In-Time principle in two directions: traditionally to the input supplier and specifically to the client of one's own service.

timely delivery of raw materials

The first mode of application will be fairly obvious. Many service providers use tangible goods when producing the service. Thus, JIT may be applicable when these "raw materials" are bought. The timely delivery of these raw materials can minimize procurement prices. In addition to this, one can strive to improve input materials, or the achievement of zero-defects may be desirable (no loss of materials bought).

appointments made are kept on time

In order to make the JIT principle work for the client, it is essential that appointments made are kept on time. This principle must work if the required consumer participation during the servuction process is bigger, rather than smaller. A late delivery will immediately cause waiting times and costs for the consumer. As seen from the service-providing matrix point of view (Chapter Two), the necessity to make JIT deliveries grows when three features are found to be present to a larger degree: the service is performed by people (to the average consumer, having to wait for a cash dispenser is perceived as less irritating than having to wait an equal amount of time at a counter); the service is aimed at people and the service can only be provided with the consumer being present (this required presence makes the consumer aware of what delays are like); and custom-made services must certainly be delivered on time (delays will lead to negative perceptions of quality).

Service
practice
13-12
JIT at the
amusement
park

Amusement parks do not have an infinitely large capacity. By managing the influx of visitors, they can try to optimize the number of these visiting the restaurant and reduce the rush in attractions by guiding the visitor along set routes. There are camera systems to monitor and relay any bottlenecks quickly to make adequate reactions possible. Here, without knowing it, consumers themselves see to it that they arrive at their destination "just in time". They maximize their own entertainment, whereas the amusement park is able to accomplish a full-capacity occupancy without any undesirably long waits.

CO-MAKERSHIP

co-makership

Co-makership can be described as a long-term cooperation between the supplier and the client based on mutual trust. However, not every form of cooperation immediately becomes a form of co-makership. One could say that the issue of co-makership is present if the relationship is marked by a certain degree of cooperation and integration concerning logistics (in which the just-in-time principle, in particular, is often mentioned); quality (these arrangements should lead to the delivery of the correct goods and services); and development (in the field of know-how when developing the final good/service).

Co-makership is relatively important in business to business services. The ultimate goal of co-makership is to improve the competitive position of both parties. This is in their mutual interest – doing things together. Partly, co-makership is the result of out-sourcing activities.

In principle, services form fertile soil for long-term cooperation in the form of co-makership. The basic principle of production and consumption, being inseparable during the interactive consumption, already implies the necessity of cooperation. The client's desire for more quality combined with more comfort cannot be achieved without long-term cooperation. This cooperation results in or must result, in the end, in a certain degree of cooperation based on a continuous relationship.

cooperation based on a
continuous
relationship

An important aspect here is that both parties consider each other as equal partners in the relationship, and that the number of cooperating partners that can be labelled as co-makers stays within limits. A certain degree of exclusivity will be appreciated by both parties. For example, a software company seconding personnel to a large institution over a long period has clear advantages above other colleagues. These are, for instance, lower costs – due to improved coordination; improved quality control (personnel has been informed about company procedures); more possibilities for product differentiation; and confidence in supply and distribution.

exclusivity

In fact, co-makership is a form of contracting-out (outsourcing). Co-makership can also be described as a form of (commercial) enterprise in which one does not focus on short-term sales or transactions, but on long-term cooperation.

RELATIONSHIP MARKETING

relationship marketing

Relationship marketing is geared to create ongoing relationships between suppliers and clients. The term "ongoing" means that the continuation of the relationship has priority. The service outlet plays an important role in keeping the customer. The importance of keeping the relationship often increases when the service tends to become custom-made. However, the fact is that not every contact the service provider of a custom-made service engages in will benefit, by definition, from such a long-term vision. Many contacts are a one-off occurrence. Signing a mortgage-deed at a notary-public or having an undertaker arrange a funeral is such a rare occurrence that for most entrepreneurs maintaining continuous relationships with the ultimate consumer is not profitable. For many standard services (salary accounts, telephone services), we can speak of a continuous relationship. Generally speaking, supplier and client benefit from relationship marketing provided the market satisfies the following conditions:

- changing to a different supplier or client brings about high switching costs; and
- the market is unstable, which is accompanied by a high degree of insecurity.

The ultimate goal of this intensive form of contact is to increase loyalty and retention, to improve the quality of the service and distribution during the process and by realizing permanent and fairly intensive relationships between suppliers and clients.[31]

ACCEPTING TECHNOLOGICAL INNOVATIONS IN DISTRIBUTING SERVICES

success or failure of technological innovations in distributing services

In Chapter Eleven, we mentioned a few reasons why innovations in service might succeed or fail. Many of those innovations have to do with the way in which services are distributed. That is why we will have a closer look at some of the reasons for success or failure of technological innovations in distributing services. In many cases, these innovations substitute human labor by machinery or new, automated procedures working without or with less personnel than before.

"negative consumer behavior"

A number of direct and indirect causes can be given why consumers do not accept a particular innovation of a high technological nature in the distribution of services.[32] This type of behavior may be called "negative consumer behavior" since consumers do not do what they are expected to do (at least, according to those who invented and applied the innovation).

direct causes
cognitive reasons

affective reasons

environmental reasons

Direct causes can be of a cognitive nature, an affective nature or due to the environment. Cognitive reasons may be, for instance, a perception of: lack of control; a higher risk; a lower self-efficacy; a greater effort to be made; or a longer waiting time. The affective reasons can be formulated as consumers feeling more lonely, having fear of an interaction with a machine, or, having a negative attitude towards dealing with a machine and preferring a person (because one likes to interact with people, or one does not want to contribute to increasing unemployment). Environmental reasons could be that the machine is out of order, that customers do not have the correct

indirect causes coins to pay, or that the machine is located in a dark or unfriendly spot. Indirect causes have to do with the supposed (or not supposed?) flexibility, complexity and reliability of the machine or new way of working. Also, past experiences contribute to accepting the innovation or not. Service practice 13-13 illustrates all this.

Service practice 13-13 Accepting innovations

In a joint French-Dutch research project with respect to the acceptance of machines selling railway tickets (instead of buying them at the counter), it appeared to be necessary to make a distinction between structural-non-users and incidental-non-users.

The structural-non-users found it easier to buy a ticket at the counter, favored personal contact with front-office employees, found machines a threat to employment, perceived a high risk that the machine would not work well, felt the machine could not be tailored to their specific needs and found the machine (and the queue) threatening to privacy.

The incidental-non-users mostly did not use the machine due to a lack of coins. (N.B. the machine worked only when coins or credit cards were used; banknotes could not be used.)

13.7 CORE, AUGMENTED, STANDARD AND CUSTOMIZED SERVICES

As in every chapter on the marketing mix in services, we will conclude with an application of the issues discussed in our typology of services. Our reasoning is summarized in Figure 13-7.

standard core services Standard core services often have a strong concept built around a core service and are quite easy to duplicate. Sometimes, they look like a commodity that must be available everywhere. This eases the way to growth and increases the (already high degree of) coverage. Often, cost-leadership in distributing the service (or at least low cost servuction processes) is needed here. This is partly possible because consumers have to travel; the burden of these costs is on them. Standardization is the issue. The choice of the location is important, since traffic must be present or easy to create. Easy accessibility to the consumer is a pre-requisite. Often, single-service/multi-site situations are the issue for these convenience services, being available via intensive distribution. Price competition will follow logically.

customized augmented services Customized augmented services are the opposite of the above standard core services. Here, exclusively tailor made core and additional services are offered via one or just a few locations. Quality and image are very important here. Key success factors will hinge upon communication, designing the servuction process, participation of the customer and expertise of the employees (personal relations). Often, the service provider travels to the customer, like the lawyer or the account manager of the bank. The services are very focussed on a specific target group of customers (like Northern Trust). Exclusive distribution of these "speciality" services is the issue. The total offering will often contain a bundle of specialized services offered from one or a few outlets: a multi-service/single-site (or just a very few sites) strategy is applied. Consequently, distribution coverage is low and the location choice is not the most important issue.

The other two types of service strategies are between these two extreme forms. In both cases, a kind of service differentiation is the issue via a selected number of outlets or the number of services offered (e.g. to escape from price competition). That determines the selectivity of the distribution of these "convenience and shopping services" (in the case of standard augmented services) and "shopping and speciality services" (in the case of customized core services).

One might expect the service provider to travel to the customer in the case of the customized core services. Then, a high degree of distribution coverage is not that necessary as is also the case with the exact choice of location. The opposite is probably the case for standard augmented services. Then, customers have to travel, in most cases, to the service provider, which needs, consequently, quite a high degree of distribution coverage; the decision about the exact location is then important.

Figure 13-7
Core, augmented,
standard and customized
services

Distribution	Standard core services	Core services	Standard augmented services	Augmented services
Interaction	customer travels	supplier travels	customer travels	supplier travels
Genetic strategy	low cost	differentiation	differentiation	focus
Distribution strategy	intensive distribution	selective distribution	selective distribution	exclusive distribution
Kind of service	convenience	shopping & speciality	convenience & shopping	speciality
Strategic alternatives	single-service/ multi-site	single-service/ single-site	multi-service/ multi-site	multi-service/ single-site
Distribution coverage	high	low	high	low
Choice of location	important	less important	important	less important

SUMMARY

The intangible nature of services raises some specific issues with respect to distributing services. This affects its contribution to creating value and excellent services in a particular way. On the one hand, the non-storability of services seems to cause a serious problem. On the other hand, the direct contact between customer and service provider can also be regarded as an opportunity since there is hardly any need to think about "storing services". In both cases, organizing the distribution of services is the central issue in this chapter. This can be transformed into the question of delivery of services, e.g. making them available at a particular place in the local environment, domestically or internationally. Usually, this place is a physical place. But even that common notion is challenged today. Changes in information technology offer opportunities to distribute services in such a way that the customer does not always need to be physically present in delivering services, nor the service provider. Especially in the delivery of services internationally, this may prove to be an attractive idea. In the distribution channel, intermediary institutions are not always necessary any longer. Many forms of direct and indirect distribution may occur simultaneously (and may be a source of potential conflict).

The organization's objectives (e.g about their market orientation) determine the specific distribution goals set. Naturally, distribution strategies can be categorized by the well known concepts of intensive, selective and exclusive distribution which hold for convenience, shopping and speciality services. This chapter also shows how this distinction can be applied to our typology of standard core services, standard augmented services, customized core services and customized augmented services. In turn, it was shown how this coincides with the distinction between single and multi-site, single and multi-service and single and multi-segment distribution strategies.

In practice, these purely strategic alternatives present themselves in a hybrid form. In Figure 13-5, these multi- and single-site, service and segment strategies are linked to the four service strategies that can be developed on the basis of the famous Ansoff-matrix. Penetration and multi-site are then combined, while service and market development strategies go along with multi-service strategies and, respectively, multi-segment strategies. Diversification occurs when a combination of these strategies is looked for. Changing positions in this figure can be dangerous when it results in creating a more diffuse image of the service provider that is not clear to the customer.

In distributing services, a company should answer the question "who travels to whom". The answer determines to a great extent the importance of the location decision to the service provider which, in turn, affects the final servicescape characteristics, especially the atmospherics. The analog method, regression analysis and spatial interaction models can be used to determine the actual spot where the service firm will have its outlet, given the strategic and distribution objectives. These methods can be used to forecast sales at particular locations for the new outlet.

Distributing services is a dynamic phenomenon. Innovations occur quite regularly in this area. They partly affect the "physical" part of the distribution function (availability) and partly the communication and information function of distributors/middlemen/intermediaries. Many of these innovations are based on new opportunities offered by information technology, as for instance Internet, call centers and customer service (as it is developed at the interface of marketing and logistics). This also leads to a new notion of the network-concept. Other innovations discussed refer to franchising, Just-In-Time deliveries, co-makership and relationship marketing. Not all consumers or customers accept immediately these innovations. The reasons for showing this "negative consumer behavior" can be labelled as having a cognitive, affective and/or environmental nature. Consumers must see the benefits of the new way of distribution and the links with the existing service.

QUESTIONS

1 What is so special about distributing services? In what way, if any, is this affected by (innovations in) information technology?
2 What makes the complexity of a service environment grow?
3 What kind of distribution strategies do exist? Why will hybrid forms emerge?
4 In what way are these distribution strategies linked to "coverage"?
5 What types of concentration can be found in various networks?
6 What factors determine the choice of a particular service outlet's location? How could such decisions about an excellent location be modelled?
7 Why are the servicescape and atmospherics important in determining service quality?
8 What reasons can be found to explain why innovations in distributing services are not accepted by customers?
9 What is the difference in distribution strategy between standard core services and customized augmented services?
10 In what way can the distribution strategy of Northern Trust be related to the two types of internationalization strategies to be applied by service firms (market seeking or client following)?

ASSIGNMENTS

1 Describe the concept of "co-makership" and position it in the classification matrices from Chapter Two.
2 What can be concluded when you compare Figures 13-5 and 13-7?
3 Make a comparison of the factors determining success and/or failure in new service development (as mentioned in Chapter Eleven) with the factors mentioned in this chapter for not accepting innovations in distributing services. What differences and similarities do you find? What do you conclude from this for getting new services well distributed and accepted by consumers?
4 Why would a market oriented service provider aiming at delivering excellent service quality start a call center (on its own or in cooperation with other firms)?
5 Relationship marketing has been discussed in this chapter with respect to distributing services. Add what has been said on that topic to what you knew about relationship marketing until now.
6 Search for service firms in your own country as excellent examples for the various positions in Figure 13-5. Why do they excel at distributing services?
7 Governmental services and services provided in (and by) your local city have to be distributed. How is this distribution organized? What shortcomings do exist? When would these services be provided in an excellent way? Does deregulation add to a better distribution and availability of these services?

Case: ON THE MOVE[33]

UTS Europe was founded in 1992 as a holding company, having UTS Germany, UTS Netherlands and North American Van Lines as its founding members. Members own shares in the organization. As of 1996, 74 companies from 16 European countries and North American Van Lines are the members. They have 110 locations in these European countries and over 800 agents in the USA and 200 in Canada. UTS is organized in regions and countries. It is a unique network of individual relocation service providers, servicing individual households as well as companies (for example, UTS is the mover for European moves of all employees of one of the biggest multi-nationals). The member companies are managed by their owners and, therefore, quality and care in daily performance are the focal point of their attention. The Board of UTS consists of one woman and eight men coming from Germany, Belgium, Scandinavia, The Netherlands, the United Kingdom and the United States of America. The main office responsible for the overall management is located in The Netherlands.

Companies that want to join the UTS group must be quality oriented and show commitment to providing top-class service to customers and UTS colleagues. Members have to adhere to the Operating Policy of UTS Europe and the Code of Conduct. UTS is certified by EN 29002, ISO 9002 and BS 5750. The main office is ISO 9001 certified, which includes the design and development of all systems, services and projects.

UTS Europe is the holding company, providing many services to its members. In this respect, the UTS computer network is of vital importance. It is used for planning, tracking and tracing all removals. It contributes to the flexibility and competitive strength of UTS. It avoids having trucks travel only partially loaded and offers the opportunity to find co-loads or return loads. In that way, trucks and crews are used more efficiently. Moreover, UTS offers its members an attractive insurance program and a recognizable house style. Also, a sophisticated, computerized program is available, ensuring timely payments between shareholders and generating substantial savings on bank charges. Moreover, UTS offers all kinds of innovations to its member companies, one of them being PROPAC.

PROPAC is a foam injected, high density container. The concept is simple. The local UTS company packs household goods into PROPAC containers at the origin address, and then transports the containers to the regional UTS terminal for transfer to the destination city. From there, a UTS company in the new city delivers the containers to the final address. The advantages of this system are, amongst others, exclusive use for the customer, guaranteed pick-up and delivery dates, less handling, easy to store, banded and sealed for security, no mixing up of smaller shipments, durable and environmentally friendly.

According to Cor Wismeijer, managing director of UTS Europe, the moving industry in Europe will face a lot of threats and opportunities over the next decade. Some of these challenges are:

- it will no longer be economical nor allowed by governments to transport goods over long distances (e.g 500 kilometers) by truck;
- transport by rail and water will become more important;
- imports of disposable materials will be restricted and expensive; and
- communication systems are important to plan, track and trace shipments.

In this environment, UTS has to accomplish its mission:
"UTS is an innovative international moving organisation built upon the talents of motivated people who work together in order to exceed client expectations. Our mission is to be totally committed to quality, achieve a sustainable competitive advantage and to earn lasting customer relationships."

QUESTIONS

1 In one of its brochures, UTS says: "The new and unique UTS network ensures that, wherever you are moving, we can provide the personal care and support you would expect from a local company, backed up by the stability, advanced technology and economies of scale that only a truly international organization can guarantee. Local knowledge combined with international experience, the best of both worlds, to offer our customers the smoothest of all possible moves."
   Explain whether UTS can make this claim come true.

2 To what extent does information technology allow UTS to deliver the services they intend to deliver?

3 Do you think UTS can manage differences in national cultures well in its organizational structure? Explain.

4 Do you think UTS is well equipped and prepared to meet the challenges of the next decade? Explain.

5 Search for UTS members in your home country; what are their strengths? If you do not have UTS members in your country, search for other movers and compare their way of working to UTS. What can you conclude from that comparison?

ENDNOTES

1. This Service practice is based largely on Rob Westgeest's MBA thesis, Maastricht University, 1995.

2. See for instance Chapter Ten on managing demand and supply. A recent overview is given by Bitran and Mondschein, 1997.

3. Probably this extreme situation is not realistic when the service provider has established long term relationships with the other organizations in the channel. This will depend partly on the kind of relationship management being practised between the middlemen and the service provider.

4. See for instance: Hudson in Wall Street Journal, June 1 1995; Quelch and Klein, 1996.

5. Such a conflict also occured amongst others in the struggle between Fidelity Mutual Funds and Charles Schwab, king of the discount brokers, who wanted to halt the selling of some of Fidelity's most popular funds like Magellan and Contrafund (see Wyatt, 1996).

6. We will discuss the impact of location choice more extensively in section 13.5.

7. Kehoe and Buckley, 1996.

8. Schrameyer, 1998 discusses Macropolis. He also indicates the founders of Macropolis will start a Europe wide consultancy agency on Internet retailing (for retailers who want to start Internet retailing). So, even Internet calls for new intermediaries.

9. Bateson, 1992.

10. Sasser, 1976

11. Samuels, 1996.

12. Coyne and Dye, 1998, p. 101. This section is based to a large extent on this Coyne and Dye article.

13. Guglielmo, 1996.

14. This Service practice is taken from Schumer's 1996 article.

15. Abrahams, 1994.

16. See an article in The Economist: Delays can be expected, July 27, 1996.

17. Bitner, 1992.

18. Bitner, 1992.

19. Rubel, 1995. It is remarkable to see that mobile banking is more or less outdated in Europe, while it is an innovation in the US to serve particular market segments better.

20. In his textbook on retail management, Ghosh, 1994, discusses retail location decisions extensively in Chapters Eight and Nine. Citations have been taken from pp. 249-313.

21. Ghosh, 1994, p. 303.

22. Ghosh, 1994, pp. 308-309.

23. This section is largely based on Jur Smit's, 1998, MBA-thesis.

24. This definition is based on Kotler, 1994 (and slightly adjusted).

25. Darden, Erdem and Darden, 1983; Baker, Grewal and Parasuraman, 1994.

26. Donovan, Rossiter and Nesdale, 1994.

27. This definition is based on Martineau, 1958, and Joyce and Lambert, 1996.

28. This section is heavily based upon Van Goor, 1992.

29. Morrison and Roberts, 1998.

30. This case is taken from Passport, the inflight Sabena Magazine, November 1996, p. 46.

31. More on store loyalty can be found in Reed, 1998; Reynolds, 1995; Macintosh and Lockshin, 1997; Diller, 1997. See also our previous discussions of relationhip marketing and brand loyalty.

32. This section is largely based on Karin Verschuren's MBA thesis, Maastricht University, 1996.

33. This case is based on FIDI speech by Cor Wismeijer, november 1995; Business Report 1995/1996; UTS brochures; Otto van de Vijver's article on UTS in ELAN, February 1995.

CHAPTER FOURTEEN

PRICING

This is the final chapter in our series on the marketing mix.
It is about pricing – the fifth instrument of the services
marketing mix; this will enable you to:

- *understand the relationship between an organization and pricing objectives;*

- *formulate a number of pricing objectives according to the type of organization;*

- *explain terms like demand fluctuations, level-capacity strategy, price bundling and segmented pricing;*

- *understand the essence of costs made by the company and consumer;*

- *interpret the relationship between price, quality and type of service;*

- *comprehend why the value of a service is linked to quality and price;*

- *apply value strategies (satisfaction based, relationship and efficiency pricing);*

- *price profitably for different services;*

- *recognize the more intuitive pricing tactics which are used in practice and be able to explain how these fit within the underlying theoretical principles of this chapter; and*

- *improve intuitive pricing by applying the theory as outlined in this chapter.*

LEFT: *Value for money on food, beverages and accessories*

14.1 INTRODUCTION

*Service
practice
14-1
Club Med: the
impact of price
changes*

The France based Club Méditerranée Group consists of Club Méditerranée SA and Club Med Inc. both offering vacation villages, hotels (amongst others City Club), cruises and tours in Europe, Africa and South America respectively, North and Central America, Asia Pacific and Indian Ocean. Moreover, Club Aquarius ("cheaper" vacation villages in France), the Maeva Group (vacation apartment rental and time sharing real estate in France) and Valtur (vacation villages in Italy) are part of the group.

Club Med faced two consecutive years with losses but turned into profit in the year 1993-1994. As stated in their annual report, the group re-focussed on its core business, brought operating costs under control, and reduced its debt. One of the important factors leading to these results is the occupancy rate. That performance indicator increased from 62% to 67% for the whole group. "Taking the Europe-Africa zone, which accounted for 49% of 1992-1993 sales, a combination of price cuts, restructuring of supply, and advertising focussing on price, boosted occupancy rates considerably."[1]

The number of hotel days consumed in Group villages rose 6.3% to 9,206,200. Volumes were up in all sectors. Due to capacity cuts made by the Group in 1994 the overall occupancy rate increased by more than 5% to 67.13%.

Analyzing occupancy rates by zone, the most striking feature is that they grew in each of the different sectors:

- with a 66% rate, Europe-Africa reverted to an occupancy rate more consistent with capacity in this sector...;
- Club Aquarius registered a very healthy occupancy rate of 72.95%. It had a particularly satisfactory winter season, and further significant performance improvement will be hard to achieve in the coming years...;
- in North America, the occupancy rate edged up 2% to 68.26%. Most of the improvement stems from the adjustment of hotel capacity during the summer...;
- in Asia, the number of hotel days rose by more than 13%. In addition to the very good results of the new Bora Bora village, the Sahoro (Japan) and Cherating (Malaysia) villages both turned in excellent scores. Moreover, the recently-opened Lindeman Island village in Australia was named Best Hotel, 1994, in a survey of tourist industry consultants.

Further, the annual report states: "Operating costs fell by approximately FRF 150 million in 1993-1994. A substantial portion of this improvement stems from efforts to refine the Club's offering, by closing certain villages, and rescheduling opening and closing dates for others in response to demand. This has led to a slight cut in accommodation capacity (down 4% in Europe and Asia, and down 2% in North America).

Result: a clear fall in costs, a 7% rise in occupancy rates on increased volumes, and savings that the Club has passed on to GM's (Club Med´s name for their customers) in the form of price cuts of up to 15%. The average price of a vacation was down 3% for the year as a whole."[2]

Club Med's policy of changing its product mix (focus on core business) and decreasing prices (focus on costs) is well known in mature markets to increase volume and sales. In order to be rewarding in the long run, flexibility in pricing and thus costs is essential at all times.

The title of this chapter may be a little confusing, because the term price is seldom used in the service sector. More often, we find terms like premium (insurance), rent (cabin), fare (railway), honorarium (legal advice), rate (tourist guide) and tariff (barber). Despite all these different names, the fact remains that a customer has to pay for most services. The marketing term "price" will be our starting point, whereas service providers often use other terms.

Demand, the costs of a service and competition including substitution factors, all three are of major importance when setting the final price. This chapter looks at the demand for a service from different points of view. Attention is paid to demand elasticity and demand fluctuations. The text also discusses the level-capacity strategy, price bundling and segmented pricing as possible options. The effect of a price decrease or increase on the revenues will be measured with the index of ARGE (Asset Revenue–Generating Efficiency). In considering the costs, the pricing issue will not only deal with costs incurred by the organization, but also, being a major characteristic of a service, with the costs incurred by the consumer. A third price-affecting factor, competition, will be discussed briefly. It will include some comments on substitution – an important consideration while pricing services. Next, combined strategies for pricing will be introduced. Subsequently, in separate sections, pricing over the service life cycle; the relationship between price, cost and quality; value strategies as well as setting prices for different kinds of services will be discussed. Figure 14-1 provides an overview of this chapter on pricing services.

14.2 STRATEGIC OBJECTIVES AND TYPES OF ORGANIZATIONS

In the service business, pricing is an important management tool, to achieve the objectives of the organization. Matching supply and demand in a service firm is also an essential part of pricing. Not every service provider is free in setting the price to the same extent. The organization's strategic objectives partly determine the freedom a service provider has in setting the price. The firm's strategic objectives are general aspirations toward which all activities are directed, not only pricing.[3] Essential in *pursue profits* setting the price is whether an organization does or does not pursue profits.

Figure 14-1
Chapter outline

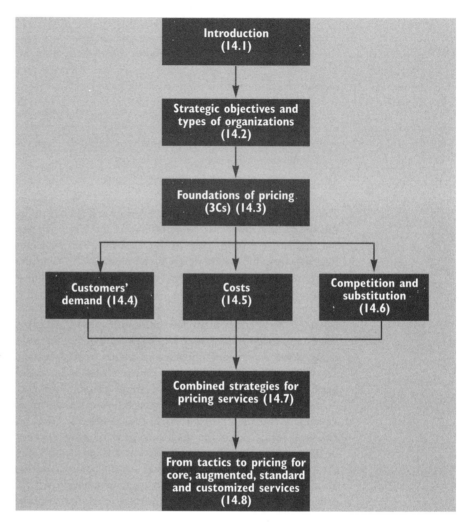

Therefore, the type of organization strongly influences the extent to which price-setting is free. Prices or price increases in public organizations are often fixed by law. It is obvious that the market structure will also determine the service provider's scope to set prices.

In addition, service providers may widely differ in their marketing strategy, work and, for example, in their ethics. Therefore, their pricing objectives will vary as well. The relationship between the type of organization and their strategic objectives, therefore, determines the price strategy and price setting (= tactics).

objectives Every organization pursues one or more objectives with its pricing policy. A service provider may offer its services at a high price, while other producers offer the same service at a low price. They may, however, have the same corporate objective in view, namely continuity or the same objective to the customer in terms of providing value for money. Chapter Two distinguishes between services subject to public regulation;

services subject to formal self regulation in a particular industry; and services subject to regulation of the market place. For each of the three types of service organizations, we can distinguish different pricing objectives.[4]

services subject to government regulation

Within services subject to government regulation, non price factors often carry great weight. This category of services involves the following pricing objectives: social/political desirability; survival, mostly non profit; and, prestige: a high price results in much prestige (or vice versa, a low price indicates low prestige). The price of services like education, health care and public transport is, in many countries, determined by public regulation. The social and political motives can be so strong that the price cannot be justified economically. A service that falls within this category,

cost price

may be offered below cost price permanently, if politically or socially desirable, as the following examples show. In many countries, education is compulsory until the age of sixteen. Enlarging access to education is often the main reason why education is free. In Israel, the education of "Ulphan" is also free. "Ulphan" is a teaching program for learning Hebrew for immigrants and kibbutz-volunteers. In most countries, information for tourists is organized by the government and (till now) freely available.

self-regulating services

The second category, self-regulating services, pursues not only pricing objectives, but also tries to give the industry an outstanding image. Its pricing strategy aims at building a permanent relationship with customers. Therefore, this industry pursues the following pricing objectives for all the companies in the industry: survival-continuity is still essential; maximum actual profit or revenue must not damage the relationship with the customer; industry image and a fixed percentage return on investment (ROI). As these types of organizations involve self-regulation to a certain extent, examples include lawyers and (chartered) accountants, and today to a lesser extent airlines (IATA). Service industries which use self-regulation as an important ingredient of pricing vary strongly from country to country. The effect, at the individual company

stable and fair prices

level, is that agreement on pricing should result in stable and fair prices. In this philosophy, the interest of both parties – the supplier and the buyer – needs to be taken into account. One big disadvantage of formal self-regulation is that market forces play (almost) no role of importance. Of course, this category involves the high risk of a cartel forming and the setting of prices based upon the cost structures of the least efficient members of a profession. In many countries, the government's competition policy tries to put an end to this. The European Union performs a very active

anti-trust policy

anti-trust policy, sometimes more active than in some member countries. Also, the US government is actively involved in anti-trust policies.

prices set by the market

In the third category of services, where prices are set by the market, price is a tool which can be used for many reasons. The number of objectives is therefore larger. Of course, this category also involves survival, maximum actual profit and a fixed percentage ROI, depending on the actual market structure. In the free market, a service

fight close competitors

provider will, in addition, use the price as a weapon to fight close competitors. In this market-oriented situation, we see, for instance, the following objective: realizing the position desired in relation to the competitor. Of course, the possibilities of positioning a service in terms of price depend on the price-elasticity of demand and balancing demand and supply throughout the year. Prices of vacations are a good example. The price for a vacation during peak periods may be five times higher than during the less busy times. The aim of these different prices is to stimulate demand in off-peak periods and to slow down demand during peak periods. Services where price is subject to regulation of the marketplace include many commercial service providers: banks, private clinics, private schools or maintenance services, etc. Despite the free character of these professions, regulation is growing in this sector in the form of industry wide organizations. Prices for car repairs with official dealers in many countries, for example, are mainly set in accordance with guidelines from the car dealer association or importer. The primary objective of these guidelines is to provide *assurance* assurance for consumers. As these guidelines become more effective, and therefore have to be observed, a certain degree of self-regulation arises automatically.

14.3 FOUNDATIONS OF PRICING

From the previous section, it is clear that a service provider may pursue different objectives with regard to price. Especially in market-oriented firms, the service provider must carefully consider the market situation and hence must think and operate in a clearly market-oriented manner. Thus, if a service provider wants to perform a market-oriented pricing policy, the price must be based on the so-called pricing triangle:[5]

pricing triangle

- value to consumer (or demand factors);
- costs; and
- competition, including substitution factors.

foundations of a pricing strategy These factors affecting price – the so-called foundations of a pricing strategy – are visualized in Figure 14-2. These are the three Cs – the customers' demand schedule, the cost function and the competitors' price. Only when a service provider has a clear understanding of these three fundamentals, can the limits of the field within which the service provider has to set his price, be defined roughly. A possible upper limit of price can be determined by a clear understanding of how demand has developed in the past, whereas the lower limit of the price is determined by the organization's costs. However, a service provider should always take into account the costs incurred by consumers themselves. The final price must be set between these limits. Even then, the general impact of competitors, their specific potential reaction to the price set and their own pricing objectives should be taken into account.[6] Given the three Cs and the price objectives, an organization is ready to select a price. The following *three Cs* sections discuss the three Cs as a base for pricing.

There are several reasons for the complexity of pricing services. First, the back office and front office processes are often entangled. Both are used for the whole range of services. This applies in particular to service providers with high fixed costs. It complicates the attempt to specify exactly the cost price of individual items. Typically, when calculating correctly it may happen that one service (partly) subsidizes the other. For instance, in a bank, consumer loans subsidize unprofitable domestic transfers; in an insurance company, life insurance may compensate for less remunerative

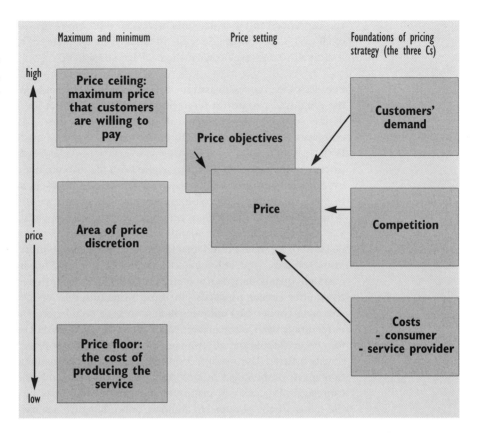

Figure 14-2
Key factors influencing
price decisions

Service
practice14-2
Customers,
competition
and costs

In a new simple wooden small café at the brink of a ski slope in Borovets, Bulgaria, one of the authors of this book noticed (early in 1998) that he paid for a pancake 2,000 Leva (US $1.20) the first day and Leva 1,500 (US $0.90) the next day. As a 25% price cut is quite large, the author was curious about the reason for this sudden action. He asked the entrepreneur why he had lowered the price for pancakes so drastically. For a while, the man looked puzzled by this unexpected question. Then, after some thought, the owner, a young clever man in his late twenties, said that the café was simply not selling enough pancakes. In addition, he explained that the café still obtained an attractive margin at Leva 1,500. However, again after some time, he added, there were two other important aspects. Firstly, the prices of pancakes in surrounding cafés (Leva 2,000 in a teahouse at 20 meters distance and Leva 1,500 in a café at 500 meters). Second, he explained that, in his place, the sale of pancakes (often to youngsters) is closely related with the turnover of drinks (at normal prices). This young entrepreneur shows us in a nutshell the important basics of pricing: demand, costs and competitors' offer.

car insurances; and in restaurants meals can offer lower net margins (after deduction of all costs) than drinks. Second, "the intangible character of the service itself makes it difficult to understand what the package consists of".[7]

Because of the intangible nature of services, it is important to introduce two concepts: the price transparency of services (which can be high or low) and the transparency of the service utility (which can also be high or low).[8] The term transparency embraces the customer's insight in the various cost and quality components. When both types of transparencies are low, the service provider has the most freedom to set prices. In the opposite position, where both features are high, customers will know everything about prices and quality. Hence, price differences must reflect differences in costs or quality. Otherwise, customers will switch to other, cheaper, suppliers. When services are quite homogeneous (as is the case in particular service industries like airlines on the North Atlantic route), price is used as a means of competition. Because of its standardized character, the service can be more easily compared with other services. And, although customers may not have full insight into the various costs and quality, they may perceive the transparency of price increases because many rivals offer similar packages. In those situations, the service firm should stress its

special or (preferably) unique selling points (or even better: unique service points) to differentiate itself in the market place. As an example, market research may reveal that for certain people the safety-image of an airline and not price is the main reason for buying a ticket. The marketeers of Quantas, Australia's national pride, with a reputation as one of the safest airlines in the world, could use this factor in their advertising campaigns. Especially in mature markets unbundling may be a solution to enhance the transparency of rates. In addition, unbundling (in a sense a form of product differentiation) alone – or in combination with market segmentation – enables established firms to protect their market share against low-cost producers.

At the same time, it is important to remember that pricing in the service sector is less influenced by cost than it is by the customers' perception of "value" or "worth".[9] In all instances, it is essential to realize that quality and price are linked together, indicating the value of the service to the customer. Len Berry (1995) shares with us in his book *On Great Service* two interesting thoughts about value:

> "A service strategy captures what gives the service value to customers. To forge a path to great service, a company's leaders must define correctly that which makes the service compelling."[10] ... "An excellent service strategy offers customers genuine value; it gives customers more for the costs they incur."[11]

These phrases about value show that "you get what you pay for". This applies in particular to customized services, but also standard services and augmented services, which are new to a consumer. Services are difficult to assess. And, because these merely intangible products are typically not homogeneous, a buyer cannot always determine the quality of a service beforehand. This applies especially with regard to

services that customers are not familiar with or those services having little search attributes. Here, price will be often used as an indicator of quality. In such cases, the expectation of a consumer about the quality is largely based on the price. A lower price will often raise lower quality expectations than a higher price. If we keep in mind that "you get what you pay for", the price of a qualitatively good service should not be necessarily low. "In order to optimize service pricing, the service provider may use his cost generators as a price bottom; however, the actual pricing is better determined by matching the customer's 'value' determinants."[12]

For internationally oriented service firms pricing is mostly determined locally. The Economist's annual "Big Mac" comparison, indicating the value of currencies, is a good example of this. However, globalization of demand and supply make prices increasingly comparable and thus transparent. Service firms feel this impact especially in industries such as consultancy and Internet services. Also, in Europe the appearance of the euro contributes to a more transparent landscape of tariffs.

globalization

transfer pricing

In international business, transfer pricing is a hot issue, next to the risks incurred in fluctuations in exchange rates. One issue hinges upon the way how transfer prices are computed. Another issue refers to which country should sales and profits be assigned when a subsidiary in country A gets a job to be performed in country B where the company also has a subsidiary? Apart from international transfer pricing, the same question arises when two business units or subsidiaries within one country are dealing with each other. Complex administrative systems can be developed to settle these issues in great detail or a system of splitting fees may be used. Some international banks have developed sophisticated shadow accounting systems to calculate the profit contribution of each subsidiary to a (flow of) deal(s). Whereas local or international accounting rules or fiscal policies may require a different registration, it is

optimize the resources of the whole organization

important for the service firm to optimize the resources of the whole organization instead of the separate units (sub-optimization). By recognizing the individual input of each unit the organization motivates its staff in the various collaborating units and not just the unit where the profit or deal is organized for accounting or fiscal reasons. This is also a way to lower tax payments – by booking profits in countries with low corporate rates. In order to prevent their countries receiving a fair slice of the profit, tax authorities around the globe are now focussing on this issue. It implies that,

internal and external prices

increasingly, companies have to justify their internal (intra-company) and external prices. Tracing the contribution of each unit motivates the employees; it also stimulates networking within the organization. Other service firms choose to split fees through the regular accounting system or by allocating a service fee of i.e. 10% to the subsidiaries initiating or hosting the deal (or project). They believe this direct approach is often more effective than dividing sales and profits in a detailed way between these units (for instance based on "hours spent on the job"). However, in these matters, it is important to remember that the service firm still pays full attention to the customer and does not forget the customer here by paying too much attention to the internal accounting. Of course, in order to avoid sub-optimizing the organizational goals, employees' networking should always be recognized by management and should be rewarded for these efforts properly.

14.4 CUSTOMERS' DEMAND

price elasticity of demand

Having insight into the degree of price elasticity of demand for a particular service is a must for any market-oriented organization. In general, we assume that if a service is elastic, a relatively small price decrease leads to a substantial increase in demand for that service. A price increase results in a relatively large drop in demand for this service.

$$E(p) \ = \ \frac{\% \ \text{Change in quantity demanded}}{\% \ \text{Change in price}} \ = \frac{\Delta \ Q/Q}{\Delta \ P/P}$$

For a service provider, it is desirable but also very difficult to understand exactly if and how responsive demand would be to a change in price. It takes a lot of research to get a clear understanding of consumer's behavior. This research is not feasible or profitable for many small service providers. Subjective estimation of customers' price sensitivity may solve this problem. Also, adding services focussing on aspects that

enlarge personal loyalty

enlarge personal loyalty (see also Chapter Two) via personal contacts often result in inelastic behavior. If prices are somewhat lower elsewhere, customers won't drop the supplier.

Price elasticity becomes even more relevant in the case of standard core services without too many complexities for the customer. Customers can compare the service with competitors' offers and the number of substitutes for the service are larger than for a customized augmented service. In general, we assume that price elasticity of a service increases as: the service is more a standard service (a "commodity"); the service includes not too many customized augmented services; the number of substitutes is larger; and/or the price covers a relatively larger share of income per household.

search, experience and credence attributes

Price elasticity of demand can be related to the search, experience and credence attributes of a service: "... demand is more likely to be elastic for services in which the salient attributes are search attributes. Moreover, the costs of switching from one service provider to another will be lower relative to the gains from switching for search-based attributes than for experience/credence attributes".[13] As stated earlier, considering recent pricing movements in such diverse industries as airlines, fast food, holiday packages and credit cards, we expect that demand is probably more elastic for standard and core services than for augmented and customized services. In addition, price elasticity will be higher when these services are at the top of the service life-cycle, as is so in mature markets, or when they can be considered as commodities with a high brand parity.

DEMAND FLUCTUATIONS (PREDICTABLE OR RANDOM)

Besides fluctuations in total demand as a result of price changes, a service organization faces other demand fluctuations. Demand for a service may vary for other reasons

demand fluctuations

than just price changes.[14] To a certain extent, demand fluctuations occur because services are perishable: they cannot be stored. Even with electronic services such as the Internet the rest of the world experiences longer waiting times; at the moment America switches on in the morning. Somehow, there must be a way to manage all these demand fluctuations. In theory, demand fluctuations are divided into: predictable demand fluctuations and random demand fluctuations.

predictable Demand fluctuations are predictable, if demand varies as a result of the time factor. As a result, a service provider may not be able to meet demand during peak periods or, at the other extreme, faces excess capacity during offpeak periods. Here, successfully managing demand is essential; it may strongly affect the perceived quality in the eyes of the customer. We will show how demand and supply affect the perception of the buyer, by discussing two capacity terms. With regard to the capacity to manage demand for services, note the distinction between: maximum capacity (the maximum level of demand an organization can handle) and optimum capacity (the level of demand at which optimum service is delivered).

maximum capacity If actual demand exceeds the maximum capacity, a part of demand may be lost. The service provider has no capacity left to serve all the customers. In this situation, the service organization has to deny service. This poses the risk that business is lost and customers switch to competitors. When actual demand is somewhere between optimum and maximum capacity, the service provider is able to serve all customers. In this situation, however, there is a risk that customers perceive a deterioration in the quality as a result of waiting times or irritation caused by other clients. In the ideal
optimum capacity situation, demand equals optimum capacity, which is best for the customer's quality perception and value for money. When demand is below optimum capacity, consumers may be affected negatively. Empty seats, for example, may cause doubts about the quality of the service.

time In many service industries, demand depends strongly on the time factor. Demand levels for, e.g. public transport vary by time of day, day of week and season of year. In peak times, prices are high, but travel quality is low. In off-peak times, prices are lower and travelling is much more comfortable. Other service organizations that face demand fluctuations as a result of the time factor are: utilities where the level of demand in winter is higher than the level of demand in summer and mail services which have peak times during the periods before Christmas, St Valentine's day and holidays.

random If the typical cycle pattern of demand fluctuations is random, demand comes from different consumer groups at one time. Hotels are faced with business travellers, tourists, people attending conferences, etc. Since the behavioral patterns and expectations of these groups vary highly, total demand may be divided into different separate market segments. In pricing, however, it is desirable to aim at one primary target group. The wrong mix of target groups may lead to discord. This is especially true when it is difficult to separate market segments, in case a price differentiation or price discrimination policy is used.

capacity-improving strategies

A service provider will have to manage both types of demand fluctuation. This can be accomplished by capacity-improving strategies, but also by using the price as a tool to match demand and supply (due to the price elasticity).

LEVEL CAPACITY STRATEGY

level capacity strategy

differential pricing

discriminatory pricing waiting lists/ reservation systems, complementary services, alternatives

The level capacity strategy aims at producing a better match between demand and supply by affecting demand. For years, the tourist industry has been used to regulating demand. Low prices are set to attract tourists during off-peak periods, whereas during peak periods the price is much higher. The use of different pricing strategies is just one tool of the level-capacity strategy the service provider can apply. The other "tools" include: differential pricing (based on different cost prices, for example, by providing augmented services along with the standard service) or discriminatory pricing (the same service is sold at different prices which are not based on similar differences in costs); maintain the price, but develop waiting lists/reservation systems, which can shift demand from peak to off-peak periods; and/or develop complementary services, which attract customers during off-peak periods and/or provide alternatives to waiting customers (e.g. sports clubs with a sauna or beauty salon). A package of different services offered at one, new all-in price, is a kind of price bundling.

PRICE BUNDLING

price bundling

Two or more services bundled at a particular price (which is often lower than the total price of all the services separately) is called price bundling. A fly-drive arrangement for one price or a hotel arrangement including sightseeing tours at a special price are examples of price bundling.[15,16]

fixed costs

relationship

complementary theory of consumer surplus reservation price

Bundling in general and price bundling particularly, can be discussed both from the suppliers' and from the customers' point of view. For this (pricing) strategy to work, there are two basic conditions:[17] a cost structure, where fixed costs cover a relatively large share of total costs (this will be the case especially in services where a high degree of capital is involved); and a relationship between, or interdependence of, the services on the demand-side. If such a relationship does not exist, it is no use trying to benefit from bundling. In micro-economic terms, these products or services must be complementary to one another. Then, the theory of consumer surplus in which consumers are willing to pay more for the bundled services than for each separate service, holds. The reservation price for the bundle will exceed the sum of the reservation prices for each of the separate services.

customer's perspective

From the customer's perspective, the following arguments can be given in favor of bundling. If bundling results in stronger and better relations with the supplier, the customer will have the opportunity to have more and better contacts with the supplier to express needs, wants, desires, problems, solutions, etc. In terms of transaction costs, buying a bundle from one supplier may save costs in terms of time and information search compared to situations where multiple suppliers are used.[18] On the other hand, such a growing dependence may be a disadvantage to customers and their freedom of choice. Finally, in cases where customers lack the skills to assemble the various parts of a service, "pre-fab" bundling may help them to overcome these difficulties and/or reduce perceived risk.[19] For example, start-up airlines often ask for guidelines in buying an initial service bundle at the start of the operation with the aircraft because they do not possess large engineering departments or maintenance and repair departments.

supplier's perspective From the supplier's perspective, bundling can be seen as one of the main opportunities open to them to develop and maintain relationships with customers. It creates a higher degree of loyalty and prevents customers from switching. But, bundling will also offer opportunities to reduce costs by decreasing the heterogeneity in products and services offered because they are now in more or less standard bundles. The micro-economic perspective, as mentioned before, indicates that total sales can increase compared to the unbundled situation. Bundling can also be a means of upgrading the firm's offer when higher quality services are added. In fact, the mere situation of bundling may increase the quality perception by the customer. This can also be the case when bundling improves product performance. It is important to know how well and quickly these bundles can be imitated by competitors. In industrial markets, changes in the physical product itself are quite easily and quickly imitated by competitors. Consequently, these changes do not have much impact on the initiator's market share or profits. However, competitors face severe problems in reacting quickly to companies improving service based around their products. For now, the initiating firms are benefitting from higher market share and profits.[20]

unbundling As the opportunity to bundle exists, sometimes unbundling might be necessary and also desirable. A strategy of unbundling may be useful in maturing markets. In mature markets, customers will be more price sensitive than in earlier stages of the life cycle. Customers will possess more information about services, less perceived risk will exist, transaction costs will be lower due to this experience and the risk of self-assembling will be less. Also, the need for standard bundles of services will decrease.

differentiate On the other hand, we can also argue that bundling could be a means for a company to differentiate itself from its competitors in mature markets as well. Adding more services to products can be successful in that respect and a means to implement the firm's market orientation. We have seen that it can be applied to strengthen relationships or prevent customers from switching. These are severe problems in mature markets. So the arguments about unbundling in mature markets are mixed, in our opinion.

pure bundling

mixed bundling Price bundling may occur in a number of forms. If bundling occurs to such an extent that the services cannot be bought separately, it is pure bundling. One may think of a tailor made augmented service belonging to a core service. Both services are sold as a package and, therefore, cannot be bought separately. Mixed bundling occurs when services can be bought as a package but also separately. Mixed bundling takes two forms: mixed-leader and mixed-joint bundling.

Service practice 14-3 Aviation – a mature market!

In many respects, the aviation market today is a very mature market. Large airlines have huge engineering departments with enormous amounts of information and knowledge about aircraft and the supporting services needed (prevention, maintenance, repair, training of pilots, etc.). The market for all of this kind of aircraft support has become highly competitive. The OEM (original equipment manufacturer), as well as many third party maintenance firms, are active in this market.

In such a competitive market, service bundling is considered an attractive issue by OEMs, especially when an airline possesses planes from different manufacturers, like Boeing, Airbus and Bombardier. Now, bundling can be used to keep customers and create bundles of services that fit to specific needs of an aircraft during its life cycle. Tailor made service bundles should then be developed. This could be a way to escape from price wars in this service market.

mixed-leader bundling

Mixed-leader bundling means that a buyer gets a discount off the price of a second service, if this is bought together with a leader service. The price of the leader service can be defined as: P(b1). In the bundling, P(b1) is still 100% and thus the same as the price, which would have been paid if the service was bought separately. P(1) denotes the separate price. In a formula, we get P(b1) = P(1). The price of the second service is lower, than the price which would have been paid, if the service was bought separately. In a formula, that is: P(b2) < P(2). In conclusion, for mixed bundling the following formulae apply:

$$P(b1) = P(1) \quad \text{and} \quad P(b2) < P(2).$$

mixed-joint bundling

Mixed-joint bundling occurs when the package price is lower than the total price of the individual services. Customers do not know exactly where the price difference is to be found, and it is, in fact, irrelevant to them. For mixed-joint bundling, the following formula applies:

$$P(b1,b2) < P(1) + P(2)$$

The extent to which this form of bundling really works depends largely on the economies of scale, which can be accomplished by stimulating demand and, of course, on how consumers value the bundling (and do not consider it as an unattractive form of cross-selling).

With regard to the price of a service bundle, consumers benefit from a bigger search efficiency when a service bundle is characterized by search attributes and demand is elastic. There is no need for the customer to search after two separate services. Services that are characterized by experience and credence attributes will, if bundled, profit from the service provider's images – provided that the image is positive. In addition, price elasticity of a service determines the choice of the type of price

price elasticity

bundling (mixed-leader or mixed-joint). To choose the mixed-leader bundle, the leader service must be elastic. To choose the mixed-joint bundle, demand for both services must be elastic.

Service practice 14-4 Fire or travel insurance?

As an example of price bundling, assume an insurance company is offering two services:

- a fire insurance at a price of 9, or P(1) = 9
- a travel insurance at a price of 5, or P(2) = 5.

Now, this insurance company is offering these two products as a package at a price of 12, or P(b1, b2) = 12.

Four potential customers are willing to pay sequentially the following maximum prices for each service separately:

- P(1) max. reflects the maximum price that each customer is willing to pay for the fire insurance;
- P(2) max. reflects the maximum price that each customer is willing to pay for the travel insurance.

We assume that each customer will buy the service, as long as the price does not exceed the maximum price. In a formula that is P(1) < P(1) max. and/or P(2) < P(2) max., the four customers' preferences are as follows:

	P(1) max.	P(2) max.	P(1,2) max.	Buying if service is offered: *separately*	*bundled (package)*
Customer 1	8	6	14	only 2	1 and 2
Customer 2	10	4	14	only 1	1 and 2
Customer 3	8	4	12	nothing	1 and 2
Customer 4	6	3	9	nothing	nothing

In the above situation, customer 1 will only buy service 2, because service 1 exceeds his maximum price (9 > 8). Customer 1 will, however, accept the package offer, because its price is lower than the maximum price he was willing to pay for the whole package. As we said, this example was based on the following assumptions:

- P(b1, b2) = 12 and
- P(1,2) max. = 14

The following applies for customer 2:

- P(1) < P(1) max.;
- P(2) < P(2) max.; and
- P(b1,b2) < P(1,2) max.

If each service is offered separately, customer 2 will thus buy the fire insurance: the price of the travel insurance exceeds his maximum price. If the services are offered as a package, customer 2 will buy both insurance products.

SEGMENTED PRICING

segmented pricing

In order to optimize profit, the pricing strategies discussed are most profitable if directed towards clearly defined market segments. Segmented pricing looks first and foremost at the question whether different market segments are willing to pay different prices. Segmented pricing and level capacity are both strategies aiming at the same area: matching supply and demand by effectively applying the price instrument.

price differentiation

separating the segments

In employing the price differentiation tool, marketeers need to be careful. Then, segments need not only be defined clearly; they also have to be separated. Bateson distinguishes six conditions to be fulfilled if a firm wants to apply price differentiation and discrimination successfully.[21] These criteria also indicate that separating the segments (and keeping them separated) is not an easy task. These are:

- different groups of buyers must value the service differently and respond differently to price;
- management should be able to identify the segments and approach these segments with various tariffs;
- buyers should not have access to lower or higher segments;
- the size of the segment should be large enough;
- the costs of price differentiation (or price discrimination) must not be higher than the expected additional revenues; and
- price differentiation (or price discrimination) should not be confusing to the potential buyers.

market segment perceives the values

benefits

With segmented pricing – a form of value (based) pricing – prices are founded on how a market segment perceives the values of a service (package). The cornerstone of this approach are the benefits buyers expect to receive from an intangible product. Value pricing, covering the total benefits to a customer, consists of the value of the core benefits and a premium for "surround" (= the additional or augmented) benefits.[22] In some countries, price differentiation is allowed; price discrimination not.

For service industries with high fixed costs, such as transport, hotel, amusement parks, (movie) theaters and hospitals, segmented pricing is often essential. Within the airline industry, it is common knowledge that business travellers prefer to return home before the weekend or at least on a Saturday. For that reason, most airlines offer substantial lower rates to travellers if they include a Saturday night in their journey when applying segmented pricing. Airlines and hotels, utilizing pricing tactics, differentiate distinctly between "holiday passengers" and business travellers. Holiday or leisure travellers are often prepared to make advance commitments, accept varying quality levels, are quite flexible in location and destination, are indifferent to prestige, have a high price elasticity and stay for a long time.[23] The opposite holds for most business travellers. However, exceptions to the rule always exist and require tailor made offerings.

Segmented pricing enables a company to develop profitable pricing strategies.

Potential customers who are less price sensitive, or more costly to serve, or less well served by competitors, can be charged more without the loss of buyers who the firm can serve more profitably at a lower price. In addition to the initial segmentation of the customers, it is crucial to keep them segmented. It requires creative tactics that keep markets separated while avoiding illegalities. In this context, Nagle names seven remunerative pricing tactics, that have been shown to be effective. The examples prove that these tactics are highly relevant to services marketing. The pricing tactics are based on the following seven segmentation variables (as an eighth option we have added membership):[24] buyer identification; purchase location; time of purchase; purchase quantity; service design; service bundling; metering; and membership.

Buyer identification

The challenge here is to obtain information about the segments and to identify the (prospective) buyer in many respects. Sometimes, segmenting is easy. Barbers charge different prices for short and long hair because long hair is usually more difficult to cut (price segmenting in combination with activity based pricing). They also cut children's hair at substantially lower rates because parents view home haircuts as acceptable alternatives to costly barber cuts for their children (price segmenting under influence of substitution factors; activity based pricing would lead to a price that is too high). For barbers, simple observation and experience are an easy guide-

buyer identification

line. In other service industries, buyer identification is not so easy. Sound marketing research is needed to identify price sensitive market segments. This aims at inducing buyers of any product or service to reveal their price sensitivities. Sometimes, sales-people are in the best position to judge the proper tariff in a sales talk. Within the limits set by management, they then evaluate the well-known price affecting factors, such as demand, competition and costs, and set the final charge. Examples include (after-sales) service contracts and consumer services where management has delegated some authority regarding pricing to contact personnel.

Purchase location

different prices at different locations

In a wide range of service industries it is common practice to charge different prices at different locations. In some countries, dentists, doctors and lawyers tend to set prices according to their clients' price sensitivity. A doctor treating patients in a hospital may demand a different remuneration from a patient in the doctor's private clinic. Client switching from the higher-price to the lower price location is mini-mized by differences in the convenience, ambience, or prestige value of different locations.[25] For instance, in the lodging industry, hotels may offer rooms – which are of the same size or even larger – outside the main building at lower rates. Many countries put legal constraints on geographical price differences. Price dumping – offering services under the integral cost price – typically aimed to undercut local suppliers, is forbidden in most countries.

Time of purchase

pricing by time of purchase

Customers in different markets may buy at different times. Firms use this information for pricing by time of purchase. Theaters segment their markets by offering midday matinées at deep discounts. Chinese restaurants in residential areas have cheap lunches on their menu while having the same food priced higher during dinner time.

Tickets on airlines and railways are less expensive during off-peak times. Hotels in city centers offer weekend-packages to families or couples at substantially lower rates than during week days. The purpose of all these service providers is to attract price-sensitive people to use seats or beds otherwise unoccupied. The effective use of this strategy assumes that the other customers (who are, in principle, more price-sensitive) cannot that easily arrange dates or work schedules to take advantage of the cheaper offers. The motto "once the plane has left, the chance to earn has gone" counts in most "fixed assets" dominated service industries. The crux for these service providers is to find market segments or niches which are of sufficient size and price sensitive

occupancy rates

to get high occupancy rates. In this context, fixed capacity costs are important for setting prices at peak times. However, as the cost of capacity up to the amount used at peak times is mostly unavoidable, fixed capacity costs should be ignored when deter-

variable operating costs

mining prices in non-peak periods. In non-peak periods, variable operating costs, such as fuel for aircraft, food ingredients for restaurants, electricity and cleaning costs after a performance in movie or a stay at a hotel, should be used in profitable decision making.

Purchase quantity

Tour operators purchasing high volumes of rooms in hotels and seats in aircrafts are naturally offered lower rates than ordinary people renting one room or buying a few tickets. Banks quote big enterprises lower interest rates for their loans than small

quantity discount

businesses or consumers. Quantity discount tactics are commonly used in the service sector and include volume discounts, order discounts, step or block discounts and two-part pricing:

volume discounts

- volume discounts are aimed at retaining business of large customers and promoting volume;

order discounts

- order discounts encourage customers to place fewer (infrequent) large orders instead of small (frequent) orders;

step or block discounts

- step or block discounts seduce customers to buy more services as every next block of volume is bought at a lower price (these discounts do not apply to the total quantity purchased);

two-part pricing

- two-part pricing consists of separate charges to consume a single service. For example, amusement parks sometimes have an entry fee plus a ticket charge for each ride (at i.e. the incremental costs), car rental companies have a daily rate plus a mileage charge and racket clubs have an annual membership plus a charge on

heavy users

court time.

In each of these cases, heavy users pay less than do light users for the same service since the fixed price is spread over time.

Service design

Some of the most effective segmentation strategies involve offering different versions of the service with hardly any or no difference in production costs. In particular, with standardized or semi-standardized services, there is frequently little or no cost differ-

service design

ence in the different versions. Segmenting by service design is easy when selling services such as air travel, because the seller can easily limit resale of the service. If airline tickets were not issued to specific passengers, firms would soon spring up to buy discounted tickets in advance for resale to businessmen closer to departure times.[26]

Service bundling

bundling   Both customers and suppliers can benefit from bundling as a tactic for segmented pricing. Manufacturers or retailers bundle goods with (free) services. Shopping malls offer free parking for one hour. Restaurants combine menu items into fixed-price dinners. Concert halls bundle diverse concerts into season subscription tickets. The reasoning for bundling is obvious. Service providers try to increase their profits while aiming at the same time to strengthen their relationship with the customers by offering more products at the same time. The price of the bundled service should be (perceived as) lower than the sum of the separate items. This advantage and the convenience are both significant benefits to the purchaser.

On the other hand, the service provider may sell more without bundling, optimize its yield management and also enjoy the benefit of convenience. Generally, bundling is optional. Thus, customers can purchase the service also separately, although at a higher total price. Again, the challenge for the supplier is to find a homogeneous group among the prospects that is large enough to justify separate services or bundled services.

Metering

metering   Metering segments buyers by usage. By offering car rentals with metering, customers are attracted by hiring a car for convenience rather than for long distance trips. Free mileage offerings typically attract a category of drivers that travel longer distances.

Membership

membership   Finally, we mention membership. At the scale of temporary versus permanent relations between clients and organizations in Chapter Two, membership is one of the most permanent. Members of all kinds of clubs, profit and non-profit organizations pay their fee periodically. Frequently, the core service is free. Members then have to pay for additional services in full or may obtain them at a lower rate. In some instances, membership of an organization features privileges such as "ensured" tickets for a concert or sports event.

The attraction of a membership relation between the service provider and the client lies in coverage of the (fixed) costs. First, management know beforehand the (basic) income contributed by the members. On this basis, it is much easier to plan activities and therefore control costs. Not unimportantly, receiving money prior to activities (cost) speeds up the cash flow of the service provider and is an enormous second benefit in terms of membership relations. Long-term contracts for annual research activities are an example of "membership" in the market research industry.

ARGE: ASSET REVENUE–GENERATING EFFICIENCY

asset revenue-generating efficiency
ARGE index   To understand the effects of price fluctuations on revenues, the values of ARGE might be helpful. ARGE stands for "asset revenue-generating efficiency" and measures the extent to which the organization's assets are achieving their full revenue-generating potential.[27] The ARGE index is composed of the yield percentage and the occupancy rate.

yield percentage

The yield percentage reflects the extent to which the maximum price is received. To compute this percentage, the actual price is divided by the maximum price. The maximum price can be seen as the highest posted price. If a group is offered a 20% discount off the maximum price, the yield percentage is 80% or 0.8. Of course, the yield percentage can only be computed if the highest posted price is known.

occupancy rate

The second component, the occupancy rate, reflects the extent to which total capacity is used. If the capacity utilization rate is 50% or 0.5, only half of the hotel beds, or seats are sold. Such occupancy rates are important in cost accounting, setting prices and calculating break-even points. There are three ways to derive an index of ARGE (see Figure 14-3).

Figure 14-3
Three ways to
calculate ARGE

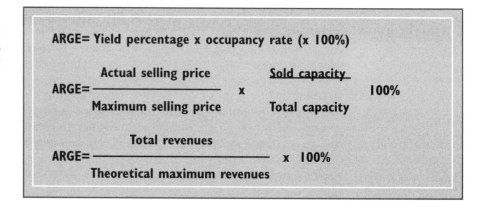

If a service provider has a number of options, the ARGE index may be useful to make the right choice. Of course, a service provider has to consider other variables as well, for instance: the costs incurred by the consumer should be the same; the relationship between direct and indirect costs of the service provider; and the relationship between total costs and revenues of the service provider.

14.5 COSTS

consider the costs

Now that we can map demand for services, it is time to consider the costs. Here, the price elasticity and demand fluctuations in relation to the costs are an essential factor for establishing profitable prices. At the start of this section about costs, it is essential to realize that for most service providers, especially those offering standard services, competitive cost advantages are essential. The service provider can reduce (service) unit costs through the efficient organization of its internal structure. It can do so by organizing its operations to exploit economies of scope, scale and experience. Controlling costs is an ongoing activity in any successful company. It must be a continuing process because various parties are involved, including both employees and external suppliers, who have a vested interest in seeing certain costs go up.[28]

Three pricing methods are often used in services in which different kinds of "costs" play a role: cost-plus pricing; rate of return pricing; and direct costing or variable costing.

cost-plus pricing

In cost-plus pricing, the firm determines the price by adding a (standard) mark-up to their costs (full costs or a part of all costs). Thus, the costs of a company determines the price, ignoring demand and competition.

rate of return pricing

The aim of rate of return pricing or target return pricing is to achieve a given rate of return on investments (ROI) or assets. ROI represents the required rate of return or the cost of capital. It does not fully represent a "cost approach".

direct costing
contribution margin

Direct costing centers on the difference between the selling price and variable costs, called the contribution margin. This margin is used to see whether a particular selling price contributes to cover fixed costs. If this is the case in the short run, the order can be accepted. This basis of setting prices is often referred to as "marginal costing". Charging a price based on a variable cost price within the company's market may quickly spoil the market in the long run. For, all consumers prefer a lower price than a price based on full cost. Direct costing is a very specific method not really suited for

in specific situations

calculating selling prices in general. It may work very well in specific situations. It is best suited to evaluating orders or assignments only on a short term perspective. For, not all costs are met. The "lower price" may spoil the market. It may even do harm to the service company itself. Clients will expect to pay the same price for all future business. Then, fixed costs will not be met, resulting in long term losses to the firm (and competitors). This approach is often used to increase short term occupancy rates. The Club Med and airline industry examples indicate that higher occupancy rates often affect profits in a positive way. Occupancy rates are therefore one of the important factors determining total costs and thus profits. The breakdown of

occupancy rates

occupancy rates (i.e. by analyzing this ratio in terms of regional zone, business unit, season, place of living of guest, location or route) in a world wide service organization will reveal where problems lie or where opportunities are present.

For a better understanding of the impact of total costs on prices, examining the costs incurred by the consumer, and the costs incurred by the service provider, are both necessary. The section concludes with a special method to determine costs made during the servuction process where both parties interact: activity-based costing.

CONSUMER COSTS

When accountants talk about costs, they usually mean amounts of money. A consumer of a service, however, faces costs other than just monetary costs. This is particularly so when it concerns services requiring the presence of a customer, services directed at the customer as a person and services of which the level of participation-intensity can be classified as high (or active). The single fact that a customer needs to be

cost and effort on the
consumer's side

present during a service delivery requires cost and effort on the consumer's side, in order to be present at the location where the service is delivered. Therefore, in determining consumer costs, a service provider has to take into account more than *monetary costs*

just its own financial costs. Besides monetary costs, the following costs may be incremental: opportunity costs; physical costs; sensory costs and psychic or mental costs.[29]

opportunity costs

Opportunity costs are the "costs of the alternative foregone". In money terms, it may be, e.g. a new car instead of a holiday abroad; a night at the theater instead of a dinner in a restaurant. Time costs incur during the total consumption process. In other words, they are part of the opportunity costs, expressing that a customer is bound by time during consumption and therefore must leave other alternatives.

physical costs

Physical costs occur when a consumer has to make physical efforts to make use of a service. These costs are sometimes hard to measure, because it is difficult to draw a line between physical effort and physical relaxation (a benefit).

sensory costs

negative external effect on consumption

mental costs

Sensory costs are all inconveniences perceived by our sense-organs throughout the service delivery. We can think of the smell of a hospital, exposure to draught, cold or heat. Irritating colors or noise nuisance are also included. Economists would call these a kind of negative external effect on consumption. Costs are closely connected with feelings of insecurity, which increase the perceived risk to such an extent that they are called mental costs. A consumer may be confronted with these costs before, during or after the service delivery. A service provider must be alert to these mental costs, because consumers may decide not to use the service, if the perceived risk is too high. For many people visiting a dentist, taking away feelings of fear is more important than the bill.

the total costs the customer has to incur to get a particular value

In the end, a service provider may economize his own costs, while (partly) shifting them on to the customer. The question is whether a consumer is willing to pay for it, considering the new quality-price relationship. The consumers themselves also have to invest in the service delivery. All these costs should be taken into account to determine the total costs the customer has to incur to get a particular value.

Service practice 14-5 The bill, please?

From the costs described, it is clear that the total costs of a service can be significantly higher than the monetary costs (= expenses):

- an independent management consultant who goes to a hairdresser during working hours does not only pay for a fancy haircut. The consultant also incurs opportunity costs because he or she is loosing income.
- Visiting a dentist will cost a patient – besides the dentist's bill:
  - travelling expenses and time;
  - physical costs (keeping one's mouth open for half an hour); and
  - mental costs (fear), which may be considerably high for some patients.

SERVICE PROVIDER COSTS

fixed costs
variable costs

A service provider's costs take two forms, fixed and variable. Fixed costs are costs that do not vary with servuction levels or sales volume. Variable costs do vary with servuction: variable costs increase as production or sales volume increases. Many costs are only fixed over a range of sales. Outside this range they vary. In other words, these costs are neither entirely fixed nor entirely variable: they are semi-fixed. In order to make the right pricing decision, management should consider these types of costs – whether they are variable, fixed or semi-fixed. Costs related to new equipment needed in service processes, e.g. a cash register in a fast food restaurant or in a hotel, are often semi-fixed. One cash register and one server may perform a certain number of transactions per hour. However, beyond that number an additional cash register (semi-fixed costs) and server (flex time/variable costs) may be necessary to ensure quality during the service encounter.

semi-fixed

Two commonly used pricing methods based on costs are: markup (cost-plus) and target-return pricing. To illustrate both methods, assume a beauty salon had the following costs and sales forecast:[30]

Variable costs per treatment	$5
Total fixed costs	$100,000
Expected sales of treatments	10,000

The total costs of a treatment (or unit) are now:

$$\text{Unit cost} = \text{variable cost} + \frac{\text{fixed costs}}{\text{unit sales}} = \$5 + \frac{\$100,000}{10,000} = \$15$$

Next, suppose the beauty salon wants to earn a 25% markup on sales. The shop's markup price can be calculated by:

$$\text{Markup price} = \frac{\text{unit cost}}{(1 - \text{desired return on sales})} = \frac{\$15}{1 - .25} = \$20$$

markup pricing

The beauty salon makes a profit of $5 per treatment. Markup pricing is simple. Although the method neglects many other considerations, it is still frequently used by lawyers, accountants and other professionals.

Target-return is a cost-pricing method that focusses on a desired return on investment (ROI). Assume the owner of the beauty salon has invested $800,000 in the company and wants to achieve a return of 25% percent ROI or $200,000. The target-return price is now verified by the following formula:

target-return price

$$\text{Target-return price} = \frac{\text{per cent ROI x invested capital}}{\text{unit sales}} = \frac{.25 \times 800,000}{10,000} = \$20$$

The beauty salon will only obtain the desired ROI of 25% if it can sell 10,000 treatments during a certain period.

break-even volume

In order to get a better feeling for what happens if this volume cannot be reached, the entrepreneur can prepare a break-even chart. Given the costs and the market price to be set, we can compute the break-even volume. At the break-even volume, neither profits nor losses are made. In fact, the break-even volume relates demand-side costs to organizational costs. In the long term, the service provider will at least have to achieve this revenue or sales volume. The formula presents the sales volume at which the service firm breaks even.

$$\text{Break-even volume} = \frac{\text{fixed costs}}{\text{price} - \text{variable cost}} + \frac{\$100,000}{\$20-\$5} = 6,666 \text{ treatments}$$

Figure 14-4 illustrates the impact of fixed (and semi-fixed) costs on a break-even point. It shows that the beauty salon with 10,000 treatments has a profit of

$50,000 = 10,000 \times \$20 - (\$100,000 + 10,000 \times \$5)$.

Assume that, with a sales projection of 12,500, the semi-fixed costs will increase with $40,000. As a result, the beauty salon achieves less profit with 2,500 more treatments, namely

$47,500 = 12,500 \times \$20 - (\$140,000 + 12,500 \times \$5)$.

In other words, the beauty salon, like most companies, has an optimal scale of operations. It means that the sales can only be increased to a certain point. Afterwards, additional (semi) fixed costs have to be met before the enterprise can reach its next optimal scale of operations.

Figure 14-4
Break-even chart for determining target return price and break-even volume

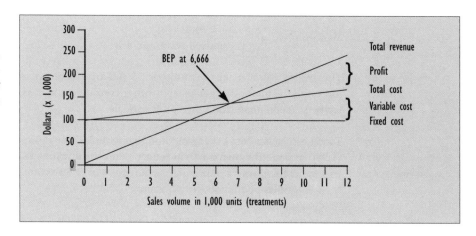

ACTIVITY-BASED COSTING

activity-based costing   Activity-based costing (ABC) differs from other costing systems in its allocation of indirect costs.[31] ABC not only results in more accurate cost prices but also provides better insight into the cost structure as well as into the cost-causing factors.

cost-drivers   Information about these cost-drivers is essential in determining whether to separate or bundle standard services and customized augmented services. Putting it simply, ABC traces the costs of services through all the service-generating activities. This method relates activities to costs. Then, it becomes important to have an adequate

value chain   insight in those activities leading to the strategic cost drivers in the value chain.[32]

activities   Because ABC is based on activities, costs are also collected per activity. These activities are the key in this approach to cost calculation. Lately, ABC has become more accepted – also among auditors – as a valuable method within the group of cost-oriented approaches.

Service practice 14-6 What you eat is what you pay: yes or no?

In many restaurants, the prices of the food on the menu are determined by the principle of What You Eat Is What You Pay. That is, in fact, a traditional costing method, where the prices are based on the price of ingredients. Direct costs (= ingredients used) are increased by a percentage to cover the indirect costs (the kitchen, waiters). A price increase of shrimps will result in a price increase of a shrimp-cocktail – an increase in wages will have no impact on the price of that particular cocktail. Of course, in the long run, all costs must be met. Consequently, the shrimp cocktail price will increase as part of an overall increase in prices. This way of reasoning also assumes that the more ingredients are used, the more time it takes to cook and serve the cocktail.

ABC looks more closely at the indirect activities associated with providing the cocktail or any dish. Preparing a cake with 65 candles takes more time than preparing a cake with just 14 candles. Serving both cakes is similar in terms of activities, time and cost.

ABC collects costs on the basis of activities, not on the basis of food.

thorough analysis of the activities involved in producing a service   On the basis of a thorough analysis of the activities involved in producing a service, dynamic production processes of services can be mapped (see also the blueprints in Chapter Ten). Expensive activities may be reconsidered: is it still necessary to perform them? Should they be priced differently? Analyzing and reconsidering activities related to the production of the service (especially from an IT perspective) is called business process redesign. Competitors and the positioning of a service relative to these competitors may also play a role in the process of dropping particular activities or augmented services.

14.6 COMPETITION AND SUBSTITUTION

competition and substitution

In setting the price, competitors also must be taken into account. Thus, competition and substitution are the third pillar of basic pricing. Here, we recall our concept of market orientation, consisting of customer orientation and competitor orientation, which is applied here to pricing. It reminds us of the attitude of the young café owner in Borovets, continuously scanning his competitive environment.

lower limit

upper limit

In the long term, the final price must be set above its costs (lower limit). On the other hand, the price must be set below the level at which consumers are not willing to buy the service. In other words, the price elastic behavior of buyers determines the upper limit. After this point, buyers prefer the competitors' offer. The costs and time connected to reservation prices should be taken into account here. To be able to determine this upper limit, those suppliers customers perceived as competitors must be identified. The identification may take place in terms of the service offered or the needs that the service fulfils as perceived by the customer. Starting from positioning models, competition occurs when the same service is offered at the same level of standardization and complexity. Examples of price setting of standardized services are "going-rate pricing" or "me-too pricing". In these markets, where services are rather homogeneous and the number of suppliers is high, service providers cannot afford to price higher or lower. A higher price will result in a loss of revenue, whereas a lower price will lead to an unintended price war. The last is especially true in so called oligopolistic markets where a few suppliers dominate the market. Commonly used and easy to apply is competitive parity pricing, where prices are set by those of the market leader.

purchaser's total monetary and non-monetary costs of substitution by doing it oneself

Without doubt, building your own car or mobile telephone is not a feasible alternative to buying. However, in services business, substitution counts as a kind of competition. In many industries, it is still a realistic option. As a consequence, the purchaser's total monetary and non-monetary costs of substitution by doing it oneself instead of buying the service should be taken as a benchmark in pricing. Firms may shun investment bankers doing their own acquisitions. Others cut down on middlemen by brokering big mergers face to face. Supermarkets can also decide whether to give away or sell the scanning data collected at their points-of-sale. Parents may decide to cut their children's hair themselves instead of paying the barber. The prices of gardeners, mutual funds and take-aways are also frequently compared with do-it-yourself. The increase of leisure time, the application of new technology in the garden, kitchen and on-line information to enhance stock-picking, may involve important changes for the respective service providers.

Customized and augmented services aim more at those segments where demand for a service is (more) inelastic. In addition, the costs of these services are often higher. It provides better insight into the actual costs of a service and makes it easier to attune the price to the costs (for example, by using an activity-based costing system). Organizing and managing the service delivery process, personnel and communication are the tools that can be used to distinguish a service organization from its competi-

competitive bidding

sealed bid pricing

tors. In this situation, "competitive bidding" is often used as a pricing method. A buyer compares competitors' offers and prices and will then make a choice. A special form of competitive bidding is sealed bid pricing. This method is, for instance, mandatory for public-funded services contracts. Tender documents of World Bank or EU-contracts indicate, normally, the weight of prices within the overall judgement of the service offer. Thus, the chance of winning, i.e. a consulting contract increases when the firm submits a lower price than competitors. The next section will show that a consumer does not automatically choose the firm that made the cheapest offer. Typically, the combination of the three basics – demand, costs and competition – determines the final price.

14.7 COMBINED STRATEGIES FOR PRICING SERVICES

Three concepts of combined price strategies complete this chapter. These are: pricing over the service life-cycle; quality, costs and price; and value strategies.

PRICING OVER THE SERVICE LIFE-CYCLE

four phases of the life-cycle

A service, like any product, passes through four phases of the life-cycle: development, growth, maturity and decline. Applying this knowledge to pricing services produces the following tips for improving profitable decision making.

Market development

first phase of market development

price insensitive

During the first phase of market development, buyers are to a great extent price insensitive because they are not aware of the service benefits. Price sensitivity may stem from substitution. Buyers may decide to do it themselves instead of purchasing the new service. The access to market volume is buyer education. At this stage, the marketeer should be informed about the firm's overall strategy. A differentiated service strategy, as a cost leadership strategy, may also have its impact on pricing issues. Even for universal banks offering both standard and customized services to the same market segment at the same time, this knowledge is important. Internal objectives, for both competition and market, will determine which service (line) differentiation counts and for which service (line) cost leadership is the predominant factor.

skimming strategy

penetration pricing

A skimming strategy is remunerative if there are clearly divided sizable segments that value the service more highly than other segments. This price discrimination or price differentiation approach allows the firm to reap early profits. As imitation is relatively easy in most service industries, penetration pricing can be used quickly to obtain a large market share before competitors wake up. Penetration pricing is an appropriate policy for establishing and exploiting industry-wide cost leadership. In markets which are not price sensitive, penetration pricing will not enable a firm to gain enough of a share to achieve or exploit a cost advantage. In those circumstances, *neutral pricing*

loss leading pricing

neutral pricing is the most appropriate pricing strategy. At the same time, this strategy can still be quite consistent with the successful chasing of cost leadership.[33] Sometimes, penetration pricing results in loss leading pricing. Of course, loss leading pricing can be only applied in the short term. Typically, it aims at building a defensible market share or cross-selling other services. Penetration is not the right strategy if the real demand (during peak times or more permanently) is larger than anticipated. Often, at this initial stage, operational systems cannot handle the demand. In conclusion, there is generally no need to apply penetration pricing, other than in the case of preventing competitors entering the market or enlarging their market share.

Market growth

market growth

Promotion, personal experiences or feed-back from the first users (innovators) spread the information about the service and its features more broadly. Combined with the entrance of new – previously lagging – large competitors, prices tend to be from stable to downwards. In particular, this is true if market growth is limited, capacity constraints are limited and buyers are price sensitive. However, adding features, auxiliary services and differentiating the core service from competitors may still strengthen the profit margins during this phase.

Market maturity

mature markets

By now, repeat sales are material for the cash flow. Most buyers are familiar with the service. In industrialized countries, many service industries operate in mature markets. Banks, insurance companies, health services and lodging are all facing saturated demand and rivalry. Service practice 14-7 provides more insight into the way in which service suppliers are pricing this longlasting stage in the life cycle of a service (line).

Service practice 14-7 Pricing services in mature markets: health care and armored services

In California, providers of health care in competitive and potentially competitive metropolitan areas are reshaping their systems, cutting costs and developing new relationships with their clients instead of entering into price wars. They redefine their roles and strive to be a value-adding partner rather then offering a commodity service. Choosing to add value promises a more rewarding and viable future.

Loomis Armored Inc., is a company handling people's money, in the United States. It offers risk transfer type of arrangements for banks and commercial institutions to safeguard their materials in transit and keep their employees safe. By defining core business in this way, Loomis Armored Inc. planned to improve its depressed results by setting the three following objectives:

- raise prices for high-risk services or get out of those businesses;
- hold costs constant; and
- reduce risk from all exposures.[34]

In a mature market, the drive towards lower prices, a lower cost base and a more diverse supply will need an integrated marketing-mix approach in order to avoid diffuse images and to protect the market share of the established firm.

Decline

final phase of decline

During this final phase of decline, suppliers are leaving the battlefield. The need to reduce prices further now depends heavily on the remaining competition, the demand and the internal cost structure of the firm. In most service industries, flexibility at the supply side is now a necessary element to meet demand and keep costs low.

QUALITY, COSTS AND PRICE

value based pricing

trade-off

higher consistent quality levels

The transcendent vision of quality in Chapter Five involves high quality costs. Quality viewed from this angle is defined as "the best" or "very good". On the contrary, value based quality-orientation implies less costs. Value based pricing mostly refers to choices, choices whether the increase in quality is still worth the effort in the eyes of the buyer. Here, the trade-off is between quality and price. Striving for excellent quality implies costs which should be incorporated in the price. Thus, focussing on higher quality often leads to price increases or rates higher than those of the competition. As a consequence, it creates openings for limited service providers ("no frills") in mature markets. Therefore, the real challenge for established organizations in all service industries lies in striving for higher consistent quality levels during the whole service offering process while at the same time reducing overall costs. Revenue management or yield management is a crucial management tool for achieving these objectives. Algorithms are at the heart of revenue (yield) management designed to optimize decision making. Higher math gives service firms new power.[35] Algorithms are a part of life. From recipes and tax forms to computer programs, any systematic, step-by-step set of instructions for solving a problem is an algorithm.

Service practice 14-8 Algorithms at American Airlines

American Airlines (see also the case at the end of this chapter) was one of the first to install yield management computer systems in its industry. " It could plug in data about every seat on every route, then manipulate it to see what would happen when variables were changed. That information helped American to discover that it could charge high rates to business fliers and create a radical system to fill empty seats: Super Saver fares. That forever changed the airline industry..."

"At the highest level, algorithms juggle the hundreds of thousands of variables in an entire airline system to tell managers how to better route their planes and price tickets. They calculate in a split second how to route a phone call in nationwide telecommunications... Hotels increasingly are using it to get the most for each room. That's why rooms cost different amounts, depending on when you stay and why you're there. TV broadcasters are just beginning to use yield managment algorithms so they can charge the most possible for commercials in prime time spots and fill in the rest with bargains. Utilities and cruise lines are trying to yield management."

Revenue or yield management software are increasingly using algorithms to go for near-perfect solutions instead of perfect solutions. Managing demand and supply goes further than pricing alone: also, Hastings Books, Music and Video in Amerillo, Texas says specialized software (such as Campbell Software) has reduced the time customers stand in line by 40% and saved 2% on labor costs.[36]

Quality and costs

costs of quality

In Chapter Five, the costs of quality were discussed on the basis of the total (quality) cost which occur during the course of delivering excellent or poor quality. There, we saw that excellent quality requires relatively high costs of inspection and prevention. Poor quality results in high internal and external costs of recovery. Also, a firm rendering poor quality may be confronted with lost orders. It is possible to link these cost categories. For instance, organizations can diminish the chances of recovery costs by spending more on inspection and prevention. Prevention costs reduce the chances of developing deviations in quality and, if expenditures on prevention are sufficient, inspection costs may eventually decline. Spending more money on these assessment activities results in a relatively high percentage of quality deviations discovered internally, within the walls of the organization. This may avoid troubles in the market and expense. Shortcomings detected at an early stage entail less expenses for the organization than quality shortcomings showing up at a later stage during the service delivery. The conclusion is that by reserving more financial resources for

prevention

prevention activities, not only inspection, but also internal and external costs may fall (and therefore rates can be decreased).

optimizing total quality costs

The ultimate goal of quality control and quality cost reporting is optimizing total quality costs. How this should be obtained is not always clear. Roughly speaking, most of the literature distinguishes between two basic views on the optimum level of quality costs:[37]

- School I favors the idea that the optimum level of quality costs is a trade-off between prevention costs and assurance costs, on the one hand, and failure costs, on the other hand.
- School II believes that the optimum level can be achieved by zero defects.

School I

School I is based on two extremes, namely:

- the proven reality that poor quality is uneconomic; and
- the unproven theory that perfect quality is also uneconomic.

optimum level

The latter theory is based on the assumption that perfect quality implies extremely high prevention costs and assurance costs. The most important representative of this school is Juran. His thesis is that when an organization has not realized the optimum level, the total quality costs can be decreased by spending more on prevention and assessment. These savings do not continue indefinitely. At a certain moment, the costs spent on prevention and assessment will outstrip the savings on fixing costs (failure costs). As a result, this school proposes that investing more in quality does not pay. So, there is a limit to quality as the costs involved become too extreme, it makes no sense to strive for perfect services. According to Juran, the optimum level of total quality costs is to be found somewhere between these two extremes (see Figure 14-5).

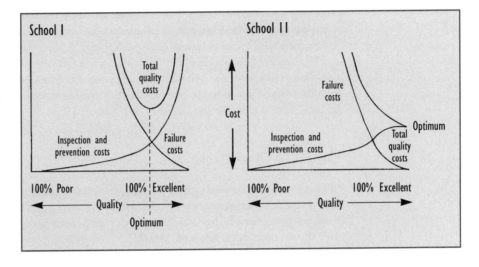

Figure 14-5
Two visions of
quality costs

School II

School II, favoring the zero-defects approach, doubts the underlying principles of School I. In their opinion, striving for zero defects can be in the (economic) interest of a (service) organization. Many advocates of this school are found in Japan. It is based on the principle: every failure is one too many. The name given to this school *zero defects* is therefore "zero defects".[38] They believe that a permanent process of gradual improvements will, in an efficient way, result in "perfect quality". Thus, they presume *100% quality level* that the optimum level of quality costs is achieved at a 100% quality level. This vision takes the line that, influenced by new technologies, perfection or excellent quality at a consistent level can be reached without extreme costs. Figure 14-5 shows the zero-defects approach in a model.

market oriented
organization

Both schools have the right to speak. However, a market oriented organization would have to aim at zero defects.[39] The progress in technology, the increasing competition and demanding buyers force the market oriented firm to deliver faultless services. The increasing technology component in many services, especially standard services, does indeed bring a zero-defects model within reach. In the first instance, this strategic choice will need to be coupled with additional investments and time consuming changes in the organization. The style of management probably needs to be adjusted as well. Such an organization would have to strive at effective internal communication and empower personnel to be able to solve operational problems occurring during the service offering. A less hierarchical organization structure with fewer layers is often the outcome.

Quality and price

positive relationship
between price and
quality

In economic theory, it is assumed that there is a positive relationship between price and quality.[40] This positive relationship will last for as long as consumers are well informed about the prices and the quality attributes. However, this is hardly ever the

price as a quality indicator

case. Some companies benefit from the fact that consumers use the price as a quality indicator. When such companies combine high prices with poor quality, they are cheating the customer. This may seem a lucrative business in the short run – in the long run it will result in losses. The customer will drop the organization and not think of buying there again. This way of behaving is contrary to the vision of relationship management and creating loyalty.

net value

In the long term, a service provider should ensure that the perceived benefits exceed the total costs as perceived by the customer. A consumer can only become satisfied if the "net value", after the performance, is positive.

VALUE STRATEGIES

The value of a trip depends strongly on the reason for that trip. A honeymoon will be more valuable to a consumer than a business trip. This point of view is therefore not based on costs but on the value of a service as perceived by a customer. Zeithaml gives the following definition of "value":[41]

- value is a low price;
- value is what is desired;
- value is quality, that I get for the price; and
- value depends on what I give and what I sacrifice.

value

In many cases, value is a very personal reflection of what people assess as good or bad. So, value, or what one is willing to pay, is very subjective. It may even deviate from actual costs, for instance.

Service practice 14-9 Value, price and knowledge

One of this book's authors once did a small scale qualitative experiment in the hotel industry. After a wonderful weekend in a great resort, he asked the other members of the party what they thought the whole weekend would cost and what they would be willing to pay for it. Although many MBAs were in the group and often stayed in hotels, they had severe difficulties in guessing what the costs would be. They mentioned some figures regarding what they were willing to pay for the weekend and all their figures were far above the actual bill: ranging from 125% to 200%.[42]

Such value based pricing strategies can be attractive to service providers given that they know their costs, have efficient operations, provide excellent service and the service is hard to assess by the customer in every detail.

Lovelock based the notion of "net value" on the difference between all perceived benefits minus the perceived costs,[43] including non monetary costs. The perceived benefits may increase or decrease as the (social) image is positive or negative.

Berry and Yadav suggest "three distinct but related pricing strategies for capturing and communicating the value of a service: satisfaction-based, relationship, and efficiency pricing".[44] Each of these pricing strategies utilizes one or more of the concepts already discussed in this chapter. The difference, however, is the starting point, which is now value, meaning benefits for "burdens endured" (monetary and non-monetary costs). In this sense, marketing thinking is shifting from trying to maximize the service firm's profit from each transaction to maximizing the mutual profit from each relationship.[45] The value strategies can be either applied separately or in a combination.

benefits for "burdens endured"

Satisfaction-based pricing

This pricing strategy is focussed on alleviating uncertainty. Well known ways to diminish the feeling of uncertainty while offering intangible products are: service guarantees (for example, promising delivery within a certain time or return of money if the buyer is not satisfied with the performance); and benefit-driven pricing, which focusses on pricing the aspect of the service that directly benefits the buyer – for instance, pricing the information instead of the search time with on-line databases. Benefit driven pricing allows people to do business in a "one-off" fashion. Here, an illustration shows the transactional pricing of investment banks. The idea of transactional pricing, in contrast to relationship pricing, is that a deal should be profitable at once and not return a positive net income to the service provider over an extended period of time. By taking the company through the whole process and underwriting the deal (buying the securities at a certain price), the investment banker offers certainty and diminishes the risk of losing (financial) face to the prospect. The benefit-driven approach also becomes crystal-clear in success-fee pricing and incentive pricing. Reducing the uncertainty and perceived value for the client (during pre-purchase phase) goes hand in hand with the profiting from real benefits (post-purchase phase).

benefit driven pricing
transactional pricing
relationship pricing

Service practice 14-10 Uncommon price policy of lawyers

An uncommon price policy is followed by the lawyers at Wilson, Sonsini, Goodrich & Rosati, Silicon Valley's other power élite. It represents promising start-ups for free until clients can pay legal bills. As a consequence, the lawyers' firm is tied to the success or failure of their clients. The gamble has paid off handsomely, with such success stories as Sun Microsystems Inc. In addition to the normal legal type work, they dole out the kind of financial advice usually expected from bankers or venture capitalists. The firm invests in start-ups and takes them public. They maintain a current portfolio of some 500 client companies, including Logic Corp and Synopsys. Between 1990-1995, the firm took more than double the number of high-tech companies public than their nearest competitor, according to Securities Data Co., representing semi conductor companies and the top three disk makers. Its vast representation of venture capitalists and underwriters makes it an incomparable business network.

"Venture lawyers" will offer to work for little or nothing, betting that when a start-up company gets big enough to generate large legal bills, it will stick with whom they know. Accounting firms handle a venture-blessed start-up for a few thousand dollars; they charge their Fortune 500 clients millions. In the same way, "venture landlords" lease at a discount.[46]

success-fee

In applying success-fee pricing, it is the service provider that shares in the benefits for its client. An IT-consultant or lease company could link its (increased) price – according to some agreed formula – to demonstrated results in performance and/or savings.

incentive pricing

In utilizing incentive pricing, it is the customer that benefits by means of a bonus or reduction on the fee. For health insurance policies, this can be achieved by participating in activities (i.e. prevention visit or excercizing programmes) or non-participating (i.e. no smoking of cigarettes). In many service industries, there are still opportunities for both types of pricing tactics.[47] In using flat-rate pricing, the service provider diminishes the risk for the purchaser by offering one flat price. This type of pricing is attractive to buyers if they do not know beforehand how often the service will be needed and/or the service is labor-intensive. Examples include long term service contracts for machinery and computers, legal services and tourism.

Relationship pricing

As customer relationships become more remunerative over time, the focus is on entering into, maintaining and enhancing the relationship with (potential) profitable clients. To optimize profit, it is crucial to base price considerations, manage costs and concentrate efforts of all parties within the firm on those customers offering the best potential profit over the relationship's life-time.

relationship pricing

Detailed information about clients and their "value" contribution is essential to focus time (and attention) of management, front and back office on these important clients. Loyal, profitable customers and their long lasting relationships are lucrative for any firm. They also decrease the substantial costs connected with acquisition of new customers. Long-term contracts and/or price bundling are at the core of relationship pricing. To establish a profitable relationship, both parties need to answer crucial questions. What do the service provider and client expect from each other? Which non-price factors also determine the "price" of the relationship? In this framework, "price" should be seen much broader than just costs and returns. Therefore, our key idea behind relationship pricing is to convert "shoppers" into "loyals" by adding (relevant) value to the client.

Some services are billed as a lump sum at the start or at intervals. These services are very attractive because the fee is paid before the service is performed. Naturally, this constitutes a marketing policy aimed at an on-going formal relationship.

Efficiency pricing

efficiency pricing

This is the last value pricing strategy mentioned by Berry and Yadev, 1996. "Understanding, managing, and reducing costs are the cornerstones of efficiency pricing. Some or all of the resulting cost savings are passed on to customers in the form of lower prices. To be effective, the leaner cost structure must be difficult to imitate in the short term. Furthermore, cost savings passed on to customers must genuinely enhance their value perceptions. Cost trimming that results in less expensive but unsatisfactory service will not be successful."

14.8 FROM TACTICS TO PRICING FOR CORE, AUGMENTED, STANDARD AND CUSTOMIZED SERVICES

Bearing in mind the variety of services and the differences in freedom of price setting, it is now time to incorporate the service classification from Chapter Two and the one at the beginning of this chapter. Our classification revealed four kinds of services. With regard to price and quality, a number of conclusions can be drawn.

price of standard services

As a result of competition and often high priced elasticity, the price of standard services is based mainly on the company's costs including, among others, full costing, Activity Based Costing, markup (cost-plus) pricing and target return pricing; in spite of their single focus on costs the two last mentioned methods are still used frequently in the service sector. These pricing methods give the company an initial impression about the final price.

customized augmented service

However, if services are added, there is more room in price setting. If a customized augmented service leads to a high degree of differentiation, even a more than proportional increase in price is possible. Mostly, adding (peripheral) services means a less transparent price for the buyer. Trust in the service provider is, however, more than necessary; otherwise the customer will not perceive a fair price and will feel cheated. A good example of an open price strategy (and also benefit-driven pricing incentives to the client) is Lease Plan, a leasing company operating predominantly in Europe and Australia, offering fixed operational leasing rates for cars. By keeping track of all costs, Lease Plan will return money to customers when actual costs are lower than the projected costs. This approach stimulates organizations – as it concerns mainly company cars – to economize in the usage of their cars. Thrifty drivers then contribute to the credit notes their companies are receiving from the leasing company. This "open" (transparent) method of calculation has proved to be a successful marketing tool in the international expansion of Lease Plan.[48]

The greater the number of services added to a core service, the more differentiated the pricing of an augmented service can be. In this case, the perceived quality strongly depends on the price: higher quality indicated by a higher price. As a result

psychological price

of the absence of search attributes, the price of such a service will be a psychological price (see also Figure 14-6 – this figure is also a summary of what has been said about pricing for various services throughout this chapter).

To illustrate price determination in practice, we will now discuss briefly some important considerations influencing pricing in two cases. First, Service practice 14-11 shows how in a business to business world, auditors apply pricing. Second, Service practice 14-12 proves that the market forces in the holiday industry require a carefully calculated bundling-offer.

Figure 14-6
Selected methods of
pricing and different
services

	Standard core services	Customized core services	Standard augmented service	Customized augmented service
Consumer costs: - Monetary - Non-monetary	high low	low high	high low	low high
Price elasticity	elastic	inelastic	Rather elastic	very inelastic
Relevance quality attributes	search	search, experience and credence	search and experienced	search, experience and credence
Price bundling method	mixed leader/ mixed joint	pure bundling	mixed leader/ mixed joint	mixed joint
Price discrimination	effective	not possible	effective	sometimes possible
Price based on competition	going-rate	less relevant	going rate	less relevant
Price setting	cost accounting	psychological	cost accounting psychological	psychological
Quality perception price	low	high	low	high

Service
practice
14-11
Charges of
auditors

Sometimes, all or many firms in one industry have the same pricing strategy. This is also the case in CPA firms, as Michael Morris and Donald Fuller report on the American situation.[49] The data in this case is based on a study these two authors did in the Orlando, Florida region. 71 questionnaires were returned from a survey among the managing partners of 268 certified public accounting (CPA) firms. Some of their main findings are presented in the following tables.

Table 14-1 Levels of importance when setting price
(% reflects those respondents considering the item to be the most important one in setting prices)

Profit objectives	39.1%
Estimating and covering costs	17.4%
Customer price sensitivity	8.7%
Ethical considerations	7.2%
Prices of other services offered	7.2%

It appeared that two thirds of the respondents either do not set pricing objectives or do so informally. Where objectives are established (= in one third of the cases) they hinge upon a wide variety of reasons, as shown in Table 14-2.

Table 14-2 Frequency ratings for common price objectives

Short-term profits	84.3%
Be competitive	82.4%
Long-term profits	81.2%
Billings	73.9%
Attract new business	64.7%
Encourage demand for services	44.8%
Image	43.3%
Market share	14.4%

In terms of demand considerations, about 70% of the managing partners perceive their clients to be price sensitive. The quality and timeliness of the work was cited by 42% of the respondents as the key factor affecting customer price sensitivity. Other factors mentioned included the availability of substitutes (18%) and client perceptions of task complexity (14%). Moreover, a mere 21.5% of those responding saw price as an effective tool for managing demand even though clients are perceived as price sensitive. Furthermore, a moderate number of firms (32.4%) explicitly used price as an indicator of service quality. This is in spite of the large number who indicated that quality is a key determinant of price sensitivity.

It also appeared that CPA firms demonstrate a preoccupation with costs in their pricing practices, as well as a general lack of strategic direction. Most firms charge a rate which is a multiple of the effective hourly rate paid to the staff member involved. Pricing flexibility is fairly limited in these firms. There is moderate reliance on such tactics as bundling or using the price of one service to help sell other services. Price changes are infrequent and some attempts are made to vary fees according to the buying situation (type of services rendered, size of the account, length of time a particular customer has been buying from the firm, volume of services purchased by a customer).

In the past, public accountants found most pricing decisions easy, based on cost principles, charging a reasonable profit margin and checking if fees were roughly in line with major competitors. That was the custom. For clients both large and small, it was not done to require invoice specifications (a major source of complaints about accountants). Today, in most countries the picture for big audit firms is more diverse. The common external audit has become a mature market. Technology and competition have changed the lives of accountants. As in the advertising industry, some large companies may organize contests between audit firms for contracts lasting several years. Then, the art of bidding or tendering also becomes important. Purchase specialists also prove to be successful in re-negotiating lower fees with auditors as part of their overall job of decreasing operational costs for their clients. At the same time, entrepreneurs and smaller firms often require more frequent access to their accountants, even during evenings and weekends, a feature that is not always offered by the larger audit firms. On the pricing front, large accountant groups react with reductions in fees, opt for long term contracts with fixed flat (hour) prices (or lump sums) as well as offering customers more transparency of rate structures. In consumer services too, pricing strategies change over time, as in the case of the Fiesta Hotel in Costa Rica.

Service practice 14-12 "Todo Incluido" at the Fiesta Hotel in Costa Rica [50]

People like to know how much they have spent before they leave. Kids asking for another coke or ice-cream leaves parents not sure of their expenditure. Therefore, Ticos (the affectionate nickname of Costa Ricans) and foreigners require all-in prices for their stay at the Fiesta Hotel in Puntarenas (Costa Rica). It was this consideration, in the first place, that forced management to change its pricing policy. The Fiesta Hotel has 310 air-conditioned rooms. It contains three swimming pools, Jacuzzis, gym, tennis courts, four restaurants, three bars, a disco and a casino. Meeting and convention facilities are part of this resort, which advertises itself as "everything under the sun". "Take an extremely high dose of fun in the sun and become Fiestaholic". The resort focusses on vacationers and companies. Fiesta vacationers typically belong to the middle class: families including young children and/or teenagers. The business segment consists mainly of local companies and regional organizations organizing seminars and small conventions. Up till 1997, for most tourists having booked their trip abroad, in particular Germans, the hotel had already offered all inclusive rates. The demand driven cry for "todo incluido" (all inclusive) prices became apparent during 1996. Especially, the Ticos spending their weekends or mid-week days at the Fiesta resort asked for a total price covering all food and beverages. Events such as aerobics, water games and children's activities were already free. A second force triggering the change in rate structure was the competition of Hotel Playa Tambor, the beautiful but less centrally located, 800 room resort offering, at that time, "all inclusive" rates. Playa Tambor, part of a Spanish owned hotel chain was heavily advertising its offer via radio stations listened to all over Costa Rica. Although less important, a third reason was the impact of studies in the tourist sector showing that an all inclusive service package could reduce staff by up to 30%. Although wages in Costa Rica are still low in comparison with many Western and Eastern countries, wages are an important cost factor in the Costa Rican lodging industry, like everywhere. As personalized service forms an important element of the total offering, the Fiesta management did not plan to cut staff to the bone. Besides, the staff morale was very high. People are proud to work for Fiesta. Every day, they are taught that the client is the main asset and that the employees are the second most important asset of the resort. In such an environment, it is difficult to fire staff without losing the motivation of the remaining staff resulting in deteriorating quality offered to the public. For this reason, it was decided to keep the labor-intensive Italian and Fish restaurant open, in addition to the large self-service buffet.

As service is a key feature of Fiesta, management also decided to retain the waiters and waitresses serving tea and coffee during the meals.

> Up till 1997, the Fiesta prices were as follows: breakfast US $6, lunch US $10 and dinner US $12. As is common in the restaurant business, these rates were mainly based on the costs of food plus a margin. The dinner rate in the central restaurant, for example, consisted of three main dishes each including either meat, fish or chicken. The exact price was then based on the experiences of the hotel of the average number of guests choosing certain menus. In all basic choices, it was profitable. Even, in most cases, if people chose combinations of expensive food ingredients, the outcome was positive.

Before summarizing we would like to recall the story of the young café owner at the ski slope in Borovets (Bulgaria). As it proved, pricing is still very much done intuitively, based on "trial and error" or, what the Germans call "Fingerspitzengefühl". As entrepreneurs in emerging markets and large service providers in mature markets, such as Club Med, experience continuously, the falling ("pricing wrongly") can hurt and rising ("pricing rightly") can be healing ("the profits").

SUMMARY

This chapter centers on price. Because of the close client/producer linkage and the fact that the production process serves various products, pricing services is complicated. It is also more difficult for the client to judge tariffs. Pricing strategies and pricing depend strongly on the organization's objectives. Three types of service organizations can be distinguished here: services subject to public regulation; services subject to formal self regulation; and services subject to regulation of the marketplace. The pricing objectives arise from this classification. Pricing objectives may vary from social or political desirability to a fixed ROI percentage or matching supply to demand. Lots of other factors also play a role in setting the final price. One of these factors, for instance, is cost. Service-related costs can be incurred by the consumer and by the service provider. The consumer's costs consist of monetary costs and non-monetary costs (physical, sensory and mental costs).

Price setting can also be affected by price bundling. This is especially useful for service organizations,

because, in this way, a part of the fixed costs can be shifted on to the customer. Moreover, it may reduce perceived risk.

Naturally, customer driven thinking requires producers to include price sensivity while formulating price policies. For this purpose, estimates of the elasticity of demand is a beneficial tool. Services for which demand is highly elastic are often not especially complex to the customer and mostly chosen on the basis of search attributes. Services for which demand is inelastic are often chosen on the basis of experience and credence attributes.

Segmentation is an obvious guide to profitable pricing. Provided the segments are homogeneous, sustainable and large enough, segmented pricing may be based on buyer identification; purchase location; time of purchase; purchase quantity; product or service bundling; service design; metering and membership.

When the price is used as a tool to regulate demand

and supply, differential pricing and/or discriminatory pricing are involved most of the time.

Service organizations whose demand is inelastic will often try to differentiate services as a competitive tool. Pricing in mature service markets requires special knowledge.

Research has not yet shown the exact relationship between (perceived) costs, quality and price. There are two views on the optimum level of quality costs. Some favor the idea that the optimum level of quality costs is a trade-off between, on the one hand, prevention costs and assurance costs and, on the other hand, failure costs. Others favor the zero-defects approach. Also, the assumption is made that the influence of price on the perceived quality is growing as a service is less standardized. Thus, pricing and quality are interrelated to a high degree.

In this relation, value is the key issue. The value concept, meaning benefits for "burdens endured" (monetary and non-monetary costs). The prospect's perception of "value" or "worth" is essential in understanding profitable decision making in the service sector. It is winning through value-oriented marketing. Value strategies for services pricing embrace satisfaction pricing, relationship pricing and efficiency pricing. Applying relationship marketing in pricing implies that a relationship should be profitable for both parties, the supplier and the buyer.

In services, the delivery process is of utmost importance. Therefore, activity based costing will always be a useful way to calculate costs in a service firm. A market oriented service firm should not only look at their own costs at a particular occupancy rate, but should also take into account the costs the customer has to pay to "enjoy" the service.

QUESTIONS

1 What are the basics of pricing?
2 In what way will a service firm's market orientation ideally be reflected in its pricing policy?
3 In what way does price add to the quality value of a service?
4 What is the essence of price bundling? What arguments are in favor or against bundling in mature markets? What are the advantages and disadvantages of price bundling to both customers and service providers?
5 Could one also apply price bundling as part of a level capacity strategy?
6 During which stages in the service life-cycle is price-based competition most successful?
7 What does ARGE mean? Why is it useful to apply this concept?
8 Why should the price be based on the service triangle?
9 What has been said about relationship marketing and pricing in this chapter?
10 What is the essence of ABC? Why can it be useful to service industries?

ASSIGNMENTS

1 List three services with a high pricing transparancy. List three services with a low pricing transparancy. What do both types of pricing transparancies imply for the supplier's freedom to determine prices?

2 Add "what has been said about pricing and relationship marketing" to what you already know about relationship marketing. How does that all fit together?

3 Why could one prefer ABC over other cost accounting systems in services? Explain your answer.

4 Which techniques of segmented pricing do you know? Give, for two techniques, a service example of a situation in which you would recommend use of these methods.

5 Give examples of services and circumstances where either costs, demand, competition/substitution or a combination (of the three) would prevail.

6 See Service practice 14-11. If we assume that these CPAs really desire to be market oriented in rendering bundles of customized augmented services such as accounting and management consultancy, then

- characterize the CPA's pricing practices;
- evaluate their current market orientation and their pricing practices;
- list pricing practices that do not seem to be applied here;
- recommend (new) pricing strategies and objectives;
- compare the pricing practices of these CPAs and the recommended pricing strategies practices with those performed by CPAs in your own country or state.

7 See Service practice 14-12. Evaluate the reasons forcing the management of the Fiesta to change their price strategy.

Case: AMERICAN AIRLINES AND YIELD MANAGEMENT: AN IDEAL COMBINATION![51]

The objectives in the airline industry are demanding: maximizing revenue, minimizing costs, high customer satisfaction and creating loyal passengers are examples every airline embraces, including American Airlines. But times are changing the way these objectives are achieved.

American Airlines started, at the beginning of the sixties, a study directed on controlling the revenues stemming from the reservation system. In view of the scope and complexity of the issue, American Airlines developed a number of models dividing the issue into three easier to control sub-issues: booking (in particular "over-booking"), allowing discounts on tariffs and traffic management. Traffic management is the control process of reservations of passengers between place of departure and place of destination, via various stop-overs, in order to maximize revenues. The answers to these sub-questions were combined and, for a long time, they have determined the reservation system.

For a number of years now, US airlines have been subject to an intensive price war. One of the consequences of deregulation has been the replacement of public regulation by the rules of the free market. The withdrawal of government has resulted in a highly competitive environment. It has forced the management of American Airlines to monitor the short-term revenues very closely.

Small airlines have been forced to leave the market place. Also, for the big mega-carriers it has been difficult to operate profitably every year under the immense pressure of aiming at low costs and high revenues.

Another consequence is the change in determining prices. Tariffs are based more on cost techniques than market considerations. This change in the legislative environment affected pricing. In the past, tariffs were heavily influenced by the authorities. At present, while setting prices, the competition and the wishes of the consumer should be taken more into account. What is even harder to map, is that the prices and demands fluctuate over time.

Finally, this fading away of governmental bodies fixing prices has ended up in a more concentrated industry. It seems that the concentration has resulted into higher entry barriers, making it more difficult for newcomers to enter the market. As one of the reasons to amend airline regulation was to create more opportunities for new startups, the intention of the deregulation has partly failed.

As a result of the emerging rivals and the calculation of tickets on the basis of cost techniques, American Airlines has been focussing, for the last twenty years, increasingly on minimizing costs and maximizing revenues. A system that has been utilized for this purpose is yield managment.

Applying the definition of yield management to the airline business, one could say: at how long before departure, should tariffs be altered, according to demand, in order to optimize the revenue? Yield management provides airlines with the opportunity to find the right balance between occupancy rates and pricing, enabling them to obtain most profit. With the assistance of yield management, better information is generated for the management on the basis of which better decisions can be made.

American Airlines and yield management

In fact, yield management tries no more than to accomplish what American Airlines already wanted to achieve, since the sixties, by controlling the three sub-issues: over-booking, allowing discounts and traffic management; namely, providing a quality service at a price as profitable as possible in the long term.

For many years, decision makers at American Airlines have played around with their selling rates, by granting discounts and taking too many reservations for a particular flight ("over-booking") in order to maximize turnover. However, management do not need to juggle with ticket prices to increase sales and thus profit. By allocating supply and demand optimally, a profit increase will be accomplished, benefiting both the client and American Airlines.

Revenues

An airline such as American Airlines has an average of 1,500 flights daily with 220 seats on board in eight booking classes. The planning of these seats starts 330 days before departure of the plane. The planning will be monitored at various moments and adjusted. With the allocation of seats via yield managment, American Airlines has realized an additional revenue of 5-10%. This implies an advantage of $1.4 billion in three years' time. Besides which, management expects an additional yearly revenue of $500 million in the future.

Every day, there are occasions when managers consult the system. The management also knows that they could allow discounts 24 hours before departure, if:

- the occupancy rate is below 95% and
- the decision will increase ARGE.

The maximum sales for one flight, Amsterdam–New York, is theoretically $330,000. The capacity sold 13 hours before the flight amounts to 205 seats. At that moment, a tourist party requires six places for a tariff of $1,150 per seat. In this type of situation, management heaves a sigh of relief, because with the help of the system a decision can easily be made according to the company's guidelines.

On the basis of this information, it could be concluded that American Airlines optimally utilize yield management. The implementation of yield management has been a far reaching change. However, the airline has clearly reaped the fruits of their decision. So, one could speak about an ideal combination between the airline and its approach.

Currently, service providers in many industries are applying the yield management approach. Typically, at present, yield management is exercised with the assistance of algorithms, allowing up to hundreds of different variables to be used to optimize pricing decisions.

QUESTIONS

1 Classify the services of American Airlines in our service typology in Chapter Two.
2 Describe how the system of overbooking of reservations operates.
3 Formulate a number of problems a manager of American Airlines can solve with the support of a good yield management system.
4 Estimate the additional revenue American Airlines generates, if you know that through the operation of the system 0.001% of the seats, which are incorporated in the system, can be sold for $150.
5 In addition to yield management, American Airlines can also apply various other forms of capacity management. Please, give some examples.
6 Argue whether American Airlines has to reckon with a high or low price elasticity of demand?
7 What kind of monetary and non-monetary costs does a passenger need to take into account for a flight?
8 What is the occupancy rate before the request for the six seats? What is the revenue percentage if American Airlines honors the proposal if you know that all other seats have been sold for the maximum price? What will then be the sales realized? Calculate ARGE via three methods. Has the manager taken the right decision?
9 Answer question 8 again, but now in the situation 210 seats have been sold.

ENDNOTES

1. Club Méditerranée, Annual Report 1993-1994, p. 13. More on Club Med is presented in Chapter Fifteen.
2. Ibid, pp. 16-17.
3. Nagle, 1987, p. 7.
4. Nagle, 1987, p. 7 and Cowell, 1984.
5. See, also Lovelock, 1991, pp. 236-245.
6. Consumers' demand and costs can not always be separated. For the sake of clarity, we will discuss them in a separate section, however.
7. Normann, 1991, p. 125; see also Chen et al., 1994.
8. Simon, 1992.
9. Normann 1991, p. 126.
10. Berry, 1995, p. 62.
11. Berry, 1995, p. 66.
12. Normann, 1991, p. 126.
13. Guiltinan, 1987.
14. Lovelock, 1991, pp. 32-33.
15. Price bundling is just one of the means firms can use to implement bundling. Bundling can also be regarded as a cheap, low risk form of innovation (Eppen et al., 1981; De Brentani, 1995; Simonin and Ruth, 1995). Then existing products and services are combined in a new bundled form.

    Bundling can also be seen as a form of standardization. When services are completely tailor made and/or new, it is hard to convince the prospective buyer about the (benefits of the) new service, especially when it is hard to assess the new service on search attributes. A bundled form of services may provide the customer with more attributes or tangibles. Then the purchase decision may become easier to the customer.

    Bundling can also be seen as a way to strengthen relationships with customers by providing them full packages of products and accompanying services. In this respect, Eppen et al. (1991) even discuss the concept of "loyalty bundling" as a form of bundling primarily aimed at preventing customers to switch.
16. Much of this section is based on the MBA thesis written by Coos Groot, 1995.
17. Guiltinan, 1987, p. 352.
18. Paun, 1993.
19. Paun, 1993, p. 30.
20. See, for instance Lemmink and Kasper, 1994.
21. Bateson, 1995, pp. 366-376.
22. Payne and Clarke, 1995.
23. Adapted from Rutherford, 1995, p. 102.
24. Nagle, 1987, pp. 175-176. To a large extent, this section about segmented pricing, is based on Chapter 7 of Thomas T. Nagle.
25. Nagle, 1987, p. 158.
26. Nagle, 1987, pp. 158-162.
27. Lovelock, 1991, pp. 122-127.
28. Nagle, 1987, p. 217, see for a more detailed explanation of the importance of competitive cost advantages and internal/external cost efficiencies, see Nagle, Chapter Nine.
29. Compare for example Lovelock 1991, p. 236.

30. The idea for this example is based on Kotler, 1991, pp. 483-485.

31. Roozen, 1991.

32. Porter, 1985; Govindarajan and Shank, 1989.

33. Nagle, 1987, p. 153.

34. Health Care Strategic Management, Volume 14, Issue 5, May 1996; Business Insurance, Volume 30, Issue 17, April 22, pp. 130-131. The information from both sources has been adapted on the basis of UPI Company data.

35. Under this headline, Kevin Maney writes in the popular paper USA Today, Friday, 2 January 1998, pp. 7a-8a, a brief essay about the impact of algorithms on various industries and the effects on our daily life.

36. These quotations, and Service practice 14-8 are from Kevin Maney, USA Today, 2 January 1998, p. 8a.

37. See, for example De Heer et al., 1990, pp. 27-33.

38. Crosby, 1983.

39. See Simon and Hartog, 1993.

40. See for example Steenkamp, 1993a.

41. Zeithaml, 1988.

42. The great resort was Hotel Vaalsbroek in The Netherlands.

43. Lovelock, 1991.

44. Berry and Yadav, 1996.

45. See also the recent books and courses of Philip Kotler in which this idea has been worked out.

46. Business Week, 8 May, 1995 and The Economist, January 1997.

47. See for more information about success-fee pricing and incentive pricing Normann, 1991, p. 130.

48. Lease Plan is a fully owned subsidiairy of ABN AMRO in The Netherlands.

49. See Morris and Fuller, 1989.

50. By Piet van Helsdingen, based on a company brochure, stay at the hotel and interview with one of the employees.

51. This case has been written by Monique Dijkstra, student, Free University, Amsterdam.

CHAPTER FIFTEEN

IMPLEMENTATION AND CONTROL

After studying this chapter you should be able to:

- *discern the unique problems of implementation and control of the marketing strategy in a market-oriented service firm;*

- *formulate ways to avoid these problems and/or solve them;*

- *position the problems of implementation and control within the framework of the SERVQUAL-model;*

- *discern the importance of accurately formulated corporate and marketing objectives;*

- *realize that these goals set the framework for the financial and non-financial criteria for evaluating actual service performance;*

- *fine tune the various elements of the marketing mix in services;*

- *determine how demand and supply can be matched;*

- *define the role of the consumer, the contact personnel and the rest of the personnel in the service encounter;*

- *see the need to apply the concept of internal marketing in easing the implementation of high quality service strategies and tactics;*

- *define and measure performance in service industries;*

- *control strategies and activities in market-oriented service organizations: and*

- *take notice of a stepwise plan to introduce strategies which can increase quality and/or market orientation.*

BELOW: *Hotel Vaalsbroek*

15.1 INTRODUCTION

Service
practice
15-1
Amtrak ready
to fly high by
challenging
the airlines [1]

After being left for dead, Amtrak – a US railway company – is back with a new campaign, "Experience the Freedom", and the goal of taking business away from the airlines. Amtrak was forced to cut routes and service frequency by 16% in 1995 because of severe cutbacks in federal subsidies. Funding dropped from $392 million in fiscal 1995 to $185 million in fiscal 1996, according to the US Department of Transportation. Some travel experts wondered whether the rail service could survive the long-term. The campaign began with national TV and radio spots, designed to ensure Amtrak's viability. The adverts were being supplemented by national promotions tied to the release of the Walt Disney video, *The Aristocats*. Coupons enclosed in the package allowed kids to ride free with their parents or grandparents on Amtrak. Bob Herring, senior director of marketing for Amtrak, said the focus of the campaign was "to communicate the on-board experience on Amtrak and its personal freedom benefits, which are sociability, relaxation, and a no-hassle travel experience".

Amtrak is trying to compete with airlines by borrowing some of their successful practices. It has advance-purchase requirements and cancellation penalties on many discount tickets. Like airline adverts, the Amtrak campaign focussed on specific routes instead of generic services. Amtrak's first TV ad campaign specifically featured the Empire route, which links New York City with Albany and western New York. Amtrak introduced the Frequent Rider incentive prgram for its Empire and Metroliner (New York to Washington, DC). George Warrington, CEO of Amtrak's Northeast Corridor, said the program is designed to reward travellers for taking the train. For two round-trips or four one-ways in a three-month period, travellers could earn 20% discounts at Clarion Hotels and other Choice properties, 20% discounts at thousands of restaurants nationwide, and Empire or Metroliner Club Class upgrades. Four round-trips or eight one-ways earned 10% discounts at Bloomingdales up to $160, or a half-hour's worth of domestic long-distance phone calls from MCI, and a $25 Amtrak travel certificate. At least five round-trips or 10 one-ways earned travellers discounts of 25% to 50% on Royal Carribean cruises plus a cabin upgrade, a free six-month subscription to one of five outdoor recreational magazines, and one free Empire or Metroliner weekend ticket.

Amtrak has also concentrated on adding features to its trains including room service, showers, and private TVs in some sleeper cars. The Viewliner, the newest train car, has showers on board. The sleeping compartments in the Viewliner now have a second berth of windows for the top bunk so that riders don't get claustrophobic. The Viewliner is a new generation of rail car and the first completely designed by Amtrak, said Jim Loomis, owner of Loomis & Pollock, a marketing agency in Honolulu and author of *All Aboard: The Complete North American Train Travel Guide*. Amtrak's new Club Class includes deluxe seating (separate section, bigger seats, more room), hot towels, complimentary newspapers, free meals and beverage, including a glass of wine, served by an attendant, and use of the Metropolitan lounges in New York, Washington, DC, and Philadelphia. The new Custom Class is defined as deluxe seating with a free newspaper and nonalcoholic beverage. It is available only on the Empire and Northeast Direct (Boston to Newport News, Va.) lines.

By adding the new program and features, Amtrak hopes to earn enough money to pursue its long term strategy and have a major chance of survival.

Amtrak has selected Canada's Bombardier and France's GEC Alsthom to build high-speed trains for the Northeast corridor. They are expected to spend $750 million on the development of the trains, due to be in service by 1999. The challenge is to market the current rail service and increase the customer base now so that the high-speed rail program can build on that success.

"The one problem with Amtrak is that when something good is offered, people don't know about it because the marketing support isn't there," said Scott Leonard, assistant director, National Association of Railroad Passengers (NARP), Washington DC. Leonard said he has heard of many cases in which citizens didn't even know that Amtrak served their towns. "This concentrated marketing effort of specific routes should try and take care of that problem," he said.

Another problem with Amtrak is that until last year it had not been entrepreneurial, said Ron Kilcoyne, transit manager of Santa Clarita Transit, Santa Clarita, Calif., and a train expert who has worked with NARP. "Any new train route came either at the behest of states... or if some congressman wanted a train," he said. Amtrak was not in control of its future. "Nobody at Amtrak went after markets," said Kilcoyne. "Trains would be cut if there was a budget problem."

To focus on marketing, Amtrak has changed its management structure. Three regional strategic business units in Philadelphia, Chicago, and the West Coast are responsible for local service. Every train line has a product manager who is responsible for all the marketing and services. Kilcoyne said the West Coast unit has developed a more entrepreneurial spirit to try to find new markets. "There's a vast, vast potential for intercity rail travel," he said "You have to look beneath the surface."

In this chapter, we deal with a number of subjects about the implementation and control of a marketing strategy in a service organization. In previous chapters, we have discussed many issues of a strategic and tactical nature, including its implementation. Some hints were given, deemed relevant to efficient implementation. The issues at stake in this chapter will mainly be ones which have not been discussed before. They are about implementing and controlling the service marketing effort and the final stages of the marketing planning process aimed at accomplishing the goals set. Some features of breakthrough service providers have not been discussed yet. A more detailed overview of the characteristics of these kinds of service providers (what they think and actually do and how they do it) may function as a benchmark other service providers may use for comparison purposes. That is why we discuss them here at the beginning of the chapter on implementation and control.

breakthrough service providers

Breakthrough service providers are characterized by many features.[2] They "regard the relationships in a service encounter as a series of mutually reinforcing concepts (higher quality and higher productivity, lower costs and higher customer loyalty, etc.). They concentrate on producing services of the highest value to customers, taking into account quality in relation to price and other customer costs of service acquisition; and focus marketing and service delivery efforts on building the loyalty of existing customers while also attracting new ones. They measure both customer and server expectations and meet or exceed both, recognizing the self-reinforcing relationship between server and customer satisfaction."[3] It appears that these service providers

mission

define their mission in terms of the customer benefits to be produced for a clearly defined segment, to meet (or exceed) their needs by specifically defined services and

relationships

service delivery systems. Close relationships are the basis for having so much information about these customers and talking to them about the service offering and

loyalty
profit chain

service quality desired. That sets the basis for creating loyalty and repeat purchasing. The profit chain, recognizing the close links between customer loyalty and customer satisfaction, on the one hand, and employee loyalty and satisfaction, on the other, is a

excellent service quality

valuable tool for providing information about the cost of excellent service quality and productivity. It also demonstrates the cost of poor quality.

communication

Information technology is not only important in having relevant data about the customer but also in matching demand and supply. Short and informal communication channels and lines of decision making are necessary in order to be flexible and react quickly to changes in the DRETS factors. This calls for a flat

empowerment

organization with empowered people. They can only exercise that high degree of empowerment when they are aware of the framework within which they have the freedom to decide. Consequently, the mission, strategy, customer benefits, service quality, etc. must be known in order to do so. This comes back to our view of the

market-oriented service-providers

characteristics of the market-oriented service providers from Chapter One:

> "Such a culture is characterized by a sincere concern/care about people (customers and employees), high ethics, results or goal oriented, long term orientation, risk taking, empowerment and, pragmatically, meeting customer needs. This is reflected in thorough market knowledge, clear and internally well communicated target group specific marketing goals, developing new services, manager's role model, better relative quality of services and after sales services, and an excellent cooperation and exchange of market information between departments."

The marketing strategy and the marketing mix can be used to give content and meaning to the relationships the service organization and the customers want to establish, maintain, enhance and, if necessary, want to end. Many issues have turned out to be important in these relationships in order to assure excellent service quality.

key success factors

Managing all of them properly, effectively and efficiently is a complex task. The key success factors for the service firm have to be identified, implemented and controlled (via the relevant key control variables) to meet the goals of (= create value for) the stakeholders, e.g to accomplish customer satisfaction, employee satisfaction and profits for the shareholders. Then, the basics for the marketing strategy and competitive positioning can be formulated and implemented.[4]

personal relationships

retention rates

Personal relationships have proven to be very effective (but often also very costly) in service industries. However, the mere fact of introducing the function of "account manager" is not sufficient to create loyal customers and high retention rates; more needs to be done to make the whole organization market oriented and work in a market oriented corporate culture. In many service businesses, the professional (be he or she a doctor, dentist, veterinarian, lawyer or accountant) has to change attitudes in order to cope with the laws of the market today (face competition, advertise, etc.). They have to realize that their own professional (technical) quality is often not the decisive factor in determining service quality.[5] A recent study about marketing relationships in personal banking in New Zealand revealed "the personal banker strategy facilitates the development of customer-bank relationships – where customers are satisfied with their personal banker's performance. Contact with personal bankers builds positive perceptions and word of mouth, yet is not significantly correlated with retention. This is perhaps indicative of the complexities and depth of relationships. The ability of banks to further implement the relationship approach is jeopardised by a number of factors: lack of adequate training in personal banking, large customer numbers per personal banker, and inability to calculate accurately customer profitability. These all suggest that banks in New Zealand are not building the capabilities required to fully operate on a relationship basis."[6] However, these banks are not the only ones facing difficulties in implementing a relationship strategy. A UK study about the relationships between a bank and their business customers who require low cost basic banking services, such as making and receiving payments by cheque (a special target group of business customers), revealed various deficiencies in their retention practice.[7] Possible solutions to overcome these shortcomings are: formulate explicit targets for retention; differentiate the customer retention marketing mix from the mix used in customer acquisition; focus attention not only on satisfying customers but also on the profitability of the relationship; obtain from customers valuable information to improve the relationship; and check whether the customer(s) really do want an intense relationship with the bank (the intensity may vary per customer or target group). In an international context, relationships may even expand onto another continent. The different dimensions of national culture will play an important role here: access to high status managers and informality in relationships will be different in countries with a high or low power distance, or in cultures characterized as individualism or collectivism. Comparing the relationship marketing programs of two groups of banks in Hong Kong (those whose country of origin is in Asia or outside Asia – western banks) showed "the well recognized belief that the concept of relationship marketing in the western context is treated as a structured, systematic and corporate issue while the Asian culture treats the relationship as more a personal issue, "Guanxi"."[8] This indicates that for Asians the relationship is not only built on the business context, but on the personal context as well. In other words, differences in culture are significant in the content of the concept of relationships, in the formulated relationship marketing strategy, in its implementation, and, thus in the way it can be controlled.

human resources management

The importance of people in the servuction process (and thus the close interface with human resources management) has been stressed on many occasions. They also contribute to the content of the relationship in market oriented service companies. We have stressed the close links between customer satisfaction and loyalty and employee satisfaction and loyalty. Commitment to quality, the brand or to the firm is important here. It has been shown that managers who are committed to service quality are more likely to empower their employees via behavior-based criteria. Customers' perceptions of service quality can be increased by increasing employees' self-efficacy and job satisfaction, and by reducing the employees' role of conflict and ambiguity.[9] Commitment of employees may be enhanced via internal marketing, for instance. Targeted communication (internal as well as external) about corporate values, goals, strategies, actions, new plans, etc. will help employees to identify themselves with the company. The communication climate in the organization is decisive here: how an organization communicates is probably more important in this respect than what it communicates. Openness, honesty and participation in decision making are relevant and "hard" factors with respect to organizational identification.[10] In the end, organizational commitment will be enhanced. These issues closely resemble the openness dimension and people orientation in a market oriented corporate culture.

commitment of employees

communication climate

organizational commitment

As was said before, HRM (recruitment, training, assessment, career development and rewards/incentives) is an important part of company activities in order to be or become market-oriented. This part of the managerial activities should be considered in close relationship to the company's organizational system (structure and processes), its information system (the generation and dissemination of information and the memory function), its planning system (target definition, monitoring the environment, choice of alternatives, etc.), and its controlling system (the comparison between target and actual performance, and the analysis of variance/deviations).[11] In this way, the whole process of strategy development, implementation and control fits into a systems approach of organization. It labels the areas where changes should be made in order to deliver excellent service quality and be market oriented (if deemed necessary).

organizational system
information system
planning system
controlling system

In Chapter One, the practical aspects of a market-oriented strategy and culture are mentioned. In describing the classification of services in Chapter Two, we looked at the question – what does a particular choice in this classification mean for the way of working in the organization. For example, increasing the degree of customer participation in the service delivery process has consequences for the way the customer has to act and the way the service provider can control this process. Other elements in front office employees' behavior are stressed when choosing a high quality service. Analyzing the whole service of delivery from the point of view of the technical, functional and relational quality and the quality dimensions belonging to them. When developing the different steps in the delivery of these three service qualities, different subjects have already been mentioned which might ease its implementation and control. Next to this, the chapters on the marketing mix in service organizations contain a lot of practical issues related to implementing and controlling them. One could think of:

- the notion of considering employees as part-time marketeers and consumers as part-time employees;
- the notion of the external and internal orientation of the employees and the triad of the employees;
- the content given to the service attitude and the leadership style in a service organization;
- the analysis of the total service delivery process by means of, e.g flow charts and blueprints;
- the strategic and tactical service concept as such;
- the process and organization of developing new services, new service processes and their implementation;
- the stages in the processes of dissatisfaction management;
- the strategic choice for a location of the service outlet;
- the innovations in distribution;
- the basis on which the selling price is determined (particularly the price strategies and activity based costing);
- the relationship between the service quality dimensions and the communication policy; and
- the guidelines for an effective communication campaign.

In Chapter Eight, we touched upon the idea that internal marketing can be applied at a strategic and an operational level. This can, for example, be done on the one hand, to create and implement a market-oriented culture or, on the other hand, to encourage the acceptance of new ideas and concrete activities. The notion of internal marketing will be discussed more thoroughly in this chapter (section 15.6).

We will also discuss a few more subjects which are either completely new or which integrate with previous topics. With respect to the part on implementation in this chapter these will be:

- the link between relationship marketing, implementation and control (section 15.2);
- the characteristics of the marketing mix elements for each of the four types of services we have developed will be put together to show the (need for) coherence between them (section 15.3);
- marketing services in mature markets (section 15.4);
- some general issues which can hinder or prevent implementation and which a service-provider therefore has to avoid (section 15.5);
- matching demand and supply (section 15.8);
- solving and/or preventing the problems by which gaps arise in the SERVQUAL-model (section 15.9); and
- the service encounter where contact personnel and customer meet each other and shape the service delivery process (section 15.7).

With respect to the part on control, this chapter discusses, amongst others, the relationship between control, strategy and the service concept (section 15.11) and measuring performance in services (section 15.10). This is all visualized in Figure 15-1.

Figure 15-1
Chapter outline

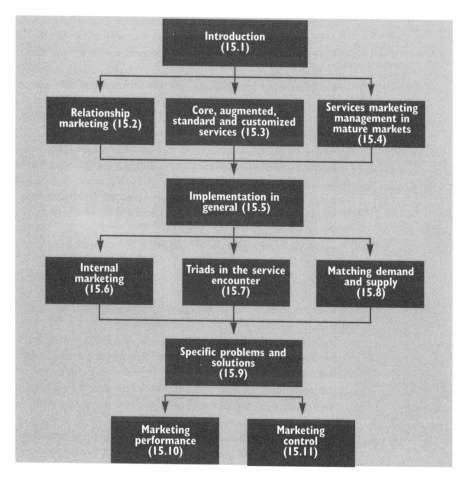

15.2 IMPLEMENTATION, CONTROL, RELATIONSHIPS AND MARKET ORIENTATION

making strategies work

Implementation refers to what Thomas Bonoma, 1985, once called "making strategies work".[12] Making plans is only one part of the deal. Secondly, these plans have to be implemented into the organization and, finally, they have to be executed properly. The implementation and execution is possibly more difficult than making plans in a service organization, since a service organization depends heavily on people (employees and participating customers), resources, (core)competences, possibilities and routines. Now, one has to actually accomplish the plans formulated behind the desk. Then, it will be seen whether the plans are built logically, e.g. whether all parts really fit together. The chosen strategy, the desired relationships (intensity and target group) and the accompanying marketing mix of the service organization should be in line with one another, at least they should not be contradictory. This sounds self-evident, but is hard to achieve. Often, the employees (and customers) have to perform new activities or work in different ways than before. This may cause some degree of resistance which the organization has to cope with.

Control refers to influencing the service delivery process in such a way that the chance to accomplish the specified strategic and operational goals will increase. This often requires having the right information about the actual (quality of the) service delivery process in order to take corrective action (when needed) on time.

The stages of implementation and control belong to the last phases of the planning process in both the external and internal marketing planning process discussed in Chapter Eight. The focus here, however, is on the lower part of Figure 15-2.

15.3 CORE, AUGMENTED, STANDARD AND CUSTOMIZED SERVICES

The four types of services developed in our classification scheme, in Chapter Two, have been elaborated upon in Chapter Eight with respect to the strategic characteristics of these four groups of services. In each chapter on the marketing mix, we have elaborated upon the characteristics of each of those four services with respect to

overall picture

each element of the mix. Here, we will put all of them together to show the overall picture of the characteristics of each of those four services. It must be now shown whether the parts are consistent to one another, one of the major issues in implementing strategies.

Our classification of services hinges upon two dimensions, namely: the degree of customization (between standard and customized services); and, the degree of differentiation (between core and augmented services). This is shown in Figure 15-3.

The characteristics of each of these four types of services have been discussed in Chapters Eight, Ten, Eleven, Twelve, Thirteen and Fourteen.[13] The results are summarized in figures in those chapters. Here, we will combine all those separate figures into one overall figure: Figure 15-4. This overall figure will be elaborated upon now.

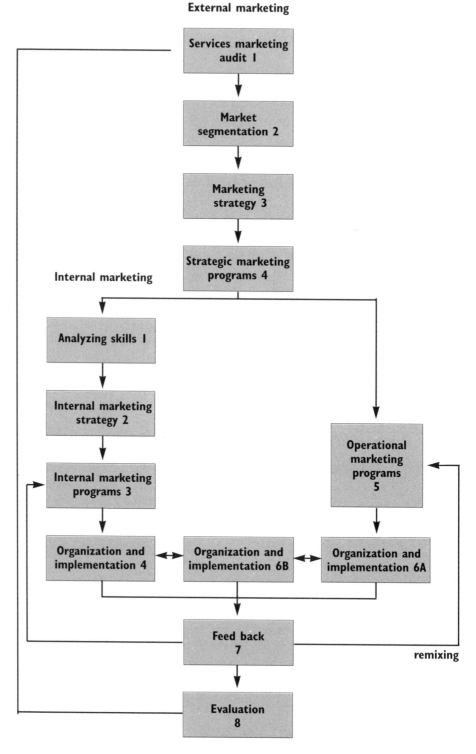

Figure 15-2
*Implementation and
control in the external
and internal marketing
planning process*

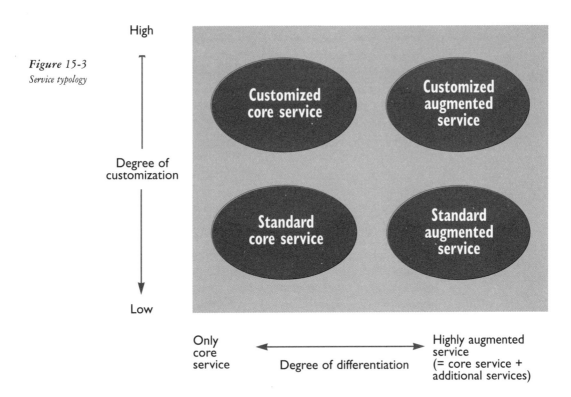

Figure 15-3
Service typology

STANDARD CORE SERVICES

standard core services   Standard core services are usually characterized by large scale cost effective production. This is possible due to its standard character of serving an unsegmented market (or very large segments in a market). It is a typical production line organization (also in terms of empowerment) for the front office employees. The standardization in work procedures are high and (top) management exercises direct control. Relatively low skilled jobs are present.

The services offered consist of a wide but not so deep assortment of core services including some (simple) facilitating services. Brands are not that relevant in this mass market (they may become more important in order to differentiate from competitors in mature markets or when these services become "a commodity"). Personal contact in the service encounter is quite low (often replaced by computers and machines: ATMs). Advertising and direct marketing are appropriate means of communication between service provider and customer/client. These convenience services are provided via intensive distribution. The choice of the location to which the customer has to travel is an important issue. Prices are quite elastic. Monetary costs are high to the customers while the non-monetary costs are quite low.

Figure 15-4
Four genetic service strategies in detail

	Standard core services	Standard augmented services	Customized core services	Customized augmented services
Key success factors	cost efficiency	cost efficiency more complexity	differentiation to unique client/ segment relationships	highly differentiated complex
Offering	standardized	standardization and some standard additional services (not so complex)	standardization and some differentiation (quite complex)	specialization unique services added to core (very complex)
Market focus	broad no/hardly any segmentation	broad some segments	narrow very specific segments defined	very narow individualized personalized
Kind of contact personnel	contactors	modifiers contactors	contactors modifiers	modifiers
Role (top) management	direct control	supporting initiating	direct control supporting	initiating coaching
Standardization in work procedures	high	moderate	high	low
Type of empowerment	production line	job involvement	production line suggestion involvement	high involvement
Strategic services concept	core and facilitating services	core and facilitating services	core and facilitating and supporting services	core and facilitating and supporting services
Assortment	not wide, shallow	broad, undeep	not wide, deep	broad, deep
Service process: - personal interaction - capacity management	low contact chase demand	high contact level capacity	low/middle contact chase demand	high contact level capacity
Advertising	appropriate. Communicate message internally and externally	appropriate, but relatively expensive, especially for starting organizations	very appropriate for big organizations. Aim internally and externally at differentiaion by aditional service delivery	appropriate. Mainly aimed at quality and image

Figure 15-4
Continued

Personal selling	mostly inappropriate. Only used when explanation is required	mostly inappropriate. Only used when explanation is required	crucial. Service delivery process often is personal selling	service delivery process is initialized by personal selling
Sales promotion	can be used in several forms	can be used in several forms	can be used in several forms	only as image support
Word-of-mouth and public relations	important	important	essential	essential
Direct marketing	effective when big (general) database and mailing lists are used	effective when big (general) database and mailing lists (of the organization itself) are used	effective when small – mostly local – mailing list is used	effective when small specific mailing list is used
Interaction	customer travels	supplier travels	customer travels	supplier travels
Distribution strategy	intensive distribution	selective distribution	selective distribution	exclusive distribution
Kind of service	convenience	shopping and speciality	convenience and shopping	speciality
Strategic alternatives	single-service/multi-site	single-service/single-site	multi-service/multi-site	multi-service/single-site
Distribution coverage	high	low	high	low
Choice of location	important	less important	important	less important
Consumer costs: - monetary - non monetary	high low	low high	high low	low high
Price elasticity	elastic	inelastic	rather elastic	very inelastic
Relevant quality attributes	search	search, experienced and credence	search and experienced	search, experienced and credence
Price bundling method	mixed leader/mixed joint	pure bundling	mixed leader/mixed joint	mixed joint
Price discrimination	effective	not possible	effective	sometimes possible

Prices based on competition	going-rate	less relevant	going-rate	less relevant
Price setting	cost accounting	psychological	cost accounting/ psychological	psychological
Quality perception price	low	high	low	high

Figure 15-4
Continued

CUSTOMIZED CORE SERVICES

customized core services

Customized core services are standardized services which are differentiated to a certain extent to meet the needs of some specific segments in the market. This differentiation, via some facilitating and/or supporting services, is used to give deeper meaning to the relationship intended between service provider and customer. Standardization in work procedures is high, although some form of personal involvement of front line personnel is at stake. Top management not only exercises direct control but also has a supporting role. The personal interaction during the service encounter is low to medium. The assortment of services offered is not wide, but deep. This fits quite well into these shopping services offered via a selective distribution strategy. Prices are probably not so elastic and the quality perception of prices is quite high.

STANDARD AUGMENTED SERVICES

standard augmented services

Standard augmented services are dominated by the standardization character. Again, cost efficient production of these services is at stake. Differentiation via some standard additional, facilitating service leads to this kind of augmented service. Some broad market segments have been defined for which this offering is intended. The standardization in work procedures is moderate, empowerment is taking place via a high job involvement and a supporting or initiating role of top management. The assortment of these convenience and shopping services is broad but not so deep. Selective distribution via a multi-service multi-site policy and high contact personal interaction are crucial in the servuction process. This explains why personal selling and quite high labor skills are crucial here. Prices are rather elastic and the quality perception of prices is low, mainly because of the dominant feature of standardization within these augmented services.

CUSTOMIZED AUGMENTED SERVICES

customized augmented services

Highly differentiated, complex services consisting of a core service plus a wide variety of facilitating and supporting services defined for a very specific market segment or even individual customers, are the main features of the customized augmented services. Highly qualified and empowered front office employees, coached by their top managers provide services without hardly any strict or standardized work procedures. They perform the role of modifiers, have high contact situations during the service encounter and "sell and market" the services personally. These specialty services are offered via a strategy of exclusive distribution. The service organization does not have that many outlets. However, in each outlet a multitude of services can be "produced". Psychological pricing is at stake, the quality perception of prices is high (meaning a higher price will be regarded as providing better quality because experience and credence attributes play a crucial role here).

15.4 SERVICES MARKETING MANAGEMENT IN MATURE MARKETS

maturity phase

scissors movement

processes

improving sales and lowering cost

In many developed countries, the maturity phase is currently visible for services as diverse as external audits, car rental and consumer banking. At this stage, the level of personnel costs is crucial. Companies have to be alert to avoid what is called the scissors movement: the percentage of operating costs is growing faster than the percentage of operating revenue. As the so called Limited Service Supplier (LSP) enters the market and win a market share, it may be even necessary to lower the absolute level of the operating costs. The services marketing instrument processes is now gaining importance. Efficient providers with established brand names are less sensitive to low cost producers when they can redesign their processes efficiently. Improving sales and lowering cost simultaneously is the goal (sometimes easier said than implemented) in order to survive in mature markets.

product

LSP's

distribution

promotion

pricing

In the maturity phase, the mix-instrument product points to branding, innovation and unbundling (in a limited number of cases, bundling may enhance customer loyalty). A viable option may be to distinguish fully between standardized and customized services. Both product concepts should be made clear in the mind of the buyers. At this stage, the wish to compete with LSP's may lead the GSP to a choice of different distribution channels, mostly available to the same client. In finance, the consumer may choose customized services (i.e. advice on mortgages or investment advice) at one moment while, the next moment, he or she uses a LSP such as an Internet provider to assess the account, to order shares (discount brokerage) or to transfer money. Thus, established service organizations are opting for multiple distribution channels. In many service industries, the "24-hours" economy is taking off. Every consumer may choose at which moment he or she wants to consume. Dependence on location is on its way back. For example, in insurances, at least one distribution channel (i.e. accessable by telephone or PC) is always available. We may eat a pizza at the restaurant, take away or choose to have it delivered at home at 12 o'clock midnight. Typically, promotion is centered on below-the-line activities (i.e. direct mail and price actions). Another, above-the-line, focus is on branding. For instance, a strong brand name will ensure that the Website of a reputable GSP will be preferred over an (unknown?) LSP. However, in order to preserve its market share against the new and old order the organization should be prepared to cut its tariffs. Also, at this stage, value pricing is gaining importance. The three value strategies: satisfaction based, relationship and efficiency pricing, are attractive options to avoid a complete price war. In the event that supply does not form an obstacle "flat" rate, such as that recently introduced in the USA by telephone and Internet providers form an attractive tactic to lure business from other suppliers. Similarly, as shown in the airline industry and standardized banking services, smaller suppliers with lower cost structures than GSP's are becoming more competitive. This requires big enterprises with high fixed cost structures – which are developed over the years – to react. Thus, cutting costs and simultaneously increasing sales are becoming central to the survival of the company. At corporate level, strategic partnering, implementing flexitime schemes, cutting staff levels, outsourcing and spinning off non-strategic units are common reactions. By offering cheaper alternatives to the client, i.e through own low cost limited service providers (LSP's as owned strategic business units) or partnerships, the established institution tries to strenghten its relationship with the client. Mergers and/or acquisitions – striving to simultaneously remove competitors and increase economies of scale – are viable possibilities for growth at the expense of the other market players in mature markets.

mergers and/or acquisitions

In conclusion, the large firm tries to protect its market share in mature markets via many internal and external measures. All of them have not only to be invented, formulated but also implemented.

15.5 IMPLEMENTATION: GENERAL PROBLEMS AND SOLUTIONS

strategy development and implementation mutually influence each other

One has to realize that in implementing a newly developed strategy (or changing an existing strategy) development and implementation cannot be seen apart from each other: strategy development and implementation mutually influence each other. This seems to be self evident, but in practice we unfortunately see that it is not or is insufficiently taken into account. That is one of the most important reasons why the implementation of a new strategy may fail. What has been developed on one level in the organization might serve as a limiting factor for the next level in the hierarchy. Therefore, it is possible that, when at the beginning of the strategy development process or at the planning process the involvement of those who have to execute the strategy is decreased, implementation ultimately will not be possible. To avoid these problems, a well-balanced combination of top-down and bottom-up communication is absolutely necessary. Other causes which can hamper the implementation of new or altered marketing strategies are: unclear or non-existent goals or objectives; top management does not (completely) support the new plans (or insufficient commitment and/or resources); the culture and/or the structure of the organization prevent implementation (for example, when there is insufficient linking-up with the means, possibilities and routines in the service process to realize the new position); those who have to decide on and those who have to execute the strategy cannot overlook the consequences of their decisions.[15]

top-down and bottom-up communication hamper the implementation

In 1998, the *Financial Times* quote Philippe Bourguignon, the new CEO at Club Med, who had brought many ideas with him from his time at Euro Disney and Accor, a French hotel group. Reshaping the organization was necessary because Club Med had not made real money for five years. "The main lesson from Disney was its ability to stimulate ideas and talent while applying rigorous management," he said. "We have to let the villages be a bit crazy, fun and provocative, but manage them properly." He understood the importance of marketing. Pricing strategies and yield management were essential in putting Club Med back into the black. Club Med would be focussing more on the Club Med brand. That included a huge increase in advertising, combined with an effort to redefine the group's image, which he said had been locked into the 1970s. There would be a fresh appeal to younger clients. "It's less about eroticism than sensuality, and also – which is not a traditional Club Med value – about freedom and autonomy," he said.

Mr Bourguignon has another quality which will prove to be essential in the months ahead: his apparently enormous enthusiasm for the product, and his willingness to roll up his sleeves and spend time talking to employees. At the inauguration of the Club Med's Varadero village in Cuba, he had no hestitation in disguising himself as a waiter, and taking part in a song-and-dance routine.

He needs to tread carefully to preserve what he argued is the greatest source of Club Med: its *gentils organisateurs*, or staff. Yet he promised in the first month of 1998 to find Ffr150m ($25m) in productivity savings over three years; he did not rule out staff cuts. Under his management, a substantial change at top levels has already taken place. At the centre of his strategy is the attempt to refocus the business on its core middle-of-the range "three trident" villages. While some visitors to the villages become loyal, many of them visit Club Med only one or two times more and then do not return. The inconsistency of services and quality at different sites is the main cause for this type of loyalty, according to Mr Bourguignon. Therefore, some 74 villages will be renovated in the next three years, at a cost of Ffr 1.8bn. The separate Aquarius brand will disappear, and its villages become Club Med sites.

Mr Bourguignon has the support of his largest investors. However, the *Financial Times* questions whether he can gather similar support from staff and customers.

Several studies have been done about some other more general problems which occur when implementing a strategy. In implementing, e.g. quality management in service organizations, a short term policy is often harmful. [16] The advantages of quality management often become evident only in the long term and not in the short term. This problem can be solved by introducing a long(er) term orientation in the organization. Then, the organization will not only rely on the short term and financial indicators to measure effectiveness and efficiency (measuring success and results in the short term). This, for example, also means that the variable part of the wages of, for

short term policy

instance, sales representatives, sales people and marketing managers will not only be determined by the monthly or quarterly turnover, but also by behavioral variables like customer satisfaction, brand loyalty and other long-term standards. This fits into a culture of market orientation which is characterized by a clear long term orientation.

culture Also, the necessity of a high degree of consistency in the culture of a service organization should be recognized.[17] This agrees with our remarks on small differences in subcultures within a service organization. This cultural problem could be an essential problem, especially in developing a marketing policy in and for governmental organizations. Other factors that hinder the implementation of a marketing strategy aimed at high quality service provision are the lack of knowledge of perceived quality and the problems that might be encountered in translating the externally required quality into the necessary internal quality (and, the other way round, when looking at the internal strengths of the service provider).[18] Often, more attention is given to external quality than internal quality, forgetting that the weakest part of the chain (e.g. internal service quality) determines the quality of the whole value chain, and thus external quality.

Service practice 15-3 The strategic power of internal service excellence[19]

"Over the past decade, most efforts in organizational change have focussed on the higher profile activities, such as serving the external customer. But more than 40 per cent of the workforce and 45 per cent of the payroll of most large companies are comprised of **internal service units** – those groups whose primary task is to supply services to others within their own firm. The quality of these services, delivered so early in the value production chain, sets an absolute ceiling on the possible quality of final goods or services to the external customer. Nevertheless, despite the size and importance of these internal service functions, they all too often perform quite poorly in many organizations."

dynamics of the service process It may also be the case that the dynamics of the service process itself are insufficiently taken into account. Expectations change over time and the service provider has to know the cause of the ascertained difference in quality. A stepwise plan with the following phases can help in overcoming or avoiding such shortcomings:

1. a thorough analysis of the factors determining customer's quality perception (for example, the dimensions of the service quality: 18, 10 or 5;
2. management and employees actually have to be involved in defining and operationalizing the organization's quality and market orientation. As stated in Chapter Ten, this means that they have to be able to have the opportunity to and be motivated to accomplish this;
3. open communication about quality and market orientation between customers, personnel and management is fundamental, also in connection with the management of customer expectations;
4. market orientation and quality have to flow throughout the organization and require continuous attention; and

5. continuous monitoring and measuring the quality of service delivery and market orientation with customers and employees.[20]

We believe internal marketing can also be used as a means to encourage the smooth implementation of new strategies or new ideas.

15.6   INTERNAL MARKETING[21]

internal marketing

The concept of internal marketing first appeared in articles in the late 1970s and early 1980s.[22] Since then, several articles and books have been written about this subject. Many issues are also common in the field of HRM.[23] As stated in Chapter Eight, at a certain point of time in the marketing planning process, the internal side of the organization must be ready and well equipped to execute the plans for the external market. Here, we will discuss how internal marketing may contribute to that end.

All the attention paid to the subject of internal marketing can be explained by increased competition in many markets and the growing need for customer orientation.[24] The increase in competition makes the role of the boundary-spanning personnel more important, especially in the service sector.[25] Other causes for the growing interest in internal marketing are its potential for easing the implementation of marketing strategies and the on-going urge for cost reduction and quality improvement.[26]

DEFINITION

exchange processes

Marketing is aimed at the creation of exchange processes that satisfy individual and organizational objectives. External marketing usually deals with exchange processes with, and therefore with the demands of, external customers. Inside an organization there are exchange processes as well. Most of these processes have a similarity with the exchange processes between the organization and its external environment. Like the exchange processes with the external environment, it is also important to know the demands and wishes of customers inside the organization. In the first publications on the subject, internal marketing was described in quite a narrow definition:

> "Internal marketing means applying the philosophy and practices of marketing to people who serve the external customer so that (1) the best possible people can be employed and retained and (2) they will do the best possible work."[27]

boundary spanning role

From this definition, it follows that the employee who has a boundary spanning role between organization and customer is therefore exposed to the same marketing practices as the external customer. These employees can therefore be regarded as an internal customer of the organization, but they are not the only internal customers. There are more exchange processes within an organization. There are, for instance, the exchange relationships between the various departments. In later definitions this and other aspects of internal marketing get more attention.[28] In the definition, there should be attention to the attitude and behavior of the organization and its personnel with regard to the external environment as well as to the internal exchange processes. This leads us to defining internal marketing as:

> The process of planning and executing marketing activities aimed at the creation and improvement of exchange processes within the organisation, with the objective of accomplishing organizational and personal objectives and processes in a more efficient and effective way.

three important
statements

In this definition, three important statements emerge:

1. internal marketing is applied to exchange processes within the organization;
2. it deals with HRM activities, for which internal marketing instruments are used; and
3. it is a process of planning and executing aimed at satisfying the objectives of both parties in the service encounter (if we apply it to service organizations).

strategic level
tactical level

There are two levels within the internal marketing concept: the strategic and the tactical.[29] At the strategic level, conditions are established for the execution of the internal marketing concept (planning). The tactical level is concerned with the adjustment around certain activities (execution and fine tuning). Most of the exchange processes will have both a strategic and a tactical dimension, only the intensity of each will differ with the type of exchange. Therefore, the different exchange processes will be described first.

FOUR TYPES OF EXCHANGE PROCESSES

Four exchange processes can be found. The exchange process between the organization and the employees, which is concerned with the employment and motivation of the employees, has already been mentioned. Next, there are three other types of exchange processes. First, the one between top management and the departments of an organization; the second is between departments, and the last is the one between the management of the department and its employees (see Figure 15-5). Of course, this figure may differ per firm (especially between small and large ones).

Exchange processes between the organization and the employees

the organization and
the employees

The first goal of internal marketing in the exchange process between the organization and the employees is recruiting those employees that best fit the organization and the tasks to be performed (corporate image plays a filter role in this respect). A second goal is to motivate the employees to generate the highest possible effort in realizing the organizational objectives. Both refer to the organization's input of labor, knowledge, skills, etc. To recruit the right personnel and to motivate them, the service organization will have to offer the personnel a set of benefits. These include not only a job and a salary but also the possibility to gain knowledge, personal development and responsibility. In return, the (prospective) employee sacrifices leisure time, but

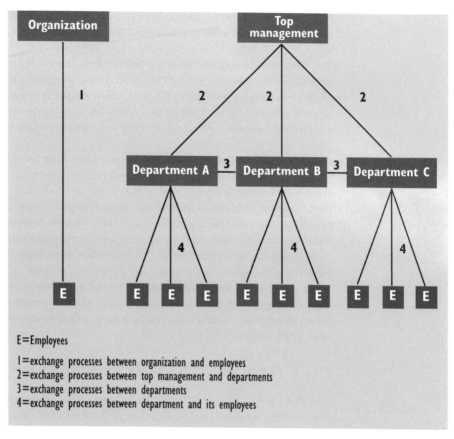

Figure 15-5
The four types of
exchange processes
in internal
marketing

E=Employees

1=exchange processes between organization and employees
2=exchange processes between top management and departments
3=exchange processes between departments
4=exchange processes between department and its employees

displays motivation, dedication and involvement by accepting the responsibility offered. The efforts made by organization and employee should be well-balanced (actually and perceived).

Exchange processes between top management and the departments

top management and the departments

The main goal of the exchange process between top management and the departments or middle-management is to create conditions in order to ensure good business practice. Most of these exchanges are of a hierarchical nature instead of market driven. Top management offers a business mission, objectives and policies. The top management also offers responsibility for the quality of the processes within the organization to the departments. This can be considered as the framework in which the empowered employees can work. In return, the departments have to accept the mission, the objectives and the policies, and face the responsibilities for the actions and performance of their departments.

Exchange processes between the departments

between departments

Exchanges are also taking place between departments. First, there are the exchanges in the primary production process. Here, there are exchanges between typical staff departments and line managers. The primary process deals with the actual delivery of services. The objective of internal marketing here is to stimulate efficiency and effectiveness. Excellent cooperation and exchange of information between departments is a typical feature of market-oriented organizations.

The exchange processes between departments resemble the exchange processes with the external environment. Therefore, it is not surprizing that the same marketing principles can be applied here. It is a matter of matching demand and supply between internal suppliers (who have to be market-oriented on this internal market as well) and internal customers (who, e.g. set their own standards for excellent service quality).

Exchange processes between the department and its employees

department and its employees

The fourth group of exchange processes is between the department and its employees. These exchange processes deal mostly with the subject of coordination, leadership (coaching) and the allocation of tasks and budgets. The goal of internal marketing here is to improve the attunement, and with that the efficiency, effectiveness and team-attitude. The management of the department offers the employees a more explicit job specification (usually more explicit than agreed on in the contract), including responsibilities for a task and participation in the decision making process of the department. Some other offerings are departmental culture and loyalty from one's colleagues. The department, in return, gets the employees' dedication to the department and to colleagues, which results in responsibility for their actions and the employees' loyalty.

FOUR GROUPS OF INTERNAL MARKETING TOOLS

tools

Now that the four groups of exchange processes have been described, the instruments or tools that might be used to influence and smooth the exchange processes will be presented. These are summarized in Figure 15-6. The internal marketing tools can be put into four groups, each one related to the four exchange processes. These are: the personnel management tools, the organizational tools, the internal market tuning tools and the management tools.

Personnel management tools

personnel management tools

The personnel management tools can be linked to the exchange process between organization and employees. The tools are: job and salary (in all its varieties), the possibility to gain knowledge and the organizational career possibilities. They are aimed at facilitating hiring, keeping, and motivating employees. To ensure the organization hires "the right employee", management will have to formulate its wishes, requirements and offerings. Recruiting and selection can be carried out on the basis of these trade-offs. It is a means of assuring that the company has the right "input" of employees. Once the employees are hired, it is important that they are and will be motivated to perform their tasks. If employees are willing to extend/increase their knowledge, the service organization can use tools like training, conferences, seminars and the like. In order to offer career possibilities, the organization could start a career planning policy completed eventually by a management development program. A quite different tool is introducing an internal commissioner (ombudsman) for personal affairs. This independent employee should guarantee that all employees are treated equally, and handle and investigate employees' complaints.

Organizational tools

organizational tools

Organizational tools are tools that can influence exchange processes between top management and the departments. These tools help create an environment in which the service firm can function. The mission statement and the written organizational objectives (top management's vision) are the basis for management and clear communication. A second instrument is the organizational structure. The structure not only sets the hierarchy, it also determines the structure of formal and informal meetings and thus the means of communication. It partly determines what skills are needed within the organization. The organizational structure can be used, e.g. as a segmentation criterium, on which basis it is decided on who is entitled to certain information. A third tool is organizational culture. Culture determines to a large extent the way things are carried out in the organization. For instance, culture partly determines how managers handle their staff, how problems are to be solved, how people cooperate and how the customer is treated. That is why we have paid so much attention to the link between market orientation, HRM and corporate culture in services in previous chapters. Two other tools can also be used: an internal complaint registration and a suggestion box (idea box).

Internal market tuning tools

internal market tuning tools

Internal market tuning tools can be used to attune the departments' wishes and needs. These tools are basically the same as the marketing tools used for external markets. In departments, internal markets exist with internal clients, whose wishes and needs should be satisfied. Examples of tools are internal market research, internal market segmentation, internal and external mass-communication and personal selling. Internal transfer-prices and (in)formal relations will already exist.

Management tools

management tools

Management tools are those tools used not only to influence the exchange processes between the department's management and employees, but also for the exchange processes between top management and departments. Most tools can be characterized as communication tools. Three kinds of communication can be mentioned here: oral, written, and using audio-visual equipment.[30] Within the oral communication type, it is possible to differentiate between three sub-groups: formal communication (e.g. meetings), informal (e.g. talks in the hall-way) and personal mass communication. Within these groups, there are several possibilities to communicate. Written communication can also be performed in different ways. The media could contain memos, corporate bulletins, and publications. There are also function descriptions, manuals, etc. Audio-visual communication can also be presented in different ways, using television (evenutally via satellite), video, audio-tape and/or computers (especially in the international firm). Other instruments that can be used as management tools are employee opinion surveys and management style (which may vary, e.g from authoritarian to coaching, leading to different degrees of empowering employees).

The specific tools and offerings should be balanced one way or another. That leads to the "exchange balance" in Figure 15-6. This figure also reveals which tools and exchange processes apply the most (+++) or the least (+) at a particular level.

Figure 15-6
*Overview of relevant
issues in internal
marketing*

Exchange process	Tools	Exchange balance		Use mainly	
		Offerings	Returns	Strategic	Tactical
Organization and individual employees	Personnel management tools	Job and salary Knowledge (training) Responsibility Career opportunities	Giving up leisure time Dedication Motivation and involvement Accepting responsibility	+ + +	+
Top management and departments	Organizational tools	Mission statement Objectives Policies Responsibilities Control instruments	Acceptation Results Being accountable	+ +	+ +
Department and other departments	Internal market tuning tools	Raw material/semi-manufactured articles Final products/ services	Internal transfer prices cooperation	+ +	+ +
Department and employees	Management tools	Job descriptions Participation in decision making Responsibility Working atmosphere Colleague loyalty Back-up and attendance	Dedication Motivation Results Acceptance of responsibility Colleague loyalty	+	+ + +

+++= Very appropriate   ++= Appropriate   +=Not very appropriate

PLANNING INTERNAL MARKETING

The third important aspect of the definition of internal marketing is the process of planning internal marketing. To make use of internal marketing in the best possible way, objectives should be set, just like external marketing. Once these are defined, one should determine the marketing strategy to be followed. Setting strategies includes determining tools to be used and the way results will be measured. Factors that might influence the planning process are: the nature of the objective; the complexity of the objective; the importance of the exchange; the size of the target group; the location of the target group; the employee's own position in the organization; and the cost of executing the internal marketing strategy.

It is important to note that this internal marketing process should be finished just before the new strategy is brought to the external market. Then, the organization itself is – internally – prepared.

15.7 TRIADS IN THE SERVICE ENCOUNTER

resistance

The previous section dealt with internal marketing as one of the means of smoothing over the implementation of new ideas and new ways of working in a service organization. To convince employees of the necessity of these new ideas, ways of working, strategy, procedures, service encounter, etc. it may be that some resistance has to be overcome. The way these changes and new plans are communicated, largely determines their acceptance (i.e. resistance to accept it). Individual employees may differ in their acceptance of these new issues. These changes in the service encounter may impose new demands on employees and customers. Otherwise, the new way of working in the service encounter (new roles, script, etc.) will not work. Therefore, we will look at some specific requirements with regard to people interacting in this service encounter that may enhance the chance of a successful implementation. As a starting point for our discussion we take the "service triangle".

THE SERVICE TRIANGLE

service triangle

The service triangle consists of the following three actors: the service organization, the contact personnel (front office) and the customers. In managing this triangle it is important to find a good balance in the mutual relations between these three actors. According to our values, a sound relationship between the internal organization, personnel and customers with respect to the servuction process will enhance the implementation of the marketing strategy. The forms that "customer" and "personnel" take in this triangle will be elaborated further.

THE TRIAD OF THE CUSTOMER

customer's role in the service encounter

With respect to the customer's role in the service encounter, concepts like "interactive consumption", "customer participation in the service delivery process", "presence", "participation requirement", "intensity of participation", "customer involvement" and "customer loyalty" were discussed. In Chapter Four, the term "involvement" is put into slightly different words. Discussed are what customers themselves shall, can and want to do during the service delivery process, taking into account the "perceived risk" with which they are confronted (their capacity, opportunity and motivation to participate in the service delivery process). These three questions (a triad) are important to the subject of this section. By means of these three questions, the three parts of the service triangle can be better tuned to each other. It concerns the following three questions with respect to the customer:

able to participate

motivated to participate

opportunity to participate

- to what extent are customers able to participate in the service delivery process?
- to what extent are customers motivated to participate in the service delivery process?
- to what extent have customers the opportunity to participate in the service delivery process?

In this process, the relationship of the customer with the service provider will become more clear when we recognize that customers can also be regarded as "part-time employees" of the service provider. This indicates they "work" for the service provider or at least "take over some work".[31]

THE TRIAD OF THE PERSONNEL

In Chapter Ten, we mentioned the characteristics of the service attitude, leadership in a service organization and the internal and external orientation of all employees. It was concluded that it is important to look at the capacity, opportunity and motivation to perform in a market-oriented way. In other words, the following three questions are relevant to the employees:

able and the opportunity to work in a market-oriented way?

- to what extent are the employees able to work in a market-oriented way?
- to what extent are the employees motivated to work in a market-oriented way?
- to what extent do the employees have the opportunity to work in a market-oriented way?

front office/contact personnel

Concerning the service encounter, these questions have to be adjusted for the front office/contact personnel in the service organization. Then, the questions read as follows:

- to what extent are the contact employees able to work in a market-oriented way?
- to what extent are the contact employees motivated to work in a market-oriented way?
- to what extent do the contact employees have the opportunity to work in a market-oriented way?

The relationship of the contact personnel towards the customer and the market is expressed even more emphatically by the term "part-time marketeers". This shows the importance of the marketing function contact personnel fulfil in their relations with the customer. That is where and when the relationship marketing is performed.

front office and back office employees

The distinction between all personnel and the contact personnel in a service organization is not mutually exclusive. Therefore, it is better to distinguish between contact personnel and the rest of the personnel. Then, there is no more overlap. This is similar to the distinction between front office and back office employees.

THREE TRIADS TOGETHER

In market-oriented service organizations, it is important that both customer and service provider know what is expected from them in the roles that they play. However, it goes without saying that good links between the different triads discussed in this section will prevent (or solve) many implementation problems. Amongst others, the "squeezing in" of the terms "part-time employee" and "part-time marketeer" should make this possible. Next to this, the servuction process indicates that not only excellent links between customer and contact personnel are required during the service encounter, but also that an excellent link between front office and back office is necessary in order to accomplish the goals set for excellent service quality. The implementation of a market-oriented marketing strategy in a service organization aimed at providing the excellent service quality expected by their customers will therefore be enhanced when:

are able
- the contact employees and the back office personnel are able to work in a market-oriented way and the customer is able to participate in the service encounter;

motivated
- the contact employees and the back office personnel are motivated to work in a market-oriented way and the customer is motivated to participate in the service encounter; and,

have the opportunity
- the contact employees and the back office personnel have the opportunity to work in a market-oriented way and the customer does have the opportunity to participate in the service encounter.

This is depicted in Figure 15-7.

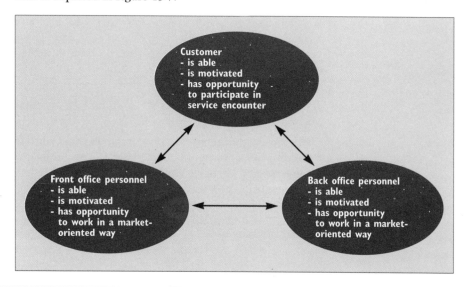

Figure 15-7
Three triads facilitating the implementations of a market-oriented marketing strategy in a service organization

Finally, we would like to make two comments. First, the implementation will be easier if the capacity, motivation and opportunity of the three actors are more in line with one another. Secondly, the term "being able or capable to" is, in Chapter Ten, illustrated by the words "being mentally and physically able". This can be further complemented by saying that the three actors should possess the means, resources, possibilities and routines to accomplish the service during the service encounter. That this is not a mere slogan is because of the fact that one of the causes of Gap 3 in the SERVQUAL-model refers to an incorrect fit of people, jobs and supporting equipment.

15.8   MATCHING DEMAND AND SUPPLY

Matching demand and supply is a crucial issue in the service sector where it is usually not possible to create stock. It is a major determinant of profitability. In other chapters, we discussed some issues about capacity management (what can be done to control demand patterns as well as supply: occupancy rates and capacity utilization), waiting times (i.e. situations where demand is higher than actual supply at that very moment) and its consequences.[32] In fact, all parts of the marketing-mix in services, and the relationships a service provider wants to have with its clients, can be used in matching demand and supply.

matching demand and supply

Service practice 15-4 Capacity management and loyalty

James Heskett, Earl Sasser and Christopher Hart state that insight into demand relationships is crucial in capacity management, for instance in the airline industry.[33]

"Airlines have probably spent more time studying the intensity of customer preferences than firms in other service industries. Their work and what they conclude from it is instructive. Even though Delta Air Lines, for example, has devoted a great deal of effort into building customer loyalty among business travellers through quality of service, frequent flyer incentives, and other means, its management knows that if it does not have a flight departing within an hour of the desired time, it will lose targeted business travellers rapidly to competitors who do. All of its efforts have probably only increased this measure of 'loyalty' from perhaps 30 to 60 minutes, because the intensity of customer preferences for flying Delta instead of one of the competitors only applies in the abstract, not when it comes right down to available departure times."

These preferences of business travellers are completely different from pleasure travellers who – most of the time – do not have problems with a, little, longer waiting time. "This helps explain why business travellers drive most airline capacity scheduling systems."

In previous chapters, the concepts of "chase demand" and "level capacity" were introduced. They are also mentioned in Figure 15-4 and can be implemented in highly different situations:

chase-demand
- "The chase-demand alternative is often selected where demands are highly volatile and unpredictable, the cost structure can be managed on a highly variable basis, and there is a ready supply of relatively low-skilled labor for jobs requiring limited training."

level-capacity
- "In contrast, level-capacity strategies may be employed where demand is less volatile and more predictable, the consequences of a poorly performed service are serious, and the need for expert providers requiring substantial training (or expensive, complex, specialized equipment) high."[34]

breakthrough service providers
The size of fluctuations in demand, the speed of these fluctuations and their predictability as well as the cost structure, the cost of poor service quality and the cost of lost business are important issues in determining whether we have to employ a chase-demand or a level-capacity strategy. Breakthrough service providers, confronted with volatile, unpredictable demands (as with chase-demand strategies) modify these strategies by, for instance, "maximizing service delivery during peak periods, using part-time employees or renting/leasing equipment, cross-training employees to perform two or more jobs with different demand patterns, sharing capacity among businesses, and increasing consumer participation in the delivery of service. In addition, through advanced facility planning, excess capacity of hard-to-change features may be built into service facilities when they are constructed. Finally, even if none of these possibilities exists, humans are able to deliver what we often call superhuman efforts for short periods of time."[35]

operating responses
Operating responses that can be made to the problems of managing chase-demand or level-capacity strategies refer to, amongst others, the percentage of peak business that will be covered by the base capacity, the division of labor, the required level of labor skills, the job discretion, the compensation rate, the working conditions, the training required for each employee, the amount of supervision required, and the type of budgeting and forecasting required. This is summarized in Figure 15-8.[36]

specific rules
Breakthrough service providers apply some specific rules in managing demand and supply. First of all, they attack these problems of managing demand and supply by managing both demand (through marketing, pricing, or demand inventorying practices) and the capacity to supply a service simultaneously. Forecasting demand is a matter of knowing what is the rhythm of doing business in a particular industry. In forecasting demand, breakthrough service providers track demand patterns by capturing data for both actual customers and those who were not served because of capacity problems, using it as input data to superior revenue control information systems. With respect to the design of capacity, they determine facilities of "optimum" size, look for ways to design flexible capacity by utilizing "floating" personnel, contracted services, high levels of organizational spirit, etc. in addition to estimating demand. In seeking ways to minimize customer waiting time during peak periods of demand, they alter the customer's waiting experience through diversions that the customer finds relevant and useful, including the involvement of the customer in the service, with or without economic incentives.[37]

Figure 15-8
Conditions encouraging
chase-demand and
level-capacity strategies
and characteristics of
some operating responses

Condition encouraging:	Chase-demand	Level-capacity
Size of fluctuation in demand	large	small
Speed of fluctuation in demand	fast	slow
Predictability of fluctuation in demand	unpredictable	predictable
Cost structure	highly variable	highly fixed
Cost of poor service	low	high
Cost of lost business	high	low

Operating responses	Chase-demand	Level-capacity
Percentage of peak business covered with "base" capacity	low	high
Division of jobs	high	low
Labor skill level required	low	high
Job discretion	low	high
Compensation rate	low	high
Working conditions	sweat shop	pleasant
Training required per employee	low	high
Amount of supervision required	high	low
Type of budgeting and forecasting required	short-run	long-run

professional service
firms

Professional service firms working in very competitive environments are often faced with severe and increasing competition and thus lower prices. In such a situation, they have to deliver excellent quality in ever more shorter times to perform the assignment. At the same time, their employees also expect "value in their jobs" otherwise it will be difficult for the firm "to keep them on board".[38]

15.9 SPECIFIC PROBLEMS AND SOLUTIONS WHEN IMPLEMENTING AT THE STRATEGIC AND TACTICAL LEVEL

strategic and tactical implementation

In order to provide more practical information about implementation topics we will make a distinction between the strategic side and the operational side. It is more or less similar to the distinction between long term and short term. This issue has been discussed in relation to the planning process and the service concept. In our discussion on the SERVQUAL-model, such a distinction has not been made explicitly. Here, however, we do make such a distinction in order to get a better insight into the problems with strategic and tactical implementation and the options for a solution.

PROBLEMS

strategic level
operational/tactical level

The gaps in the SERVQUAL-model arise at different levels in the service organization. The subjective quality judgement of the customer (Gap 5) is determined by the other four gaps. Gap 5 results from gaps which have a more strategic character (Gap 1 and 2) and gaps which have a more tactical nature (Gap 3 and 4). For, we assume, the parts with the labels "management perceptions of customer expectations" and "translation of perceptions in specifications of service quality" correspond predominantly with the strategic level in the service organization. The parts with the labels "actual service delivery" and "external communication" can mainly be regarded as the operational/tactical level of the service delivery (see Figure 15-9).

Figure 15-9
Problems with implementation at the strategic and tactical level

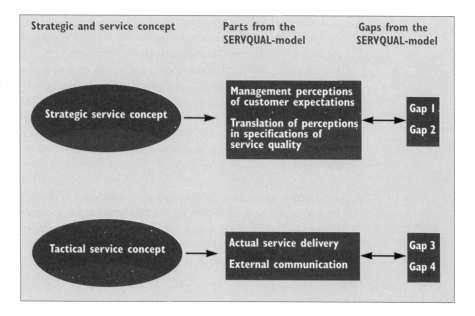

causes of problems

The four gaps which together determine the subjective judgement of the quality of service delivery (Gap 5), are mentioned in Chapter Four which also contains the causes of problems in service delivery. These causes can be regarded as the causes of implementation problems. In other words: Gap 1 and Gap 2 mainly apply to problems with the implementation at a strategic level, whereas Gaps 3 and 4 mainly reflect problems with the implementation at a tactical level.

SOLUTIONS

solution at the strategic level

The solutions for problems with implementation at the strategic level (and for preventing them) mainly imply creating a culture of market orientation and quality awareness in the organization. In this respect "all noses have to point in the same direction"; the whole organization has to be deeply convinced of this.[39] A clear commitment and role model of top management is essential in this area.[40] Moreover, the following strategic solutions are valid: formulate clear marketing and quality objectives (then this can be communicated internally and, consequently, employees will know what is expected from them and know where they stand); create an organization as flat and as informal as possible; collect more and better (reliable) market information (e.g via more quantitative market research and more qualitative, intensive contacts with the market through, for example, the boundary spanning role and an external orientation of the employees); encourage more and mutual cooperation, information-exchange and bottom-up communication between persons and departments (the idea of the internal customer); and make an accurate mapping of the complete service delivery process via blueprints, flow charts and service maps.

solution at the tactical level

In solving (and preventing) problems with implementation at the tactical and operational level, much practical advice can be given. This is often situational specific. In general (amongst others), the following solutions can be mentioned: perfect working conditions, atmosphere; teamwork; perfect mutual fit between knowledge, ability, personal skills, jobs and supporting equipment/technology; delegation of responsibilities and empowerment; selection, recruitment and training of employees, taking into account strategic requirements; do not promise too much in communications; promise what can be realized; communicate first internally before externally (then employees are informed and are not surprised by customers who already know about special offers or new services). This is summarized briefly in Figure 15-10.

leadership skills

Leadership skills that encourage the solutions to both these implementation problems are an overall view of the business, setting a clear strategy and goals (not being clouded by daily work), highly developed analytical capabilities and a result-oriented approach for the achievement of excellence, in addition to the leadership skills mentioned in Chapter 10.[41]

Figure 15-10
Solutions for problems
with implementation at
the strategic and
tactical level

Strategic level	- culture of market orientation and quality awareness
	- clear objectives
	- flat and informal organization
	- more and better market information
	- cooperation, information exchange and bottom-up communication
	- mapping the process
Tactical level	- working conditions, atmosphere
	- teamwork
	- fit person, job and equipment
	- delegation and empowerment
	- selection and training
	- realistic promises

15.10 MARKETING PERFORMANCE IN SERVICES

The implementation of the marketing strategy and tactics will lead to a particular performance. How can this performance be measured in order to check whether the goals set are accomplished? This latter issue is relevant with respect to the control of the marketing performance in services, and will be discussed in the next section. Here, we will pay attention to measuring performance as such.

measuring performance

Usually, performance is defined in financial and quantitative terms like sales, market share, profitability, return on investment and the like. One may wonder whether this applies to the service business as well.[42] Especially, when the creation of service quality and added value is important, the performance of the service organization should be measured in terms directly associated with those concepts, for instance total value added or value added per employee, respectively service quality or return on quality.[43] In the return on quality approach, a model has been developed to allow managers to determine where and how much they should spend to improve customer satisfaction and service quality, and the likely financial impact of those expenditures.[44]

return on quality

Service practice 15-5 European retail performance indicators

The Oxford Institute of Retail Management (OXIRM) provides overviews of the financial performance of leading European retailers annually.[45] They present data (that can be used as a kind of bench mark) on turnover; total assets; profit margin; asset turn; return on total assets; day's stock; day's cash cycle; sales per employee; profit per employee; employee cost as a percentage of sales; sales per square meter; profit per square meter.

We would like to add to that a measure lacking in this overview – the added value per employee. Figure 15-11 reveals some of the leading European retailers from the OXIRM database on each of these criteria.

final outcome
causes that affect these
final outcomes

specific features of
services

In defining and measuring performance in services, like retailing, it seems not only relevant to look at the final outcome but also at the determinants or causes that affect these final outcomes: that does justice to the process character of service delivery and the service encounter. Or, should we go even further and ask an even more fundamental question, do the specific features of services (its intangibility, the service encounter, the crucial role of employees and customers, etc.) give rise to defining and operationalizing performance and productivity in a different way? When we focus so much on key success factors in general or market orientation and service quality in particular, these issues should also be reflected in measuring service industry performance. But how? Should the performance then be measured (and controlled) in terms of image/reputation, relationships with key customers, quality, satisfaction, customer friendliness, advice, information, timely execution, competence, trust, participation in the service encounter, etc.

Service
practice
15-6
How Germans
and Americans
rate
their banking
services [46]

A 1996 study by California State University and the Fachhochschule Hamburg tested the conventional wisdom that the US is a much more customer-centered and service-oriented society than Germany. Students collected data in Southern California and in the Hamburg area to that end. "The overall findings indicate that Americans expect and receive better banking service than do their German counterparts. This difference is illustrated by the much more extensive banking hours in the US. But the consistently greater performance gap across the items suggests a higher level of dissatisfaction with banking services for the American sample. Better service performance may not lead necessarily to more satisfaction if it creates ever higher expectations." (And, as Service practice 9-1 illustrates, Germans are not that satisfied about financial service providers, but they might have lower expectations about these services' quality.)

A more in-depth analysis revealed: "Overall, Americans had higher expectations for banking services than did Germans. The only item for which Germans had a significantly higher expectation was competence concerning investment services. Americans tended to use other types of advisors in their investment decision making and did not expect their banks to be especially strong in this area.

One of the biggest differences between the two groups was that Americans held much higher expectations for state-of-the-art services and technical support, such as banking by telephone. The great divergence on this might be caused partly by the high price of local telephone service in Germany, which is about 10c per minute, the cost of a long-distance call in the US.

The Americans rated trust and friendliness as the two most important attributes of excellent banking services, while the Germans wanted competent investment advice and timely execution of service." ... "The Americans rated their banks somewhat higher than the Germans did. Of the major regional US banks, Wells Fargo was given the best overall evaluation, while Bank of America received the worst." .... "In Germany, Deutsche Bank was the most highly rated major bank, followed by Dresdner Bank and Commerzbank. The Sparkassen or

> savings banks received many high evaluations, but also many low ones, suggesting a financial love-hate relationship. Customers really liked the down-to-earth attitude of Sparkassen employees, but were very disappointed with the quality of the information they received by mail."

An answer to the questions raised about the uniqueness of performance measurement in service businesses may be given by focussing on the measurement indicators of the final results, i.e.:

- competitiveness (relative market share and position, sales growth, measures of the customer base);
- financial performance (profitability, liquidity, capital structure, market ratios);

and topics about the determinants of these results, i.e.:

- cost traceability;
- internal and external service quality (the 18, 10 or 5-dimensions of service quality);
- service flexibility (specification flexibility, volume flexibility, delivery speed flexibility);
- resource utilization (productivity, efficiency. The utilization of equipment is an important issue in services determining actual profitability – see our cases on Club Med and the quarterly figures of airlines and their percentage of capacity utilized in Service practice 15-8);
- service innovation (performance of the innovation process and of individual innovations); and
- motivational and reward systems.[47]

quantitative and a qualitative nature financial and a non-financial background

From this overview, it becomes clear that a wide spectrum of topics can (or must?) be used in measuring service performance. They have a quantitative and a qualitative nature as well as a financial and a non-financial (behavioral) background (see also Service practice 15-7).

combined use of a wide variety of instruments to measure corporate performance in services

The combined use of a wide variety of instruments to measure corporate performance in services comes also to the fore in a US study by the International Benchmarking Clearinghouse.[49] The study that revealed CEO's in service businesses like insurance, banking, transport, retail consumer services, utilities, health, consulting and the government mostly use the following measures:

- profitability (net operating income or contribution, budget variance, ROE/ROC/ROI/ROA, revenue, revenue growth, after tax net income);
- customer satisfaction (customer satisfaction surveys, competitive comparisons, customer perception of service, complaints/complaint resolution, on-time delivery, customer retention, inactive accounts, customer acquisition, customer loyalty, profit per customer, expenditure per customer);

Figure 15-11
Retail performance
in Europe

Retail performance indicators 1993/1994	Top four	Lowest four
Turnover	Carrefour (Fr) Promodes (Fr) Ahold (Neth) J.Sainsbury (UK)	Magazine zum Globus (Swi) Allders (UK) Pao de Acucar (Port) Stockmann (Fin)
Total assets	Carrefour (Fr) Migros (Swi) Pinault Printemps (Fr) J.Sainsbury (UK)	Massa (Ger) Stockmann (Fin) Pao de Acucar (Port) Allders (UK)
Profit margin	Benetton (It) Great Universal Stores (UK) Marks & Spencer (UK) Boots (UK)	GIB (Bel) Asda (UK) Massa (Ger) Dixons (UK)
Asset turn	Kwik Save (UK) Massa (Ger) Ahold (Neth) AVA (Ger)	La Rinascente (It) Sears (UK) Benetton (It) Great Universal Stores (UK)
Return on total assets	Kwik Save (UK) Douglas Holding (Ger) Marks & Spencer (UK) Benetton (It)	GIB (Bel) Asda (UK) Massa (Ger) Dixons (UK)
Day's stock	Tesco (UK) Wm. Morrison (UK) J.Sainsbury (UK) Pao de Acucar (Port)	Kingfisher (UK) Benetton (It) Groupe André (Fr) Eroski (Sp)
Day's cash cycle	Pryca (Sp) La Rinascents (It) Standa (It) Pao de Àcucar (Port)	Groupe André (Fr) Sears (UK) Benetton (It) Great Universal Stores (UK)
Sales per employee	Eroski (Sp) SOK (Fin) Promodes (Fr) Colruyt (Bel)	John Lewis (UK) Boots (UK) Burton Group (UK) Sears (UK)
Profit per employee	Benetton (It) Kesko (Fin) Great Universal Stores (UK) Marks & Spencer (UK)	GIB (Bel) Asda (UK) Massa (Ger) Dixons (UK)
Employee cost as percentage of sales	Kesko (Fin) SOK (Fin) Kwik Save (UK) Pao de Acucar (Port)	El Corte Inglés (Sp) Douglas Holding (Ger) Migros (Swi) Horton (Ger)
Sales per square meter	Migros (Swi) Tesco (UK) Carrefour (Fr) Wm. Morrison (UK)	La Rinascente (It) Storehouse (UK) Kingfisher (UK) GIB (Bel)

Figure 15-11 *Continued*	Profit per square meter	Marks & Spencer (UK) Dixons (UK) Wm. Morrison (UK) Tesco (UK)	Eroski (Sp) Horton (Ger) Standa (It) La Rinascent (It)

Service practice 15-7 Marketing pays off!

In the UK, a study has been done to develop an understanding of what elements of marketing strategy were associated with differences in performance between financial service companies. The researchers used a wide variety of criteria to have the companies participating in the study evaluated by experts in the financial world.

"The findings discount the argument that the poor performance of the UK financial services sector has been the result of moving away from the traditional way of doing things, with too great an emphasis on aggressive competition and too little on traditional prudence. However, this research suggests that this has not been the case. The better performing financial service companies are characterized by a greater emphasis on control of costs and profitability and by greater selectivity in targeting their customers. For the better performing companies, the argument that financial service companies are engaging in irresponsibly aggressive competition can be dismissed. However this does not imply that the better performing companies are concentrating on the traditional virtues of financial services. Selectivity and profit orientation are keystones of the marketing concept. Thus the research suggests that it is through successful application of the marketing concept that the better performing companies have achieved their position."[48]

- workforce issues (employee satisfaction, employee turnover, cost of benefits, suggestions, inclusion in incentive programs, diversity targets, safety results, training amount or cost, health or cost of health, job rotation);
- market place (market share, target market penetration, service development cycle time, share of customer, number of new services, presence in distribution channel);
- productivity (labor productivity, cost per unit of service, inventory turns, equipment utilization);
- quality (cycle time, error rate/sigmas, supplier performance, training/competency, cost of poor-quality, score on quality assessment, scrap/rework, supplier profile); and
- community and environment (community involvement, public image, corporate citizenship evidence, environmental results).

market, workplace, financial perspective

Again and again, we see that in services performance is and must be measured from three perspectives, namely the market (=satisfying the customers), the workplace (=satisfying the employees), and a financial perspective (=satisfying the owners). All these measures are needed to measure the performance in the process of delivering *balanced score card*

excellent service quality.[50] In fact, they all fit into the four categories of the balanced score card developed by Robert Kaplan and David Norton. The balanced score card links performance in four areas to one another, namely a financial perspective, a customer perspective, an innovation and learning perspective and an internal business perspective. "The balanced scorecard allows managers to look at the business from four important perspectives. It provides answers to four basic questions:

- how do customers see us? (customer perspective);
- what must we excel at? (internal perspective);
- can we continue to improve and create value? (innovation and learning perspective): and
- how do we look to shareholders? (financial perspective)."[51]

The score card tracks the key elements of a company's strategy, from continuous improvement and partnerships to teamwork and global scale. For our purposes in service industries, we maintain that it is important to explicitly add a fifth perspective, the employee's perspective (satisfaction, turnover, etc.). This could be a part of the "internal perspective" but should not be overlooked.

employee's perspective

Elaborating on this idea of the balanced score card, it is important to realize that a proper fit should exist between the service company's strategy and the performance measurement system. (In general, this fits into the well known fact of searching for the perfect configuration of – turbulence and dynamics in the – environment, strategy, culture, structure and control system of an organization). Consequently, the relative weight of each of the four (or five) components of the balanced score card may differ as a strategy of cost leadership, differentiation or focus is implemented. So, it may vary according to the accents given in the market-oriented strategy, the specific combination of these general strategies and, e.g. the present position in the life-cycle of the market in general or the particular service. "Whereas the financial perspective is important regardless of strategy, the different market strategies should emphasize one of the other perspectives: customer focus, internal analysis, or innovation." Therefore, the name of the balanced score card could be changed to the strategic scorecard.[52] The following can be said with respect to the other four boxes in Figure 15-12. Product leaders emphasis the innovation perspective (the development of new services as such and innovations in the servuction process); the figure shows how that could be operationalized in the performance measurement and evaluation system. "Customer-intimate businesses naturally focus on understanding the customer and its perception of the value of the product or service offered. But this goes far beyond tracking the traditional indicators of profit margin, sales growth, market share, and customer satisfaction.".... "Brand champions also emphasize the customer perspective in their performance measurement systems. Because in this strategy the concept of "customer" has more meaning at the market or market segment level than at the individual customer level, performance measurement for brand champions differs from that for customer-intimate businesses. The challenge for brand champions is to develop a system for assessing brand equity." (Chapter Eleven revealed the importance of brands and images in services.) .... "Operationally excellent businesses emphasize the internal perspective because of their

strategic scorecard

focus on efficiency…, have taken a process focus with an emphasis on throughput-oriented measures, where time is often a key metric."[53] As a conclusion, we may state that all the measurement issues mentioned in this section fit into the five boxes of the strategic scorecard in Figure 15-12. Once the dominant strategy type is determined, the key success factors and the key performance indicators or key control variables must be defined.

Figure 15-12
The strategic scorecard

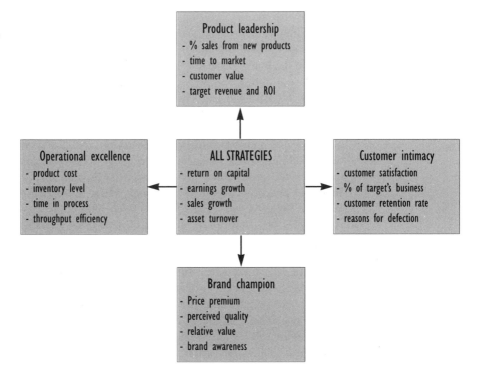

15.11 MARKETING CONTROL

control in services

In the preceding section, we raised the question about whether the characteristics of services had a special impact on defining performance and productivity in services. Here, we can pose a similar question with respect to control in services: "All service characteristics … have direct implications for the notion of controllability. First, the involvement of customers as co-producers may increase the unpredictability of outcomes of the service process and have a negative impact on the extent to which one can evaluate employees based exclusively on controllable events. Second, the uncertainty regarding individual performance levels may contribute to the difficulties of determining what is attributable to individuals' actions and what results from factors unrelated to differences in capability. Finally, the often complex web of interdependencies between individual employees and between employees and customers may complicate the identification of who has control over what and even further who to hold accountable."[54] What impact does this all have, for instance, on the responsibility structures in a service organization? Moreover, both the customer and the front office employees will search for ways to control the service encounter themselves. Much depends on the clarity of roles and the responsibility (or empowerment) given to the front line personnel (e.g. the absence of role conflict and role ambiguity).

activity based performance measurement

With respect to the pricing strategies to be used in services, we discussed activity based costing (ABC) as a proper way to determine the cost of a service operation (as an alternative to direct costing or full costing). When ABC is applied, activity based performance measurement has to be based on process costing, focusing on the activities performed and the costs attached to those activities. This requires a perfect insight in the whole process of service delivery.[55]

Once the performance of a service organization can be measured, it becomes possible to control this performance, and to compare objectives or budgets with actual outcomes. This can be done by just comparing the two or by a simple analysis of variance in which one looks for the explanation for the differences found. The necessary feedback can then be provided and corrective actions (if needed) can be taken. It then becomes necessary to control the efforts efficiently and effectively by means of all kinds of organizational structures and processes. A service organization should not forget to explicitly pay attention to their personnel (their service attitude, leadership style, knowledge, ability, skills, etc.), hence human resource management (HRM).

measured, evaluated and assessed

The objectives have to be formulated emphatically (for example, in terms of service quality for a market-oriented service-provider). The objectives have to contain criteria which can be measured, evaluated and indeed assessed. Then, it will be possible to decrease the possible differences between goals set and actual realizations (the correcting actions needed) and to increase the chance that the goals set are achieved. This does not mean that only financial criteria can be used; non-financial, behavioral criteria can also be used, as we have repeatedly discussed.

output
input
"throughput"

formal control mechanisms
informal control mechanisms
key control variables

The factors which will be used in controlling a service organization will refer partly to the output of the organization (for example, the number of policies closed, train tickets sold and customer satisfaction). They will also refer to the input used - (professional skills of employees, equipment, etc.) and to the "throughput" (how does the service process work, the service attitude; in short, the functional and relational quality). Another important distinction that has to be made is the difference between formal control mechanisms (focussing on the abovementioned input, throughput and output measures) and the informal control mechanisms (self-control, social control, control via, e.g. colleagues, and cultural control; control via the existing corporate culture).[56] Moreover, the service company should not only define its key success factors, but also its key control variables (they may be different).

feedback

An important part of this control process is measuring, just like giving feedback. Control and giving feedback can take place on a formal and/or informal basis with the help of processes and structures which characterize the service delivery and the whole organization of the company.

marketing control

In the preceding parts, we made a distinction between the strategic and the tactical/operational level. This distinction can also be made for control. This all leads us to defining marketing control as:

> Marketing control in a service organization consists of processes and structures which are aimed at influencing the marketing strategy and the marketing tactics in such a way, that the chance to reach the specified goals will be increased.[57]

learning organization

The concept of the learning organization plays an important role in control processes and also in market-oriented cultures. In fact, it refers to the development of knowledge or insights that have the potential to influence behavior, leading to behavioral changes that lead to improved performance.[58] One can think of two types of learning,

adaptive learning

adaptive learning and generative learning. Adaptive learning is the most basic form of learning. It occurs within a set of recognized and unrecognized constraints that reflect the organization's assumptions about its environment and itself. Generative

generative learning

learning occurs when the organization is willing to question long-held assumptions about its mission, customers, capabilities, or strategy. Organizational learning is a process including the acquisition of information, the dissemination of information and the shared interpretation of this information. All this may affect both the organization's strategy and tactics. In turn, it affects both the definition of the organization's market orientation at a conceptual level and at an operational level where all kinds of activities are performed by employees and customers in the service encounter.[59]

MARKETING CONTROL AT THE STRATEGIC LEVEL

ensuring that the mission and the strategic objectives are achieved

Here, the focus is on the structures and processes aimed at ensuring that the mission and the strategic objectives are achieved. Therefore, the organization will not just have to find some important criteria, but have to pay special attention to the critical success (and control) factors. These are, for example, the image/reputation, relationships with key customers, service quality, or the unique internal capabilities and routines positioning the service organization in such a way that it is hard to imitate. These factors will therefore give the organization a competitive advantage.

culture

The specific strategic content given to the organization's market orientation is another issue at stake. Here, informal control mechanisms related to the role of corporate culture and the relevant dimensions of a market-oriented corporate culture are crucial. Input control with respect to selecting and recruiting the "right" persons fitting to the organization's goals and way of working is also important. It is self-evident that the

planning

whole planning process as such can be used for control purposes. Planning is one of the ways to formally guide the organization. The service marketing audit provides a lot of information. This demonstrates, amongst others, to what extent customers think that their desired service quality is achieved; to what extent the specified goals for turnover, market share, profit, etc. are reached. Importantly here, are internal measurements on the organizational culture and the opinions of employees of their own

service marketing audit

service attitude. The service marketing audit or other research shows how customers think about this. Partly, these are subjects for which the organization has applied internal marketing in implementing the proper strategy and activities.

MARKETING CONTROL AT THE TACTICAL LEVEL

that the tactical objectives are met

short-term concrete activities

This has to do with the processes and structures aimed at ensuring that the tactical objectives are met. Now, especially, the control of short-term plans (annual plans) and all sorts of concrete activities play a central role: e.g. the realized output per service or market segment or the way in which the service is delivered. It hinges mainly upon formal mechanisms of throughput and output control. Although we talk about a different level here, we still come across the technical, functional and relational quality. Examples of this tactical control are the effectiveness of a particular short term promotion campaign, the number of times a phone rings before the contact personnel answers it and the utilization of capacity/occupancy rate per quarter.

Service practice 15-8 Greater utilization of capacity pays off!

In 1994, the 220 international airlines (being members of IATA) "processed" 8% more passengers. Their capacity increased by 5%. The average occupancy rate increased from 65% in 1993 to 68% in 1994. Such an increase made them all almost profitable again.

Lufthansa realized a 70% occupancy rate in passenger travelling in 1994. They were very enthusiastic about that since it contributed to their profits.

Northwest Airlines had (till 1995) an all time high profit in the fourth quarter of 1994, thanks to the efforts the employees had made, and an occupancy rate of 65.2% (compared to 63.9% in the equivalent period a year before).

Due partly to price actions (temporary price discounts), KLM's occupancy rate for passengers was 78% in March 1996, compared to 73.3% in March 1995. Unfortunately, the occupancy rate for freight decreased in that period from 75% to 71%.

MARKETING CONTROL AND OUR TYPOLOGY OF SERVICES

classification of services

The specific content which can and shall be given to marketing control in a particular service organization also depends on the turbulence and competitiveness of its environment and the classification of services. This latter issue implies control partly depends on the strategic positions taken by the service provider in the different service matrices (Chapter Two). It goes without saying that control mechanisms aimed at the behavior of contact personnel need to receive much more attention when service delivery is more labor-intensive than in the case of a largely automated service delivery process.[60] The possibilities to guide the service delivery process will be completely different in service encounters with intensive customer participation than when the customer hardly participates. For standard services produced via low cost servuction processes, the control mechanism will be different from that for very differentiated, customized services. The opportunities to rationalize or standardize service delivery processes will determine the control mechanism as well; these will be more output related in the case of standardized services.[61] We can state, in general, that as the service process is more labor-intensive, the organization will have to use more control mechanisms consisting of elements concerning contact personnels behavior. Then, the focus is on indicators referring to the throughput in the service delivery process to improve the functional and relational quality. There are, for example, waiting times before one is helped or before a damage claim is paid, friendly treatment, errors in letters and so on. Travelling times will be an important aspect in controlling a service delivery in which the service provider visits the customer.

The consequence of these views is that the control mechanisms in a service organization also will have to be adjusted when the service provider takes another position in the different service matrices in Chapter Two. Minor changes will probably not have many consequences for control, fundamental changes, however, do. The strategic scorecard has to be adjusted as well.

SUMMARY

This chapter discusses subjects belonging to the last phases of the planning process.

Implementation not only refers to developing the marketing mix in services according to the service provider's mission, goals and strategy "on paper" in such a way that all parts logically fit together. In fact, implementation hinges upon actually "making strategies work" and making relationships come true. In other words, the required investments in equipment and employees should be completed, employees should be convinced of the new strategy, plans, actions, ways of working, etc., accept them and act accordingly. The resulting performance should be measured. The specific features of services (intangibility and the like) impose special requirements on these measurements as such and, in particular, with respect to assessing the performance achieved, also affects the way performance can be controlled. Since the service encounter and the processes that take place in it are crucial to providing services and delivering excellent service quality, measuring and controlling this process and the activities of the actors (front office personnel and the customer) should be crucial elements in measuring and controlling this performance. So, throughput measures are relatively important here, next to input and output measures. Also, informal control mechanisms can be applied.

The added value can be looked at from three points of view: the customers', the employees' and the owners' point of view. The balanced score card or the strategic scorecard are useful means to that end.

Many problems in implementation appear to be obvious. Maybe they are so obvious that often it is forgotten to pay attention to them. The distinction between strategy and tactics implies that the causes for these problems and their solutions can be found at both levels. Also, control should be exercised at a strategic and a tactical level. Much insight into the performance of a service organization can be obtained by combining the following issues:

- the idea of putting Gap 1 and 2 from the SERVQUAL-model (the strategic side) versus Gap 3 and 4 (the tactical side);
- the strategic and tactical problems with implementation;
- the causes for both these groups of problems;
- the solutions to both these groups of problems;
- the control at the strategic and tactical level.

Special attention is paid to solving and preventing problems with implementation in the service encounter where the customer and the employee interact. These problems can be avoided when:

- the contact personnel and the other employees are able to work in a market-oriented way and the customer is able to participate in the service delivery;
- the contact personnel and the other employees are motivated to work in a market-oriented way and the customer is motivated to participate in the service delivery; and
- the contact personnel and the other employees have the opportunity to work in a market-oriented way and the customer has the opportunity to participate in the service delivery.

A very important means of accomplishing this is the application of the so-called internal marketing. Then, four different exchange processes with the accompanying tools can be distinguished.

Matching demand and supply is essential to the success of a service organization. The occupancy rate of the existing capacity clearly impacts on the service firm's performance, especially its profits. It is interesting to see what breakthrough service providers have come up with to cope with this problem in benchmark studies. Another example of the integration of all issues discussed in this book is given by integrating all the characteristics of our four service types into one coherent picture: standard core services, customized core services, standard augmented services and customized augmented services.

In marketing control, financial as well as non-financial and behavioral variables can be used. As such, planning and the way the marketing department is organized, are also means to (formally) control the marketing performance. Marketing control is also dependent on the positions the service provider takes in the service matrices in Chapter Two.

QUESTIONS

1 What is the essence of implementation and control with respect to the marketing strategy and activities in a service organization?

2 Do you think the content of each of the four columns in Figure 15-4 fits logically with one another? Explain.

3 What is the link between Figure 15-4 and 15-8? What similarities do you see? What can you conclude when you compare both?

4 What can be said about planning internal marketing when the views on that topic in this chapter and in Chapter Eight are compared?

5 This chapter defines three triads in the service encounter. Describe them. Why would a perfect fit between them facilitate the implementation of new ways of dealing with the customer?

6 What is unique to measuring performance and exercising control in service businesses?

7 What are the main characteristics of breakthrough service providers? How do the remarks about breakthrough service providers in this chapter link with the discussion about these service providers in Chapter Eleven? How do the characteristics of breakthrough service providers fit into the characteristics of a market-oriented, excellent service quality providing service organization (as developed throughout this book)?

8 What is unique to marketing services in mature markets?

9 In previous chapters, many (18, 10 or 5) dimensions of service quality have been mentioned. How are they related to the implementation problems mentioned in this chapter?

10 Why is it crucial to realize that quality is in the eyes of the beholder?

ASSIGNMENTS

1 Do you think that the plans Amtrak has made and the way these are implemented (see Service practice 15-1) will contribute to their long-term survival? Explain.

2 What would you suggest that Mr Bourguignon does in order to get the support from the staff and customers necessary for the changes to be successful (see Service practice 15-2 and the Club Med story in Chapter Fourteen).

3 Throughout this book, many examples and data have been presented about accounting firms in different countries. Collect all this data and put it together into one report.
What can you conclude about marketing and CPAs? Given these findings, what would you recommend CPAs do to become really market-oriented in strategy and daily activities?

4 Chapter Four contains a number of causes underlying the implementation problems at the strategic level (Gaps 1 and 2 of the SERVQUAL-model) and at the tactical level (Gaps 3 and 4). Put these causes in a diagram distinguishing between the strategic and tactical level.

5 Combine Figures 15-9 and 15-10 with the findings from assignment 4. Make one overall figure out of it. What can you conclude from that scheme?

6 How could marketing control be exercised in a service organization at the strategic as well as at the tactical level? Put these findings in a new column in the figure you developed in assignment 5. What can you now conclude about the relationships between implementation problems, its causes, the solutions and the control mechanisms at the strategic and tactical level?

7 Put all the measurement issues/criteria mentioned in section 15.10 into the strategic scorecard. What can you conclude?

Case: THE RUTAS DE AL-ÁNDALUS: THE ANDALUSIAN HERITAGE PROGRAM: GRANADA '95 [62]

... Legend has it that when Granada fell to the Catholic monarchs, Boabdil, the last King of the Nazarenes, wept as he left the Alhambra...

... his mother then addressed him with a remark that later became famous: "You are weeping like a woman for what you were incapable of defending like a man"...

Al Ándalus

Al-Ándalus is the name of the Muslim state founded by the Arabs when they invaded the Iberian peninsula at the beginning of the 8th century. Almost eight hundred years were to pass before Spain was again united under the Catholic monarchs, Ferdinand and Isabella, in the 16th century.

Muslim Spain was a country where three religions – Muslim, Jewish and Christian – lived in peaceful harmony. All three groups somehow influenced the development of the Al-Ándalus civilization. Spanish Muslim scholars spread the philosophy of ancient Greece, used compasses to open new sea routes, taught numbers by the decimal system, devised new ways to irrigate the fields and produced paper for their learned books. Traces of Al-Ándalus survive today in many Spanish customs, in architecture, and in the Castilian language.

Under the rule of various emirs Al-Ándalus became the most advanced country in the Western world. Its economy and industry flourished and it became a cultural center that would later contribute to the enlightenment of Europe.

Andalusian Heritage

The idea of the Andalusian Heritage tours was the brainchild of Jerónimo Paez, a lawyer from Granada who is passionately interested in the Arab culture in Spain. The project was designed to bring the splendors of eight centuries of Al-Ándalus culture and history to the notice of the general public. The initial idea was that these tours would complement the 1995 World Skiing Championships in Sierra Nevada (which were cancelled at the last minute due to a lack of snow). His inspiration to develop these tours was also based on the success of tours that followed the historic Road to Santiago.

In 1994 a team of Jerónimo Paez and other historians and experts on Andalusian culture developed a preliminary proposal. Jerónimo Paez later hired a group of marketing experts to study this new service and asked for their advice on how to market it. Because time was short, market research studies were done among experts only. These experts had a thorough knowledge and understanding of the tourism market in Spain, Andalusia and Granada.

The general aims of the project were to popularize the Andalusian Heritage, making it readily understandable and accessible to the millions of people who made up the target public. This could be done by focussing on the cultural and artistic riches of Granada and its surroundings. As a side effect, these tours could strengthen the regional tourist industry by offering alternatives to standard tourist routes. An additional aim was to cultivate the image of Granada as a symbol of dialogue and solidarity between Europe and the Arab world.

Every year, two million people visit the Alhambra in Granada. Because the Andalusian Heritage tours begin or end in Granada, 400,000 tourists a year (20% of all visitors) was expected to be a reasonable objective as the number of tourists taking one of the many tours offered.

The Concept

In more concrete terms, the Andalusian Heritage was defined as a cultural project aimed at creating a greater appreciation of the Andalusian civilization: its culture, its natural settings, its humanistic traditions, and shaping an awareness of its importance to the history of Europe. The Al-Ándalus civilization spread from Granada throughout Andalusia to other parts of Spain, Morocco and Portugal.

The Andalusian Heritage project consisted of two complementary operations. On the one hand, there is the cultural tourism and, on the other hand, making the culture more popular among the public.

The cultural tourism part focused on retracing the paths followed by travellers in Al-Ándalus 12 centuries ago. Making the culture more popular could be achieved through exhibitions and publications. The Andalusian Heritage exhibitions are organized in different cities in order to introduce visitors to Andalusian art and civilization and the Heritage project in general. The exhibitions, to take place between April 16 and July 16, 1995, were as follows:

NAME OF THE EXHIBITION	PLACE
Al-Ándalus and the Mediterranean	Algeciras y Cádiz
The Scientific Heritage of Andalusia	Ronda
The Bazaar: Economics and Traditional Arts in Al-Ándalus and Morocco	Jaen
Music and Poetry in Southern Al-Ándalus	Seville
The Andalusian Heritage: A Romantic Image	Almuñécar
Water in Al-Andalusian Agriculture	Almería
Islamic Art in the Kingdom of Granada	Granada
Andalusia in America: the Overseas Connection	Huelva
Andalusian Architecture. Documents for XXIst Century	Córdoba
Spanish-American Mudejar architecture: From Islam to the New World	Málaga
Andalusian Residential Architecture (XIIth and XIIIth centuries)	Murcia
The Aromas of Al-Ándalus	Granada
Andalusian Horses	Jerez de la Frontera

The Andalusian Heritage publications included work both written specifically for the project and recently-recovered historic texts. They aim to introduce readers to the world of Al-Ándalus. Here, we can think of books like (only in Spanish)

- *Unas palabras preliminares* by Antonio Domínguez;
- *Naturaleza y Ecología* by Joaquín Molero;
- *Gastronomía. El sabor de Al Andalus* by Pablo Amate;
- *Historia del arte y arquitectura* by Ignacio Henares; and
- *Granada en la literatura* by Manuel Villar.

The Rutas de l-Andalus: retracing the paths of history

The Rutas de Al-Ándalus are a series of 12 itineraries that historically linked 10 key cities in Al-Ándalus. Individual visitors and groups can now retrace the steps of travellers before them, journeying to historic sites, drinking in the natural beauty of the region and enjoying a select program of recommended entertainment, shopping and gastronomy. The Al-Ándalus routes were inaugurated on April 1, 1995 and remained open in the year 1995 until July 31. The Al-Ándalus routes are:

- The Washington Irving route (Seville-Granada);
- The route of the Caliphate (Córdoba-Granada);
- The route of Leo Africanus (Almeria-Granada);
- The Alpujarras route (Almeria-Granada);
- The Ibn Battuta route (Málaga-Granada);
- The route of the Almoravids and Nasrids (Bailen-Jaen-Granada);
- The route of the Almohades and the Nazaríes (Navas de Tolosa-Granda);
- The route of al-Idrisi (Algeciras-Granada);
- The route form Puerta Elvira to the Alhambra in Granada;
- The route from Mirador de San Cristobal to Alcázar Genil;
- The Ibn Al-Jatib route (Murcia-Granada); and
- The Münzer route (Murcia-Granada).

Being an open travel alternative, the Rutas de Al-Ándalus start in Granada and cover sites of scenic and cultural interest, shaping an understanding of the past and giving tourists an enjoyable opportunity to experience Andalusian history at first hand.

The open travel alternative means travellers choose their own routes and the amount of time they will spend on it. They follow the footsteps of travellers of yore, visiting the sites mentioned in their writings.

In covering sites of cultural and scenic interest, people interested in Andalusia's cultural heritage may visit the area's history and monuments. People interested in outdoor activities may actively visit the area's natural scenery.

The routes depart from various points (like Almeria, Murcia, Málaga, Seville, Jaen, Córdoba, Algeciras, Marrakesh (Morocco) and Silves (Portugal)) and end in Granada: the last capital of Al-Ándalus.

Well-guided tours of towns or strolls through history, historic buildings, mosques and churches, museums, exhibitions and other places of interest shape an understanding of the past.

Experiencing the legendary hospitality of the Andalusian people and discovering the culinary attractions, the shopping opportunities, and the cultural traditions of the places on the routes make it an enjoyable opportunity.

Experiencing Andalusian history at first hand can be achieved via seeing and experiencing a paradise of refinement and perfection, getting acquainted with what was an economically powerful, cosmopolitan and tolerant civilization. Local performances,

Arab baths and the general atmosphere all add to that experience.

Segmentation

Potential visitors with interests in culture and nature were classified into several groups. These visitors may come from the Andalusian area, the rest of Spain, or, outside Spain (mainly Germany, Belgium, France, Great Britain and The Netherlands). In general, two groups of visitors can be distinguished. However, each group can be divided into three subgroups. At first, the distinction is made between the visitors specifically interested in the Andalusian Heritage program and the current visitors to Andalusia.

The visitors specifically interested in the Andalusian Heritage program are highly motivated by an interest in culture and nature. Mainly, they should be sought (and found) in Spain itself and the other European countries mentioned. Attracting the higher quality visitors among them would be very interesting since they would be a segment with great purchasing power. However, they would ask for high quality hotels, restaurants, transportation and the like, which should be available then.

The current visitors not only stem from the rest of Spain and those European countries mentioned but also from the Andalusian area itself. Within this group, the segment with a great interest in culture and nature should be searched for.

Each of these two groups can be further analyzed to determine their willingness and need to

follow specific itineraries, visit landmarks and exhibitions. Visitors interested in touring the area are the most likely to follow an itinerary such as that offered by the Andalusian Heritage program and make trips of either 2-3 days or longer (7-14 days). They are very interested in culture and nature and make their own travel arrangements. The visitors of landmarks are lodged in Andalusia and tend to be very dynamic. They move around within the immediate area and outside of it, making their own arrangements or travelling with an organized group. The people who take excursions from the town where they are based, follow round trip itineraries and visit natural landmarks and scenic beauty spots to a large degree. Tourists visiting exhibitions spend their days visiting monuments, museums, cathedrals and exhibitions. They always return to their home base.

The Rutas de Al-Ándalus: positioning

The principal specific differentiating features of the Rutas de Al-Ándalus are:

- they showcase the Andalusian civilization, whose level of development in the Middle Ages and influence on the formation of Europe are not yet fully appreciated;
- they bring history to life by presenting cultural and scenic attractions in their proper context, recounting tales told by figures of the epoch, or retold by travellers who followed in their footsteps;

- they give travellers a chance to get to know the present day inhabitants. Visiting smaller towns and lodging in villages makes it easier to get acquainted with the people and participate to a certain extent in their daily lives; and
- they offer total freedom and safety. The Rutas de Al-Ándalus are open itineraries. Travellers are absolutely free to design their routes as they go along, travelling always in a perfectly safe country (Spain).

The Rutas de Al-Ándalus have a number of advantages over other culturally-based travel proposals:

- European travel : the culture is closer to the traveller's own; and
- travel outside of Europe: travellers are often forced to choose between mass tourism or danger.

To sum up: the Rutas de Al-Ándalus are practically "The only chance to journey to a 'different' (non-Christian, 'exotic') but accessible civilization with the same guarantees of safety as can be expected in Europe today".

Designing the core service in more detail

In order to make the ideas more concrete, the Andalusian Heritage management team was developed. One of their duties was to assess the ideas in four respects:

1. the places that make up the route were selected: the places to be included on the route were selected and the mile- stones on each route identified in order to facilitate analysis and assessment of the route as a whole;
2. tourist activities were defined: three groups of tourist activities are defined on the basis of information gathered about the cultural and scenic highpoints of each route: cultural, nature-based and additional activities were defined and described;
3. all other possible activities on each route were catalogued: the information collected included all the activities available in the towns along the route as well as at intermediate points; and
4. all towns and routes were assessed in terms of activities, infrastructure and tourist ser- vices: activities, infrastructure and tourist services were evalu- ated in both quantitative (e.g. number, capacity) and qualita- tive terms (= inherent value to the Heritage program, its uniqueness, etc.). The following rankings were assigned:
   A. a "must" on the route;
   B. a recommended stop on the route; and
   C. an optional stop on the route.

Designing additional services

In addition to the core service just described, particular services were designed to assist travellers in each one of the spots along the route. They come together with the augmented service of the Andalusian Heritage program. Among these additional services are services in Granada itself and on all other sites along the routes. Additional cultural activities in- clude, e.g. visits to museums and churches, strolls along historic routes and cultural events (con- certs, plays, etc.). Additional nature- based activities refer to hikes in scenic countryside, studying flora and fauna and adventure sports in scenic settings.

In Granada and all the gateways to the routes a special system of signs marking the routes and their specific points of interest was established. Information booths were introduced where travellers can get information about exhibi- tions and other activities included in the Heritage program; they can plan their own routes, and can receive the special passport designating them as Al-Ándalus travellers. On all other sites along the routes, a special system of signs marking the routes and their specific points of interest was introduced. Moreover, an informa- tion and support system has been developed enabling travellers to:

- understand and experience the Andalusian civilization through Heritage program attractions and events arranged in every stopping place;
- purchase heritage products as well as the typical products and handicrafts at every stopping place;
- reserve necessary accommoda- tion for the night and trans- portation; and
- get their special Al-Ándalus passports stamped.

In places where two or more routes converge, the sign and information systems are particu- larly important as they help travellers stay on their chosen routes or, if they have not yet made their choice, provide information about all the available alternatives. The information system is also very important in terms of taking care of hotel reservations and transportation arrangements in the spots recommended for overnight stays.

Conceiving these additional services was the first step. Next, they had to be made concrete. So, implementation programs had to be made to develop the sign system (size, color, lettertype), the information booths (sites, software, information up-dates, etc.), a range of high quality Andalusian Heritage products, an information and reservation service for accommodation and transportation, training programs for tourist information personnel, and, graphics and other visible material like brochures, audio-visuals, videos, a guide to tourist services, counter displays, logos, signs and other material for use along the routes, a catalogue of Andalusian Heritage products and recommended shops; panels and posters.

QUESTIONS

1   Do you think the basic concept of the Andalusian Heritage tours has been worked out and implemented well? Explain. What would you skip or add to achieve the general goal of popularizing the Andalusian Heritage, making it readily understandable and accessible to millions of people?

2   What has been done to ensure that excellent service quality will be provided? Do you think the measures taken are sufficient? Explain. What should be done?

3   Taking this segmentation, positioning and service into account, how would you market the Andalusian Heritage tours in Spain and abroad?

4   How would you encourage Spanish and foreign visitors who have already taken one or two tours and who are satisfied about it, to come back to take more tours (and hopefully all twelve)?

5   What kind of actions would you take to measure and control all the organizations and people involved in the Andalusian Heritage, to make it a great success?

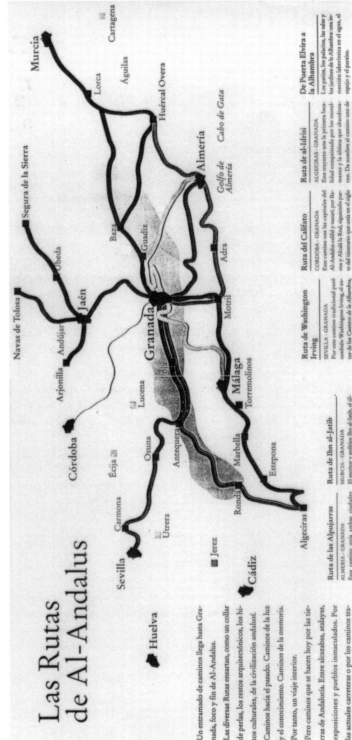

ENDNOTES

1. This Service practice is based on Rubel, 1996.
2. Heskett, Sasser and Hart, 1990, pp. 260-275.
3. Heskett, Sasser and Hart, 1990, p. 260.
4. See also Hooley, Saunders and Piercy, 1998, especially chapters 17 and 18.
5. Bell and Fay, 1991.
6. Stewart and Colgate, 1998, p. 275.
7. Buttle and Ahmad, 1998, p. 255.
8. Lai Man So, 1998, pp. 236-237.
9. Hartline and Ferrell, 1996; Wetzels, 1998.
10. Smidts, Van Riel and Pruyn, 1998. See also Mathieu and Zajac, 1990, or, Mowday, Steers and Porter, 1979.
11. See also Homburg and Becker, 1998.
12. Bonoma, 1985.
13. This section is largely based on Rob Thomas' (1995) MBA thesis.
14. Jack, 1998. This Service practice is an addition to the Club Med story in Chapter Fourteen.
15. e.g. Bonoma, 1985.
15. Reuyl and Willenborg, 1993.
17. Webster, 1991.
18. Roest and Verhallen, 1993.
19. Hayes, 1996, p. 15.
20. These five steps stem originally from Roest and Verhallen, 1993. We have adapted them slightly.
21. This section is largely based on a report written for the NIMA (the Dutch Marketing Institute) by Wolter Kloosterboer (under supervision of Dr Jos Lemmink and Prof. Dr Hans Kasper). This report is based on his MBA-thesis about Internal Marketing, University of Maastricht, 1992.
22. See amongst others Berry, 1980.
23. We will not go into the debate about the difference between HRM and internal marketing. To us, it is important to show that the insights from the marketing field can be applied to the field of HRM for instance in encouraging a smooth implementation of the proposed plans.
24. See, respectively Diller, 1991 Grönroos, 1990b.
25. Sasser and Arbeit, 1976; Berry, 1980.
26. See, respectively Piercy and Morgan, 1991, Gummesson, 1987b.
27. Berry, 1980, p. 26.
28. Gummesson, 1987b; Stauss and Schulze, 1990.
29. Grönroos, 1990b.
30. See also our chapter on communication where many basics in communication have been discussed.
31. This may also mean we could regard the decision not to serve a customer anymore as a kind of firing the customer. Attracting new customers could be regarded as a way of "hiring" part time employees. This would be another way of applying concepts from HRM via internal marketing in the service sector.
32. This section is largely based on Service Breakthroughs, 1990 by James Heskett, W. Earl Sasser jr. and Christopher Hart.
33. Heskett, Sasser and Hart, 1990, pp. 140-141.
34. Heskett, Sasser and Hart, 1990, p. 150.
35. Heskett, Sasser and Hart, 1990, pp. 152-155.

36. The authors of this text have based their Figure 15-8 on Table 8-1 from Heskett, Sasser and Hart, 1990, p. 151 but also made some modifications to it.

37. Heskett, Sasser and Hart, 1990, p. 268.

38. For more on strategic management in professional service firms, see Løwendahl, 1997.

39. See also Kasper, Van Lit and De Ruyter, 1998.

40. See also Hartline and Ferrell, 1996; Bonoma, 1985.

41. Dahlgaard, 1998.

42. Edvardsson, Thomasson and Øvretveit, 1994.

43. Rust, Zahorik and Keinigham, 1995.

44. Research is forthcoming to validate this model empirically. That is why we cannot elaborate on the empirical findings obtained (see Rust, Zahorik and Keinigham, 1996a).

45. Bob Vause, the author of the article containing these data, holds it "should be noted that the sample of companies excludes several of the German retail giants – Metro, Tengelmann, Rewe and Aldi – as well as a number of French groups including Intermarché, Leclerc and Auchan together with other private continental companies where it is difficult to obtain strictly comparable figures." "The data presented are" ... "not designed as a 'ranking' of retail companies..." "They, however,"... "provide insights into the comparative financial characteristics of retail trading across the continent."

46. Witkowski and Kellner, 1996.

47. Fitzgerald, Johnston, Brignall, Silvestro and Voss, 1993; Brignall and Ballantine, 1996. In their article Stan Brignall and Joan Ballantine, 1996, develop twelve hypotheses about new ways to measure performance in service businessess. Because they do not report on an empirical test of these hypotheses, we will not go deeper into it.

48. Speed and Smith, 1997, p. 338.

49. Thor, 1996.

50. See also Kullvén, 1996.

51. Kaplan and Norton, 1992, p. 72; see also Kaplan and Norton, 1993.

52. Slater, Olson and Reddy, 1997, p. 40.

53. Slater, Olson and Reddy, 1997, pp. 40-42.

54. Modell, 1996, pp. 62-63.

55. Holzer, 1996. Edward Holzer's Moret-prize winning MBA thesis contains a perfect overview of ABC (its content, ABC as a decision making tool, activity based control, and Activity Based Management by benchmarking). However, it is not explicitly applied to the service sector. Due to the present lack of knowledge in this field, we cannot solve all these problems about control in service organizations. However, we can mention some general issues deemed relevant in controlling the performance in service organizations.

56. The basics about control in a marketing setting are presented in Jaworski, 1988. A comprehensive overview of management control is presented in Merchant, 1995. Insight into the accounting and control implications of the various characteristics of services, is still rare. Sven Modell, 1996 recently developed a framework to that end. However, this framework has not been tested yet; that is why we will not elaborate on it here. See also Suchanek, 1998.

57. This definition is based on an overview of the literature on management control. Arjen Kampf, Hans Kasper and Fred Vlotman, 1994, made such an overview in order to come to a framework of marketing control.

58. Our discussion on the concept of the learning organization is largely dependent on the Slater and Narver 1995 article on Market Orientation and the Learning Organization and the MBA thesis of Miranda van Golde, 1996.

59. This idea stems from the MBA thesis of Judith van der Hulst, 1996.

60. This sounds self-evident. However, one could also say the opposite. In high-tech service encounters, the few things that front office employees do are so critical to the final service quality, that control should focus on employees' behavior to a very large extent (the machine will do its work automatically).

61. Schwenker, 1989.

62. Case prepared by Josep Chias, PhD., Professor of Marketing Management, ESADE, Barcelona, with help of research assistent Iñigo Soler. The case was translated from the Spanish by Patricia Mathews and edited by Hans Kasper.

BIBLIOGRAPHY

Aaker, David A. (1991), *Managing Brand Equity: Capitalizing on the Value of a Brand Name*, The Free Press, New York.

Aaker, Jennifer (1997), Dimensions of Brand Personality, *Journal of Marketing Research*, vol. 34, August.

Aaker, Jennifer and Susan Fournier (1995), A Brand as a Character, a Partner and a Person: Three Perspectives on the Question of Brand Personality, *Advances in Consumer Research*, vol. 22.

Abbott, L. (1955), Quality and Competition: an Essay in Economic Theory, Columbia University Press, New York.

Abell, Derk (1980), *Defining the Business: the Starting Point of Strategic Planning*, Prentice-Hall, Englewood Cliffs, NJ.

Abrahams, Paul (1994), Keeping the Customer Satisfied 24 Hours a Day, *Financial Times*.

Adler, N.J. (1983a), Cross-Cultural Research: The Ostrich and the Trend, *Academy of Management Review*, vol. 2.

Adler, N.J. (1983b), A Typology of Management Studies Involving Culture, *Journal of International Business Studies*, vol. 2.

Agres, Stuart J. and Tony M. Dubitsky (1996), Changing Needs for Brands, *Journal of Advertising Research*, January/February.

Ahmed, Sadrudin A. and Alain d'Astous (1994), Comparison of Country-of-Origin Effects on Household and Organizational Buyers' Product Perceptions, *European Journal of Marketing*, vol. 29.

Al, Debra (1997), *Dienstenbranding*, GVR-monografie, Genootschap voor Reclame, Amsterdam.

Alsem, Karel Jan and Janny Hoekstra (1994*), De Marketingorientatie van het Nederlandse Bedrijfsleven* (The Marketing Orientation of Dutch Companies), SUM Research Report, Groningen University, Groningen.

Alsem, Karel Jan and Janny C. Hoekstra (1995), Frappante Omgang met Marketing: een Kwantitatief Onderzoek onder Nederlandse Bedrijven, *Tijdschrift voor Marketing*, January-February.

Anderson, J.C. and B. Weitz (1992), The Use of Pledges to Build and Sustain Commitment in Distribution Channels, *Journal of Marketing*, vol. 29, no. 1.

Andriesse, F.G. and Freek F.O. Holzhauer (1994), Kredietbank succes met retentiemarketing, *Tijdschrift voor Marketing*, vol. 28, maart.

Ansoff, H. Igor (1965), *Corporate Strategy*, McGraw-Hill, New York.

Assael, Henry (1987), *Consumer Behavior and Marketing Action*, Kent Publishing Company, Boston.

Axtell, Roger E. (1991), *The DOs and TABOOs of International Trade*, John Wiley, New York.

Baker, Julie and Michaelle Cameron (1996), The effects of the Service Environment on Affect and Consumer Perception of Waiting Time: an Integrative Review and Research Propositions, *Journal of the Academy of Marketing Science*, vol. 24, no. 4.

Baker, Paul (1994), *Europe in 1998*, ERECO, BIPE Counseil, Paris.

Baker, J., Grewal, D. and A. Parasuraman (1994), The Effect of Store Atmosphere on Customer Quality Perceptions and Store Image, *Journal of the Academy of Marketing Science*, vol. 77, no. 7.

Barksdale, Hiram C. and William R. Darden (1972), Consumer Attitudes toward Marketing and Consumerism, *Journal of Marketing*, vol. 36.

Barksdale, Hiram C., Perreault Jr, William D., Arndt, Johan, Barnhill, J., French,W.A. Halliday, M. and J. Zif (1982), A Cross-national Survey of Consumer Attitudes toward Marketing Practices, Consumerism and Government Regulations, *Columbia Journal of World Business*.

Barlow, R.G. (1992), Relationship Marketing - The Ultimate in Customer Services, *Retail Control*, March.

Barrington, Stephen (1998), Canadians Show Knack for Selling Online Banks, *Ad Age International*, January.

Bart, Christopher K. (1997), Sex, Lies and Mission Statements, *Business Horizons*, November-December.

Bartlett, C. and S. Ghoshal (1987), Managing Across Borders: New Organizational Responses, *Sloan Management Review*, vol. 4, no. 7.

Bateson, John E.G. (1985), Perceived Control and the Service Encounter, in Czepiel, John A., Solomon, M.R. and Carol F. Surprenant (eds), *The Service Encounter: Managing Employee/Customer Interaction in Service Businesses*, Lexington Books, Lexington, Mass.

Bateson, John E.G. (1992), *Managing Services Marketing*, The Dryden Press, Orlando, second edition.

Bateson, John E.G. (1995), *Managing Services Marketing, Text and Readings*, The Dryden Press, Orlando, third edition.

Beek, van, W.J., Rademaker, P., Ridder W.J. de and F.M. Rochar (eds) (1993), *Kijken over de eeuwgrens, 25 fascinerende trends* (Looking beyond the end of the century, 25 fascinating trends), Stichting Maatschappij en Onderneming in samenwerking met de Stichting Beweton.

Behara, Ravi S. and Richard B. Chase (1993), Service Quality Deployment: Quality Service by Design, in Sarin, V. Rakesh Ph.D., *Perspectives in Operations Management*, Kluwer Academic, Norwell, MA.

Bell, John D. and Michael T. Fay (1991), From the Gentleman to the Marketer: the Changing Attitudes of the Professions in New Zealand, *International Journal of Advertising*, vol. 10.

Benito, Gabriel R.G. and Lawrence S. Welch (1994), Foreign Market Servicing: Beyond the Choice of Entry Mode, *Journal of International Marketing*, vol. 2.

Berkowitz, Eric N., Kerin, Roger A. and William Rudelius (1986), *Marketing*, Times Mirror/Mosby College Publishing, St Louis.

Berry, Leonard L. (1980), Services Marketing is Different, *Business Magazine*, May-June.

Berry, Leonard L. (1995), *On Great Service, A Framework for Action*, The Free Press, New York.

Berry, Leonard L. (1997), Branding the Store, *Arthur Andersen Retailing Issues Letter*, Center for Retailing Studies, Texas A&M University, vol. 9, no. 5, September.

Berry, Leonard L., Conant, Jeffrey S. and A. Parasuraman (1991), A Framework for Conducting a Services Marketing

Audit, *Journal of the Academy of Marketing Science*, vol. 19, no. 3.

Berry, Leonard L., Lefkowith, Edwin F. and Terry Clark (1988), In Services, What's in a Name?, *Harvard Business Review*, September-October.

Berry, Leonard L. and A. Parasuraman (1991), *Marketing Services, Competing through Quality*, The Free Press, New York.

Berry, Leonard L. and A. Parasuraman (1993), Building a New Academic Field - The Case of Services Marketing, *Journal of Marketing*, vol. 69, Spring.

Berry, Leonard L. and A. Parasuraman (1997), Listening to the Customer - The Concept of a Service - Quality Information System, *Sloan Management Review*, vol. 38, no. 3, Spring.

Berry, Leonard L. and Manjit S. Yadav (1996), Capture and Communicate Value in the Pricing of Services, *Sloan Management Review*, Summer.

Berstell, Gerald and Denise Nitterhouse (1997), Looking 'Outside the Box', *Marketing Research*, Summer.

Berthon, Pierre, Hulbert, James M. and Leyland F. Pitt (1997), Brands, Brand Managers, and the Management of Brands: Where to Next?, *Report no. 97-122*, Marketing Science Institute, Cambridge, MA.

Besig, Hans-Michael, Maier, Michael and Anton Meyer (1996), Markenstrategien im Finanz-Marketing-Beispiel: Privatkundengeschäft der Bayerischen Hypotheken- und Wechsel-Bank AG, in Dichtl, E. and W. Eggers (eds), *Markterfolg durch Marken*, Wechsel-Bank, München.

Bharadwaj, Sundar G. and Anil Menon (1993), Determinants of Success in Service Industries, *Journal of Services Marketing*, vol. 7, no. 4.

Bhattacharya, C.B. (1998), When Customers Are Members: Customer Retention in Paid Membership Contexts, *Journal of the Academy of Marketing Science*, vol. 26, no. 1.

Bitner, Mary Jo (1992), Servicescapes: the Impact of Physical Surroundings on Customers and Employees, *Journal of Marketing*, vol. 56, April.

Bitner, Mary Jo, Booms, Bernard H. and Mary Stanfield Tetreault (1990), The Service Encounter: Diagnosing Favorable and Unfavorable Incidents, *Journal of Marketing*, vol. 54.

Bitner, Mary Jo and A.R. Hubbert (1994), Encounter Satisfaction Versus Overall Satisfaction Versus Quality: The Customer's Voice, in *Service Quality: New Directions in Theory and Practice*, Sage, Thousand Oaks.

Bitran, Gabriel and Susana Mondschein (1997), Managing the Tug-of-War Between Supply and Demand in the Service Industries, *European Management Journal*, vol. 15, no. 5.

Blackmon, Douglas A. (1996), UPS, Feeling Boxed In, Stages its Own Coming Out, *The Wall Street Journal Europe*, 18 September.

Blackston, Max (1992), Beyond Brand Personality: Building Brand Relationships, in *Brand Equity and Advertising: Advertising Role in Building Strong Brands*, L. Erlbaum Ass, Hillsdale NJ.

Bloemer, Josée M.M. (1993), *Loyaliteit en Terredenheid*, Ph.D., Maastricht University, Data Wyse, Maastricht.

Bloemer, Josée M.M. and Hans D.P. Kasper (1995), The Complex Relationship Between Consumer Satisfaction and Brand Loyalty, *Journal of Economic Psychology*, vol. 16.

Bloemer, Josée M.M. and Hans D.P. Kasper (1998), The Effect of Satisfaction and Involvement on Loyalty, *Working Paper*, University of Maastricht, Maastricht.

Bloemer, Josée M.M. and Jos G.A.M. Lemmink (1992), The Importance of Customer Satisfaction in Explaining Brand and Dealer Loyalty, *Journal of Marketing Management*, vol. 8.

Bloemer, Josée M.M., Ruyter, Ko de and Karin A. Venetis (1995), Kwaliteit en Tevredenheid in de Dienstverlening: Kop, Munt of Dubbeltje op zijn Kant?, *Jaarboek 1994-1995 Nederlandse Vereniging van Marktonderzoekers*, De Vrieseborch, Haarlem.

Boerkamp, Ellis J.C. and Marco Vriens (1993), Het Meten van Kwaliteit bij Diensten: een Vergelijking van Alternatieve Meetprocedures, *Tijdschrift voor Marketing*, vol. 29.

Bolton, Ruth H. and James H. Drew (1991), A Longitudinal Analysis of the Impact of Service Changes on Customer Attitudes, *Journal of Marketing*, vol. 55, January.

Bonoma, Thomas V. (1985), *The Marketing Edge, Making Strategies Work*, The Free Press, New York.

Booms, Bernard H. and Mary Jo Bitner (1983), Marketing Strategies and Organizational Structures for Service Firms, in Berry, Leonard L., Shostack L. and G.D. Upah, (eds), *Emerging Perspectives on Service Marketing*, AMA, Chicago.

Booms, Bernard H. and Jody L. Nyquist (1981), Analyzing the Customer/Firm Communication Component of the Services Marketing Mix, in Donnelly, J.H. and William R. George (eds), *Marketing of Services*, American Marketing Association, Chicago.

Boulding, William, Kalra, Ajay, Staelin, Richard and Valarie A. Zeithaml (1993), A Dynamic Process Model of Service Quality: from Expectations to Behavioral Intentions, *Journal of Marketing Research*, vol. 30.

Bouts, J.M. (1989), Het Buitenlandse Merk, *Tijdschrift voor Marketing*, vol. 23, no.12.

Bowen, David and E. Lawler III (1992), The Empowerment of Service Workers: What, Why, How, and When, *Sloan Management Review*, Spring.

Bowes, Elena (1998), Brits Add on Savings Accounts, Mortgages to their Grocery Lists, *Ad Age International*, January.

Bradley, Frank (1995), The Service Firm in International Marketing, in Glynn, William J. and James G. Barnes (eds), *Understanding Services Management, Integrating Marketing, Organisational Behaviour Operations and Human Resource Management*, John Wiley, Chichester.

Brady, Diana (1995), *Asian Wall Street Journal Weekly*, 4 December.

Brentani, Ulrike de (1995), New Industrial Service Development: Scenarios for Success and Failure, *Journal of Business Research*, vol. 32, no. 2.

Brignall, Stan and Joan Ballantine (1996), Performance Measurement in Service Businesses Revisited, *International Journal of Service Industry Management*, vol. 7, no. 1.

Bruhn, M. and B. Bunge (1994), Beziehungsmarketing - Neuorientierung für Marketingwissenschaft und - Praxis? *Arbeitspapiere des Instituts für Marketing an der European Business School*, no. 15, Rheingau.

Buchanan, Richard W. (1996), *The Enemy Within, Actions that Self-destruct Companies, Customer Service and Jobs*, McGraw-

Hill, Sydney.

Buckley, Peter J., Pass, C.L. and Kate Prescott (1992a), *Servicing International Markets, Competitive Strategies of Firms*, Blackwell, Oxford.

Buckley, Peter J., Pass, C.L. and Kate Prescott (1992b), The Internationalization of Service Firms: a Comparison with the Manufacturing Sector, *Scandinavian International Business Review*, vol.1, no. 1.

Burgmaier, Stefanie (1997), Nebenbei erledigen, *Wirtschaftswoche*, 24 April.

Buttle, Francis and Rizal Ahmad (1998), Loving, Retaining and Losing Customers: How National First Bank Retains its Corporate Direct Customers, in Per Andersson (ed.), *Proceedings 27th EMAC Conference*, Stockholm, vol. 1.

Buzzel, Robert (1968), Can you standardize multinational marketing?, *Harvard Business Review*, November.

Canziani, Bonnie Farber (1997), Leveraging Customer Competency in Service Firms, *International Journal of Service Industry Management*, vol. 8, no. 1.

Capps, Alison (1997), Professional Services - Are They Getting the Brand Right?, *Admap*, July/August.

Carman, James and Eric Langeard (1980), Growth Strategies of Service Firms, *Strategic Management Journal*, vol. 1.

Carr, Steven D. (1996), The Cult of Brand Personality, *Marketing News*, 6 May.

Cateora, Philip R. (1996), *International Marketing*, Irwin, ninth edition.

Cetron, Marvin J. (1994), An American renaissance in the year 2000: 74 trends that will affect America's future - And Yours, *The Futurist*, March/April.

Chen, L.J., Gupta, A., W. Rom (1994), A study of price and quality in service operations, *International Journal of Service Industry Management*, vol. 5, no. 2.

Chernatony, L. de and M.H.B. McDonald (1992), *Creating Powerful Brands: the Strategic Route to Success in Consumer, Industrial and Service Markets*, Butterworth-Heinemann, Oxford.

Clemmer, Elizabeth C. and Benjamin Schneider (1993), Managing Customer Dissatisfaction with Waiting: Applying Social-Psychological Theory in a Service Setting, in Swartz, Teresa A., Bowen, David E. and Stephen W. Brown (eds), *Advances in Services Marketing and Management*, vol. 2, JAI Press.

Club Mediterrane (1994), Annual Report 1993-1994.

Cooper, Robert G. and Ulrike de Brentani (1991), New Industrial Financial Services: What Distinguishes the Winners, *Journal of Product Innovation Management*, vol. 8, no. 2.

Cowell, Donald (1984), *The Marketing of Services*, Heinemann Professional, Oxford.

Coyne, Kevin P. and Renée Dye (1998), The Competitive Dynamics of Network-Based Businesses, *Harvard Business Review*, January-February.

Crimp, Margaret (1985), *The Marketing Research Process*, Prentice-Hall, London, second edition.

Cronin, J. Joseph Jr and Stephen A. Taylor (1992), Measuring Service Quality: A Reexamination and Extension, *Journal of Marketing*, vol. 56.

Cronin, J. Joseph Jr and Stephen A. Taylor (1994), SERVPERF versus SERVQUAL: Reconciling Performance-Based and Perceptions-Minus-Expectations Measurement of Service Quality, *Journal of Marketing*, vol. 58.

Crosby, Larry A. and Nancy Stevens (1987), Effects of Relationship Marketing on Satisfaction, Retention, and Prices in the Life Insurance Industry, *Journal of Marketing Research*, vol. 24, November.

Crosby, Philip B. (1983), *Quality is Free*, McGraw-Hill, New York.

Cuneo, Alice Z. (1997), Marketer of the Year, *Advertising Age*, 15 December.

Cunningham, Lawrence F., Young, Clifford E., and Moonkyu Lee (1997), A Customer-Based Taxonomy of Services: Implications for Service Marketers, in Swartz, Teresa A., Bowen, David E. and Stephen A. Brown (eds) *Advances in Services Management*, vol. 6, JAI Press, Greenwich CON.

Czinkota, Michael R. and Ilkka A. Ronkainen (1995), *International Marketing*, The Dryden Press, New York, fourth edition.

Daems, Herman and Sietze W. Douma (1989), *Concurrentiestrategie en Concernstrategie*, Kluwer, Deventer.

Dahlgaard , Jens J. (1998), *Profile of Success, European Quality*, vol. 5, no. 1.

Danaher, Peter J. and Jan Mattsson (1994), Customer Satisfaction During the Service Delivery Process, *European Journal of Marketing*, vol. 28, no. 5.

Danaher, Peter J. and Roland T. Rust (1996), Indirect Financial Benefits From Service Quality, *Quality Management Journal*, vol. 3, no. 2.

Darden, W.R., Erdem, O, and D.K. Darden (1983), A Comparison and Test of Three Causal Models of Patronage Intentions, in Darden, W.R. and R.F. Lusch (eds), *Patronage Behavior and Retail Management*, North-Holland, New York.

Dart, Jack and Kim Freeman (1994), Dissatisfaction Response Styles Among Clients of Professional Accounting Firms, *Journal of Business Research*, vol. 29.

Davenport, T. and W. Nohria (1994), Case Management and the Integration of Labor, *Sloan Management Review*, Winter.

Davenport, T. and J. Short (1990), The New Industrial Engineering: Information Technology and Business Process Redesign, *Sloan Management Review*, Summer.

Davis, Frank W. and Karl B. Manrodt (1996), *Customer-Responsive Management, the Flexible Advantage*, Blackwell, Cambridge MA.

Day, George S. (1990), *Market Driven Strategy, Processes for Creating Value*, The Free Press, New York.

Day, George S. and Robin Wensley (1983), Marketing Theory with a Strategic Orientation, *Journal of Marketing*, vol. 47.

Day, Ralph L. and E. Laird Landon Jr (1976), Collecting Comprehensive Complaint Data by Survey Research, in Beverley Anderson (ed.), *Advances in Consumer Research*, vol. III, Association for Consumer Research, Cincinnatti.

Deal, Terrence E. and Allan A. Kennedy (1982), *Corporate Cultures: The Rites and Rituals of Corporate Life*, Addison-Wesley, Reading MA.

Diamantopoulos, Adamantios and Susan Hart (1993), Linking Market Orientation and Company Performance: Preliminary Evidence on Kohli and Jaworski's Framework, *Journal of Strategic Marketing*, vol. 1.

Dibb, Sally, Simkin, Lyndon, Pride, William M. and O.C. Ferrell (1994), *Marketing, Concepts and Strategies,* Houghton Mifflin, Boston, second European edition.

Dibb, Sally, Simkin, Lyndon, Pride, William M. and O.C. Ferrell (1997), *Marketing, Concepts and Strategies,* Houghton Mifflin, Boston, third European edition.

Dick, A.S. and K. Basu (1994), Customer Loyalty: Toward an Integrated Conceptual Framework, *Journal of the Academy of Marketing Science,* vol. 22, no.2.

Dijk, Nico M. van (1990), Don't You Also Hate Having to Wait, *Paper,* Forschungsinstitut für anwendungsorientierte Wissensverarbeitung, Abteilung Mathematik VII, Universität Ulm, Ulm.

Dijk, Nico M. van (undated), To Wait or Not To Wait: Is That The Question?, *Paper,* University of Amsterdam, Amsterdam.

Diller, H. (1991), Entwicklungstrends und Forschungsfelder der Marketing-organisation, *Marketing ZFP,* vol. 3, no. 3. Qartal.

Diller, H. (1994), *Beziehungsmanagement und Konsumentenforschung,* Arbeitspapier no. 32, Universität Erlangen-Nürnberg, Betriebswirtschaftliches Institut.

Diller, H. (1997), Forschungsbericht AMarken- und Einkaufsstattentreue, *Marketing Newsletter,* June.

Diller H. and M. Kusterer (1988), Beziehungsmanagement: Theoretische Grundlagen und exploratieve Befunde, *Zeitschrift für Forschung und Praxis,* vol. 10, no. 3.

Dobree, J.S. and A.S. Page (1990), Unleashing the Power of Service Brands in the 1990s, *Management Decision,* vol. 28, no. 6.

Donovan, R., Rossiter, J.R. and Nesdale, M.G. (1994), Store Atmosphere and Purchasing Behavior, *Journal of Retailing,* vol. 70, no. 3.

Douglas, Susan P. and C. Samual Craig (1983), *International Marketing Research,* Prentice-Hall, Englewood Cliffs.

Douglas, Susan P. and C. Samuel Craig (1995), *Global Marketing Strategy,* McGraw-Hill, New York.

Duboff, Robert S. and Lori Underhill Sherer (1997), Customized Customer Loyalty, *Marketing Management,* Summer.

Durgee, Jeffrey F. (1988), Understanding Brand Personality, *Journal of Consumer Marketing,* vol. 5, no. 3, Summer.

Dwyer, Robert F., Schurr, Paul H. and Sejo Oh (1987), Developing Buyer-Seller Relationships, *Journal of Marketing,* vol. 51, no. 2.

Edgett, Scott (1994), The Traits of Successful New Service Development, *Journal of Services Marketing,* vol. 8, no. 3.

Edvardsson, Bo, Thomasson, Bertil and John Øvretveit (1994), *Quality of Services, Making It Really Work,* McGraw-Hill, London.

Eiglier, Pierre and Eric Langeard (1987), *Servuction,* McGraw-Hill, Paris.

Endewick (1989), The Internationalization of Service Firms, *Advances in Strategic Management,* vol. 9.

Eppen, G.D., Hanson, W.A. and R. Kipp Martin (1991), Bundling New Products, New Markets, Low Risk, *Sloan Management Review,* no. 7.

Erramilli, M. Krishna (1992), Influence of Some External and Internal Environmental Factors on Foreign Market Entry Mode Choice in Service Firms, *Journal of Business Research,* vol. 25.

Erramilli, M. Krishna and C.P. Rao (1990), Choice of Foreign Market Entry Modes by Service Firms: Role of Market Knowledge, *Management International Review,* vol. 30, no. 2.

Erramilli, M. Krishna and C.P. Rao (1993), Service Firms' International Entry-Mode Choice, a Modified Transaction-Cost Analysis Approach, *Journal of Marketing,* vol. 57, July.

European Business Handbook (1995), Kogan Page, London.

Faes, Wouter and Cyriel van Tilborgh (1984), *Marketing van Diensten,* Kluwer, Antwerpen/Deventer.

Feinberg, Richard A., Ruyter, Ko de, Trappey, Charles and Tzai-Zang Lee (1995), Consumer-Defined Service Quality in International Retailing, *Total Quality Management,* vol. 6, no. 1.

Firestone, Sidney (1983), Why Advertising a Service Different, in Berry, Leonard L., Shostack, Lynn and Upah, G.D. (eds) *Emerging Perspectives on Service Marketing,* AMA, Chicago.

Firth, Michael (1993), Price Setting and the Value of a Strong Brand Name, *International Journal of Research in Marketing,* vol. 10, no. 4.

Fisher, Andrew (1996), German Banking and Finance, *Financial Times,* May.

Fisk, Raymond P. and Stephen J. Grove (1995), Service Performances as Drama: Quality Implications and Measurement, in Kunst, Paul and Jos Lemmink (eds), *Managing Service Quality,* Paul Chapman Publishing, London.

Fisk, Raymond P., Brown, Stephen W. and Mary Jo Bitner (1993), Tracking the Evolution of the Services Marketing Literature, *Journal of Retailing,* vol. 69, Spring.

Fitzgerald, Lin, Johnston, Robert, Brignall, Stan, Silvestro, Rhian and Christopher Voss (1993), *Performance Measurement in Service Businesses,* The Chartered Institute of Management Accountants.

Fitzsimmons, James A. and Mona J. Fitzsimmons (1994), *Service Management For Competitive Advantage,* McGraw-Hill, New York.

Flanagan, J.C. (1954), The Critical Incident Technique, *Psychological Bulletin,* vol. 51, July.

Flipo, Jean-Paul (1986), Service Firms: Interdependence of External and Internal Marketing Strategies, *European Journal of Marketing,* vol. 20, no. 8.

Floor, Ko and W. Fred van Raaij (1989), *Marketing Communicatie Strategie,* Stenfert Kroese, Leiden.

Ford, David (1984), Buyer/Seller Relationships in International Industrial Markets, *Industrial Marketing Management,* vol. 13, no. 2.

Ford, David (ed.) (1990), *Understanding Business Markets,* Academic Press, London.

Ford, David (1997), *Understanding Business Markets: Interaction, Relationships and Networks,* The Dryden Press, London, second edition.

Fornell, Claes (1992), A National Customer Satisfaction Barometer: the Swedish Experiment, *Journal of Marketing,* vol. 56, January.

Fornell, Claes, Johnson, Michael D., Anderson, Eugene W., Cha, Jaesung and Barbara Everitt Bryant (1996), The American Customer Satisfaction Index: Nature, Purpose and Findings, *Journal of Marketing*, vol. 60, October.

Fromm, Bill and Len Schlesinger (1994*), The Real Heroes of Business ... and Not a CEO Among Them*, Currency/Doubleday, New York.

Garvin, David A. (1988), *Managing Quality, the Strategic and Competitive Edge*, The Free Press, New York.

Gaski, John F. and Michael J. Etzel (1986), The Index of Consumer Sentiment toward Marketing, *Journal of Marketing*, vol. 50, July.

Gemünden, Hans Georg (1985), Perceived Risk and Information Search: a Systematic Meta-Analysis of the Empirical Evidence, *International Journal of Research in Marketing*, vol. 2, no. 2.

George, William R. and Leonard L. Berry (1981), Guidelines for the Advertising of Services, *Business Horizons*, vol. 24, (May-June), no. 4.

Geyskens, Inge and Jan-Benedict E.M. Steenkamp (1995), An Investigation into the Joint Effects of Trust and Interdependence on Relationship Commitment, in Bergadaa, Michelle, Ph.D, *Proceedings of the 24th EMAC Conference*, Paris.

Geyskens, Inge, Steenkamp, Jan-Benedict E.M., Scheer, L.K. and N. Kumar (1996), The Effects of Trust and Interdependency on Relationship Commitment, *International Journal of Research in Marketing*, vol. 13, no. 4.

Ghosh, Avijit (1994), *Retail Management*, The Dryden Press, Orlando, second edition.

Gnoth, Juergen (undated), An Essay on Branding Tourism Services (The New Zealand Way), *Paper*, Department of Marketing, University of Otago, New Zealand.

Golde, Miranda M.N. van (1996), *Marktgerichtheid, een Uitdaging om te Leren*, MBA thesis, University of Maastricht, Maastricht.

Goor, A. van, a.o. (1992), *Fysieke distributie: Denken in toegevoegde waarde*, Stenfert Kroese, Leiden.

Gotta, Manfred (1989), Dienstleistungs-Produkte als Marken-Persönlichkeiten, *Marketing Journal*.

Govindarajan, Vijay and John K. Shank (1989), Strategic Cost Analysis: The Crown Cork and Seal Case, *Journal of Cost Management for the Manufacturing Industry*, vol. 2, no. 4.

Grant, Robert M. (1991), The Resource-Based Theory of Competitive Advantage: Implications for Strategy Formulation, *California Management Review*, Spring.

Green, Paul E., Tull, Donald S. and Gerald Albaum (1988), *Research for Marketing Decisions*, Prentice-Hall, Englewood Cliffs, fifth edition.

Grifford, Jr, Dan (1997), Brand Management, Moving Beyond Loyalty, *Harvard Business Review*, vol. 75, March-April.

Grönroos, Christian (1982), *Strategic Management and Marketing in the Service Sector*, Research Report 8, Swedish School of Economics and Business Administration, Helsinki.

Grönroos, Christian (1990a), Relationship Approach to Marketing in Service Contexts: the Marketing and Organizational Behavior Interface, *Journal of Business Research*, vol. 20.

Grönroos, Christian (1990b*), Service Management and Marketing*, Lexington Books, Lexington MA.

Grönroos, Christian (1993), Towards a Third Phase in Service Quality Research: Challenges and Future Directions, in

Swartz, Teresa A., Bowen, David E. and Stephen W. Brown, *Advances in Services Marketing and Management*, vol. 2.

Groot, Coos (1995), *Bundling Customer Services in International Industrial Markets*, MBA Thesis, University of Limburg, Maastricht.

Grove, Stephen J., Fisk, Raymond P., and Mary Jo Bitner (1992), Dramatizing the Service Experience: a Managerial Approach, in Swartz, Teresa A., Brown, Stephen W. and David E. Bowen (eds), *Advances in Services Marketing and Management*, vol. 1.

Gruen, Thomas W. (1997), Relationship Marketing: the Route to Marketing Efficiency and Effectiveness, *Business Horizons*, November-December.

Guglielmo, Connie (1996), Here Come the Super-ATMs, *Fortune*, 10 October.

Guiltinan, J.P. (1987), The Price Bundling Services: a Normative Framework, *Journal of Marketing*, vol. 51, April.

Gummesson, Evert (1987a), The New Marketing - Developing Long-term Interactive Relationships, *Long Range Planning*, vol. 20, no. 4.

Gummesson, Evert (1987b), Using Internal Marketing to Develop a New Culture - the Case of Ericsson Quality, *The Journal of Business and Industrial Marketing*, vol. 2, no. 3, Summer.

Gummesson, Evert (1991), Marketing-orientation Revisited: the Crucial Role of the Part-time Marketeer, *European Journal of Marketing*, vol. 25.

Gummesson, Evert (1993), *Quality Management in Service Organizations*, International Service Quality Association, New York.

Gummesson, Evert and Jane Kingman-Brundage (1992), Service Design and Quality: Applying Service Blueprinting and Service Mapping to Railroad Services, in Kunst, Paul and Jos Lemmink (eds), *Quality Management in Services*, Van Gorcum, Assen/Maastricht.

Häkansson, Hakan (1982), *International Marketing and Purchasing of Industrial Goods*, John Wiley, New York.

Halinen, Aino (1994), *Exchange Relationships in Professional Services; a Study of Relationship Development in the Advertising Sector*, Published Dissertation Project, Sarja/Series A-6, Turku School of Economics and Business Administration, Turku.

Hamel, Gary and C.K. Prahalad (1994), *Competing for the Future*, Harvard Business School Press, Boston MA.

Hammer, M. (1990), Reengineering Work: Don't Automate, Obliterate*, Harvard Business Review*, July-August.

Hammer, Michael and James Champy (1993), *Reengineering the Corporation*, Harper Collins, New York.

Harris, P. and McDonald, F., (1996), European Business and Marketing: Strategic Issues, Paul Chapman Ltd, London.

Hart, Christopher W.L. (1988), The Power of Unconditional Service Guarantees, *Harvard Business Review*, vol. 66, July-August.

Hart, Christopher W.L., Heskett, James L. and W. Earl Sasser, Jr (1990), The Profitable Art of Service Recovery, *Harvard Business Review*, vol. 68, July-August.

Hartline, Michael D. and O.C. Ferrell (1996), The Management of Customer-Contact Service Employees: an Empirical Investigation, *Journal of Marketing*, vol. 60,

October.

Harverson, Patrick, Winning Abroad by Staying at Home, *Financial Times Exporter 12.*

Harvey, Michael and Jack. J. Kasulis (1998), Retailer Brands - The Business of Distinction, *Arthur Andersen Retailing Issues Letter*, Center for Retailing Studies Texas A&M University, vol. 10, no. 1, January.

Hattink, Robin J. (1995), Merken en Merkenbeleid binnen Dienstenmarketing, MBA thesis, University of Limburg, Maastricht.

Hauser, John R. and Don Clausing (1988), The House of Quality, *Harvard Business Review*, May-June.

Hayes, Richard D. (1996), The Strategic Power of Internal Service Excellence, *Business Horizons*, July-August.

Haynes, Paula J. (1990), Hating to Wait: Managing the Final Service Encounter, *Journal of Services Marketing*, vol. 4, no.4, Fall.

Heer, A. de, Ahaus C.T.B. & Vos A.M.A.M. (1990), *Kwaliteitskosten, wat baat het?*, Kluwer Bedrijfswetenschappen, Deventer, second edition.

Helgesen, Sally (1990), *The Female Advantage, Women's Way of Leadership*, Doubleday/Currency, New York.

Hellman, Pasi (1994), The Internationalization of Finnish Financial Service Companies, *International Business Review*, vol. 5, no. 2.

Helsdingen, Piet J.C. van (1982), Produktbeleid en overheid, *Research memorandum 1982-4*, Vrije Universiteit, Economische Faculteit, Amsterdam.

Hentschel, B. (1990), Die Messung wahrgenommener Dienstleistungsqualität mit SERVQUAL: Eine kritische Auseinandersetzung, *Marketing ZFP*, vol. 4.

Herk, Hester van and Theo M.M. Verhallen (1995), Equivalence in Empirical International Research in the Food Area, *Paper*, Second Conference on the Cultural Dimension of International Marketing, Odense University, Odense.

Herrington, J. Duncan, Lollar, James G., Cotter, Michael J. and James A. Henley Jr (1996), Comparing Intensity and Effectiveness of Marketing Communications: Services versus Non-Services, *Journal of Advertising Research*, November/December.

Heskett, James L. (1986), *Managing in the Service Economy*, Harvard Business School Press, Boston MA.

Heskett, James L. (1987), Lessons in the Service Sector, *Harvard Business Review*, March-April.

Heskett, James L., Jones, T.O., Loveman, Gary W., Sasser, W. Earl Jr, and Leonard A. Schlesinger (1994), Putting the Service Profit Chain to Work, *Havard Business Review*, March/April.

Heskett, James L., Sasser, W. Earl Jr and Christopher W.L. Hart (1990), *Service Breakthroughs, Changing the Rules of the Game*, The Free Press, New York.

Heskett, James L., Jones, Thomas O., Loveman, Gary W., Sasser, W. Earl Jr, and Leonard A Schlesinger (1994), Putting the Service Profit Chain to Work, *Harvard Business Review*, March - April.

Heskett, James L., Sasser, W. Earl Jr and Leonard A. Schlesinger (1997), *The Service Profit Chain, How Leading Companies Link Profit and Growth to Loyalty, Satisfaction and*

Value, The Free Press, New York

Heuvel, Jan (1993), *Dienstenmarketing*, Wolters-Noordhoff, Groningen.

Hill, Richard (1992), *We Europeans*, Europublications, Brussels.

Hite, Robert E., Fraser, Cynthia and Joseph A. Bellizi (1990), Professional Service Advertising: the Effect of Price Inclusion, Justification and Level of Risk, *Journal of Advertising Research*, September.

Hoekstra, Janny C. (1993), *Direct Marketing*, Wolters-Noordhoff, Groningen.

Hoffman, D.L. and T.P. Novak (1994), Marketing in Hypermedia Computer-Mediated Environments: Conceptual Foundations, *Working Paper*, Owen Graduate School of Management, Vanderbilt University, Nashville.

Hoffman, K. Douglas and John E.G. Bateson (1997), *Essentials of Services Marketing*, The Dryden Press, Forth Worth.

Hofstede, Geert (1991), *Cultures and Organizations, Software of the Mind*, McGraw-Hill, London.

Holmlund, Maria (1997), *Perceived Quality in Business Relationships*, Ph.D. Swedish School of Economics and Business Administration, Helsinki.

Holzer, Edward L. (1996), *Activity-Based Management, More Than Just the Step Beyond ABC*, Stichting Moret Fonds, Rotterdam.

Holzmann, Kathy (1996), Leasing operations catalyze capital equipment purchases, *Development Business*, 16 October, vol. 9.

Holzmüller, Hartmut H. (1995), *Konzeptionelle und Methodische Probleme in der Interkulturellen Management- und Marketingforschung*, Schäffer-Poeschel Verlag, Stuttgart.

Homburg, Christian and Bern Garbe (1996), Industrielle Dienstleistungen - Lukrativ, aber Schwer zu Meistern, *Harvard Business Manager*, no. 1.

Homburg, Christian and Jan Becker (1998), Market-oriented Management: a Systems-based Approach, in Per Andersson Ph.D., *Proceedings 27th EMAC Conference*, Stockholm, vol. 3.

Honomichl, Jack (1995), Marketers Value Honesty in Marketing Researchers, *Marketing News*, vol. 29, no. 12.

Hooley, Graham J. (1992), *Marketing in the UK*, Aston Business School, Birmingham.

Hooley, Graham J., Saunders, John A. and Nigel F. Piercy (1998), *Marketing Strategy and Competitive Positioning*, Prentice-Hall, London, second edition.

Huang, Jen-Hung (1994), National Character and Purchase Dissatisfaction Response, *Journal of Consumer Satisfaction, Dissatisfaction and Complaining Behavior*, vol. 7.

Hudson, Richard L. (1995), New Barclays Service Banks on Internet Growth in Europe, *Wall Street Journal*, 1 June.

Hui, Michael K. and John E.G. Bateson (1991), Perceived Control and the Effects of Crowding and Consumer Choice on the Service Experience, *Journal of Consumer Research*, vol. 18, September.

Hui, Michael K. and David K. Tse (1996), What to Tell Consumers in Waits of Different Lengths: an Integrative Model of Service Evaluation, *Journal of Marketing*, vol. 60, April.

Hulst, Judith van der (1996), *Het Beheersende Vermogen van Marktgerichtheid*, MBA thesis, University of Maastricht, Maastricht.

Hurts, Floris and Piet-Heijn van Mechelen (1997), Portfolio-management voor Dienstenmerken, *Tijdschrift voor Marketing*, vol. 31, October.

Hutt, Michael. D. and Thomas V. Speh (1992), *Business Marketing Management, a Strategic View of Industrial and Organizational Markets*, The Dryden Press, Orlando, fourth edition.

Interview-IPM (1974 and 1981), *Consumentisme, een onderzoek naar de consument in een veranderende samenleving* (Consumerism, an investigation to the consumer in a changing world), Schiedam, Amsterdam.

Ivasncevich, J.M. (1994), *Management: Quality and Competitiveness*, Irwin, Burr Ridge, Ill.

Jack, Andrew (1998), Redefining Sun, Sand and Sangria, *Financial Times*, 28 January.

Jahoda, G. (1980), Theoretical and Systematic Approaches in Cross-cultural Psychology, in Triandis, H.C. and W.W. Lambert (eds), *Handbook of Cross-cultural Psychology*, vol. 1, Perspectives, Boston, MA.

Jain, Subhash (1989), Standardization of International Marketing Strategy: Some Research Hypotheses, *Journal of Marketing*, vol. 53.

Jallat, Frédéric (1993), *Innovation Management in the Consumer Services Sector: An Empirical Study*, ESCP Groupe, Paris.

Jallat, Frédéric (1994), Innovation dans les Services: les Facteurs de Succès, *Décisions Marketing*, no. 2.

Janssen, Ringo (1996), *The Internationalisation of Business Services, Satisfying Clients Through Relationship Marketing and Service Quality*, MBA thesis, University of Limburg, Maastricht, The Netherlands.

Jaworski, Bernard J. (1988), Toward a Theory of Marketing Control: Environmental Context, Control Types, and Consequences, *Journal of Marketing*, vol. 52.

Jaworski, Bernard J. and Ajay K. Kohli (1993), Market Orientation: Antecedents and Consequences, *Journal of Marketing*, vol. 57, July.

Jeannet, Jean-Pierre and H. David Hennessey (1988), *International Marketing Management*, Houghton Mifflin, Boston.

Jeannet, Jean-Pierre and H. David Hennessey (1995), *Global Marketing Strategies*, Houghton Mifflin Company, third edition.

Johnson, Gerry and Kevin Scholes (1988), *Exploring Corporate Strategy*, Prentice-Hall, London.

Johnston, Robert (1995a), Service Failure and Recovery: Impact, Attributes and Process, in Swartz, Teresa A., Bowen, David E. and Stephen W. Brown (eds), *Advances in Services Marketing and Management*, vol. 4.

Johnston, Robert (1995b), The Determinants of Service Quality: Satisfiers and Dissatisfiers, *International Journal of Service Industry Management*, vol. 6, no. 5.

Joyce, M.L. and Lambert, D.R. (1996), *Memories of the Way Stores Were and Retail Store Image*, International Journal of Retail and Distribution Management, vol. 24.

Judd, V.C. (1987), Differentiate with the 5th P: People, *Industrial Marketing Management*, vol. 16.

Juran, J.M. (1974), Basic Concepts, in Juran, J.M., Gryna, F.M. and R.S. Bingham (eds), *Quality Control Handbook*, McGraw-Hill, New York.

Kahn, Barbara E. (1998), Dynamic Relationships with Customers: High-Variety Strategies, *Journal of the Academy of Marketing Science*, vol. 26, no. 1.

Kampf, Arjen J., Kasper, Hans and Fred W. Vlotman (1994), Plaatsbepaling van marketing-beheersing, *Working Paper*, University of Maastricht, Maastricht.

Kapferer, Jean-Noël (1995), *Les Marques, Capital de l'Enterprise*, les Editions d'Organisation, Paris, second edition.

Kaplan, Robert S. and David P. Norton (1992), The Balanced Score Card - Measures That Drive Performance, *Harvard Business Review*, January-February.

Kaplan, Robert S. and David P. Norton (1993), Putting the Balanced Score Card to Work, *Harvard Business Review*, September-October.

Kapoor, Harish C. and Elise Truly Sautter (1995), Self Service: a Cross Cultural Perspective, *Proceedings Winter Conference American Marketing Association*, Chicago.

Kasper, Hans (1992), *Classifying After Sales Services, a Framework for Comparative Testing of Services After the Sale*, Seminar International Organization of Consumer Union, The Hague.

Kasper, Hans (1993), *The Image of Marketing: Facts, Speculations and Implications*, Working Paper 93-104, Faculty of Economics and Business Administration, University of Limburg, Maastricht.

Kasper, Hans (1994), Some Trends in Distribution and Retailing in Europe, in Urban, Sabine Ph.D., *Europe's Economic Future, Aspirations and Realities*, Gabler Verlag, Wiesbaden.

Kasper, Hans (1995), The Essence of a Market Driven Corporate Culture: Theory and Empirical Evidence, *METEOR Working Paper 95-009*, University of Maastricht, Maastricht.

Kasper, Hans (1997a), *Corporate Culture and Market Orientation in Services: a Matter of Definition and Communication*, in Arnott, David, Shaw, Veronica and Robin Wensley (eds), Progress, Prospects and Perspectives, Proceedings 26th EMAC Conference, Warwick.

Kasper, Hans (1997b), Remote Service Delivery, Information Technology will Alter the Distribution of Service - if Customers Cooperate, *Marketing Management*, vol. 6, no. 3, Fall.

Kasper, Hans (1998), Corporate Culture and Market Orientation: First and Preliminary Result, *Working Paper*, University of Maastricht, Maastricht.

Kasper, Hans and Josée Bloemer (1997), Cultural Closeness: a Matter of Structure and Care, From 18 Case Studies, *Working Paper*, University of Maastricht, Maastricht.

Kasper, Hans and Jos Lemmink (1988), Perceived After Sales Service Quality and Market Segmentation, in Blois, Keith and Stephen Parkinson (eds), *Innovative Marketing - a European Perspective*, Proceedings of the XVII EMAC Conference, Bradford.

Kasper, Hans and Jos Lemmink (1989), After Sales Service Quality: Views Between Industrial Customers and Service Managers, *Industrial Marketing Management*, vol. 18.

Kasper, Hans, Lit, Arjan van and Ko de Ruyter (1998), Alle Neuzen naar de Klant, *Tijdschrift voor Marketing*, vol. 32, June.

Kasper, Hans and Sigrid Peters (1993), Triads and Dyads in the

Marketing - R&D Interface: a Meta-analysis in Terms of a Service Rendering Relationship, *Working Paper 93-104*, University of Limburg, Maastricht

Kasper, Hans, Lit, Arjan van and Ko de Ruyter (1998), Op Weg naar een Marktgerichte Onderneming, *Working Paper*, University of Maastsricht, Maastricht.

Keaveney, Susan M. (1995), Customer Switching Behavior in Service Industries: an Exploratory Study, *Journal of Marketing*, vol. 59, April.

Kehoe, Louise and Neil Buckley (1996), Wal-Mart to Launch Online Shopping in Microsoft Link, *Financial Times*, 13 February.

Kelley, Scott W. (1992), Developing Customer Orientation Among Service Employees, *Journal of the Academy of Marketing Science*, vol. 20, no. 1.

Kelley, Scott W., Hoffman, Douglas, K. and Mark A. Davis (1993), A Typology of Retail Failures and Recoveries, *Journal of Retailing*, vol. 69, no. 4.

Killough, James (1978), Improved Pay-offs from Transnational Advertising, *Harvard Business Review*, July/August.

Kloosterboer, Wolter (1992), *Interne Marketing, een Inventariserend Onderzoek*, NIMA, Amsterdam.

Kohli, Ajay K. and Bernard J. Jaworski (1990), Market Orientation: The Construct, Research Propositions, and Managerial Implications, *Journal of Marketing*, vol. 54, April.

Kohli, Ajay K., Jaworski, Bernard J. and Ajith Kumar (1993), MARKOR: A Measure of Market Orientation, *Journal of Marketing Research*, November.

Koopmans, A.J. and M.F. Versteeg (1989), De Rol van het Industriële Merk: case-story IBM, *Tijdschrift voor Marketing*, vol. 23, no. 12.

Kordupleski, Ray, Rust, Roland T. and Anthony J. Zahorik (1993), Why Improving Quality Does not Improve Quality, *California Management Review*, vol. 35, Spring.

Kostecki, M.M. (1994), *Marketing Strategies for Services; Globalization, Client-orientation, Deregulation*, Pergamon Press, Oxford.

Kostecki, Michel (1996), Waiting Lines as a Marketing Issue, *European Management Journal*, vol. 14, no. 3.

Kotler, Philip (1991), *Marketing Management, Analysis, Planning, Implementation and Control*, Prentice-Hall, Englewood Cliffs, seventh edition.

Kotler, Philip (1994), *Marketing Management, Analysis, Planning, Implementation and Control*, Prentice-Hall International Editions, Englewood Cliffs, N.J., eighth edition.

Kotler, Philip (1997), *Marketing Management, Analysis, Planning, Implementation and Control*, Prentice-Hall, Upper Saddle River, NJ, ninth edition.

Krapfel Jr R.E., Salmond, D. and R. Spekman (1991), A Strategic Approach to Managing Buyer-Seller Relationships, *European Journal of Marketing*, vol. 25, no. 9.

Krubasik, Edward (1988), Customer your Product Development, *Harvard Business Review*, November.

Kuin, Harry (1998), Y&R's Brand Asset Valuator, Biedt Zicht op Sterkte Merken, *Adformatie*, no. 6, 5 February.

Kullvén, Hakan (1996), Performance Measures for Service Processes, in Edvardsson, Bo, Brown, Stephen W., Johnston,

Robert and Eberhard E. Scheuing (eds), *Advancing Service Quality: a Global Perspective*, Proceedings of QUIS 5, Karlstad.

Kumar, N., Scheer, L.K. and Jan-Benedict E.M. Steenkamp (1995), The Effects of Perceived Interdependence on Dealer Attitudes, *Journal of Marketing Research*, vol. 32, no. 4.

Kurtz, David L. and Kenneth E. Clow (1998), *Services Marketing*, John Wiley, New York.

Lacity, Mary C. and Rudy Hirschheim (1993), *Information Systems Outsourcing, Myths, Metaphors and Realities*, John Wiley, Chichester.

Lai Man So, Stella (1998), Factors Influencing the Implementation of Relationship Marketing in the Banking Industry: an Empirical Study in Hong Kong, in Andersson, Per Ph.D., *Proceedings 27th EMAC Conference*, Stockholm, vol. 1.

Lambert, S.J., Chen, K.H. and C. Joyce (1996), Overhead Cost Pools, *Internal Auditor*, vol.53, no.5.

Langerak, Fred, Peelen, Ed and Harry R. Commandeur (1995), De Voelhoorns Aangescherpt, *Tijdschrift voor Marketing*, vol. 29, no. 7/8.

Lapin, L.L. (1988), *Quantitative Methods for Business Decisions with Cases*, Harcourt Brace Jovanovich Publishers, San Diego, fourth edition.

Larson, R.C. (1987), Perspectives on Queues: Social Justice and the Psychology of Queueing, *Operations Research*, vol. 35, no. 6.

Laulajainen, Risto (1991), Two Retailers Go Global - The Geographical Dimension, *The International Review of Retail, Distribution and Consumer Research*, vol. 1, no. 5.

Lazarus, David (1997), This Year's Model, *Marketing Week*, 12 June.

LeClerc, France, Schmitt, Bernd H. and Laurette Dubé (1995), Waiting Time and Decision Making: Is Time Like Money?, *Journal of Consumer Research*, vol. 22, June.

Leeflang, Peter S. H., Alkema, S., Rosbergen, E. and Marco Vriens (1992), De Markt voor Accountantsdiensten in Nederland, De Aanbodzijde van de Markt voor Accountantsdiensten, *Maandblad voor Accountancy en Bedrijfseconomie*, vol. 66, April.

Leeflang, Peter S.H., Heyboer, A. and F.J. de Jonge (1992), Marketing Planning in de Nederlandse Bedrijfspraktijk, *Onderzoeksmemorandum nr. 507, Instituut voor Economisch Onderzoek, Faculteit der Economische Wetenschappen*, Rijksuniversiteit Groningen.

Lehmann, Alex (1993), *Dienstleistungsmanagement, Strategien und Ansatzpunkte zur Schaffung von Servicequalität*, Schäffer-Poeschel Verlag NZZ, Stuttgart.

Lehmann, Donald R. (1998), Customer Reactions to Variety: Too Much of a Good Thing, *Journal of the Academy of Marketing Science*, vol. 26, no. 1.

Lele, Milind M. and Jagdish N. Sheth (1987), *The Customer is Key, Gaining an Unbeatable Advantage through Customer Satisfaction*, John Wiley, New York.

Lemmink, Jos G.A.M. (1988), Klachtenmanagement: Blauwdruk en Onderzoeksresultaten, Working Paper, University of Maastricht, Maastricht.

Lemmink, Jos G.A.M. (1991), *Kwaliteitsconcurrentie tussen Ondernemingen*, Proefschrift Faculteit der Economische Wetenschappen, Rijksuniversiteit Limburg, Datawyse, Maastricht.

Lemmink, Jos G.A.M. (1992), Metingen ten behoeve van Kwaliteitsmanagement: een kritische beschouwing van het SERVQUAL model, *Jaarboek Nederlandse Vereniging van Marktonderzoekers*, Haarlem.

Lemmink, Jos G.A.M. and Ravi Behara (1992), Q-Matrix: A Multi-dimensional Approach for Using Service Quality Measurements, in Kunst, Paul E.J. and Jos G.A.M. Lemmink (eds), *Quality Management in Services*, Van Gorcum, Assen, Maastricht.

Lemmink, Jos G.A.M. and Hans Kasper (1988), Het Meten van de Service-Kwaliteit en Implicaties voor het Marketing-Beleid, in *De praktijk van denken naar doen*, Bundel National Marketing Congres, NIMA, Amsterdam.

Lemmink, Jos G.A.M. and Hans Kasper (1994), Competitive Reactions to Product Quality Improvements in Industrial Markets, *European Journal of Marketing*, vol. 28, no. 12.

Lemmink, Jos G.A.M, Rohs, Rene L.E.J. and Jos M.C. Schijns (1994), One-Price-Selling en de relatie met de autodealer, *Tijdschrift voor Marketing*, vol. 28, no. 12.

Levitt, Theodore (1980), Marketing Success Through Differentiation - of Anything, *Harvard Business Review*, January-February.

Levitt, Theodore (1983), The Globalization of Markets, *Harvard Business Review*, May-June.

Lewis, Barbara R. (1991), Service Quality: an International Comparison of Bank Customers' Expectations and Perceptions, *Journal of Marketing Management*, vol. 7.

Liljander, Veronica and Tore Strandvik (1995), The Nature of Customer Relationships in Services, in Swartz, Teresa A., Bowen, David E. and Stephen W. Brown (eds*)*, *Advances in Services Marketing and Management*, vol. 4, JAI Press, Greenwich CON.

Loosveld, Alain (1991), *Het Marketing Planning Proces voor Industriele Diensten*, MBA thesis, University of Limburg, Maastricht.

Lovelock, Christopher H. (1983), Classifying Services to Gain Strategic Marketing Insights, *Journal of Marketing*, vol. 47, Summer.

Lovelock, Christopher H. (1991), *Services Marketing*, Prentice-Hall, Englewood Cliffs, second edition.

Lovelock, Christopher H. (1995), Managing Services: The Human Factor, in Glynn, William J. and James G. Barnes (eds), *Understanding Services Management; Integrating Marketing, Organisational Behaviour, Operations and Human Resource Management*, John Wiley, Chichester.

Lovelock, Christopher H. and George S. Yip (1996), Developing Global Strategies for Service Businesses, *California Management Review*, vol. 38, no. 2, Winter.

Løwendahl, Bente R. (1997), *Strategic Management of Professional Service Firms*, Handelshojskolens Forlag, Copenhagen.

Macintosh, Gerrard and Lawrence S. Lockshin (1997), Retail Relationships and Store Loyalty: a Multi-level Perspective, *International Journal of Research in Marketing*, vol. 14.

Maney, Kevin (1988), *USA Today*, 2 January.

Mangold, Klaus (1997), Produkt und Dienstleistung, Kombination auf High-Tech-Ebene, *Absatzwirtschaft*, no. 8.

Martin, Peter (1998), What's in a Name?, *Financial Times*, 26 February.

Martin, W.B. (1986), Measuring and Improving your Service Quality, *Cornell Hotel and Restaurant Administration Quarterly*, vol. 27, May.

Martineau, P. (1958), The Personality of the Retail Store, *Havard Business Review*, vol. 36.

Mathieu, J.E. and D.M. Zajac (1990), A Review and Meta-Analysis of the Antecedents, Correlates and Consequences of Organizational Commitment, *Psychological Bulletin*, vol. 108, no. 2.

Merchant, Kenneth A. (1995), *Control in Business Organizations*, Ballinger, Cambridge.

Meurs, Anjo (1995), *Country of Origin Effects: are They Different for General and Product/Service-specific Country Images?*, MBA thesis, Rijksuniversiteit Limburg, Maastricht.

Meyer, Anton and Frank Dornach (1996), *The German Customer Barometer 1995 - Quality and Satisfaction, Yearbook of Customer Satisfaction in Germany 1995*, German Marketing Association e.v., German Post AG, Düsseldorf, Bonn.

Meyer, Anton and Tom Tostmann (1995), Die nur erlebbare Markenpersönlichkeit, *Harvard Business Manager*, no. 4.

Miles, G.L. (1993), Why Airtransport is Taking Off, *Inernational Business*, September.

Miller, John A. (1977), Studying Satisfaction, Modifying Models, Eliciting Expectations, Posing Problems and Making Meaningful Measurements, in Keith H. Hunt (ed.), *Conceptualization and Measurement of Consumer Satisfaction and Dissatisfaction*, School of Business, Indiana University, Bloomington IN.

Mitchell, Alan (1997), Preaching to the Converted, *Marketing Week*, 5 June.

Modell, Sven (1996), Management Accounting and Control in Services: Structural and Behavioural Perspectives, *International Journal of Service Industry Management*, vol. 7, no. 2.

Mohr, Lois A. and Mary Jo Bitner (1995), The Role of Employee Satisfaction with Service Transactions, *Journal of Business Research*, vol. 32.

Möller, Kristian E. and David T. Wilson (eds) (1995), *Business Marketing: an Interaction and Network Approach*, Kluwer Academic, Boston.

Morello, Gabriele (1988), Business requirements and future expectations in competitive bank services: the issue of time perception, in *ESOMAR, Research for Financial Services*, Milano, Italy.

Morello, Gabriele (1993), *The Hidden Dimensions of Marketing*, Vrije Universiteit, Amsterdam.

Morgan, Neil and Nigel Piercy (1993), Marketing in Financial Services Organization: Policy and Practice, in Teare, Richard, Moutinho, Luiz and Neil Morgan (eds), *Managing and Marketing Services in the 1990s*, Cassell, London.

Morgan, R.M. and Shelby D. Hunt (1994), The Commitment-Trust Theory of Relationship Marketing, *Journal of Marketing*, vol. 58, no. 3.

Morris, Michael H. and Donald A. Fuller (1989), Pricing an Industrial Service, *Industrial Marketing Management*, vol. 18.

Morrison, Pamela D. and John H. Roberts (1998), Matching Electronic Distribution Channels to Product Characteristics: the Role of Congruence in Consideration Set Formation, *Journal of Business Research*, vol. 41, no. 3,

March.

Mowday R.T., Porter, L.W. and R.M. Steers (1982), *Employee-Organizational Linkages*, Academic Press, New York.

Mowday, R.T., Steers, R.M. and L.W. Porter (1979), The Measurement of Organizational Commitment, *Journal of Vacational Behavior*, vol. 14.

Murphy, Ian P. (1997), Amex Looks Beyond Satisfaction, Sees Growth, *Marketing News*, 12 May.

Murray, Keith B. (1991), A Test of Services Marketing Theory: Consumer Information Acquisition Activities, *Journal of Marketing*, vol. 55, January.

Nagle, Thomas T. (1987), *The Strategy and Tactics of Pricing, A Guide to Profitable Decision Making*, Prentice-Hall, Englewood Cliffs.

Narver, John C. and Stanley F. Slater (1990), The Effect of a Market Orientation on Business Profitability, *Journal of Marketing*, vol. 54, October.

Neijzen J.A. and M. Trompetter (1989), *Kwaliteitszorg in Dienstverlenende Organisaties*, Kluwer Bedrijfswetenschappen, Deventer.

Nillesen, J.P.H. (1992), *Service and Advertising Effectiveness*, Universiteitsdrukkerij Rijkskuniversiteit Groningen, Groningen.

Normann, Richard (1984), *Service Management: Strategy and Leadership in Service Business*, John Wiley, Chichester.

Normann, Richard (1991), *Service Management: Strategy and Leadership in Service Business*, John Wiley, Chichester, second edition.

O'Farrell, Patrick N. and Peter A. Wood (1994), International Market Selection by Business Service Firms: Key Conceptual and Methodological Issues, *International Business Review*, vol. 3, no. 3.

Oliva, Terence A. and Richard Lancioni (1996), Identifying Key Traits of Good Industrial Service Reps, *Marketing Management*, vol. 4, no. 4, Winter/Spring.

Oliver, Richard L. (1993), A Conceptual Model of Service Quality and Service Satisfaction: Compatible Goals, Different Concepts, in Swartz, Teresa A., Bowen, David E. and Stephen W. Brown (eds), *Advances in Services Marketing Management*, vol. 2, JAI Press, Greenwich.

Oliver, Richard L. (1997), *Satisfaction: a Behavioral Perspective on the Consumer*, McGraw-Hill, New York.

Onkvisit, S. and J.J. Shaw (1989), Service Marketing: Image, Branding, and Competition, *Business Horizons*, January/February.

Øvretveit, John (1992), *Health Service Quality*, Blackwell Scientific, Oxford.

Palmer, Adrian (1994), *Principles of Service Marketing*, McGraw-Hill, London.

Palmer, Adrian J. (1995), Relationship Marketing: Local Implementation of a Universal Concept, *International Business Review*, vol. 4, no. 4.

Palmer, Adrian (1997), Principles of Service Marketing, McGraw-Hill, London, second edition.

Papadopoulos, Nicolas and Louise A. Heslop (eds) (1993), *Product Country Images: Impact and Role in International Marketing*, International Business Press, Binghamton NY.

Parasuraman, A. (1995), Measuring and Monitoring Service Quality, in Glynn, William J. and James G. Barnes (eds),

Understanding Services Management, John Wiley, Chichester.

Parasuraman, A., Berry, Leonard L. and Valarie A. Zeithaml (1990), An Empirical Examination of Relationships in an Extended Service Quality Model, Working Paper 90-122, *Marketing Science Institute*, Cambridge MA.

Parasuraman, A., Zeithaml, Valarie A. and Leonard L. Berry (1985), A Conceptual Model of Service Quality and its Implications for Future Research, *Journal of Marketing*, vol. 49.

Parasuraman, A., Zeithaml, Valarie A. and Leonard L. Berry (1988), SERVQUAL: A Multiple Item Scale for Measuring Customer Perceptions of Service Quality, *Journal of Retailing*, vol. 64.

Parasuraman, A., Zeithaml, Valarie A. and Leonard L. Berry (1994), Alternative Scales for Measuring Service Quality: a Comparative Assessment Based on Psychometric and Diagnostic Criteria, *Journal of Retailing*, vol. 70, no. 3.

Patterson, Paul and Muris Cicic (1995), A Typology of Service Firms in International Markets: an Empirical Investigation, *Research Paper*, Services Marketing Unit, Department of Management, University of Wollongong, NSW, Australia.

Patterson, Paul and Muris Cicic (1996), Modelling Service Firms' Export Behavior: An Empirical Investigation, *Paper*, Michigan State University.

Paun, D. (1993), When to Bundle or Unbundle Products, *Industrial Marketing Management*, vol. 22.

Payne, Adrian (1993), *The Essence of Service Marketing*, Prentice-Hall International, London.

Payne, Adrian and Moira Clarke (1995), Marketing Services to External Markets, in Glynn, William J. and James G. Barnes (eds), *Understanding Services Management*, John Wiley, Chichester.

Peelen, E. (1989), *Relaties Tussen Consument en Aanbieder*, Ph.D, Haveka, Alblasserdam.

Peter, J. P. and Jerry C. Olson (1993), *Consumer Behavior and Marketing Strategy*, Irwin, Homewood Ill., third edition.

Peters, Monique A.M. (1997), Brand Personality in Services, *MBA thesis*, University of Maastricht, Maastricht

Peters, Thomas J. and Richard H. Waterman (1982), *In Search of Excellence: Lessons from America's Best-Run Companies*, Harper and Row, New York.

Petrof, John V. (1997), Relationship Marketing: the Wheel Reinvented, *Business Horizons*, November-December.

Petty, R.E. and J.T. Cacioppi (1986), *Communication and Persuasion: Central and Peripheral Routes to Attitude Change*, Springer Verlag, New York.

Piercy, Nigel and Neil Morgan (1991), Internal Marketing - The Missing Half of the Marketing Programme, *Long Range Planning*, vol. 24, no. 2.

Pirsig, Robert M. (1987), *Zen and the Art of Motorcycle Maintenance*, Bantam Books.

Plummer, Joseph T. (1985), How Personality Makes a Difference, *Journal of Advertising Research*, vol. 24, no. 6, December/January.

Poiesz, Theo B.C. (1989), *De Transformatie van een karikatuur*, Tilburg University, Tilburg.

Poiesz, Theo B.C. and W. Fred van Raaij (1993), A Psychological Approach to Relationship Quality in Industrial Markets, *Papers on Economic Psychology*, no. 117,

Erasmus University, Rotterdam.

Porter, L.W., Steers, R.M., Mowday, R.T. and P.W. Boulivan (1974), Organizational Commitment, Job Satisfaction, and Turnover Among Psychiatric Technicians, *Journal of Applied Psychology*, vol. 59, no. 5.

Porter, Michael E. (1980), *Competitive Strategy, Techniques for Analyzing Industries and Competitors*, The Free Press, New York.

Porter, Michael E. (1985), *Competitive Advantage*, The Free Press, New York.

Post, H.A. (1992), Internationalisatie van Dienstverlenende Ondernemingen, *Maandblad voor Accountancy en Bedrijfseconomie*, vol. 66, September.

Price, Linda L., Arnould, Eric J. and Patrick Tierney (1995), Going to Extremes: Managing Service Encounters and Assessing Provider Performance, *Journal of Marketing*, vol. 59, April.

Pruyn, Ad Th.H. and Ale Smidts (1993), Consumentenreacties bij Wachtrijen: Literatuuroverzicht en Studiebevindingen, *Tijdschrift voor Marketing*, vol. 27, no. 9.

Quelch, John A. and Lisa R. Klein (1996), The Internet and International Marketing, *Sloan Management Review*, Spring.

Quinlan, M.R. (1991), How Does Service Drive the Company? Success in Services Means More than Just Pleasing the Customer, *Harvard Business Review*, November-December.

Raaij, W. Fred van and Theo M.M. Verhallen (1994), Domain Specific Market Segmentation, *European Journal of Marketing*, vol. 28, no. 10.

Rathmell, J.M. (1974), *Marketing in the Service Sector*, Winthrop, Cambridge MA.

Ravindran, A., Philips, D.T. and J.J. Solberg (1987), *Operations Research: Principles and Practice*, John Wiley, New York.

Reed, David (1998), Card Games, *Marketing Week*, 22 January.

Reuyl, Jan C. and Gijsbert B.W. Willenborg (1993), Aspecten van Kwaliteit en Kwaliteitsmanagement in Service-organisaties, *Maandblad voor Accountancy en Bedrijfseconomie*, vol. 67, no.12.

Reynolds, Jonathan (1995), Database Marketing and Customer Loyalty: Examining the Evidence, *European Retail Digest*, OXIRM, Summer.

Riddle, Dorothy I. (1992), Leveraging Cultural Factors in International Service Delivery, in Swartz, Teresa A., Bowen, David E. and Stephen A. Brown (eds), *Advances in Services Management*, vol. 1, JAI Press, Greenwich, CON.

Ries, Al and Jack Trout (1986), *Marketing Warfare*, Plume, Penguin Group, New York.

Riezebos, Rik, De Vries jr, Wouter and Eric Waarts (1996), *Miles Mania, van Gratis Weggevertje tot Electronisch Sparen*, Wolters-Noordhoff, Groningen.

Roest, Henk C.A. and Theo M.M. Verhallen (1993), Kwaliteit als Commerciële Strategie, *Maandblad voor Accountancy en Bedrijfseconomie*, vol. 67, no.12.

Rogers, Jerry D., Clow, Kenneth E. and Toby J. Kash (1994), Increasing Job Satisfaction of Service Personnel, *Journal of Services Marketing*, vol. 8, no. 1.

Roozen, Frans A. (1991), Activity Based Costing, in *Handbook of Management Accounting*.

Roth, Martin S. and William P. Amoroso (1993), Linking Core Competencies to Customer Needs: Strategic Marketing of Health Care Services, *Journal of Health Care Marketing*, 20 November.

Rubel, Chad (1995), Banks Go Mobile to Service Low-income Areas, *Marketing News*, Summer.

Rubel, Chad (1996a), Pizza Hut Explores Customer Satisfaction, *Marketing News*, 25 March.

Rubel, Chad (1996b), Amtrak ready to fly high by challenging the airlines, *Marketing News*, 6 May.

Rucci, Anthony J., Kirn, Steven P. and Richard T. Quinn (1998), The Employee-Customer-Profit Chain at Sears, *Harvard Business Review*, vol. 76, January-February.

Rust, Roland T., Zahorik, Anthony J. and Timothy L. Keinigham (1995), Return on Quality (ROQ): Making Service Quality Financially Accountable, *Journal of Marketing*, vol. 59, April.

Rust, Roland T. Zahorik, Anthony J. and Timothy L. Keinigham (1996a), *Service Marketing*, Harper Collins, New York.

Rust, Roland T., Zahorik, Anthony J. and Timothy L. Keiningham (1996b), New Developments in Return on Quality (ROQ), in Edvardsson, Bo, Brown, Stephen W., Johnston, Robert and Eberhard E. Scheuing (eds), *Advancing Service Quality: a Global Perspective*, Proceedings QUIS 5, ISQA, St John's University, Jamaica NY.

Rutherford, Denney G. (1995), *Hotel Management and Operations*, Van Nostrand Reinhold, second edition.

Ruyter, Ko de (1993), *Dissatisfaction Management, a Study into the Use of Consumer Dissatisfaction as a Source of Management Information by Organizations*, dissertation, University of Twente, Enschede.

Ruyter, Ko de and Hans Kasper (1997), Consumer Affair Departments in the United States and the Netherlands, *Journal of Consumer Policy*, vol. 20, no. 3.

Ruyter, Ko de, Kasper, Hans and Martin Wetzels (1995), Internal Service Quality in a Manufacturing Firm: a Review of Critical Encounters, *New Zealand Journal of Business*, vol. 17, no. 2.

Ruyter, Ko de and Norbert Scholl (1995), *Kwalitatief Onderzoek*, Lemma, Utrecht.

Ruyter, Ko de, Lemmink, Jos, Wetzels, Martin and Jan Mattsson (1997a), Carry-Over Effects in the Formation of Satisfaction: the Role of Value in a Hotel Service Delivery Process, in: Swartz, Teresa A., Bowen, David E. and Stephen W. Brown (eds), *Advances in Services Marketing Management*, vol. 6, JAI Press, Greenwich.

Ruyter, Ko de, Wetzels, Martin, Lemmink, Jos and Jan Mattsson (1997b), The Dynamics of the Service Delivery Process: a Value-based Approach, *International Journal of Research in Marketing*, vol. 14.

Samuels, Gary (1996), Snowbird Bank, *Forbes*, 4 November.

Saporito, Bill (1995), Going Nowhere Fast, *Fortune*, 3 November.

Sasser, W. Earl (1976), Match Supply and Demand in Service Industries, *Harvard Business Review*, November-December.

Sasser, W.Earl and S. Arbeit (1976), Selling Jobs in the Service Sector, *Business Horizons*, vol. 19, June.

Schefczyk, Michael (1992), Operational Performance of Airlines: an Extension of Traditional Measurement Paradigms, *Strategic Management Journal*, vol. 14.

Schiffman, Leon G. and Leslie L. Kanuk (1987), *Consumer Behavior*, Prentice-Hall, Englewood Cliffs NJ, third edition.

Schijns, Jos M.C. (1996), Measuring Relationship Strength for Segmentation Purposes, in Parvatiyar, A. and Sheth, J.N. (eds), *Contemporary Knowledge of Relationship Marketing*, 1996 Research Conference Proceedings, Center for Relationship Marketing, Emory University, Atlanta.

Schijns, Jos M.C. (1998), *Het Meten en Managen van Klant-Organisatie Relaties*, Ph.D., University of Maastricht, Maastricht.

Schrameyer, Hugo (1998), Virtueel Winkelen Krijgt Eigen Europees Informatiecentrum, *Adformatie*, 2 April.

Schreurs, Jean-Pierre (1992), *International Retailing, Ambition, Skills and Knowledge*, MBA thesis, University of Limburg, Maastricht.

Schriver, Steve (1997), Customer Loyalty: Going, Going, ..., *American Demographics*, September.

Schumer, Charles E. (1996), Let the Credit Cards Compete, *Financial Times*, 4 August.

Schwartz, Karen and Ian P. Murphy (1997), Airline Food is No Joke, Marketers Improve Menus to Please Passengers, *Marketing News*, vol. 31, no. 21.

Schwenker, Burkhard (1989), *Dienstleistungsunternehmen im Wettbewerb; Marktdynamik und Strategische Entwicklungslinien*, Deutscher Universitätsverlag, Wiesbaden.

Scott, Don R. and Nicholas T. van der Walt (1995), Choice Criteria in the Selection of International Accounting Firms, *European Journal of Marketing*, vol. 29, no. 1.

Segal-Horn, Susan (1993), The Internationalization of Service Firms, Advances in Strategic Management, vol. 9, JAI.

Semenik, Richard J. and Gary J. Bamossy (1993), *Principles of Marketing, a Global Perspective*, South-Western Publishing Co., Cincinnati OH, second edition.

Sharma, D.D. (1994), Classifying Buyers to Gain Marketing Insight: a Relationships Approach to Professional Services, *International Business Review*, vol. 3, no. 1.

Shemwell Jr, Donald J. and J. Joseph Cronin Jr (1994), Services Marketing Strategies for Coping with Demand/Supply Imbalances, *Journal of Services Marketing*, vol. 8, no. 4.

Sheth, Jagdish N. and Atul Parvatiyar (1995), Relationship Marketing in Consumer Markets: Antecedents and Consequences, *Journal of the Academy of Marketing Science*, vol. 23, no. 4.

Shimp, Terence A, and Subhash Sharma (1987), Consumer Ethnocentrism: Construction and Validation of the CETSCALE, *Journal of Marketing Research*, vol. XXIV, August.

Shostack, G. Lynn (1977), Breaking Free From Product Marketing, *Journal of Marketing*, vol. 41, April.

Shostack, G. Lynn (1987), Service Positioning Through Structural Change, *Journal of Marketing*, vol. 51, January.

Sikkel, Dirk (1993), SMART, een diagnose-instrument voor de kwaliteit van dienstverlening, in *Jaarboek Nederlandse Vereniging van Marktonderzoekers*.

Simon, Hermann (1992), *Preismanagement*, Gabler Verlag, Wiesbaden, second edition.

Simon, Martin (1995), *De Strategische Functietypologie, Functioneel Denkraam voor Management*, Kluwer BedrijfsInformatie, Deventer.

Simon, P.V. and J.J.H. de Hartog (1993), Ook Kwaliteit Kent Zijn Grenzen, *Rendement*, July/August.

Simonin, Bernard L. and Julie A. Ruth (1995), Bundling as a Strategy for New Product Introduction: Effects on Consumer's Reservation Prices for the Bundle, the New Product, and its Tie-in, *Journal of Business Research*, vol. 33, no. 3.

Singh, Jagdip (1990), Voice, Exit, and Negative Word-of-Mouth Behaviors: an Investigation Across Three Service Categories, *Journal of the Academy of Marketing Science*, vol. 18, no. 1.

Slater, Stanley F. and John C. Narver (1994a), Does Competitive Environment Moderate the Market Orientation-Performance Relationship?, *Journal of Marketing*, vol. 58, January.

Slater, Stanley F. and John C. Narver (1994b), Market Orientation, Customer Value, and Superior Performance, *Business Horizons*, vol. 37, March-April.

Slater, Stanley F. and John C. Narver (1995), Market Orientation and the Learning Organization, *Journal of Marketing*, vol. 59, July.

Slater, Stanley F., Olson, Eric M. and Venkateshwar K. Reddy (1997), Strategy-based Performance Measurement, *Business Horizons*, July-August.

Smart, Tim (1996), Jack Welch's Encore. How GE's Chairman is Remaking his Company - Again, *Business Week*, 28 October.

Smidts, Ale, Riel, Cees van and Ad Pruyn (1998), The Impact of Employee Communication on Organizational Identification, in Per Andersson (ed.) *Proceedings 27th EMAC Conference*, Stockholm, vol. 3.

Smit, Jur (1998), MBA thesis, University of Maastricht, Maastricht.

Soest, Iwan P., van and Wal, Jacques van de (1995), Global Industry Survey: Telecommunications, Internal Report, ABN AMRO Bank, Amsterdam.

Soons, Jolande (1995), *Tevredenheid en Ontevredenheid bij Diensten*, MBA thesis, University of Maastricht, Maastricht.

Speed, Richard and Gareth Smith (1997), Customers, Strategy and Performance, in: Meidan, Arthur, Lewis, Barbara and Luiz Moutinho (eds), *Financial Services Marketing, a Reader*, The Dryden Press, London.

Spoon, Kathleen (1996), How to Ruin a Beautiful Relationship, *Marketing News*, 9 September.

Stauss, Bernd (1991), Internes Marketing als personalorientierte Qualitätspolitik, in Bruhn, Manfred and Bernd Stauss (eds), *Dienstleistungsqualität: Konzepte-Methoden-Erfahrungen*, Gabler, Wiesbaden.

Stauss, Bernd (1994), Internal Services: Classification and Quality Management, *Paper* presented at the QUIS 4 Conference, Newark CONN.

Stauss, Bernd and H.S. Schulze (1990), Internet Marketing, *Marketing ZFP*, vol. 3.

Steenkamp, J.E.B.M. (1993a), Kwaliteit van diensten, Enige inzichten uit de Economische Theorie, *MAB*, no. 12.

Steenkamp, Jan Benedict E.B.M. (1993b), Ethnocentrisme bij Europese Consumenten, *Tijdschrift voor Marketing*, vol. 27, December.

Steenkamp, Jan-Benedict, E.M. and Marnik G. Dekimpe

(1997), The Increasing Power of Store Brands: Building Loyalty and Market Share, *Long Range Planning*, vol. 30, no.6.

Steenkamp, Jan Benedict E.B.M., Verhallen, Theo M.M., Gouda, J.H., Kamakura, W.A. and Th.P. Novak (1993), De zoektocht naar de Europese consument: heilige graal of kansrijke missie?, *Tijdschrift voor Marketing*, vol. 27, September.

Stewart, Kate and Mark Colgate (1998), Marketing Relationships and Personal Banking, in Per Andersson (ed.), *Proceedings 27th EMAC Conference*, Stockholm, vol. 1.

Storbacka, Kaj (1994), *The Nature of Customer Relationship Profitability - an Analysis of Relationships and Customer Bases in Retail Banking*, Ph.D. Swedish School of Economics and Business Administration, Helsinki.

Storey, Chris and Christopher J. Easingwood (1996), Determinants of New Product Performance, a Study in the Financial Services Sector, *International Journal of Service Industry Management*, vol. 7, no. 1.

Strandvik, Tore (1994), *Tolerance Zones in Perceived Service Quality*, Swedish School of Economics and Business Administration, Helsingfors.

Strandvik, Tore and Veronica Liljander (1994a), A Comparison of Episode Performance and Relationship Performance for a Discrete Service, *Paper*, Third Services Marketing Workshop, Berlin.

Strandvik, Tore and Veronica Liljander (1994b), Relationship Strength in Bank Services, in: Sheth, Jagdish N. and Atul Parvatiyar (eds), *Relationship Marketing: Theory, Methods and Applications,* 1994 Research Conference Proceedings, Emory University, Atlanta.

Strandvik, Tore and Kaj Storbacka (1996), Managing Relationship Quality, in Edvardsson, Bo, Brown, Stephen W., Johnston, Robert and Eberhard E. Scheuing (eds), *Advancing Service Quality: a Global Perspective*, Proceedings QUIS 5, ISQA, New York.

Suchanek, Mireille A.M.F. (1998), *Exploring the Sales Control Function, Control Systems That Drive Business Excellence*, Ph.D., University of Maastricht, Maastricht.

Suchard, H.T. and M.J. Polonsky (1991), A Theory of Envirnomental Buyer Behaviour and its Validity, in *Proceedings American Marketing Association Educator's Conference,* Chichago.

Swan, John E. and I. Frederick Trawick (1994), Determinants of Industrial Purchaser Delivery Service Expectations and Satisfaction: an Ethnography, *Journal of Consumer Satisfaction, Dissatisfaction and Complaining Behavior*, vol. 7.

Swartz, Teresa A., Bowen, David E. and Stephen W. Brown (1992), Fifteen Years After Breaking Free: Services Then, Now and Beyond, in Swartz, Teresa A., Bowen, David E. and Stephen W. Brown (eds), *Advances in Services Marketing and Management*, vol. 1.

Szmigin, I.T.D. (1993), Managing Quality in Business-to-Business Services*, European Journal of Marketing*, vol. 27, no. 1.

Tapscott, Don (1996), *The Digital Economy, Promise and Peril in the Age of Networked Intelligence,* McGraw-Hill, New York.

Taylor, Shirley (1994), Waiting for Service: the Relationship Between Delays and Evaluations of Service, *Journal of Marketing*, vol. 58, no. 2.

Taylor, Steven A. (1995), Service Quality and Consumer Attitudes: Reconciling Theory and Measurement, in Swartz, Teresa A., Bowen, David E. and Stephen W. Brown (eds), *Advances in Services Marketing and Management*, vol. 4, JAI Press, Greenwich.

Teas, R. Kenneth (1993), Expectations, Performance Evaluation and Consumers' Perceptions of Quality, *Journal of Marketing*, vol. 57, October.

Tettero, Jozef H.J.P. and Jos H.R.M. Viehoff (1990), *Marketing voor Dienstverlenende Organisaties, Beleid & Uitvoering*, Kluwer Bedrijfswetenschappen, Deventer, second edition.

Thams, Robert (1984), *How do you Determine which Quality Aspects are Worth Extra Attention?*, Research International, Stockholm/Amsterdam.

The Economist (1996), Delays Can Be Expected, 27 July.

Thomas, Rob (1995), *Duidelijkheid in het Marketingplanningproces voor diensten*, MBA thesis, University of Maastricht, Maastricht.

Thor, Carl G. (1996), Corporate Performance Measures in Service Industries, in: Edvardsson, Bo, Brown, Stephen W., Johnston, Robert and Eberhard E. Scheuing (eds), *Advancing Service Quality: a Global Perspective*, Proceedings of QUIS 5, ISQA, St John's University, Jamaica NY.

Treacy, Michael and Fred Wiersema (1995), *The Discipline of Market Leaders*, Addison-Wesley, Reading MA.

Triplett, Tim (1994), Brand Personality Must Be Managed or It Will Assume a Life of Its Own, *Marketing News*, vol. 28, no. 10.

Upshaw, Lynn B. (1993), *Building Brand Identity: a Strategy for Success in a Hostile Market Place*, John Wiley, New York.

Usunier, Jean-Claude (1992), *Commerce entre Cultures: Une Approche Culturelle du Marketing,* Presses Universitaire de France, Paris.

Usunier, Jean-Claude (1993), *International Marketing, a Cultural Approach*, Prentice-Hall, London.

VanderMerwe, Sandra and Michael Chadwick (1989), The Internationalization of Services, *The Services Industries*, January.

VanderMerwe, Sandra and Douglas J. Gilbert (1991), Internal Services: Gaps in Needs/Performance and Prescriptions for Effectiveness, *International Journal of Service Industry Management*, vol. 2, no 1.

Varadarajan, P.R. and Thirunarayana (1990), Consumers' Attitudes towards Marketing Practices, Consumerism and Government Regulations: Cross-national Perspectives, *European Journal of Marketing*, vol. 24, no. 6.

Vause, Bob (1995), European Retail Performance Indicators, *The European Retail Digest*, OXIRM, Spring.

Veendorp, Saskia (1989), *Globalization of Marketing Approaches, a Literature Study. Analyisis of Globalization Activities in Seven Companies and Interviews with Employees within the ABN Bank*, ABN Bank, Amsterdam.

Venetis, Karin A. (1995), Professional Service Quality Perception During Business-to-Business Service Relationships; Differences over Relationship Development, *Working Paper*, University of Limburg, Maastricht.

Venetis, Karin A. (1997), *Service Quality and Customer Loyalty in Professional Service Relationships: an Empirical Investigation into the Customer-based Service Quality Concept in the Dutch*

Advertising Industry, Ph.D., Univsersity of Maastricht, Maastricht.

Venkatraman, N. (1994), IT - Enabled Business Transformation: From Automation to Business Scope Redefinition, *Sloan Management Review*, Winter.

Ven-Verhulp, Marleen van der, Wels-Lips, Inge and Rik Pieters (1995), Critical Service Qualities: A Cross-Sector Analysis, *Paper*, presented at the XXIVth EMAC Conference, Paris.

Verschuren, Karin (1996), *Waarom maakt een consument geen gebruik van technologische innovaties in de dienstverlening*, MBA thesis, University of Maastricht, Maastricht.

Vijvers, Otto van de (1995), UTS, *Elan*, February.

Viscusi, W., Vernon, John M. and Joseph E. Harrington, (1992), Economics of Regulation and Antitrust, D C Heath, Lexington.

Vogels, René J.M., Lemmink, Jos G.A.M. and Hans Kasper (1989), Some Methodological Remarks on the SERVQUAL Model, in Avlonitis, George J., Papavasilou, N. K. and A. G. Kouremenos (eds), *Marketing Thought and Practice in the 1990's*, Proceedings of the XVIII EMAC Conference, Athens.

Vogler-Ludwig and Hofmann (1993), *Business Services in Market Services and European Integration: Issues and Challenges*, European Economy, Social Europe, Commission of the European Communities, No. 3.

Vries jr, Wouter de, Kasper, Hans and Piet J.C. van Helsdingen (1997), *Dienstenmarketing* (Services Marketing), Stenfert Kroese, Houten, second edition.

Wackman, D.B., Salmon, C.T. and C.C. Salmon (1987), Developing an Advertising Agency-Client Relationship, *Journal of Advertising Research*, vol. 26, no. 6.

Wakefield, K.L. and J.G. Blodgett (1994), The Importance of Servicescapes in Leisure Service Settings, *Journal of Services Marketing*, vol. 8.

Walt, Nicholas van der, Scott, Don and Arch G. Woodside (1994), CPA Service Providers: a Profile of Client Types and Their Assessment of Performance, *Journal of Business Research*, vol. 31.

Weatherly, Kristopher A. and David A. Tansik (1993), Tactics Used by Customer-contact Workers: Effects of Role Stress, Boundary Spanning and Control, *International Journal of Service Industry Management*, vol. 4, no. 3.

Webster, Cynthia (1989), Can Consumers be Segmented on the Basis of their Service Quality Expectations, *Journal of Consumer Research*, vol. 3, Spring.

Webster, Cynthia (1991), A Note on the Cultural Consistency within the Service Firm: The Effects of Employee Position on Attitudes toward Marketing Culture, *Journal of the Academy of Marketing Science*, vol. 19, no. 4.

Webster Jr, Fred E. (1992), The Changing Role of Marketing in the Corporation*, Journal of Marketing,* vol. 56, October.

Webster Jr, Frederick E. (1994), *Market-Driven Management, Using the New Marketing Concept to Create a Customer-oriented Company,* John Wiley, New York.

Westgeest, Rob (1995), *Verkoop van mobiele communicatie via de detailhandel*, MBA thesis, University of Maastricht, Maastricht.

Wetzels, Martin G.M. (1998), *Service Quality in Customer-Employee Relationships, an Empirical Study in the After-sales*

Service Context, Ph.D., Univsersity of Maastricht, Maastricht.

Wierenga, Berend and Peter A.M. Oude Ophuis (1997), Marketing Decision Support Systems: Adoption, Use and Satisfaction, *International Journal of Research in Marketing*, vol. 14, no. 3, July.

Wijngaarden, J.H. van and M.I. van Thienen (1994), Value for Money; Accountants, Waar Blijft het Advies, *Controllersvizier*, no. 4.

Wilson, David T. (1990), Creating and Managing Buyer-Seller Relationships, *ISBM report 5-1990*, Penn State University.

Wilson, David T. (1995), An Integrated Model of Buyer-Seller Relationships, *Journal of the Academy of Marketing Science*, vol. 23, no.4.

Winston, Clifford (1993), Economic Degruglation: Days of Reckoning for Microeconomists, *Journal of Economic Literature*, vol. 31.

Witkowski, Terrence and Joachim Kellner (1996), How Germans and Americans rate their banking services, *Marketing News*, vol. 30, no. 21, 7 October.

World Bank (1994), *World Competitiveness Report 1993*, Oxford University Press, New York.

World Bank Policy Research Report (1995), Bureaucrats in Business; the Economics and Politics of Government Ownership, Oxford University Press, Oxford.

World Development Report (1993), Investing In Health, Published for the World Bank, Oxford University Press, Oxford.

World Development Report (1994), Infrastructure for Development, Published for the World Bank, Oxford University Press, New York.

World Development Report (1995), Workers in an Integrating World, Published for the World Bank, Oxford University Press, Oxford.

Wright, Lauren K. (1995), The Effects of Service Type on New Service Success, in Swartz a A., Bowen, David E. and Stephen W. Brown (eds), *Advances in Marketing and Management*, vol. 2.

Wright, Peter, Pringle, Charles D., Mark J. Kroll (1992), *Strategic Management, Text and Cases*, Allyn and Bacon.

Wührer, Gerhard A. (1995), Quality Positioning in the Austrian Banking Industry: a Benchmark Case Study, in Kunst, Paul and Jos Lemmink (eds), *Managing Service Quality*, Paul Chapman Publishing, London.

Wyatt, Edward (1996), Why Fidelity Doesn't Want You to Shop at Schwab, *The New York Times*, 14 July.

Yorke, David A. (1988), Developing an Interactive Approach to the Marketing of Professional Services, in Blois, Keith and Stephen Parkinson (eds), *Innovative Marketing – a European Perspective,* Proceedings XVII EMAC conference, Bradford.

Zeegers, R. (1998), *Adformatie*, 6, 5 February.

Zeithaml, Valerie A. (1981), How Consumers Evaluation Processes Differ Between Goods and Services, in Donnelly, J.H. and W.R. George (eds), *Marketing of Services*, American Marketing Association, Chicago.

Zeithaml, Valarie A. (1988), Consumer Perceptions of Price, Quality, and Value: a Means-End Model and Synthesis of Evidence, *Journal of Marketing*, vol. 52, July.

Zeithaml, Valarie A. (1990), Communicating with Customers

about Service Quality, in Bowen, David E., Chase, Richard B. and Thomas G. Cummings and Associates, *Service Management Effectiveness, Balancing Strategy, Organization and Human Resources, Operations and Marketing*, Jossey-Bass Publishers, San Francisco.

Zeithaml, Valarie A. and Mary Jo Bitner (1996), *Services Marketing*, McGraw-Hill, New York.

Zeithaml, Valarie A., Berry Leonard L. and A. Parasuraman (1988), Communication and Control Processes in the Delivery of Service Quality, *Journal of Marketing*, vol. 52, April.

Zeithaml, Valarie A., Berry, Leonard L. and A. Parasuraman (1993), The Nature and Determinants of Customer Expectations of Service, *Journal of the Academy of Marketing Science*, vol. 21, no. 1.

Zeithaml, Valarie A., Berry, Leonard L. and A. Parasuraman (1996), The Behavioral Consequences of Service Quality, *Journal of Marketing*, vol. 60, April.

Zeithaml, Valarie A., Parasuraman, A. and Leonard L. Berry (1990), *Delivering Quality Service, Balancing Customer Perceptions and Expectations*, The Free Press, New York.

Zinken, Karin (1995), *Der Einfluss von (Un)Zufriedenheit auf das Verhalten, insbesondere im Dienstleistungsbereich*, MBA thesis, University of Limburg, Maastricht.

INDEX

Note: Page references in *italics* refer to tables and illustrations.

ACKNOWLEDGEMENTS

The Publisher wishes to thank the following who have kindly given permission for the use of copyright material.

Page 5	KLM	Reprinted by permission of KLM Airlines
Page 6	Service practice 1–1	Reprinted with permission from "Going Nowhere Fast" by B. Saporito, April 3, 1995 Fortune Magazine
Page 36–40		Reprinted from Oct. 28, 1996 issue of Business Week by special permission, copyright ©1996 by the McGraw-Hill Companies
Page 43	Alltel	Reprinted by permission of Alltel
Page 71	Star Alliance	©1997 Wilhelm Schultz
Page 85	Figure 3–3	From World Development Report 1995: Workers in An Integrating World by World Bank. Copyright © 1995 by The International Bank for Reconstruction and Development/The World Bank. Used by permission of Oxford University Press, Inc.
Page 91	Figure 3–4	From Bureaucrats in Business: The Economics And Politics of Government Ownership by World Bank. Copyright ©1995 The International Bank for Reconstruction and Development/The World Bank. Used by permission of Oxford University Press, Inc
Page 107	Table 3–1	Reproduced from Advertising Age
Page 108	Table 3–3	Reproduced from Advertising Age
Page 113	Table 3–6	Reproduced by permission of Eurostat
Page 126	Figure 3–5	Reprinted from Van Soest and Van de Wal 1995
Pages 129–134		Reprinted by permission of Paul Chapman Publishing from P. Kunst and J. Lemmink, Managing Service Quality, 1995
Page 143		Reprinted by permission of Radisson SAS Hotels
Pages 170–197		Reprinted with the permisssion of The Free Press, a Division of Simon & Schuster, Inc from MARKETING SERVICES: Competing Through Quality by Leonard L. Berry and A. Paramsuraman. Copyright ©1991 by The Free Press
Pages 177–178		Reprinted by permission of Marketing News published by American Marketing Association, Ian Murphy, 1997, vol. 31, p.14
Page 181	DHL	Reprinted with permission of DHL
Pages 184–186, 189–191		Reprinted with permission of The Free Press, a Division of Simon & Schuster, Inc from Managing Quality: The Strategic and Competitive Edge, by David A. Garvin. Copyright ©1988 David A. Garvin
Page 190	Service practice 5–6	Reprinted with permission from Services Marketing Today, vol. 10, no. 3, June 1995 published by American Marketing Association
Page 199	Figure 5–3	Reprinted by permission of Journal of Marketing, published by American Marketing Association, V.A. Zeithaml, L.L. Berry, A. Parsuraman, The Behavioral Consequences of Service Quality, 1996, vol. 60, April, pp31–46
Page 202	Service practice 5–11	R. Johnston, "Determinants of Service Quality", International Journal of Service Industry Management, 1995, vol. 6 no. 5 pp53–71, Reproduced by permission of MCB Press
Pages 213, 215–219, 282–283		Reprinted with the permisssion of The Free Press, a Division of Simon & Schuster, Inc from DELIVERING QUALITY SERVICE: Balancing Customer Perceptions and Expectations by V. Zeithaml, A. Paramsuraman, L.L. Berry. Copyright ©1990 by The Free Press
Page 226	Service practice 5–17	Reprinted by permission of Marketing News published by American Marketing Association, C. Rubel, Pizza Hut Explores Customer Satisfaction, March 25, p.15
Page 228	Figure 5–8	From Health Service Quality, J. Øvretveit 1992. Reprinted by permission of Blackwell Science
Page 241	SAS Data Mining	Reprinted by permission of SAS Institute (www.sas.com)
Pages 242–243	Service practice 6–1	Reprinted by permission of Marketing News, published by the American Marketing Association, J. Honomicl, Marketers Value Honesty in Marketing Researchers, vol. 29, no. 12, 1995, p.H27
Page 264	Holiday Inn	Reprinted by permission of Bass Hotels & Resorts
Pages 265–266	Parkroyal	Reprinted from Guest Comment Form
Page 276	Service practice 6–11	Reproduced by permission of Research for Marketing Decisions 5th edition, Green, Tull/Albaum
Page 281	Service practice 6–13	Reprinted by permission of Journal of Marketing, published by American Marketing Association, C. Fornell et al, vol. 60, Oct., pp7–18
Pages 297–299		Reprinted by permission of Marketing News, published by the American Marketing Association, K. Schwartz and I. Murphy, May 12 1997, p.6
Page 303	Andersen Consulting	Reprinted with permission of Andersen Consulting
Pages 337–338		Reprinted by permission of Journal of Health Care Marketing, published by American Marketing Association, M.S. Roth and W.P. Amoroso, Linking Core Competencies To Customer Needs, Summer 1993, pp49–54